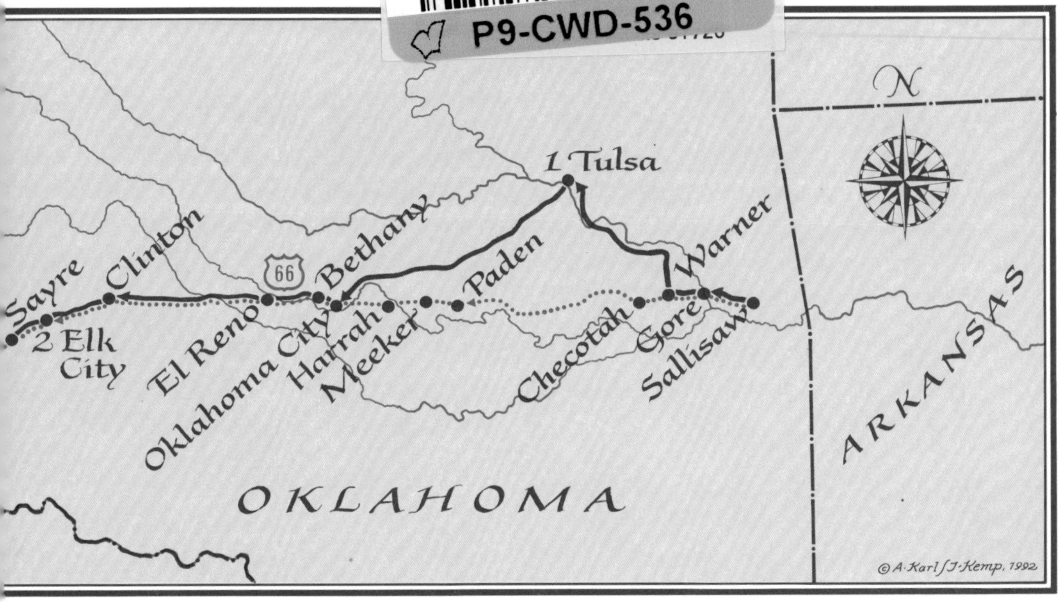

N

1 Tulsa

Sayre Clinton 66 Bethany Paden Warner
2 Elk City El Reno Oklahoma City Harrah Meeker Checotah Gore Sallisaw

ARKANSAS

OKLAHOMA

© A. Karl / J. Kemp, 1992

Colorado R.

ARIZONA

NEW MEXICO

Little Colorado R.

66 Gallup Albuquerque 6

Flagstaff Joseph City
Winslow Holbrook

Miles
0   75

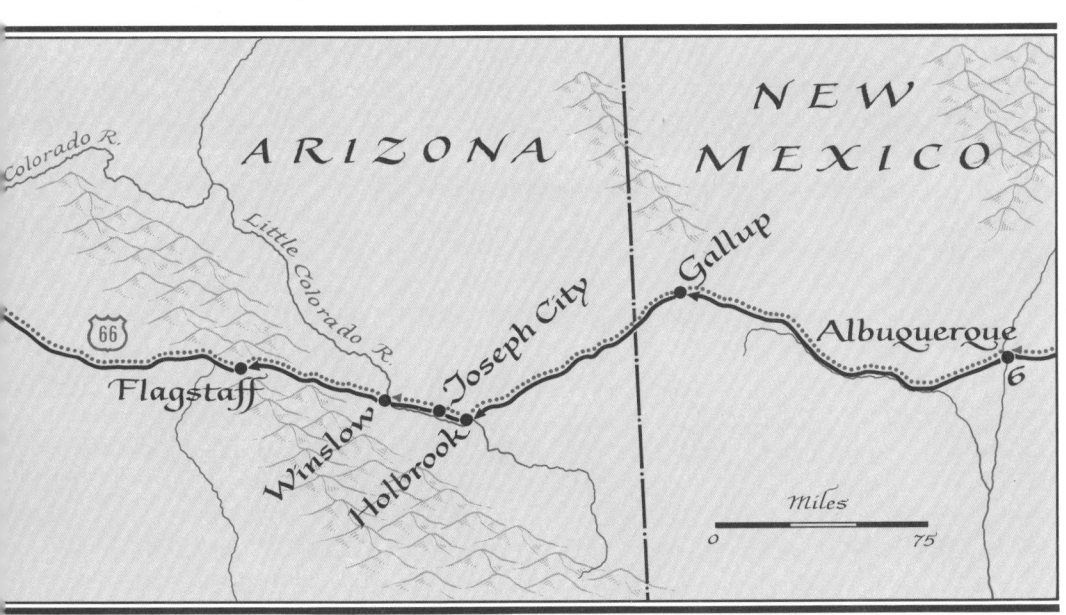

8. They cross the bridge into California.

9. Oca wades in the Pacific.

10. They camp out.

11. "Twin Pines" Ranch.

The Journey of the Tathams, August 20-27, 1934
◄———

The Journey of the Joad Family in John Steinbeck's The Grapes of Wrath
◄·············

ALSO BY DAN MORGAN

Merchants of Grain

Rising in the West

RISING
IN THE
WEST

**THE TRUE STORY
OF AN "OKIE" FAMILY
FROM THE GREAT
DEPRESSION THROUGH
THE REAGAN YEARS**

DAN
MORGAN

ALFRED A. KNOPF   NEW YORK 1992

THIS IS A BORZOI BOOK
PUBLISHED BY ALFRED A. KNOPF, INC.

Copyright © 1992 by Dan Morgan
Endpaper maps copyright © 1992 by Anita Karl
All rights reserved under International and Pan-American Copyright
Conventions. Published in the United States by Alfred A. Knopf, Inc.,
New York, and simultaneously in Canada by Random House of Canada
Limited, Toronto. Distributed by Random House, Inc., New York.

Library of Congress Cataloging-in-Publication Data
Morgan, Dan.
Rising in the West : the true story of an Okie family from the Great
Depression through the Reagan years / Dan Morgan.—1st ed.
p.   cm.
Includes bibliographical references.
ISBN 0-394-57453-2
1. Tatham family.   2. Migration, Internal—United States—History—
20th century.   3. Rural families—United States—History—20th
century.   4. United States—Social conditions—1933–1945.   5. United
States—Social conditions—1945–   6. Oklahoma—Biography.
7. California—Biography.   I. Title.
CT274.T39M67   1992
979'.03'0922—dc20
[B]   89-45314 CIP

Manufactured in the United States of America

FIRST EDITION

TO EDDIE, BILL, TEMP, AND GENERAL

AND IN MEMORY OF PHYZZIE

CONTENTS

Illustrations follow page 298.

THE TATHAMS

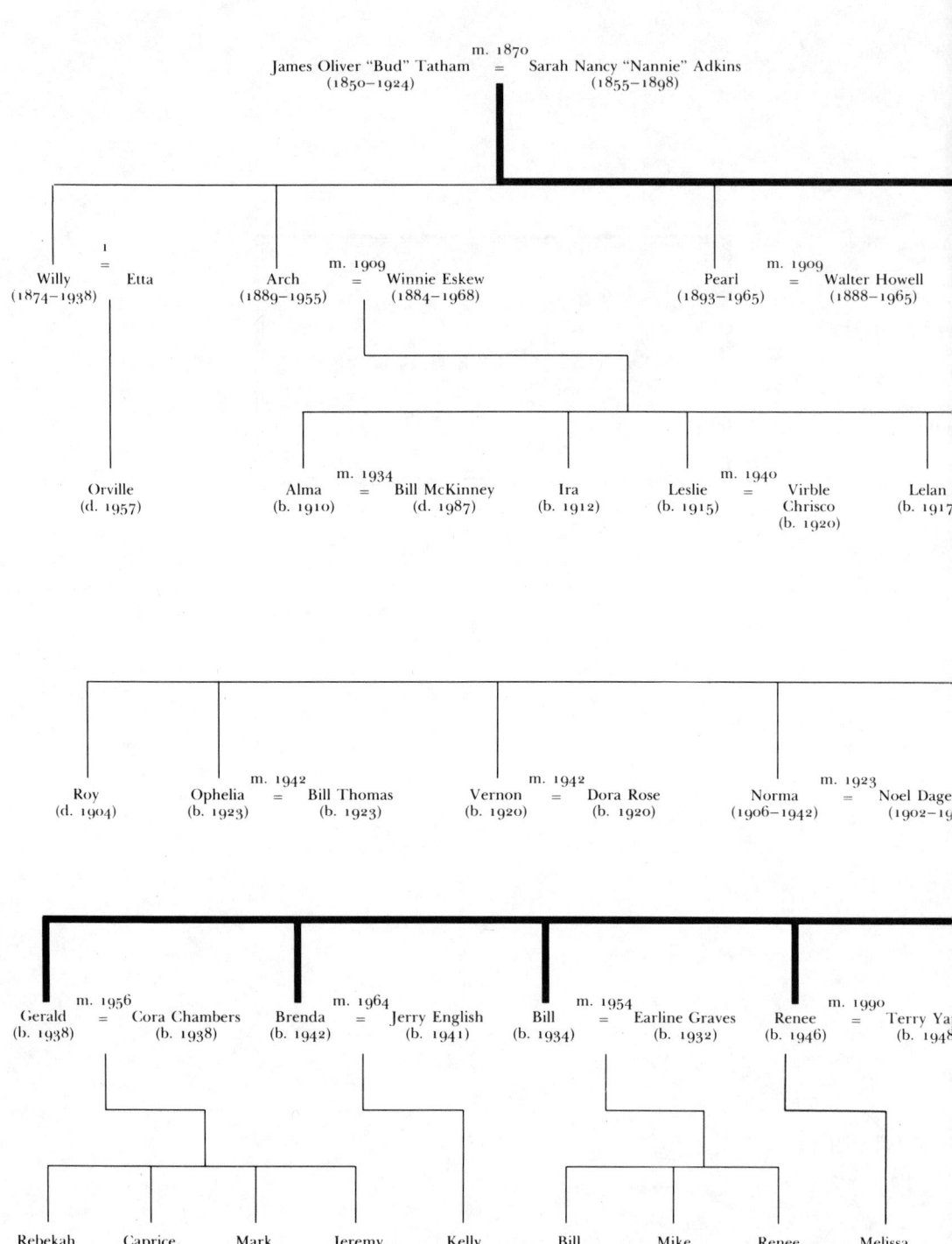

James Oliver "Bud" Tatham   m. 1870   Sarah Nancy "Nannie" Adkins
(1850–1924)   =   (1855–1898)

Willy   Etta   Arch   m. 1909   Winnie Eskew   Pearl   m. 1909   Walter Howell
(1874–1938)   =   (1889–1955)   =   (1884–1968)   (1893–1965) =   (1888–1965)
         1

Orville   Alma   m. 1934   Bill McKinney   Ira   Leslie   m. 1940   Virble   Lelan
(d. 1957)   (b. 1910)   =   (d. 1987)   (b. 1912)   (b. 1915)   =   Chrisco   (b. 1917
                                                                                                (b. 1920)

Roy   Ophelia   m. 1942   Bill Thomas   Vernon   m. 1942   Dora Rose   Norma   m. 1923   Noel Dage
(d. 1904)   (b. 1923)   =   (b. 1923)   (b. 1920)   =   (b. 1920)   (1906–1942)   =   (1902–19

Gerald   m. 1956   Cora Chambers   Brenda   m. 1964   Jerry English   Bill   m. 1954   Earline Graves   Renee   m. 1990   Terry Ya
(b. 1938)   =   (b. 1938)   (b. 1942)   =   (b. 1941)   (b. 1934)   =   (b. 1932)   (b. 1946)   =   (b. 1948

Rebekah   Caprice   Mark   Jeremy   Kelly   Bill   Mike   Renee   Melissa
(b. 1961)   (b. 1963)   (b. 1966)   (b. 1968)   (b. 1968)   (b. 1954)   (b. 1958)   (b. 1964)   (b. 1981)

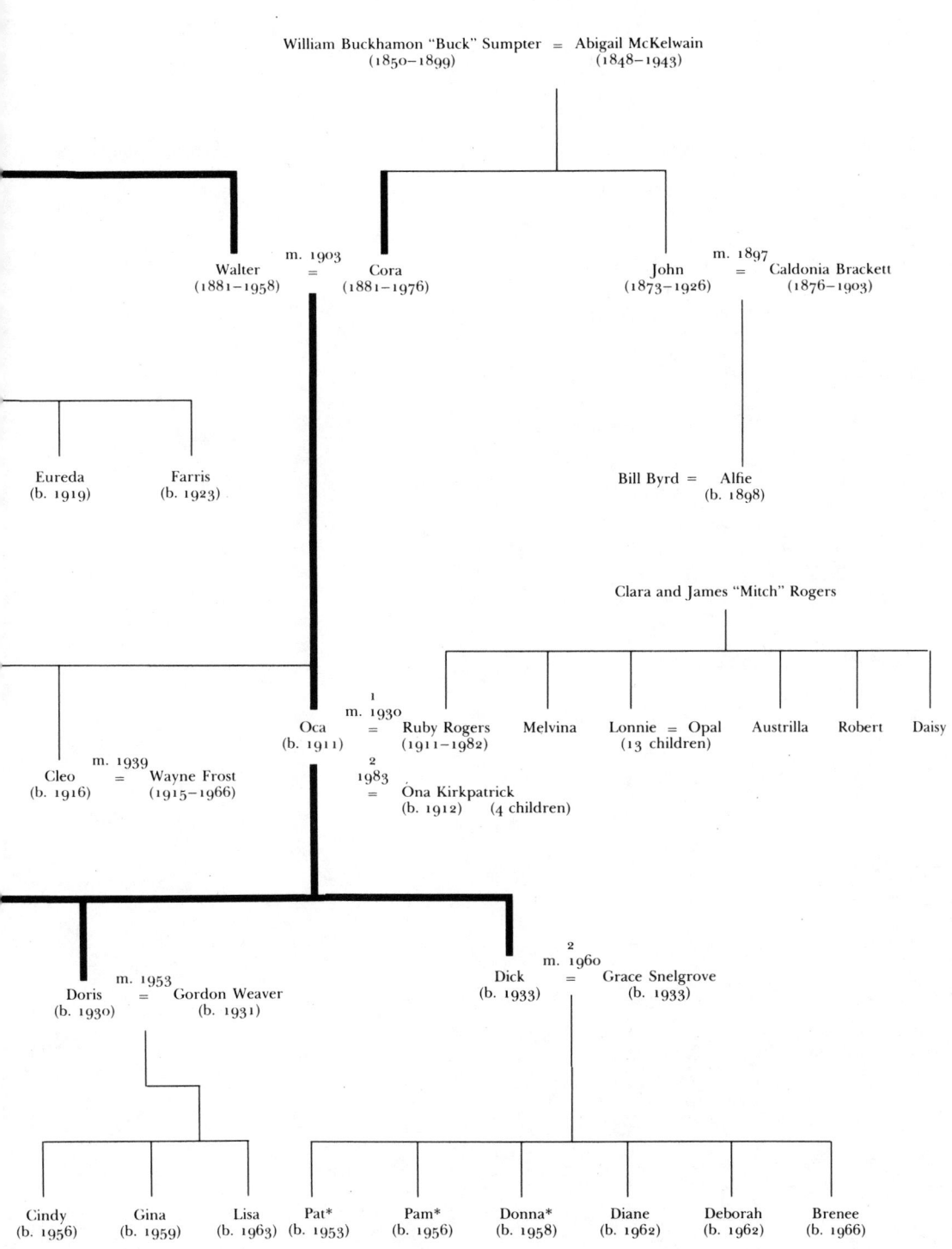

William Buckhamon "Buck" Sumpter = Abigail McKelwain
(1850–1899)   (1848–1943)

Walter   m. 1903   Cora   John   m. 1897   Caldonia Brackett
(1881–1958)   =   (1881–1976)   (1873–1926)   =   (1876–1903)

Eureda   Farris   Bill Byrd = Alfie
(b. 1919)   (b. 1923)   (b. 1898)

Clara and James "Mitch" Rogers

                                              1
                                        m. 1930
Oca   =   Ruby Rogers   Melvina   Lonnie = Opal   Austrilla   Robert   Daisy
(b. 1911)   (1911–1982)   (13 children)
                                              2
                                        1983
Cleo   m. 1939   Wayne Frost   =   Ona Kirkpatrick
(b. 1916)   =   (1915–1966)   (b. 1912)   (4 children)

                                                              2
                                                        m. 1960
Doris   m. 1953   Gordon Weaver   Dick   =   Grace Snelgrove
(b. 1930)   =   (b. 1931)   (b. 1933)   (b. 1933)

Cindy   Gina   Lisa   Pat*   Pam*   Donna*   Diane   Deborah   Brenee
(b. 1956)   (b. 1959)   (b. 1963)   (b. 1953)   (b. 1956)   (b. 1958)   (b. 1962)   (b. 1962)   (b. 1966)

*Grace's children adopted by Dick

I FIRST READ *The Grapes of Wrath* in the spring of 1955. The book made me dream of the open road, and when classes let out that year I took to the highway with a friend in his '52 Ford in search of the America that John Steinbeck had so powerfully described.

It wasn't long before we found it. We were driving west on a desolate stretch of old U.S. 40 in Kansas when two forlorn hitchhikers hove into view. We pulled over and in got Mac and Dude. He was thin as a stick and needed a shave; she had a beautiful warm face, but she bulged in the wrong places, the telltale sign of a poverty diet. After a couple of sandwich stops at which Mac and Dude waited in the car—they were "not hungry"—we deduced that they were penniless.

For the next six weeks we traveled together, two down-and-out migrants and two Ivy Leaguers, as unlikely a crew of farmhands as anyone could imagine. But the relationship worked. We had the car. Mac and Dude knew the timetable for the ripening of crops across the West and, in return for transportation, pointed us toward orchards and fields with fruit and vegetables ready for picking.

In younger days, Mac told us, he had played the drums in the dives of St. Louis. Then the booze and the drugs and the wild women had got him and he had slipped into seasonal farm labor. Somewhere along the way he had met up with Dude. It was a "road" marriage. Mac still had problems with the booze, as we discovered after a quart bottle of Budweiser had turned him mean, but Dude kept him off it most of the time. He was the streetwise man from the honky-tonks who wore a suit coat into the orchards; she was the soft-spoken country woman who had taken him in tow. She bore a remarkable resemblance to Jane Darwell, who played Ma Joad in Darryl F. Zanuck's Twentieth Century-Fox film *The Grapes of Wrath*. Now and then, she sang us songs in a bell-clear soprano—the "sweetest voice this side of heaven," Mac called it.

While we camped out in our sleeping bags or rented cheap motel rooms, Mac and Dude bedded down in the Ford. To pay our way, we worked in the apples in Ogden, Utah, the cherries in Emmett, Idaho, and then headed for the hops in Oregon. The hopyard that was our destination beckoned like a beacon as we headed toward the Cascades. Mac had once worked at the operation. The money would be good and the work not too demanding, Mac assured us with a jaunty confidence that increased the closer we got. We splurged on T-bone steaks in expectation of the paychecks we would soon be drawing. But when we reached the hopyard, it was shut. No doubt there had been a crop failure or some shift in the economics of beer production of which we were completely ignorant. We drove on in silence.

We had better luck in the Willamette Valley north of Salem, where we found work at a migrant camp across from a bean field. We shared a windowless shack of weathered boards with three other families and paid five dollars a week for the privilege. It had a small gas stove and sink; toilets were in another building.

The camp was for whites only. Mexican pickers and their families squatted in tents and cars along the edge of a nearby bean field. When quitting time came in the fields, whites and Mexicans went in separate directions. The camp looked as if it had been left over from the set of Zanuck's movie. I half expected to see Henry Fonda, as Tom Joad, come striding down the dusty, rutted street past piles of old tires, rusted-out jalopies, barefoot children standing in dark doorways and stubbly faced men leaning against old pickup trucks.

My buddy and I each earned about four dollars for a day of agonizing bending, picking, and squatting in the beans. Mac and Dude did somewhat better, the Mexicans better still. Happiness was the day the field boss handed us hoes; for that day, at least, we would be paid by the hour for weeding and chopping.

Hard as the work was, it was only an adventure for the two of us from the East. We could drive away in the Ford anytime. And when our money began to run low, we left Mac and Dude in the fields and drove into Salem to check things out. We quickly found cannery jobs that paid union wages to pack cherries in big barrels of salty brine. We drove back to the labor camp to give the good news to Mac and Dude: there were jobs in town. But Mac looked crestfallen. "They won't hire Okies," he said. That night at the cannery we looked around. Sure enough, none of the workers looked like the migrants at the camp.

The next weekend we drove out to visit Mac and Dude. They were gone, headed south, we were told, but nobody knew just where. We never heard from them again.

FOR YEARS AFTERWARD I would think of Mac and Dude and wonder about the people in *The Grapes of Wrath*. And in the spring of 1984, with more than twenty years behind me as a professional journalist, I set out to satisfy my curiosity. I started in Sallisaw, the eastern Oklahoma town where Steinbeck's fictional Joads begin their journey. The country around it is rolling and wooded, hardly the "dust country" described in the novel. But I soon learned that hundreds of families from around Sallisaw had indeed gone out to California in the great Okie migration of the 1930s. They had not been "dusted out" or even "tractored out" by the arrival of labor-saving farm equipment. They had simply drifted out, a family or a community at a time, often thinking it would just be temporary because they were poor and desperate. With the help of Loris Dickey, a longtime resident who had worked on a county history, I began to meet people who had made the trek to California or had relatives who had. The notes I took at the time reveal the common thread of desperation that ran through their experiences:

"Was 17 when drove out with parents . . . tied carrots . . . claims to have met Steinbeck at farm . . . would box for his supper and a cot . . . drove old Nash . . . broke down in Arizona . . . got to a 'shade tree mechanic' . . . picked cotton in '35. . . .

"Went with Jim in Sept '35 . . . 10 kids . . . Ed stayed . . . raised potatoes, melons . . . boss of farm . . . no work for women except shipyards . . . bought 40 acres back here in '39 . . . sold 30 in '42 for $100 and old car . . . 75 turkeys lost to fever. . . .

"Barbara was 16 . . . ma and dad went, so had to go . . . parents were sharecroppers . . . went into tire business . . . had done that in okla . . . they went back to field work to make money."

And, finally, a comment that seemed particularly revealing: "Woman says wouldn't have missed it . . . better there than here . . . no job for anybody."

I met a schoolteaching couple who had made more than forty trips to California since the 1930s to cut grapes, visit relatives, and "have a ball." In the early years, Oklahoma accommodated itself to California's agricultural timetable by letting its schoolterms run through the summer and then let out in fall, just in time for the California grape and cotton-picking seasons. The schoolteaching couple told me they got twelve cents a pound for a lug of grapes and could take in twenty dollars a day in California. The $500 they earned was for "clothes and land." The rest of the year they lived off their teaching money.

After a few days I had collected a notebook full of names: relatives, friends, ex-husbands, long-lost sweethearts, all Californians now. I was ready to head west.

CALIFORNIA SEEMED a long way off to Oklahomans in the 1930s, but no more. Air travel and the interstate highways have made it an easy journey. One can go from Sallisaw to California in two days of hard driving now. The only hazard is the crushing boredom of Interstate 40, which bypasses the towns, the people, the roadhouses, the smells of country evenings, everything. I-40 has replaced Highway 66 for the greater good of commerce and efficient travel but to the regret of the romantic. The old road had the character of a good tenement building in a closely knit neighborhood of corner groceries and watchful grandmothers. The new one has all the personality of a modern suburb.

In places, the old highway still runs playfully alongside its big brother. It has much more fun. It passes right by homey diners and truck stops where farmers gas up their tractors and runs out through country that is close enough for a motorist to smell the hay and hear a dog bark. Elsewhere the old road has been unceremoniously buried under the new interstate.

I-40 crosses the famous Dust Bowl where 66 did, in the Texas panhandle, but a motorist might not know it. The winds still blow and the sandy soil is still eroding, but technology has transformed the region into one of the most drought-resistant agricultural areas in the country. Deep plowing and the centrifugal pump have beaten the drought cycle, though there may be a reckoning someday when the great subterranean aquifer is pumped dry.

One day in New Mexico I parked alongside the interstate and scrambled up a steep, stony slope in search of what I had been told was a tiny section of the original Highway 66. I reached a level place but saw nothing until I looked down and realized I was standing on it! Half buried in sand, covered with weeds and grass, were loose pieces of crumbling concrete. I picked up a chunk and examined it. From down below came the swish and hum of traffic on the interstate. Thoughts of people and dreams and stories and time swirled through my head. Here lay the bridge that finally connected the South to the West—that brought cotton and poverty and old-time religion and the Jackson, Bryan, Roosevelt politics of the common man into the dry valleys of California. Highway 66 had changed America forever, creating the Sun Belt—a greater South—by uniting the Old South with the New West. Now, its work done, it was going back to sand and pebbles.

AT THE OTHER END of the bridge, I met the Tatham family that was to become the principal subject of this book. The Tathams were not migrant "fruit tramps" who followed the crops year in, year out, like Mac and Dude. Rather, they were more like the Joads and the majority of those who left the Southern and Southwestern states during the hard times. Properly speaking, they were immigrants, with a good deal in common with the Europeans who flocked to the United States in the nineteenth and twentieth centuries. They wanted permanent jobs and homes, and California simply seemed like the best opportunity for getting them. When the same chance presented itself in the improving postwar economy of Oklahoma, a good many Tathams went right back home and stayed.

My first contact with the California family was with Bill Tatham in Fresno. He told me later he thought I just might be a private investigator—he was in the middle of several lawsuits—until he checked out my credentials. After that, I had a green light. Over the next five years I conducted hundreds of hours of interviews with Tatham relatives in California, Arizona, and Oklahoma, as well as with their business associates, friends, pastors, and dozens of Okies who entered and exited the Tatham orbit over the previous half century. Later, when I decided to add several chapters about the second family that plays an important role in the book, the Tacketts, they were equally open, accommodating, and generous.

This is their story, but it is my book. Under my agreement with the subjects, I retained full control over the contents and was free to interview whomever I chose. In return for that I agreed to let them see the manuscript before publication and to consider any suggestions they made. As a result of this process, I made one small change in wording about an event involving a Tatham who is now deceased and agreed to omit one piece of information that involved a member of the family who is not central to the story and was not a party to the main agreement I had with Bill and his father.

Wherever they are, I hope Mac and Dude will approve.

THE TRUCK

Walter Tatham, b. 1881, Carroll County, Mo.

HIS WIFE Cora Tatham, b. 1881, Joplin, Mo.

THEIR CHILDREN Ophelia, b. 1923, Miami, Okla.
Vernon, b. 1920, Collinsville, Okla.
Cleo, b. 1916, Brushy, Okla.
Oca, b. 1911, Brushy, Okla.

OCA'S WIFE Ruby, b. 1911, Collinsville, Okla.

THEIR CHILDREN Doris, b. 1930, Collinsville, Okla.
Dick, b. 1933, Gore, Okla.

RUBY'S HALF-BROTHER Dewey Rogers, b. Okla.

OTHERS Jim Anderson, b. 1912, Okla.
Bill Elbertson, b. 1914, Okla.
Arley Land, b. 1914, Okla.
The Nurse
Her two sons

PART ONE

CHAPTER ONE

GOIN'

OCA SWUNG THE TRUCK off the gravel highway and tasted the chalky white dust of the section road seeping up through the floorboards. The vehicle rattled across Drake's Prairie, stirring up a cloud of white powder that just as quickly settled back on the weeds and wildflowers.

Ruby held Doris and Dick close. "We're coming to Granpa's directly," she said.

Oca steered the truck past flimsy box houses with tar paper peeling over cracks and crooked stovepipes rising through rusty sheet-iron roofs. Here and there a strand of barbed wire, sagging from its burden of vines and honeysuckle, stretched between a pair of crooked fence posts.

It had been tricky weather all year. The Arkansas River had flooded in March, spreading a layer of mud and debris over the bottoms. A storm had hailed out a goodly amount of the cotton. And then the dry spell had settled in. Now a boy could cross the river at the sandbar and scarcely wet his shins. Nigger Creek was dry, and the renters were driving their cows six miles to drink. The cotton looked a dead loss.

August, thought Oca. It had a way of burning the fool ideas right out of a man and showing him the truth that the prairie hid in other seasons with its neighborly customs and settled routines of plowing, planting, churchgoing, and courting.

DRAKE'S PRAIRIE, rising gently away from a river bend six miles west of Sallisaw, had been a refuge for Tathams off and on since they'd come to the Indian Territory from Missouri in nineteen hundred and two. In-laws and relatives were always farming there. When the oil fields and smelters up around Tulsa slacked off and a man couldn't make a dollar cutting wood, why, there was always the prairie, where at least you wouldn't starve.

The prairie was really the closest thing to a home place Oca had. His dad, Walter Tatham, a restless drifter who moved from smelter to mine and back to the prairie, had been there this time since the fall of 1932. Walter's kid brother Arch had helped them find ten acres to rent and put up a box house—a frame of one-by-twelves set on cinder blocks.

Oca's mom, Cora Tatham, hadn't wanted to come back to the prairie from Claremore, which had electricity. Oca's kid sisters, Cleo and Ophelia, nicknamed the box house "the orphan's home," it seemed so drab and poor compared to what they'd had in the electric-light towns east of Tulsa.

The prairie was a whole other world from the mining towns around Miami, Commerce, and Picher, Oklahoma, where ambulance sirens screamed and pimps and whores plied their trade. Back on the prairie, there was no electricity for Cleo's phonograph, no gas for cooking, just a wood stove and kerosene lamps and a "typhoid" well out back.

But the prairie was everything that the mining towns were not: it was old-time, neighborly, and religious. At night you could sometimes hear banjos or fiddles over the creek or a good loud gospel chorus. A farmer could tell who was coming up the road by the gait of the team. When a farmer took ill during cotton chopping, his friends and family turned out to hoe it for him.

The talk among the farmers was pleasant and familiar. How much meat had such-and-such family laid away in the smokehouse? Had the potatoes sprouted in the root cellar? What was to be done about the field mice eating the roots clean out of Brother So-and-so's celery patches? Was that new heifer fresh?

People kept their butter cool in springs, made their lard from hogs they butchered themselves, and bought their flour and sugar in hundred-pound bags. When they killed a chicken, they kept the feathers for pillows. They went to Sallisaw Creek for wash day. The women took along rub boards and cast-iron pots for boiling clothes, and if the weather was good enough, they brought picnics and children hit the swimming hole.

Life was regular. You could just about tell the seasons by the sounds. The chink of plow blades striking stones meant spring. Summer was quiet, with crops laid by and so many of the men off in the wheat harvest in Kansas or working in the zinc mines up north. Wagon wheels squeaking in their spindles was the sound of fall and of another cotton crop rolling to the gins.

The Lord provided when the weevils got the cotton. Oca's mother, Cora, sent her daughter Ophelia to the creek for crawdads and gathered wild onions for omelets. She hatched baby chicks in an incubator. And when she needed meal for corn bread, she sent her husband to the mill with a load of corn, with Ophelia riding atop, and had a turn ground. The miller kept part of the grind in payment, and on the way home Walter traded some of the rest for groceries at Butler's store.

Winter was hog-killing time. After the hog was stuck and bled, everyone helped to heave the carcass into a tub of scalding water so its hair and bristles could be scraped off. Arch cut off the fat and put it in fifty-pound tin cans to be melted down for lard. The best part of the carcass was smoked or sugar cured. The rest was salted down for salt pork. Oca's mother saved bacon drippings and fat from the cooking, boiled them down, skimmed off the fat, and made soap in a pan. Ophelia loved the way her hair shined after her mama had washed it with her own lye soap.

People made their own entertainment. After work, a farmer might light up a "tailor," a tailor-made cigarette rolled with Bull Durham or his own homegrown tobacco. Young folks met after church at "the corners," and the sparkier ones might slip off on horseback to take in a picture show in Vian, chancing a whipping if they were caught.

The prairie had a grammar school, a store, a telephone switchboard. But more than anything, it was the Free Holiness church that made Watts a real little community instead of just a settlement of huddled, struggling renters.

The Holy Spirit had swept the prairie years before. Since then it had been just as the Tathams' neighbor Floyd Bagley would later tell

it: "Once Pentecost gets into a family, it just *keeps* gettin' in." Most of
the Tathams and their closest friends and in-laws had the Holy Ghost.
Cora had been saved, sanctified, and blessed with the Holy Spirit
before almost any of them. Oca's Uncle Willy, the one who'd lost the
leg in the mining accident, was Jesus Only. Norma, Oca's older sister,
had brought her husband to the Lord, and he'd made an Assemblies
of God preacher. Oca himself had just been saved at a little colored
church in Vian.

Not his dad, though. Not Walter Tatham. Walter had tried and
tried to get the Holy Ghost, but it wouldn't come. Just when he'd
think he had it, he'd smack his thumb with a hammer trying to drive
a nail, and out would come a cuss word. That would be all it took to
persuade him he just wasn't as good as Cora or Arch or the others
whose sin had been cleaned right out by the Holy Ghost. And after
a while he kind of quit trying.

So Walter stayed home when Cora and the children went off to
the Watts Church for meeting. They liked a preacher there who
could "shake a building," who could "take the hide off a sinner,
preachin' *hard*." Pastor George Land was one who could. It was nothing to see a woman sixty years old, roused by Pastor Land or "Uncle
Dave" Brewer, shouting and dancing in the Spirit. It was said that
Charlie Floyd from Sallisaw—whom the papers called Pretty Boy—
wanted his funeral preached by Uncle Dave.

Pentecost was a whole way of life. Oca's Aunt Winnie wouldn't
call a doctor or take her children to one; when her son's toe was
pinched clean off by a horse's hoof, she wouldn't so much as apply
kerosene, the cure in those parts for cuts and lacerations. Instead,
she prayed for healing, and her prayers were answered: the wound
healed cleanly. If Pastor Land couldn't come to the sickbed, people
sometimes sent for Elder Pool, the colored preacher from across the
river. Then Elder Pool would drive up in his black Cadillac and pray
and clap his hands and speak in tongues till daylight. Visiting kin on
the prairie, Oca had seen people "go into a thicket to where they
were pretty well hid in the shade. They'd have a place. If you got
close you could hear them calling out to God."

It was scriptural, Oca believed. The Bible said, "Cry out to the
Lord and make a joyful sound." And they did, in their homes, in the
fields, and at the frame church at Watts. Farm families would hear
each other praying at night, that was how close the box houses were.
Floyd Bagley would wake after midnight and hear them. "Mama,"
he asked, "don't people ever *sleep* around here?"

Or a person could be driving a team down a section road and suddenly hear voices, and a dozen or so women would be down on a little bluff by the river, holding a prayer meeting and glorifying God.

At haying time, men would come in all sweating and dirty, wash their hands, and sit down to dinner. Some would ask a blessing: "Father, we thank you for the food. We pray your blessing upon it in the name of Jesus, A-men." And sometimes they'd sing a hymn or read a chapter from the Bible.

In summer, people from the Holiness and Pentecostal churches in all the country around would gather for brush arbors. Men would fell a couple of small trees, strip the branches, make poles, fashion some cross members, and cover them with boughs to keep out the sun. Then people would come in their wagons or jalopies from miles around. The women had box suppers or home-canned fruit and pies. After dusk, the younger ones went to sleep in the wagons and the worship would begin. Sometimes a traveling preacher preached by the light of kerosene lamps. Plenty of people came after a real day's work in the fields, weary and ripe for the Lord. The potluck would fill them with plenty of fire. Oca saw them run right down the aisle, preaching and crying, tears streaming down their faces. People got close to the Lord there, and many a doubter came under the power, threw himself to the ground, and asked God to convict him of his sins then and there, while his friends and neighbors shouted, "Hang on, brother," or "Turn loose, brother," or just "Praise the Lord."

OCA PULLED UP at his Uncle Arch's place, and everyone got down.

Oca and Ruby had been married going on four years. He was twenty-three, she twenty-two, still young in years but old, really, in a place where men and women grew up fast (and wore down fast, too). Her pale, soft face was welcoming and gentle. Her black hair fell back on her shoulders in ringlets. Those ringlets were the first thing Oca had noticed about her, sitting behind her in church, and they had captured his heart before he ever saw her face.

Oca was short but powerfully built and handsome. He had the jutting McKelwain chin of his mother and grandma, but scarcely a hint of the Cherokee from his grandfather's side. The Cherokee came out in his sister Cleo, who was dark as a half blood. A snapshot of him taken in a Tulsa photo gallery showed him wearing a gray felt hat, a trace of a smile just starting to curl his mouth. It was the face of a worldly-wise town man, not a farmer, a face that looked as if it knew the ropes in the rough industrial towns east of Tulsa and had the confidence that came from passing their tests of manhood.

Then, too, he stepped too quick and jaunty to be taken for a slow-walking country man.

He swung little Doris out after him while Ruby stayed in the truck cradling Dick, the baby.

Then he stopped and listened hard. Arch was a whistler, and in a moment Oca heard the whistle coming from a patch of cane.

"Com'n see m'new truck," called Oca.

It wasn't really new. He'd been doing the rounds of the junk stores in Tulsa and spotted it on a used car lot. It was a Chevrolet, nineteen and twenty-nine, with a wood-frame cab and a flatbed. Nothing special, Oca thought. The '29 model didn't have fancy things like double rear wheels to take heavy loads. But he turned on the engine and it sounded good enough.

The dealer had wanted fifty dollars. Oca didn't have it, but it was Depression times, and the dealer was ready to bargain. "Well, how much *have* you got?"

"Nothing."

"Well, do you have enough for the *sales tax*?"

Oca figured. Penny on the dollar. Fifty cents. He had seventy-five. It would leave just enough to buy a couple of gallons of gas. "You got yourself a *deal*," he said.

So they wrote up a contract. Fifty dollars and twenty-four in carrying charges. A stiff finance charge, and the dealer insisted on holding the title. But Oca got the truck.

Long before that day, Oca had decided that cars and trucks and things like that could help him get ahead. When he was just a small boy he'd stare at the colored neon sign in front of the car dealer's. BUICK, it flashed. Then it flicked off and spelled it out one letter at a time: B, U, I, C, K. That sign was so shiny and up-to-date that it got him thinking and dreaming.

When he was twelve, his dad got a secondhand Model T Ford touring car. Walter couldn't drive and didn't much want to learn, so he told his oldest son to try. The little boy got behind the wheel, started up, and bounced along right through a wheat field, while his sister Cleo squealed for joy in back. And when he got it back to the house, his dad climbed up and they headed out onto the highway. It was the grandest feeling Oca Tatham had ever had. He was sure of himself, working the three pedals for reverse, forward, and full speed ahead. It came so naturally he felt he could have taken it all the way to Kansas City.

It was different for his dad. Walter Tatham had grown up handling horses, mules, and wagons, not gas engines, and he never did get the hang of a power vehicle. Driving a car down a hill in eastern Oklahoma once, the brakes locked and he took out several railings on the bridge at the bottom. When he finally got the thing stopped, Walter climbed down and Oca slid over behind the wheel. That was pretty much the end of Dad Tatham's driving days.

But for young Oca it was just the beginning. When he was seventeen and living in Collinsville, he and his dad got a Model T Ford roadster. Oca painted it blue, polished it up, kicked his right foot up on the dashboard, and drove down Main Street admiring his reflection in the plate glass windows. He rigged up a whistle on the exhaust hitched to a wire that came right up under the driver's seat. The town's policeman never did figure that one out.

It was a wonder he didn't kill himself. One day after church he took off in the Model T in pursuit of Ruth Johnson, a local girl. His car was outfitted with clincher tires, held onto the rims with air pressure. Ruth's Model A had something else. They came racing down to the one-way bridge over the creek with Oca trailing. Oca told the story on himself. "I had the ears just pulled back on that old Model T Ford, and, man, I went over that bridge and took the turn and rolled three of those clincher tires right off their rims and they went off into a pecan grove."

Primitive as those old cars were, they could go. Once he came down to the Illinois River west of Gore, "flyin' low," thinking there was a bridge at the bottom, but there was none, and the Illinois was flooded. The car floated across while his dad, a great talker, fell stone silent. She started up on the other side, and Oca knocked the bearings off her before they reached Tulsa.

UNCLE ARCH TOOK OFF his cap and walked silently around the Chevy, just whistling. At last he looked up and said, "Wehhhlll."

"I'll need twenty-four dollars to pick up the title," said Oca quietly.

"Wehhll." Now Arch was thinking ahead. "I know a man who needs his hay hauled to Marble City. We can start tomorrow."

Oca climbed back into the truck and drove to his parents' place. He told them, "I've got a truck. If we can get enough people to go in on the gas, we're goin'."

He and Ruby had talked about it even before they married. They were sitting by a country road one day when Oca said, "You know something? If I can ever get enough money together to get out of here, and I can get to California, I'll make it. And you know what? I'll have a home for you." He was just thinking of a little place with one or two rooms.

That had been in 1929. They were eighteen, with eight years of schooling, but no steady jobs. They'd almost left then and there. Instead they'd married, had the two children, and stayed close to their parents. He'd worked at a dairy, driven a truck, dug coal, cut wood, done some peddling, and even engaged in a little bootlegging. And what did he have to show for it? His "home" was a transient hotel in Gore, and now a third child was on the way.

It was hard country. If you knew what was good for you, you didn't stop for a body stretched across the highway at night. That was the oldest trick of the hijackers and highwaymen who came down from the Ozark foothills. Oca had run right over a "thing" like that one night, and his dad had told him to keep right on going and not go back to see what had made the thump. On the prairie, at least, the Christian people kept the gamblers and bootleggers thinned out, but the outlaws controlled the back country and sheriffs entered at their peril.

Men died young in those parts. His Uncle Arch had been grazed by a bullet down on his knees praying in church, and his dad carried a pearl-handled pistol in his suitcase. It was hard country, and it turned men hard. Oca didn't necessarily approve of the outlaws or believe all the stories they told about the generosity of Charlie Floyd. But he thought he understood what drove them.

He thought: *Some people just got fed up with living the way they had to live, and they went ahead and lived a different way, bootlegging or doing whatever they had to do. The state was crooked, and every county was up for fraud. The politicians were tied in to payoffs, and if you knew the right guy you could have anything. Many a time he was fed up to the neck, and he knew that was what drove a lot of the guys to crime. They give up and say, "I'll get it some other way." And one reason they did was they had a bad situation with that den of thieves in Oklahoma City. Why, instead of going out to help the poor with highways and all, they stole it for themselves.*

There was a way out.

The year Roosevelt was elected, Oca landed a job working on a section of the new 66 Highway in Rogers County. He worked all the hours he could, sometimes twenty-four at a stretch, shoveling dirt on the freshly poured cement so it didn't dry too fast in the sun. There weren't many jobs like that, and the sorriest-looking fellows hung around waiting for someone to drop so they could take up his shovel.

"They're waitin' for your job if you burn out," Oca had whispered to Ruby's half brother, Dewey Rogers, who worked alongside him. "Just keep steady, don't quit, don't fool aroun'."

The sweat ran into their eyes and their mouths went salty, but they didn't drop. And as that cement strip got longer every day, Oca started thinking about the places up ahead, the red clay country, the plains, the mountains, those dry big deserts, and then the place at the very end of the road people in those parts called "Californy."

WALTER TATHAM was ready. He'd always been a mover. There was no stopping him when the moving urge got him. "We're luffin' off to God's country, Squaw," he'd tell Cora. They'd soon be heading for greener pastures, and he'd have a cattle ranch for them. Sometimes she'd cry, but when Walter Tatham got one of his "movin' spells" there was no changing his mind. Then Cora, knowing it was all just talk, would dry her tears, pack up her sewing machine and possessions, and off they'd go.

So the day after Oca came by to say that this time he was "goin'," Walter went to Vian and told the man who'd sold him some milk cows on credit. "We're goin' to California, but we're not leavin' to beat the debt," Walter told him. "The cows are stayin' here."

"Good luck in Californy," said the man. It was the Depression. People had to be flexible.

Cora was ready, too. This was her son's move, not her husband's, and it seemed to have more of a direction to it. She could fix as good a pot of crawdaddies and souse as any farm woman. Living on Drake's Prairie she managed the food and took milk to a baby who was starving down the section road. But the prairie was not her place. She was a town woman, progressive, really, for her time—a mother who wept when her daughter Cleo quit school because the money was not there for the books.

The only thing that could have held Cora back was her own mother. Cora's father, a Cherokee half blood, had been resting in his grave in Brushy Cemetery going on thirty-five years, and Cora's mother, Abigail, was alone. But Abigail Sumpter was progressive, too, and didn't want to hold her family back.

Cleo couldn't wait to go. She missed electricity and dreaded the Oklahoma twisters that came on so suddenly. The sky would turn black and they'd hurry home, the horses nervous and the first fat raindrops cratering the dust in the road. If there was time they went to the Callahans' cyclone cellar, but sometimes the storm came on too fast and her dad would brace the door of the box house with furniture and make Cleo and Ophelia get between mattresses and comforters in case the house burst. There were no tornadoes in California.

So it was decided. Now it was only a matter of raising the money to spring the title to the truck, so they could leave the state. Arch took Oca to work in the hay from dawn till after sundown, raking long rows of new-mown prairie grasses into little stacks, then feeding them into a mechanical baler that worked with a spring-fired plunger. When that was done, they loaded the bales onto the truck until the cargo seemed ready to topple. The prairie grass was light, but by the time the cows were settling under the oak tree, Oca was tired.

It didn't take the word long to spread all along the section roads. Soon it was the talk at Butler's store. Oca Tatham had a truck and was going to California. He needed people to help with the gas.

Not many from Drake's Prairie had been out to *California*, though most had been *places*.

California seemed far away as the moon to most of the renters. You didn't move unless somebody you knew moved, and not many had gone that far in 1934. People said, "Ocy, do you know how far it is out there? It's a long ways to Cali*for*ny, do you know that?" Or, "What'd you do, Ocy, hit an oil well?"

Jack Smith was Oca's friend, and he was doubtful, too. "Californy? Why that old truck won't make it out of the county," he said, and he was only half kidding.

All Oca said was, "I'm goin'. The only thing that'll keep me is if I can't get enough together to buy the gas." And soon, his confidence got to be catching.

Jim Anderson was a farmhand down in the bottom. He was twenty-two years old and had seen a little of the world. He'd soldiered at Fort Sill, he said, and afterward he'd gone west with buddies to pick bolls. Living down in the bottom, he'd got the chills—maybe a light case of malaria. Jim figured if he had to die, at least California would be a warm place to do it in. Oca gave him a place on the truck.

Jim was a talker, and sometimes when he talked he did a sort of chicken strut, walking in a circle, snapping his head around hard when he changed course to keep his eyes riveted on the fellow he was talking to, maybe kicking at the dirt. "If you're going to Californy, I'll pay to ride with ya," said Jim.

Oca said fine. But he kind of thought Jim had other reasons for wanting to come along. Jim just might be a little sweet on his kid sister Cleo, Oca thought.

Arley Land, the pastor's brother, put in for a place. The Depression had taken his job with an oil company, and he'd come down to work on the farm his wife's dad rented in Henryetta. But they didn't have much luck there, and when the old man died in 1933, they'd pulled stakes and moved to Sallisaw to be near relatives. They tried to make a crop on the prairie, but it didn't work out. They had a baby to care for, and by the summer of '34, Arley was ready to try anything. Oca took him aboard because he needed a driver. Arley was too poor to pay.

Bill Elbertson, a quiet farm boy from the other side of town, was coming.

Dewey Rogers was, too. He was a good worker but penniless and unschooled. He'd stayed home to help his father farm and couldn't read or write a single word.

Then there was a woman they remember just as "the nurse." She had a job in L.A. and had come with her two children to visit relatives in Oklahoma. She could help pay for gas.

Oca and Walter bought new lumber and made sides for the flatbed. Then they built two long seats. They ran canvas over the top and stretched it down over the sides so that it could be raised and lowered to keep the sun out and let the cool wind from the highway in. Oca got a barrel to keep cool water in and scrounged a thirty-gallon drum for gasoline.

On August 19, a Sunday, everything was finally set. Cora sliced up some potatoes and fried them, then cleaned the skillet and set it aside for the trip. She gathered some more potatoes and put them in a sack for the journey. Then she went into the garden one last time. The sugar-cured bacon from last winter's hog killing was all used up, so she sent Vernon and Cleo for the salt pork she'd stored in Arch's smokehouse. She put the pork in a big tub of water to soak out the salt and have it ready to pan-fry on the road. Then she sent Cleo out to wring the necks of a couple of chickens. Cleo hated the smell from the scalding, so Cora plucked the birds herself, then cut them up, fried them, and put them aside.

Ruby was busy with the babies. She was set on keeping Doris clean on the journey. She and Oca watched the sun going down over the branch. Oca's dad had told Arch that they'd be back by Christmas, but Oca had made up his mind up differently. Another baby was coming in December. That baby would be born in an easier place.

They started toward noon Monday. People straggled in with bedding and bags. There would be sixteen men, women, and children in a truck no bigger than a henhouse. There was Walter and Cora and their youngsters—Cleo, eighteen, Vernon, fourteen, and Ophelia, eleven. Oca and Ruby had their two: Doris, three, and Dick, sixteen months. Then there were the men, Jim Anderson, Bill Elbertson, Arley Land, and Dewey Rogers, and the nurse and her two boys, who were waiting in Sallisaw. Between them all, they had less than fifty dollars, not counting the twenty-four Oca would have to hand over in Tulsa to claim the truck title they'd need to cross state lines.

Oca climbed in behind the wheel. Ruby and the little ones got in next to him. He started up the Chevy and headed it out the section road. Lord, it was dry. Unless they got rain soon there wouldn't be a second hay crop. The cotton, what was left of it, was burned and brown, almost the way it was after the stalks had wintered in the ground.

As they went past John and Irma Callahan's, Cleo remembered the fun they'd had at singings there, and how they'd brought fudge and cookies. Arch's boys had come, and the Lands and the Brashears. Somebody would always have a guitar and they'd start with cowboy songs. But pretty soon out would come the Hartford Music Company songbook, and Riley Brashears would lead them in a gospel hymn. Ruby would sing along, and Oca, when he was there, would listen, though he was no singer.

They made the big bend around Drake's Cemetery, passing the shortcut that boys would dare each other to take at night. Then they were up on the 64 Highway, heading for Tulsa.

"Promise to tell me, Walter," Dewey Rogers said earnestly. "Promise to tell me when we get to *Californy town!*"

CHAPTER TWO

TUMBLEWEED

IN THE FIRST PART of the twentieth century eastern Oklahoma was a kind of third world republic, fabulously rich in resources, but corrupt, dangerous, and sorely lacking in well-functioning institutions. Around Tulsa, in the oil and gas fields, zinc smelters, and lead mines at the edge of the Great Plains, a sprawling American Ruhr arose about the time that Oklahoma became the forty-sixth state in 1907. All the characteristics that North Americans half a century later would associate with new and underdeveloped states in Africa and Latin America were present there then: a reliance on foreign capital, volatile prices of the commodities in the ground or grown above it, a floating rural proletariat, wild land speculation, serious health problems related to industrial pollution, a scarcity of medical services, tremendous extremes of wealth and poverty, bouts of martial law, and death and terror squads of several political persuasions.[1]

Tenant farmers and hill people and their families tramped between mine, smelter, refinery, and farm as the fortunes of some commodity rose and fell according to the vagaries of the world economy. Communities disintegrated only to be reconstituted in the peculiar conditions of the mining camps and then dissolved again as the industrial boom that started in 1914 gave way to bust and finally to the Great Depression.

In the generation between statehood and the crash of 1929, a breed of flinty rural individuals confronted the complex economic and social machinery of the industrial United States. They were conscious of being drawn into "progress" even as progress was pulling away at an accelerating pace. And they knew only too well what was happening, for they were a drifting, mobile people and could see with their own eyes. Even the smallest hamlet had train service and the Tin Lizzy was soon to appear.

In these anarchic, unsettled conditions, people fashioned their own worlds around their families, their church communities, and the mythic exploits of outlaws roaming the Ozark hills. The embroidered tales about bank robbers suited the general attitude of a people who did not believe that the organized system of politics and government was designed for their benefit. Charlie Floyd of Sequoyah County captured the populist imagination, as did lesser figures who were said to have built bonfires out of the foreclosure papers they plundered from the mortgage companies.

At the end of the nineteenth century, strange, populist religions began to find a following in the mining camps and tenant farms of the South and its border. Churches and religious movements had always been a stepping-stone into organized America. The Great Awakening of the 1740s, frontier revivalism, the founding of frontier churches by Baptist farmer-preachers, Methodist circuit riders, and Campbellite pastors—all provided a way for scattered people living on farms, on hillsides, and in gullies to establish ties of belonging beyond their clans and extended families. The churches were, in that sense, a training ground for participatory democracy. But by the end of the nineteenth century, the principal Protestant denominations had abandoned common people in the backcountry. The Indian Territory was still essentially a field for missionaries, and in drought-ravaged parts of Kansas next door people were "begging for the Gospel," according to a Presbyterian preacher there, "because of their poverty and the embarrassed state of the Presbyterian Board of Home Missions."[2]

Into the void stepped Holiness and Pentecostal preachers, setting a spark to a tinder-dry prairie. The flames blazed up in many places undergoing the stresses of changing times: the backcountry of the Appalachians and Ozarks; remote valleys of Arkansas, Kentucky, Virginia, and Tennessee; mining towns in Kansas and Oklahoma; the East Texas oil patch; the poorer districts of Detroit, Cincinnati,

Akron, Chicago, and Los Angeles, where Southern whites and blacks adjusted to the time clocks of the new automobile and auto-parts plants. The awakenings infiltrated the textile towns of the Piedmont and the lumber camps of Georgia and Louisiana. And they spread to migrant tenant farmers in the tent cities of Tulsa and zinc miners in the Oklahoma-Missouri-Kansas district.[3]

At the dead center of the experience offered by these unfamiliar new sects was the Holy Ghost operating mysteriously—secular observers would say magically—through visions, dreams, signs, wonders, insights, and intuition. The sects followed the distinctive teaching that all Christians should seek a mystical religious experience *after* conversion, called Baptism in the Holy Spirit, and that the believer might then receive one or more of the supernatural powers known in the early church, including instantaneous purification from sin, the ability, as God's intermediary, to cast out demons, discern evil spirits, sense the presence of disease in others, heal through the power of prayer, resuscitate the dead, and speak in tongues (glossolalia). They found support for their beliefs in the teachings of the English theologian John Wesley, and in the twelfth chapter of Paul's First Letter to the Corinthians: "Now concerning spiritual *gifts*, brethren, I would not have you ignorant . . ."

Before the century was over, these teachings, which at first appealed mainly to the deprived, inspired a "charismatic renewal" movement among Catholics, Episcopalians, and other hierarchical, mainstream denominations. It spread to millions in the educated classes and the unaffiliated all over the world.

Immediately after 1900, however, the special focus of Pentecostal sects was on speaking in tongues as the "initial evidence" of one's having been baptized by the Holy Ghost. The source for their doctrine was the second chapter of the Acts of the Apostles, which describes how Jesus' disciples gathered on the feast of Pentecost soon after the crucifixion and "suddenly there came a sound from heaven as of a rushing mighty wind, and it filled all the house where they were sitting. And there appeared unto them cloven tongues like as of fire, and it sat upon each of them. And they were filled with the Holy Ghost, and began to speak with other tongues, as the Spirit gave them utterance."[4]

The fiery imagery of Pentecost distinguished it from the cooling, water imagery of the Baptists, and appropriately so. Pentecost was not for those literal and linear-minded who were forever trying to decipher nature, reduce matters to numbers, or write schedules and owners' manuals. The holy rollers, as the early Holiness followers were called, touched on a world that was not usually imagined by the awake mind—a world constantly illuminated and warmed by the glow of miracles. They responded to emotion, personality, charisma, and narrative. And they were ready for excitement, stimulation, even glamour, and were quickly bored.

Holiness and Pentecostal people saw things collectively that would have seemed lunatic if reported by any one individual. Whole congregations observed tongues of fire darting over their heads or pillars of fire leaping all the way to the church roof. They saw healing to confound modern medicine, saw people brought back from the dead. And in the collective sight of the congregation, the world was lit by a kinder light.

Yet the same individuals who spoke in tongues, experienced healing, read the signs in a deer crossing a cornfield, and saw flames shooting down from heaven could jury-rig a truck, fix a motor, and repair a wagon with baling wire. This resourceful pragmatism was perfectly consistent with a wholehearted belief in miracles: both grew out of everyday experience. To unsettled people, life seldom "made sense." It demanded constant improvisation and was never predictable. Everyone lived on the thin edge. A baby went to sleep healthy and died of fever before morning. Locusts descended on a wheat crop and destroyed it in a twinkling. Holy roller religion was for conditions in which no two days were ever the same and there was no one "right" way of doing things.

Outside commentators considered the holy roller tabernacles and brush arbors backward and inward-looking, an understandable oversimplification. Like Jews carrying the Torah into a new land, the faithful in the frontier towns did tote bits and pieces of their old world into their new tabernacles and storefronts—their seemingly arcane interpretations of the Bible, their customs, their music and songs. The communities were insistently separate. Yet there was a powerful tension between that separateness and the strong attraction that people in transition felt toward what is new and modern. They were moving toward a different future, one that they would come to share comfortably with millions of other Americans, but they recognized that surviving the journey would require a concentrated inner focus, a marshaling of internal resources. The paradox of holy roller religion was that it instilled the self-confidence to master the world even as it held it suspect and apart.

.   .   .

THE STATE OF OKLAHOMA was not quite four years old when Cora Tatham gave birth to Oca on June 21, 1911, in a log house on Brushy Mountain, up behind Sallisaw. It was a thinly settled semiwilderness with blackberry and sassafras thickets so dense a mother could lose track of a child if he wandered fifty yards from the house. Its stony soil made for poor farming, and the community was sorely lacking in social amenities. "Just a bunch of old Indians," Cora would say of it ever afterward. There was a post office, a school with eight grades open April until October, a cemetery, and a church shared by Baptists and Methodists, for which there was no regular pastor. The inhabitants lived mainly in one-room log houses. Children learned their alphabets by studying the "wall paper,"[5] the newspapers glued over boards or logs to keep out wind and snow. Some earned a grubstake hacking ties for the railroad. The existence of a local Anti-Horse Thief Association testified to the kind of country it was: the hollows and thick woods of the Cookson Hills to the north were a notorious hideout for outlaws.

Cora's family, the Sumpters, had been on Brushy Mountain for several decades when Oca was born. Cora's mother, Abigail, a McKelwain born in Tennessee, had come over to the Missouri country with her widowed mother after the Civil War. She felt strongly attracted to the handsome, dark-complexioned young man driving one of the wagons, and he to her. His name was Buck Sumpter, and after they were married, he prospected for lead around Joplin, paying farmers a royalty to let him dig his strip pits. Their daughter Cora Bell was born there in 1881. Eventually, Buck moved the family to Hot Springs, Arkansas, in hopes that the mineral waters would cure his rheumatism. But he had no liking for the bright lights of the spa town and worried that city life would ruin the morals of Cora and her four sisters. To protect them from such influences he brought his family to the community called Brushy, on Brushy Mountain in the Cherokee Nation.

There may have been a second reason for coming to such a God-forsaken place. Buck Sumpter's mother was a full-blood Cherokee whose own mother, it was said, had perished on the Trail of Tears. In Missouri, "half-breed" was still a term of opproprium, and Buck's father had made the boy promise always to live as a white man—to "pass" if he could. It was a burden of sorts, but in the remoteness of Brushy, where most of the residents were of Cherokee blood, he could just be himself.

Whatever attractions the boy on the wagon had had for Abigail, she was as different as could be from her taciturn husband. She was a spirited, jut-jawed woman who enjoyed company and lively talk, and followed politics and the shenanigans on Wall Street in the Kansas City *Star*. If the *Star* wasn't available, she made do with the Tulsa *World*. Her other fondness was for the corncob pipe she'd smoked since a doctor prescribed inhaling herbs to improve childhood asthma. Only after she lost her teeth did she switch from the pipe to Peachy Plug chewing tobacco.

Buck died at the age of forty-nine in 1899, at a time of upheaval in the Indian Territory. The Curtis Act, passed by Congress a year earlier, had set a deadline of 1906 for the end of tribal government. Proof of one's Indian bloodline was about to become a requirement for property ownership throughout the Cherokee Nation. Under an agreement with the federal government that the tribal elders reluctantly signed in 1900, all the tribal lands were to be divided up among those citizens of the Nation who could claim a Cherokee blood connection. The test was not onerous. A single ancestor six generations back sufficed, so Buck could easily have qualified. But Buck, remembering his promise to his father, did not try to establish his bloodline.

His only son, John Sumpter, was too resourceful a man to let the opportunity for free land pass, however. John had only six grades of schooling, but he could draw up a plan for a building, gauge the values of things, and make friends. When other farmers ran out of corn, John Sumpter would always have a turn left for his animals. Whether out of love or shrewdness or a combination of the two, in 1897 John was wed under Cherokee law to Caldonia Brackett, whose parents lived close by at Brushy. The slenderness of her Cherokee ties evidently did raise some initial objections when it came to admitting her to the rolls to qualify for the free land. Once the issue was settled in her favor in 1902, John selected a modest acreage for his wife and children on Drake's Prairie, named for Seymour Drake, a Yale-educated Yankee trader who after the Civil War used his connections with certain leading Cherokees to establish a trading post on the Fort Smith–Fort Gibson stagecoach line. In his heyday Drake ran hundreds of cattle over the prairie grasslands above the Arkansas River.

Drake's Prairie made for better farming than Brushy. John's father-in-law, Benjamin Brackett, took some land adjacent to that which John Sumpter had selected, as did many others from Brushy. Just before statehood John shrewdly (though to no avail, it would turn out) signed a lease with an oil and gas company for test wells on his daughter's allotment property.

John's choice of the allotment land was the occurrence that brought the Tatham and Sumpter families together, for it was about the time that John was completing the arrangements, probably in the spring of 1902, that Walter Tatham arrived from Missouri with his father, "Bud," his brothers, Willy and Arch, and his sister, Pearl.

THE TATHAM STORY up to that point had been a kind of Everyman's diary of America. Walter's ancestors were pioneer farmers who had followed the main path of westward migration out of Virginia, through the Cumberland Pass into Kentucky and thence into the upper Mississippi Valley. They were good, honest people who had lived for several generations in and around the same community on the northern side of the Missouri River in Carroll County, Missouri.

The Tatham story was that of thousands of other pioneer farmers: it was remarkable overall, yet long stretches of it were the ordinary stuff of plantings, harvests, weddings, deaths, and births. For generations it would be a matter of pride to Tathams that Walter's grandfather, Thomas Tatham, had soldiered with the Union Army in the Civil War. Yet Thomas's service was unheroic. He never saw combat, for he was discharged after a few months with a serious case of malaria contracted at a camp in Chillicothe.

One had to go back to Virginia in the closing decades of the eighteenth century to find a direct Tatham ancestor of true storybook dimensions. He was John Thomas Tatham, a real Indian fighter and pioneer in the most dangerous English frontier of the time, the slender, picturesque Valley of Virginia. Life in the wild valley between the Blue Ridge and the Appalachians required courage. Settlers lived in fear of Indian raids and were far away in both distance and culture from the English communities along the Chesapeake Bay. Some scholars have suggested that a uniquely American outlook first developed in the Valley of Virginia.

When John Tatham arrived there sometime in the 1760s, it was accessible only by a few rivers and by the wagon road that ran down from Philadelphia through the German country of western Pennsylvania. John was an Englishman who probably came by river from the Chesapeake Bay settlements, where Tathams descended from a family of seafarers had been residing since early in the seventeenth

century. Evidently he divided his time between fighting Indians and
keeping up his wife's farm, located on a branch of the Catawba Creek
near present-day Fincastle, right alongside the Philadelphia wagon
road. He received a land warrant for his service as a sergeant in the
French and Indian Wars of 1755–1762 and may have been among
the Virginians who staved off an attack by Chief Cornstalk's Shawnee
warriors in the woods on the Ohio River at Point Pleasant on October
9, 1774. Late in his life, he was drawn into the new round of frontier
warfare set off by the resistance of the Indian tribes to American
expansion along the Ohio River.[6]

The backcountry settlers were a rough lot of Scots, Scotch-Irish,
and Germans, with only a smattering of English, and the valley's
distance from the British commercial centers on the Chesapeake Bay
made it a breeding ground of American patriotism. John Tatham, the
Englishman, displayed his American loyalties by keeping a wounded
Continental soldier for ten months during the Revolution.

Isaac Tatham, born about 1800, appears to have been John's son
by a late second marriage to the widow Mary Adkins. Whatever
happened to John—presumably he died in Virginia shortly after
Isaac's birth—it appears that his second wife made her way west with
Isaac in the company of her Adkins in-laws, stopping for nearly a
generation along the Green River in southern Kentucky. Sometime
in 1823, probably after the corn was harvested and the roads were
frozen hard enough for travel, a party of Adkins and Tathams moved
west to make yet another new start, this time in Missouri. They
stopped in Boone County, a bustling new settlement on the north
side of the Missouri River, and Isaac and his family remained there
for at least two years before moving on to less settled country upstream. He chose a place on the north side of the river, near Wakanda
Creek, beneath the bluffs marking the edge of the prairie.

On February 4, 1833, Isaac Tatham and at least one of his Adkins
kin were present when local citizens met at the Carey house on Wakanda Creek to establish a government for the new county of Carroll.
The county clerk was ordered to issue six blank licenses for ferries,
six for vendors of merchandise, six for retailers of "spirituous li-
quors," and three for peddlers of clocks and other wares. When the
meeting resumed the next day, Isaac was offered the post of county
assessor but declined. His half brother William Adkins was picked
for the county's first grand jury, and another half brother, Roland
Adkins, was selected for the second.[7]

And there he and his descendants remained for three generations.

Tathams appear to have been been typical Carroll County folk— friendly, easygoing, and moderate in matters of politics and religion. A recurring aspect of the Tatham character was a knack for latching onto people of greater initiative and enterprise. As Tathams and Adkins moved west, it plainly was the Adkins who led the way, finding land in Kentucky and probably reconnoitering in Missouri as well. But that political acumen may have only partially compensated for what some in-laws suggest was another Tatham quality, a certain passivity and willingness to accommodate to circumstances. As the years passed, Tathams began to describe themselves to the census taker not as farmers but as "tenant farmers" and "farm laborers" and their livelihood as "working out." When the population grew and they found the good land occupied, some drifted away to become chicken pluckers at a processing plant in Atchison, Kansas.

WALTER WAS JUST twenty-one when he moved to the Indian Territory in 1902. There was not much to hold him in Missouri. His mother, Nannie Tatham, had burned to death in 1898 when the hem of her dress caught fire. Not too long after that, Walter had had the run-in with local bullies that proved decisive for his future. Country bullies were no laughing matter. Away from the watchful eye of town policemen, they could terrorize farm communities. According to the story that was handed down, Walter and his brother Willy encountered them when they were all on horseback one day. In the fracas, Walter stabbed one of the bullies with a barlow knife. The boys duly reported the incident to their Uncle George Tatham, a local justice of the peace. "Leave the county now and just keep ridin'," George advised. "Go to Oklahoma and that's the end of it." Walter did what he was told, and not long afterward he came back for the rest of the family and took them down to the Indian Territory.

It might have been a foreign country. In Carroll County, the Tathams had been on the westernmost edge of eastern farming, in the rich, deep soil of Missouri's corn and hog country. People could see their neighbors' places and have a sense of connection to a broader world through the chilled-steel plows and farm equipment coming from John Deere, and from the river and rail traffic that carried goods east and south. Tathams were not at all like the tumbleweed people of the Cotton Belt, the Scotch Irish and the hangers-on who were never more than loosely attached to the land. Tathams, like the Germans with whom they coexisted in central Missouri, stayed put generation after generation. But when the family took the train south into the Indian Territory, they crossed an invisible boundary and entered an unorganized land of cotton, fundamentalist religion, and unsettled people.

The Tathams came first to a place called Harrisontown, on the edge of Drake's Prairie. It was named for John Harrison, who himself had come there from Carroll County's Wakanda community and who may have been the connection for Walter. Like Wakanda, Harrison was a farming community on the north side of a major river.

By then, the communities around Sallisaw had been filling up for several decades with a drifting population of poorer whites, displaced farmers, and others with no set destination—people who were "goin' " but with no clear idea of where.

One Sequoyah County settler, James Diffee, lost his father to bushwhackers in Tennessee near the end of the Civil War. He crossed the Mississippi with his mother, settled in the Arkansas hills, and later drove his cattle to Sallisaw.

Frank and Martha Roark came down from Walnut Grove, Missouri, in 1898. They had their four children and all their possessions in a covered wagon. An Indian policeman evicted them from their squatters' camp inside the Cherokee Nation. Frank cleared out in a hurry and went on to Sequoyah County, where he was left in peace.

The widow Priscilla Ramey left for the Indian Territory from Murfreesboro, Tennessee, in the late 1880s "in search of land and a better life." She came to Sequoyah County.

Berry Norman and Susan Creed drove their wagon from Virginia, to South Carolina, to Texas, and finally came to the Arkansas River bottom before 1900.

Jacob and Sallie Dyer left Georgia because the soil was too "acid" and they had lost their slaves. They got a foothold in the Price Chapel community on Brushy Mountain by working for a Cherokee.[8]

The frontier to which these pioneers came was like no other. Whites had limited rights and a second-class status in the Indian Territory. The dry, open, western half of the future state had been brought under United States control through a series of land runs and lotteries that parceled it out to white settlers after 1889. But the eastern half of the territory presented legal and political problems for those riding the statehood bandwagon. Sovereign domain was vested in the Five Civilized Tribes, the Cherokees, Chickasaws, Choctaws, Creeks, and Seminoles, who had been forcibly removed from their homelands east of the Appalachians before the Civil War. As railroads were built in the Territory, whites had drifted in to squat on land or work for Indian landlords. Eventually, the poorer white settlers far outnumbered tribal members, but could not legally obtain title to land.

The solution for Walter was to latch onto somebody better connected, and that somebody was John Sumpter. John needed help farming his new allotment properties on Drake's Prairie and he took a liking to the pleasant young Missourian who laughed and joked and told stories, yet still put in a good day's work. "I've got the finest-looking man you've ever seen working for me," he told his sister Cora. When she met Walter at a pie supper at the schoolhouse on Drake's Prairie, she agreed.

They were cut from different cloth. Cora had a sharper edge. With her piercing eyes and jutting chin, she resembled her mother Abigail. And she had piercing, uncompromising frontier values to go along with her features, no doubt a result of her strict moral upbringing in the extreme isolation of Brushy and the early responsibilities thrust on her by her father's untimely death. But opposites attracted. They were married in 1903.

That same year, tragedy struck John Sumpter. He lost both his wife and an infant son. When he remarried in 1907, he again chose a Cherokee-blooded bride, Frances Clapp. He called her "Frank" and built her a fine frame home on her allotment land on Brushy Mountain, with a round front porch ornamented with fancy gingerbread molding. He put up a barn, cleared enough land to grow a few acres of cotton, planted apple, plum, and pear orchards, and sold the fruit to local dealers. He also found time to look after the land on Drake's Prairie and help W. D. Mayo run his all-around food and merchandise store in Sallisaw. Walter and Cora came up to live in the log house behind his home and sharecrop his land. Cora kept up an okra garden, and John's apple orchards always produced a heavy crop, which he stored away in a cool cellar with a sweet, pleasant smell. In the living room was real leather furniture.

Exactly how Walter supported his family in the ensuing years is not entirely clear. He was working in the wheat harvest around Norman, in western Oklahoma, when their second child, Norma, was born there in 1906. (A first child, Roy, had died soon after birth in 1904.) The Sumpters and the Tathams were people who took care of their own. Cora seems to have been a natural-born nurse and caretaker for younger members of the family. Arch and Pearl were only fifteen and eleven when she married Walter. Cora cared for them as if they were her own. It was said she cut up her wedding dress to make school clothes for Pearl.

The sharing of home and hearth by several generations was

plainly evident in the Tatham and Sumpter living arrangements in 1910. Abigail Sumpter was living with Walter and Cora in the log house behind John and Frank Sumpter's place, while Walter's dad was living with Pearl and her new husband close to Drake's Prairie. Next door to them was his son Arch Tatham, with his wife and baby daughter.

John Sumpter was clearly the center of the Tatham and Sumpter clans then living in and around the Sallisaw area. In 1911, Arch and his new family moved up from Drake's Prairie to Brushy Mountain, closer to John.

The baby Oca arrived in 1911. He had none of his sister Norma's dark, Indian looks. Physically he resembled his mother more than his dad. Possibly Cora named him Josiah, which might explain why he was soon being called by the easier nickname "Oca."

Five years later Cleo Abigaile Tatham was born on Brushy. Cora was only a few months' pregnant with her, and this time John Sumpter sent for a doctor. The premature infant was given little hope, but in those frontier conditions, one did everything possible to save a baby. Cora directed that the child be placed on the kitchen table where it could be warmed by the stove and cleaned; helping hands dipped cotton balls in olive oil and gently dabbed the baby's frail body. Then Cora told them to wrap the tiny infant in flannel up to her chin and brought her to her mother. Cleo could not nurse, but Cora squeezed milk from her nipples into the baby's mouth. Then the tiny thing was gently lifted into her brother's white, woolen stocking cap to keep warm. After a week, the baby began to nurse. In a few months it was nearly as well developed as a full-term baby.

It was, Cora was certain, the kind of miracle promised by her burning religious faith, for by then her life revolved around prayer, healing, and church. It had not always been so. The Sumpters were not overly religious. Abigail was a pipe-smoking Free Will Baptist; John Sumpter, a whiskey drinker most of his life, did not get right with the Lord until a few years before he died. Cora was Church of Christ, but only because an uncle was a Church of Christ pastor.

For Cora the change came one hot summer evening on Brushy Mountain. There was a holy roller meeting at the little country Methodist Church, and Cora and Walter decided to go along with friends to poke fun at "the show." As they neared the church, they heard singing. Cora's daughter Ophelia remembers her mother relating how they had looked in the windows and how "Mama said, 'I'm going in.' . . . So the women went in and sit down and the men were to the window of the church. Mama, she got in there and heard this preacher. He was full of the power of God and he preached a sermon to make your hair raise on your head. Made you examine yourself to see if you were really, truly, born again, and she sat there and all she had ever known when she grew up on Brushy was the preacher coming through on a horse and preaching some Sundays."

This preacher was different. He had the Holy Ghost and spoke in tongues. Banjo lamps with long stems and round globes full of kerosene cast a dim, yellow glow over the interior of the church. Some danced up to the altar, or shuffled up and knelt in groups, men with their arms around each other's shoulders, women falling, "slain in the spirit." Kneeling there on the hardwood floor, they made a strange, collective moan, while the pastor pleaded with them to "Pray through," or "Let go."

Ophelia said, "All those people watching that came with her and all them making fun and everything, Mama was standing there, hanging onto that bench, dying to go down. She felt the Holy Spirit drawing her down to that altar to repent of her sins, and so when all the rest of them laughed, she knew that's what she needed. She needed forgiveness for her sins, and so the next night she went back to do it again."

After that, Cora would kneel and pray at home every night, often in tongues. She would be conscious of making sounds, but had no sensation of controlling her speech. In letting go, out came a childlike babble, sometimes followed by wailing sobs. Hearing this, it was difficult not to feel the presence of the supernatural.

Nowhere was the message more warmly received than on Drake's Prairie. An itinerant evangelist by the name of John Himer had arrived there (some say he floated down the Arkansas River on a raft) about 1909; he put up a tent and began holding meetings. Himer said he was a Nazarene, one of the sects formed after the Methodist Church had expelled troublesome "Holiness" factions from its ranks in 1894. The Nazarenes considered themselves true disciples of John Wesley, the founder of Methodism. They believed in "heart purity and perfect love" and in a second, dramatic religious experience after conversion that eradicated the sins of the sinner: the "second definite work of Grace." At first the Nazarenes accepted the distinguishing characteristic of Pentecostalism, that speaking in tongues provided the initial evidence of the purifying second experience, which they also called the baptism by the Holy Ghost. But by the time Brother Himer had arrived on Drake's Prairie, the Nazarenes had rejected tongue speaking, as had many other Holiness sects, fearing the emphasis on it left too much of an opening for chicanery and "cheap Grace."

Himer grafted several of these doctrines together and preached the "triple cure," in which conversion was to be followed by the shattering second experience that purged sin and a sinful nature and then by the baptism of the Holy Ghost, as evidenced by speaking in tongues. Himer's revival caused a sensation. Skeptics spread the word that Himer was a hypnotist. But as local farmers came and saw their friends and neighbors fall under the power, the doubters dwindled. By some accounts, the Nazarene elders sent another evangelist to undo the apostasy of the "tongue speaker," but when he arrived on the prairie, he, too, was won over.

In 1918, a plain clapboard church was built near the schoolhouse in Watts on Drake's Prairie. It was Free Holiness, a sect that espoused an amalgam of Pentecostal and Holiness doctrine. Not everyone on the prairie went to it. John Sumpter, for one, was never swayed. Some Sunday evenings there were more people and pranksters outside than in, gawking at the girls and cutting the bridles of worshipers' horses. But the church exerted an almost gravitational pull, and there were nights when some sinner would suddenly find himself hurtling across the threshold as if pulled by a magnet, his life changing forever, helpless to resist, and seemingly no longer in control of his or her actions.

Arch Tatham and Winnie Eskew married the same year as Brother Himer's revival, and it was soon clear that Winnie, then twenty-five, and four years older than her husband, would be one of the strongest converts. She refused any medical care and would not allow her children to receive any, either. All her life she suffered eye and back problems. Eventually, curvature of the spine gave her a hunched look, but she accepted that as God's will.

People said of Drake's Prairie that it was the "prayin'-est place in all Oklahoma." The religious people there felt caught up in a vivid, day-to-day drama in which the Devil battled the forces of the Lord. The sky seemed to hover a notch or two lower than in other places. A deer crossing a field at dusk was "a sign." A hawk cruising high above the forest might be "a warning" in which to read the hand of Providence. "And I will show wonders in heaven above, and signs in the earth beneath. . . ."

Say a person promised to give up smoking, and the Devil got to work on him. One man was down at Nigger Creek drawing water when the Devil hopped up on a log and told him he wasn't *about* to give up his habit. A mighty struggle ensued. The man tied himself to a tree with a long rope and ran as fast as he could until the line ran out and hurled him to the ground. The third time he did it the Devil went away.

The sect on the prairie was strengthened and empowered by denial. There was a kind of rabbinical quality to its culture. A good Christian, like a good Orthodox Jew, was defined through adherence to prohibitions requiring tremendous commitment and character. Though they remained part of the broader community around Sallisaw as farmers, craftsman, or laborers, they were set apart by their dress and conduct. A Holiness woman did not cut her hair because the Bible said a woman's hair was her glory. Some Holiness women accepted the doctrine that there should be no sex except for procreation; others sought to simplify the way they lived, making their own dresses from simple cloth, while the men shunned adornments such as neckties.

Baptism by the Holy Spirit was not only a spiritual event but also a rite of passage through which younger people entered the tightly knit fellowship of the churchgoing circle on Drake's Prairie. The church bound together families and linked generations through an almost daily round of meetings that were alive with the anticipation of unexpected conversions, healings, tongue speakings, and admonishments by the preacher of some brother or sister who had strayed from the strict code.

The Holy Spirit changed lives. Holiness people spoke of "burying that ol' Devil for good." Cleo one day would put it another way. To be filled with the Holy Spirit, she said, was to be "like a car with a new battery."

THE TATHAMS might have gone on farming, subsisting, reproducing, and worshiping around Sallisaw forever if World War I had not come along to change their lives. The war caused a boom in the oil and gas refineries, the factories, and the lead and zinc mines north and east of Tulsa. On Brushy, almost everyone felt the call.

Sallisaw, unlike the boomtowns, was a thriving little example of stable metropolitan America. Main Street had a row of three-story red-brick buildings facing the Missouri-Pacific Railroad tracks. It had electric lights, three drugstores, a steam laundry, a movie house, a photo studio, three barbershops, an ice plant, a job printing plant, eight general stores, four hotels, a bottling factory, two lumberyards, a brick high school, three hardware stores, three restaurants, and two railroad stations. Sallisaw, the Chamber of Commerce modestly noted in a 1919 pamphlet, was "a city splendidly governed by competent officials," a "good place to rear and educate a family," and was inhabited by "3,200 of the best people on earth." But rural places such as Brushy and Drake's Prairie lived at that time apart from the town, except for the Saturdays when people caught rides in. In the sticks, there was seldom a veterinarian, a doctor, or even a hardware store. The preachers, tinkers, and drummers passed through but did not stop for long. Cars began to make an appearance—kerosene lamps were hung on the front for night driving—but there was no electricity, no indoor plumbing, and no tractors. The prairie wouldn't get a party line telephone until the 1920s. People shopped at Butler's store, which met the test of being up-to-date: it had a gas pump to service the occasional automobile.

The oil and gas fields were part of a surging new America, a kind of industrial frontier which drew renters off the farms by the tens of thousands. Life there was unlike that in Brushy or Sallisaw. The gas fields and mining towns were more like gold rush camps than communities. They had electricity, uniformed policemen, and doctors. But life had a raw quality. There were no building codes, not much indoor plumbing, and frequent epidemics. And churches were outnumbered by saloons and brothels. A large group of Tathams and Sumpters went to work in the oil fields and lived at first in a tent city on the bank of the Arkansas River west of Tulsa. The frenzy touched off by Glenn Pool, a great oil strike in 1905, had scarcely abated. Walter laid pipe for the Oklahoma Natural Gas Company and was able to hammer together some boards for a house of his own in an empty lot on the outskirts of Tulsa. Cora took in boarders from the gas fields. It must have been a good enough dwelling, for the children remember a piano. But houses in those days were improvised shelter more than valuable assets. Walter eventually took an old oil-field wagon and a team of horses as payment on the house.

The pipelaying work ended shortly before the Armistice, and then Walter and Arch landed jobs at the Bartlesville Zinc smelter in Collinsville, a case study of Oklahoma's boom and bust cycle. The smelter began operation in 1911 under the ownership of the interests controlled by the Guggenheims, the wealthy German-Jewish industrialists. Four years later it was reputed to be the largest zinc smelter in the world[9] and well positioned to exploit the wartime arms industry, since zinc, a component in brass alloys, is used in making artillery cartridges. Collinsville's population soared from 1,300 in 1911 to 8,000 in 1917. "So liberal are wages received and the pay days so regular that the people of this city never suffer hard times or 'tight money,' " wrote the *Daily Oklahoman* about Collinsville on September 23, 1917.

Thirty-four days later most of the smelting blocks closed temporarily due to an unexpected shortage of the natural gas to run the smelter. From then on production was intermittently interrupted. In 1921, the smelter shut down forever. Walter, who arrived soon after the difficulties began, bought a modest house with his savings from the gas fields. It had an outdoor toilet, but running water indoors and Cora's first modern appliance: a gas stove. The crowded conditions were generally unhealthy. Oca and Norma contracted typhoid, and the whole family had a light case of smallpox. But a job was a job, and the Tathams stayed almost four years. The children went to school on Smelter Hill, and in 1920 Cora had a new baby boy, Vernon.

In 1921, when the gas shortages forced a permanent shutdown, Walter found a buyer for his house and moved the family to Miami, Oklahoma, where he found a job in a lead mine. But when Cora came back on the train to get their money out of escrow, she found the bank padlocked. It was bankrupt, and they had lost their savings.

The S.S.&G. mine in Miami, where Walter got his job, held a particular dread for the whole family. On the morning of December 13, 1919, Walter's brother Willy had been working several hundred feet underground when he heard the telltale cracking and snapping of wooden props. "Run, boys," he shouted. The other men made it to the opening of the shaft, but the cave-in crushed Willy's right leg. They freed him and hauled him to the surface in the bucket, where an ambulance from the Todd Undertaking Company took him to Picher Hospital. Doctors amputated his right leg at the knee. Family legend had it that Willy instructed the doctors not to cut the boot, for it was new. He was outfitted with a wooden leg and given a job in the S.S.&G. office. That was workmen's compensation, 1919-style.

Walter and Cora did what they could to help Willy when they came to Miami in 1921. Willy's first wife, with whom he had had four children, was in a mental institution. His second wife died in 1923, leaving him to care for their son as well. Cora served as mother to several of these many children, and there was a steady traffic on the streetcar between the two households.

The mining towns were ugly, dangerous, and unsanitary. Horse-drawn ore cars raced from mine to rail depot and sometimes got mired in the mud of the unpaved streets. Pyramids of chat—gravel and dirt from the digging—rose next to the tall, weathered super-structures that enclosed the mine shafts and buildings where the extracted ore was cleaned. Malarial mosquitos bred in the stagnant pools of brackish mine water, which covered acres of what had once been a gently undulating, treeless prairie.

In 1910, the *Engineering and Mining Journal* had described the mines in the Joplin, Missouri, area as "highly dangerous and unsani-tary," adding, "We should not be surprised if mining in the Joplin district were really as dangerous as work in an arsenic factory."[10] The risks of roof cave-ins, hydrogen-sulfide gas that caused temporary blindness, careless use of explosives, and silicosis were ever-present. Mine health and safety improved somewhat after 1915, but silicosis, malaria, and injury still took their toll. In 1919, fifty miners died and 15,000 were hurt in mine accidents in Ottawa County alone.[11]

The Tri-State District was going through a classic colonial experi-ence. Outsiders provided the capital, and the environs supplied a cheap, docile labor supply. The robber barons Jay Gould and John D. Rockefeller visited Joplin with an eye to investing, and Gould wondered "how a district so rich in natural resources, and of so considerable development, had so long escaped his notice and that of his lieutenants." Rockefeller looked over the ground to see if it would fit into his scheme to control prices of lead ore and by-products. Neither invested. Instead, it was British, Swedish, and lesser-known East Coast mining syndicates that ultimately came in.[12]

Dangerous as the mines were, they paid well. Walter took out his first interest in an automobile, a Buick. They were moving up in the world. But at a price. Cora lived in fear that her husband would have a fatal or disabling accident of the kind that had crippled Willy. Cleo never forgot listening to the sound of ambulances racing to the mines and wondering if they were for her dad. When someone had been killed or hurt, the family would hear about it at supper from Walter, and the meal of beans and corn bread would be a somber one. Some days Walter started out for the mine but quickly returned: he had seen a black cat or some other omen. Cora did not fault him.

The death of Walter's father, Bud, in 1924 gave Walter the excuse he needed to leave the mine. He and the family accompanied the coffin back to Carroll County, Missouri, for burial. It was spring, and the Missouri River was in an ugly mood when they crossed on a flatbed skiff. Relatives met them on the Wakanda side. The horse-drawn wagon pulling the coffin got mired in mud up to its axles and had to be pulled out. Finally, they made it to the Methodist Church that Nannie and Bud had attended in the old days. It was shuttered by then, many of its parishioners having moved or died. But it had been Bud's wish that the service be held there and that he be buried in Adkins Cemetery, next to his wife. It was cold inside. Pigeons roosted in the eaves, leaving their droppings on the pews below. And Cleo, then eight years old, wept to think that her granddaddy was going off to heaven from a place like that.

Walter stayed in Missouri for a year, working on an apple and wheat farm in Lexington. After a season he moved the family again, this time to Carterville, Missouri, to gouge lead from abandoned mines.

John Sumpter died unexpectedly in 1926. His death was a great blow to Cora, and when the Tathams went back to Sallisaw for the funeral, they decided to stay on for a while after. Arch was already renting on Drake's Prairie, and Walter found ten or so acres to rent on the Gober Place.

His timing was poor, as was so often the case. Cotton farmers had enjoyed a boom in the war decade, but then England reopened its trade with traditional suppliers such as India and prices fell below fifteen cents a hundred weight. By 1926, the situation had somewhat improved, but hard times revealed truths about growing cotton in marginal conditions that the farmers had not recognized before. Drake's Prairie lay near the northern limits of the cotton-growing belt. There were barely two hundred days between the last and first frosts of winter, the absolute minimum for growing cotton. The boll weevil had arrived during the war decade, and there were problems with bitterweed in wet years.

Time passed and the better land close to the Arkansas River was acquired by more affluent farmers, including several who were not Indian, while the less fertile land sloping away from the river stayed with the original allotment holders. As cotton prices tumbled, mortgage companies in Sallisaw and Fort Smith, Arkansas, began to own more and more of that land as well.

The fortunes of old Seymour Drake were a barometer of the changes. After statehood, the onetime overlord of the prairie was left with only a narrow, 240-acre strip of bottomland along the Arkansas River, which was allotted to his part-Indian children. He retired to Sallisaw, but in 1919, at eighty, he moved back to a farmhouse on

Drake's Prairie to try a comeback. Within two years, cotton prices had broken, and in 1925 Drake gave up. A mortgage company foreclosed on his farm holdings and he moved back to Sallisaw, where he died in 1928.

Farmers on the prairie preferred to rent rather than sharecrop, which meant that they furnished their own mules, horses, seeds, and equipment, and gave the landlord a quarter of their cotton and a third of their grain. Like most Drake's Prairie renters, Arch Tatham usually went to work in the oil fields or at the wheat harvest in July or August. Sometimes he went off to shuck corn. If the money was good, he might stay over and leave Winnie and the children to take in the cotton crop. In winter, Arch and his oldest sons dug coal out of a damp slope mine near the river and sold it in town. His son Ira would go in on his hands and knees because he was still small enough and plant a charge of black powder in the seam. They sank air holes and set off the charges. When the smoke cleared Arch and the boys shoveled the coal into the car, paid a royalty to the farmer on whose land they were mining, put the coal on their wagon, and took it to Vian to sell.

It was nothing new for people to tramp off somewhere to get money: the new thing was how far they were going. At first you could hardly notice. After cotton was in on Drake's Prairie, some fellow would pack his wife and kids in a truck and go off to pull bolls in western Oklahoma. When he came back he'd have a few dollars for tires or shoes, maybe even some for bananas and oranges from town. Farther west, the weevils weren't as bad and the harvest came later because there was less rain. Then a few people began going farther, to Arizona and even California. Cotton was on the move, and it was pulling them. People felt it across the whole Cotton Belt.

Walter stayed on Drake's Prairie two seasons. In 1927 he took out seventy-five dollars' worth of credit for seed and other necessities, but when he harvested his crop that fall, he couldn't pay up, and he headed back to the industrial district to earn money to pay off the debt. There was no job for him at S.S.&G., so he hired on with another mining outfit and the family found a place to live in Commerce. But one day he came home early. He looked pale and scared. He sat down at the dining-room table and was quiet for a few minutes.

"I've had a warning," Walter said.

Just what the "warning" was he never did reveal, but it frightened Cora.

"It's a sign," she said. "Don't you go to that mine today."

Walter did not go back to the mine that day or ever. He was only forty-six years old, but something had given out in him. He never again held a steady job for long. For a while they lived in Tulsa, where Oca worked at an open-air fruit stand and Walter rode the back of a garbage truck hauling scraps from the hotels to local pig farmers. Cleo remembers her dad bringing home "finds" from the garbage truck—hotel silverware that had been thrown out along with the steak bones and potato skins.

Then, in 1928, Walter purchased some secondhand furniture and rented a "tax title" house back in Collinsville, a town that had had more than a whiff of the coming Depression after the closing of the BZ smelter. The local government was holding dozens of houses for nonpayment of taxes and was leasing them for a few dollars a month. Walter arranged to have a man with a truck drive him and their things to the tax title house, but on the way, while Walter was lying under the truck changing a tire, a car hit the vehicle, knocking it off the jack and raking it across his face.

Cora got the news from a relative. Frightened as she was, she made the children put on their best clothes to go to the hospital. Ophelia never forgot the "hole" in her dad's nose and how disappointed he was that there was no money for a plastic surgeon.

Oca went to the accident site and collected what was left of their belongings. Knives and forks and spoons were scattered, and clothes were blowing away in the fields or were ruined on the highway. He retrieved what he could.

Walter went to recuperate at his brother Willy's so as not to be an added burden for Cora, and she and the children moved into the tax title house.

The December after the accident, Oca brought in a small Christmas tree, and they decorated it with strings of popcorn and homemade decorations made from tinfoil. Oca scrounged some cast-off toys from the Salvation Army and came tramping onto the porch pretending to be Santa Claus, while they made Ophelia hide her eyes. When Oca stamped off he'd left a pile of toys under the tree.

AS SO OFTEN HAPPENED when things turned bad, it fell to the wife to hold things together. The Tathams' oldest child, Norma, had married and left home at seventeen, and Oca could fend for himself, but there were still three young Tatham children at home, and Cora was looking after one of Willy's. It was common enough. In hard times, a woman had more options than a man. She could mend or launder clothes, take in boarders, tutor schoolchildren. She had ready, useful tools: a sewing machine, a washer, a stove on which to cook food for boarders. Cora made clothes from patterns she saw in magazines. She kept a garden and nursed a sick sister. When the family moved to Claremore in 1931, she took in laundry from the Oklahoma Military Academy. Cora and Cleo blued the shirts, starched the uniforms, and dried them on a line. Cora invested in an electric washer with a ringer and two washtubs. The collars and cuffs had to be very stiff. Cleo ironed the jackets and pants, and Cora made sure the cuffs and collars were extra stiff.

She had the equipment and the skills. But in addition to that, Cora was a naturally progressive woman. As a woman who did so much of the hard work, she appreciated the modern conveniences. She was also a Sumpter. Her brother John had never been one to look back at the old times and the old ways. That showed in his work as a cattle inspector in charge of enforcing the new laws requiring the dipping of cattle against hoof-and-mouth disease. To backcountry people, the dipping pits represented the suspect magic of science and the hated authority of government. Independent-minded cattlemen hated the dips and threatened to dynamite them, but John posted a relative with a shotgun at the pits and prevented trouble.

John Sumpter defended the new order. Walter Tatham, on the other hand, was buffaloed by it much of the time. He didn't drive a car and was uncomfortable in the new world of bosses and laborers that he found in the industrial district. He liked his freedom and feared the responsibility of being a boss. Being a boss meant accounting for pay, accounting for hours, and being accountable to bigger bosses.

He was generous with what he had. Back in Collinsville, Walter gave food from Cora's table to the hungry children who came begging at the door—or bought them shoes when he had money. But within the Sumpter family, it was observed by one of Cora's Sumpter nephews that "Cora corralled them and pulled things together." Her deepening religious convictions, which Walter did not share, were perfectly consistent with her belief in personal betterment and her approval of the newfangled modern comforts available in the industrial towns, but not yet on the prairie. Religion was not for the backward, but for the imaginative and curious individual, who looked for something beyond the predictable litany of stories and customs arising out of a closed circle of kin and community. Church afforded a connection to a bigger world, a link to broader associations beyond oneself and to new ideas and possibilities.

Time and again, religion entered families through the women, and the Tathams were no exception. Arch Tatham's mother-in-law, Ida Eskew, had been one of the first to get the Holy Spirit on Drake's Prairie. (Her husband, Roland, was "anything but" religious, according to one of his daughters. He did not approve of holy rollers, and there were angry scenes when Mother Eskew gathered up her brood to go to the Watts Church. But Roland Eskew was not averse to being prayed over whenever he took sick.) The Free Holiness church eventually was known as the "seven sisters" church for the seven Eskew daughters who attended it. Four of the seven spoke in tongues. One, Nettie Brashears, shared the pastorship for many years.

Arch's initial reluctance to follow his wife, Winnie, on religious matters put a strain on them. It aggravated him that when the children were ill with whooping cough she would take them to church instead of to a doctor. Not that he fought her on it. He would hitch up the buggy and drive the sick children off to meeting, but sometimes he couldn't restrain himself: "Well now, if you can heal these kids, pray the Lord that He'll tighten those ol' buggy tires out there," Arch would say loud enough for people to hear.

Winnie prayed about her man's religious recalcitrance. Sometimes she would slip off to a place near the creek, and Arch would wonder what she was up to. Once he sneaked up and listened.

"Lord," he heard her cry, "You'll have to do something with Arch, 'cause I can't stand it any longer . . . either save him or do somethin'."

He was afraid when he heard that. What if the Lord *did* do something—the way he seemed to do whenever Winnie prayed for a sick child? Back at the house, he spoke up.

"Now, Winnie, I heard you a-prayin' and I heard you tell God either save me or kill me."

"Well, I can't stand any more—but I didn't quite say that."

"Well, if you promise not to ever pray for Him to save me or kill me, I'll go to church with ya." Arch kept his promise to his young wife. And not long after that he, too, got the Holy Ghost, receiving the baptism of the Holy Ghost.

Men were losing their power and authority, so women picked up the leading role in Oklahoma families—and often as not in Pentecostal pulpits, though that would change in a few decades.

At the same time as Himer's revival meetings on Drake's Prairie, stories of miraculous healings and other "works of the Holy Spirit" were circulating widely in Oklahoma.[13] A boy was bitten by a water moccasin but was reported saved through prayer. Bootleggers in Tillman County in 1909 were said to have destroyed their stills, and rustlers returned cattle, pigs, and chickens to their rightful owners after coming under the power of revival. Anderson Cathey, who lived on a ridge near Tahlequah, "prayed through" to the Holy Spirit and "got power I didn't know I had." Cathey testified how he "came up from the ground preaching a sermon in tongues with my arms lifted to the heavens."

At a meeting in Tulsa, Mrs. J. C. Ament claimed to have been "instantly healed" of blindness and stomach and back trouble. By 1912, there were three Pentecostal missions in Tulsa, and it was reported that "the power of God is falling." A Holiness evangelist known as "Uncle Tom" reported that "before he could tell the people that they couldn't have Pentecost they *got* Pentecost."[14]

By the 1920s, bitter doctrinal disputes divided many of the competing sects and denominations in the Pentecostal and Holiness denominations. Cora's church in Collinsville originally had been affiliated with one of the Holiness groups, but when Dan Sallee came up from Sallisaw and became pastor, he brought it into the Assemblies of God, the fastest-growing white Pentecostal church. Cora attended Assemblies of God churches in Collinsville, Miami, and Claremore. Norma's husband, Noel Dagenette, became an Assemblies of God preacher in Miami. And on Drake's Prairie, Drury Callahan left the Watts Church in 1927 and started Sallisaw's first Pentecostal "work." It, too, was associated with the Assemblies of God.

The doctrine that Cora followed, like so much else in the faith, was rooted in Wesleyan theology, but shaped by American conditions. It held out the possibility of "entire sanctification," or total purification from sin in this life. Entire sanctification implied a character of almost saintly dimensions. The entirely sanctified were seen as having been fully immunized against sin, though it was left to the believer to frame the definition of what sin was.

The Assemblies of God rejected the doctrine of entire sanctification, and there were other unresolved differences between the sects. Yet they were united by a common belief in the possibility of miracles, especially healing miracles. Healing was a glue that helped keep the sects from destroying themselves in the fire of their own disagreements.

Cleo was five years old when she got her first healing. The Tatham family was living in Collinsville, when she developed a painful earache. Cora sent Norma to get Brother Dan Sallee, an Assemblies of God preacher. Cora and Norma kneeled in a corner while Brother Sallee prayed over Cleo, asking the Lord to heal her.

In an instant, Cleo said, her ears "quit."

"You're healed, dear, aren't you?" asked the preacher with a smile. He placed a coin in her palm and closed her fingers around it. "Now run to the store and get you somethin'."

Cleo was sure that prayer also saved her in her bout with typhoid the year her dad was farming on Drake's Prairie.

Norma had come from Miami on the train to join the watch around the sickbed. Cora held Cleo's hand and prayed, while the child tore at the sheets and her fever rose to 106.

A doctor came from town to examine her. "If that girl gets well it will take a higher power," he whispered to Cora.

"Run to the church and bring the pastor," she directed Norma.

A service was in progress, but Norma went straight to Pastor George Land and said, "Cleo's dying, Mama wants you to come and pray."

Pastor Land stopped the service. "We'll all go," he said.

Uncle Dave Brewer came along, and the two preachers fell on their knees at Cleo's bedside and began to pray in tongues. Cleo dimly heard Uncle Dave rebuking the fever.

Cleo slept, only to awaken in "a brand-new land." Her mother fed her strained oatmeal and buttered bread, fresh-baked and still warm from the oven. Cora was still afraid that Cleo's high fever "took her brain," but Cleo's mind was clear as a trout pool.

"God drove the fever away," the pastor told Cleo. "You got an instant healing."

Cora Tatham was a "prayer warrior" who prayed for the sick at marathon all-night sessions that left her exhausted. This was no Sunday morning devotional prayer. It was Olympian. A prayer warrior used up calories the same as an athlete.

And yet, unlike her sister-in-law Winnie, Cora Tatham did not hesitate to call a doctor. Her mother had sent her off to care for sick people around Brushy, and she could "pull people through things other people had died with," said her daughter Ophelia. One of Cora's sisters was married to a dentist. Entire sanctification or not, she was no fanatic. She was a woman of common sense. A Sumpter.

OCA WAS ONLY seventeen when Walter had the accident, but he was no child. The mining and smelting towns knocked the child out of boys early. Transportation for an Oklahoma youth was often an empty boxcar with old metal wheels worn out from having the skids put on too often. Boys "walked the plank"—a board laid across a deserted mine shaft—or dropped live chickens down the shafts. They pinched dynamite caps and tossed them into the ponds of mine water. And as they grew older they matched their wits against the railroad bulls, hopping off and on the freights in displays of daring and putting up with rough rides that "beat a boy's insides out," Oca said.

Oca learned to wrestle. Anything went except eye gouging. Choking and holds that produced painful cramps were allowed. The contestants went until one of them had had enough. Oca had powerful legs and went for scissor grips around an opponent's chest or neck that cut off his wind. Since it was unmanly to quit, the loser in those matches could be roughed up pretty badly. In more serious fights, he learned to get what he called "an equalizer"—a brick or a piece of wood.

Boys learned never to show hurt or pain and to keep an open account with the rest of the world. Once in Carterville, a man whacked the side of Oca's horse with a dry cornstalk. The popping sound startled the horse, and it bucked Oca off. He landed on his head, and wondered if his neck was broken. But falling off a horse was a disgrace, and Oca concealed what had happened when he got home.

The remedy was to square accounts—with the world. He got another man to ride the horse. "Kick her up, bust her one!" yelled Oca. The horse took off and ran right through Carterville, but the man stayed on. Oca regretted that he hadn't had a dry cornstalk to pop.

In Collinsville, he joined the group of boys who sought amusement and entertainment in girls, cars, practical jokes, and tests of manhood. When he dressed "western," his tastes ran to the lavish— a black cowboy hat and dressy leather cowboy boots. He always took a dare, sneaking into a movie or cadging free meals from friendly waitresses.

Cleo called him a "cat on wheels."

One time he outfitted himself in the best gray suit he could afford, got a wool cap with a felt visor to match, and went cruising in a Model T Ford Roadster with the exhaust that could whistle. It seemed to Cleo that all the girls were sweet on her older brother. An acquaintance, Clifford Greenwood, remembers him as a "smooth talker." He sized up Oca as a fellow who was not overly "struck on work" and who had no more ambition than the average seventeen-year-old single man.

But Oca worked when he could. He could handle a team of horses—"shake those lines and talk to them, raise a hair on their back with a whip, and really get a lot out of them." He drove a team of horses hauling rocks, worked in a brickyard, cut wood, dug coal.

Oca told Cleo that he had his heart set on marrying a rich Indian—one of the wealthy oil or mineral-rich Quapaws or Osage they sometimes saw in the back of chauffeur-driven limousines. He told her, "I'm going to buy myself a western outfit and marry one of them wealthy Indian gals and have one of them big automobiles."

Instead he married Ruby, who was dirt poor too.

He'd seen her in church that first year back in Collinsville in 1928. Clifford's brother Lon Greenwood was going with Ruby's sister. Oca didn't have a car of his own, so he rode along in Lon's 1924 Model T Ford when Lon called on the sister.

Ruby was an attractive, quiet young woman whose oval face radiated warmth. There was just a hint of the enigmatic Choctaw from her mother's side in her small, quick smile. Ruby was a woman of few words, but she missed very little. She came out of hard times, same as Oca. Her mother's first husband had been shot dead in a quarrel, and Clara had then married James Rogers, a tenant farmer who raised cotton for seed and sold milk and butter in Bartlesville. They called him Mitch.

The Rogers lived on a farm near Collinsville with a house full of kids—four daughters and two sons of their own and older siblings from earlier marriages. Mitch was a hardworking farmer who believed chores should take precedence over schooling in the lives of his young daughters. Like Oca, Ruby had dropped out of school to help. But Ruby was progressive, too. She learned to play the pump organ and was working at a drugstore in Collinsville when Oca started dating her.

It was an on-again, off-again courtship. He took her for fast rides in whatever car he could lay his hands on. One time he was showing off around a curve when the hydraulic brakes gave out and the car took off across a man's yard, just missing the front porch. Oca and Ruby were married on May 26, 1930. Neither of them was quite nineteen, and they didn't have money for a church wedding. Oca shelled out three dollars for a marriage license at Pryor, Oklahoma. Then he got a Baptist preacher to come to his parents' place in Collinsville and say the right words over the fence. Late that fall their first child was born in his parents' home. They named her Doris. She was a great joy, but her arrival added new financial pressures. It was a year after Black Tuesday, and the Depression had begun.

While they were all living in Collinsville, Oca was almost arrested for helping himself to coal from a pit outside the town of Skiatook. Oca and Walter had presumed it was abandoned. They worked in freezing water up to their knees as they broke off hunks of coal with sledgehammers and stakes. At night at home, Oca would stand his frozen pants up as if they were made of tin.

One day someone at the filling station told Oca that men had come to arrest him for stealing coal. The coal pit, it seemed, was only idled by the Depression. He took off for Seminole for a few days, and the police arrested some other people. The mine had squared accounts, even if it had the wrong culprits.

Walter and Cora moved to Claremore in 1931, and Oca and Ruby followed. It was a better town than Collinsville, they thought. Even in hard times it attracted a lively tourist trade, drawn to the birthplace of Will Rogers and to the hot sulphur waters of its spa. Vernon peddled strings of candied popcorn in the lobby of the Will Rogers Hotel and saw Rogers himself once on one of those occasions. But now the shadow of the Depression had grown darker. Businesses were closing, and families did what they had to do.

Only the liquor business seemed unaffected by the Depression. Oca and Walter noticed that bootleggers never went broke. And everyone had a bootlegging story to tell.

One cold winter day, Cleo went outside to get the clothes out of the washtub and pulled out a bottle a neighbor had tossed into the tub when the police came after him. Walter Tatham dabbled—but only dabbled—keeping a makeshift still by their bathtub while they had lived in Collinsville. Walter told Ophelia that if "men" came she should lock herself in there and pour the liquid down the drain.

But it was Oca, not Walter, who had the required nerves. In Claremore, he delivered the "groceries" to a lawyer on Main Street. He'd put two half-gallon jugs at the bottom of a brown paper bag, cover them with apples and potatoes, and walk right down Main. "Ooooh, he's gonna get in trouble," Cora would say. But she never tried to stop him.

The penalty was a year and a day in jail. That was what worried Cora, not the principle of the thing. She was "death on liquor," but Prohibition was an abstraction—part of a web of legalisms imposed by government, from the outside, with plain people often bearing most of the burden. Sober conduct was right conduct, but she made a distinction between that and what the law required. The liquor trade, legal or illegal, served mainly the "upper crust"—lawyers, doc-

tors, people with money—not religious people. If they wanted to go
to Hell, so be it.

So when Oca got into bootlegging, Cora looked the other way.
He gave it up only when the heat was on. His Uncle Arch, visiting
from Sallisaw, heard the sheriffs talking on the corner and tipped
him off. "Son," he told Oca, "you better get out of town. I heard 'em
talkin' about a guy who's peddling whiskey and I think they got your
number."

Oca headed for Drake's Prairie and laid low. When he felt it was
safe, he came back and took the road job on Highway 66. He moved
Ruby and Doris to their first apartment and acquired a yellow Packard
touring car with leather upholstery.

In the fall of 1932, Walter and Cora Tatham cast their votes for
Franklin D. Roosevelt for president, and Oca, just twenty-one, did
the same. Tathams had been Republicans since Thomas Tatham had
served in Mr. Lincoln's army, but the times called for change. "Maybe
he can pull it out," said Walter without enthusiasm. They moved
back to Drake's Prairie soon afterward, the family's eleventh move in
fifteen years, and with few jobs in the mines and refineries, it looked
to be one of the last.

Before leaving Claremore, Walter gave away Cora's sewing machine, the symbol of her economic independence and status. The
deed was too pointed and too devastating to have been inadvertent.
It undermined the role she was assuming as the family's principal
provider. For Walter it was an understandable protest, even if a petty
one. She never forgot it. "That old Indian was mad," Cleo would
chuckle years later. "She cried. She could have gone on a war dance
right quick."

Oca moved to Gore, not far from Drake's Prairie, where Dick,
their second child, was born on April 14, 1933, while they were living
in a transient hotel and Oca was driving a dump truck on a highway
job. In their free time, they went over to Drake's Prairie to see his
parents.

The Tatham clan had an influential connection in Sequoyah
County. John Sumpter's daughter Altie had married a tough, mean
man called Bill Byrd. Some said Bill must have married her for her
allotment on Drake's Prairie because he never treated her well. But
Bill had a flair for politics, and in 1932 he was elected county sheriff.
It took a brave man to run for that office. Much of the county lying
in the Ozark foothills was simply not under the control of the law,
and no sheriff was foolish enough to venture very far into those

Cookson Hills. A previous sheriff, Perry Chuculate, had been killed in a 1926 shootout with a notorious outlaw gang, the Kimes Brothers.[15] The brothers were captured, but Matt Kimes was later freed by a carload of men with sawed-off shotguns and went on to rob and plunder in eastern Oklahoma until he was taken again.

Bill boasted that he would arrest Charlie Floyd if he got the chance. But it seemed to Oca that Bill was tougher on the poor Indians whom he found with a few bottles than he was on the real outlaws. The Arkansas line was just twenty-five miles from Sallisaw, and with the end of national Prohibition in December 1933, it became a crossing point for smugglers carrying liquor into Oklahoma, whose towns, under local option, remained mostly dry. Bill confiscated his "cut" from the smugglers and sold it or used it himself.

Bill Byrd took a liking to Walter and Oca, and deputized them to keep order around the Watts Church when services were under way. But Walter would have nothing to do with Bill's liquor raids. "If I couldn't bother his cronies I wasn't going to bother those poor old men whose children will starve if they go up for a year and a day," he said.

One day Oca pulled up in front of Bill's house. "Hey, come out and see my load of apples."

He reached down into the apples and pulled out a jug. Bill slid into Oca's truck, and the sheriff and his deputy enjoyed a few swigs.

OCA HADN'T YET GIVEN his heart to the Lord, and he was nearly twenty-three years old. By the time he married Ruby he'd tried "a little bit of everything"; even after he was married he wrestled with every bad influence that Depression-era Oklahoma could throw at a young man. The Devil used his weakness for women. "He knew how to work on me and work on me good," said Oca. "I'd go to church and there'd be a pretty gal. I'd look and I'd pray right there, dear God, help me to make it. And Ruby sittin' right beside me!"

He felt like a moral failure. He wasn't living up to the standards of his Christian mother or of his wife. He would not be a good father the way he was going. Sometimes he thought to himself that he didn't deserve a woman like Ruby. He would think: *Eternity is from now on and you're not ready to meet God. You are going to end up in Hell sure as the world. You will split Hell wide open, the way you are living. You are doomed for Hell.*

Heaven and Hell were not abstractions to him. He believed in eternal damnation—believed in it totally, without reservation. And he was headed for it, no doubt about it. At times he would consider making a deal with the Lord. He thought to himself: *Wouldn't it be playing it smart to get on God's side? If you want to play it smart, you'll turn to God. Oca, you've got nothin' to lose, you're doomed for Hell anyway.*

But then some new temptation would come along.

He'd end up dead or in jail, he figured, if he kept chasing women, drinking, driving fast, and skirting the edge of the law. Being a deputy sheriff in Watts, working for Bill Byrd, put him on the "right" side of the law, but only in the eyes of the law. In the eyes of local people, it might just make life more dangerous.

One Sunday evening in 1933 outside the Watts Church, Oca arrested a troublemaker. As usual, a group of drunks had assembled to make noise and cut the horses' bridles. "You're under arrest," said Oca, grabbing a fellow by the lapel and jerking him hard. To Oca's surprise, the man went like a lamb. Oca slid into the backseat of a car with his prisoner, keeping him covered with a revolver, while a friend drove them to the county jail.

There were plenty of opportunities for sin within riding distance of the Watts Church. One house up on Highway 64, which was within a mile of the school, was known for dances and wild parties that occasionally ended with a shooting or stabbing.

The change in Oca's life happened suddenly—as such things often did. Oca was at a revival at a "colored" church in Vian, a few miles up the Arkansas River from Sallisaw, late in 1933. In those days blacks and whites of the Pentecostal persuasion shared pastors and churches, and black ministers like Elder Pool would sometimes come to minister to the sick on Drake's Prairie. The Vian Church served a concentration of blacks who lived around Sand Town bottom, south of Vian.

Oca's recollection of his conversion is oddly sketchy. Was the pastor a woman, as one friend of the Tathams recalled? Or was that not the case, as Oca contends? Was Ruby present? He is unsure on that point. But something powerful happened that evening—on that point relatives and friends are all agreed. His life changed.

He arrived in a roguish mood and decided to have a little fun with Gaylord Land, an earnest farmer who was married to one of the Callahan sisters. Gaylord looked so holy happy and innocent, thought Oca, that he might as well shake him up.

"Come on, Gaylord boy, you sure do cover up good around your wife," said Oca when he had sidled up to him.

Gaylord stared at him.

"Come on," Oca persisted, "You know you're just as guilty as sin. If your wife knew the truth about you it'd be too bad for you."

Gaylord's eyes were getting big, and he backed away. "Oca, you need the Lord."

"Why don't you level with her, Gaylord?" asked Oca, speaking confidentially, but loud enough for Gaylord's wife to hear.

"What?"

"You know *what*," Oca said loudly. By now, Gaylord's wife was staring hard at her husband. "Get it out in the open, man. It's the only way."

Oca checked to make sure he'd produced the desired effect and swaggered into the church. When the revival service started Oca felt himself starting to regret the cruel trick. Why had he done that to poor Gaylord and his good wife? He was a rotten, no-good character all right. He thought of Ruby and their two children and of their miserable poor lives. He recalls whispering a prayer: *Now is the moment, Lord. Cleanse me. I want to live for You. I can't do it alone, Lord. Share my burden, Father.*

Then the deacons were standing over him, asking, "Brother, wouldn't you like to know the Lord?"

They took him by the arm, he says, and he bowed his head and wept. After that, he was suddenly one of those most involved in the services at the Watts Church, "tarrying" at the altar to help the saved break through to the second experience of sanctification.

He hadn't cried for a long time before that night in Vian, but after that, he did cry. The Lord was breaking him, making him soft, he said, bringing what he called "a washing and a cleansing." The more he wept, the better he felt. It "seemed like the Holy Spirit come in and helped me to be a 'will overcomer' and to help me grow," he said.

Oca did not speak in tongues. But he and Ruby would pray together "in the Spirit." They would feel the Holy Spirit coming in, cleaning them and giving them confidence. They would raise up their hands and "tears would pour in praise to the Lord. We reacted with tears . . . tears of repentance and joy."

He went up to Claremore for a revival and testified and witnessed to some of the boozers and bootleggers he'd known. "The guys that I boozed with and all on the street down there, where they carried whiskey up and down the street in a paper sack with apples and potatoes on top—I stood there and testified to them that the Lord had come into my heart and cleaned my life up, you know, and let the people know publicly what God had done, because the scripture says that we have to come to him publicly, before everyone."

He "turned about-face," he said. But it didn't happen all at once.

"I found out that that didn't destroy the temptation. I found out that the enemy was always at hand to point out some good-lookin' gal or whatever, but I learned that by being a Christian you learned to be an overcomer, and to be an overcomer you had to get rid of that thing, and never yield."

MORE THAN EVER, the family counted on the western Oklahoma cotton crop to tide them through the winter. In the fall of 1932, Oca had showed up on the prairie in a stripped-down school bus, an outlandish vehicle with no windshield, homemade seats, and a bed in the back, and taken his cousins Ira, Leslie, and a friend to Elk City to pick bolls. Oca was not good at it and drove home, but the cousins went on to Texas, where they slept in hay barns. When he was ready to come home, Leslie "blinded a passenger" train—hanging on up front where the steam from the coal-fired engine kept him concealed. After switching trains a couple of times he hopped off a few miles from his home.

In the fall of 1933, Oca drove west to pick bolls again, taking Ruby and Cleo along. Ruby had the two babies with her. They slept on cotton sacks in a shack the farmer provided. It was cold and windy. In the fields, Ruby was a fast picker, even when she had to drag Doris along on a cotton sack.

Cleo was not used to the red clay soil of western Oklahoma. It got into everything, and they hadn't brought washtubs and rub boards. When they got home to Drake's Prairie before Christmas, Cora built a big fire and boiled the clothes.

Oca's cousin Ira, they learned, had ridden the freights to Los Angeles and found a job washing dishes "for eats." But he didn't stay long. Homesick and lonely, he'd soon headed back to Drake's Prairie.

ON MAY 23, 1934, three months before the Tathams set out for California, Clyde Barrow and Bonnie Parker were killed in an ambush on a farm in Arcadia, Louisiana. The authorities put the riddled car on a flatbed truck and took it on a tour of Oklahoma, Missouri, and Texas as a lesson about the futility of crime. The exhibit pulled in big crowds, but it was not at all clear that the people drew the intended lesson. On their travels through Oklahoma, Bonnie and Clyde had been given food and water by Okies along the road.

As for the Floyds' boy Charlie, he was still at large.

CHAPTER THREE

THE HIGHWAY

THEY COASTED ALONG in the moonlight, through the dry country rising out of the rangelands to the passes through New Mexico's Sandia Peak. Out behind them the highway unfurled slowly, a glowing white satin ribbon twisting lazily before flattening out and disappearing into the receding blackness.

Oca slept fitfully on the lumpy feather mattress. Around him were cardboard suitcases and cooking gear, bedrolls, boxes of pans and glasses, a gas stove, a water barrel, a drum of gasoline, towels drying on a line, jackets and coats swinging on hangers—a whole Salvation Army showroom traveling west at forty miles an hour. And curled around, under, and between were slumbering men, women, and children.

Oca listened to the sound of the truck motor. Two and a half days and eight hundred miles out of Sallisaw, he thought. And not a single flat!

He dozed, then woke with a start and listened to the sound of the engine again. The Lord must be with them. How else could he have sweet-talked the people at the truck place in Tulsa into letting him have the title to the Chevy? Well, he wasn't figuring on beating them out of their money. His mind raced far ahead to a town called McFarland, a name he'd heard from a friend of Cleo's, a Mr. Rowland.

" 'Round McFarland they need people to work, and they pay good," Mr. Rowland had said. A family could work in the cotton and grapes in the fall and go on to the lettuce in Salinas and the Imperial Valley all winter.

Mr. Rowland had mentioned something else, too. The state gave you commodities to live on if there was no work. Oca wasn't keen on welfare since he'd gone down in Collinsville to ask for it one time. He'd stood in line for his $2.75 worth, but men were pushing and shoving, and he figured it wasn't worth getting killed for a little flour and potatoes, so he'd walked out.

But in California, he'd been told, they made it easy. "You know how much they give the people on welfare a month? You know, *each one*?" Mr. Rowland had asked, and then told him. Oca thought, If a country will do that for you, it can't be all bad. If he couldn't get a job, the family could live better on welfare in California than working steady in Oklahoma.

Still, he worried. He was no cotton picker. Ruby could pick twice his share, but now Ruby was having the new baby. He'd try, but the way he picked wouldn't make them much.

He envied his dad, a happy-go-lucky guy who never seemed to worry and who left the worrying to his wife. He was happy now, on the move, heading west. It had been nothing but "by grannies this" and "by dogies that." It was no trouble at all getting Walter Tatham going. He was a kidder who'd kid you to death.

"How much money you carryin', Walter?" somebody'd asked before they'd gone ten miles. That was Walter's cue. He had two wallets, one for his money, when he had some, and another empty one he called "the world."

Walter pulled out "the world" and just said, "I ain't got nothin' in the world." And everybody laughed at that joke they'd heard so many times before.

Oca was surer than ever that Jim Anderson was sweet on Cleo, but it did Jim no good. After Jim told a story, Cleo would stare right through him and sing, "There's nothing in this world that I don't know," as if to say that Jim Anderson acted like he knew too much.

Out beyond Tulsa, Highway 66 had been just two lanes of white cement creeping through a hundred crowded main streets and over dozens of railroad crossings. It really wasn't more than a lot of little roads hooked up with detours and ninety-degree turns to make what they called a national highway.

Going up and down the hills between Tulsa and Oklahoma City, they'd become part of the road. The truck was small and it was slow, and you could smell the prairie grass and hear the animals in the barns and stare at the dogs that came out to bark. On the bit from Sapulpa to Bristow to Stroud to Chandler, tongues of earth as red as copper ore lapped onto the highway. There were fields with big rolls of hay, clapboard farmhouses, dead oak trees, big whitewashed barns, a sign that said "Cow Creek," and main streets with tall, flat-fronted, red-brick buildings with stores on the ground floor.

Just before Oklahoma City, they got into flat wheat country, with oil derricks sticking up out of stubbly fields. Then they were driving past the State Capitol, where rows of oil rigs swaggered up the avenue in front as if they were going to march right in. Oca thought: *The dirty crooks, those politicians with their big Cadillacs and their millions of dollars of tax money, taking all that money and seeing people starving! Well, they didn't realize that the people they pressed down—the down-and-outers with nothing to eat—were some of the happiest people in the world.*

Then the country opened up into the Great Plains, vast and hazy, with wisps of cloud hovering over the horizon.

They had dinner on a wide shoulder off the road.

"Slice 'em thin so they cook fast," Cora told Cleo, who was peeling and cutting potatoes. The men gathered stones and wood and built a fire in a pit. Ruby cleaned and washed Doris and Dick with water from the barrel, while Cora cut strips of salt pork and threw them in with the sliced potatoes on an iron skillet. When the fire was hot they laid the skillet on a grill and let the spuds cook until they were browned and crisp. Cora put ground coffee from a tin in the bottom of a big pot and boiled the water and grounds together. There was the aroma of coffee and the smell of cut hay.

Squinting into the sunset, the men talked about the Chevy's tires, the chance for work in McFarland, the price of eggs, the merits of Spam. Then the women boiled the dishwater, cleaned the cooking gear and stowed it away. "We ain't gonna make California if we set here all day," said Walter, who figured they'd reach Gallup, New Mexico, in two days if their luck held out.

They'd ridden on, passing roadside campfires of families just like themselves. One river after another had fallen behind them: the Illinois, the Grand, the Verdigris, the Arkansas, the Canadian. Late that night they'd crossed the Washita. And then the stars and the moon went out, and it stormed a Plains storm, big lightning flashes and big drops of rain plopping against the windshield.

That was enough for Cora. "We're not going to be out in this truck and them clouds. We'll find a cabin," she declared.

They'd pulled into a place with roadside cabins at Elk City, where Oca and his cousins had picked bolls. After a few hours' rest they went on.

The land had turned into weed-covered sand dunes with an occasional clump of gnarled dwarf trees, and then it was Texas panhandle country, the dry prairie, hot and windy.

They knew about the dusters. The windstorms sucked the topsoil up and blew it hundreds of miles. They'd started in 1932. There'd been more the next spring, and then had come a big one in November 1933. In May, the radio had reported a duster that vacuumed the dirt up into the air in Montana and Nebraska and dumped it down on vessels hundreds of miles out at sea.

Near Amarillo, they'd seen dead cattle on the range, and some places you could only tell what the crop was supposed to be by a few cornstalks sticking out of the parched, sandy soil. But what they were scared of most wasn't drought but twisters. Thunderstorms had followed them across the plains, and that afternoon they'd stopped early and put up in a grain elevator in Texas. A friendly Texan offered them shelter in a railroad bunkhouse.

The next morning they'd left Texas behind, and then the sandburs and goatheads in New Mexico got the kids when they ran off the road to play.

OCA WAS LISTENING to the engine as the preacher's brother headed the Chevy up into the mountains. He worried about Arley's driving. That evening they'd stopped and slept a few hours under a bridge by Santa Rosa. When it came time to leave, Oca had felt too worn down to drive.

The brakes were gone. "It ain't got synchromesh," Oca told Arley. "You gotta double-clutch her into low . . . match the gears . . . wind the motor up just right. Don't let her pull down." Lord forbid that Arley would need the *brakes*.

Arley didn't look as if he liked it, but he'd climbed up and taken the wheel. They'd rolled through tumbleweed and sagebrush country that looked spooky in the moonlight, and passed little ranch houses. Poor people same as us, Oca thought. Then he dozed off.

He came awake. He heard the engine labor as they climbed. A

windmill reared up on the left. Then a little town called Edgewood and a sign, "Last filling station before Sandias."

The Chevy rose up into the canyon, losing speed. And now Oca could hear something wrong. They were slowing down, and he heard the preacher's brother trying to ease her into low. The truck made a hard, groaning sound as Arley tried to shift down. Slower and slower, and then the engine stopped, and they were rolling back.

There was no noise. Bill Elbertson and Jim Anderson cussed quietly. There was still no noise. Oca heard Arley fiddling with the gears and heard him pump the brakes. It was still quiet. Then there was the sound of gravel crunching under the wheels, and then BANG, as the truck bounced off the road and down the hill, striking big mountain boulders as it went.

Cora Tatham was wailing. "Lord save these people."

"*God*-darned," yelled Jim Anderson up front.

Walter rolled out and gave the gas drum a push out the back and into the ravine. Dewey leapt clear and went running ahead, down the hill, with the truck bouncing after him. Then it was smashing against rocks. Bill Elbertson jumped clear on the passenger side, and Jim came right behind him. The running board caught Jim square in the seat of the pants as it turned, and it knocked him right in the air—he came down so hard that his shoe heels were sliced clean off. With a final, loud crash, the Chevy was on its side and people and bedrolls flew out onto the rocks and cactuses.

Oca had landed hard on his right arm. He rolled over, holding his arm against his chest, knowing it was broken.

Ophelia had been asleep on a mattress when things went wrong and when she woke up next to a big rock all she could think was "Snakes!"

A shout: "You there, Ocy?"

"Ruby, honey!"

There was Ruby, unhurt. "Where's the baby?" she cried.

"Ain't you *got* him?"

"Oh, Lord help us. Where's Dick? *Where's my baby?*"

They were dazed, wandering around, checking their cuts and bruises and looking for baby Dick. Then they heard a muffled cry from under the truck's sideboards. Jim Anderson, none the worse for his flight skyward, was a skinny fellow but strong and wiry, and now he began to lift the truck. There came a popping and cracking of sideboards. More hands heaved, and they pulled the child free. It was a miracle. Dick was sleepy but unhurt.

Then Walter said, "Mama's buggered up bad."

Cora was sitting on a rock and her foot looked as if it had been sliced down to the bone with a sharp butcher's knife. She'd need help.

Jim and Vernon headed up in the direction of barking dogs. On the way they met a big woman wearing nothing but a housecoat. You could play shirttail poker on that thing, thought Jim. He whispered to Vernon, "Careful of them dogs, they look like they'd bite a hole in your britches."

"That place is death on trucks," said the woman. "I save my old sheets to bandage up the folks what's banged up down in that canyon." And she went hurrying on to the wreck with her sheets trailing behind, and Jim and Vernon went on to a store a quarter mile down the road to buy vinegar for the cuts.

Back at the wreck, the pain spread up Oca's arm. His hand was swollen and twisted.

Just then Bill Elbertson slipped up behind him. "You ought to have that took care of," he said. "I've got fifteen dollars. Take that and get it set proper."

But Oca shook his head. "We'll need that for gas."

He hadn't hurt so much since the old gray mare tossed him on his head in Carterville after she'd been popped with a dry cornstalk. But he'd never been to a hospital in his whole life and wasn't going to start now. He locked the fingers of both hands together, put his knee against them, and pushed. He could feel bone and ligaments sliding back into place.

Jim and Vernon came back with vinegar for the cuts, and the woman was bandaging with her bed sheets. "I helped many a person when they come down through here," she said. "That's just what God lets us do—help the people that have these wrecks."

People had stopped in a car and were offering to take Cora to the hospital in Albuquerque. But she was wailing, "How will I ever get with my folks again?"

"We'll get with you again, just take her easy," Walter said to her as she went off in the car.

BY SUNUP, the situation looked a little better. A rancher's mule team had pulled the Chevy up on the highway again, and the others had built a fire. You could see the morning sun catching the tops of the peaks and turning the canyon a soft sort of blue, but mostly they were looking at the damage. Their bedding and cooking gear was scattered. The windshield was gone, and that wooden cab they'd worked so hard to put together was smashed. Still that old Chevy was Okie-tough. The engine ran and there were no leaks and not even a flat.

Oca went over and sat by Ruby.

She was very quiet. "Will we go back to Oklahoma now?" she said.

"We ain't goin' back," he said. "We ain't got nothin' to go back *for*."

Ophelia sat by the roadside and worried. They were on a mountain a long way from Oklahoma, with snakes and scorpions crawling in the rocks, a bunch of poor people in ragged clothes. Where was her mother? What would people think of them?

They weren't a bunch of hoboes. They were decent people. But how would anyone know? The truck looked a wreck. The men had built a sort of lean-to on the back with the canvas and lumber that was left. They had stubbly beards and looked worn out.

She felt ashamed. Oh, they'd always been poor since her dad's accident. She remembered making her tablet of Big Chief Five writing paper last and last by using the back of each page when the front was filled. Yes, they were poor. But not sorry. They'd always had furniture and clean clothes. Her mother had sent them to school dressed beautifully. She could work off a pattern in a magazine and had sewn in shops in Tulsa where they sold wedding gowns—that was how skilled she was. She'd made Cleo a coat with a fine fur collar. Cleo had worn it on Drake's Prairie, not to put on airs but to show off her mother's handiwork.

Sitting on the highway, now, Ophelia wondered how people would know that.

THEY STARTED UP again shortly after noon. Halfway down the mountain, they passed a bus with Cora in it coming the other way. The hospital had sewn up her cuts and sent her back to look for the family. The driver put her off, and she limped over to her people. Poor little Mama, thought Ophelia.

They were almost to Gallup before the mood lightened a little.

They crossed the Continental Divide. "Now it's downhill all the way," said Oca.

Dewey Rogers got them laughing again when they stopped at a filling station. He had poured himself four glasses from a big barrel of ice water before Oca saw the sign that said, "Ice Water 5 Cents a Glass."

"Can't you read that sign?" Oca asked crossly.

"Nope," said Dewey.

"It says five cents a glass. Now you get away from there."

It was too late. The filling station man wanted his money. Dewey didn't have it. He was broke.

"That man hasn't got a cent to his name," said Oca, who wasn't about to fork up for him.

The filling station man grumbled and told them to move on. When Dewey came out of the restroom, Oca told Arley to pull out and keep the truck just ahead of Dewey. They went a quarter of a mile up a long hill before Oca said stop.

"You just about . . ." panted Dewey. "You just about run off and left me."

"Well, you hadn' oughta stayed in that restroom so long," Oca yelled back.

"What would you a-done if we *had* left you, Dewey?" asked Walter.

"I'd a-lived," he pouted.

They stopped in Gallup, bought bread and bologna, fixed a meal, slept, went on. Before they knew it, the Chevy was humming on into Arizona. Past Flagstaff, where the air was fresh and cool, they slid down into the Mojave Desert. Sitting up front, the men felt the heat off the hood and wished they still had a windshield.

Beyond Oatman, Arley stopped the truck and they all got out. They were on a bluff above the Colorado River gorge with the river meandering below. The muddy, reddish stream was bordered by willows and sycamores. On the other side was a dry desert broken up with tabletop mesas and sunken plateaus: California.

The descent to the Topock Bridge was narrow and steep, and they were scared. The Chevy's brakes were shot. The gears would have to do the braking.

"I'm not gettin' in there with Arley," said Cora. It was decided. Arley would drive the truck down alone and the others would walk. They did—a ragged band of unshaven men in overalls, barefoot children, a pregnant woman carrying her infant son, a middle-aged woman half hobbling, half being carried, a young man with his arm in a sling: survivors of Highway 66, limping the last few miles toward California, one step at a time.

Arley made it. The Chevy went rat-tat-tatting by and glided to a gentle stop at the bottom.

They camped close to the river, within sight of California. In the middle of the night, a rainstorm and flash flood forced them out and sent them stumbling to cover, dragging soggy bedrolls behind them. A bright morning restored their sagging spirits.

"You got any cotton sacks with you?" asked a uniformed man at the inspection station at the bridge.

"Our cotton burned up in Oklahoma, mister."

"Cotton mattresses?"

"Just feather."

The man climbed into the back of the truck and took a quick inventory of the ramshackle contents.

"Go ahead," he said, scowling at the battered cab. They rolled into California, through one of the bleakest gateways in the world. Beyond the town of Needles, a subtropical oasis of palms, cotton-woods, tamarisks, and pepper trees, they climbed up into the bleached hills and entered the Mojave on the California side. It was nothing but a bleak plateau furrowed by gullies and pockmarked by dry lake beds. Only an occasional cactus or creosote bush—or the burned-out hulk of a car—broke up the gray-brown landscape.

Dewey Rogers stared at the bleak sight. "Walter," he said at last, "you told me a-way back there we was in Califorrny. But I thought we was goin' to Califorrny *town*."

"Well, Dew, they have towns in California, but there ain't no 'Califorrny town.' "

At Barstow, a desert frontier town with five-and-dime stores, beauty parlors, and cocktail bars along the main avenue, Okie travelers had to choose. Straight ahead on Route 466, beyond more miles of dry country, were the Techachapi Mountains, Bakersfield, and the San Joaquin Valley with its miles of golden farms. Southwest on 66 was San Bernardino, Riverside, Orange County, Los Angeles. Straight ahead were grapes and cotton. Southwest were orange groves, fruit orchards, plants, and packing houses.

Destinies were set by the decision to go left or straight. Someone would say, "Folks come back says they's done with oranges in Hemet," or "Fella says they need swampers in Delano," and that would determine the direction of a family for half a century. The Drake's Prairie crew planned to head for L.A., but only to drop off the nurse and her boys. After that they would be bound for McFarland, in California's central valley.

They reached the outskirts of Los Angeles near daybreak, and the nurse and her boys disappeared forever.

"Where to now?" asked Arley.

"Keep her goin' to the Pacific Ocean," said Oca.

Oca knew many who'd come back from California and had never seen it. It was the narrowness of country people, Oca thought. He planned to see the ocean first thing.

Arley kept the truck on 66 through Hollywood and Beverly Hills and reached the end of Santa Monica Boulevard. They piled out and stared at the huge expanse of gray water. Then they ran barefoot across the cool sand, flinging off shoes and socks, and waded in. Oca rolled up his pants and walked into the water, cradling baby Dick in his good arm. Ruby walked in up to her ankles, holding Doris's hand. They turned and stared back at Cleo as she snapped a picture of the four of them with her Box Brownie. Cleo borrowed a pair of Jim's overalls and rolled them up to the knees and came in, too.

When the fun was over, they piled in and headed north on Highway 99. They camped at Gorman, a town near the pinnacle of the narrow, switchback "grapevine" road over the coastal range. The next morning, they started out again, with Oca using his one good arm to ease the Chevy down the treacherous incline. Suddenly, there was the valley. A gauzy haze covered its gold-brown floor. Off to the east were the snowcapped peaks of the Sierras catching the morning sun. Below them Highway 99 cut straight through toward Bakersfield.

Down on the valley floor, they passed through country where herds of cattle and sheep grazed. Hardly a word passed. Back away from the highway oil derricks rose from the hog wallow. The place was an arid, bleached desert dotted with sagebrush. Tumbleweed blew across the narrow road. Only the occasional clump of wild poppies added a dash of color to the drabness.

At Bakersfield, their anxiety eased a little. They were in the kind of country that was familiar to them now: spindly oil towers hovered over cotton and alfalfa fields, just like Oklahoma. At a little dirt road with a sign and an arrow that said "Shafter," they pulled over for a stop, hoping to calm their nerves. There was a café across the street and outside it a truck piled high with wooden lugs of grapes. Several men leaned against it. Oca had never seen such grapes. They were fat as a man's thumb, and they came in big bunches.

He sidled up to the husky man who seemed to be the driver.

"Wonder if I could buy some of them grapes for my women and children over there," Oca asked.

The man reached over the side of the truck and handed Oca several large bunches. There's enough grapes there to fill a bushel basket, thought Oca. That would take all the money they had.

The man eyed Oca curiously. "No charge," he said, figuring the Okie was broke.

The grapes were sweet and plump. Rolled between thumb and forefinger, they felt springy. And as they pulled off bunches and reached for more of the sweet fruit, their moods changed. They all felt it finally. This was California.

North of the Shafter turnoff, they saw trays of raisins drying in the sun and more fields of cotton. The cotton looked about ready, and Oca thought there were many more dots of white than in Oklahoma.

Toward midafternoon they pulled the truck into McFarland and walked around. It was a tiny farming community, smaller than Sallisaw, one of those places where folks on Main Street kept an eye on new arrivals.

A fellow was soon studying their license plates. "You boys from Oklahoma, I see. Where you comin' from?" he asked in a familiar-sounding drawl.

"Sallisaw."

"Why, that's *my* home."

It was a Mr. Lessley, and he was happy to see them. After they'd exchanged gossip, he told them they'd find plenty of work north of town.

Oca pulled out again and headed up 99 a few miles until they came to a ranch entrance on the left. A four-by-four laid across two posts formed a western-style gate with a sign on it in green letters: "Twin Pines Ranch."

Oca turned in and drove up the long dirt road to a modest farmhouse with shade trees. A man came out and spoke to him. "My name's Calvert," he said. "I can use you fellas."

He was a farmer with a spread of cotton to pick. His wife came out and talked with the women.

They camped right there that night. Mr. Calvert had said he'd have places for them tomorrow, and they could work in grapes until his cotton was ready.

It was August 27, in the year 1934. They counted money. Between them they had just a few dollars. They laughed and joked, and the men talked about going to town. Cora got out the two-burner, and the children went down to Mr. Calvert's pond to draw water. Ruby washed Baby Dick. The next day they'd start.

PART TWO

CHAPTER FOUR

THE VALLEY, 1934

THE SOUTH was late reaching the West.

For more than two centuries before the Okies began to pour into California, white, English-speaking people from the British Isles had been drifting south and west across the American continent, filling, but not really transforming, a world of woods, swamps, prairies, and plains with a particular outlook and character.

They were a kind of tumbleweed, blown from one marginal area to another. Many of their ancestors were the Scotch Irish who had come through the Delaware Bay ports in the five decades before the American Revolution and trekked down the Great Wagon Road running by John Tatham's Catawba Creek farm. By 1740 some of these wanderers had crossed the James River. By 1800, they had worked their way deep into the Georgia and Carolina Piedmont. Growing population, cattle disease, and the taking of more and more land for cotton cultivation persuaded many of them to press on. Some went through the Appalachian gaps, drifted down the rivers of Tennessee, crossed over the Mississippi River to Cape Girardeau, and made their way from there to the Ozark highlands. Others drove their small herds of cattle and hogs west through the forests of longleaf pine along the Gulf Coast all the way to East Texas. They slashed and burned their way west, leaving it to nature to restore the forests, just as they would one day leave it to time to heal the fragile grasslands that they so recklessly plowed up at the edges of the High Plains.

Cotton forced the pace of migration. The better-financed cotton planters or their agents let enterprising pioneer farmers prove out undeveloped land, then assembled their tracts from the most promising small holdings. Having sold his land, the small farmer either moved on in search of a new stake or retreated to a few inferior acres farther back.[1]

The Civil War brought loss, displacement, and homelessness on a scale never before known by the people of the South. A common figure on the rutted southern wagon tracks long after 1865 was the Civil War widow moving somewhere with her children.

Then, in the 1870s, a great exodus out of the Deep South began. Its cause was not a sudden calamity, but a slow, economic squeezing of plain people. Farmers were victims of the crop lien system, in turn a product of the South's financial collapse. The region's capital, its slaves, had been lost. Banks being few, farmers turned for credit to the local "furnishing merchant," a storekeeper with a connection to a banker or a supplier in the North, pledging the proceeds of their next crop against seed, calico cloth, and other urgently needed goods. Each year, they tried to "pay out." But as cotton prices declined and the interest rates grew more usurious, they fell behind, until "the man" took away their farms and whatever shred of dignity they once had. They became landless tenant farmers.[2]

The road was the escape valve, as it always had been. Those for whom the new conditions were intolerable packed their belongings on a mule cart, scrawled "GTT" for "Gone to Texas" on their weathered boards, and left. They crossed the Mississippi River and carried on through the piney woods and eventually to the western limits of the Cotton Belt. Some pressed on right into the hills of Comanche country and began to farm the fragile grasslands that would one day blow into dust. They could go no farther; beyond there were Indians, insufficient rainfall to grow cotton, and no roads.

Eventually, some of the Southern drifters reached the Indian Territory, a last resort.

There was a passive quality about the whole enterprise, an absence of a plan. People were nudged on by a general dissatisfaction with conditions, not so much by the pull of opportunity as American myth would claim. Many thousands of Scotch-Irish immigrants doomed their descendants to lives of transiency simply by their poor choice of land. They often selected the poorer sandy soils because they were easier to work and more familiar to them than the richer gumbo and lime soils of the lowlands, for which their tools and technology did not seem right.[3] The poorer soils were adequate at first, for the firstcomers tended to be cattle herders, not farmers. But as the crowding forced them to give up those ways and farm, the stony, sterile soil condemned them to a poor existence.

Considering that they were movers, they could be curiously inflexible. They tended to be good improvisers but poor innovators. The tumbleweed culture produced few inventions that the rest of America would adopt. Yet they had "Ulster iron," a flinty, proud, stoic quality. When conditions became intolerable they exercised their ultimate right as Americans—the right to move on. In America one could always just say, "To hell with it, I'm going."

The whites who moved into the Greater South beyond the Mississippi were a mixed group of former cotton farmers, highland hunters, tobacco growers, and farm laborers. They were "rednecks," "hillbillies," "crackers," and "mudsills." But as they moved west, the differences became blurred. They had their own notions of freedom and community. They would not be told what to think, and they trusted their own experience more than the science that came to them from on high—from "upper crust" and know-it-alls. Their suspicions of higher authority meant that they created a patchwork of minimalist authority everywhere they went. And the more isolated they were, the more elaborate and complex became the doctrines and ideologies springing up in seemingly primitive, isolated conditions. Populism, Pentecostalism, Landmarkism, the Two-Seed Doctrine of Calvinism—intricate religious and political revelations—each grew from the grass roots up.

They were intensely collective about some matters and joined together at camp meetings, logrollings, and barn raisings. When a neighbor took ill, they often chopped his cotton and fed his livestock without asking a thing in return. But they were no Yankees settling in Ohio, laying out the lines of future towns, planning the schools and courthouses before the first harvest was in. They were no Germans, no thrifty, accumulating *Bauern* who came to the dairy and corn country of the Middle West, built sturdy barns with broad beams, and were buried in the same cemeteries with their forebears, generation after generation.[4] Nor were they Quakers, born organization men who built a thriving society in Pennsylvania before the Revolution. The tumbleweed of the Cotton Belt were not even the poor Irish huddled close in Boston's North End, dreading the thought of the great American outback where people could not see their neighbors. The Irish were a bloc; they could get a hearing for their interests.

The first significant exodus *out* of the expanded South was of blacks moving north in the 1880s and 1890s. That migration continued at a trickle until a second great northward surge in the 1940s and 1950s, when the labor of sharecroppers began to be replaced by the mechanical cotton harvester.

For whites, the early migration patterns were complex. Until the decade of 1910–1920, whites tended to move mainly within the region—from Alabama, Mississippi, and Georgia to Texas in the 1870s, for example, and from Missouri, Arkansas, and Appalachia into Oklahoma in the 1890s and early 1900s. White migration out of the South generally followed the black pattern: Appalachian Southerners went north to answer the call of Henry Ford and of companies making the products of the new automobile age.

This migration was something of an anomaly in the history of American population movements. The typical direction of migration had been due west. New Englanders went to settle in New York State and later in the northern parts of Ohio, Illinois, and Indiana. Virginians moved through the Cumberland Gap to Kentucky, southern Ohio, Illinois, and Indiana and eventually to Missouri. In the 1870s, northern Midwesterners and immigrants arriving in New York headed straight west to the wide-open expanses of the Great Plains. A steady stream of migration to the Pacific Northwest and California followed the same general pattern from the 1870s on. The major traffic consisted of Germans, Scandinavians, Yankees, and old-stock farmers from the upper half of the country—Missouri, Iowa, Illinois, and Indiana—crossing the plains by rail to make a fresh start on the other side of the Rockies.

Not until the 1920s was there a comparable, even noticeable westward traffic in the lower part of the states. Before that, there was nothing much to go *to* on the other side of the dry southwestern deserts and rugged mountains. Most of Arizona and southern California was semiarid and unfit for agriculture. Roads were not much more than desert tracks, and cars were unreliable. Beyond the West Texas hill country, Southerners faced physical and psychological barriers.

That began to change in the 1920s, even before the industrial slowdown of the Depression and layoffs in the North. Southern traffic going west began to pick up as a result of better cars, better roads— and the success that a particular variety of long-fiber cotton known as Acala was beginning to have in the irrigated San Joaquin Valley of California. Acala cotton, which was developed and perfected in Mexico,[5] was suited to California's extreme climate and it resisted the boll weevil. The yield per acre was considerably higher than that of the varieties cultivated in Texas and Mississippi. Shipped by rail to eastern textile mills, the longer-than-average fiber was prized for its strength on the spindle. Prodded by the U.S. Department of Agriculture and a transplanted South Carolina farmer by the name of W. B. "Bill" Camp, Acala cotton cultivation by big land companies and farmers spread rapidly around Bakersfield. In Arizona, enterprising men ripped out the cactus and scrub, plowed the fields, and planted different varieties of cotton. As cotton took hold, poor whites followed the crop they knew so well in Georgia, Alabama, Mississippi, Louisiana, Arkansas, Oklahoma, and Texas.

KERN COUNTY, CALIFORNIA, to which the Tathams came, was just another frontier—another marginal place on the long march of white Southerners going west. It covered thousands of square miles and was roughly the size of Rhode Island, yet in 1920 it had only five incorporated townships, including Bakersfield; a decade later its population was still only 82,570.

Kern County was at the southernmost end of a vast elliptical bowl, 385 miles long and an average of only fifty miles wide, running from the edge of the Mojave Desert to the cool rain forests of northern California. The southern half of this "central valley," the San Joaquin Valley, extended from Bakersfield to Stockton. On the east, standing like a rampart, was the rock-ribbed Sierra Nevada range. On the west was the gentle, golden-gray rise of California's coastal range.

Once the valley had been a kind of American pampas, too dry for anything except cattle ranching and wheat farming. At the end of the nineteenth century, however, the wheat empires that had ruled the valley died out and were replaced by an irrigated agriculture of orchards, vines, and vegetables. Semiarid desert though it was, the valley's "east side" was blessed with a bounteous supply of water that made possible the development of a wondrous kind of farming. First, streams cascading down the west slopes of the Sierras and into the valley could be tapped, using crude mud dams or, later, more sophisticated techniques. As if that were not enough of an endowment, nature bestowed on the east side something even more wonderful: for farmers without access to the stream water, there was a vast aquifer so near the surface that as late as the 1920s farmers still dug "pits" instead of wells into which they could lay a simple pump. From McFarland to Visalia the question was, "How deep is your pit?" The pump would be located at the high point of one's gently sloping land, and the water it brought up would run into ditches that watered an entire farm. As the water table declined, gas and electric pumps were introduced. By 1920, with the great federal irrigation projects still far in the future, there were 4 million acres of irrigated farmland in the San Joaquin Valley. Forty acres was still a good-sized farm any-where in America, but in California, forty irrigated acres was a real spread. It could sustain a respectable orchard or vineyard, produce two or three crops of vegetables a year, or yield a decent crop of cotton. All that was needed to turn out crops with the regularity of products moving off an assembly line was irrigation water.

Although the water made it possible, it was the real-estate industry that pushed the pace of development, as it always did on American frontiers. Land companies shaped the social and cultural develop-ment of the valley's east side. Between 1880 and 1900, they carved agricultural subdivisions, called "colonies," out of the old wheat ranches and sold off homesteads to one immigrant group after an-other. The developers sought homogeneous populations of immi-grants for each colony so that compatible, hardworking ethnic groups would make a successful adjustment. The colony system facilitated bloc sales, and each colony acted as a magnet for newcomers.

The colonies were bunched along the east side because of water. Water companies such as Fresno Canal and Irrigation laid out roads and town centers, planted trees, and established nurseries for the culture of raisin grapevines. The former wheat ranches were divided into twenty-acre plots; towns and groups of farmers formed irrigation districts to arrange for the distribution of water, mainly from rivers. By 1920 there were more than a hundred such irrigation districts, each wielding considerable political and economic power.[6]

The colonies and homesteads attracted an extraordinary range of immigrants: Armenians, Swedes, Danes, Italians, Portuguese, "Volga River" Germans, Russians, Croats, and Serbs. Finns fleeing Russian oppression settled in Reedley. Molokan Russians, who broke away from the Russian Orthodox church, arrived in Los Angeles after grueling trips through the Panama Canal or over the Andes; land dealers came to their churches in Los Angeles and sold them spreads in Kerman. There were German Mennonites in Dinuba; Armenians on the east side of Fresno and Fowler; Portuguese dairy farmers from the Azores in Caruthers, Biola, Raisin City, and Los Baños. There were Greeks and Italians. Japanese preferred the higher eleva- tions of Reedley, Sanger, and Fowler for their lemon orchards. Cro- atians settled in Reedley and Sanger and grew grapes. The rural valley became a patchwork quilt of nationalities living in communities that were every bit as separate as the ethnic quarters of big American cities. And, of course, farmers of older American stock came from all over the United States to try their hand at agriculture California style.

All of this was set in place before the Okies arrived. And so, as a people they found themselves with all the familiar disadvantages of latecomers: like the Scotch-Irish arriving in Pennsylvania in the eighteenth century to find Germans occupying the most desirable farms, the Okies found that the best land was occupied. Once again, the Southern element was "marginalized." The oil-field and agricul- tural jobs were in the southernmost parts of the valley. There, most of the land was owned by huge oil, land, or corporate farming compa- nies. The Okies became a surplus labor force and were pushed back— into tent cities, labor camps, or, most often, Okievilles on the "wrong side" of the railroad tracks in the farming towns.

FOR THE TATHAMS, time would soften the harder memories of those first months in the valley, however. Recalling those first weeks years later, Oca said: "We were so excited. Our spirits were high. It was an opportunity, we could buy clothes. There was a great world out there ahead of us, you know. We said, 'Boy, this is the land of plenty, this is great.' Go over to the orange belt there and there's oranges left in the trees after they'd pick 'em, and you helped your- self. Why, we couldn't believe it. You go out in the grape vineyards there and those great big blue grapes, you could eat all you wanted. The farmer, he didn't say anything."

Others in the family remembered that the cotton was "big" and pulled out of the burrs easier than Oklahoma cotton did without cutting the hands. Cora, Walter, and Cleo could do eight hundred pounds a day, which made eight dollars. Even Oca, with his bad arm, and Ruby, in the final term of her pregnancy, made money.

Clear, cold water came up out of the ground and ran along the

sides of the cisterns that stood on every quarter section. Walter liked
to put his hands in the freezing liquid until they ached, then help
himself to a drink. "Oh, Sis, isn't that the finest?" he said to Ophelia.
She thought it tasted better than the Drake's Prairie well water, which
was rumored to run down from the cemetery.

Cleo recalled how Vernon's chills from the malaria stopped. Mr.
Calvert had told Cora the grapes would cure them, and it seemed
that they did.

Oca never tired of one particular story, which he used to sum up
the incredible bounty of his new home. It was about a Sunday trip
he and the family took to the Tagus Ranch, the huge peach-growing
operation that had been the scene in 1932 of a strike by its predominantly Mexican workers. Oca pulled in to look at the packing sheds,
where trucks were loading up with boxes of peaches.

"Sir, would you sell us some of those peaches on the floor?" he
asked.

"*Sell* them to you? You see those stacks of boxes and the trucks
out there hauling them away?"

"Yeah."

"They're all going to be dumped. Culls. Too big."

"Too *big*?"

"Yep. You talkin' about buyin' 'em. The more you can take with
you the fewer we'll have to haul away."

Oca backed the truck up, and they loaded up a few boxes.

Driving down the highway afterward, Oca worried. "You know
what?" he said. "That guy felt sorry for us and caused me to steal
them peaches. He set me up to help us. You know they wouldn't give
up peaches like that." Only later did he learn that the growers
dumped part of the crop to keep prices up. Ruby canned so many
peaches that time that her old camp stove caught fire.

Mills Calvert, the owner of the forty-acre Twin Pines Ranch, and
his son-in-law Pete Holgren, who had a ranch on the east side of
Highway 99, were small operators who treated the new arrivals from
Oklahoma well. The Calverts had arrived from somewhere "back
east" right after World War I, planted barley, and then switched to
cotton when the Acala strain was introduced in the early 1920s. Pete
taught public school; Mrs. Calvert taught Sunday school at the
Church of the Brethren in McFarland.

Walter and Cora and their family lived in the "block house" on
the Calvert place. It had a gas stove, running water, and a toilet. Oca
and Ruby, their children, and several of the men from the truck lived

in a "tank house" on the Holgren property. Atop the house was the water tank that fed the farm's gravity irrigation system. It had a dusty wood floor and was attached to a small wooden cabin with enough room to put down bedrolls and set up an eating area with orange crates for furniture.

For all the talk in later years about the excitement of those early weeks, it was not an easy time. Cleo woke at night worrying about her mother: Cora had a "real bad tired look," she thought. Cleo pushed it away by imagining a better day, when her mother would live in a place where she never had to work. She'd have her own furniture and Walter wouldn't sell it or make her move.

Cleo was right to be concerned. Cora's foot didn't heal properly, and the cotton field was no place for a fifty-three-year-old woman with an infection. Still, Cora went almost every day and made her three hundred pounds, same as her husband. Once a week she went to Bakersfield to get her foot bandaged.

Ruby was six months pregnant when they arrived, but she had to go to the fields. They had the two babies to feed, and Oca was a slow picker even without his bad arm. He worked on a neighboring farm picking raisins the first few days at Twin Pines, before the Calverts' cotton was ready. The job had stretched and pulled every muscle until the pain ran from his neck to his toes. He and Cleo had worked together, she leading the team that pulled the wagon, he pulling wooden trays off the back and turning the grapes into new trays so the sun dried them on all sides. The sling on his arm kept him from bending over and flipping the trays like the others, so he'd had to slip to his knees and put his head down even with the ground to get leverage on the trays.

"C'mon, bud, you take the horses and I'll turn," she told him after a while.

In the cotton, Ruby's fingers flew as she worked her way down the rows. While Doris ran along beside her, Ruby deftly extracted the lint from the boll and stuffed it in her sack. When baby Dick got fussy, Ruby dragged him along with her on a cotton sack.

Mexican and Filipino families would usually be weighing their first sacks of the day by the time they started. Full of coffee and breakfast, people were sociable in those first few hours. By ten, the temperature would be close to a hundred degrees, and they saved their breath.

They'd stop fieldwork in midafternoon, but Cora Tatham's work didn't end then. She fixed dinner for the family and Bill Elbertson and Jim Anderson, who were bunking with them. By the time she and Cleo had finished with the cooking and washing up and had started a tub of hot water for the clothes, it was after ten.

CALIFORNIA NEVER CEASED to astonish them.

As long as they were in the cotton fields or around the cabins, it was just like home. But when they left the ranches and tested the less familiar territory of the farming towns, the results were unpredictable.

That first week in California, Jim Anderson, Bill Elbertson, and Dewey Rogers caught a ride to nearby Delano, where they sampled the dives and beer joints along Glenwood Avenue. They liked one with music and Mexican señoritas in low-cut cocktail dresses, but found they weren't welcome. When the Mexicans drew knives, Dewey ran the four miles back to the Twin Pines Ranch, cutting across cotton fields to save time. He was asleep with the covers up when the others got back.

People did things differently in California. It was strange to find stores open on Sundays, and church was different, too. Delano had an Assemblies of God church, but Cleo thought it was more "high-polished" than the Assemblies churches in Oklahoma. They went to a service there soon after they came to Twin Pines Ranch, and what happened astonished them. The pastor rebuked a woman for speaking in tongues. "Just a minute, sister, you're out of order. I'll take care of that part," the pastor had said. At that church, it seemed to Cleo, the pastor "told the Holy Spirit when to stand up and sit down."

Years later, Oca remembered that experience with considerable discomfort: "We, being new Christians and unlearned, really had never been taught very much about baptism of the Holy Spirit. Later on, we found out, you see, that [our way] was a little bit wild and we learned to appreciate [the church in] Delano and realized that *we* were out of order. They were doing it according to what Paul's teachings were, you see. He said not to be more than two or three at the very most speaking in tongues, and each one of them to be interpreted, you see. In some of the little churches, you know, they just made a play thing out of this and didn't do it scripturally and the Assemblies of God tried to keep it in line and in order—the Bible said let everything be done in decency and in order. Well, if you're talking, you're speaking and somebody happens to try to give a message or speak in tongues during that time, they're out of order, see. The yelling—and the thing was that we were such down-and-outers, let's face, really down-and-outers, and had just got there and were a little out of place."

The family did not go back there for some time. Instead, they began going to Pentecostal services in an old Grange hall in McFarland where they could be themselves.

Yet California helped them along. The children came back from school telling Cora they didn't need to bring their lunches, the school provided those. Walter huffed: "What's wrong with 'em? Don't they think we can pay for the lunch?"

Cora sent them back with sandwiches several more times before Ophelia told her, "Mama, this is California. They get a free hot lunch every day."

Not long afterward the welfare woman showed up in the cotton field and asked for Mr. Tatham. She was from the Bakersfield office of the Federal Transient Service, one of the first of the New Deal programs. "No, we're doin' just fine," said Walter, when the woman asked if they needed help. "Don't need no help. We're workin' every day and payin' off our debts, doin' right good."

The woman seemed unconvinced. "Well, I'll tell you, we'd be glad to help. I'd like to give you some grocery orders—you don't need to take money."

They found out that it had been Ophelia's spindly legs that got the welfare people on them. Cora had tried everything to make her daughter gain weight. She'd had stomach troubles, possibly caused by an allergy to milk, but she wasn't starving. Even so, Walter had nothing against putting in for a load of commodities. "I'll take anythin' they want to give me, me bein' a heathen," he told Oca with a chuckle.

He'd been following the 1934 campaign for governor of California, and liked the style of the Democratic candidate, Upton Sinclair, who was running under the banner of EPIC-End Poverty in California. Oca drove Walter to Bakersfield in the Chevy truck, and they picked up food, new mattresses, comforters, and quilts. "We thought we were doing great—*but they didn't*," said Ophelia. "So they said, 'Come to Bakersfield.' And so somehow or another we went down to Bakersfield, and they gave us an order or something where you could take it to any store you wanted to go to and trade. Mama would bring beautiful big loads of gorgeous groceries, things we hadn't bought before, little extras and stuff. It was really nice. She'd bring that home and we thought that it was the greatest thing on earth. We thought that it had to be nearer Heaven than anything for people to want to help you like that, you know, and to give you things when you were doing *good*."

OUT IN THE COTTON FIELDS and around their cabins, the Tathams reconstructed the self-contained world of family and friends that had sustained them in Oklahoma. Cora's nephew Ray Sumpter, who had a job as a mechanic in Sacramento, came down to visit. And one day, a fresh contingent of Oca's cousins from Drake's Prairie showed up. They'd driven out in a '29 Chevrolet and picked up thirty-day car tags at the border. They bunked with Cora and Walter at the block house or put down folding cots under a shade tree.

There was always plenty to talk about after the picking was done. On the night of October 22, they gathered around a radio to hear the news that Charlie Floyd had died in a gun battle with special agents of the FBI and members of the East Liverpool, Ohio, police force. The accounts in the Los Angeles *Times*, with their innuendos about her friends the Floyds, made Cleo "mad as fire." (Back home in Oklahoma, sheriffs had to put up roadblocks when thousands of mourners and souvenir hunters hoping to get a piece of the casket converged on the cemetery where Charlie was being interred.)

Walter kidded the Sallisaw bunch, especially a redheaded youth called Perry. "Boys, I want to tell you the cheapest way to get to Oklahoma," he told several of them while they waited at the scales. "It won't cost you no gas and you can save all your money for food."

"Goll-y. How's that?"

"Get you a bicycle."

"Wouldn't that be kind of dangerous?"

"Well, here's what you do: put Perry on the back and use his head for a taillight."

"Aw, my hair's not that red."

"Yes it is, Perry. That hair of yours will glow in the dark."

Evenings, Cleo and Vernon went over to a cabin where an old woman was dying of cancer and sang her Gospel songs. Her son had wanted to leave her in Oklahoma, near loving relatives who could make her last days comfortable. But he couldn't find work, and she had to eat, even if she was dying. So he'd been obliged to bring her with him to California. They sang "Sing Aloud the Savior's Love" until tears streamed down the old woman's face and she reached up her hands and clapped for joy.

The first California Tatham was born on the morning of December 13 in the tank house at Browning and Peterson roads. Gladys and Pete Holgren called a doctor from Delano, and he came out from town to assist. They named the child William Ray Tatham in honor of the doctor, William Smith. The birth certificate issued a few days later listed Oca as having been a "ranch laborer" for eight years—but unemployed since October.

A few weeks after Bill was born, Walter took his family back to Oklahoma. There was little work left to do around McFarland, and he was worried about selling his cows in Sallisaw. The cousins had pulled out in November in time to beat the deadline on their thirty-day car tags. They'd all accomplished something. Walter had sent back the money to pay off what he owed on his five cows, and Oca had paid off the money for the truck. Cleo had used her earnings to buy a secondhand two-seater Studebaker with a "California top"—a hard roof but rear windows like those in convertibles. Arley had sent money home so his wife, Myrtle, could come out on the Greyhound bus and bring their baby daughter.

But they were homesick now. Cora wanted Oca and Ruby to come with them, but Oca was dead set against it. They could not afford to buy the new baby clothes they would need for the Oklahoma winter. They would stay in California.

"Son, there's no telling what will happen to you out here," Cora said. "You'd better come home with us."

"I don't have a home back there," he said, thinking of the transient hotel in Gore where Dick had been born.

Walter went down to the relief office in Bakersfield and stocked up on relief commodities one last time—sugar, coffee, flour, fruit, and staples—and loaded them in the trunk of the Studebaker.

"I got enough here to open a country store," he told Oca.

Ophelia and Vernon were sick, so Walter sent them with Cora on the train. Walter, Cleo, Arley and his wife and child, and Dewey Rogers piled into Cleo's Studebaker. Walter still couldn't drive, so Arley took the wheel again, and off they went to Oklahoma.

It was a melancholy parting.

The valley had turned cold and damp. Some days the fog rolled in over the brown fields and made the tank house damp. Oca was discovering what all farm laborers in California learned sooner or later: the money was good if there were work, but it drained away in the off-season so that a man or woman would have to start again from scratch as soon as picking began again.

That was why so many farm workers were on the move, always pursuing the next job, going from the Imperial Valley to Bakersfield to San Jose, never having enough time to put the children in school or develop community ties.

After the cotton season, Oca worked when he could with a Filipino contractor, tying grapes or doing other odd jobs in the local vineyards. But mostly he lived off relief.

Nothing in his experience had persuaded him to look at government as a friend. He'd known a man in Oklahoma with a grocery store who was repacking relief flour and selling it for cash. Oca had started to put in for relief himself just that one time in Collinsville.

But relief was different in California, and as winter came on, he needed to feed his family. In California the Relief office treated them like decent people. "They treat you almost like a *customer* down there," he told Ruby when he came back from Bakersfield with a new mattress, some blankets, and a "family box" of canned milk, ham, and flour.

One day when they had nothing else to do, Oca and Jim Anderson wrote a poem and sent it to Walter Tatham back in Sallisaw.

> We eat oranges by the pack,
> Don't you wish you had a sack?
> And if your California groc'ries last till June,
> You'll have to fast morning, night and noon.
> And in your mind, you'll be coming back soon.
> But you'll be there until your doom.
> If your hogs are fat as rails,
> Put your lard in a ten-pound pail,
> And hang the rest on a shingle nail.

They chuckled to think of Walter reading it in the ice and cold. He'd written to say that his commodities had spoiled by the time he'd reached Texas.

But the poem was mostly bravado. Oca was out of work. The Chevy truck had one flat after another, and he finally traded it for a '31 Chevy sedan. It was a good-enough deal, but a car was not a truck that could make you money. After six weeks of going to the relief office, he realized he had to make a move.

The family drove north to a place called Knights Landing, in the irrigated rice, wheat, bean, and sugar beet country above Sacramento on the Sacramento River.

Oca had heard about it from some Filipino farm workers. He was too broke to pay for gas, but the man who ran the filling station gave him a tank on credit.

The farmers around Knights Landing drew their irrigation water from the Sacramento River, so the main growing season was in the winter and spring when the river was running full.

The rainmakers were going when Oca and the family pulled in at one of the large farms.

"You got any work for an able-bodied guy?" he asked the foreman when he found him.

"You mind working nights?"

"No, *sir*. I'll work any ol' time."

"Well, we got work all right. Minding rain machines."

"Okay. When can I start?"

"Why, buddy, you can start right now." Then the man paused and looked at him coldly. "Say, you folks ain't *Okies*, are you?"

Oca was not going to lie, but he wasn't about to pass up a chance for a steady job.

"Mister," he said, "you give me that job and you won't be sorry for one minute. We're honest, hardworking people."

"Well, Okay. But we don't hire no *Okies*. Them people'll rob you blind. We put our bagged beans and rice out on the road and them folks come along in trucks at night and steal her away."

It was a reminder to the Tathams of their immigrant station. "Okie" was soon to become a derogatory term. Private citizens and public officials would, over the next few years, blame the Okies for crime and lawlessness, disrupting the public schools, overburdening the hospitals and social services, draining the state budget, and creating a communist menace. Okies would be derided as dirty, lazy, immoral, disease-ridden, lawless, and fanatically religious. In short, bigoted Californians ascribed to Okies all the inhuman characteristics once assigned to Irish, Polish, Italians, and Jews arriving in the urban centers of the North.

The situation called for a shrewd tactical response. The successful Okie had to have some of the qualities of the guerrilla fighter, blending into his surroundings and calling as little attention to himself as possible. It did not take Oca long to master the art.

They rented a damp old houseboat pulled up on the riverbank next to a drawbridge. Oca went to work every night, when the sprinklers were turned on. His job was to move the long aluminum pipes at regular intervals. The pay was good—ninety dollars a month. After a couple of months he moved into a house and got Ruby her first washing machine and himself a '32 Ford roadster with a V-8 engine.

Pretty soon, Walter Tatham joined them. The wandering urge

had gotten to him again—the women had paying jobs back in Sallisaw, Cleo in a grocery and Cora in a sewing room, but there was not much paying work for able-bodied men. He came out on the train. Then two cousins who'd been with them at Twin Pines Ranch, Ira and Lelan Tatham, showed up. They'd ridden the freights out on the southern route, passing through El Paso on their way to L.A., hopping a freight train up the valley to Sacramento. Their brother Leslie, just twenty, stayed in Oklahoma long enough to help his dad plant the cotton crop before he came out, too.

The cousins boarded for a while with Ruby or bunked with Jim Anderson, who'd come up from McFarland with them. Oca helped them get jobs on the sprinklers. Some of the farmers and foremen cussed Okies, and it was best not to say too much. Oca told them to keep quiet about where they came from, and he made sure he kept his own Okie brogue under control so it wouldn't give him away.

He'd had a side job for a while moving bags of grain. Not being used to handling fork lifts, he'd cut open a grain bag by mistake and the boss had started in on him.

"You Okies are no better than a bunch of stupid dogs," he shouted. He was cussing and yelling, until Oca told him he didn't take that from anybody, and walked off the job.

One day, Ira almost did give them away. They were working on a big one-cylinder engine with a flywheel that pumped irrigation water.

"Hand me that tap," said Ira.

Oca looked up at the crew chief to see if he'd heard. He had. "Tap nothing," the man said. "That's not a tap, it's a nut." Oca winced. Tap was what they said in Oklahoma; it was "taps and bolts" back in the old Southwest. Hardware shops had little boxes that said "T-A-P-S" in Oklahoma, but not California. They were Okies—that was what the boss was surely thinking. He left them alone, though.

Keeping one's "Okie brogue under control" was the tactical act of an immigrant in a new country. Okies arriving in California made all kinds of smart compromises like that. Lots of them ditched their Oklahoma car plates as quickly as they could, others just kept their mouths shut. They were the opposite of the "fighting Okies" who were forever getting in scrapes defending the honor of the old country against slurs and insults. Their behavior only made them bigger targets, and strengthened the stereotype. It was smarter to keep a low profile. Oca knew how to playact when it served his purposes.

Leslie got work driving a three-cylinder diesel tractor and Ira got work on farm machinery. But the steady jobs at Knights Landing came to an end in the summer of 1935. The cousins were all single men, and moving on was all part of their adventure in California. But for Oca, a family man with three children, it meant that hard times were beginning again.

He tried picking fruit in Marysville, but there were too many people going after too few jobs, and the pay was poor. Marysville was the first place that Oca saw large encampments of fruit tramps, and it scared him. Before they ran out of money, Oca packed the family in the car and they drove back to McFarland in a convoy with Ira and Leslie, who had cars of their own.

They were able to get a shack by the tank house on Pete Holgren's ranch. After a year in California they were exactly where they'd started, but conditions for pickers were worse. When the Tathams arrived in 1934, California farmers were short of hands because the state had been paying the way home for Mexican pickers. It was cheaper than paying relief.[7] But in the spring of 1935 the situation was worsening for transient workers. Relief clients were dropped from the rolls and ordered to report to the fields to work, thanks to lobbying by the Associated Farmers Organization, representing California's growers and corporate farms. The Associated Farmers wanted able-bodied pickers in the fields and relief rates kept below farm wages.[8] That April, the Federal Emergency Relief administrator in California acquiesced. In May, 2,396 persons were "turned over" to the growers by relief agencies in the San Joaquin Valley.[9] Later in the year, President Roosevelt would direct the federal government to withdraw its direct relief, and Washington ended the Federal Transient Service, which had been charged with helping interstate migrants. Within months, California discontinued aid to persons who refused to return to their home state of "legal residence" after the harvest.

It seemed to Oca that more men were sleeping along the railroad tracks in Delano and that there were more hobo jungles along the ditch banks with tents and lean-tos smelling of kerosene, hog fat, and fried food. Highway 99 thronged with beat-up cars that had barely gasped their way over the mountains from Barstow, full of mattresses, beds, boxes, and windswept, lean, leathery people with gaunt, hungry faces.

Ruby worried about the health of the children. Children of farm workers suffered many life-threatening maladies: diarrhea, pneumonia, boils, impetigo, whooping cough, heat stroke, meningitis, tuberculosis, red measles, and "valley fever," or "desert bumps," a serious skin disease that produced bumps and boils. Polio was rampant.[10] And there was very little that could be done against these afflictions. Antibiotics and vaccines for diphtheria, lockjaw, tetanus, and polio had not yet been perfected. Ruby boiled the children's clothes in a washtub and tried to keep them away from children with body sores— the telltale sign of impetigo. Dick, just two, sometimes ran high fevers and had swollen neck glands that Ruby soothed with a "Denver mud poultice," a patent medicine available at drugstores. She prayed that her children would be spared more serious illness, and she scrubbed and washed them whenever she could. She considered it shameful for children to have lice, but Doris and Dick got lice. Ruby soaked the children in a bath with a strong solution, and if the lice were still there after the dunking she doubled the strength of the solution.

The cotton was not yet ready when they returned to the Holgren ranch, but they couldn't wait for work, so Oca drove the family to Shafter to pick potatoes. They lived in a tent at the edge of a potato field, cooked on a camp stove, and spread blankets and bedrolls on the ground. By day the thermometer crept up to 110 degrees; at night it fell to the sixties, and the tent got cold. When they returned to the Holgren ranch, little Bill was feverish. They took him to Dr. Smith in Delano, who prescribed some medicine and sent him home. By the next morning, the child was having difficulty breathing. Mrs. Calvert came by to offer assistance.

"You'd better get him to a hospital," she said when she saw the baby's blue pallor.

"He's too far gone," cried Oca. "If God don't undertake for him right now, he's gone."

The baby was breathing with difficulty, and what Oca called a "death sweat" had popped out. Oca pressed his forehead against the dusty floorboards and prayed. "Spare him, Lord," he begged.

Then he stood up and looked at Ruby and Mrs. Calvert. "He's healed, I know it," he said. "We don't need any medicine now." The baby was still blue and sweating, but Oca felt flooded with joy. In a short while, the baby breathed easier. Bill would live.

Years later Oca would say he'd taken the Lord on as a partner then and there. "It was the first of so many things that I couldn't handle that He handled for me. I had to rely on Him. I didn't have an education, I couldn't rely on my knowledge of things. I didn't have opportunity the way I was brought up. He handled it for me."

CHAPTER FIVE

THE HORSE TRADER I

EVERY FARMER in the backcountry had a little of the horse trader in him. In a small rural county, there were always shortages of this and surpluses of that. Cash-poor farmers bartered, taking a saddle for a mule here, a coat for a pair of boots there.

Eventually, some would find that they were better horse traders than farmers, and they began to do it for a living. The professional horse trader served an essential purpose. In town, prices were posted and fixed, set by stores that held a monopoly. In the backcountry, price was "discovered" through bargaining. Riding the perimeter alone, the horse trader made a market in the sticks.

The renter or sharecropper was too tied down by his cotton crop and his livestock to know about the prices of milk cows and bridles in the next township. But the horse trader was always on the move, roaming, questioning, pricing, listening, weaseling information— spotting things. His capital was the software of humanity—rumors, sources, tips. He used his ears, and he circulated, letting his eye wander ceaselessly across the full spectrum of commodities, goods— and possibilities.

The rural South was a particularly fruitful habitat for the horse trader. Its economy was underdeveloped and fragile. The predominant architectural feature was the box house, the renter's board shack, the perfect symbol of transience and turnover. (Some renters hauled their boards with them to their next farm.) People made do by jury-rigging, as the tottering jalopies heading west clearly showed. Every farmer knew uses for things that had never been intended by their makers. Nothing was ever unwantable. In such a society the horse trader—the lone, itinerant economic actor conjuring up value with little more resources than his own imagination—prospered. He bought castoffs cheap and sold them where they were "short," based on his knowledge of "book value"—an article's rock-bottom intrinsic worth. A saddle's book value was, for example, what he could get for the cut-up leather.

Trading required very special qualities, especially a fearlessness and a supreme self-confidence. Most people thought and thought about their purchases, hesitating, figuring, calculating. They had to imagine exactly how some article could be used, how long it would last, what it would be worth in five years. The best of the horse traders acted—*then* he imagined. If the price was right, he knew, some use would turn up or he would let his wide circle of contacts find a use that had never occurred to him.

As long as he could *understand* what he was buying, of course. The horse trader believed in keeping it simple. If a deal was getting too complex—or too big—or if it required a specialist or a training manual to explain it, he backed away fast. It had to make sense.

A good horse trader had to be part salesman. He had to appear outgoing and optimistic, not morose or shifty, for it was his personality that put him into a bargaining situation. A good country peddler was like a good preacher. His sermon was optimism and hope and a better day tomorrow. A trader knew the words that could turn a few worn-out pieces of clothing into joy and opportunity. Partly it was technique, but mostly that ability came from temperament, instinct, and personality. He could create an atmosphere in which information came spilling out and opportunities suddenly presented themselves.

Yet under the banter would be an extremely shrewd mind working very fast, one that had already discounted the existing situation and moved five steps ahead, where it patiently lay in wait. For example, the horse trader might seem to volunteer all sorts of information about himself or what he was selling, when in fact he was giving away very little of real importance. At the same time, a good horse trader never asked direct questions, for they could reveal the gaps in his knowledge and weaken his position in the bargaining. He was a master of indirection, who could squeeze all the information out of another man without him knowing he had given away a single thing.

Once the bargaining began, he was not a man of sentiment. Some poor dirt farmer might be parting with his favorite cow or best saddle, but to the horse trader it was just a deal. This extremely focused quality could make him seem a hard man. Indeed, the horse trader's mind was not expansive or speculative. He wanted to know everything he thought he needed to know—but not a whit more. He was all business. The trading man couldn't afford to *need* people, for he had a hard job to do. A man who needed to be liked or loved would not have the mettle. Almost by definition, the great horse trader had an enormous capacity for self-sufficiency. He did not need to be needed. Otherwise, he would forever be reviewing the details of the last deal and worrying that he had got the best of the other man. And there was one thing a horse trader could not do, and that was go back and offer to renegotiate.

Some thought the horse trader was unscrupulous. In fact, he followed a particular, technical code of ethics. He never lied, but he wasn't obliged to say any more than he had to. He wasn't required to volunteer, for instance, that a certain horse was balky on hills. But there was no place in the community of horse traders for the man who would say absolutely *anything* to make a sale. In time, such people ended up dead, in jail, or simply shunned—a sorry fate for the trading man.

The horse trader's city cousin was the junk man. Both professions operated on the assumption that in twentieth-century America almost nothing was ever quite worn out. Cars, clothing, and radios wended their way down through the class structure, from the wives of rich Tulsa oil magnates to secondhand shops in small towns to poor tenant farmers, until eventually they were broken up or ripped apart and sold in pieces. The secondhand store and the junkyard were the grand bazaars of the American class structure, the points at which class as well as merchandise was mediated.

A great junk man was an artist and a creative force. His real assets were his fertile imagination and a good set of ears. He could imagine markets, and if *he* couldn't, he used the ideas of others. A good idea was something carried on the wind, like word of a good price for a used carburetor.

The junk man operated on a simple yet sophisticated theory of economic value: the sum of the parts is worth more than the whole.

The great junk men in New York, Boston, Chicago, and Los Angeles had an eye for *breakup value*. They were masters of deconstruction, of dissolving things into their useful parts. A used car might work perfectly well. The junk man disassembled it without ceremony, selling the radiator, engine block, and fenders to recoup his initial investment and making a profit on what was left.

Decades after Oca went to California, the economic theory of the junk business caused a revolution in the ownership of huge corporations. The financial experts who bought conglomerates, dismantled them, and sold them off piece by piece were celebrated for brilliant business acumen. In fact, they were doing no more than what their fathers and grandfathers had done, except that in many cases they were not doing it nearly as well.

THE THREE TATHAM BROTHERS, Walter, Arch, and Willy, were forever pricing buggies, cultivators, horses, sewing machines, cows. Willy Tatham, according to his niece Cleo, had been a professional trader of horses, and his brothers were enthusiastic amateurs.

One Sunday in church, the story went, Arch Tatham had edged up behind a neighbor and whispered: "If today was tomorrow, what would you take for that cultivator?"

Walter Tatham had sold Cora's favorite milk cow when they lived on Brushy Mountain. "If the man who got that cow shows up here I'll put buckshot in his britches," huffed Cora. That was years before he gave away her sewing machine.

But the profits never stuck to Walter. According to Cleo, he gave his money away—to a friend in need or, in later years, a grandchild. Willy told Cleo this about her father: "Walter Tatham can get more ahead in the least time of anybody I ever saw in my life. And he can get rid of it quicker."

It was his son, Oca Tatham, who was the real horse trader.

"He'd have pulled the shoes off his feet and sold them if he thought he could get a deal," Cleo said.

Oca had the gene. His fingers itched to make trades. He started peddling before he was a teenager, swapping a bicycle for a saddle horse and things like that. He even inherited the peculiar family trait of selling the belongings of one's close relatives. One day when his kid brother Vernon was at school, Oca traded Vernon's suit for a dog.

When he was a little older he told his cousins from Drake's Prairie: "If you're out workin' on a job, you could miss a deal."

One of the first deals he could remember was when he was a teenager living in Collinsville and saw a wolf pup tied up outside a store. "You want it, you can have it," said the store manager, seeing the boy's interest.

Oca muzzled the animal, thumbed a ride to Tulsa, and went to Woolworth's, where he sold it to a man who offered him fifteen dollars cash. Oca was home before dark. He thought about that afterward. He'd made as much money in four hours as a dairy hand could make in two weeks.

He was drawn to the thrift shops, junkyards, and used car lots of Tulsa. Rich oil and gas people tired quickly of their playthings. He picked up a cast-off fur coat from the Salvation Army for fifty cents and traded it to a woman for a twenty-five-pound sack of popcorn. There's a lot of eating there, Oca thought, and I can't eat the coat.

Automobiles were a drug on the market in the Depression. Sometimes Walter chipped in to buy cars with his son. With a car you could get round, make deals—or make a trade. Oca was driving a well-used seven-seat Cadillac touring car in Collinsville before he was married. He took out the rear seat and used the big vehicle to haul fruit and nuts between Collinsville and Kansas City. Nobody was harvesting the pecans in the Caney Fork River bottom because the farms had been lost for nonpayment of taxes. Cora and Cleo and Oca and a Sumpter cousin shook them down and loaded the nuts into the back of the Cadillac. Oca and Walter sold them at the outdoor markets in Kansas City, stocked up on apples, and sold the apples back in Collinsville.

Oca purchased cowboy boots and clothes for a few dollars at a Tulsa thrift shop, tucked them into the back of a Model T he was driving, and peddled the clothing to farmers around Claremore.

"What'll you give me for these boots and hats?" he asked a farmer who seemed interested.

"I can't give you anything except them three bull calves," said the farmer.

It was a deal. Oca and the farmer took two-by-fours and made a box in the back of the Model T. Somehow they stuffed the calves in. Oca drove to a slaughterhouse in Claremore and sold them for veal for fifteen dollars. That was a handsome profit for a day's work.

It seemed to his cousins living on Drake's Prairie that Oca always showed up in different vehicle, which he'd bought for a few dollars or traded for a horse or some clothing. Once he came visiting in a Moon car, a sleek rig with hydraulic brakes, a rumble seat, and a long shiny hood. He would trade a horse for a truck if it looked like a good deal. After the road job on Highway 66, he purchased a dump truck with bald tires and used it on another job around Gore. When the job was done, he traded the truck for a team of sorrels outside the blacksmith shop in Vian, where folks came to trade and talk.

Oca remembered it well because he got stung on the trade and had a good laugh at his own expense:

"A guy said, 'How would you like to trade that truck for my team of sorrels?' One of those sorrels was gorgeous. Looked like I'd be tradin' a Model T for a Model A. I looked that horse over and thought must be something wrong with that horse—some horses broke wind, which meant they couldn't get breath. I asked if the horse would work. He said sure, he'd made a crop with her.

"We started out from town prancing. When we hit the first hill I found out why the guy wanted to get rid of it. He either went full speed ahead or he stopped. I could use line pretty good. I realized, Well, that horse's spoiled, it's gonna take time to work that horse out. So when we hit a grade I just said, Go ahead, run up this mountain, go ahead. I'll work you down where you won't want to run so. Well we went all the way back in the mountains that way and came back the same way."

One hot September day in 1935 in California, not long after Bill's pneumonia, Oca walked out of the cotton field by McFarland and never went back. The story would be told many times in the family and became part of Tatham folklore. Oca was emptying his cotton sack at the scales when he overheard some other pickers talking. "They's selling potatoes for fifty cents a hundred over at Wasco," he heard.

"You can buy potatoes for *how* much?"

"Fifty cents a hundred pounds."

"You mean *good* ones?"

"I mean good."

"You gotta be kiddin'."

"Naw, I was just over there. You can buy all you want for fifty cents a hundred."

Oca didn't hesitate. Potatoes in his neck of the woods were selling for at least a dollar a hundred. You didn't have to be a genius to see the possibilities for arbitrage. Oca handed in his sack and told the crew boss he was done for the day. Then he climbed into his old Chevy and drove the thirty miles to Wasco.

He had four dollars, enough to buy eight sacks. He stuffed six of them into the Chevy and tied two more to the front fenders. Loaded with eight hundred pounds of spuds, the vehicle creaked, but nothing broke and Oca climbed in.

The dollar a hundred around McFarland and Delano was for culls that were too small or knobby to pass inspection. The potatoes he'd just bought were No. 2 rounds, good ones.

It was almost dark when he drove into the ditch-bank camp of some migrant cotton pickers. Women were busy over camp stoves and tubs of dishes, and men leaned back against the fenders of jalopies and scraped the last of the potatoes and gravy off plates.

"Hey, look what I got. Beautiful potatoes. What you been buyin' those culls for?"

They heard the familiar Oklahoma accent and sauntered over.

"You buy mine from the middle not the top," he said, slashing a sack lengthwise with a knife. "See? No culls."

By the time he'd finished that night he'd sold all eight sacks and made four dollars' profit, same as a couple of hard days of cotton picking. He did it again the next day and the next. Pretty soon he had a routine. When Ruby went to the cotton field, he'd drive to Wasco and load up. He'd bring the sacks of potatoes back to the shack on the Holgren ranch, stack the potatoes inside, then go back for more. He'd do this until his money ran out. He could double his money on each trip.

After quitting time in the fields he'd load the Ford with potatoes and drive north. The weary pickers in the camps along Highway 99 were glad to see a peddler. He wouldn't waste time. He'd make his sales pitch, take his money, and leave. When he'd sold his load he'd head home for another.

Oca was too busy to dwell on the plight of the poor migrants and farm workers he traded with. It didn't pay to think too much about it, and a trader just didn't have the time. Some days he kept going till early in the morning. He'd wake people in their tents and sell them potatoes. The pickers would come out, rubbing their eyes, barefoot, hobbling through the sand and cockleburs, and Oca would give them the sales pitch: "No culls." He "sold from the middle."

At times the wooden shack at the Holgren ranch creaked and groaned from the weight of potatoes stacked from floor to ceiling. Oca worried the joists would split.

His daughter Doris remembers the "potato house" being "filled with potatoes. We had a place to sleep and a teeny little kitchen. Probably had no paint. I mean it was probably something that nobody would have wanted, but remember, we didn't have anything. We were starting from zero. As far as clothes or furniture or anything, I mean we were just existing, we probably didn't have furniture, and it was important to have a place to put those potatoes, so I remember ceiling-to-the-floor potatoes stacked in there. And he'd go out selling them. He'd go out and sack them and bring them in and sell them."

Oca made twenty dollars some days while friends and relatives from Oklahoma were sweating all day in the cotton fields to make two or three. Within six weeks he had enough money to order a gunmetal gray 1936 Ford pickup truck from the dealer in Delano. His cousin Ira and Ruby went to pick it up—Oca was out trading and couldn't spare the time.

It was a beauty, and it opened up new possibilities. He could pack in a lot more potatoes, and soon he was running potatoes up to country stores, taking care to steer clear of bigger towns where they might ask to see a peddler's license. He added crates of oranges and onions to the sacks of potatoes stacked up in his house and started hauling culls to ranchers for hog feed.

Then one day, the bottom dropped out of the potato market. The cotton season ended, people who'd worked a whole season were broke, and Oca had a houseful of unsold spuds. As he made his rounds, his eyes roamed over the old radiators, tires, batteries, and wheel rims that littered the camps. He didn't want to skin up his new pickup with that stuff, but his potatoes would be sprouting soon if he didn't sell them.

"What are you going to do with all that iron?" he asked.

"We don't know."

"I'll give you a sack of potatoes for it," Oca said.

It started all over again. Oca would buy some stoves, clean them up, paint them, put in new wicks, and sell them to families who had come to look for winter work in the vineyards.

"What was popular then was three-burner and two-burner kerosene stoves, hot plates, just a little stove, a little oven. And I would buy those, take them and clean them up, give them a good working over, and have a really good-looking stove. And the same thing with the oven. Paint them and all, have them looking nice. Anything they had in camping supplies, I'd buy and then turn it around. And they were glad to get it. So I caught them coming and going. I'd trade if they didn't have but a couple of hens. I think I traded for two or three pigs and a few hens one day. You couldn't go wrong 'cause you could eat 'em. It wasn't a pleasant situation; it was a necessary situation. Some people were doing without."

The pile of old radiators, wheel rims, and bedsprings that piled up in the yard of the potato house attracted the interest of a Jewish junk dealer from L.A. who took out four crisp ten-dollar bills and counted them out on the hood of Oca's pickup.

"Take that money and if you get a good buy on stuff, get it, and I'll buy it from you," he said.

Oca had never seen the likes of that. That junk dealer was advancing him forty dollars, knowing he might never lay eyes on him again! After a few weeks of doing business, Oca began to think he could win the Jewish junk man for the Lord.

Before Christmas 1935, Oca rented a place in Delano. The Holgrens wanted the place for farm workers, and they knew from the pile of junk that Oca was moving into other things. Ruby left the orange crates behind for the new tenants. She figured they could use a "kitchen set."

Their new home was at 1223 Glenwood Avenue, half a block west of the Southern Pacific Railroad tracks—on the "wrong side" but within walking distance of the Delano packing sheds. There was a Filipino church next door and it was "full Gospel" Pentecostal, not Catholic. Down the street was a barbershop, a five-and-dime, Pete's Saloon, and a Filipino market. Farther down was the red-light district, with beer joints and a whorehouse.

Their place was a good-sized frame house that rested on cement blocks, with a second-story, screened front porch and a fenced backyard with a shed where Oca could store his junk. Oca got it for ten dollars a month. It had electricity, a tiny kitchen, and a flush toilet off the back porch. Ruby took in boarders—single men with jobs— and put them on the second floor. The whole Tatham family slept on the first floor.

There was a driven, sleepless quality about Oca in those first months in Delano. Doris would look out in the evening and see her dad sorting glass and aluminum and cast iron by the light of a street lamp. His eyes always seemed bloodshot, and he had a squint.

There were nights when he was in the yard until two in the morning, he recalled, "separating iron, beating cast iron away from the other iron, separating steel, takin' all the aluminum off a motor and all the brass and copper and everything, and putting it in one pile. I had a light bulb I was workin' by. I was doin' all those things like that, start every morning and end up with a load of junk. Because I had to do it. I didn't let up, I just kept going. There was no place to quit."

Doris remembers, "He worked lots of hours. He would run instead of walk. He was a young man going somewhere, and he was always conscious that he didn't have a fine education and that he had to work more carefully and work harder."

His son Bill remembers Oca chasing people who'd come in from the back alley to steal furniture from the junk shed: "I remember them buying hogs and slaughtering them in the backyard. I remember them hanging them up and cutting them open."

When the authorities made a bonfire of abandoned cars in a field by Delano, Oca was ticketed for crossing the fire line to check out the salvage possibilities. He made a deal for the scrap when he went to the station to pay his fine. No deal was beneath his dignity. He moved into the niches nobody else cared about. In 1936, he set up Tatham's Tire Shop and Wheel Exchange on High Street and began dealing in used tires and rims. He promoted it aggressively, painting the shop's name on the side of the Ford pickup and adding some advertising logo for a Ford dealer.

Balloon tires were replacing the harder, high-pressure tires, and farmers couldn't get enough of them. Oca went to the auto shops in Bakersfield and scrounged wheels and rims that had been bent in wrecks. Back at Tatham's Tire he'd straighten the wheels and regroove worn tires with a hot iron. Then he'd rig farmers' cotton trailers with secondhand balloon tires.

It didn't work every time, as a customer who came in with an Austin sports car found out to his dismay. Oca said, "We put Model A twenty-one-inch spoke wheel tires on it, took his hubs, and welded his hubs into the Model A wheels. That meant he never could put others back anymore. They were so big he couldn't turn a corner, and he had to put it in low gear to run the thing. It'd just get up and fly in second gear. The guy would have to back up to turn the corner. It just destroyed the car."

Within two years of settling in Delano, Oca bought several flatbed trucks and an eighty-five-horsepower semitrailer and hired a couple of drivers. He learned to talk the language of the bosses at the packing sheds and ranches around Delano. He put his smaller trucks to work at nearby potato farms, providing a driver and swamper to haul the partially filled potato sacks to the sheds for grading.

He was a scrapper who occasionally tested his wrestling skills in matches at the sheds. He remembers, "I knew where to get 'em and just what to do. And I used my legs as well as my arms, and I'd get a 'cramp hold' on a guy and just cut his wind off, you know." He became "tougher than a boot." More important, his wrestling feats caught the attention of shed bosses who hired the trucks for hauling No. 1 potatoes, melons, or hay to Los Angeles.

On these runs to L.A., he could not resist the auctions and second-hand shops. After he and the driver had delivered the potatoes or hay to the market, they would swing around to a sale or poke around. Oca noticed that the Hollywood crowd discarded their belongings almost as quickly as the oil and gas magnates of Tulsa. Cabinet radios purchased for a dollar in L.A. could be sold to farmers and foremen in Delano for a good markup.

That was his "luxury" trade, but he did not neglect the low end of the market. He brought back mattresses, bedding, and furniture and sold them to the transients who worked on the ranches. Pretty soon there was too much for him to sell on his own, so he opened his first store in a vacant motion picture theater in the melon-growing community of Buttonwillow and had a Pentecostal preacher friend mind it. For a while he operated two other stores in Shafter and Delano under the logo Bargain Center Furniture, and put his dad in charge.

He was building a network of connections. He did his banking at First National Bank of Delano, which was run by Loren R. Billings, a legendary, six-foot-six man who was reputed to have shot a bank robber dead. Billings, who had a loud voice, intimidated and fright-ened many of the Okies who came in looking for a loan. Even Oca felt a little intimidated by him. In those days, small-town bankers made loans on the basis of character assessments. The loans were Billings' judgment of Oca's character.

The local blacksmith let him use his shop at night to convert his trucks to flatbeds or to rig up sideboards, depending on the job. The owner of the Delano lumberyard let him take whatever boards he needed over the fence at night and keep his own list of what he'd used.

Oca understood that imagination, energy, and nerve could create value—and he never needed an elaborate education to convince him otherwise. He had that readiness to roam, to seek out the niches that others overlooked or disdained, and an eye for the value in society's disposables.

Walter Tatham said of his son, "He was born when hogs was high—everythin' he touches turns to money."

He floated like a bee above the economy, pollinating a transaction and then moving on. He never stuck to something that didn't work, and he usually abandoned things that *were* working before everyone else. Once a line of business became overcrowded with franchised dealerships or heavily regulated by government inspectors, he would be long gone.

Oca seldom had a plan, but he always had a premise: if it was cheap enough, there'd be a market. Over the years he applied that simple maxim again and again to horses, cars, junk, land, houses, schools, and hospitals. It led him into new activities ahead of most other people—and out of them just as fast.

But it looked easier than it was. Would-be emulators found they didn't have the knack. His cousin Orville, Willy Tatham's son, envied Oca's success peddling spuds. Orville was thrifty and hardworking and had saved enough to acquire a 1936 Ford pickup just like Oca's, but he was reluctant to scrape up his beautiful new pickup or break the hundred-dollar bill he carried in his shoe.

"Try it," Oca coaxed. Orville broke his bill reluctantly and bought some potatoes. But right away he ran into problems. Trying to sell to the pickers during the heat of the day when they were busy in the fields, he found few takers and complained to Oca: "You got me to sell potatoes, and now I've broken my hundred and I'm stuck with them."

Oca took him out that night and demonstrated how to "sell from the middle." Orville improved, but he wasn't a peddler.

Oca understood in a way that Orville never did that money could work for you, same as a mule or a truck. Oca borrowed to the hilt, from the bank, from friends, from relatives, leaving himself and Ruby only the bare minimum to live on.

His borrowing showed self-confidence. The truly self-reliant didn't sock money away "for a rainy day." To borrow was to make a personal wager with the lender that one could get a higher return. Oca's borrowed money never went for food, or socks, or a new car, but only to invest in Oca Tatham and his business ventures.

He sometimes borrowed back his truck drivers' wages. Among the drivers, Oca did not have a reputation as a big payer, but he always paid them back. He borrowed fifty dollars from his cousin Leslie for a used Studebaker. After he fixed up the upholstery and cleaned it, he sold it for a profit and paid Leslie off with interest.

"Oca could make more money trading than working with his hands," said Leslie. Ira said Oca "was always connivin', he was a hustler." Their pastor, Jay Fuller, saw Oca as a "go-getter," and his wife said Oca "borrowed money from us a lot when he didn't have any. He'd come by and want to borrow whatever my husband could let him have. He was in the trucking business and sometimes he was in between jobs and waiting for his money and then he would see if we had any we could loan him. And then, of course, he'd pay it back, you know. It was just a struggle."

Every loose dollar Oca and Ruby had went for food, clothing, or the offertory plate. Ruby made do with secondhand. Oca said, "My wife went to the Salvation Army and bought men's suits and got the beautiful material out of them and made those kids some fine suits of clothes and they were good ones."

Maxine Kooken, a Delano neighbor, remembers Ruby being almost penniless because their money was tied up. "She called me and asked me if I would come over and take her out to an old farmer who owed them some money," Maxine said. "She didn't have anything in the house for the kids to eat, and they'd be home for lunch. So I went over and got her, and we went out. I don't know what the fellow owed her or anything about it, but he did give her fifty cents. And so we came back to the grocery and I think got a can of pork and beans and a loaf of bread. Seemed like she got about three canned items. But I remember the pork and beans and the bread."

Ruby looked after the boarders they kept upstairs on Glenwood. Doris said, "Mother did the sewing, mending, cooking, washing, and ironing, and she washed on a washboard with big tubs of water with blueing in it. She did all the washing for all these men, and she fed them breakfast and dinner and packed their lunches. They paid ten dollars a week for room and board during that time, and she did everything. To come out on this she had to do a lot of canning and a lot of cooking, and after the children and everybody was asleep at night she would do the ironing. Sometimes she would iron until two and she'd have to get up at four to start breakfast so they could get out in their trucks."

Ruby began to wear rubber stockings for her varicose veins, and Maxine Kooken remembers her suffering from "a lot of sick headaches. I went over and helped her, and she'd be so sick with the head."

In the first year in Delano, Ruby canned lots of damaged fruit that Oca brought home from the packing sheds. They'd load the pickup with fruit and dump it into big washbasins full of hot water to make the skins come off. Doris would sit and help her mother peel.

OCA WAS NOT of the school that held to a belief that poverty glorified God. John Wesley stressed love, emotion, "heart purity," and a simple life-style, but he acknowledged that "religion must necessarily produce both industry and frugality, and these cannot but produce riches."[1]

In that respect, Oca was a California version of John Hull, the self-made blacksmith's son, shipowner, and prominent citizen of the Massachusetts Bay Colony who believed that "religion included seizing the main chance, and sin was synonymous with wasted opportunities." Since God was absolute Lord of all things, an individual had a duty to the Almighty to improve what he had.[2]

Still, it took Oca time to learn that a Christian had to be patient. He wondered: *Why am I still poor? If other Christians had good shoes, why do I have to wear pasteboard inner soles and shine the uppers—and the soles gone on them? Why, Lord?* He was paying his tithes, attending church regularly, and praying. But he was still struggling financially.

Finally, he figured it out: the Lord simply wasn't ready for him to be rich. He hadn't been proven. He said, "When you give and are faithful at a time when God tries you and you come through, and God feels like He can trust you to do it, why *then* He'll give it to you."

To Oca, there was no contradiction between his search for material opportunities and membership in a strict church that foresaw the imminent demise of this world. The Bible left ample room for the Christian entrepreneur, and Oca had an individualistic approach to business and God alike. Sometimes it seemed as if he had taken the Lord in as a kind of business partner.

Sometimes he'd pull the truck over on a shoulder outside a town and pray to God to help him sell the spuds. He'd tell the Lord he'd worked a town in every direction and gone as far as he could go, and now he needed His help. Then he'd start up the car and go looking for people to buy potatoes. And God would be right there advising, encouraging, warning about dangers and pitfalls.

Doris remembers her parents "taking it to God" when they were unsure about business decisions. Her father "felt a sense of direction in some of his businesses and decisions because he and Mom would pray. It made him feel safe to go ahead and do something. And if he felt he was, 'checked by the Holy Spirit,' as he called it, a door would close. He would realize that he wasn't supposed to do that and something would let him know. In all that, he realized that God's wisdom was far superior to man's, and he depended on his relationship with God to direct him in a lot of things."

If he came home from an auction at which his bid had not been accepted, Doris said, "He wasn't devastated—because God did not mean him to have it." But if his bid *was* accepted, it was a sign that it was part of God's plan. Oca listened to the Lord's business advice. He said of at least one major business transaction, "The Lord gave me the price."

Oca left it in God's hand whether he would succeed. It was God's Plan—the Puritans called it Providence—whether a particular enterprise would be profitable. Looking back on those years, he said, "God knows a-way ahead of time what's going to happen and He actually prepares *for* it, whether we believe it or not. He prepares everything in advance, so that things happen just in their right time."

But this did not mean that a Christian could sit back and wait for the phone to ring. When a person walked out into the world confident that something good would happen, he demonstrated faith. And then usually something good did happen. He knew from his own answered prayers. "I was just facing a brick wall. I mean, it looked like I'd caved in. And I told Ruby, 'We're going to have to pray.' Right there in the living room we knelt down and I'll never forget that prayer. 'Dear God, I've tried to be faithful with my finances and my givings. I've hauled lumber for churches free. I've done things that really I wasn't able to do, but I did them anyway, for the church. Now, God, I've went as far as I can go, done everything possible to find a job and there's no jobs to find. I feel now it's time, Lord, for You to do what You said You'd do: You've said You'd bless me. Now, Lord, You take over because I've come to the end of the road. You furnish the job."

"We've got a job," he told Ruby after he got up from the floor. And sure enough, that very same day he walked over to Main Street in Delano and got work for his trucks hauling sand for the construction of the new Purity Market. The lesson was clear: "Was God going to have to lead me by the nose? Or make the guy come over and hunt me up? No, He expected me to have enough faith to go over and talk to somebody."

DORIS TURNED SIX their first year in Delano. She got a nickel-a-week allowance and worried all week about how to use the money. Ice cream was best but was gone in a jiffy. So she'd compromise on a sucker, some gum, and a pencil that would last her for a month.

It was a bittersweet time—sweet because they were poor but could see some prospects but bitter because there was sadness and loss and life was still very hard.

The Lord didn't bring a miracle every time trouble arose.

On July 5, 1936, Ruby gave birth to their fourth child, a boy they named Oca Junior. As always, a new baby was an occasion of great joy. And in its own way, the selection of the name was a sign of confidence and hope for the future. It suggested continuity. Cora, who by then was living with Walter and their family some blocks away, came over to help Ruby with the older children and fuss over her new grandson. But the child was sickly from the start.

In late October, an intestinal flu swept through the valley, taking the lives of hundreds of children. They would run fevers, develop diarrhea, go into convulsions, and die. It was the worst epidemic that the doctors at Kern County General Hospital in Bakersfield had confronted, and they seemed helpless to deal with it. Nothing seemed to change the course of the sickness. The doctors fell back on the only remedy known, rice water and tea.

Ruby's brother Robert and his family had just come out from Oklahoma in the fall of 1936 when their baby got it. Within a day or two, it hit the baby of Ruby's sister Melvina. Both children died within the week. Little Oca took ill at almost the same time, on a Friday in late October. A week later—the same week that Franklin Roosevelt was elected to a second term as President of the United States— Oca Junior died. The death certificate attributed the cause to severe malnutrition resulting from diarrhea. Ruby dressed him and put him in a small open casket, over which the family kept an all-night vigil at the Glenwood Avenue place. Someone got out the Box Brownie, and Ruby, Oca, and Doris took turns holding the dead child while each member of the family had a last picture taken with him. Click, click, click went the camera as the other children stood numbly by.

The three babies were buried close together in Delano Cemetery, a peaceful place west of town surrounded by wheat fields. One of the other two families—Oca could not remember which one—used the foot of little Oca's grave for their baby. They could not afford a burial plot of their own.

CHAPTER SIX

IMMIGRANTS

FROM 1936 UNTIL PEARL HARBOR, farm families from Sequoyah County, Oklahoma, piled onto jalopies, trucks, buses, and trains and headed for a tiny farm town along Highway 99 in California. "Sallisaw took Delano without firing a shot," cracked an old-timer.

Oca Tatham was no Joseph Smith leading his people across the Utah desert to a new promised land. He was too busy pursuing his own interests to care whether anyone followed or not. But he *was* a kind of Okie Seropian. The Seropians were Armenian brothers who had come to Fresno in the early 1880s and, by succeeding in the raisin- and fig-packing business, showed the way for thousands of their countrymen to follow.

To a good many people on Drake's Prairie, Delano meant a new gunmetal gray Ford pickup truck that appeared on their section roads around Christmas 1935. Oca and Ruby had driven back in it to be with their parents after those first successful months as a peddler of potatoes and junk. He made sure to display it on the prairie, and the new truck spoke volumes to the renters and sharecroppers. A fellow who hadn't amounted to much when he left Drake's Prairie in

August 1934 was doing all right for himself in a place called Delano fifteen months later.

The following spring and summer was droughty on the prairie and some farmers just gave up. The exodus began. From Drake's Prairie came Smiths, Lands, Littlejohns, Eskews, Callahans, Bracketts, Wessons, Brannams, Andersons, Sparks, and Tathams. Ben Callahan ran a round-trip taxi service, carting a load of folks to Delano, resting a day, then carrying another load back over the Tehachapis to visit relatives in Sequoyah County. Soon neighbors from Mule's Head Bottom were comparing notes outside the Purity Market on Delano's Main Street, and folks from the Free Holiness church at Watts were working in California side by side at Joseph DiGiorgio's packing sheds or at his vast Sierra Vista ranch east of town.

Cora and her three youngest children had stayed around Sallisaw while Walter was in Knights Landing with Oca. Walter was back in Oklahoma again in time for Oca's Christmas visit and braved a snowstorm to see Norma after her fourth and last child was born. By then Walter had had enough of winter and of Oklahoma. In early 1936 he loaded his family into Cleo's Studebaker and had Cleo drive them to Delano for good. Arch Tatham followed later in 1936. His oldest boys already were in Delano; Arch's family lived for a while on a corner lot in "Jap town," a few blocks from Oca and Ruby, then got a cabin on the DiGiorgio ranch with running water and electricity but no inside bath. Compared to what many were living in, it was a palace. There were grapes all around. Soon Oca's Aunt Pearl and her husband came from Oklahoma and found jobs running a hamburger stand in town.

The same four Tathams who had left Missouri for the Indian Territory in 1902—Walter, Willy, Arch, and Pearl—were all living within a few square miles of each other in and around Delano. By the end of 1937, most of Oca and Ruby's relatives and friends, except for Norma, had left Oklahoma and were living within a few blocks. Ruby's parents had quit farming in Oklahoma and took up residence in a homemade trailer with plywood siding on the back of Oca and Ruby's lot on Glenwood, and Ruby's brothers and sisters were also close by.

The exodus divided some families. Most of the Sumpters stayed in Oklahoma. John Sumpter's son Ray had gone to California before anyone else, in 1924, and after Cora joined Oca in Delano in 1936, her sister Myrtle and husband followed. But that was about all. Sumpters were doing all right in Oklahoma. It was the Depression: people with jobs or decent situations didn't risk change.

The migration divided Arch Tatham's in-laws, the Eskews, about equally between California and Oklahoma. Typically, jobs were the main reason. One Eskew woman stayed put because her husband had a steady job with the Arkansas and Oklahoma Gas Company. But often it was the women more than the men who were ready to move. The men sometimes felt overwhelmed by California and its modern ways. But the women, who bore the brunt of the cold winters, children's sicknesses, and lack of medical care, were ready for something better. In Oklahoma, they likely as not supported their families by taking in laundry, or keeping boarders, or nursing the sick when their husbands couldn't get jobs in the depressed economy. In California, there was a better chance that their husbands could find a job.

Hoeing cotton on the Twin Pines Ranch one day in 1934, Cleo Tatham told her father, "Dad, one of these days I'm going to be twenty-one, and then I'm never moving again."

"Aww, you live under my roof, if you're forty you'll mind," said Walter.

"I'm here," she said firmly. "I'm sick of moving. I'm satisfied here, so I'm going to stay."

"Aww, if we go, you go."

"No sir, when I'm twenty-one years old I'll decide. And I *have* decided. I'm never going to leave Delano."

Once a decision had been made to go to California, people took whatever transportation was available.

Leslie Tatham was a strapping, slow-talking twenty-year-old when he rode the freights out to join his cousin Oca in Knights Landing in 1935. When the MoPac train came through, he hopped aboard and rode it all the way to Osawatomie, Kansas.

"We were heading west through Kansas and just near sundown I jumped off and got me a little something to eat and climbed back on. Then sometime in the night in western Kansas, when they stopped at some little burg that wasn't hardly on the map, they put a bunch of us off right at the street crossing. By that time, I knew what a highball was: when they give two whistles, they's fixing to take off. They just pulled that string and let that whistle blow. When that thing highballed, I saw there was two railroad bulls—brakies, they called them—I just took off around the edge of the depot in the stockyard and run about two blocks. As we started circling back the train began to pick up speed, and there was a brakie runnin' alongside the train, and he hollered, 'Don't catch that train, I'll shoot you.' But I was going to California. I caught it anyhow.

"I got on the train and walked around behind some oil cars, and he come up behind us and got up on top and walked to where the oil cars were. I was gettin' scared, then because we was doin' forty, fifty miles an hour and I was scared he'd come up there and shoot us. I didn't know anything about what they'd do to you. I was just a kid. But he set down there a little while, and we was ridin' an oil car that had a rail around it where you could hook your arm around.

"About daylight way out in western Kansas in the corn and wheat country, it went off onto a switch for a passenger train coming the other way. When it did we three guys got off and got into this corn about knee-high over across the fence, and two guys came from the back and one from the front. Well, there was three against two. So when it highballed and started getting back on the track, I just started runnin' up through that field of June corn. When this brakie got to the switch I looked back and those two guys were headin' 'em off. I caught hold in the middle of the train and rode it on into Colorado, where a few Spanish got on. By the time we got to Pueblo there was two hundred sitting on top of the train like blackbirds. In one boxcar, guys were throwing bowie knives at the side of the car. I still had my five dollars tucked away. I rode it into Sacramento. When I got there I busted my five-dollar bill and ate a good meal. It was dangerous in a way. In another, it was cheap transportation."

Oca's Okie friend Jack Kooken came out the traditional way. He'd been born in the former Cherokee Strip, the dry wheat and cotton country just east of the Dust Bowl. His granddad came there from Kansas in the boomer days, but the family's land had been sold or lost somehow, so Jack's dad sharecropped. Jack considered farming, but when he'd walk through a field of broomweed or poke around in the sand hills and cocklebur patches wondering how he could ever grow crops *there*. Soon after Jack married Maxine, his dad gave him forty dollars and two tires and told him to go to California. It was 1937. Jack bought a '28 Chevy Roadster for $7.50. He said, "I didn't have the money to buy side glasses for that car, so I took them curtain windshields off another car and then got an orange crate, made me a sideboard one on each side, and soldered the glass up a little bit and set the sideboard in, and then I'd roll it up and thataway it'd be all closed up. That's what we came to California in."

They headed west at thirty-five miles an hour, eating bread, bologna, and beans and sleeping in barns and farmhouses. "We were afraid of a holdup," Jack admitted.

Jack tried tying grapes at the Franzi Winery in Ripon, but he made grannies instead of square knots and they let him go. They went on to Reedley and found the uncle of a man who farmed near them in Oklahoma. He was now a big man in the automobile business, and he arranged for Jack to go to work at a Chevy garage he owned in Delano.

"We'll put you to work," said the manager when Jack reported the next Monday morning, "but we can't pay you no money."

That was fine with Jack. He wanted to show he could work. And after a while they put him on the payroll at seventy-five dollars a week. When he drew his first paycheck he put twelve in the bank. Jack saved his money and kept his mouth shut. When he'd hear people cussing Okies, he didn't let on he was one. He ditched his Oklahoma plates as soon as he got the chance, for he knew he wasn't going back to the dust country.

Dwight "Buck" Dodson, one of Ruby's boarders hailed from Missouri's Bootheel. He'd hopped a freight one day in 1936 and come to Stockton. Young and penniless, he'd floated around picking beans and living in a "hobo jungle," where men chipped in to buy a few pieces of meat and some potatoes for a common stewpot. A contractor came by and hired them to pick cherries and live in a barracks full of Italian workers, who gave the Okies a hard time. But in the cherry orchards, it was all for one and one for all.

Buck said, "I was standing on a sixteen-foot ladder poking cherries off the top. There was a little four-inch bolt that holds the end of the ladder to the stand it sets on and it broke. I came right down through the tree, breaking off branches as I came. When I hit I had both arms full of cherry limbs. The owner was right there and said, 'Fire that man.' But those Italians come down out of their trees and they was all gonna go. So they talked it over for a while and decided we could go back."

Work was pretty scarce. Buck made his way to Delano for the 1937 grape and cotton harvest. He picked up a day hire here and there, until one day he ran into Walter Tatham in a cotton field. He slept at Walter's for a while, then moved to Oca and Ruby's.

The trip west could be a dangerous undertaking. Coming out in 1936, Walter Tatham and his family ran into dust storms so thick that patrolmen were stopping cars. They took refuge in a roadside guest cabin, but even with the doors and windows shut they had to cover their noses and mouths with damp handkerchiefs to keep from breathing the dust. Afterward they could write their names on the dinner plates.

On New Year's Day 1937, Leslie Tatham was bringing a load of people from Drake's Prairie in a pickup truck rigged with a "home-made top—two-by-twos and canvas." Eleven people were aboard, including his mother Winnie, and several children. A little way out of Las Cruces, on Highway 80, a passenger car coming the other way drove them off the road. An axle snapped and the pickup flipped. Winnie broke her collarbone, and there were plenty of bruises and chipped teeth. A hotel in Las Cruces put them up for free, and a doctor came over and set Winnie's collarbone. Leslie called Delano, and Orville Tatham drove eight hundred miles in his pickup to fetch them.

The lure of California was simple: cash money. Throughout most of the 1930s, California's unemployment rate was nearly as high as Oklahoma's—in 1937, 11.8 percent as against 13.6 percent. But the pay was better in California, and for agricultural labor it was much better. Daily pay for field work averaged $2.70 in California compared with only $1.30 in Oklahoma on January 1, 1937.[1]

Outside Tulsa, the state of California erected a billboard that said: "No Jobs in California. If you are out of work keep out! No state relief available for non-residents." It didn't stop many. Some 96,742 migrants from Texas, Missouri, Oklahoma, and Arkansas came in 1936, 104,976 in 1937, and close to 120,000 in 1938.[2] Only a tiny number of the Oklahomans, perhaps no more than 2 or 3 percent, came from the westernmost six counties of the state, where the black blizzards were creating the Dust Bowl.[3] It wasn't dust that was causing the migration, but a larger economic breakdown. In the 1930s thousands of people moved away from America's industrial areas and cities and back to small towns and rural villages. Sallisaw, a rural center and a cotton-ginning town, saw its population *increase* during the decade from 1,785 to 2,140. Half the population was under twenty-one years old. The movement back to the farms and small towns was driven by desperation, but it did not alleviate the economic pressures. California, which now had lots of cotton, along with many other crops with which Oklahomans were less familiar, was the escape valve.

Around Delano, the main attraction for the Tathams and dozens of other Sequoyah County families was the DiGiorgios' 9,000-acre Sierra Vista Ranch with its vineyards, vegetable crops, and packing sheds. Joseph DiGiorgio, the son of a Sicilian lemon grower, played an important role in the Tatham saga. He had left home at fourteen and within a decade was operating a fleet of banana boats out of New York City. He arrived in the Bakersfield area in 1919, a millionaire still in his twenties. Long-staple Acala cotton was about to be introduced, and more powerful pumps and artesian wells would soon inaugurate the era of large-scale irrigated farming. The huge farms that DiGiorgio laid out near Arvin and Delano became models for the valley's budding "industrial agriculture."

A lot of the countryside in those parts was still only good for cattle and dryland wheat farming. A few descendants of the Russian immigrants who had reached the valley in the 1880s came to hack away at the poor, alkaline land west of Bakersfield. To the east, wheat fields stretched all the way to the Sierra foothills. Rainfall was sparse, and the Kern and Kings rivers were too distant to provide irrigation water. Then came artesian wells and the first small plots of fruits and vegetables.

East of Bakersfield the undeveloped land was cheap, and in 1922 Joseph DiGiorgio acquired several thousand acres there. It had to be cleared, leveled, and planted, and some of the grapevines did not work out well, but DiGiorgio sent experts to Europe to bring back other varieties. Thompson Seedless eventually accounted for a quarter of the total, for that variety grew well in the local soil and climate. By the 1930s, the DiGiorgios' Earl Fruit Company managed twenty-seven farm properties of its own and leased another eleven holdings. It owned eleven packinghouses and shipped 1,000 freight-car loads of produce annually. It had its own crating and boxing company and controlled two wineries, including the largest in the United States. Earl Fruit also owned the Baltimore Fruit Exchange and held interests in fruit auction houses in Chicago, New York, Cincinnati, and Pittsburgh.[4] At the packing plants around Delano, lines of trucks discharged cargos of watermelons, eggplants, onions, potatoes, peaches, melons, prunes, almonds, peas, grapes, raisins, and cotton. Inside, dexterous hands and fingers stacked, sorted, washed, tied, and cut the incoming produce. And in the surrounding fields, trucks, tractor-drawn sleds, and other specially adapted machinery stirred up clouds of dust above the heads of the armies of pickers.

The Sierra Vista Ranch outside Delano was the agricultural equivalent of a Piedmont textile mill. It anchored the whole economy of Delano, McFarland, and the country around, providing hourly employment for as many as 1,800 people in peak seasons. It operated like a factory, with a rigid hierarchy of foremen, subforemen, irrigators, pruners, swampers, truck drivers, handymen, and pickers. It had its own labor camps for single men, segregated by race and nationality. There were two "Jap" camps, a "Filipino" camp, a "Mexican" camp, and an "American" camp. Field-workers were usually under a boss of their own nationality and ate their own national cooking prepared by a cook of their nationality in their own mess hall.

Because so much of the Sierra Vista Ranch was devoted to vineyards that required year-round attention, it sustained a more stable force of agricultural labor than ranches in some of the other valley towns. Arch Tatham and his family were fortunate to be living there, for after the picking, packing, and processing of grapes came winter pruning, spring hoeing, irrigating, and other caretaking of the 6,000 acres of vines.

Oca Tatham was one of the few men in Delano from Drake's Prairie who never worked in the DiGiorgio fields or sheds. For most of those arriving from the Sallisaw area, the way into California led through the Sierra Vista Ranch. Arch, Leslie, and Alma's husband, Bill McKinney pruned, cut, and swamped grapes there. Cora Tatham worked in the packing sheds. Leslie worked through the whole grape cycle. Wine grapes grew on low vines, and harvesters had to work on their haunches or knees, cutting the bunches and placing them in lugs. The hazards were sunstroke, wasps, cuts from the knife, and bellyaches from eating grapes, but it paid five cents a lug. Picking table grapes started each morning after the dew was off, which made for a short day. Harvesters "picked by color," leaving the greener bunches for later, and placed the bunches in "field packs." In winter, Leslie pruned and tied vines and clipped cuttings for new plants. He and Jack Smith wrapped potato sacks around their legs to keep warm. From March until the grapes started ripening they irrigated. Eventually, Leslie was promoted to swamper, which involved picking up the boxes and field packs of grapes or raisins that were left in the fields by the harvesters. Driving paid a few cents more an hour, but it still seemed to Leslie that ranch management had it set so that whatever the work was it usually came out to $2.50 a day. For the women who were not too busy washing, cooking, and scrubbing for their husbands and children, there was shed work. Cleo and Cora graded potatoes in Wasco and Shafter and tomatoes in Delano. In early winter, Cleo got a job at a pea shed behind the Chevy dealer in Delano. The peas were graded in refrigerated sheds. Cakes of ice were stacked along one wall, and the women wore long underwear to keep warm.

Though California agriculture operated on an industrial scale, Delano was still a small town—a kind of blue-collar factory town. The year-round population was only a little over 9,000 at the end of the

1930s. Yet it encompassed ethnic diversity that was more like that of a big city than a small farming community. Mexicans had predominated in the fields until the arrival of the Okies, and many still worked in the crops. The Filipinos who lived in a large dormitory at the Sierra Vista Ranch and around Delano, had been actively recruited to help solve the agricultural labor shortage in California resulting from the 1924 Exclusion Act that restricted Japanese emigration. But in 1934 quotas were imposed on Philippine workers, too.

The house on Ellington Street that Walter and Cora Tatham rented was in a neighborhood of Russian Americans—"big old muscled-up things with beards," Cleo remembers. "Japtown" was only a few blocks from Oca and Ruby's house on Glenwood, and next door was the Filipino Church. The agricultural elite was made up of a mixture of Italian and Croatian Americans, the latter group mostly from the sunny Adriatic island of Hvar. The success of the DiGiorgio family had inspired the Croatians, grape growers who had settled around Reedley and Sanger, to buy Delano farmland at Depression-era prices. Families named Caritan, Zaninovic, Radovic, and Pandol were to become the "big farmers" around Delano after World War II.

There were tensions in this patchwork of ethnic groups and economic classes. "My right hand was sore the first three years I was in California," said Jim Anderson, referring to his fights in defense of the honor of Oklahoma.

Okies joked among themselves that they worked for "the wops" (and later, when Croatian Americans controlled more of the vineyards, the "sons of Vitches"). Once, three Filipino men pushed their way into the house on Glenwood Avenue when Oca was away and asked Ruby to come with them to the Philippines. She was ironing, and had the hot iron in her hand when the men entered. She raised the iron up, and they took off. But considering everything, there was remarkably little friction. Leslie had "worked with Spanish people" picking cotton in western Oklahoma and did not find it strange to work side by side with Mexicans in California. Doris had a Japanese friend at school. Sometimes Tathams attended the Filipino church next door, the Assembly of the First Born.

Okies in Delano had no illusions about their position in the social hierarchy. Most of them still lived west of Highway 99 and the railroad tracks; the bankers, ranch owners, and businessmen lived on the east. At school, Ophelia was aware of "the 400 Club," which she said comprised pupils from the established class. She said, "They just felt like they were a little better than people who worked for a living.

Any native Californian looked down on Oklahoma. My mother was thrifty, and our clothes were as nice as some of those kids. I was friends with girls in the Four Hundred Club. But some of the Okies were green as grass."

Ophelia's friend Clara Matthews remembers the 400 Club, too: "We were Okies. There was a lot of us there, and we'd get together. We were meant as the underperson, the underdog. We called them 'the Four Hundred'—the elite, them that had nicer clothes. They were managers of J. C. Penney and stores in town. They lived in the town. I could go to their parties. But the Four Hundred could go skating and skiing in the mountains. I couldn't go."

Yet Doris considered "Okies" to be the hoboes or the panhandlers at the station several blocks away, not Tathams. "We made a joke of it that we were Okies," she said, for you could be born in California and still be Okie if you were "lower-class or very poor" or if you were not dressed as well as the other kids. Ruby made sure the children *were* well dressed for school, and Oca let them know he did not approve of slangy Okie speech and poor grammar. The Tathams considered fieldwork as just a transitional stage until they could find regular work and afford a permanent home. An entirely different class of people were truly "migrants," following the sun and the next crop. A migrant field-worker might start the year picking peas in the Imperial Valley in February and March, then be at Nipomo in April and Alameda County in June, involved in different fruit jobs in the summer, grapes and cotton in Fresno and Kern County from late August to December, before starting all over again. Some went to pick apples in Washington as well. Within the family, that class of migrants were called "fruit tramps"—and sometimes "Okies."

The Tathams and their friends knew many people who were in dire economic straits. It was estimated that 3,881 families in Kern County were in "squatters' camps in 1937. The infant mortality rate hit a shocking 108 per thousand."[5] "I don't know how some people lived," said Buck Dodson half a century later. "Sometimes I still feel pretty bad about that. I got acquainted with people who couldn't get a job even though they had six or seven in the family. I could always go to work. I was kind of heavy, could operate trucks and tractors. I could work most anytime."

Within the Tatham circle, the "Okie problem" was seen more as many thousands of individual problems rather than one big one. Tathams and their relatives were managing, through a combination of strategies that involved enterprise, energy, resourcefulness, and mutual help. They were not opposed to relief—Walter Tatham, in fact, had supported the socialist Upton Sinclair in 1934. In 1939 Walter was an enthusiast for "Ham 'n' Eggs," a ballot initiative to distribute thirty dollars in scrip every Thursday to each needy Californian over fifty.[6] Ham 'n' Eggs was soundly trounced. Most Tathams saw too many people pulling themselves up by their bootstraps to believe that government aid was the only hope. Within the Okie community, there were always some who made the effort, others who slipped behind. Indeed, the material differences within single families was often wider than those in the Okie population as a whole.

Whatever their place in the local Okie pecking order, Oca and Ruby still lived firmly within the cultural boundaries of the world of Texans, Oklahomans, Arkansans, and Missourians. Their home on Glenwood Avenue was the center of an extended family of cousins, grandmothers, nieces, and nephews that was every bit as encompassing as the one that had existed on Brushy Mountain, or Collinsville, or Drake's Prairie. When Ruby gave birth to her fifth child, Gerald Tatham, in August 1938, the baby had three generations of family close by to care for him. Cora Tatham weaned the baby with a "sugar teat" of sugar balled up in a handkerchief. Ophelia, who was fourteen the year Gerald was born, came to baby-sit. And when Ophelia herself took ill with the chills, Ruby's mother Clara Rogers came over from the wooden trailer across the lot and applied hot towels to her chest all night. For good measure, a brother-in-law of Ruby's made her drink a potion of orange juice and whiskey.

Ruby and Oca's boarders were all Okies in the inclusive sense of that word. There was Bill Elbertson from Sallisaw, Buck Dodson from Missouri, Herman Morgan from Oklahoma, and another driver from those parts by the name of Gilbert Lewis. There was a large Oklahoma contingent in the schools and by the 1940s a number of Okie churches. Frequent trips "home" kept ties to Oklahoma alive. Cora Tatham went home once a year to see her mother Abigail. Leslie Tatham went back every year but one between 1936 and Pearl Harbor.

In farming communities up and down the valley, Okie culture began to make itself felt in churches, saloons, and country music. The radio singer Lloyd "Little Mac" Combs from Oklahoma "made local hearts melt with his guitar and cowboy ballads."[7] Woody Guthrie was at a squatters' camp in 1935 when two young girls transformed the mood of discouragement by singing to an audience that quickly grew to several hundred, "Takes a worried man to sing a worried song . . ." When Guthrie himself began to sing on a Los Angeles radio station, he was deluged with mail. "You sing the songs I used to sing forty years ago," wrote one admirer. By 1937, most California radio stations were carrying at least one singing cowboy.[8]

The singers had their fans among the Tathams. Walter Tatham always turned on the cowboy station while he was getting his biscuits, gravy, and eggs. He hummed cowboy songs, like "Cattle Drive," and yodeled and sang. Oca's brother Vernon listened to the Sons of the Pioneers and tried to copy the yodeling style of his idol Jimmie Rodgers. After he got a guitar he'd strum "Tumbling Tumbleweeds" or "Louisiana Moon" in a sweet tenor that indeed sounded like that of Rodgers himself.

Almost every Oklahoma boy dreamed of owning a new guitar. Vernon's heart pined for a rosewood number he saw on sale at a music store in Bakersfield, but it was ninety dollars with the case and he was making three dollars in the cotton. Something about the upright, honest young man impressed the salesman, though, for one day he drove out to Delano and stopped at the address that Vernon had left.

"Are you ready to buy that guitar?" he asked Vernon. "Give me five dollars down and you can pay me off month by month." Vernon threw in his old guitars, and they had a deal. He never missed a payment.

Corny humor and pranks were as much a part of Oklahoma life as the strum of guitar strings, and Okies transported this style to California. When Herman Morgan married Clara Matthews, friends "shivareed" them, an old backcountry Southern tradition derived from the "charivari" wedding night pranks practiced in the north British borderlands.[9] For Clara, it meant a rough ride in a wheelbarrow right down the middle of Main Street with Herman pushing against the traffic while his fellow truck drivers egged him on. That wasn't enough, so the boys rigged their marriage bed with an electric fence charger, but Herman found the hot wires before he and Clara climbed in.

Southwesterners made themselves the butt of their own humor most of the time, their favorite themes being poverty and gullibility. The boarders at the Glenwood Avenue place joked about a truck driver who asked a waitress, "How much is the soup if I furnish my own crackers?" Oca found something very funny in the true story about another waitress who charged him a nickel to warm up his coffee. Buck Dodson told about a man who owed him money. "He'd get his paycheck and walk up the street paying off. He never got to me—I was on the wrong side of the street." Okies felt that they were on the wrong side of the street most of the time, but it helped to joke about it.

Walter Tatham outdid them all with his jokes and pranks. One spring day when he and others were thinning the young cotton plants with their hoes, the farmer took Walter aside. The man had come out from Texas himself, and was soft-spoken and polite. Nodding in the direction of a young man named Melvin he said, "Mr. Tatham, if you could just talk to him real nice and tell him to leave a little more of my cotton, I'd be obliged to you."

Walter sidled over to Melvin. "You see that guy who come out here a while ago?"

"Yeah."

"Do you know he said he was going to make you hoe this whole field over for the way you've been choppin' his cotton away. At half price."

Melvin threw down his hoe and said, "I'll go right down there and whup him."

"You know what?" continued Walter. "I'd advise you to stay away from that guy. That man's been a Texas Ranger, and he's killed a lot of the Mexicans down there on that Texas border. You get into it with him, and he wouldn't think any more about killin' you than he would one of them Mexicans."

Walter let Melvin fume a while and then told him what the rancher had really said. "I was only kiddin' you about that stuff," he said. "You know, if we go near a drugstore tonight I'm going to have to take you in and buy you a big milkshake."

As much as music, humor, and church, marriage cemented and perpetuated the Okie culture. On trips home to Oklahoma men found women of their own kind to marry, or they married Oklahoma women who'd come to California.

Oca's cousin Leslie Tatham had long had his eye on a young woman back in Sallisaw, but she was only fifteen and pretty young for matrimony when he first took notice. But when he went home for Christmas in 1939, he met her again at a service at the Assemblies of God church in Sallisaw. They were married three weeks later, and he brought her out to Delano to live on a "tent platform" on the Sierra Vista Ranch. Later they stepped up to a real honeymoon suite: a boxcar with a water faucet and outdoor toilet.

Men and women from the same locale in Oklahoma met half a continent from home and tied the knot.

On one visit to Drake's Prairie, a woman friend told Cleo that her son was in California and was "kind of lonely." When Cleo got back in Delano, the son came to call. Wayne Frost, a Missouri-born man with some Blackfoot Indian in him on his mother's side, liked Delano and he liked Cleo. He got a job in Delano with the railroad earning thirty-eight and a half cents an hour. Cora Tatham gave him a room to board in in her house. On the first of December 1939, they married.

THE SEQUOYAH COUNTY contingent in Delano had come to California to work. It wanted nothing to do with politics or labor unions—or government labor camps, for that matter.

Difficult as life often was, many were finding their hopes being slowly fulfilled. Oca's cousin Ira had been making $12.50 a month farming for somebody on Drake's bottom. When he came out to Knights Landing in 1935, he made that much in just three days and learned skills as a tractor driver as well. Ira and his brothers Leslie and Lelan all had their own cars, and their dad was earning steady money at the Sierra Vista Ranch.

"Sierra Vista was the best place for people when you came from a place where you couldn't get a job," said Cleo.

Oca had his businesses, and others were getting jobs as drivers or mechanics. Women worked at the packing sheds to bring in extra money. Ruby's sister Daisy worked at the five-and-dime.

Arch had been a property owner back in Oklahoma, and he doubtless intended to become one again. It was not long before his wife, Winnie, invested in a small property in Delano. Leslie and his new wife did the same.

Those who came to California in the late 1930s had no choice except to work; they were not eligible for relief under the more stringent eligibility requirement that the state, under political as well as fiscal pressure, was establishing. But unlike the Japanese, Filipinos, Mexicans, and others who had been in the fields, the Okies were white Americans. It was more difficult to intimidate them with threats of "exclusion" or deportation though the relief agencies tried sending some back where they had come from. For most of them, independent individualists that they were, the fields were a temporary stopover; the idea of unionizing to improve conditions did not have much appeal.

Those from eastern Oklahoma came from a region that had shown little interest in improving economic circumstances through collective action. The Tri-State District had been a target of the International Workers of the World and of the Socialist Party from the early 1900s on. Socialist leaders such as Eugene Debs and Mother Jones were frequently to be found there, holding political camp meetings and drumming up support for their cause of improving the lot of the working man. The IWW established a local in Joplin, Missouri in 1906. However, the IWW had little success when its six hundred members struck for better conditions and a dollar more a day on June 10, 1910. The operators foiled the action with strikebreakers. In June 1915, 3,000 walked out; the mineowners shut down for two weeks and threatened a permanent lockout. Within three weeks, they had broken the strike, and the union did not recover for twenty years.[10]

In fact, the Tri-State District lead and zinc miners were known to be difficult to organize. So notorious was the antiunion sentiment among the workers that the *Engineering and Mining Journal* wrote on July 10, 1915, that Joplin was "noted for its freedom from unionism and independence of the men, who have been notorious strike breakers in Colorado." Some of the miners had been small-time prospectors and saw themselves as having more in common with the operators than with union radicals. As part of a fluid proletariat, most were recruited from the small tenant farms of the Ozark foothills and could fall back on relatives or tenant farming if need be.

Even so, the DiGiorgio Corporation took no chances. It was "probably the strongest foe of unionization in California."[11] The Sierra Vista Ranch utilized a caste system to divide workers by ethnic group and reduce the chances that white American workers would be polluted by the unionism of Filipinos, Mexicans, and other foreigners. Tathams were unable to recall any trouble when they were working in Delano. An in-law recalls a couple of sit-down strikes in the area, but they were wildcat actions that ended quickly when a particular grievance was eliminated.[12] Field-labor militancy subsided with the arrival of the Okies. Two bloody and violent labor engagements, in 1936 and 1937, took place far from Delano, the first at Salinas's lettuce-packing sheds, the second at Stockton's canneries. Okies were involved as strike*breakers* in both cases. In fact, Okie strikebreaking was so apparent during the Stockton strike that the local union's secretary-treasurer expressed fears that Filipino strikers would use "other methods" (meaning vigilantism) to deal with the imported whites who were undercutting their efforts.

The "red" tint of the farm-labor unions cooled any sympathy the Okies might have had for them. When the United Cannery,

Agricultural, Packing and Allied Workers of America voted in 1937 to join the Congress of Industrial Organizations, CIO policymakers in Washington assumed that a potentially violent new phase of labor trouble was brewing on the farms and braced for it.[13] As with the earlier Cannery and Agricultural Workers Industrial Union, the leadership of UCAPAWA was dominated by Communists, but that proved to be much more of a hindrance when mobilizing Okies than Mexicans or Filipinos. Okies were susceptible to the growers' propaganda about "Communist Generalissimos" in UCAPAWA.[14] Only a Madera cotton strike of 1939 lasted for more than a few days before it collapsed. By the end of 1939, UCAPAWA's membership amounted to no more than 2,500 or 3,000.[15]

From one end of the valley to the other, Okies were indifferent, even hostile to most organizing efforts. A Farm Security Administration official in the Sacramento Valley noted: "There is absolutely no organized labor movement among the farm laborers in this district. . . . Our campers . . . seem to shy away from the idea."[16] Some families were too hard-pressed and desperate to think of unions. Others simply wanted no part of them. "Rural Americans that they were, their ideologies conformed, not conflicted, with the ideology of their exploiters," the historian Walter Stein has written. "Only by late 1940 did some of California liberals become aware that the theories of the Depression decade did not apply to the Okies."

Oca had no love for the union workers who had a monopoly on unloading produce that he trucked to San Francisco and, under union rules, charged him for two hours' work when they'd put in an hour and a half.

Self-reliant Tathams "weren't rich, but we could hold our heads high," said Cleo. The federal government opened a labor camp in Shafter in 1936, a short drive from Delano, but Tathams wanted no part of it. Cleo's cousin Leslie saw plenty of people who *looked* poor. But he figured that if they used a "little water and soap and rub board" they would have looked better. Members of a wheat-harvesting crew that his brother Lelan worked on were surprised to learn that Lelan was from Oklahoma.

"You'll see poor people who have a little get-up-and-go about 'em, you know," he told them.

CHAPTER SEVEN

THE CHURCH

THEY BUILT A CHURCH.

Jay Fuller, their bantamweight reformed gambler of a preacher, went into the cotton fields around Delano and pleaded with people he knew to lay aside something toward it. Cleo "hit the fields early and late" and met Brother Fuller's challenge.

Land was cheap, and two small lots were purchased at the corner of San Juan Avenue and Kern Street in McFarland. Oca Tatham, Jay Fuller, and Buck Dodson went in trucks and picked up used lumber on Alameda Street in Los Angeles. They pulled the nails out and Happy Martin sawed the boards into proper lengths. Volunteers hammered and painted. The roof was up in a single day. The Pentecostal Church of God of McFarland was a reality.

It wasn't Notre Dame Cathedral. They couldn't afford a hardwood floor at first, and people fell down onto sawdust. But it was theirs. Oca said, "It was our church. . . . We owned it. We went out and picked cotton to earn money for it. Everybody was as excited as if it had been a cathedral. It was our church where we could worship out of the weather."

To round up a congregation Brother Jay held street meetings in

McFarland on Saturday night. The hardware store let him plug in an electric loudspeaker, and Lowell Syers plucked a guitar as Jay shouted to shoppers to gather 'round. The commotion attracted families in old jalopies and field-workers from the ranches. Jay begged them to make room in their hearts for Jesus and follow him to the church on San Juan Avenue.

The church welcomed all comers. Jay Fuller's wife, Helen, said, "We never made any special doctrine of fighting other churches, we always felt we were all in the body of Christ. My husband did not preach against their churches and all that kind of thing." Oca was "a great hand to testify and witness to the boys . . . a real soul winner," said Jay. Sometimes Oca drove out to the camps where he'd been selling potatoes and picked up folks for church. Their clothes might still have dust and cotton lint on them, but that was all right. The deacons wore striped overalls. You were welcomed even if you were poor and didn't have clean Sunday duds or two dimes to rub together.

Doris remembers the mingling of joy and sorrow at those meetings: "They had a hard life, and the church they went to was always joy and talking about joy. It was sort of like how the colored people felt, the slaves, they were very religious, but it was a sad, moaning sort of thing, always asking the Lord to help instead of praising the Lord and being thankful. It was hard for them because they were just so needy. It was because there was no security except in the Lord. That's why they all went to church often, that's really all they basically knew, they didn't know where the next meal was coming from."

Helen Fuller said, "They came because there was a lot of spirit in that church and it was a going thing." And sometimes because there was food and hot water. Hungry, dirty men sometimes came to the door of the parsonage, and Jay and Helen Fuller fed them, let them use the tub, and gave a bedroll and a corner of the church to those who were truly penniless, of which there were a great many. Sometimes Jay and Helen did not have enough food themselves; still they shared. After the men left, Helen scalded the tub and scrubbed it down with Purex to get rid of lice.

THEY WERE MAKING HISTORY.

In 1935, the modern Pentecostal movement was only a few decades old, and its life span had been so full of sect-creating battles that it was often difficult to detect the large outlines of what was occurring. But along California's irrigation frontier, in the wide-open inland country, the movement came into its own. There, the holy roller tabernacle and the country-music honky-tonk became symbols of a transplanted culture.[1]

American Pentecostals had followed a backwoods trail. Most scholars, looking for the movement's origins, are led back to the reaction against "respectable" Protestantism in the latter part of the nineteenth century. The strongest backlash was among American Methodists. Concerned that the fire had gone out of their denomination, Methodist bishops after the Civil War initiated a Holiness movement to renew its ardor. Holiness Associations were established in many communities to restoke the fires. But the bishops soon lost control of what they had started. Many of the Holiness Associations turned against comfortable, middle-class Methodist congregations. Soon Holiness healers were traveling around the South and Midwest, holding revivals and ever more shrilly criticizing the easy ways of mainstream churches. In 1894, Holiness "fanatics" were expelled by the Methodist Conference. Many of these "come-outers" went on to ignite independent Holiness sects such as the Nazarenes.

The champion of the Holiness sects was John Wesley, the great English preacher of the eighteenth century. Wesley, Oxford-educated and a member of the Church of England, was no commoner. But in seeking a richer spiritual life than was provided by the Church of England, he showed the way for Protestants to partake of a deeper religious experience. Wesley had read the Catholic mystics and undergone a series of episodic experiences, and out of that came his belief in a postconversion experience, or "second blessing."

Methodism, as it was called, because it required of its practitioners a systematic approach to a holy life, spread first to the churchless British working class, and then to the American frontier, where it seemed especially at home. Wesleyan religion seemed right for people bent on self-improvement and opportunity. It was optimistic, joyous (its motto was "heart purity and perfect love"), and democratic. Wesleyanism rejected the Calvinist and Puritan notion that man is fundamentally sinful and corrupt as long as he lives.[2] Wesley suggested, rather, that sin could be gradually overcome and finally eradicated in *this* life, by anyone, through free will. Wesleyan belief extracted a price. The deterministic Baptist soul was "in repose," but the Wesleyan soul was restless, self-questioning, demanding, and straining to be better. Although the Wesleyan disciple knew that anyone could find God's grace through faith, he or she knew that it could be lost just as quickly.

The effort to recapture the Wesleyan fires after the Civil War took place in a far less hopeful setting than had existed previously. American soil was stained with fraternal blood, science was casting doubt on the absolute truth of scripture, and the rise of cities and factory towns seemed to be spreading vice and corruption across America. The Holiness divines, many of whom were poor, crippled, or afflicted in some way, had a vision of Jesus returning to earth to smite the wicked and impose his kingdom by force. This vision— which they all felt had come to them straight from Heaven—recast and exaggerated certain Wesleyan doctrines, but retained much of the core. Christians should seek a transcendent experience *after* con-version, subsequent to which they could hope to be endowed with the supernatural gifts (the Greek *charismata*) described by Paul in his First Letter to the Corinthians. After 1906, the hallmark of explicitly Pentecostal denominations, as opposed to Holiness ones, was their doctrine that speaking in tongues was the initial proof that a Christian had been baptized by the Holy Spirit.[3] Many of the Holiness sects ultimately rejected this, and Baptists never accepted it. A doctrine claiming supernatural powers for twentieth-century sinners seemed arrogant and wrong to most Baptists, since such powers could easily be used for deception, chicanery, and "cheap grace."

Yet the world was changing. William James had begun to explore the subconscious mind in his writings about religious experience; Sigmund Freud would soon attempt to decipher the unconscious world of dreams. And in truth, much of American evangelical history had a Pentecostal flavor to it. The backcountry had always been full of folk magic, séance, and ritual brought by settlers from the North British borderlands and by African slaves and former slaves. In any case, it was not surprising that religion in a democracy should give such a prominent place to the miraculous, for the miracle could be experienced by the plain citizen as well as the aristocrat.

Pentecostal-like influences, some clearly taken from the folk cultures of Africa, could be seen in black churches in the nineteenth century, including nominally Baptist ones. In 1783 an escaped American slave by the name of George Lyle founded a church in Jamaica that was Baptist in name only. Lyle had heard John Wesley's hymns and knew of his translations of the Catholic mystical writers. His church in Jamaica became a place where Wesley's ideas on ecstatic experience fused with the influences of Africa and the Caribbean.[4] After Emancipation, the cross-fertilization continued in the United States, inspiring the formation of hundreds of black churches in the

South that had the good sense to identify themselves with the white South's largest denomination. The first Pentecostal denomination to be chartered as an institution, the Church of God in Christ, was founded in Memphis in 1897 by two black preachers who had come into contact with Holiness revivals. The church was led by Charles Price Jones, a preacher from Selma, Alabama, who became known for his hymns, but the dominant personality was Charles Mason, the son of former slaves. The Church of God in Christ later spread far and wide in Tennessee, Arkansas, and Mississippi.[5] Hundreds of whites were ordained by black Church of God in Christ ministers over the next few years—and this was no mere formality. Without pastoral credentials, a preacher was not eligible for a draft deferral, could not obtain discount fares on the railroad, and was not allowed to perform marriage ceremonies—one of his or her few ways to earn money.

The first white Pentecostal sect appears to have grown up around a strange misfit preacher and to have been scattered across the country thereafter by equally marginal and strange figures. Charles Fox Parham was a sickly rheumatic who ran a small Bible school in Topeka, Kansas, in the closing years of the nineteenth century. Parham had been in contact with radical elements of the Holiness movement, such as Alexander Dowie, ruler of Zion City, a faith-healing community north of Chicago that became famous all over the world. Parham's heart attacks and illnesses frequently were followed by intense religious experiences, and he was receptive to the mystical side of Wesleyan religion.[6]

After events at the Bible school in 1901 in which several claimed to have spoken in tongues, Parham started his Apostolic Faith Church in Topeka. He then held revivals and started churches in the lead-mining towns on the Kansas side of the Tri-State District. In Galena, Parham held meetings and conducted healings in a tent and then, as the crowds grew, in a warehouse. The revival continued night and day all winter long, and hundreds were baptized in the freezing waters of nearby Spring River. Many received "the baptism" and gave evidence of it by speaking in tongues. Several Apostolic Faith churches sprang up in and around many of the towns in which Walter and Cora lived between 1917 and 1932—including Carthage, Missouri, and Miami, Oklahoma.

The coming together of the black and white conflagrations raised the temperature close to the boiling point. In Houston, where Parham had gone to preach in the new oil-field camps, he met William Seymour, a half-blind black preacher of Holiness persuasion who was working in Houston's missions. Seymour accepted Parham's religious tutoring and then went on to Los Angeles, where in 1906 he helped launch a three-year-long revival that lit a Pentecostal fire across the entire nation.

The Azusa Street revival was an extraordinary event, even by the inflamed standards of an American revivalist tradition that included George Whitefield's preaching in the Great Awakening, the great revival attended by 25,000 people at Cane Ridge, Kentucky, on August 6, 1801, and countless smaller subsequent movements. Seymour's meetings were held in a former horse stable converted into a makeshift church at 312 Azusa Street, in a seedy quarter of wholesale houses dispersed around a stockyards complex. A tombstone shop was just up the street.

A cold-eyed Los Angeles *Times* reporter described "wild scenes" of the "sect of fanatics" and called Seymour "an old colored exhorter" whose "stony optic" (glass eyepiece) hypnotized unbelievers. Old "colored mammys" were seen to "gurgle wordless talk" in a frenzy of religious zeal. Yet some visitors claimed that they could feel a "supernatural atmosphere" as far as two blocks away. Blacks, whites, Chinese, Mexicans, and Jews prayed and chanted side by side. Men and women testified, shouted, wept, danced, went into trances, spoke and sang in tongues. As the fervor built, strange new exertions were reported, such as "treeing the devil." Mediums and fortune-tellers hung around the edges of the crowds or set up shops nearby. And all this extraordinary interracial fervor occurred half a generation before middle-class whites were swept up by enthusiasm for black jazz, though jazz is often credited with being the first widespread black influence on white American culture.

Some were appalled by what they saw: whites and blacks touching each other and praying together, white people "imitating the crude negroisms of the Southland." Even Parham was shocked when he visited, and denounced the "chattering, jabbering and sputtering." But some skeptics came away feeling that they had witnessed an extraordinary event. One hardened newspaper reporter left as a convert to the new "religion of Pentecost."[7]

From Azusa Street, the word spread as the participants returned home. One burning bush on a prairie might not have set a prairie fire, but a thousand burning bushes—a thousand revivals linking the backcountry and the back streets—was not so easy to extinguish. Preachers used storefronts, warehouses, tents, brush arbors, street corners, and city parks. These holy rollers were greeted with rotten eggs, jeers, intimidation—and unexpected acts of simple kindness. An early Pentecostal pastor in a northern city, arrested for disturbing the peace with loud worship services, was bailed out by the neighborhood brothel owner.[8]

What was happening rose above every "ism" in the American vocabulary. "No instrument that God can use is rejected on account of color or dress or lack of education," said one pioneer.[9] The poor, the sick, the elderly, and the uneducated all had a place at the altar—indeed, in the pulpit.[10] At the Azusa Street revival, "the color line was washed away by the Blood," according to Frank Bartleman, a leading chronicler of the revival.[11] Evangelist Aimee Semple McPherson, who founded her own Pentecostal denomination in the winter of 1917–1918, had her first success among impoverished, illiterate blacks and whites. In Key West, Florida, she said: "All walls of prejudice are breaking down, white and colored folks to the altar together, white and colored joined hands and prayed, people so hungry after God that color is forgotten even here in the Southland." Jonathan Perkins, a Methodist minister who attended Pentecostal services in Wichita, Kansas, in 1909, went away disgusted over the failure of those in charge "to keep niggers in their place," but fourteen years later, Perkins was converted and issued a sorrowful comment on his previous behavior. "God broke me over the wheel of my prejudice," he said. Integrated meetings were commonplace even in the Deep South, though Fred Bosworth, pastor of a Pentecostal church in Dallas before and after 1912, was beaten by local whites for befriending blacks. Watson Sorrow recalled integrated meetings in parts of Georgia.[12]

Pentecostal churches forbade membership in any organization, including the Ku Klux Klan. One sect, the Pentecostal Holiness Church, formally repudiated the Klan in 1925 as "un-Christian and un-American"[13] and this at a time of growing Klan power and terror. The official organ of the Assemblies of God declared, there "may be true Christians in the Klan" but if so, they are "severely misguided."[14]

Yet somehow the moment passed. By 1914, black and white Pentecostals were separating to form their own denominations, and though women held a place in Pentecostal pulpits well into the 1960s, they were eventually relegated to supporting roles. Still, while it lasted, integrated Pentecostalism offered a remarkable vision of men and women, blacks and whites coming together.

It must also be said that the early years of black and white Pentecostalism were characterized by extreme factionalism and sectarianism, which expressed fundamental doctrinal differences as well as struggles for leadership. Terrible quarrels broke out over the nature of the Holy Trinity, an issue that has plagued Christianity from the very beginning, and for a time it seemed that a unitarian faction calling itself "Jesus Only" would dominate Pentecostalism.

There was bitter dispute about entire sanctification, the doctrine holding that sin could be instantly eradicated by the Holy Ghost. That one led to the formation of the Assemblies of God as a "voluntary fellowship" in Hot Springs, Arkansas, in 1914, bringing together at least five different Pentecostal camps, including ones from as far away as Illinois and Ohio.[15] The Hot Springs convention rejected entire sanctification and instead adopted the doctrine that the attainment of grace was a gradual, lifelong process. Aside from comporting with what many people simply considered to be plain common sense, it was shrewd strategy. For it sidestepped the controversial claim that a mortal could be completely purified of his or her sin in one blazing instant. This compromise on doctrine made the denomination more hospitable to Baptists or former Baptists who had been raised to believe in man's inherently sinful nature. The men at Hot Springs also may have sensed that other, more generalized dangers lurked in the doctrine of entire sanctification. Any belief system in which the individual not only claimed perfection, but also reserved to himself or herself the right to define what perfection was, was vulnerable to the fanatic.

The Pentecostal Church of God, the denomination to which the church in McFarland belonged, likewise rejected entire sanctification. The split put Oca at odds with his mother, Cora, but for Oca there was no question of accepting her doctrine. It was right for her because she, a woman and a mother, was possessed of near-saintly qualities. Oca knew he was not perfect. Though a member of a religious movement strongly influenced by Wesley, he had something of a Baptist temperament. Although he had been saved and sanctified in Oklahoma, he felt that entire sanctification was unachievable, for every day was a new struggle. He was "still Oca Tatham" and "felt the devil would pester me every day if I didn't keep my eyes on the Lord. You don't put him away. We don't get cleaned up once and forever and then live above sin for the rest of our lives without going back to the Lord and saying Lord forgive me, I spoke to this guy kind of sharp or I showed anger, or I did this to my brother or this or that. . . ."

The issue, however, was only a small sore point in the family. Oca kidded his mother when she lost her temper, implying that she was losing her sanctification. Cleo, who was also Pentecostal Church of God, nonetheless defended her mother's position. Being entirely sanctified didn't mean never getting mad—"because Jesus got mad—it meant not sinning." Cleo saw these battles as "itty-bitty matters."

In the San Joaquin Valley, Pentecostalism first made headway in Fresno. The Azusa Street revival had burned itself out by the end of 1909—just about the time that a severe recession was ending. Soon afterward some Pentecostal "works," as the faithful called their small buildings, sprang up in Fresno's "Colored Town" west of the railroad tracks. Then, toward the end of World War I, William E. Opie, a white man who had witnessed Azusa Street, came to Fresno and put up a tent on an empty lot. Opie had given up a job as a railroad engineer to spread the message. Finding progress rather slow, he joined forces with a black preacher by the name of Cotton, whose wife, Mother Cotton, was a fiery activist with the local Church of God in Christ. Opie's tent—which a local Baptist preacher called a "seat of demons"—was splattered by tomato-throwing hooligans and eventually blew down.[16] But Opie, who had a gift for prophecy and healing, persisted. Eventually his Thomas Avenue Mission became Bethel Temple, Fresno's first full-fledged white Pentecostal church.

Aimee Semple McPherson inspired the little movement at a big revival at Fresno's civic center in January 1922. She came back several times after that, always helping to bring new recruits to Opie's church. By the mid-1920s it had eight hundred members, and others had broken away to form another Pentecostal church, the Full Gospel Tabernacle (later called City Center), which became affiliated with the Assemblies of God. The Full Gospel Tabernacle, housed in a big wooden barn of a building in town, was led by A. G. Osterberg, an ambitious organizer who dispatched crews of "Christian Crusaders" and musicians to the small churches between Fresno and Bakersfield.

Another early church leader in Fresno was Otto Pauls, a Kansan who had grown up in the Mennonite Brethren before turning Pentecostal. As down-and-out Dust Bowlers arrived in the 1930s, Pauls and his wife, a fiery sermonizer in her own right, moved back across the tracks and ministered to street people in storefront missions, turkey sheds, and a building at Fourth Street and Washington Avenue that had once been a bakery. Pauls called it Calvary Tabernacle. By 1935 it had gained enough of a following among local Swedes, Germans, and Okies for Pauls to consider building a real church. To organize the job the congregation called on Murrell Coughran, a

Texan whose family had moved to Fresno early enough to have attended Aimee Semple McPherson's revivals there.

Coughran had been saved and baptized by the Holy Spirit when he was only eight years old. He had been one of the first foreign missionaries for the Assemblies of God, when the hardships of that duty often meant sacrificing one's life to disease or hostile natives in faraway places. Coughran returned in broken health from a posting in India.

He was a showman and improviser who organized what may have been Fresno's first "brush arbor" camp meeting. People gathered branches of birch and ash from the banks of the San Joaquin River, covered saplings with palm branches—a California innovation—and held a meeting. Fresnans had never seen anything quite like it. Coughran brought in a Salvation Army band and kept the prayers, music, and gospel singing going nonstop. Soon after that, Calvary Tabernacle was completed at First Street and Nevada Avenue: an unadorned, wood-frame building with plain white clapboards and a belfry housing a bell rescued from an abandoned country school. Coughran filled the front of the church with people who could sing and make music with accordions, guitars, banjos, saxophones, harmonicas, trombones, and trumpets—anything, he said, that made a "joyful sound unto the Lord." One man played a fiddle, another the saw, still another the washboard. Young people were encouraged to strum or blow. Coughran himself played saxophone and slide trombone, accompanied by his wife on the banjo or at the piano. It was, he believed, "the liveliest music in town."

The lack of sympathy that the Assemblies had shown for its missionaries had left Coughran with less than warm feelings toward the denomination, and he saw to it that Calvary Tabernacle was chartered as an independent church. Coughran himself took out credentials with the Pentecostal Church of God, an affiliation that established the connection between his church in Fresno and the small churches going up in the farm towns in the valley.

For the Pentecostal movement, the Dust Bowl migration to California was a new kind of opportunity. Until the 1940s, the Southern Baptist organization honored a 1912 agreement that had conceded California to the American, or Northern, Baptists.[17] The traditions of that denomination tended toward less fundamentalist interpretations of Biblical texts and were more apt to view private conduct as a personal matter in which the church should not intervene directly. Baptist churches in California were less like intimate, extended families than their Southern counterparts. So an Okie was bound to feel

35

3 - 7 -   P. 65

12-30   P. 8-39
12-31   P 39 - P 70
1-1   P. 70 - 101
1-2   P 101 - P 132
1-3   P 132 - P 163
1-4   P 163 - P 194
1-5   P 194   P 225

2 - 20 - 95   44 mins.

    513
     30

    483

        34
  14)483
     42

      63
      56

       7

"A Soldier's Home"
By Ernest
Hemingway
3.51 - P 259

ill at ease in the Baptist church in Shafter, for example. A newcomer said, "The average migrant out here is broke and can't get good clothes, so when [you] go down to church among the natives you feel they are saying, 'Here comes a damn Oklahoman.' . . . To go [to church] down here with our clothes among the high-ups and all their fine cars, it makes you naturally feel like you ain't in their class." The minister did not disagree. "The people who come to my church are the kind who like to dress up and dress up their kids, too," he said, adding with apparent satisfaction: "I know only one migrant woman who comes." A Modesto resident characterized that town's Pentecostal church as a "crazy house" in which people were "standing and shouting like wild Indians." A Kern County grower complained that the churchgoers "pray and sing so loud and furious all hours of the day and night" that they should not be permitted "in any ordered community." Said the Reverend Grover Ralston of Bakersfield, "We do not talk their language." The Reverend E. M. Keller of Fresno declared: "Emotional types and then some! They do not fit into our present California churches, other than those of their type."[18]

By the late 1930s, Pentecostal Churches of God had sprouted in Wasco, Tracy, Earlimart, Taft, Porterville, Shafter, Modesto, Stockton, and Bakersfield, and a publication called *Pentecostal Young Peoples Association Witness* carried news of the activities in the Pentecostal Church of God organizations in farming towns from the Imperial Valley to Salinas:

> We are glad we can report victory from Earlimart . . . the Lord is truly blessing our little assembly.

> We are glad to report that Tracy is still on the firing line for our Lord and Saviour, Jesus Christ. There has been some remodeling on our building in the past month and we are expecting to finish in the near future. Our Sunday school is growing and we are praising God for the new people He has sent in and the new ones He has saved.

> We are very happy to report victory in our little church by the road in Gilroy. We are very proud of the nice group of young people who are so willing to do their part. We also thank Him for a wonderful orchestra.

One by one the victory reports came in from Pentecostal churches in the towns where Okies were settling. From Laton came word that the new church was painted and electric lights were in. "Our Sunday school attendance is growing and the sinners are becoming more interested." From McFarland, Nellie Robertson reported that thirty children had been present for a Sunday Bible "drill" and "two precious souls were saved." She added: "Bro. Fuller gave a talk [to the youth group] and used the scripture where the lad gave to the Lord his five loaves and few fishes, bringing the thought what God could do with our PYPA [Pentecostal Young Peoples Association] talent."

A church in Shafter put up a sign: "Pentecostal Gospel Mission Old Time Revival." The pastor, a Mrs. Edwards, played the xylophone at Sunday meetings. There was also a piano, snare drum, and tambourine. One of the titles in its songbook was, "There Is no Depression in Heaven."[19]

After his own church was completed, Jay Fuller took leave from his congregation to preach a revival in Corcoran, a few miles north on Highway 99. "We got enough people saved to buy the lots and buy the material," he proudly recalled many years later. Oca Tatham hauled the lumber to Corcoran in the back of one of his trucks.

Pastor Fuller's personal story testified to the church's power to change an individual.

He had grown up dirt poor in Comanche County, Texas, only a few counties away from where Lyndon Johnson was born in the same year, 1908. Two counties over, the populist Farmers Alliance had held its first meeting in 1877. When Jay's father died his mother took the children to Arizona, where she worked in the cotton. She was a very religious woman, and a son and an adopted daughter became Pentecostal preachers before they were twenty.

Jay, like Oca, was a late convert. For a while, he operated what he called a "booze joint" in Mesa, Arizona. He was a card sharp who claimed he could tell each card by its "feel." But not even a skilled gambler could survive without going out to work in the early Depression. He moved on to California, where he picked cotton and fruit to supplement his gambling earnings.

Jay's winnings never stuck to him long, for he generally lost at cards whenever he got "loop-legged" drunk. Jay was "preached into conviction" by Bill Morefield, a Pentecostal pastor who couldn't read a word. Working in the grape vineyards around Dinuba after his first exposure to Morefield, he sensed the presence of Morefield close to him.

Jay Fuller was one of those drawn to the stirring Pentecostal meetings at McFarland's Grange Hall. It was not a regular church, but it served the purpose. A Free Pentecostal preacher, M. V. Walker, rented it for meetings, and farm workers came from the ranches all around. On the particular occasion when Jay attended, Walker had brought in a battling evangelist by the name of M. D. Townsend, a strapping ex-prizefighter who boasted of having once boxed a heckler into accepting the Lord. Townsend pulled Jay the rest of the way to the Lord and "the old life left me like a freight train leaves a tramp," he said.

Jay soon hit the road himself as an itinerant preacher. When he came back to McFarland, he lived in a room at the back of the Grange Hall, preaching and helping all he could. In 1936, when Oca and the others began building their church, they asked him to be their pastor.

Many of those on the move from Oklahoma, Texas, Missouri, Arkansas, and Kansas gathered at the Grange Hall. Oca and Ruby were regulars; other families came and went. Typical of these were the Kirkpatricks and the Syers. The Kirkpatricks came from Roff, Oklahoma. They had moved to Mesa in the late 1920s with their seven daughters and a son and farmed twenty acres of cotton and corn. Ona, one of the daughters, could handle a cultivator before she was sixteen. When she wasn't helping her dad she "worked out," hoeing, chopping, and picking cotton for other farmers. In 1929, the Kirkpatricks and their friends the Syers moved on to California in search of work. It was common for families to team up like that. They were simply doing what the Tathams and Adkins had done two centuries earlier.

Ona eventually married Lowell Syers, whom she'd met at a Pentecostal church in Mesa. Their first child was born while Lowell was picking cotton in McFarland in 1930. The second came while the couple were living at a dairy farm and Lowell was working in the grapes at the Sierra Vista Ranch. Ona and Lowell followed the crops. Lowell cut lettuce in Watsonville, picked peaches at Kingsburg, harvested garlic near Monterey Bay, and canned peaches in Live Oak. Ona worked in packing sheds when she could. They crisscrossed the path of Oca and Ruby, living for a while on Peterson Road near McFarland. In fact a Kirkpatrick daughter and her husband moved into the "potato house" on the Holgren ranch right after Oca and Ruby vacated it.

One thing that kept drawing the Syers and Kirkpatrick families back to McFarland and Delano was Pentecostal fellowship. Lowell's mother was a strong Pentecostal Christian, and Ona had been saved in Mesa. But the existing Pentecostal church in Delano, the Full Gospel Church, was the one that had not felt right to Oca and Ruby when they attended it fresh from Oklahoma. Later, Oca learned that the Assemblies of God were trying to create a less-improvised kind of meeting, in which speaking in tongues and other outbursts would be "in order." Oca accepted that, but at the time, he took their reception as a sign that the Delano church disapproved of down-and-outers of their ilk.

OKIE RELIGION generally was viewed with a mixture of disdain, amusement, and concern by the New Deal bureaucracy of social workers and transient camp managers, as well as by intellectuals and writers. John Steinbeck in *The Grapes of Wrath* depicts Pentecostal religion in a highly negative light and the only good preacher as one who has given up the trade. New Deal bureaucrats often seemed to view Okie religious feelings as a bad habit that needed to be broken before Okies could move on to another phase. Holy rollers and prayer healers greatly annoyed the management of the government transient camps. One official expressed fears that the sects were "productive of fanaticism and irrationalities which can seriously disturb the general social equilibrium."[20] The Marysville camp manager discouraged Pentecostal preachers from visiting by refusing to let them take up collections. The Arvin camp manager justified his open disapproval of a sect that believed in divine healing on the grounds that it could lead to the spread of communicable diseases. On the other hand, one of the "healthy" activities favored by the camp managers was amateur theatricals—which clashed with the religious code of many Southerners.

Evidently, Pentecostal and other fervent religion was seen by social reformers as standing in the way of molding Okies into a more progressive force in California politics. In fact, religion gave a form to the Okies' thoroughly confused situation and helped stabilize thousands of them. Not only that, the new churches dealt with some of the same problems that the reformers were addressing. Pentecostal and Holiness churches forged communities that helped the poor and needy, though their principal purpose was to win souls for Jesus, not to provide charity. And they opened educational and leadership opportunities to people who might not otherwise have had them—for example, in at least two hundred and fifty Bible schools formed in the twentieth century.[21]

The views of the social reformers were a reminder to Okies that they had come to a new kind of place, one in which secularism was not only strong but also respectable. In Oklahoma, little of importance was not religious, the Ku Klux Klan included. In California, religion was considered more of a private matter; one could be a leading citizen and never go to church. Indeed, one saw prosperous and highly regarded individuals living lives untouched by religion or its disciplines, and one could see the evidence everywhere that the government was not the tool of the churches. Stores were open on Sundays, and there was no local option against liquor. The first social activism of some Okies in California was directed not at growers but at store owners who extended their Sunday hours.

Nonetheless, politics posed a dilemma for a people who were renouncing this world as wrecked and wicked. Some Baptist and Pentecostal preachers were involved with farm labor strikes, but they were the exception. Most, like Jay Fuller, wanted no part of politics, and many who did leaned toward the conservative side. When influential Pentecostal pastors did speak out, they sometimes seemed torn between their conservative opinions and a conviction that there was no place for good Christians in politics. When A. G. Osterberg came to Delano in October 1934 to speak on "Christian Politics," he first said he was "not interested in politics, only as it applies to religion," but then launched into an impassioned defense of the U.S. Constitution as "the greatest document in history" and condemned Upton Sinclair, the Democratic candidate for governor, in no uncertain terms: "I cannot see how Christians can support Upton Sinclair, a man who if one tenth of his promises were to come true, would indeed bring the Millennium before half of us, preachers and all, would be ready." Evidently, however, the Sinclair candidacy was a hot issue within the Pentecostal community, for Osterberg acknowledged that "some in my church have been foolish enough to believe the vague promises of this man. In fact, I know of two deacons who almost caused a riot in their church."[22]

The church communities in the San Joaquin Valley towns found themselves exposed to new and unfamiliar political influences and material blandishments. Exactly because of that, it took uncommon character and commitment to participate fully in a Pentecostal community. It took a "toughness of temper, [a] strenuous self-disciplined sense of commitment, soul-searching and self-testing, seriousness of purpose, intensity of will, [and] determination."[23]

What held it all together was not doctrine, but fellowship and intensity. Members gave "sacrificially" to their churches. Buck Dodson saw Ruby put all the Tatham household money in the offertory plate one night when Oca was away. (The next day there was a check in the mail for thirty dollars—a truck insurance rebate she had forgotten was due.) Ruby, said Oca, "wasn't the woman who would say, 'You gotta think about your kids first.' She would never say that, never. She said, 'If you feel that way about it, just go and give it to Him.' "

The Pentecostal Church of God was considered somewhat "easier" than the Assemblies of God, mainly because it allowed divorced individuals to become pastors in some circumstances. Jay Fuller was not a "condemner," but he was no liberal either. His church forbade drinking, smoking, and gambling and frowned on dancing, bowling, attending motion picture theaters, mixed bathing, the wearing of jewelry or fancy apparel, the wearing of men's apparel by women, and the cutting or permanent waving of women's hair. A church member did not wear earrings or makeup, although a dab of face powder was considered acceptable.

When Doris was in the sixth grade in the Delano school, Oca and Ruby forbade her to wear gym shorts to a county track meet in accordance with church rules. "I had to tell my teacher that I would wear a short dress," Doris said. "Well, you can imagine how that looked with my underwear showing. I was very embarrassed. I was the only one there like that. I don't think my dress was so short that it was indecent, but I think back now, thinking how much better I would have looked, you know, in a pair of shorts that fit on a little girl. So from then on I was allowed to wear gym shorts."

One preacher refused to perform marriage ceremonies for divorced individuals, saying "Go back and get your *first!*" That was perhaps not so extreme, for in the 1930s many Episcopalian ministers refused to remarry the divorced. But the same pastor refused to pray for little Dick Tatham, who was suffering from painfully swollen neck glands, because Ruby and Oca had been treating the child with Denver poultices. Seeing this resort to the "medical arts," he told Oca, "I won't pray for the baby, brother, but I will pray for you—you're the one needs prayer for letting your wife put that poultice on." Oca considered such men "fanatics."

It was common for Pentecostal children to make an early commitment to Christ. Doris was five when she "gave my heart and life to God" on the way home from a service at the Pentecostal Church of God. "I made a decision to give my heart and serve Him and be in fellowship with Him." Either that night or some other she recalled Jay talking about Hell. "I didn't want to go to Hell. I decided to go to Heaven that night. And he told us how to do it: we had to repent of our sins and accept Jesus as our Savior and ask him to come into our hearts. So I went up to the altar when the sermon was over. And I knew at that moment I was a Christian, and never anytime since then has there been any doubt." It would be another five years, though, before she received the baptism of the Holy Ghost while attending church with her grandmother Clara Rogers at the Full Gospel church in Delano.

Radio was a great boon to the spread of the Pentecostal movement everywhere. The Tathams and their friends listened to the broadcasts of Sister Aimee McPherson from her Angelus Temple in Los Angeles. Pastor Roy Ogan of Bakersfield, one of the most influential Pentecostal pastors in the valley, had his own radio program. Ogan, an ex-convict, delighted his Okie listeners with stories of his prison days in Oklahoma. He took prisoners for weekend furloughs so they could go to church. He spoke the language of Okies, just as the country and western singers who were beginning to make their names on local radio stations did. Jay Fuller preached a Sunday afternoon radio sermon from Bakersfield.

Plenty of people within the Tatham orbit were not church members. Few of the upstairs boarders were. Jim Anderson sometimes went to outdoor meetings with the Tathams, but not to church. "If I'd went into a church house the devil would leave," he joked. But all of them were impressed by the religious commitment of the Tathams and others in their circle.

Busy as he was, Oca would say that he "never got too busy for God." Church members greeted each other as "brother" and "sister." Social life and family life revolved around church activities. There were church summer camps in the Greenhorn Mountains at which the McFarland contingent met groups from other Pentecostal Church of God churches up and down the valley. People looked after each other the way they would members of a family. Ona Syers ironed Pastor Fuller's shirts before his wedding to Helen.

Marriages often took place within the church community. Oca's cousin Ira married Fern Wiley's niece. Rosie Hubbard, who played the piano, married one of the Callahans from Drake's Prairie. And so it went. Oca's cousin Leslie was "resaved" in the church at San Juan and Kern. He'd been "born again" at the Free Holiness church on Drake's Prairie, but it hadn't stuck. He kept "runnin' with the same crowd, datin' the same girls," as he put it. He lived like that for about eight years and "couldn't find peace." But after he and Virble were married he said to her, "We might as well start goin' to church. . . . So we went, and she got right in, but it took me a little longer to get started again."

The pastor represented the congregation, as if he had been elected—as indeed he had been, in a manner of speaking. It was important to everyone in the church community that the pastor be well situated, that he have a decent home and a car that wasn't rattle-trap. Oca and Ruby gave money to Jay Fuller when they had any, for, after all, they had also borrowed from him when they were needy. Oca helped Jay by making him part owner of one of his trucks.

The wedding of Jay and Helen on the night of July 5, 1936, was a milestone for the local Pentecostal community. The bride, according to the Delano *Record*, wore "white taffeta fashioned princess style with a roll collar. She wore white accessories and carried a bouquet of red roses." Afterward Jay drove away with his bride for a two-week honeymoon in his brand-new 1937 Ford. The Delano *Record* reported that Helen's going away suit was of green linen, with a pink blouse. The write-up was so detailed that one reading it years later could not but wonder if the reporter had his tongue in his cheek for the benefit of the *Record*'s larger, non-Okie readership. Probably the article simply reflected the editor's realization that along with the fruit tramps who passed through town, a growing number of newcomers were planting more permanent roots in the community.

The wedding was the crowning event at the statewide meeting of the Pentecostal Young Peoples Association, attended by more than seven hundred people. Among those present at the ceremony for Jay were Roy Ogan and M. D. Townsend. Ogan's son served as ring bearer. Ona Syers was a bridesmaid, and her oldest daughter, Ione, was flower girl. The child wore a pink ruffled dress and carried a pink basket.

However the write-up may have been meant, one and all in the Pentecostal community took it as a welcome sign of recognition. Fifty years later, those attending still had vivid recollections of the day. Ona Syers recalled it so well that she was able to correct a tiny error in the report of the Delano *Record*. Ione, she said, had worn a yellow dress, not a pink one.

ON THE EVE of the Second World War, the Pentecostal Church of God was the second largest church in McFarland. Sunday school attendance was above three hundred. The public high school scheduled sports and extracurricular events so as not to conflict with the church's program since so many of the community's youth were involved in its activities, and the local Methodist minister unable to rally his flock for Sunday night meetings, sometimes worshiped there.

Yet it was still an unsettled time for the Tathams and their friends. Walter and Arch's brother Willy had died of a heart attack in Delano at the age of sixty-four in October 1938. He had come to California to retire and rest, leaving a dairy job in Joplin. The shock of transition took its toll.

Another casualty was the marriage of Cora and Walter Tatham. It wasn't completely unexpected. The marriage had been shaky for some time. The fact that Cora found herself more at ease in California than Walter no doubt widened the gulf between them. Walter was a restless charmer and a gadabout. Cora was a religious woman who had known too much hard work and was frustrated by Walter's ways. His constant moving had "worn her down," said Ophelia. Then, too, little things had made Cora question his feelings for her. She hadn't wanted to move back to Drake's Prairie in 1932, but Walter had more or less forced her to, and she had never forgotten how he had given away her sewing machine. It seemed to Cleo that when her father got to California, he "slipped." Walter loved Cora in his own way, but it was hard for him to feel good enough for a woman with such rigid Holiness views about men and sex. Walter believed in true love and was forever playing matchmaker for the confirmed bachelors and old maids who drifted into his orbit. Cora's strength made it hard for her to indulge a husband whose self-confidence had been damaged by his failure as a provider.

He had been coming and going all his life, and this time, after thirty-five years of marriage, he just stayed gone. He had asked Cleo to drive him off somewhere to sell some furniture that he'd loaded on a truck. Cleo knew what was really going on, and she slipped over to tell Oca.

"I'm not takin' him," said Cleo, who knew that Walter could not drive himself.

"Don't you do it," Oca agreed. "You come by here and tell him you are going to tell us good-bye and when you get here whirl that truck around and jump out."

Cleo did just as Oca told her, and when she jumped out she took the keys with her just to be sure. Walter couldn't drive away, the truck stayed put, but Walter did not return home.

For a while, Cora moved over to Oca's house, and then she found a place to rent, moved the children and the furniture into it, and took in boarders. Cora didn't believe in divorce, and Walter had no desire for one: he visited her on holidays and at family reunions for the rest of his life. Vernon, who was eighteen, quit high school and went to work full-time on the Sierra Vista Ranch to help support his mother. And Arch came over from the Sierra Vista Ranch to offer his sister-in-law what comfort he could. Cora had been a mother to him when he was just a boy in Oklahoma.

Not long after the separation, Cora learned that Norma had cancer of the uterus. Her husband, Noel Dagenette, drove her and their four children to Delano, where Cora took them in. Noel, who'd been preaching for the Assemblies of God in Oklahoma, was slipping back into the drug addiction that had plagued him early in life. It turned out he was using morphine meant for his wife.

As Norma's suffering worsened, the family decided to seek divine healing for her at Aimee Semple McPherson's Angelus Temple. Oca drove her and the rest of his family there in August 1941. Doris was awed by the spectacle. Aimee made a great appearance in her robes. There was a choir and orchestra, and people fell to the ground "slain in the spirit," as deacons stood ready to catch them or cover them with blankets. Dick, eight, fell down unconscious when he saw the lady in white silken raiments. Hands lifted him up and carried him to a side room, where, he would forever remember, his childhood neck pains passed from him.

The family's joy was lessened by the apparent failure of Norma to get her healing. Her pain was too great for her to go to the altar to receive Sister Aimee's personal blessing. After the service, they carried her back to the car. But by the time they got back to Delano, it appeared that a miracle had indeed transpired.

Oca said, "We came home and the cancer turned loose and passed out of her. Mama put it in a jar of alcohol, and the cancer smell was gone. She peeled potatoes and helped my mama, and talked about buying a washing machine."

For several weeks, Norma's condition seemed to improve, and Cora gave hourly thanks to God. But then the pain began again. Some of the family blamed Noel for what happened. It was bad enough that he had been stealing her morphine—picking it up at the doctors but not giving it to her. Now he planted doubts in her mind about her healing.

He was living in Bakersfield and was no longer an Assemblies of God pastor, but he visited her from time to time. After the trip to

Los Angeles, when things seemed to be going well, Noel came calling. Oca said, "Her husband went into the bedroom and told her she was going to die. He told Mama, 'Norma knows she is going to die.' He finally had her agreeing she was going to die.' And from that moment on she headed downhill.

"She'd scream out in pain, and it got to a point where medication didn't help. I remember her saying, 'Oh, Bud, oh, Bud, can't you help me?' I was so heartbroken then, I fell on the floor on my face and begin to weep. I couldn't understand, but the Bible says, 'There is a sickness unto death.' Those words you never forget."

YEARS LATER Oca reflected on what church had meant to them in the Depression.

"Did we need the church in the Depression? You bet we did. What else did we have? We had no one else to turn to. We couldn't turn to our landlords. And you know something? We were full of joy—more joyful than people whose faces were hanging down to their stomach, who *hated* Pentecost. We didn't have everything, but we had peace and joy."

CHAPTER EIGHT

WARTIME

OPHELIA AND VERNON TATHAM saw *The Grapes of Wrath* at the movie house in Delano not long after it was released by Twentieth Century-Fox in 1940. Parts of it had been filmed on location in Sallisaw in the fall of 1939. Oklahoma boosters such as the state chamber of commerce were up in arms over John Steinbeck's novel, so the studio put out a cover story that it was filming a noncontroversial movie called *Highway 66*.[1] But in Sallisaw, the local citizenry greeted the film crews enthusiastically. A few people the Tathams knew made twenty-five dollars a day loading up their jalopies and driving down Wheeler Avenue while the cameras rolled. The chamber wasn't bringing opportunities like that to Oklahoma.

The movie made Ophelia very sad. She related to the scenes of the journey, especially to the one where the Joads had to bury Grampa by the side of Highway 66. Her people had left a grandma behind, not buried in a grave, but rocking on a porch because she was too old to make the trip. Watching the movie, Ophelia understood for the first time how poor and uneducated they'd been. Vernon thought those times had been even "worse than Steinbeck made them out to be."

The movie came out in the midst of a tremendous debate in Washington and California about what to do about the migrant prob-

lem, prompted largely by Steinbeck's book. The furor forced America
to begin a slow awakening to the poverty in its midst; in that sense
the attention given to the Okie predicament set the stage for the
antipoverty and antihomeless programs enacted in the 1960s and
thereafter. New Dealers and conservative Republicans alike agreed
that there was a major problem while differing in their ideas of what
to do about it. Republicans generally argued for reduced relief and
aggressive repatriation of migrant workers to the states they had come
from. Some conservative analysts spoke of the "ominous outlook" for
the state of California and its citizens resulting from the influx of
"people of the lower fringe of humanity"[2] and argued that relief
"encouraged indolence." In 1940, Congress began to consider sweep-
ing legislation that would authorize the "resettlement" of migrants
and provide various forms of relief. Liberals, on the other hand,
called for more generous relief programs and attributed the Okie
problem to drought, Depression, and "deep-rooted unhealthy social
and economic conditions."[3]

Yet within a year after the release of the movie, a problem that
many believed would require long-term massive intervention by the
federal government had all but vanished. A defense boom that began
well before Pearl Harbor created thousands of jobs and opportunities
for able-bodied men and women. Okies, ready to work (and to fight
when the war came), quickly were hired to build bases and airstrips
or to work for hourly wages at shipyards and munitions plans. "In
the thunder of guns had been as well the jingle of cash," wrote Walter
J. Stein in *California and the Dust Bowl Migration*.

The unexpected "solution" of the Okie problem caught policy
makers off guard. In 1940, California congressman John H. Tolan's
House Committee on the Interstate Migration of Destitute Citizens
was just winding up a massive, nationwide investigation and was
preparing to introduce legislation. The most exhaustive study of
poverty in America done up to that time, it was soon gathering dust
on shelves.

The withering away of the larger problem (except for pockets of
homelessness, substandard housing, and unhealthy living conditions)
affected thinking about the nature of American poverty for some
time to come. It was remembered that the Okies had been able to
"pull themselves up by their bootstraps" through hard work and
individual initiative. Less often mentioned was the fact that this miracle was accomplished largely through an unprecedented expenditure
of federal tax dollars for defense, roads, dams, power projects, and
water projects, not only during the war but for the twenty subsequent

years as well. The Okies were the beneficiaries of the greatest infra-structure program ever undertaken by the federal government and probably by any government in the history of the world.

The Roosevelt-sponsored defense buildup began well before Pearl Harbor. In January 1939, following Germany's occupation of the Sudetenland, President Roosevelt asked Congress to approve a $1.3 billion defense budget. That was still only 14 percent of the total U.S. budget (roughly half the proportion earmarked during the later era of the cold war), but it was still much larger than in prior years. Eighteen months later, the president asked Congress to triple defense outlays in light of the grave international crisis. Then, in early 1941, nine months before Pearl Harbor, Congress authorized $7 billion of Lend-Lease aid to the European countries fighting Hitler.

As Japan grew more assertive, the West Coast became the center of defense activity. Long before Pearl Harbor, the army was con-cerned about the possibility of a Japanese attack on American terri-tory and feverishly began building bases along the Pacific coast. Naval shipbuilding was also concentrated on the West Coast. The West had millions of acres of federal and state lands that could easily be requisitioned for bases and defense plants. The boom was on.

By 1942, new arrivals from Oklahoma and Texas were going straight to defense plants or shipyards instead of into agricultural work. Growers in the central valley had to increase the pay of field and shed workers, a situation that benefited whites until the U.S. and Mexican governments negotiated an international agreement for the importation of braceros in August 1942.[4]

The military services and wartime industries provided on-the-job training, built up working people's confidence and self-esteem, and promoted entrepreneurism by encouraging innumerable small con-tractors. Thousands of people became their own bosses; millions learned how to take orders, to be on time, to work together.

The Allied victory in 1945 wasn't the end of it. Government and the private sector in California as elsewhere in the country continued on this wartime track for years. After World War II came huge dam and water projects and then, in the 1960s, the Interstate Highway program. Along with these developments in the public sector, private corporations invested tens of billions of dollars in manufacturing plants throughout the United States. These investments helped ab-sorb most of the white, predominantly Southern agricultural work force into the economic mainstream by the late 1960s. And the princi-pal beneficiaries were the class of white Southern and Southwestern farmers and laborers from which the Tathams came. The Socialist writer and activist Michael Harrington still found plenty of white poverty when he prepared *The Other America*, published in 1962. But it was hard to argue with the proposition that the enormous federal expenditures on defense and infrastructure had not been a boon.

After the mid-1960s, the investment priorities of the federal government changed. The surge of spending on public works, highway, dam, and water projects, which had provided so much assistance to the Okies, was over. Investment of that kind continued on a modest scale, but more and more appropriated funds were channeled to the high-technology sector of the defense and space industries as the Cold War escalated and the United States set its sights on putting men on the moon.

Left out of this process of assimilation of the agricultural population was one very large and significant group: the blacks. There were blacks in the Dust Bowl migration, but the major migration began after the introduction of the mechanical cotton harvester in 1948, an event that spelled the end of the Southern black sharecropper. Beginning in the 1950s, blacks headed north in very large numbers, often choosing the same urban destinations as the Appalachian white poor. The blacks were less fortunate than the Okies for three reasons. They were black and were quickly ghettoized in northern cities, which meant that they did not have the same freedom of movement and access to jobs as whites. Second, in the northern cities they were not geographically well situated to take advantage of federal spending on infrastructure programs, which tended to be concentrated in the West and in rural areas. Finally, they were not well-prepared to benefit from the shift in the federal budget to spending on high-technology space and defense programs.

Ironically, it was Southern whites who, from the mid-1960s on, benefited in particular from the new jobs and opportunities created by the large-scale corporate investment in the South that was the region's reward for abolishing segregation. Southern blacks also were helped, of course. But by the time desegregation and federal equal-employment laws really began to have an impact in the 1970s, the white agricultural and rural class had been dispersed throughout the American lower-middle and middle classes. It was ready to protect its interests politically. The Okies had got through the gate first.

OCA TATHAM lived through this history of white advancement, and was the first to say that the defense boom saved his neck. In 1939, he had several trucks and was doing better than most Okies, but the trucks were bought with borrowed money and it was all he could do to keep up with the payments. He was struggling, paying drivers, buying insurance, buying fuel, and feeding the family. Things got so bad at times that he considered selling his hydraulic jacks and spare tires to buy groceries. Small truckers in California's central valley depended on the agricultural cycle for work, but had to find work for their trucks in the off season.

When the defense buildup started, it seemed that every down-and-out trucker converged on whatever job was opening up and anything went. Oca wouldn't give payola. The first few defense jobs he applied for were "dirty, rotten, chiselin' deals, and I wouldn't pay," he said. His break came just before Christmas 1940. He headed south to San Diego to check out a report that the army was planning to carve a training center out of the lush state recreation reservation called Torrey Pines. It would become Camp Callon. Oca stopped at the home of Tom Fuller, brother of Pastor Jay Fuller, and his wife, Lola. The Fullers gave him a steak and gravy breakfast, and then they all got down on their knees and prayed for the job—"bombarding Heaven," as Oca recalled it.

The contractor told Oca to have his trucks on the job the following Monday, and Oca telephoned Ruby to have the drivers hit the road. He was flat broke, and Jay Fuller came down with the truckers from Delano and gave him twenty dollars. After that job, he got another at a training base near Santa Maria. It was a huge, sprawling project that became the army's Camp Cooke and, eventually, Vandenberg Air Force Base. But in 1941 it was still a lonely stretch of sand dunes, scrub oak, and mesa. The drivers lived in a block house with no windows. Jack Kooken still had his job at a Ford garage in Delano, but he came down weekends to work on a gray '42 Ford dump truck that he had gone in on halves with Oca. Jack was down working on a carburetor the weekend of December 6 and 7, 1941, and was washing their truck when he got the news that the Japanese had bombed Pearl Harbor. Being a practical man, he went back to work on the carburetor.

For Oca and the Okie truckers, the defense boom provided work and a draft deferment. There was no shame in deferral. In the Okie culture, the isolationist strain ran deep. Oklahoma had been the scene of violent antidraft protests during World War I, especially the Green Corn Rebellion of 1917, which involved thousands of sharecroppers who were resisting induction. In Oca's case it was more a case of having a wife and four children to support. Then, too, the whole organized mob scene of armies and war went against his individualistic, horse trader's grain. For a trading man whose life revolved around small opportunities, deals, and bargains, war was a vast waste of resources, energy, and time. He would stay out if he could. And many in his group felt just the same way.

In any case, once the shooting started, the truckers had more work than they could handle. They moved on to Merced Army Air Field, eventually to be renamed Castle Air Force Base. The contractor proved difficult. "You ain't nothing but a bunch of damn Bolsheviks," he shouted at the truckers one time when several complained that he was pocketing government money while their trucks stood idle. Things were better in Sacramento, where they hauled rock and gravel for the new runways of Mather Air Force Base. They sloshed around in the January 1942 mud while military planes landed alongside them.

By this time, they were working in a pack that included a dozen or so Okie truckers and their drivers. One of the truckers was Aubrey Crouch, from Knox County, Texas. He'd come west to Arizona in the early 1930s, stopping there to run a filling station and help a rancher pull mesquite bushes out of the desert so it could be planted in cotton. He'd pushed on to California in 1935 and become a fruit tramp.

Aubrey liked to tell how he'd been jailed for vagrancy in Fresno. He'd had a hundred and fifty dollars on him when the policeman stopped him, but the cop sent for the paddy wagon. After a night in jail he told the judge he'd come to pick cotton.

"There's no cotton in the city of Fresno," the judge had said and gave him thirty days. After a few hours of chopping wood, the guard told him to get out of town and not come back. Aubrey caught a freight straight back to Texas.

He drove a wheat combine, but he still had California fever and the jailing hadn't scared him that much. The next thing, he was in Los Angeles, installing the soundproofing on Hollywood movie sets. The five dollars a day was better than anything he could make picking crops, but he wanted to run his own business. Soon he'd cleared enough to start a mattress company.

They were still making box springs by hand and selling them in L.A. when Oca and another man stopped by for some reason. Aubrey figured that hard times were coming for the mattress business and in no time Aubrey closed up shop and bought one of the last ton-and-a-half Ford dump trucks that could be had without getting a license from the government. He caught up to Oca and Jack at Merced.

Truman Sipes had started out with this gang as camp cook, but had been promoted to driver by the time they reached Merced. He'd left his home in Norman, Oklahoma, "to see the world." He'd "highwayed it" to California after gambling away his savings and gone to work as a field hand. California had looked like paradise in 1929. Spuds were fifty cents a bag. It seemed to Truman that you could fill your pickup with groceries for five dollars.

Money was no problem for a single man who was a whirl of a cotton picker. One day he picked 678 pounds and could have hit seven hundred if he hadn't taken time to help his wife. He'd met her in a cotton patch, of course. She was fifteen—"below statutory," he admitted. She'd come out with her folks in "forty miles of Buick," Truman recounted, on a trip that was "almost like *The Grapes of Wrath*." He was twenty-one and, by his own acknowledgment, "wild as a deer." They worked in the grapes, tomatoes, and cotton and then the lettuce in Salinas. Truman was driving a tractor on a ranch around Delano when he met Jack Kooken, and Jack put him to work.

There were others. The Vassar brothers, Mack, Benny, and Arch, were entrepreneurs who owned their trucks. Rocky Ross was an independent operator like Jack. And there were drifters who came and went.

Few if any in this crowd shared Oca's religious zeal. Aubrey "left religion to my wife." Back in his home county in Texas, people on the prairie had been mainly Baptists and Methodists; the Holiness church was "in the sticks," and was attended by "backwoods people who would shout and talk in tongues and roll in the sawdust till it ran chills up and down your back." But Aubrey saw that Oca's faith instilled a focus that distinguished him from the rest of them. It didn't make Oca "crazy" as it did some, Aubrey acknowledged, and his conviction that God's will would work its way seemed to let him plunge ahead with a kind of recklessness.

To Truman, Oca seemed "all business." Aubrey admired his self-confidence. "He was enthusiastic and forward, while I was reticent," said Aubrey. Most of the Texans and Oklahomans were not in as much of a hurry as Oca. They had time to trade yarns and jokes.

Oca hired other men to do his driving and kept a "shade-tree mechanic" around to maintain the vehicles while he watched out for opportunities, studying special publications, asking questions, and ferreting out information. Oca served as a kind of subcontractor on behalf of the other Okie truckers. He was their promoter with the big contractors, Jack Kooken said. Once they had a job, Oca negotiated with the contractor and called for trucks as they were needed.

Sometimes that led to friction. Allegations that he was favoring his own trucks made Oca very angry.

"I had to remember I was a Christian who couldn't turn around and say, 'I'm gonna bust you one right in the eye,' " Oca said. "You don't handle it like that as a Christian. I was probably *tempted* to do it. But you just have to control yourself. You don't do the things every time you feel like doing—you know it's wrong."

It seemed to Jack that Oca was "playing for the big win." That may have explained why Oca ended up with several dump trucks and he, Jack Kooken, had only a half interest in one—and that one had painted lettering on the side that proclaimed "Oca Tatham Trucking."

After Sacramento, they moved on to Oregon, where the army was starting work on a training camp and gunnery school outside Medford, to be called Camp White. This time Ruby and the family left Delano and came up to join him. The Oregon interlude began on a sad note because Norma died of her cancer a month after Oca started on the job. She left three young children who needed adult care and a husband who had pretty much abandoned them. Federal men had come to pick up Noel on a drug charge at Cora's house one day, and he went off to jail.

It fell to Cora, now sixty-one, to take custody of Norma's two youngest children. In the summer of 1942, right after Ophelia finished high school—the first in the family to do so—she brought Ophelia, Cleo and Norma's children up from Delano to Oregon. They felt different in Oregon, where they were just plain white working people, not Okies. Oca bought a 120-acre farm on the edge of Ashland. It had a creek, cherry trees, corrals for horses, and small game in the woods to blast away at with .22 rifles. There was a Foursquare Gospel Church associated with Aimee Semple McPherson's Pentecostal denomination.

Ruby's and Oca's fifth child, Brenda, was born there in 1942. Soon it was a Tatham gathering, as one after another of the Delano gang arrived. Cleo's husband, Wayne Frost, got a job at Camp White, and so did Vernon Tatham. Herman Morgan came up with Clara to work for Oca again, and Walter Tatham tended the stock on Oca's farm. There must have been romance in the air, for the Oregon interlude led to matrimony for Vernon and Ophelia.

Vernon's sweetheart was Dora Rose, sister of one of the truck drivers. The Roses weren't Okies strictly speaking. Dora was born in the Nebraska Sand Hills above the Platte River, in a sparsely populated country where a different kind of culture evolved than what the Tathams knew. Dad Rose had rented a place forty miles from Rushville, the nearest town. He raised his own vegetables and meat and sold cream and milk in five-gallon cans, which the mailman picked up and took to town. They had no radio or phone. Because of the distances, they bought everything in bulk—even honey was purchased in five-gallon tins. To save coal in winter, they burned cow chips. Dora and her twin sister could milk cows when they were nine, and they had to do so on the days their dad made the eighty-mile round-trip journey to Rushville.

Mrs. Rose's recent ancestors were German and believers in a good education. But school attendance beyond the local grammar school was difficult for people living in the wide open prairies. So, in September 1934, a month after the Tathams left Sallisaw, the Roses moved west to Grants Pass, Oregon, to be near a high school.

Dora and four of her brothers and sisters completed high school while her parents worked in the potatoes or the hops and Dora went on to a "continuation school," where she learned business and advanced home skills.

She met Vernon through friends when she was twenty-two and four years out of high school and he was working at Camp White. She thought the customs of the Southwesterners were quite strange. The twangy guitar music that Vernon loved was unfamiliar and a little worldly, with its themes of love and loss and country towns—and not always of God. The Tathams ate red beans, the Roses white ones. The Oklahomans ate biscuits with gravy, because they were easy to make from their winter wheat. The Nebraskans ate hotcakes, loaves of homemade bread and lots of cakes made out of flour from their hard, spring-planted northern-plains grain. The Roses' taste for cakes over pies was a matter of simple necessity: except for a nearby orchard of chokecherries, they didn't have much fresh fruit. In the north, pies, made from store-bought apples, were a rare treat. Dora learned all about pies from Cora Tatham.

Both the Roses and the Tathams ate the ubiquitous corn bread. But Mrs. Rose used corn in ways that amazed the Southerners, for cornmeal cereal or fried mush.

Different as their backgrounds were, the Roses and Tathams had a strong bond in the church. The Roses had been "saved" at a Pentecostal revival preached by two men who came into the Sand Hills and called a meeting at the schoolhouse when Dora was eleven. Before that there had been nothing but a Sunday school for the inhabitants of twenty-five square miles of country. So many were saved and sanctified at the revival that afterward there was a church and eventually a minister. Because of the distances, church three or four times a week, as was the Southern custom, was impossible. So church usually was an all-day Sunday occasion, and when a visiting preacher came through, he tended to stay awhile and take his turn haying and shucking corn. Yet sanctification and the gifts of the Spirit were no less compelling to a lonely farmer in Nebraska than a crowded community of renters in eastern Oklahoma.

Vernon and Dora were married in June 1942. The Tathams and their friends shivareed them, running Dora down the street in a wheelbarrow and honking car horns. A few months later, Vernon was drafted and entered the medical corps.

Ophelia married Bill Thomas, who'd gone to school with her in Delano and had also come to work at Camp White. Bill's dad had been a farmer in Oklahoma and had sold meat to the crews working in the oil fields. In 1937, the Thomases came west with Bill and his two younger sisters, working at first in the cotton in Arizona and then moving on to a job in a Southern California orange grove. A month or two later they moved to Delano, where a Thomas brother was tending bar. When a brother got a job at Camp White as a carpenter, Bill Thomas and his dad followed.

Bill was glad for a chance to leave Delano, which, he joked, was full of "gamblers, hobos, fruit tramps, and child molesters." Bill had been going with Dora Rose's sister when he made the switch to Ophelia. Vernon brought Bill to lunch one day, and Bill asked Ophelia if she went to church.

"I would if a little black Ford came to pick me up," she said. That was the start of their romance.

Bill was drafted the next year. Ophelia followed him to Abilene, Kansas, in October 1943. Bill got a day off from boot camp and they found an Assemblies of God minister there to marry them. That was marriage, World War II style.

That Oregon chapter in the Tathams' lives ended in late 1942, with the completion of the base. The Ashland farm allowed for enjoyment—and a draft deferment until another government job turned up. Aubrey found government work building an internment camp for Japanese Americans in Idaho. Jack Kooken took a job at the navy yards in Stockton, California. Those few who went back to visit Oklahoma took a ribbing. "All you'll have in your backyard is peanut hulls and rabbit hair," they were told.

Within a few months, Oca and some of the gang were in Arizona, using their trucks to build runways at Kingman Army Air Field. Jack quit the defense plant in California, joined them in Kingman and bought a junker from Oca for $900. The Kingman job was just off Highway 66 in western Arizona in a blistering hot corner of the Mojave Desert. Oca and Ruby found a shack with a tin roof in the mining town of Chloride. Wild burros scavenged in their backyard at night.

One day federal marshals came out with a warrant and arrested one of the truckers for draft dodging. They put handcuffs on him and led him away, leaving his truck with the key still in the ignition. Soon after that, the truckers convoyed north again and Oca and Ruby went back to a rented ten-acre place. They'd sold the spread in Ashland. Oca staged rodeos for his boys and thought about becoming a rancher, but he soon got restless and set out with Jack to look for work.

It was early 1943. They drove through the night and pulled in for breakfast at a café in Pasco, Washington, in rugged Columbia River country. Jack looked glum. As he worked on his eggs and hashed browns, he thought about the busted universal joint on his truck back in Oregon and wondered why he always let Oca Tatham talk him into things. He was only half paying attention when he heard something that made him spin around.

"There's a big job up a ways. Military secret."

Jack was all ears. Military secret! Every independent trucker in the West knew that meant jobs.

Jack and Oca paid and drove the few miles to Richland, where the military secret was supposed to be. They had no trouble finding the headquarters of the contractor. A man came out and said they needed water trucks.

"Mister, you *got* water wagons," Oca said.

Jack eyed his friend. All they had was a bunch of battered dump trucks that had seen better days.

In Klamath Falls, they bought some steel plate and some water tanks and found a blacksmith to weld them onto the dump trucks to make workable water wagons. Then they cut holes to make a sprinkler system. Oca settled Ruby and the children in a two-story house with hardwood floors in Yakima and went to work at Hanford.

It was the most lucrative of Oca's wartime jobs. Jack, Aubrey, Truman Sipes, and many of the regulars since Mather Air Force Base were there. Trucks rolled twenty hours a day. With $1.25 an hour for a driver, gasoline, and maintenance, each truck could clear $2.75 an hour and $55 a day. Oca was running four of them.

It wasn't until the end of the war that they learned what the military secret had been. It was the Hanford nuclear site, which produced the plutonium for the weapon that ended World War II: the Nagasaki bomb. That bomb had really changed their lives.

By then, Oca was back in California and out of the trucking business. Around Christmas 1943, he sold his trucks and drove back to Delano, where he visited his mother and called on his former banker, Loren Billings, to inquire about a loan to buy a ranch. "We don't generally put people in business around here, Tatham," Billings said. "But I understand you ended up a rich man and made a fortune. All right, Tatham, you go and get your ranch and we'll see what we can do."

The conversation made Oca feel like a poor Okie again. Delano looked smaller and slower than he'd remembered. So he drove north and stopped at a real-estate office he knew in Fresno. East of town they showed him a place with a bunkhouse, corrals, and farrowing pens for hogs. It would do. He'd been reclassified 1A. He was thirty-three, had a wife and five children, and felt he'd done his part for the war effort. The Selective Service said he could get back his draft-exempt status as a farmer if he had some cows. He paid $18,000, all cash, and was in the dairy business the next day.

THE WAR WAS ADVANCING Oca's fortunes, but for the Tatham women in Delano, it brought only heartache and sacrifice.

Bill Elbertson enlisted in 1940, more than a year before Pearl Harbor. It was said he was having trouble with alcohol and women, and one day he was just gone.

Buck Dodson was one of the first called in the draft. He went in 1941.

Herman Morgan was drafted.

Pentecostal men could avoid military service in World War II. The Assemblies of God had a conscientious-objector clause in its bylaws, and objectors could legally avoid service by performing unpaid service in the Civilian Public Service camps, but few apparently did. None of the Tathams took that option.

Wayne Frost entered the service in 1943 and soon rose to sergeant. He was one of those indispensable people who really ran the army in the war—a common-sense man and a good shot, who could "clip a turkey's head off at a hundred yards."

Vernon, in the medical corps, trained at various bases, while Dora followed him everywhere she could. In 1944, he was shipped out to Europe and went to a field hospital in France two weeks after the invasion.

Vernon had chosen the medical corps because he did not want to kill, but during his training he told his commanding officer what he would do if the enemy shot at him. "If anybody shoots at me they better shoot straight 'cause if they miss I'm going to grab a rifle and shoot back," he said. Vernon felt that "the war had to be won."

Bill Thomas considered himself "a conscientious objector in terms of killing people," and he had noncombatant status. But he had tried to enlist in 1942 and was unable to do so only because his draft board's enlistment quota was filled. Like Vernon, Bill was ready to fight if necessary and almost did. He served as a clerk-typist, eventually at General MacArthur's headquarters. When Bill reached the Philippines, he was issued a rifle and told that he might be sent to the front. He did not object.

Isolationism had emerged strongly in Oklahoma and many other parts of the Southwest and in the uplands of the Ozarks and Appalachians during World War I, and the early Pentecostal movement lent an uncompromising pacifist strain to what already was a deep-grained suspicion of foreign wars in the backcountry. The Azusa Street chronicler Frank Bartleman wrote tracts against war and criticized U.S. foreign policy for being driven by greed: "The least degree of retaliation or severity will harden the affection and give a coldness and toughness in the inner life.[5] War is not God's way for the church." The American beneficiaries of a U.S. involvement in war would be "Wall Street interests, Pork Barrel administration, Brewer's Corporation, Syndicated and Monopolist, Steel Trust and Armor Plate, Powder Trust, etc., world without end."[6] Some saw in such positions a foreshadowing of the themes of nonviolent resistance in the civil rights and antiwar movements of later decades.

Pacifism, isolationism, and populism fused in these early Pentecostal stands against fighting, war, and the draft. Before World War I, A. J. Tomlinson's Church of God was so outspoken in its criticism of combatant service that it was investigated by the Department of Justice for disloyalty.[7] Charles H. Mason, one of the founders of the black Church of God in Christ, was hounded throughout his life for his pacifist views and was jailed in Mississippi for them.[8]

By World War II, however, the Pentecostal church was changing its stance. Assemblies of God pastors generally did not exert pressure for or against conscientious objection, and of the estimated 11,950 objectors who served during World War II in the Civilian Public Service camps, only 130 were Pentecostal, including a mere twenty from the Assemblies of God as of 1943.[9] The General Council of the denomination passed a resolution supporting U.S. neutrality in 1939, but it was the last such resolution it ever adopted, and once the United States entered World War II, Pentecostal leaders outdid themselves in demonstrating their patriotism. In 1942, Aimee Semple McPherson showed up at a war-bond rally in downtown Los Angeles wearing a red, white, and blue costume. In fire and brimstone sermons she rebuked Hitler and Mussolini. "How many of you would like to see Hitler covered with boils from head to foot?" she cried. "Well, I would!"[10]

Reveille, an Assemblies of God publication for servicemen, made its debut with a mailing list of 76,000 servicemen whose names were provided by Assembly pastors. More than 1,000 servicemen associated with the denomination were killed in the war, enabling a church historian to write that "the blood of the noble youth from the Assemblies of God flowed with that of all the others."[11]

To the extent that the tradition of isolationism and pacifism was kept alive, it was done so by the women.

Cora and Cleo hated the war and retained their isolationist sentiments even after Pearl Harbor. Before the Japanese attack, Cleo hoped fervently that the United States would stay out. "When you know it's going to take your husband and your boys off and you don't know whether they're coming back, I didn't want it," she said. Indeed, the peace issue made Cleo a Republican voter in 1940, the first year she could vote for President, for she knew that a Democrat, Woodrow Wilson, had involved the United States in World War I and cost the lives of thousands of American boys. Wendell Willkie, the Republican presidential candidate in 1940, courted isolationist votes, saying: "We do not want to send our boys over there again and we do not intend to." FDR, forced to respond, declared in a speech in Boston a few days before the election, "We will not participate in foreign wars and will not send our army, naval, or air forces to fight in foreign lands outside of the Americas except in case of attack."

This promise had a tremendous impact on Cleo and her circle. Cleo's father-in-law urged Wayne to vote for the President because "he won't send you boys overseas." But Wayne was skeptical. "Dad, don't believe that, that's just a bunch of election baloney—there's shiploads of boys going overseas right now."

Even after Pearl Harbor, Cleo had her doubts about the United

States' participation in the war, and she didn't hold it against anyone who looked for a way out. The war strengthened her conviction that Democratic presidents got the nation into war. Now the war had come, their men were in it, and the women were left to look after the home front.

Cora, who had returned to Delano, had the most to cope with, what with having taken on responsibility for Norma's children. She had moved into the house on Glenwood Avenue that Oca and Ruby had rented from 1936 to 1942. Cleo and Ophelia lived with her, making it five women against the world: a grandmother, two of her children, and Norma's two youngest daughters.

They adopted what Cora called a "family strategy." There was an army allotment check for Cleo and Ophelia, but with five to feed, they would have to work, too. They pooled everything. Ophelia graded potatoes at the Wasco sheds. Norma's daughter Catherine was under-age, but she put on earrings to look more grown up and worked side by side with Ophelia, at Wasco or grading grapes at the Sierra Vista Ranch, or at a variety store in town. At the sheds, Ophelia said, "The rest of us who were over eighteen worked twelve hours a day." Cora sewed and cooked for the children; then about six o'clock in the evening, she would take a truck to the packing shed and her job putting up the "fancy packs" of grapes that grocers displayed in cartons.

Soon after Wayne Frost shipped out for Europe in the 363rd Infantry, Cleo learned she was pregnant. It was joyous news, but it meant after a while quitting the sheds and minding the house. They learned to stretch what they had. Ophelia got free sacks of potatoes at the sheds. Once, when a freight train broke down, they used boxes and cans to collect shortening that was being dumped. Cora strained it into empty Fluffo jars until it was pure. Cora made the children's clothes, and Ophelia was hairdresser for Norma's girls.

Ophelia remembers their troubles drawing them closer to God. "One time Dad brought down a calf from Oregon. We didn't run to the county for aid. God seen us through and we didn't go hungry. God seen the need and He helped us. We got a house for ten dollars a month and then this woman said to Mother, 'Don't bring the rent but twice a year because it's too hard for you to walk across town.' When she took the rent, the woman says, 'You can't afford all that money, you're a widow and you're keeping these little children. You have no way for getting by. Take part of that back.' "

At the Manila Market down the street, the Filipino proprietors slipped them butter and meat when their rations cards ran out. They knew the women had loved ones fighting to liberate the Philippines.

Sometimes the women were afraid. The bracero program, instituted for the benefit of big growers such as the DiGiorgios, had resulted in a fresh influx of Mexicans, and that meant new tensions in Delano. The women on Glendale Avenue feared burglars, drunks, and the occasional visits of Noel Dagenette, who would beat on the door or sometimes beg money from a daughter.

Cora found solace in the Holiness church that Delano finally had. A Pentecostal Holiness Church of Delano had opened in a Main Street storefront in 1943. It moved to a tent on the back of the lot. In 1944, the congregation began building a church on the south end of Main Street. It was a simple structure, with painted block walls. Cora took Catherine, and sometimes Cleo and Ophelia went there instead of to the Pentecostal Church of God in McFarland. Cora Tatham was a founding member, and George Land, the old pastor from Drake's Prairie, helped with the preaching. Cleo gave her place to the preacher when she moved in with her mother.

Vernon's wife, Dora, who was working as a waitress in Delano for a while, said: "Looking at it from Granma's standpoint, because of the poverty that they were in, and they didn't have things they really needed, Granma could go to her knees in prayer and their needs would be supplied." Often Cora's prayers and Cleo's and Ophelia's *were* answered. The free potatoes and shortening seemed to Ophelia to have come from God's hand, and they saw the hand of Providence in the gifts of food that sometimes turned up on Cora's doorstep.

But the hand of Providence was working in other ways, too. Not even their prayers could keep the telegram man away. His name was Sam, and he brought the war home to the mothers, fathers, and wives of Delano.

One day in 1943, Sam delivered a telegram to the house of George Land, their friend from Drake's Prairie. When Sam left, Brother George could only weep and tell himself that the Lord never makes a mistake. His son Alvis had been killed in Italy.

On August 3, 1944, Sam stopped at the house on Glenwood Avenue. Cleo took the telegram with a shaking hand while Sam waited awkwardly.

"The Secretary of War desires me to express his deep regret that your husband, Staff Sergeant Herbert W. Frost, has been reported Missing in Action since 8 July in Italy. If further details or other information are received, you will be promptly notified. Helio, the Adjutant General."

Cleo collapsed in a chair, and Sam sat down on the front porch and began to weep.

"If I have to keep bringin' these I'll quit my job," he said. Cleo was five months pregnant.

Cora and Ophelia came back from the sheds, and they prayed together. Dora took the bus down from Medford and joined the other women in Delano.

There was not much to do but wait. Sam came again on September 30.

"Is it good or bad?" Cleo asked.

"It's good *and* bad," said Sam.

Wayne was alive, but he was a German prisoner of war.

When Wayne's brother was taken prisoner in the Philippines, there were two brothers in enemy hands on two sides of the world.

On November 11, Herman Morgan was severely wounded on Peleliu Island in the Pacific, hit by a Japanese sniper as he moved a box of ammunition. When he stooped over the sniper sent a bullet through his collarbone. It punctured a lung and came out his back. He caught pneumonia and had trouble seeing. Ophelia heard about it from Herman's wife, Clara. Clara had given birth to the Morgans' first child, a daughter, six weeks earlier.

News came that Bill Elbertson had been severely wounded while serving with the 87th Infantry in the Pacific, taking a ricocheting machine-gun round in the head.

On December 8, Cleo gave birth to a son, whom she named Jerry Wayne Frost. It was the one happy event in a sad year, but the happiness was muted, for it had been a difficult birth and Cleo was told that she would be unable to have more children.

Early the next year, Buck Dodson was taken prisoner while serving as a staff sergeant with the 106th Division during the Battle of the Bulge. He was incarcerated in camps in Germany, where his feet froze and some of the men with him died.

It was turning out as Cleo had feared, with the men being chewed up in a foreign war that President Roosevelt had promised to stay clear of.

Cleo learned through the Red Cross that her husband was being held at Stalag VIIA, in Moosburg, Germany. He was liberated by American forces in May 1945. Wayne wrote her on Red Cross stationery: "Darling, I'll be so awfully glad to see your face and know you will be tickled for I know you've worried yourself sick. Just keep your sweet little chin up."

The night Wayne was due home Cleo waited up.

There were footsteps and a knock. She flung the door open, but it was only a friend. Wayne came about four o'clock in the morning. His boots went clomp, clomp, clomp. Then there were three knocks.

"It's him," said Cleo.

Cleo handed Wayne his son. She was looking at a man who weighed a little over a hundred pounds, not the 160-pound fellow who'd gone off to war. But the war showed in Cleo, too. Her hair had been almost black when Wayne went off. Now, at twenty-nine, it was graying.

The war was over, but it would echo like Wayne's footsteps in the lives of the Tathams and their friends for a long time. Wayne's feet had been frostbitten and gave him problems. Vernon came home a changed man. In the field hospitals of Europe, following the front from France to Nuremberg, he'd taken care of dying men, men whose groins or heads or limbs had been shot away. In relating what he'd seen to Oca, his face would turn purple and his lips go white.

People who knew Herman Morgan before the war said he never was the same after. His "hole in his chest," as Oca put it—his shot-through lung—gave him problems for a long time. He was not discharged from a military hospital until October 1945 and in subsequent years developed a drinking problem that contributed to further miseries.

Bill Elbertson, who got the Bronze Star for valor, wasn't let out of the hospital until the end of 1945. He went back to Sallisaw and never returned to California to live. Cleo ran into him in 1948 on a trip back to Oklahoma. His war injury still caused him difficulty in speaking, but he greeted her happily: "Cleo, I'll not forget the days when we went to California."

Buck Dodson was released from the service and later claimed disability because of frostbite. He never returned to California either. He went home to Missouri, joined the Methodist Church, and worked with the Disabled Veterans of America.

After the war, very few people suggested anymore that the men and women who had come from Oklahoma to California in the 1930s were "of the lower fringe of humanity." Those that served were simply American veterans—at least those who lived through it were—and many of them were heroes.

PART THREE

CHAPTER NINE

DESTINIES

CALIFORNIA WASN'T FOR EVERYONE.

Thousands of Okies went out to California for only a season or two, until they could find steady work in Oklahoma. Others drifted between the two states in a kind of limbo. Oca's cousin Alma and husband, Bill, returned to Sallisaw after the war and bought a 120-acre spread outside town; a California dollar went a long way in eastern Oklahoma. But they didn't stay long. They'd left two children behind, so in 1949 they sold out and bought a small house up the road from Delano in Earlimart, all cash. Bill worked as an irrigator on the Sierra Vista Ranch.

Arley Land, who'd shared the wheel with Oca on the drive out in 1934, returned to California with his wife, Myrtle, in 1946, but his job didn't work out and they headed home again. "Everything was so strange and different from what we was used to," said Myrtle. "Everybody was different." Myrtle changed her mind again, though, and went west once more to be near a daughter after she and Arley divorced.

Oca's Uncle Arch made a permanent U-turn. He never did make a full accommodation with California. He was too much a country man in an agricultural valley that was a lot like a city, with its ethnic neighborhoods, traffic, potentially violent labor trouble, packing sheds big as factories, trains that roared through day and night. Not being a driving man himself, he hired someone to motor him, Winnie, and their youngest children back to Oklahoma in 1942. He had sold his ten acres on the prairie to an Eskew brother-in-law, and when he returned to Sequoyah County he bought the farmhouse that George Land had left when he moved to Delano. It had an *inside* wall hung on two-by-four studs, which meant Winnie could have wallpaper. Arch did some farming and worked for a coal company, but he did not have much money to show for his half-dozen years in California.

Arch's son Leslie was already back home in Oklahoma. He'd enjoyed the adventure of riding the rails to California and being a single man in the wide-open West. "Eighty, ninety dollars a month was something different for a farm boy," he said. But his new wife's family was in Oklahoma, and after Pearl Harbor they worried about a Japanese attack. Early in 1942, they sold the small piece of property they'd acquired and headed for Oklahoma.

Arch's son, Farris, back from war service in the medical corps, bought a spread to grow corn and hay. Soon he married a local woman whose dad had come to Oklahoma at the turn of the century to build the railroads.

Oklahoma's economy was slow to benefit from the wartime boom, and there was still a great deal of poverty. Depression-era misery had spread across all regions and all classes. Only a tiny percentage of people who migrated to California in the 1930s—an estimated 6 percent—came from the six western panhandle counties hardest hit by the Dust Bowl. Most came from the Cotton Belt of northern Texas and central and eastern Oklahoma, where Drake's Prairie was and where the small farming plots could not sustain commercial agriculture. Many of the Oklahomans who pulled up stakes in the 1930s were not even farmers. Perhaps not surprisingly, more professionals, proprietors, clerks, and semiskilled and unskilled laborers left Oklahoma in that period than farmers or farm laborers. These were the people confident of their ability to find work elsewhere. And large numbers of the self-reliant, religious, predominantly Scotch-Irish hill people from the Ozark regions of Arkansas, Oklahoma, and Missouri—impoverished people who had moved out of the Appalachians more than a century ago—now also moved again.[1]

But even in Oklahoma, the wartime economy created new opportunities. Leslie got a job at an army camp in Oklahoma in 1942, then learned to read blueprints in a sheet-metal and riveting course in Wichita. With those credentials he was able to get a job at the Oklahoma Steel Casting Company, making parts for PT boats. With the money he saved, he bought a small truck and invested in some property in Sallisaw.

There had many been changes in town and on the prairie between 1935 and 1945. Many of the box houses were abandoned or falling down. People had scattered—some to California, others to town, where jobs and the high school were close by.

Charlie Floyd had been in his grave in Akins Cemetery for eight years, and the Cookson Hills no longer echoed with gunfire. Bill Byrd had not run for sheriff in 1936. He tried to regain the office in 1938, but his reputation was too damaged by the stories of how he'd deserted Altie and run away with a younger woman. Altie herself had become something of a legend. Stories circulated about how she'd sold her best cow to buy a gun to shoot the other woman but had decided that Bill wasn't worth going to jail over.

It still wasn't easy making a living around Sallisaw. The small farms in Sequoyah County couldn't support the 8,000 thousand people in the county under twenty-one. Only one business had more than twenty employees in the whole county. Arch and Leslie returned to California periodically for the grape and cotton harvests, although Arch was not in the best of health. His familiar whistle had been silenced by the removal of a cancer from his lip, but he still worked. He returned to the valley one summer and worked at the Repetto grape ranch, where his son Ira was foreman.

Leslie took his family back to valley towns around Delano in 1947, 1948, and 1951 and sent his children to the local schools. The first two years, they worked in the cotton east of Pixley. In 1951, they worked on the ranch of a friend. "We had a table and cooking stove and a mattress—and some of the children had to sleep *crossways*," Leslie remembered. His wandering continued until 1953, when he finally could support himself with his carpentry in his own hometown.

There was no mystery about what had drawn Arch and Winnie Tatham back to Oklahoma. Arch wanted his own farm, and she missed the Free Holiness church at Watts. The church hadn't changed. Drury Callahan had left in the 1920s to start his own Assemblies of God Church in town, anticipating that many of the people from the prairie would be moving in, but there was still a lively congregation carrying on the old traditions. Holiness children learned to stay on their pallets as the service went on around them hour after hour and learned self-discipline and patience at long services and summer camp meetings.

Many of the descendants of the original founders were still there, including Winnie Tatham. She had a "burning testimony that the souls of all the others were fed by," a grandson remembers. "I can well recall Granny and Clara Branham and Jack Smith and Aunt Jewell. They had such a spiritual fervor that it excited you so you sat on the edge of your pew. They would shout and dance in such a beautiful rhythm that could never be learned."

Arch Tatham was not a great one for testifying or dancing in the spirit. When the spirit took him, it came out as a deep groaning and a quiet swaying.

Around the church, the prairie was changing. Fields once planted to cotton were going over to pasture and hay, leaving the rich bottomland along the river for cash crops. Something profound was happening: the prairie was returning to what it had been before the cotton. From their ridge on Drake's Prairie, Arch and Winnie could once again smell the sweet grasses after a rainstorm. From the knoll, one could see for miles across an undulating landscape that could have been painted by Breughel or described by Hawthorne: cattle or horses stood in the shade of the big oaks, and hay lay in big rolls in the fields.

The cotton had outlived its usefulness. By the middle of the 1930s, only a few gins were still operating in the county. Cotton, like the people, had moved west. With cotton gone or going, the land could breathe more freely. Briefly in the 1940s, the prairie was violated once again with the arrival of strip-mining companies digging for coal in its shallow mineral veins. Bulldozers chugged over the fields, leaving ugly spoil piles, draglines, and strip pits where water gathered after a storm. Eventually, the big machines left, too. With its soil and minerals mined out, Drake's Prairie began to heal.

As if to mark a new chapter, in 1949 Charlie Floyd's kid brother, E. W. Floyd, was elected county sheriff. He was reelected over and over again in the ensuing years and more than redeemed the family name.

MOST OF THE ORDINARY Southerners who flocked to California after the Depression were under no illusions that the streets were paved with gold. California was not yet a place of mythic stature. Europeans might believe that all Americans were rich, but all Americans did not believe that of Californians.

Pre-war California, in fact, was still a rather sleepy, almost forgotten outpost of the rich, industrial East, dependent on agriculture,
forestry, and mining, empty and undeveloped throughout large
quarters—still, in many respects, the "plundered province" described
by the writer Bernard De Voto. Towns measured their importance
by their distance from San Francisco, the state's only world-class city.
Los Angeles was not much more than a big, sunny town connected
by a few roads to the many separate and distinct communities around
it. A twenty-minute drive brought one to orange orchards and dairy
farms. There were no sprawling suburbs, only disparate villages,
many with a distinctive ethnic or cultural flavor. Orange County, a
place of farming communities initially settled by people from the
utopian Oneida Community in upstate New York, was appropriately
named. Hollywood was emerging—but more in the pages of movie
magazines than as a center of great wealth and power. The notion
that political candidates for the highest offices in America would one
day come on bended knee to Hollywood to seek money for their
campaigns would have seemed strange.

California's infrastructure was yet to be developed. Highway 99
traversed the central valley; Highway 66 went east from Santa Monica. There were dams and canals—but not many. The cornerstone
for Shasta Dam on the Sacramento River in northern California—
centerpiece of the federal government's great power and irrigation
projects—was not laid until 1938, and the large-scale canal building
did not get under way until the late 1940s.

Yet someone who was poor had always been able to live better in
California than most anywhere else in America. The climate was
good, food was plentiful, the pace of life was fairly slow, and government took an interest in the plight of the working poor. For all these
reasons, California attracted the down-and-out, the misfit, the rebel.
When the writer Eric Hoffer lived in a federal transient camp in
California in 1934, he found thirty cripples, sixty "confirmed drunk-
ards," fifty old men, twelve men with chronic diseases, four mildly
insane individuals, four fugitives from justice, and only seventy who
were "apparently normal." There was evidently nothing so new about
that. When Hoffer questioned old-timers about the early settlers and
Gold Rush pioneers, he was told that they had been much like the
present-day "Okies and fruit tramps."

Had it not been for the arrival of waves of Southerners of highly
individualistic temperament, California might well have become a
kind of American Denmark: a socialized "workers' paradise." In the
1920s and 1930s, before the Okies, California labor movements were

strong, the Communist Party was well represented among San Francisco dockworkers, and socialists such as Upton Sinclair made respectable showings running for high office.

And then came the war years, when California began finally to become *California*. The war ended a pleasant period and marked the start of a new one that was both more prosperous and less gentle. After Pearl Harbor, California was never again a sleepy backwater. Before the war, everything of importance happened on the East Coast; afterward, that was no longer so. The war seeded the state with military installations, bases, and defense plants; modern air travel put California closer to the rest of the country; now it made sense for new companies and industries to establish their headquarters—not just regional branch offices—in California. It was decades before the promise of its greatness fully ripened, but in those years the process truly began.

This new stirring in the West was felt all across America but nowhere more strongly than in the South. Nearly a million people from the Greater South, from North Florida to West Texas, uprooted themselves and went to California during the 1940s. Oklahoma's experience was typical in this regard. Returning soldiers had dreamed of their Oklahoma home while lying in foxholes, but when they got back they found that the family farm "was just another piece of dirt," as one Okie put it.[2]

After World War II, someone counted fifty-two people from Sequoyah County working in one packing shed in Delano. Red Wesson, the former county tax assessor, supervised a night shift. "Red," one of his bosses is said to have told him, "I don't care if those boys from Sallisaw come with one leg. They do twice as much work as those California birds." Red hired all the Okies he could.

Abigail Sumpter had died in Sallisaw in 1944 at the age of ninety-six, cutting one of the Tathams' main ties between Oklahoma and California. Cora Tatham still had a few Sumpter relatives in Oklahoma, but with her mother gone, there was no reason to go back. She had come to California, and now she knew that she would die in California, too.

Cleo liked everything about California, right down to the little things. "I came here to Delano because I could do better," she said. "And that's why my mother stayed. And Dad. We could have a better life. We had better health. Ophelia and Vernon were sickly, but after they got here to California, they never got sick again. Vernon never chilled with the malaria one more time. Better living and better health, that's why we stayed. We came out here to pay our debts, and we worked hard and paid them."

Jobs and opportunities were there. The federal government's huge Central Valley Project, which was building dams, canals, and power stations, meant jobs at union wages. At the same time, the water projects made it possible for central valley growers to expand production of cotton, grapes, fruits, and vegetables, which needed hands to pick. As the Cold War geared up, the defense plants of Southern California hired the skilled and semiskilled.

Wayne Frost, who was finally discharged from the service in February 1946, found a union job with Hillcrest Sheet Metal in Delano. Jack Kooken worked for a company in Stockton that made military landing craft, then in shipyards and machine shops. In 1951, he started his own diesel repair shop.

The women, in particular, liked California, and their views counted. Oklahoma women often gave the orders and took the men in tow when their confidence faltered. Oca's driver Truman Sipes landed a job in the oil fields around Taft. His wife took him to see a house for sale, but the thought of owing all that money frightened Truman, and he went straight to bed.

"Get out of that bed, we're going to raise the money to buy that house!" she commanded. They paid the thousand dollars down out of his wartime savings.

Arch Tatham's oldest son, Ira, got wartime work in a shipyard, then was foreman on a grape ranch. In 1947, he hired on to drive a bulldozer for a contractor in Ventura County. Afterward he drove the big Cats on highway, dam, and government installations from Wyoming to Catalina Island. He was thankful for a good union, Operating Engineers Local Number 12 in Los Angeles, which set his pay at $1.25 an hour to start and guaranteed health and welfare benefits and pension.

Arch's son Lelan stayed on in the West, too. In 1942, he was hired by the Delano office of a Los Angeles company that sold irrigation pumps to farmers. When there was an opening in the sales department in 1947, the company moved him to Clovis, New Mexico. Deep irrigation wells, tapping the Ogllala aquifer, were just beginning to revolutionize the dryland farming in the former Dust Bowl region of the plains, and there was a tremendous market for the pumps. Lelan stayed.

Sometimes people just slipped into becoming Californians without thinking much about it. They'd come expecting to stay only for the cotton and grapes, stay through the winter to avoid the cold, hang around for another harvest. Then a son would marry and settle down in California. Oca's friend Jack Smith had planned to go back to Oklahoma for good, but he never did. Years later, he said, "Our daughter married out here, our son went to college. We kind of got oriented to the country. The times change, people change, ideas change, and you change your plans. You have to change because nothing stands still."[3]

By the late 1940s, an Okie no longer needed to be in Oklahoma to feel at home. The familiar western accent—"ever" for "every," "far" for "fire"—could be heard in every valley town with a "little Oklahoma." The journalist Oliver Carlson reported in 1952 how "the Texas twang and the Arkansas drawl pervade discussions at the cotton gin, the filling station, the bars and the market" in Arvin.[4] By then, Okies were feeling a defiant sense of their own importance in the central valley. When Jack Kooken was ticketed by a Stockton policeman for a vehicle infraction in about 1951, Jack gave a smart answer to the officer. "I'm from the grapes of wrath," said Jack, expressing himself forcefully enough to get himself handcuffed and taken to the station. An anonymous letter in the September 18, 1946, Fresno *Bee*, cryptically signed "One of Them," declared: "People like us from the Middle West are taking over. If you will go down to the real estate offices you will find we just about own California. What we don't own we are planning to buy."

Oca Tatham distanced himself from that kind of thinking. He was not interested in seeing Okies take over. He was too much his own man for that. He just wanted to make the most of California. His circle of friends and acquaintances were mostly people from his own background—Jack in Stockton, people at the church he attended in Fresno. But, like him, they were people on the move. Oca had a limited tolerance for what passed as Okie culture—country and western music, twangy guitars, Okie brogue, and slow-moving ways. One of the points in Fresno's favor, as far as Oca was concerned, was that it wasn't Bakersfield, that capital of Okiedom, of Confederate flags flying over corner stores, of pickup trucks and country music and saloons. Plenty of Okies settled in and around Fresno, too, of course. Clovis, near the forty-acre place Oca bought at the Shields and Armstrong intersection of Fresno in 1944, could have been in Texas or Oklahoma. But Fresno was different from Bakersfield. Okies in Fresno were just another group of newcomers, taking their place alongside Armenians, Swedes, Italians, Portuguese, Serbs, Croats,

Russians, Finns, Germans, Japanese, Chinese, and Filipinos. In that sense, Fresno County was more like the real California than Bakersfield. And it had the feel that Oca liked: much of the land around it was still undeveloped, marginal—the kind of country a horse trader could feel at home.

Fresno hadn't been settled so much as designated—that was the only appropriate word for it—by the Central Pacific Railroad Company, which put a railroad stop in the middle of the "big empty" in 1872 and called it Fresno Station. In 1889, a man by the name of Frank Roeding and his son discovered how to use wasps to cross-fertilize the Smyrna fig, and the American fig industry was born on the outskirts of what was still just a dusty little town. Grapes came next. Farmers first began growing vines in their wheat fields, then dispensed with the wheat altogether. Fresno County evolved into the "raisin capital" of the world because of its climate. European curing of raisins required dipping and drying, but the long, hot, usually dry days after a California harvest allowed growers to sun-dry their grapes, cutting costs and (for reasons having to do with the chemistry of the sugar) greatly improving the shelf life of the product. The arrival of Acala cotton in the 1920s gave farmers a profitable alternative to grapes and figs, and when the Central Valley Project began providing irrigation water for the east side in the early 1950s, the agricultural future was secure.

Oca was cut out to be king in a smallish realm—and Fresno was small enough. East of Fresno, where he took up residence in 1944, there was plenty of undeveloped space and a welcome sense of possibilities—though exactly what they were Oca had not yet imagined. The spread and the cows he bought for it preserved his draft-exempt status. He loved the place, loved getting on horses bareback and showing off for his sons, and daring them to do the same. Walter Tatham lived in a bunkhouse with Dick, Bill, and Gerald; he filled their heads with bawdy Oklahoma songs and rhymes and stories about being chased by wolves back in Nebraska, and had the boys shave him "dry."

But Oca was no farmer. He found it "too slow . . . it wasn't going to make that much money." As soon as the war ended he cast around for more suitable activities. Briefly he jumped back into trucking—then jumped back out of it again when a truck broke down with a load of tomatoes and the driver called to say there was tomato juice dripping out the back. He went into the furniture game as a partner in a Fresno furniture store—and right back out of it.

His natural habitat ever since Tulsa days had been the second-hand store and the auction. He and Ruby gravitated to Just Egypt's, a junk place on North Blackstone Avenue that sold used everything. Oca was also a regular at the Cherry Avenue auction, where he bought calves and horses for his farm. He kept his ears open. Often as not, what an alert trader could pick up at a place like that was worth more than the goods, for unlike the merchandise, the information was often brand new. He checked in frequently with the Rochas, a large Portuguese-American family that owned hundreds of acres close by to his property on Shields and Armstrong. The Rochas' years in Fresno made them a fount of knowledge about the community. He squeezed information from every source, until he had the pulse of the place. Riding around with him in his car, his boys heard a running commentary about what restaurant was in financial trouble, whether a particular business was run by a good or bad class of people, where lots were cheap. He was constantly evaluating, assessing, criticizing—buildings, people, business deals. At the dinner table and on the way to church, business was the topic.

In 1946, he traded his property for a house right in Fresno, on Adoline Avenue, and the same year he bought twenty acres of undeveloped farmland east of Fresno on a country road called Maple Avenue, where he put up a house with a two-car garage and a Spanish-tile roof. When it was ready he moved the family in; Renee, the sixth and last child born to him and Ruby, arrived soon afterward.

What came next was unplanned. People were coming home from war and needed homes for new families. Oca bought undeveloped farmland cheap and made it available for homes and lots, offering it first to friends and relatives. Ophelia's husband, Bill Thomas, came back from the war and bought a lot from Oca on Maple Avenue. Bill said, "We came to Fresno to work, and Oca had these lots . . ."

Vernon and Dora lived in a tent on one of Oca's lots, near Bill and Ophelia's, until they bought an Oca Tatham lot on Shields. Herman Morgan and Clara bought a half acre from Oca on Pontiac, then purchased part of an old barracks that Oca had bought "as is" at auction. Herman hauled it to their property to make a starter house. Aubrey Crouch was back in Texas raising milo on a small ranch when Oca wrote that there was money to be made in the Fresno County building game. Milo prices were down, so Aubrey sold the ranch and came out to Fresno. Oca sold him a couple of corner lots at Shields and Maple.

Oca had picked a promising area for his subdividing. East of Fresno there was plenty of undeveloped land. There was ample land west of Highway 99, too, but the west side tended to be Mexican and black; south of town, it was said, the air was bad because of the southerly wind; and due north, in the direction of the San Joaquin River, developments were on the pricey side because the land was in valuable fig orchards.

Oca's system of subdividing relied on leverage and the smallest possible outlay of cash—of which he had little. He obtained deeds from farmers, sketched out a subdivision plan on his dining-room table, put up a few scattered houses, sold some lots—or preferably, sold the whole tract to a better-financed developer. Beyond the city limits, planning and zoning regulations were still permissive to nonexistent. A developer had to file a plan with the county if he was subdividing into more than four lots, but it was necessary only to purchase many smallish tracts from obliging ranchers to get around the requirement. The county didn't yet require curbs, and it would install streets for developers at cost.

Three of his subdivisions—Maple Gardens, Tatham Country Homes, and Rainbow Terrace—were located within a square mile bounded by Shields, Cedar, Yale, and Chestnut avenues. Maple Avenue ran right down the middle.

Oca bought and sold lots and houses like commodities. His strategy was to buy low, hold down the costs of improvements (by doing his own contracting and hiring his sons if they were available), and sell as quickly as possible. He bought several surplus buildings from the army's Camp Pinedale. He stripped them, tearing out the plumbing and lumber, cleaning and stacking it, and selling it or using it in one of the houses he was putting up. There were Oca Tatham houses with pipes and plumbing taken from one place, cabinets from another, and a thing or two from a secondhand store.

For a horse trader in real estate, the name of the game was turnover. "It was paint it, shine it, clean it up—and dump it," his son Gerald recalled. He remembers his dad telling him to go easy on the paint, he wasn't selling mansions on Park Avenue. His customers couldn't afford to buy expensive houses, and Oca couldn't afford to build them. He pinched pennies and told Dick, "It's not how much you can make, but how much you can save." Dick noticed that his dad "bought everything at auction and never paid full price for anything." To keep his properties moving, he took back notes. By the late 1940s, the transactions book at the County Recorder of Deeds showed as many as ten entries a page for Oca and Ruby Tatham. The ledgers told a story of feverish buying, selling, and taking back trusts.

He was resourceful. When the city began widening Blackstone

Avenue and selling the condemned houses, the price was right. He bought several buildings at auction and moved them to Maple Gardens—except for those he resold before he left the auction room. Everything was for sale all the time.

Oca was ready to make deals with anyone who came along, but he also had to accommodate his lenders. In those days before fair housing laws, the federal government routinely required restrictive covenants on properties receiving Federal Housing Authority loans, and an underwriting manual used by the FHA during the Roosevelt and Truman administrations included a proviso that "if a neighborhood is to retain stability, it is necessary that properties shall continue to be occupied by the same social and racial classes."

Oca said that the local FHA manager insisted that Oca's properties be restricted against Armenian Americans. Fresno had one of the country's largest concentrations of Armenian Americans in the nation, but they had trouble shaking a reputation for sharp practices in business. A March 1918 report by the California State Commission of Immigration and Housing, a document remarkable for its insight into the prevailing prejudices of the times, had pointed to "certain anti-social traits, which stand in the way of [Armenians] being easily assimilated. They are so aggressive that their ambition carries them into questionable business practices. Many report difficulty holding the Armenians to their contracts. Consequently their means of achieving success has often stirred up animosity among native-born Americans. . . . No doubt [these] traits will be lost and already some of Fresno's most highly respected cits. are Armenians."

Oca says he was caught in the middle. Whatever his opinions were of the business methods of Armenian Americans, redlining went completely against his grain as a free trader. Like any good free-market man, he wanted the largest possible pool of customers. But on his first development he did what he was told. After some Armenian Americans found out and complained, he promised never to restrict a property again.

His subdividing led him naturally, but at first reluctantly, into yet another venture. Backyard wells were providing household water when Oca entered the building game. But as the subdivision boom continued, county authorities became concerned about well pollution. Since the city of Fresno would not extend water service to the subdivisions, the developers were obliged to form privately owned water companies to serve their subdivisions from a single pumping station. They grumbled, but there was plenty of water only a few dozen feet under the surface, and a cheap, twenty horsepower electric pump could service a hundred homes. Once the systems were in, they pumped out a steady flow of cash. The valley might be a semidesert; but water meters were unheard of, and customers paid a flat monthly rate—$2.75 a month plus a surcharge for lawns and "swamp coolers," air conditioners that used water.

Eventually, there would be requirements for six-inch water mains, durable pipe, and screens to filter out sand. In the beginning, though, the virtually unregulated private water business used thin-wall steel pipe and two-inch mains. Customers sometimes complained about sand in the water, low pressure, and leaks, but as long as the system operated more or less free of problems, the owners had little else to do except mail out the bills and let the money roll in.

Oca started the Northeast Gardens Water Company in 1950. His company, and many of the other new private water companies, lay outside the jurisdiction of the city of Fresno. It was two years before he registered it with the Public Utilities Commission. He hit good water at eighty-five feet. Once the well was in, he enlisted the help of his sons and their friends from church to dig the shallow trenches for the mains. Two years later Oca built a second pumping station, and Northeast Gardens was serving 140 homes in six subdivisions east and west of Maple Avenue.

It was strictly a mom-and-pop operation, with Oca handling everything personally. Like a country doctor he was on call twenty-four hours a day. When a customer said rates were too high, Oca was apt to slip around to the house and discover that shrubs and lawn had been expanded, entitling him to a higher monthly fee. "You didn't say anything to me about putting your whole backyard in lawn and shrubbery," he would tell the customer crossly after raising the monthly charge.

Oca Tatham took no guff. During a break in service necessitated by repairs to a main, two customers found where the work was going on and threatened to give him a licking if the water wasn't back on promptly.

Oca climbed out of the ditch ready to do battle. "You haven't got guts enough," he said. "Come on, if you want. I'm gonna work you over. You're both full of wind."

The men decided not to fool with the tough little Okie. They backed off.

In Fresno, he was again the family hero—the Tatham who was uncovering all kinds of opportunities. More than any of his in-laws or relatives, he was *relating* to California through deals, contacts, and businesses. It took the others longer.

Vernon's experience as a medical corpsman in the army qualified him for a hospital job, but he'd seen all he wanted of blood and suffering. Instead he and Dora opened Tatham's Grocery at Fifth and Stanford streets in Clovis. The store was in "Beanville," a community of tiny houses, some still with dirt floors, inhabited mostly by Okie field hands and laborers. Walter came to live with them in the back of the store after Oca sold the farm with its bunkhouse at Armstrong and Shields. He minded the counter, gossiping with the old-timers who came in to buy tobacco or groceries. If a customer's child got sick, he might send over a quart of ice cream. Sometimes he went to Delano on the bus, bringing a load of groceries for Cora.

Walter Tatham kept them laughing. He still didn't drive a car and still used expressions and phrases from another world, like "burg" for town. "Where you threshin' today with that thing?" called a friend when Walter went riding down the street in Vernon's rattletrap Ford. Walter shot right back, picking up the wheat harvest metaphor: "We're headed down the road a ways, the heads is all too green around here."

The first of Vernon and Dora's three sons, Gary, was born in 1947; Terry was born in 1949 and Clifford in 1952. By the time Terry came along, Tatham's Grocery was starting to lose customers. Okie men were leaving to get jobs on the Central Valley Project. The canal building paid union scale, and many of the Tatham customers who had once done seasonal farm work moved down the valley to work on the giant water projects. Vernon finally gave up the grocery business himself and went to work at Pine Flat Dam on the Kings River. By the time his job there ended in 1951, he had enough to buy a home in Pinedale, a small community surrounded by apricot orchards north of Fresno.

Successful as Oca was, he and Ruby, with their six children, were far from rich. Every penny he had was tied up. Oca was the opposite of the Depression-scarred figure socking money away in bank accounts or insurance policies as a hedge against the return of hard times. Oca never let his money sit. He saved only to invest—in Oca Tatham. Not having a steady income or business, it was hard to get a conventional bank loan, so he turned to the grapevine, the private lending market where one borrowed money on a handshake—and when all else failed, he turned to friends and relatives. Once he borrowed $800 from his brother-in-law Bill Thomas. Bill was disappointed that when he asked for a loan from Oca, he got turned down, but that was Oca—his money was tied up. The family usually had so little ready cash on hand that when a real financial need arose, Oca sometimes sold a house or a lot to raise the money. They lived at the financial brink because everything went back into the business.

When the family turned out for church, however, everyone was scrubbed and well dressed. The boys wore ties, pressed trousers, and coats with all three buttons done up. Doris wore a suit. Renee remembers their getting chipped furniture at Ray's Salvage, which sold goods damaged in shipment, and socks from the bins at a variety store—"used ones with holes in the toes that would curl at the ends that my mother would darn and patch." Bill remembers, "We always got our clothes from Penney's, or Dad and Mom would buy second-hand clothes and make them over for us."

Doris recalled, "I never had my own drawers to put my clothes in or anything like that. When I was twelve my folks bought a cedar chest that most girls have for a hope chest. They put that in their bedroom, and all my possessions, my clothes, were in there. They weren't hung up in the closet. I was a girl with three brothers, so if there was a bedroom it would have been for them."

When Oca moved the family into a house with new wall-to-wall carpeting, Ruby felt uncomfortable with the luxury. As Doris recalls it, "Mom didn't like the idea of us doing it for her, and so we didn't stay there very long."

In fact, they didn't stay anywhere very long. Everything Oca and the family had was for sale if the price was right. That included clothes, furniture, cars, boats . . . even the roof over their heads. Doris "counted once about seventeen houses that I lived in and we never felt, 'This is our home.' We were all together as a family, but home wasn't like something we were going to pass down to our kids or any feeling like that. We'd come home Friday, pack our bags, and go off to school Monday from a different place." From 1941 to 1946, the children were in eleven grammar schools in four states.

They lived by the rhythm of their father's deals. The family would go from rather cramped quarters one week to sumptuous ones the next. When the family moved to Adoline Avenue, they were suddenly on the edge of the affluent part of town—"uptown," Gerald called it. But it wasn't more than a few months before they were out on Maple Avenue in the subdivisions. After a home on Shields Avenue burned down, they moved to a place near a dairy and then to a fine old two-story home on Clinton Avenue with a three-car garage, aviaries, and a peach orchard out back. But not long afterward they moved into the bachelor officer quarters on the former Camp Pinedale—into a part that Oca wasn't moving or tearing apart. The family room was the lobby. Later Oca converted it into a seventeen-room motel.

The children went from good neighborhoods to poor ones, from the best schools to mediocre ones, from fine cars to junkie pickups, for they had a dad who was status-blind. A house was an asset and shelter, wherever it was. He felt no emotional ties to it or any other thing, and he was as unimpressed by addresses as by fancy titles. He bragged that people couldn't tell he had money, and it tickled him when he was mistaken for the contractor at one of his developments.

Oca's only luxury was his car, a baby blue '49 Cadillac Sedanette. But he didn't get it for status. He had no pride of ownership in anything. The car was his "office"; he wanted it to be comfortable. Ever the horse trader, he eventually swapped it for what Gerald called "a big old red hog." Later he got a used Pontiac.

"Dad *had* a job," said Gerald. "It was to buy low and sell high. It kept him moving." That was Oca Tatham's way of mastering California.

CHAPTER TEN

THE VALLEY, 1950

ELDON TACKETT experienced California in an altogether different way from Oca Tatham, whom he never met. For Oca, the huge dams and canals on which the valley's economic survival depended were part of the background, like the shadowy peaks of the distant Sierras. As a man who saw the opportunities in the cracks and angles, the big picture was not of great interest. But Eldon Tackett gave himself to the interlocking system of agriculture and water that was the center of institutional California. He literally immersed himself in it, picking fruit in the orchards for a dozen years, building the life-giving canals, and finally tending the water system itself.

Oca's philosophy was "If you're out working, you might miss a deal." Eldon's was "The good worker, he gets a lot more, and they'll never bother you. Make 'em a good hand and you'll get to stay."

Eldon was nineteen when he came to the valley in 1937. He had been born in Arkansas, but had moved with his parents and five brothers and sisters to Bokoshe, Oklahoma, a little community on the Choctaw side of the Arkansas River much like Drake's Prairie and no more than twenty-five miles away from it. Joseph Edgar Jefferson Tackett grew cotton there until 1934, when he was killed by a blow to the head from a wagon spoke during a fight over a dog at a country dance. Eldon's mother was too ill to travel when her son climbed aboard his cousin's Chevy truck with a load of relatives and friends and headed west. One of the Chevy's front wheels had a habit of rolling off down the highway every few hundred miles. But the tire always made its bid for independence on a straightaway, and no harm was done.

Eldon's first base in California was Porterville, a town nestled next to the Sierra foothills on Highway 65, where relatives had been living since the late 1920s. Eldon got a job in a barn capping milo—picking the good kernels off the cob for seed. The barn was hot, there was fuzz on the grain, and the heat ate him up, but it was a start.

Porterville, in the Tulare County citrus belt, was a magnet for people from a few eastern Oklahoma communities, but it was not overrun with migrants from the Southwest. Most Okies gravitated to the cotton fields closer to Highway 99.[1] When work stopped in the groves around Porterville, people went to the coastal valleys to pick oranges.

Still, the year Eldon came out to Porterville there were eighty-eight Oklahoma-born students in the high school, the next year 128. Except for the citrus packinghouses, Porterville could have been a town in Texas or western Oklahoma. It had a red-light district called Little Tijuana and a couple of beer joints and pool halls for cowboys, ranch hands, and field-workers to whoop it up. For the more staid there was the picture show at the Monache Theatre. Saturday night everyone trooped into town to catch up on news, eye the girls, and trade tips. It was a small world. Oklahoma people in California identi-fied themselves by their hometowns: "so and so from McAlester" or "so and so from Norman." Places had stories and special associations. Sallisaw meant outlaws and Pretty Boy Floyd. Norman meant wheat. Tahlequah meant Indians. Bartlesville meant oil. But Bokoshe and Poteau, where the Tacketts came from, meant mainly poor renters and farmers.

A few months after coming west the first time, Eldon was back in Bokoshe, helping to care for his dying mother and visiting his girl-friend, Loretta Smith. The Tacketts were nominal Baptists. Loretta came from a family of Free Will Baptists. The Smiths were a big, hospitable group who owned land down the road from the Tacketts in Shady Point. They always seemed ready to share their meals with anyone who came.

Loretta grew up among strangers at the dinner table—preachers, usually, but sometimes city people who came down from Tulsa to hunt on the farm. Mrs. Smith cooked them pork and chicken. Church was the center of social life. Sundays, people would take food to church for potluck dinners and stay all day, quilting, eating the Smiths' fried chicken, singing and praying in the exuberant spirit of their denomination.

Loretta was a blond-haired young woman with merry eyes. Eldon had fallen for her when they were both just kids and too young to marry. Her mother gave her some advice about how to size up a man. "If he's good to his mother, he'll be good to his wife," she said. Eldon passed that test. He'd come all the way back from California to be with his mother while she was sick. But he was young and almost penniless and not ready to wed.

Eldon's mother died not long after he got back from California. When the weather got cold and his money ran out, he headed for Porterville again.

Eldon was a short, brick-hard young man, straightforward and direct. He loved to work hard, and it wasn't long before he was being touted by his friends as the fastest orange picker in the whole state. They bragged that Eldon could throw a ladder up a tree and be on it clipping oranges by the time it came to rest. Working in groves near the coast he set a ranch record: 130 boxes in a single day. Friends wanted to match him against another fellow who was fast and strong, but before the contest could take place, Eldon moved back to Porterville, where the growers were paying a nickel more a box. There his friends told him about a "smartie" who claimed to be the fastest apricot man in California. When apricot time came round, Eldon went to the coast and worked in the same grove as the smartie. Eldon had more boxes at the end of the day.

Picking required the mental qualities of baseball, Eldon's favorite sport. A great picker adjusted to a different crop the way a fine hitter adjusted to a new pitcher. In the oranges Eldon said he "clipped and jerked at the same time. Hold the limb up with one hand and clip so it drops into the bag. Flip them oranges in that bag, do the top of the tree first, then what they call the 'skirt.'" Lemons paid more but were slower because each one had to be ringed for size and double-clipped—once to snip it from the branch, a second time to scalp the remaining stem cleanly from the fruit. It required care and skill. Any stem left on the lemon could perforate the other lemons and turn them rotten, but if cut too deep the lemon would spoil.

Olives required still another technique. "You reach up into one of them limbs and find a bunch and just strip 'em. You pull it through and those leaves would cut your hands till your fingers bled. I'd tape my fingers before I'd go out. You get up there ten, twelve feet high on the ladder, turn around, and go backward. That ladder is touching nothing except right up at the top. They was strict on getting the leaves out. But never stop until you dump them in the box—*then* pick the leaves off the *top*."

With oranges, the trick was to leave some air in the box. "You'd *ease* 'em out of that bag, *ease* 'em out until you had a full box. You shake that box it wouldn't be full. But you let it *ease* real *easy*, there's a lot of holes in there. I'd probably gain six, eight boxes a day that way." That came to serious money by the end of a week.

Eldon took a professional's pride in his work. He owned his own tools and equipment: specialized clippers for oranges and lemons, an orange sack that could be snapped closed at the bottom, an olive bucket contoured to his stomach. He taped the orange clippers with rubber so they'd still feel soft at the end of the day.

Eldon developed the muscular shoulders and arms of a man who often made a hundred or more trips a day from the tree to the truck with a sixty-five-pound sack of oranges. His right shoulder, tanned as polished leather, got big and round as a bowling ball. But willpower was more important than muscles in the groves. By midday bodies all itched from sweat, dirt, and "whitewash"—the insect dust the growers sprayed on the Valencias.

A lot of orange pickers set a daily goal of fifty or sixty boxes and quit when they reached that number, no matter what time it was. Eldon kept going for hours more. Eulis Skinner, who was in the orchards with him, remembered his friend's stamina: "He *ran* up that ladder and run down it. He was the fastest guy I ever picked with. A hustler. He worked hard at anything. He wasn't after the money. It was just *in* him. He didn't feel heat or cold. He wore short-sleeve shirts summer and winter."

Eldon worked well with a partner. One time in the spinach a fellow demonstrated how two people working together could more than double their individual output: one cut while another boxed the leaves and picked out yellow ones—tasks that were hard for one person to combine effectively. "You have to have a buddy," the man said. "You want to buddy with me?"

"Sure," Eldon replied.

"Okay, you pack 'em and I'll cut."

Once they'd worked out their system, the boss left them alone.

"If we can stay ahead he'll never bother us," the man said. Eldon remembered that.

He wanted to work. In Porterville in late 1940 Eldon heard about labor trouble at the Rancho Sespe orchards outside Santa Paula. Mexicans had returned to the fields as Okies took better factory jobs. The growers looked vulnerable, but when the Mexicans struck at Rancho Sespe, word spread that there was work to be had. Eldon, his brother-in-law, and three others piled into a car and drove down.

The ranch was situated in the fertile, picturesque valley that penetrates into the coastal range south of Santa Barbara. When Eldon's group pulled in, deputy sheriffs were lining the road, ready to move against troublemakers. After they had been waved through, the Porterville group bedded down in a dormitory, and the next morning a truck took them to the orchards. Eldon never showed any regret over his role in that incident. He had come to California to work. Other people could look after the politics.

A few days after Pearl Harbor, Eldon went back to Oklahoma, married Loretta, and drove back through a blizzard in a '35 Chevy. They spent the winter around Santa Paula near the coast, working in the oranges, and then returned to Porterville. Friends and relatives shivareed them, Oklahoma-style, firing off shotguns and firecrackers around their cabin in the middle of the night and trying to see if they'd scare.

Eldon and Loretta moved where the jobs were—to Porterville for the Valencias, San Jose for canning fruit cocktail, Sunnyvale for cherries, then back to Santa Paula for the Navels. While other Okies were leaving the fields and looking for union jobs paying hourly wages, Eldon figured he could make more doing piecework in the orchards. All during the war years, Eldon's industriousness and Loretta's home-taught skills served them well. It was a matter of pride to both of them that they never stayed in a "camp." Like Oca and Ruby they were savers and knew how to stretch their money. In 1941, Eldon put up his first house—a tiny one on the corner of a lot next to relatives in Porterville. He did not like paying rent.

Eldon was up an orange tree at Rancho Sespe in 1943 when the boss came to tell him his wife was having their baby. They named the boy Eugene Eldon Tackett. When Gene was thirteen months old, they came back to Porterville and bought a little place on the edge of town for about $250.

Not until 1949, a dozen years after he reached California, did Eldon get the job that would lift him out of the fields for good and give him a regular job. He was hired to work on the Friant-Kern Canal, one of the key building blocks of the federal government's Central Valley Project.

At first there had been plenty of groundwater for agriculture along the whole east side of the valley from Madera to just north of Bakersfield. This water and the water from the San Joaquin, Kings, Kaweah, and Tule rivers had made it a propitious place for developers to situate the first colonies of immigrants. But by the 1930s, the water table was declining at an alarming rate. The land boom had tapered off as a result of overpricing and occasional water shortages. "Save the water table" became the rallying cry of the farmers on the east side.

The solution was obvious. Captured in the snowbanks on California's mountain peaks every winter was more water than the farmers could ever use. Much of it flowed off the mountains each spring and summer in torrents that could not be efficiently utilized and that caused disastrous floods in the plain below. A system of dams and canals would control flooding and relax the pressure on the declining water table. The California state legislature had approved the Central Valley Project in 1933 but had no money to pay for it. Five years later, however, with the Roosevelt administration committed to going forward, the cornerstone for Shasta Dam on the Sacramento River in northern California was laid.

The Central Valley Project was perhaps the most ambitious engineering project ever undertaken. It called for thirty-eight major reservoirs and scores of smaller ones, hundreds of miles of cement-lined canals, dozens of giant dams and power stations. In places, irrigation canals would flow under natural rivers. Water from one river, the Sacramento, would be used to replace water taken out of another, the San Joaquin. Aquifers made by nature over millions of years would be refilled as if they were leaky bathtubs. And, according to federal officials, it would be almost free. Eighty to 90 percent of the costs to the taxpayers would be recovered by the sale of electricity from the dams and the fees paid by the water users.

The Central Valley Project added a new element to California's mixed public-private economy. In effect, the state was ceding some of its sovereignty in return for massive federal aid. Congress would henceforth have a say in local economic decisions, such as the size of farms eligible for irrigation water. And since 1902, federal reclamation law had been clear: each individual was limited to 160 acres— double that for a farm couple. To receive water on additional land, owners had to sign a contract with the government agreeing to sell their excess land within ten years at a price determined by the Bureau of Reclamation.

Most farmers on the east side, who were to be the main beneficiaries of the initial federal water, were not adversely affected by this acreage limitation. Their agriculture, which had grown out of the colony system, historically had been on a smallish scale, with the exception of the huge corporate farms such as the DiGiorgio operation outside Delano. One made a comfortable living from irrigated farming even on a few dozen acres.

But the notion of a federal limitation on anything clashed with the prevailing outlook, self-image, and ideology of the people who ran the corporate operations and of the agricultural "wildcatters" in the south and west side of the valley. In the dry, southwest corner was an unusual breed of "farmers," with names such as Kern County Land Company, Tejon Ranch, Southern Pacific, Standard Oil, Belridge Oil, Getty, Shell, and Chevron. Around Tulare Lake, between Bakersfield and Fresno, there was another type. In the 1920s, one Colonel J. G. Boswell had bought land around the lake, and he and a few others had obtained downstream rights to the water of the Kings River, the lake's source. Within a decade hundreds of thousands of acres around the lakes were in the hands of four private entities: the Kern County Land Company, the J. G. Boswell Ranch Company, Salyer Land Company, and Miller and Lux.[2] With dikes and ditches, these companies had reclaimed much of the land from swamp, turning adversity to advantage. Boswell bought land that was underwater much of the year, siphoned off the water spilled onto the property by the spring floods, sold it to parched adjacent farms, and farmed the drained land, thereby reaping a double reward. Since Boswell, Salyer, and the others controlled the irrigation districts downstream, they had political control over any upstream developments that would threaten their legal claims, including new dams.

Farther north, but still on the arid west side of the valley, the so-called Westlands contained some of the richest topsoil in the world, dumped there by millennia of volcanic activity in California's coastal range. But rainfall was light and the water table was deep—six hundred feet down or more. Until the late 1930s, few had tried farming there: it was largely the preserve of Basque shepherds and cattlemen. But then a breed of swashbuckling Texans and Southerners arrived on the scene, the most prominent among them being Jack Harris, Russell Giffen, and Jack O'Neil, men with little education but much determination and practical judgment. Where the Southern Pacific Railroad owned every other quarter section along the right of way on the west side, it was mostly idle land. Giffen shrewdly offered to lease it for a sixth of the value of his crop (compared to the usual one-fourth on the east side). The costly groundwater, brought up from great depths, was full of boron, but it was adequate for cotton and grain, and with the big acreage and low rental fees, one could turn profits on this long-fallow land.

The Westlands and Lake Tulare superfarmers calculated the value of their land on the basis of the cost of the irrigation water for their cotton crops. These colorful wildcatters were big and strong enough to deal with the big gins and cotton brokers on their own, and for a while at least they did not look to the federal government for help. But on the east side, the small farmers could not wait. Pressure on the resource that sutained them, the aquifer, was increasing as economic conditions improved and farming expanded. Cotton acreage increased two and a half fold in Kern County in the years before 1933–1938.[3] In the 1940s, Orange County citrus growers, pushed out of their ranches by Los Angeles's urban sprawl, bought acreage in the east side and tried to make new starts. By 1946, the water table in some places was 250 feet below its original level.

The solution was the Central Valley Project's Friant-Kern Canal, which was to carry water impounded by Friant Dam on the San Joaquin River on a zigzagging 156-mile journey along the easterly edge of the valley to just west of Bakersfield. Another canal north of Fresno, the Madera Canal, had been finished earlier. The canals would stabilize the water table, east side farming, and the whole economy of the southern San Joaquin Valley.

Even as the dam- and canal-building continued, doubts were raised about the overall wisdom of this stupendous alteration of the central valley. In March 1946 Assistant Secretary of Agriculture Charles F. Brannan warned that the Interior Department was paying too little attention to "the behavior of various soils under irrigation and the ability of farm production to repay the construction and operating costs involved." He noted that there had been little discussion of drainage of the valley's irrigated soils. "Indiscriminate use of irrigation water, spreading of floodwater or use of other means of recharging ground water may be followed by serious drainage and alkali complications," he warned.[4] Brannan was merely stating what every farmer and every hydrologist familiar with the central valley knew: it was a gigantic bathtub with no drain, for underlying a million or more acres of fabulously productive farmland was a shallow layer of nearly impermeable Corcoran clay.

Brannan, who expressed the concerns of Southern and Midwestern farming interests about California's vast expansion of agricultural production, pointed out that "a number of crops presently under irrigation in the central valley, such as rice and cotton, are, from a longer-time point of view, in the surplus-production bracket." But his warnings were brushed aside. It was too late to stop the drive for federally sponsored irrigation in California. Too many economic livelihoods depended on it; too many powerful people wanted it. The Labor Department liked the jobs, the Army Corps of Engineers saw in the dam building a new post-war role, and the Federal Power Commission wanted the electricity. President Truman, a Midwesterner who was less committed to irrigated agriculture than Roosevelt had been, was too new to his job to stop it.

The Central Valley Project, whatever its shortcomings, gave a boost to thousands of Okies.

Eldon Tackett was hired by Peter Kiewit Construction Company which was building portions of the Friant-Kern Canal.

The canal work developed a culture of its own. There were "powder monkeys," "high scalers," "muckers," "sand hogs," "divers," "boot men," and "nippers." The grading, where Eldon worked, required precision work. Acres of concrete had to be poured to form the canal's sloping sides and bottom along very precisely calculated depths and widths. At the top, it was two hundred feet across.

Eldon Tackett took a craftsman's interest in the work. "You'd have to figure if there's a low place how wide the berm would be out there when it got four feet high. You'd have to build that berm up there ten feet high. Had to be level. The canal dropped six inches a mile. Fill that canal with water and the water moved so slow a man could walk ahead of it. That's why it's so crooked—to keep the elevation.

"We trimmed out two feet along the berm for the cement to be poured. The 'monegan,' they called it, went through a-diggin' that trench—can't undercut it—and left two foot for the trimmer to dig out to pour cement on. The monegan went ahead and we come behind him and finished it up for the liner and trimmer. The carpenters boxed it in for turnouts. Then here come the concrete people to pour concrete, and a different crew to do the liner.

"I was out there bareheaded, no shirt, hundred-degree weather. I couldn't hardly get my elbows together, skin was just like leather.

Back was cooked. But I had it easy, grade checkin'. All the guys liked me, and I liked them."

Eldon worked five days a week, union scale, and often picked almonds or oranges on the weekends. The canal-building job lasted close to two years, and when it was done, he landed a follow-up job with the Kiewit company on another canal job in the Black Hills of South Dakota. He packed Loretta and their son, Gene, in a car, and off they went for two years. At the end of it he turned down a job for Kiewit in Greenland and heeded the call of Oklahoma. He enrolled Gene in school in the town of Panama, but soon Oklahoma proved to be a disappointment and they all headed back to Porterville.

Eldon took a job briefly as a school janitor in Shafter before a better offer came up—a job with the pipe company that was connecting farmers around McFarland and Delano to the Friant-Kern Canal. Eldon was back in the water business. Soon after that he got a job with SMUD, as everyone called the Southern San Joaquin Municipal Utility District. SMUD was one of twenty-three quasi-public authorities contracting for water from the Friant-Kern Canal, run by an elected board but basically controlled by the local farmers. Unlike some of the east-side irrigation districts, SMUD did not have good access to river water, and the local water table had dropped from 42 to 170 feet.[5]

SMUD served 602 farms growing cotton, alfalfa, potatoes, and truck crops. Five hundred and thirty-nine were less than 160 acres, 258 less than 40. There was one corporate farm with 2,030 acres, but it was an exception, and the DiGiorgios' Sierra Vista Ranch lay just outside the district. But many of the farmers were also operating on leased land in addition to their own holdings, and corporate ownership was on the upswing. So the beneficiaries included farmers whose operations, regardless of the acreage, already amounted to large-scale businesses: the Pandols and the Zaninoviches, Croatian-American grape growers who had been in the Delano and McFarland area for several generations; several Italian families with vineyards; and Hollis Roberts, an Okie who had bought property where he had once picked grapes and cotton.

SMUD signed its first contract with the federal government in 1946, anticipating the completion of the canal a few years later. In May 1950, the SMUD directors declared their unalterable opposition to compromises with nonfarming interests that were seeking specific amounts of San Joaquin River water for recreation, fish and game, and other uses. "If the Bureau is compelled to turn out such water as mentioned in pending suits, it will jeopardize the farm economy of this district and have an adverse effect on all business and investments of untold millions of dollars," the board declared.[6]

Installation of the local water delivery system turned out to be a major headache. By the end of 1951, there were so many leaks in the concrete lateral pipes that some farmers wanted the system ripped out and replaced. Spokesmen for the contractor acknowledged in open meetings that it was "not a dependable irrigation system" and blamed faulty design. Others blamed the quality of the pipe, the freezing temperatures of the canal water, and earthquake tremors. The contractor defended the practice of dumping horse manure into the system to plug leaks and said it had been authorized by the chief engineer of the Bureau of Reclamation. A $7.7 million pipe system held together by manure!

Eldon's job on the crews that were trying to keep up with the leaks paid $400 a month, which did not leave much over after taxes and groceries. In 1953, the Tacketts moved from Porterville to McFarland. Loretta cleaned houses and took in ironing to bring in some extra. Two years later they put down money to build a house west of town.

Eldon was a bear of a worker. One Friday he and his partner fixed fifteen leaks. Sometimes he would be lowered into a pipe and would crawl through it looking for leaks and removing obstructions. In the heavy spring rains, the crews would get on the uphill side of the canal and lay sandbags to keep water from the fields from overflowing back into the canal and jamming the turnouts with sand and mud.

After a few years, SMUD gave him responsibility for one of the lines. His job was to keep the laterals and reservoirs behind him full so the farmers could draw water. He had to get the water turned on as quickly as possible when the farmers needed it, and he beat all the records. "Quicker I got up there and get him his water, better off that farmer was. So they all appreciated it," Eldon recalled.

Eldon had come a long way from Porterville. He had a home and a family and a steady job at union wages. The valley was a wonderful place for a fellow with his green thumb. He grew fresh peppers and tomatoes and whatever else was in season in his garden. There were wild rabbits to hunt in the open country, ducks and geese in the wetlands near Lake Tulare. Eldon felt a personal connection to the land. To him the water the canals brought seemed a wonderful gift of the taxpayers of America, not a God-given right of farmers. He had a clear understanding of the great machine that made inland California go. He had helped build it, and now he tended it. Without the federal water, the farmers would be nothing.

Over the years, however, he began to think of the water as a kind of poisoned fruit. Once the agricultural interests of the valley had had a bite of it, they wanted more and more. It was the end of innocence. That left him in a complex situation. He had been content to make his bed in the corporate body of agriculture and water. At first it had just been a job, but slowly the work became part of his identity. He gave everything he had to the system. He had set himself up to become disillusioned.

CHAPTER ELEVEN

IDENTITY

GERALD TATHAM felt as if he were living a double life. In the spring of his senior year in Clovis High's class of 1956, he was a soloist in the *a cappella* choir and a track star. He had been a lanky end on that fall's football team. Even his nickname was cool: "Goose," for Goose Tatum, "clown prince" of the Harlem Globetrotters basketball team.

But then there were "the greasers," the crowd he sometimes hung around with. Attending movies was near the top of his church's list of prohibited activities, but Gerald and the other greasers often went. One of his favorites was *Blackboard Jungle*, which initiated the age of rock music and ducktail haircuts. Gerald felt the spirit of what he called "the defiant times." He went along as his friends siphoned gasoline from the cars of "big shots," cruised on Fulton Street, backed into the exits of drive-in movies, and hung out at the Royal Drive-In on Blackstone Avenue.

The Royal was Clovis High's turf, which the greasers defended against carloads of kids from Roosevelt and Fresno High. The rumbles never went much beyond shoving and pushing, but tire irons and chains came out a few times. When things were slow at the Royal, the greasers would drive up to Millerton Lake with six-packs. Gerald even knew a member of the Black Velvets—a white gang from San Francisco with members in Fresno that was reported to use heroin.

He was no juvenile delinquent, though, even if his conduct seemed "wild" to a boy from his strict background. To his non-Pentecostal classmates, Gerald was just another popular athlete. What led him to his off-beat associations was mainly curiosity, a desire to learn more about what lay outside the perimeter of the Pentecostal world whose boundaries had been so carefully drawn for him by his church and his father.

In California's public schools, young Pentecostals became keenly aware that they were different. They learned what less-sheltered children already knew: that California was full of people who were Catholic, or did not believe in God, or had experienced divorce in their families. Doris first heard about Darwin's theory of evolution at Clovis High, and spoke up against it. "Some people may look like monkeys, but I wasn't descended from them," she told the teacher. But there was no real alternative then to the public schools. The deacons at the Tathams' church briefly considered forming a Christian school under Pentecostal leadership, for even then there was concern about public school influences, but the congregation did not have the resources to support such an undertaking.

Cool as Gerald pretended to be in the corridors of Clovis High, he dreaded hearing the words "holy roller," the term that outsiders used loosely to describe the enthusiastic sects of the poorer classes. He wanted to be just another teenager, not the kid from a religious sect that was always reminding its young that they were "set apart." Outwardly, he acted nonchalant when a teammate kidded him, "Come on, Tatham, save me!" But inside he was dying.

When someone did ask him about his church, he would say he went to one like the Full Gospel Church in downtown Fresno. Technically this was true. Full Gospel Tabernacle, housed in a handsome brick building, was affiliated with the Assemblies of God but was attended by a different crowd than his family's blue-collar church: teachers, government workers, store owners. It was difficult for his parents to understand his dilemma. Oca and Ruby had joined the Pentecostal culture voluntarily, but Gerald and his five brothers and sisters had been *born* into it, an altogether different experience, and it meant that, at least at first, the authority of parents and the church community had to substitute for internal motivation.

Oca was self-confident enough to believe that he could counter any outside influences on his children, but he also knew that eternal vigilance and determination were called for. Scripture provided the best parenting guide: "Raise up a child in the way he should go, and when he grows old he will not depart from it." Generally, he believed that character and shrewdness were more important than knowing lots of things out of books. Like so many from the frontiers of the South, it didn't occur to him that a formal education was necessarily an asset of great value. Instead, he concentrated on instilling ethical and moral values—honesty, honor, courage, dependability, and responsibility. He wanted jobs to be finished. When the boys quit potato-picking early, he sent them back to work in the field for the rest of the day. He admired a local Portuguese American family whose children worked alongside their parents. He expected the boys to stick up for themselves. When Gerald complained that he was being picked on by two boys, Oca straightened him out. "You go down there tomorrow and punch them right in the kisser and they'll be your friends for life," he said. "But if you come bellyaching back to me here, I'll whip you myself." Gerald followed the advice—he pushed back—and things happened just as his dad had predicted.

Oca instilled the Okie cult of toughness in the boys, buying them boxing gloves and encouraging them to slug it out in one-on-one matches, while he rooted for the smallest or youngest. He wasn't the kind of father who would patiently explain the ins and outs of escrows around the dinner table or give lessons in the proper handling of reins on a horse. His "teaching" was the message he sent by his daily activities: it wasn't necessary to have training certificates or degrees in order to make deals, buy properties, start a water company. Nobody had ever taught him how to handle horses. He just got on and did it. He found out what it took after he was aboard.

He liked the boys to take risks, and he punished lightly, if at all, for youthful escapades. When Bill and Dick smashed the headlights and radiator of a tractor during an unauthorized ride, they got off with a reprimand. When Gerald turned blue swimming in the deceptively icy waters of an irrigation canal, it was a family joke. Boys living on farms could get a driver's license at the age of fourteen, and Dick got his in 1947, when they were living in the farm country east of Fresno. He drove all over Fresno. Later, when they were no longer living in the country, Oca let fourteen-year-old Renee drive the new Oldsmobile station wagon to church, and gave her the nod to pass on a two-lane road.

But disobedience, insubordination, or dishonesty were punished without mercy, with a whipping from a peach branch or, worse, a prickly olive branch. Many times the boys heard the warning, "I'll wear out your bottom when I get back if that job isn't done."

It was the way of his people. Cora Tatham had used a little switch on her children, though Walter was too softhearted. Cora had made Ophelia "dance a tune," switching her legs until they were "striped as a stick of candy," said Ophelia. Ruby's father had whipped his girls with peach switches. Oca felt he would live to regret it if he didn't discipline the children and that corporal punishment was right. To spoil a child was to sin in one's duty to God. He didn't spare the peach branch or the belt. Sometimes he sent the children out to select a branch themselves. If it was too flimsy, they would have to go back for a sturdier one—all of which added to the drama of the event, as well as to the mounting hysteria of those about to be punished. For these were real whippings. The children were hit until they cried or until welts appeared on their legs. Dick was the most stoic and hated to cry, which meant that sometimes there was blood on his legs from the olive thorns before it was over. Bill cried quicker and got off lighter.

When Gerald was in second grade he got a memorable licking when he took five dollars from his mother's purse and treated his friends to rides at Roeding Amusement Park. Oca's suspicions were aroused by reports of his son's generosity, and he sat him down at a stool in the kitchen and obtained a peach-tree sprig from the backyard.

"Where did you get the money?"

"Picking up potatoes at the potato sheds." They had been visiting near Delano and the potato sheds were not far away, but the story did not wash.

Whack! across the knees.

The question was repeated.

"From Mom's purse."

The lashes that were due for the theft would have been hard no matter what. Because of the lie, Oca raised welts on Gerald's legs.

After these punishments were over, Oca would consider the matter closed. None of the children thought he took any pleasure from it.

OCA'S AUTHORITY over the children was direct and physical. The church's authority over them was subtle but in some ways more pervasive. Despite—and perhaps because of—the blandishments of California, Pentecostal churches in those days enveloped their youth, involving them in a round of activities that left little time for sinful behavior and shepherding them away from any behavior that deviated from the Pentecostal code.

Pentecostal youths growing up in Fresno in the 1940s and early 1950s did not drink, smoke, or dance, and the girls did not wear eye makeup. Attendance at theaters, sporting events, or bowling alleys was frowned on. This code created conflicts for the Tatham children, as the churches no doubt intended it to do, to maintain the separation of their youth from secular California. Doris, who graduated from Clovis High in 1948, did not go to school dances and rarely went to the Friday night football games that were the high point of school social life. The games conflicted with the regular Friday meetings of Christ's Ambassadors, the Assemblies of God social-service organization. Doris was a CA, and Oca put his foot down when a boyfriend invited her to the games. To Oca it was a straightforward choice: the Lord or football. Doris battled him, but it was not until his sons made the team that he relaxed his stand against Friday night at the games.

Doris, who was active in the music department of her school, remembered the post-rehearsal dance parties, when she asked the teacher to change the records so she would not have to dance. If anyone asked why she wasn't dancing she said, "Well, my church frowns on it and I just never learned." When the inevitable questions came about why, she would say, "Well, it's just a stand we've taken, it's something that's part of our belief, the things that we don't do."

"We really were a separate people," Doris said about those years. "We didn't socialize with other people. We planned our social life around this group of young people. There would be fellowship times together when we'd have potluck suppers, picnics, or whatever, and it was a time for us to have fun. We all really liked each other. There was a lot of love, and we were all in agreement on probably most everything. We didn't drink, smoke, wear makeup, do all those things. So we were alike, and when we went to school, we mixed with all these other people who were different. We were not as comfortable as we were with our own groups."

Bill and Dick graduated in 1952, four years after Doris, after exemplary high school careers. Bill was vice president of the student body and a star halfback on the varsity football team; Dick won the decathlon his junior year; both boys won the school's coveted "all-American blanket" for their athletic performances. They had worn the standard uniform of leather jackets and flattops, but that was the extent of their identification with the broader youth culture.

The church culture provided many positive experiences for young people, especially those who had a talent for music. The three Tatham boys sang in church and school musical groups; Dick played trumpet and Bill the trombone. Brenda played the piano by ear, and learned by watching the organist in church. Doris, who had an operatic voice and played the cello, was one of four "Calvary Girls" who sang on "Echoes of Calvary," a radio program broadcast live from a studio at the church. Hearts melted when she sang, "I'll hide my heartache behind a smile, I'll wait for a reason 'til after a while." Dick sang, "Don't carry that load, you'll break if you do, the Lord will carry it for you."

The Tathams slipped easily into the fellowship at Calvary Tabernacle, the church founded in the 1930s by Otto Pauls and expanded under the leadership of Murrell Coughran. There had been a succession of pastors after Coughran. The first were co-pastors Tom Fuller, Jay's brother, and Tom's wife, Lola, the couple who had prayed with Oca before he got the trucking job at Torrey Pines in 1941. The next pastor took the church into the Assemblies of God.

The congregation of 250 people included a butcher, an electrician, an air-conditioning specialist, an auto mechanic, a mailman, the owner of a small auto and electric repair shop, and small businessmen like Oca. Many of the congregation hailed from Dust Bowl states, though with a sprinkling of Swedish Americans and others. The worship style was free. As one member said, "If someone wanted to praise the Lord, they'd get up and do it."

When Claude Baldwin and his wife arrived in Fresno from Muskogee in 1952, part of a new wave of people who arrived in California after the war, the church became their home. They had come down to Fresno from working in the prunes in the Sacramento Valley and knew not a soul. They looked up churches in the newspaper advertisements and hooked up with Calvary in that way. Oca helped Claude obtain a building lot and get plumbing supplies wholesale. Claude said Oca treated him "like a brother, even though I was a poor man without a dime."

People at Calvary Tabernacle gave each other helping hands. When Oca's home was gutted by fire while the family was at service one Sunday, the church had a day for them, giving them presents of clothing and other necessities right at the altar. Doris remembers it as the "wedding shower my parents never had." The deacons sought guidance on church business at all-night prayer meetings, such as the vigil at Oca and Ruby's home on Maple Avenue. The church was struggling over a dispute between the deacons and the pastor on the issue of whether to continue the radio shows. The door was open, and people dropped in after work to kneel on the living-room floor and pray to God that the issue could be resolved in love and without damage to the church or its pastor. The radio show was dropped for lack of funds.

In addition to being held together by fellowship and a strict code, Pentecostal communities were bound up in the drama and excitement of a highly spiritual faith. The excitement rose to a fever pitch in the late 1940s with the arrival of one after another traveling evangelist who used prayer to bring healings.

Oca got what he called his first "definite healing" in the spring of 1948, after being whipped in the eye by a metal line that had caught on the upright exhaust of a tractor he was driving out behind his home on Clinton Avenue. A doctor covered the wound with an air-tight bandage but made no predictions about the eye.

The next day was Sunday; Oca and Ruby attended the concluding evening session of a five-week camp meeting event at Fresno Memorial Auditorium. The chief attraction was Kelso Glover, a well-known evangelist who broadcast from Angelus Temple. The campaign was sponsored by local Pentecostal churches and underwritten by Demos Shakarian, a Los Angeles dairyman and religious activist. Oca hoped it would get his mind off the pain in his eye, but he was fidgeting and ready to leave when Ruby suggested he go to the altar. He did as she suggested, not knowing what to expect.

"All of a sudden I felt like I was wading in the Spirit up to my knees, the spirit of the Lord, you know. And he just laid hands on me like that. And you know that pain completely went. That eye felt better, I think, than the other eye. I mean every bit of that pain left instantly. And I thought, Wow, boy, that eye don't hurt one bit. And I started taking that bandage off and Demos Shakarian liked to fainted. Scared him to death. Isn't that something? He just hadn't been around it. He knew God was healing and he just woke up to the fact that God was doing so many things. He was a very wealthy man, you know. And he was very excited, and he was underwriting that meeting. And if the money didn't come in, I think he was going to pick up the tab. So, I took the bandage off right there in front of all those people, thousands of them. My eye was not bloodshot. My eye was clear, and it felt so cool and good. The light didn't hurt it, the air didn't hurt it, nothing hurt it."

Shakarian wrote about this incident in his book *The Happiest People on Earth*: "In the sight of those 5,000 people, Tatham began to unwind the bandage. Round and round his head the layers peeled away until there was a little heap of white gauze at his feet. The innermost bandage was held with adhesive tape. He ripped it away. Two whole perfectly blue eyes stared incredulously from Kelso Glover to me. There was no scar, no bruise; Tatham's left eye was not even blood-shot."[1] The meeting broke up at midnight, having lasted eleven and a half hours.

Ruby was healed of a goiter on her neck by a country preacher in a worn, threadbare suit. The preacher had declined offers of new suits, always saying that too many who'd touched the old one had been cured. Oca was watching closely as Ruby went to the altar and the preacher "rebuked" the goiter. "That thing went down and went out and disappeared. Right there at the church. When Ruby come home she didn't have one. It never come back either."

Such events were part of a new chapter in the history of the Pentecostal movement. Divine healing through the power of prayer had always been a possible experience for Spirit-filled Pentecostals. For decades, they had witnessed healings at country brush arbors and country churches, but after 1947 they were moved to county fairgrounds and downtown civic auditoriums. They were popularized then by little-known independent evangelists, many of whom came from the unformed Southern borderlands that had been the seedbed of the earlier Holiness and Pentecostal sects. Most had been reared in Depression times and had come to Pentecost through healing experiences or as a final, desperate act of men at their wits' end. A remarkable number came out of poverty in Okie states. Tommy L. Osborn was one of thirteen children in an Oklahoma family he left at the age of fourteen to preach. William Freeman was born in a log cabin in Missouri.

Between 1949 and 1958, the heyday of the healers, they often came through Fresno, the unofficial capital of California's central valley and a mecca of the Dust Bowl migration. In a sense, they were gathering up lost flocks in the West in much the same way as the Methodist circuit riders, Presbyterian preachers, and Campbellite evangelists who had followed pioneers across the Appalachians after 1800.

Oral Roberts, the best known, was born in Pontotoc County, Oklahoma, due north of Dallas. Although his father was a minister in the Pentecostal Holiness Church, Roberts did not become especially religious until he was taken ill with tuberculosis at the age of seventeen. Soon after that his father took him to a faith healer who, according to Roberts, cured him.

Roberts claimed to have performed his first healing in 1947, using the Lord's power to remove the braces from the legs of a young polio victim at a small revival meeting in Muskogee. Exhibiting a flair for self-promotion, Roberts began to publish his own newspaper, *Healing Waters*, the first issue of which told of the Muskogee healing and offered his first book for sale. In the next few months, his small office staff answered 25,000 letters, mailed 30,000 anointed handkerchiefs, distributed 15,000 copies of the book, and sent out 90,000 copies of the newspaper.[2]

A. A. Allen, born in Sulphur Rock, Arkansas, grew up the dirt-poor son of a drunkard. His mother lived with a series of men, including a light-skinned black man named John, who was around during the boy's youth. Allen turned to drink himself and was arrested for stealing corn during the Depression. But he straightened up, was converted at a tongues-speaking, Spirit-filled church, and became an Assemblies of God pastor.[3] In 1949, he was inspired by a healing revival and began his own independent ministry. Allen became a controversial figure; he claimed to be able to raise the dead— a power he subsequently disclaimed when disciples attempted to ship departed loved ones by rail car direct to his outpost in Arizona. Allen finally had to urge the overzealous to "obey the law" and bury their dead in "a reasonable period of time."[4]

Calvary Tabernacle was important to the Fresno tent meetings. Pastor Claude Weaver, who arrived in 1949, became president of the Full Gospel Ministers Association and was an enthusiast of the big tents. In turn, the revivals were useful to the local Pentecostal churches, for the touring evangelists brought in new members and the churches divided up some of the money received at the meetings.

Oca Tatham was secretary of the board of deacons at Calvary Tabernacle and took part in the discussions about which evangelists to sponsor. The choice was not easy, for revival meetings enabled the unscrupulous to prey on the innocent for profit. While the visitors all preached for their audiences to be saved, it was the promise of miraculous events, especially healings, that drew the big crowds. The most ethical evangelists issued disclaimers. "I have no magic, I cannot heal, only God can do that, and if God is not with you there is nothing I can do," Oral Roberts said at the Fresno fairgrounds during one of his many meetings.[5] Still, many fakes were ready to exploit the upwelling of faith—"guys who came floating through in their Cadillacs," as Oca described them. Even Roberts, who came to have the second largest following of any American evangelist after Billy Graham by the end of the 1950s, came in for criticism. He was heckled on a trip to Australia, and an editor of the Denver *Post* claimed that Roberts' lieutenants kept him from interviewing some of the people Roberts claimed to have healed. In a religious movement that put such weight on the spiritual and mystical life and so little on doctrine or rigorous intellectual effort, rumors of questionable ethics were ever-present.

The Fresno revivals were gala affairs and offered an exciting break from the routine. The evangelists tried to schedule them at the end of the fall grape and cotton harvest to ensure maximum attendance by field hands, many of whom, along with Mexicans, were from the Okie states. People came night after night from all over the valley. The Tatham boys took dates. One time Gordon Weaver, the pastor's oldest son, sold hot dogs at a stand across the street.

W. V. Grant, the "plowboy preacher from Arkansas," prayed for Oca to be healed of a prostate problem at a memorable revival at Calvary Tabernacle in 1953. Oca recalled, "I remember so well, when he laid his hand on me, he just looked at me and spoke the healing in the name of Jesus. He smiled, and said, 'You want me to put my hand on you, don't you?' And he put his hand on me and I felt that warm feeling go right down to the prostate. I don't know if I ever felt it like that before in my life. I thought, Boy, what a wonderful relief." Bus loads of people came from country churches fifty miles away for the nightly meetings and "packed the church out till it squeaked." Some of Grant's meetings lasted until the sun came up. On those occasions when the meetings ended before dawn, Grant went back to wherever he was staying and prayed for the rest of the night. By the end of a two-week stay, more than four hundred persons had signed cards reporting that they had received the baptism of the Holy Spirit.

If the visiting evangelist was confident, a huge tent would be unfurled at the Fresno fairgrounds to attract people from miles around. The better-organized evangelists traveled with their own tents and sent advance men to work out advertising and other arrangements with the local Pentecostal clergy, distribute cards to be filled out by those seeking a healing, and arrange publicity.

Oral Roberts arrived in Fresno in November 1951, fresh from a triumph in Los Angeles, put up his tent, and began a ten-day revival. By then, the local non-Pentecostal clergy were becoming uneasy. Several ministers wrote to Claude Weaver to express their concern that Roberts was staging a religious "circus" and using "manipulative devices" to "steal sheep."

Oca, an usher for the revival, had the job of helping the sick and lame people who went up to seek healing through the hands of the evangelist. It gave him a chance to see with his own eyes how Roberts performed: "There was a woman with brain cancer, and I couldn't exactly see what was happening. The first time Oral Roberts touched her head, she jumped like she was shot. Then he said, 'I'm sorry, sister, anointing is in my other hand,' and he kind of reached over and slapped her. He asked if it hurt and she said, 'No.' But I felt so sorry. I thought, That poor thing. My heart went out to her because she probably didn't get healed.

"Well, the next day I drove by and stopped off at this little prayer tent they had set up that would hold about five hundred people. Something pulled me in, and I set down in the backseats. And what did I see up there? That lady rejoicing who couldn't hardly stand up in front of Oral Roberts the night before. She was telling how God had healed her of the cancer. I just set there and wept. I did. Just broke down and cried. I said, 'Lord, no wonder you wanted me coming in here, because I was doubting, and that doubt didn't help anybody.' I felt horrible to think that I was helping them up there and yet had that much doubt. If I couldn't *see* 'em healed, I didn't believe it. You've always got the enemy trying to destroy faith."

As Doris saw it, God healed to show His power and love: "The Bible talks about people seeing those things and of it making believers out of them. I think that many people saw the power of God and saw healing happening to someone in their family, their neighbor or something, and they knew it was real and it made a believer out of them. Maybe even scared the daylights out of them!"

Her brother Dick believed that if a child was born deformed, it was a result of "original sin," which had come about through the disobedience of Adam and Eve. Dick was taught that man's penalty for original sin was death, which is "why our bodies continue to get weaker and older and fall apart, and finally we're gone." But within every man was a "measure of faith" that would, under the right circumstances, enable him to obtain the gift of God's healing grace. To Dick, a world without divine healing was unimaginable. "If God said, 'Okay, I'm not going to have anything to do with healings, let 'em go,' what kind of a mess would we be in? If he just left us alone and let everything happen and there was no healing, no faith, and no hope?"

Gerald Tatham went along with his father not only to the big meetings, but also on trips to small country churches, which Oca enjoyed visiting when there was what Gerald described as a "hot revival that he liked to identify with." These churches lacked the resources or sophistication of the Fresno churches, but Oca was drawn to them over and over again. Yet for his son, the excursions were sometimes awkward: "We always rolled up in a brand-new Oldsmobile or Cadillac or something, and right away people don't like you—real quick. I used to have a lot of trouble on that." When the kids from these churches came into town for the tent meetings, Gerald would hear them talking about "the guy with the big shot for a father," and sometimes there was shoving and pushing. "You think you're better than me, poom, and then we'd start. Because of the Cadillac."

An old-style revival run by two preachers called Sonny and Sammy lasted for weeks at Highway City. Sonny and Sam were a young man and a boy playing guitars and preaching about hellfire. Oca and Ruby stood back from the demonstrative kind of worship that took place there, singing along but not joining in the often expressive gesturing and utterances. For them it was a chance just to identify quietly. Years later, when their lives had taken a different turn, Oca and Ruby continued to go back to the little churches in other places.

THE NEW GENERATION of Tathams generally stayed within the tight-knit Pentecostal community as they married and went off to college. Of the six Tatham children, four attended an Assemblies of God Bible college, and the five Tathams who married soon after school selected wives or husbands from a Pentecostal or Holiness background. Several found their spouses right at Calvary Tabernacle.

Doris met her future husband in Christ's Ambassadors. He was Gordon Weaver, the pastor's son. The Weavers were not Okies but Midwesterners who had come to California with their two young sons just before Pearl Harbor so that Claude could take a succession of pastorates in Ventura, Pasadena, Bakersfield, and finally Fresno. Gordon had been born in Chicago. His maternal grandfather had come to the United States from England to live at Zion City, Illinois, the religious commune whose world-renowned founder, Alexander Dowie, was a prayer healer and relentless enemy of the modern medical profession.[6] After the collapse of Dowie's Utopia, the grandparents became involved with Chicago's Stone Church, one of the groups that came together with others in Hot Springs, Arkansas, in 1914 to form the Assemblies of God.

Doris began dating Gordon after coming back to Fresno from several semesters at the Assemblies of God's Glad Tidings Bible Institute in Santa Cruz. The Institute, soon to be renamed Bethany Bible College, was situated in wooded acreage in the redwoods country. It was somewhat of a bold step for a young woman of her background to leave home for college, and Oca had his reservations. When Oca called her back to look after her young brothers and sisters while Ruby was hospitalized from an automobile accident, she stayed in Fresno. She and Gordon were married in 1953, in the middle of an M. V. Grant revival. The wedding rehearsal was put back until after midnight because the church was still occupied by swaying worshipers. Later, Gordon's brother, Paul, would also marry a woman from the church.

A year later, Bill married Earline Graves, whose first husband had been killed. She was from an extended family of plain, friendly religious people, Nazarenes (a Holiness denomination), who were among those drawn to the Oral Roberts meetings. The Graveses came out from Arkansas in the 1930s and picked cotton and grapes before settling in Caruthers, a one-horse town near Fresno. Mrs. Graves worked a full day at the Sun-Maid packing plant and stayed up half the night mending clothes. Earline milked cows and pumped gas at her dad's filling station, dropping out of school in the tenth grade to get married. Bill courted her at an Oral Roberts tent meeting in 1953 and took her along to Calvary Tabernacle.

Dick married a pastor's daughter. Grace Snelgrove's father had an Assemblies of God church and a radio show in Newfoundland, Canada. She attended Bethany Bible College with her first husband, and several years after he was killed in a car accident, Dick took her out on a blind date. A few months later, he met her again at a camp meeting on the Bethany campus, and this time it stuck.

Brenda Tatham married into a clan that orginally hailed from Stilwell, Oklahoma, and was somewhat infamous in those parts. Englishes, it seemed, had done a little of everything, from cattle rustling to hijacking. One English ran a dance hall and kept a still. An uncle, "Pete" English, survived after being sprayed with bullets while sauntering down a street in Fort Smith, Arkansas, but later burned to death in a suspicious fire. Brenda married Jerry English, whose dad had moved to Klamath Falls, Oregon, in the 1940s, where he swamped potatoes, worked in an orange-crate mill, and did some pastoring. Sometimes Pete would come out to visit, and Jerry would watch him make slugs for slot machines in the garage.

Jerry wanted none of that and instead went off to the Assemblies' Southern California College, where he met Brenda. Jerry took her to Oklahoma to meet her in-laws after they were married. "Keep your purse with you, and don't take your watch off at night," Jerry prudently advised his bride.

By the end of his senior year at Clovis, Gerald Tatham knew that he, too, was going to marry a Pentecostal Okie from his own kind of background. Cora Chambers's father and grandfather had come out from Missouri in the 1930s looking for work. Her dad landed a job with a mining company in Lompoc, but the family was dogged by tragedy. Cora's paternal grandfather, a colorful character who had called square dances back in Missouri, was killed when a load of pipes fell on him. When Cora was only eleven years old, her dad was drowned trying to rescue a man in a riptide off Lompoc. Cora went with her mother to live in Fresno with her grandmother and step-grandfather, who'd been converted to Pentecost at one of the revivals that followed the Azusa Street commotion. That was how Cora found Calvary Tabernacle and the Tathams.

In public school she and Gerald shared their "holy roller" secret. (Usually, Cora just said she was a Baptist to avoid a lot of questions.) But Gerald found that it wasn't just religion that set a person apart. There was also class and culture, as Gerald learned when he was briefly enrolled in Hamilton Junior High School. Through one of his deals, Oca had landed in a house on the edge of Fresno's exclusive residential district. It was just another house to him, but Gerald was suddenly embarrassed by his J. C. Penney shirts and plain shoes. The school was attended by children of doctors, lawyers, and prominent Fresno businessmen. His classmates wore white bucks, saddle shoes, and penny loafers and talked about fraternities and vacations in places that Gerald couldn't spell.

He was much happier at Clovis High. Not that Tathams were part of the upper crust even at that school. Bill had been aware of "a certain elite group at high school that we didn't belong to, but that others who were popular did belong to. They were people that were probably established socially. I didn't know who they were. They seemed to belong to the DeMolay and various clubs. We didn't belong to any of the clubs. I don't think we made an effort to join. We probably could have. Nobody ever said, 'You Okies.'"

It would have been risky to do so. Clovis High was the "school of champions" partly because it was educating so many tough farm kids whose parents came from Texas and Oklahoma. George Kastner, who eventually became principal of Clovis High, interviewed new arrivals.

"Where are you from?" he would ask.

"Midwest."

"Where, exactly?"

The newcomer would look around nervously. "Oklahoma." The word came out in a barely audible whisper.

At Clovis, Gerald saw kids "whose pants and shoes did not fit and who walked to school because their parents didn't have a car. These kids coming out from Oklahoma, they'd come with the migrant workers and farm laborers and stuff, and they were put down, you know. They didn't have neat clothes and everything and they'd fight back on that basis. Some of them had chips on their shoulders and they were ready to fight, I mean at the drop of a hat. It was sad."

Gerald always had his grandparents to remind him of exactly where he came from. Granma Cora Tatham was always ready with pies and apple butter in Delano when her grandchildren visited. Walter was full of tales and jokes. Ruby's mother, Clara, a plain farm woman who always wore aprons, loved prayer and boxing, in that order. When she was living with Oca and Ruby, the fight broadcasts brought her to the edge of her rocker, shouting and gesturing. She also spoke in tongues, sometimes right at the dinner table, and was very rigid about dress. Clara Rogers sewed lace on the end of her apron sleeves to cover up her bare arms.

Gerald didn't really think of himself as an Okie, though he knew he'd been born "outside Bakersfield," the center of Okiedom. Okie, he thought, meant real down-and-outers. But that made the identity question all the more confusing because there were some of those right in his own family.

His Uncle Lonnie Rogers and Aunt Opal simply couldn't cope with their thirteen children and, it seemed to Tatham relatives, didn't particularly try. Brenda went with her parents to bring Lonnie and Opal clothing when they were living in a place south of Bakersfield. She never forgot the sight. The pattern on the linoleum floor was worn clean out. The place was dark; one of the Rogers girls looked scared and started fixing up her hair when Brenda came in. On the way home in the car, Brenda pestered Ruby with questions: Why didn't that girl do something, pick cotton, run away, buy a nicer dress, get a job in a store? Ruby told her it wasn't quite that easy.

Ruby cried and prayed out loud for her brother and his family, but prayers weren't enough. One day Oca and Ruby called the children together and said that all those cousins were going to go to foster homes and that Ruby's brother was going to state prison at Paso Robles for child abuse.

The identity question was sharpened by trips to Oklahoma. Dick had trouble finding the bathroom on a visit to his Great-Aunt Pearl's, until he was told it was outdoors. Sometimes an Oklahoma cousin would visit Fresno. "Say you're from Dallas," Tatham cousins advised.

Renee loved visiting Ruby's relatives who raised rodeo bulls east of Tulsa and was thrilled by their strange foods—heaps of beans, potatoes, corn on the cob, and pan-baked cakes. On Drake's Prairie near Sallisaw, however, some houses still lacked running water. A woman was dying, and the wailing set up by friends and relatives seemed "eerie" to Renee. It took a while for her to figure out that "a whole pall of tartars" was a whole pile of potatoes.

As if all that was not complicated enough, Gerald had to sort out who he was within the narrower boundaries of his immediate Tatham family. He often felt the "odd man out," the towhead in a family of dark-haired people, the awkward kid who evoked giggles from his kid sisters and concerned comments from adults. "That Gerald will be dead before he's ten," sighed Granma Tatham. He'd always been mischievous: he bought a honey-tipped, red-dot cigar for some innocent boy from the church and took him down to shoot a round of pool. He smoked cigarettes and on rare occasions swigged whiskey.

At the same time, Gerald was not a bad boy. He had genuine questions about his church. The Pentecostal definition of sinful behavior, he noted, was curiously flexible. When sons became high school athletic stars, he observed, his dad relaxed his policy of no Friday night sports. The code was relaxed further when Oca bought a pool table and the church began allowing attendance at bowling alleys.

Tongue speaking was an issue that bothered Gerald—as indeed it did thoughtful Pentecostal theologians. It was the most distinctive Pentecostal practice, yet its role changed depending on the social context. On Drake's Prairie, it had been virtually required for full membership in the church community. In Delano, when Pentecostal doors were being thrown open to all, tongue speaking appears to have been viewed more as a wonderful but voluntary experience. By the 1940s and 1950s, as the dire economic circumstances eased, a more institutional Pentecostalism began to take speaking in tongues as a kind of generational rite of passage.

Oca and Ruby, Gerald could see, were not demonstrative themselves, and their children could not recall their speaking in tongues. Doris spoke in tongues when she was still very young, but her brother Bill's recollections about whether he ever had were vague. Older Tathams showed their spirituality in a quiet appreciation of the surrounding enthusiasm, and the children did so through music. Yet the pressure to speak in tongues was ever-present, and Gerald learned to answer with a noncommittal "Praise the Lord" when asked if he had had the experience. He wondered, anyway, why that automatically would make someone so holy. What about the other "gifts of the spirit" of which Paul had spoken of in his letter to the Corinthians: the gifts of spiritual insight and intuition, of wisdom, of discernment, of knowledge of God? Why did his church put so much stress on the volatile, emotional gifts, such as speaking in tongues, while downplaying those quieter, more intuitive powers? Was it to create an elite in the church?

He was sure of his dad's Christian commitment: it was "like the hair on a dog's back." But he was less convinced of the dedication of many of those his father called "fine Christians." They were people who observed the legalistic rules, but Gerald questioned whether they truly were filled with the love, spirit, and heart of Jesus.

Gerald responded to all this churning uncertainty in his last year of high school by making himself feel unfit for his church and family. He was skipping classes, flunking choir, and he had just missed being caught with a whiskey flask at a police bust at a basketball game. At night he heard his parents call his name in prayer.

Oca felt he had to win this struggle with his son. He might not be able to make Gerald love the Lord, but he could keep him in church and hope that God would do the rest. One Sunday night Gerald announced he was not going to church with the family. Gerald was taller than his dad, but Oca decided he could still take him. Oca remembered it as his "testing time, now or never, this was it." He said, "You're goin' to church tonight, don't think I can't handle you." The two stared at each other. Then Gerald's face relaxed. He went to get ready. A week later he went up to the altar and asked the pastor to help him.

Gerald heard messages from the pulpit being directed squarely at him, like the one from a pastor in San Jose just before Christmas of his senior year. The pastor had talked about the life-style of a particular confused young person, and spoken about rebellion as sin and as defiance of God. Gerald was certain the message was for him.

Blossom Day, a rite of spring at Clovis High, was held in late

March. The girls came to school in skimpy sundresses. Driving home that night after dropping off a friend, Gerald's thoughts were on the state finals of the Youth for Christ singing contest, in which he was entered. He wasn't a Christian, but he was a competitor, and he looked forward to winning. The thud woke him up. His '47 Mercury was barreling toward a loading shed next to the railroad tracks, and it was too late to stop. The vehicle burrowed under the shed, shearing off its roof and knocking Gerald unconscious. He woke up in the hospital two days later. The doctors had sewed his tongue back together, saving him the lifelong humiliation of being a tongueless Pentecostal. But he would win no singing contests for a while.

The family had been going to a little storefront church on Olive Street while they waited for the big opening of Northeast Assembly, which was to be their new church. A few weeks after the accident, Gerald went to the altar there and gave his heart to the Lord. Lola and Tom Fuller were serving as copastors. "Gerald, don't you need to come on down?" Lola called to him. He went to the altar, but he still kept back a part of himself. He wasn't yet baptized in the Holy Spirit, as it was meant by his church. He was still only a candidate.

Graduation was devastating. His grades were too poor to get him into college, and while other guys were getting Bank of America scholarships, he was wondering about a job. Even winning the all-American blanket in track was small consolation since Bill and Dick had done the same. Tathams were *expected* to be champions.

That summer Gerald got a temporary job with a water-softener company in Bakersfield. When he came back to Fresno, Producers Cotton Exchange hired him to muscle cotton bales off trucks. The work was hard and dirty, and he was the only white in a crew of blacks and Mexicans. He couldn't help thinking that he'd brought the Tathams full circle—from the cotton fields to the cotton bales in three generations.

Chapter Twelve

The Horse Trader II

"**WE KNOW LESS** about the origins of the trader than we do about the origins of the scribe," wrote Eric Hoffer in 1963.[1] "But as we watch the present goings on in the Communist world, the realization is forced upon us that trading is a form of self-assertion congenial to common people—a sort of subversive activity, undoctrinaire, unheroic and uncoordinated, yet ceaselessly undermining and frustrating totalitarian domination. The trader probably did not initiate the downfall of the ancient totalitarian systems, but he was quick to lodge himself in any cracks which appeared in the monolithic walls, and did all he could to widen them. Thus, despite his trivial motivation and questionable practices, the trader has been a chief agent in the emergence of individual freedom."

In the central valley, the natural-born horse trader lived in a complex and paradoxical relationship with government. The economy was based on agriculture, which by the 1940s depended on the federal dam and irrigation projects. The *individual* actor in the valley's economy was, therefore, a Lilliputian figure operating around the edges of the barely visible, huge state and national systems that moved California. Oca knew instinctively, however, that the big pieces of the

California universe did not fit together neatly, and he knew how to lodge himself in the crannies. Selling potatoes in the 1930s, he had avoided larger towns where peddling licenses were required. In Fresno County after the war he had subdivided in unimproved farmland outside the city limits, beyond the reach of Fresno's zoning laws. He did not register his water company with the Public Utilities Commission for two years.

His office was his kitchen table. He could change course faster than a hound dog following a scent. A "For Sale" sign on a truck would stop him in his tracks. On one trip to Oklahoma during the war, he'd taken a liking to a Shetland pony that could do tricks—play dead and kneel. He couldn't resist it for his boys and bought it on the spot. He was a thousand miles from home, and the Shetland didn't fit in his car. So right then and there he bought a GMC truck, hired two drivers, loaded the Shetland into the back, and sent the whole bunch back to the family in Kingman, Arizona.

That was just a taste of things to come. He was driving through Texas in 1951 when he noticed a bunch of International Harvester cotton pickers sitting outside a Cadillac dealership. He made a U-turn. He knew from the papers that harvesters were in short supply back home in California, but it had been droughty in Texas that year and many local farmers had held off buying. He hit it off with the Cadillac man—a Christian, as it turned out—and they made a deal: the Cadillac dealer would deliver the harvesters to Oca's vacant lot in Fresno. Oca would sell them, and split the profits. It was a splendid arbitrage. The harvesters sold at a premium in California, where dam projects had been draining away farm labor. Oca never sold another cotton harvester. The next year, he knew, there would be franchised dealers and agents and the margins would narrow. By then he was on to something else. He was still the bee pollinating many transactions, the trader moving from deal to deal.

Tatham Country Homes south of Shields Avenue in Fresno was his last subdivision. By the start of the Eisenhower administration, he figured the boom was over. He left the building game to developers with more capital and more patience with the architects, lawyers, and specialists, who were becoming necessary as city and county building ordinances became ever more burdensome.

Tatham Country Homes was one of the few things ever named for Oca and uncharacteristic in that regard. He seldom put his name on things, for that suggested a longer-term commitment. Or it suggested a need for recognition. Ego, he knew, was a great enemy of common sense.

The ad pages in the Fresno *Bee* amounted to a kind of daily auction, and he perused them "cover to cover," looking for deals on cars, tires, houses, and furniture. Every item was an invitation to excitement, risk, opportunity—and the thrill of the person-to-person deal. Every deal required a different approach, a shrewd assessment of value, of the market, of the other party's character.

His eye never rested. On family excursions to Santa Cruz, the children explored the boardwalk, beach, and amusement park. Oca wandered off to look at property and scout out bargains. One time he sent the family home in the Cadillac and put a "For Sale" sign on the trailer he'd hauled over the mountains. He spent a week trading trailers before heading home with an almost new one, an improvement on the old vehicle in which they'd left Fresno.

What drove him? What was the source of his restless, sleepless determination? Some need to compensate, perhaps. He was the oldest son of a man who had failed as a family provider. He could chuckle at Walter Tatham's ways, but he did not respect him. Years after Walter was gone, he would dismiss him coldly, saying he had been no example.

Some need, perhaps, to even the score with the world. He was a guy with eight years of schooling, which left him with something to prove, not once, but over and over again. And one needed no degree to trade. He couldn't pass up an auction. For a while in the early 1950s he and another man ran a used car auction of their own at a decommissioned movie theater at Camp Pinedale. They drove the cars onto the stage while vendors hawked popcorn and soft drinks as if the event were a picture show. But the used car game proved too shady for Oca.

He and Ruby went to auctions to buy clothes for the children, to furnish apartments they rented out, to supply two variety stores they operated, and sometimes just for fun. It was at sales run by a Fresno auctioneer named Bob Jett that Oca bought houses condemned by the highway department along Blackstone Avenue. As he built his own houses elsewhere, he used Jett's auctions to pick up stoves, sinks, rugs, and other accessories for his homes, rental apartments, and stores.

Bob Jett sold everything—buildings, clothes, objects from estates. Oca became one of the regulars who received penny-postcard announcements of a Jett auction. The regulars were a cross section of the Fresno melting pot: Americans of Armenian, Italian, Jewish, and Swedish ancestry, a few horse-trading Okies. Armenians had centuries of trading experience behind them, but Oca studied ways to outwit them. He noticed that they tended to raise their bids by a series of small increments and seemed confused when he suddenly raised his bid dramatically. By the time they recovered, the article often had been "sold to Oca Tatham."

Sometimes he worked with what was called a "by-bidder"—a straw man. His by-bidder was Jimmy Nichols, a transplanted Texan from the panhandle. Sometimes Jimmy bid for himself; other times he worked the floor for Jett, reporting bids to the auctioneer as they were signaled to him by other bidders who wanted to keep their identity secret. Oca only had to give Jimmy a fleeting nod or a wink, or twiddle his thumb, or just stare hard at him and Jimmy would register the bid to Oca. Jimmy Nichols paid Oca the auction man's highest compliment: "a first-rate scrounger who knew what to do with a dollar when he had it."

Jett did everything he could to build up excitement. If the action was slow, he might say, "Sold to Oca Tatham," even though Oca hadn't raised a finger. Oca went along with this ruse for keeping bidders alert. Jett's wife, Janet, remembers Oca and Ruby at the auctions always making sure they were getting what they had bid on, to the point of checking the number of socks in a hundred-pair lot.

The auction game was for those who could think up a use for everything—or find somebody who could. Gerald said that his dad never tired of "junking around." He would try anything—open a variety store, buy kits from which to assemble boats and go into the boat business. Some things panned out, some didn't. The perfect was the enemy of the good. A perfectionist like Gerald would want to clean a cement mixer after a job until it gleamed like chrome. Oca wanted it sprayed down quick, so they could get on to something else.

The auction game was made for the individual operator. Oca had never been one for partners, though he'd had a few. A Fresno furniture store with a partner had not worked out; neither had Lul-a-Luv, a trademarked rocking love seat which he and two partners hoped to manufacture and market. One problem was that he had his own individual style of doing business. Another was that he was more trader than investor. Lul-a-Luv would have required sales agents, marketers, and a long-term business plan—the whole network of connections that Oca shunned.

He had little use for lawyers. "If I had a deal, they blew it . . . I couldn't turn around and hire an attorney every time. I worked these things out myself. I didn't pay my money out for attorneys. If you know what you want in there, and you've got it in there, that's all anybody can do. Nothing an attorney can do but foul it up." He seldom went to court. He collected the unpaid water bills or late mortgage payments. Tathams had a reputation for being fair but "pretty rough if you owe 'em," he said. "Dad was the kind of guy who believed that if you owed a man money and couldn't pay, you ought to offer to work the debt off by mowing his lawn," said his son Bill. "If you owed him money, you'd better not drive up in a Cadillac," said Gerald.

Oca's approach to finance and banking was highly personal, in part because it had to be. "A lot of people don't know what it is to work money," he said. "I kept no money laying around." His money was always tied up in properties or investments so he never had a fat bank account, a regular job, or a steady residence to establish his credit worthiness. He was a fringe operator—a fly-by-night whose capital was tied up in the notes that he took back on properties, automobiles, and whatever else he was peddling.

The savings and loan associations backed him, but sometimes he negotiated a slightly better rate from a private lender. A loan wasn't a pile of money transferred from an institution; it was a relationship between two people. He preferred to borrow man-to-man, from people like himself—only more liquid. He liked the personal connection, and owing a person rather than a bank was a strong motivation to repay on time.

Unplanned as everything Oca did was, a logical pattern nonetheless emerged. Everything he did was bigger than the last thing—but not too much bigger. He knew fellows from Oklahoma who got ahead of themselves after they'd made their first million and lost it all. Each new step Oca made was connected to previous steps. Potatoes led to junk, which led to trucking, which led to furniture stores. Subdividing got him into water companies and small-scale mortgage banking. He used the auctions to outfit his properties or clothe the children and his business activities to help his church. It was all seamless. In 1936, he had helped to haul the secondhand lumber to build the Pentecostal Church of God in McFarland. Nearly twenty years later, he was involved in founding a new church, Northeast Assemblies of God, at the corner of Chestnut and Holland avenues on the northeast side of Fresno. Oca spotted the corner lot while driving around one day. Thinking it a fine location for a church, he pulled over, turned off the motor, and prayed. Then he went back and talked to the man with the property.

"Do you have some land you'd like to sell?" Oca asked.

The man hadn't thought about it, but he agreed to consider.
When Oca and others came back in a week, the deal was done for
$9,000. Horace Tolbert of Tolbert Auto and Electric mortgaged his
home to raise the down payment for the land and cover the cost of
the secondhand structure Oca had hauled onto the property. It was
a medical building that he'd bought near Hamer Air Field and hauled
away to use as a church. Oca, Ruby, and their daughter Brenda were
charter members, along with Baldwins, Johnsons, Hubbarts, and
Tolberts, all stalwarts from Calvary Tabernacle. In 1956, the Northeast Assembly of God opened for business. Gerald Tatham and Cora
Chambers were the first couple married there.

That was the way Oca did things: he didn't need manuals or
training courses to show him how. His inquisitiveness was equaled
by his competitiveness. He wanted the fastest car and the quickest
way to get there. When a truck he was driving got beaten by a bunch
of Fords on the hills going up to Oregon one time, he spent $2,800
on a blower that would give his GMC pickup more power on the hills.
He wouldn't be outdone by anyone.

IT WAS BOTH FITTING and ironic, given his personal views, that
many of his most profitable deals came from finding hidden value in
government cast-offs. In Delano he'd bought cars seized by the police
in fires. In Fresno, he'd acquired government surplus military barracks and stuff of all kinds from surplus stores. And it was Bob Jett's
auctioning of a huge government property that landed Oca in the
middle of the biggest deal of his life in 1957. Fresno County's Wish-
I-Ah tuberculosis sanatorium, located outside the town of Auberry,
nestled among black oak, Digger pine, and gnarled manzanita bushes
in the Sierra foothills, suddenly had become a white elephant. Antibiotics had finally won the fight against contagious TB. Jett and his
wife, Janet, viewing the facility for the first time, were amazed to find
what looked like a well-kept mountain village, with paved roads, neat
houses for doctors and nurses, hospital buildings, a maintenance
shop, and a sewage-treatment plant.

The first parcel on sale was federal land surrounding the property. About twenty people showed up, waiting uneasily for the bidding to begin. Sydney Jacobsen, a regular member of the auction
fraternity, looked around the room and was relieved to see that
Oca Tatham was not present. Tatham, he thought, would be sure
to appreciate the potential value of the property. Just as Jacobsen

was chuckling over the deal that Oca was missing, Oca and Ruby hurried in.

The bidding, which began at $3,000, proceeded slowly. Something seemed to be holding down the offers—possibly rumors spread by an unknown party that the four-and-a-half-acre parcel did not have access to county water, which went with the second parcel. Jacobsen dropped out of the bidding at $10,000, at which Oca jumped in. Janet Jett became so excited that she, too, entered a bid, but at $15,000, Janet got the message from Bob—a menacing scowl. It just wouldn't look right for the county auctioneer to knock off the property to his wife.

"Would you bid one more time," Jett pleaded with Oca.

"No," said Oca, he wouldn't bid against Janet.

"Come on. Bid just once."

"No."

"Would you bid even one hundred dollars?"

"Bob, I'll give you one more bid, and that's it. $15,100."

"Sold to Oca Tatham."

Several months later, the county called for sealed bids on the second parcel, 155 acres with more buildings, roads, and utilities. When none of the bids was deemed acceptable, another auction was scheduled. Oca's only real competitor this time was an attorney who was representing a client. Oca opened with the minimum that the county said was acceptable: $25,000. When the bids reached $26,750, Supervisor Henry J. Andreas spoke up in frustration. "It's a steal at $50,000," he said.[2] Oca added a hundred dollars.

"Sold to Mr. Tatham for $26,850," said the auctioneer.

A man rushed in and offered Oca $28,000 for the fine old sanatorium. "I don't think you've got the kind of money I'd want for that property," said Oca.

A reporter asked Oca about his plans for the sanatorium. "I can tell you one thing," he said. "It won't be a nudist colony."

His immediate concern was to raise the $25,000. The title company he used put him in touch with a man who lived out in the country, and Oca drove out to see him. The "banker" looked to Oca as if he'd spent the day picking cotton; he had an old Ford tractor out back. But he had the cash, and he made Oca the loan.

Now that Oca had the place, he had no idea what to do with it. His original thought was to resell it and get his money out with a small profit. He'd followed his rule: "When you buy 'em cheap enough, there's always something you can do." That winter he leased it temporarily to West Coast Bible College, operated by the Pentecostal Church of God.

Meanwhile he decided to sell the Northeast Gardens water company. Here was another arena in which government regulation was encroaching. As the water table declined, he had been forced to drill down another fifty feet, and soon it would be another fifty. As he saw it, the Public Utilities Commission let rates edge up to help cover the extra pumping costs, but never enough. When his real-estate broker brought him an offer of $85,000, Oca bumped it up to $100,000. The broker came back with a question from the prospective purchasers. What if the city took over the water company and didn't pay full value?

Oca gave his answer: "Tell him the price is now $125,000, and give him his deposit back."

The agent came back soon afterward with a doctor willing to pay the price. They wrote up a contract and sent it to the doctor's partners, who were also physicians. The contract came back from them with the $125,000 struck through and $117,500 penciled in.

"Tell them they no longer have a contract and the price is now $130,000," Oca instructed the broker. And that was the sum he got.

Wish-I-Ah, as it happened, became a nursing home. Oca's son Dick had learned a little about the nursing-home business while serving as youth director of a church in Portland, Oregon. Back in Fresno, he learned at the county hospital that the hallways were full of patients and geriatric wards were overcrowded. Dick had stumbled upon the beginnings of a major medical and social phenomenon. The life expectancy of Americans had been rising for decades, thanks to better nutrition, public health services, and medical technology. At the same time, the mobility of the population and its suburbanization were writing an end to the time when extended families cared for their own, under their own roofs.

In 1959, the private nursing-home business was small and undeveloped. There were "rest homes" for the affluent elderly, but poor, senile, or insane old people were mostly "warehoused" at big, locked, public facilities, "lunatic asylums," generally operated by state governments, while the poor and forgotten ones were cared for in state or county institutions.

But the system was about to undergo radical change. Congress took note that the tradition of caring for elderly or infirm relatives at home was conflicting with the life-style of the nuclear suburban family. A month after Oca and Ruby completed their purchase of

Wish-I-Ah, the federal government's Public Assistance Medical Care Program added federal dollars to the state and county funds that could be used to care for certain categories of the indigent in nongovernmental facilities—the aged, the blind, and members of families with dependent children. The payments were small and controls still fairly tight, but the program established a precedent of federal subsidies in nursing homes.

PAMCP marked the start of a new approach to the care of the elderly and the medically dependent. Policymakers, mindful that a massive demand for services lay ahead, decided that the business should be contracted out to private operators, whom the government would pay and regulate. A new government-subsidized industry was born. Two years later, in 1960, Congress approved Medical Assistance for the Aged. Six years after that came Medicaid, the most extensive health program for the aged poor in U.S. history.

Oca, with Dick's help, had spotted a new frontier of opportunity. At the point he entered, regulation was still relatively light in comparison with what was to come—though it did not seem so to Oca. When he purchased Wish-I-Ah, the California Bureau of Hospitals, which inspected and licensed nursing homes, had only twenty-six inspectors; twenty years later there were three hundred. Requirements such as round-the-clock coverage of each patient by a registered nurse were yet to be imposed.

From the outset, Oca and Ruby planned to take in primarily "program patients," for whom the county provided reimbursement through a complicated federal-state-county cost-sharing formula. They did not have the capital to build an upscale nursing home to attract private patients, so their niche was at the lower end of the market. They would happily accept patients whose families could pay, but most of their patients were to be those whom no other institutions wanted: old people with advanced memory loss, mentally disturbed derelicts, bums from the west side of Fresno, the terminally ill with no known relatives.

They did it their way, holding costs down by doing their own contracting and bringing in family and friends to help when necessary. Oca picked up washers, dryers, draining boards, five-gallon cans filled with casters for hospital beds, and other useful equipment at the Cherry Avenue auction. While a competitor invested in new hospital beds, Oca located used beds and secondhand air conditioners nicknamed "swamp coolers." From several local restaurants that had gone bankrupt, he obtained used cooking ranges suitable for commercial kitchens. At the railroad depot in Fresno, he found a commercial-size freezer and refrigerator that had been damaged in shipment and bought them at a fraction of the price of new models. Oca made a deal with the Safeway store in Fresno to buy meat at discount—getting beef that had turned brownish from exposure to artificial light in the store's meat display trays, but was still good.

The staff physician was a former Methodist missionary. Ruby was administrator and chief of nursing, in charge of hiring the nursing staff, buying the medications, and stocking the kitchen. She hired Clinton Banks, a black cook who used to work in a fishing camp in the Sierras, to do odd jobs. Herman Morgan, making a fresh start after fighting off a drinking problem, was rehired as driver and general handyman while his wife, Clara, worked as a nurse's aide. He and Clara had divorced soon after their son was born in 1951, but shortly before Oca bought Wish-I-Ah, they had decided to have another go at the marriage. Employed and under the eye of Oca and Ruby, they pulled things together for a while, and Clara even brought her dad in as a maintenance worker.

Even in those moderately unregulated days, Oca and Ruby had an enormous amount to learn. The Bureau of Hospitals approved plans, issued licenses, and made periodic inspections. The Department of Mental Hygiene certified beds designated for mental patients. Fire marshals, building inspectors, and planning commissioners had to approve plans for safety and operations. Oca and Ruby relied on their architect, Richard Waring, for advice. Waring had them study voluminous code books on nursing homes, and they pestered nurses and doctors for information about everything from the use of catheters to the treatment of bed sores and advanced senility. Oca must have learned well: at a meeting in Sacramento someone addressed him as "Dr. Tatham," a title that embarrassed him. Oca snapped, "I'm not a doctor. Fact is, I don't have a high school education."

Oca and Ruby had a real distaste for regulation. Oca saw himself in a drama in which officialdom was out to get him, but he said, "God expected me to stand up to people who would destroy me if they could." He was certain that county inspectors resented him for turning a white elephant into a going venture and were out to make him fail, and he felt he had to let the Sacramento officials know they couldn't push him around. Otherwise, he said, they would have "shoved me off the block."

Later, when the operation was under way, Oca believed that a competitor was reporting on him to the Bureau of Hospitals. "He would have liked to have broke me if he could, but I wasn't about to let him push me down. They'd do it, too. If you don't take your stand they'll put their foot on your neck and mash you under before you start. It's dog eat dog. It takes a lot of guts to stand up and look at your superiors—guys who are looking down on you—well, I let 'em know I stood as tall as they did."

Gerald took a more detached view: "Dad was raised up in a time when they didn't have permits and now you've got to have permits. He figured he would have done it the same way with or without the permits, and he didn't see why it was necessary."

Disputes with the Bureau of Hospitals inspectors often wound up in Waring's lap. Oca wanted his permits fast, and sometimes Waring was able to help: a former associate of Waring's was friends with a man from the Bureau. But sometimes unambiguous regulations left no room for negotiation. Oca, said Waring, found it difficult to accept that: "There was a little redheaded inspector for the Bureau, an ex-bosun's mate with a wide set of shoulders, and if he didn't like you he would shovel it at you. He and Oca were like two bantam roosters. Both were small battlers. At times it was almost hilarious. George would measure everything, Oca would grit his teeth."

But Waring respected Oca: "He may not have had all the patience in the world, but he was fair. Oca was not the type who would tell you one thing and then change his mind. If Oca told you something he stuck by it. If he made a mistake, he wouldn't blame us. And he never griped about paying you the difference."

Even when everything was approved, Oca was still suspicious. Now he thought the county hospital was deliberately withholding the program patients he needed to get his facility going. He fumed that the Board of Supervisors was retaliating against him for "showing up the county." Dick saw less sinister reasons. He thought his dad "may not have seen the inner workings of the county [bureaucracy]." After several days of waiting, someone from the county hospital called: "Are you ready for patients, Mr. Tatham? Can you take eight?"

"Can I take eight? I have a hospital sittin' empty here."

The rest home officially opened for business in July 1958.[3] Within a year, Oca and Ruby had opened several more buildings and were accommodating nearly 150 patients, most of them wards of the county.

It was a mom-and-pop operation. Ruby toted a briefcase to meetings with the county social-service officials. Other times she donned a gown and worked on the ward. Often she and Oca stayed overnight at Wish-I-Ah when an orderly or nurse failed to show up. And when

Oca, in Fresno, woke in the night and worried that the heat hadn't been turned up, he would dress and drive to Auberry to check on the furnaces.

Oca recruited Doris, Brenda, and Gerald to add a "human touch." The children brought birthday cakes or bars of soap and bananas for patients' birthdays, and sometimes Doris and Gerald would harmonize on "Happy Birthday" while Brenda played the accordion and then combed and put ribbons in the women patients' hair. The equipment may have been old, but patients got personal service. Oca scrawled on a Wish-I-Ah brochure: "Not that monotonous crap you *have* to eat. Here, if you don't like it, don't eat it, no argument. No argument about [using] urinals after dark." Next to a picture of Ruby, Oca scrawled a revealing comment: "the boss."

Ruby was his one lasting business partner. She had demonstrated managerial skills in 1954, when she ran two small variety stores that Oca had acquired on West Belmont Avenue, in the low-rent business district. He'd picked up the first of the two in a real-estate trade, selling the house the family was living in on East Clinton for a good price and taking back the stores and seventeen apartments at Camp Pinedale. Then he bought the second store, down the street, to make sure there was no competition. Ruby ran both, while Doris took inventory and made orders. They stocked the stores with everything from bobby socks to hard candy.

Ruby was the quiet force. She was such a quiet, behind-the-scenes person that relatives and long-time friends tended to fall back on clichés and generalities when they tried to describe her, like "the finest woman you ever met," or "Oca wouldn't have been what he was without her." She took care of the home and was the peacemaker, but she also gave her opinions on business matters. She told the children she would have loved for him to buy the property off Blackstone Avenue that later became the site of Fresno's largest shopping center. He didn't. He made the final decisions. Mainly she was the supportive woman who was always saying, "Ocy, you can do it." But Ruby was no pushover. Their son Bill remembers that just one time Oca made some suggestions to Ruby about the way she was running the variety stores. "If you spent more time in the stores you'd have a right to tell me how to run them," she replied. Bill never heard him try to second-guess her again.

The couple had the same approach to business. Bill described his parents as "really disciplined with their money; they really watched it. And they usually saved a lot on the way they did things. It wasn't just that they bought cheap. It was that when they improved it, they did it the cheapest way, too. So it sort of compounded and made the whole thing a lot better. They wouldn't pay the full price when they bought something; then, when they'd fix it up, they would figure out a way to do it wholesale."

Their economizing was legendary in Fresno's health-care community, but they were doing a job nobody else wanted. Wish-I-Ah took the low end of the valley's nursing home clientele, the "program patients" for whom the state and the county were, in effect, abrogating hands-on responsibility: old people without families, young men who had blown their minds on LSD, the terminally ill. This was a well-known pattern of immigrant ascent in the United States: filling a niche in the market that was beneath the dignity of established businessmen.

Dealing with the dead and dying was one such business. With Oca, it had been junk and used tires; now it was cast-off human beings. The work could be rewarding, but it was never easy, with death always close by and the hygiene of the old and sick to contend with. Those close to death were rolled into "the dark room," out of sight of other patients. Ruby herself bathed, cleaned, and dressed the deceased for the ride to the mortuary. Sometimes Oca "witnessed" to the dying, suggesting that it wasn't too late for them to know the Lord. Behind his back some of the other nursing-home operators called him "the preacher." But Oca was happy to have Wish-I-Ah known as the Christian nursing home. Occasionally, when people brought a sick parent or other relation up to the foothills, Oca and Ruby would pray with them. To plain religious folk from the Midwest and South, the prayers of the Okie proprietors were good advertisements. And the Tatham children, too, read the Bible or prayed with patients. Oca witnessed to patients about the "plan of salvation." One of those he recalls praying over was a double amputee with cancer. "If you got any relief, don't thank me. I couldn't heal a fly," Oca told him. "Thank the Lord for it." A few days later the man was wheeled into the dark room, his weeping wife and son with him. Again Oca talked to him and prayed, "He's got a great future in the Lord," Oca told them. "His worries are behind him." The patient died that night.

BUT HE WAS STILL a horse trader at heart. Even Wish-I-Ah was a commodity.

As soon as he had demonstrated its potential, he began trying to sell it. Two potential buyers were S. J. Morris and Ted Hardwick, who together owned a nursing home in Whittier. Oca had met them at a mental-health convention, and now he courted them avidly, buttonholing them at meetings and finally visiting them at their beach house in Laguna.

When Morris and Hardwick finally came to visit, they were surprised at the old swamp coolers and the secondhand equipment. But the beds were occupied, and Fresno County paid more per patient than Los Angeles County. The agreed sale price of $375,000 represented a tenfold increase for Oca on his investment in less than three years. Working without the help of lawyers, Oca structured a complicated deal involving a three-way escrow that would minimize his reportable capital gain—and tax exposure. It was the first of many examples of the Tatham family's ability to use complex transactions to take full advantage of the tax code. Oca came out of this particular transaction with valuable Fresno property, Wallace Sanatorium, which he got through a tax-free exchange. He subsequently sold the sanatorium to Safeway for $150,000.

Morris and Hardwick were surprised when Oca and Ruby showed up at the settlement without an attorney, but they were in for other surprises as well. When, as a goodwill gesture they presented gifts to Ruby and Oca—a gold watch for him, gold earrings decorated with garnets for Ruby—there was an embarrassing misunderstanding, and the beginning of a permanent coolness between the old and new owners. Ruby declined the earrings, saying it was against her religious custom to wear jewelry. She would be happy, she added, to receive a gold watch like Oca's. The distinction between gold earrings and gold watches was lost on Hardwick. That was not the end of it. The previous June the Fresno County Medical Society had given Wish-I-Ah a rating of excellent in an annual inspection. Oca was proud of the rating and had the document framed and hung in his home. But when the new owners took over, they found irregularities in some of the plumbing.

The friction with the new owners was regrettable, for the Wish-I-Ah sale otherwise marked a major turning point in the Tatham family fortunes. With the sale of Wish-I-Ah, Oca left the days of small-time hustling behind him. Oca and Ruby could afford now to live in a comfortable home on East White Avenue. Their daughter Renee felt as if she'd "died and gone to heaven." Ruby hired a housekeeper for the first time in her life, and they bought new rock-maple furniture.

Still, friends and relatives detected few changes in Oca. He lived as he always had lived—though he did treat himself to a powerboat and a few other things that caught his fancy. Then and always he remained deeply suspicious of his own wealth. He took Matthew 6:19 at face value: "Lay not up for yourselves treasures upon earth, where moth and rust doth corrupt, and where thieves break through and steal: But lay up for yourselves treasures in heaven."

"I was full of faults," he said years later. "But God opened doors for me. God answered prayers. We learned that we could go to the Lord, and God would take care of the problem."

BEFORE THE SALE, another Tatham family chapter ended on the cool slopes outside Auberry.

Walter Tatham had been living in a small trailer near Vernon and Dora's home in Pinedale when Oca bought Wish-I-Ah. One day he announced he was tired of being bothered by the little kids on the street and was moving to Oca's new property.

"I'll have to call Oca and make the arrangements," said Vernon.

"I need arrangements like I need a big billy goat," Walter shot back. Vernon called his brother, and they had a good laugh about the billy goat remark. Then Vernon hitched his father's trailer to his car and pulled it up to the convalescent home in the Sierra foothills. Oca gave Walter a job checking on work that needed to be done on the grounds.

Walter had the heart of a child. At the place Oca bought east of Fresno in 1944, Walter and his grandsons would ride horses and practice roping cows; when Oca returned and found the chores undone, Walter would pad the boys' pants with towels against the inevitable whipping. He amused his grandchildren with his Okie lingo and his risqué songs.

He was still a rover. Sometimes he went back to Sallisaw; other times he'd go on visits to Missouri. He was still remarkably young and handsome for his age, and he fancied himself a lady's man.

Arch Tatham died in Sallisaw in 1955 at the age of sixty-eight. He was on jury duty at the courthouse when he suffered a fatal heart attack. Arch had been a committed Christian ever since he'd heard Winnie praying to the Lord to do something about him. Not Walter. The whole family was praying for his soul. He had been on Doris's prayer list when she went off to Bible college in 1949. Now, at the age of seventy-seven, he evidently began to feel the Spirit move. A Baptist pastor began taking him to church on Sunday mornings.

One morning in 1958 at Wish-I-Ah, Herman Morgan knocked

on the door of Walter's trailer. Getting no response, he fetched Oca and together they forced open the door. Walter, it appeared, had died in his sleep. The doctor said it had been a heart attack.

Laid out in a fine funeral suit, Walter Tatham looked almost as young as the day he'd met Cora Sumpter on Drake's Prairie fifty-five years before. They buried him in Delano cemetery, close to his brother Willy and the three babies who had died only days apart in that sad October of 1936.

Years later, Ophelia forthrightly summed up her father's strengths and weaknesses: "He was a very easygoing man. He was a man that loved other guys there with him and loved playing pranks, loved joking. And when he worked, he worked hard. But my dad never was a leader. Well, in a way he was, when he just had a bunch of men around him. They hung around him all the time. But he never wanted any responsibility on the job. If they wanted to make him boss because he had a great personality and they'd love him right off, he'd quit the job before he would be boss over a bunch of people. It scared him to death. He didn't have the self-confidence, I guess."

After the funeral, Ruby, Oca, and Dora cleaned out Walter's trailer and went through his few possessions. The pockets of his overcoat were stuffed with maps.

CHAPTER THIRTEEN

GOLDWATER MAN

THE DEMOCRATIC PARTY had a record to be proud of in California's central valley. Presidents Roosevelt and Truman had promoted the great water projects that had guaranteed the valley's economic survival; Congressman B. F. Sisk, a Fresno tire dealer first sent to Washington in 1954, helped to secure federal funding of the San Luis Project, which began channeling irrigation water to the big corporate farmers on the valley's parched west side in 1963.

In the late 1950s, the Democratic Party controlled all five of the valley's congressional seats and enjoyed a huge majority among registered voters. Valley Democrats in Congress had their hands on the appropriation levers in Washington, and Democrats seemed more effective than Republicans in keeping the federal dollars flowing to farmers, agricultural cooperatives, and local businesses.

This strong Democratic base had historical roots. The European immigrants who had settled in the planned colonies around Fresno early in the century were mainly Catholics from the southern and southeastern European fruit and wine-producing regions. They felt uncomfortable with the Republican Party, which they identified with Prohibition, Protestantism, and native Californians. As they assimilated, some of these immigrants became Republicans, but mainly the

ethnic wards of Fresno, Madera, and Merced counties closely followed the Democratic voting patterns of the ethnic strongholds of
their countrymen in Chicago, Cleveland, and New York City. Politics
in Fresno County was urban politics. A Fresno politician might find
himself attending Mexican Independence Day, Armenian grape festivals, Greek Orthodox events, Portuguese celebrations, and the annual dinner of the Nisei farmers.

South of Fresno County, however, in Kern, Tulare, and Kings
counties, one met a different Democrat. Politicians there attended
country music jamborees and church suppers, not national festivals.
The politics and culture of those counties had also been shaped
by the relationship of water and population, but with different results. The southern valley was short on groundwater and rivers, so
the conditions were not good for small-scale immigrant farmers such
as those who had settled along the aquifer farther north.

Kern County was *developed* rather than settled. The discovery of
oil early in the century was followed by large-scale farming based on
big investments of capital for wells and irrigation. Vast tracts of Kern
County were in the hands of land companies, oil companies, and a
few well-financed families such as the DiGiorgios. When Kern County
did begin to attract large numbers of people in the 1930s and 1940s,
they were not European immigrants but old-stock American whites
from Southern tenant farms and the drought-ravaged plains.

There were a good many Republicans among them, more than
was usually acknowledged: hill people from the Ozark uplands; descendants of the Scotch-Irish Baptists and Presbyterians who had converted to the Whigs after 1830, as the Democratic Party became a
haven for Irish and German Catholics; northern Yankees who had
settled in Kansas; and border-state people such as the Tathams,
whose natural, frontier-Virginia inclination toward the South and the
Democratic Party had been altered by their fathers' or grandfathers'
personal experience in Lincoln's army. Still, most of the Okies were
"Democrats by birth"—people with familial ties to the party of
Thomas Jefferson, Andrew Jackson, William Jennings Bryan, and
Harry Truman. They were descendants of the poor white cotton
farmers who had drifted into Texas and the Indian Territory during
the woeful migration out of the Deep South in the 1870s; transplanted Virginians, Kentuckians, and Tennesseeans; people from
pockets of Southern culture in the Middle West, such as Missouri's
Little Dixie; Irishmen, Mormons, and members of other "out" groups
once persecuted by an establishment represented by the Republican
Party.

To describe this amalgam of people by party label, however, was not particularly enlightening. Whether Democrat or Republican, they shared, more than anything, an outlook evolved—and internalized—from hard times, lonely winters, family occasions, churchgoing, and moving. They were white, Protestant, God-fearing, populist, self-reliant, antigovernment, and suspicious of "upper crusts." They stood for all the plain folk of America who, for half a century, had been on the move out of the South and Southwest to the Far West and the North in an unprecedented migration that was transforming American culture and politics—transforming it by adding what was often a new element wherever they went. In California, the Okies found a politics conflicted between city liberals and small-town conservative businessmen. The Okies fit neither extreme. They were another factor, one that was inclined toward the populist politics of the South and the Southwest. In California, therefore, they needed to improvise workable arrangements until their unwavering Okie values bent California itself in their direction.

Tathams were "Republicans by birth," a legacy of Thomas Tatham's choice for the Union and Lincoln in the Civil War. But most Tathams tended to "vote the man," choosing the candidate who had "character" and was committed to their economic interests. They had voted as a group for FDR in 1932, and later, when Cleo Tatham married Wayne Frost (a Democrat), they tried to unite behind a presidential candidate so as not to "waste" their votes.

Oca Tatham forged a set of political beliefs that were as independent from those of most Okies as he was himself. They were the product of his unique temperament, of his special experiences as a trader and deal maker operating on the edges and in the cracks of society, and of his church. Basically, he distrusted government, which he believed threatened him, and he hated Communists, who threatened his church and its mission.

One might have thought he would have been grateful to government, but he wasn't particularly. Tathams had accepted free commodities and relief. Government relief had tided Oca's family over in the winter of 1934–1935, when he ran out of ways to feed his wife and three children. Walter Tatham supported California's 1939 Ham 'n' Eggs initiative, a welfare scheme to give each needy person thirty dollars in scrip every Thursday. (The Okie precincts voted heavily in favor of Ham 'n' Eggs, though the state as a whole had rejected it decisively.)

But that was in a different era. Oca was thankful, but he made a distinction between a temporary helping hand and the more or less permanent dole. Nothing in the Tatham experience suggested that government had the answer for people who were down and out. The best answer was work, prayer, and a good church that would steer them to opportunities undreamed of. Tathams had never stayed in a government camp. Cora Tatham had turned down Old Age Assistance to keep working at the sheds.

Oca had exploited government and its resources all his business life. Washington's huge wartime investments in western military bases and runways and the atomic bomb plant in Washington had saved his struggling trucking business. After the war, the federal power and water projects in California put taxpayers' money into the hands of the working people to whom Oca was selling houses. Without the dams and canals to create a lively valley economy, there would have been few opportunities for horse traders. And as a nursing-home operator, he depended on government payments for old, disabled, or indigent patients; tax money paid to government and dispersed by it ended up in his pocket for services provided.

Yet Oca viewed government with a jaundiced eye. It represented procedure, the deadliest enemy of the horse trader. Government was corrupt: relief flour was rebagged and sold for profit, defense contractors padded payrolls, building inspectors took bribes. Government was wasteful: it sold valuable properties such as the Wish-I-Ah sanatorium. Fraud, taxes, and intrusive inspectors sticking their noses into everything: that was government.

If such views grew out of personal observation and experiences, Oca's anticommunism had more institutional roots. The spread of communism, armed, dangerous, and implacably hostile to the Christian church, was, he believed, the greatest external danger the United States faced. Communism reversed the natural order of things by confronting missionary Christianity with its mirror image: a dynamic "religion" expanding its influence around the globe. The United States, he once told his dad, would have done better to support the Nazis in the final days of World War II in hopes of pushing the Communists back. Communism abolished private property, it fixed prices, it was full of busybodies telling people what to do, it was big and organized. Now it had won over China, Eastern Europe, and Cuba and was pressing its crusade into Cambodia and South Vietnam.

Initially, Pentecostal churchmen had taken the Bolshevik revolution with a certain equanimity, even a degree of satisfaction. The spread of communism fit nicely into the early church leaders' theories about the millennium and the end of the world. To these radicals, political movements were transitory and insignificant by definition, being "of men." Pentecostal social theory was based on the need to save the individual rather than society, so the early churches scrupulously abstained from the ideological conflict.[1]

On the other hand, Bolshevism clearly threatened territory that had previously been won, or might be won in the future, by Christianity. Thus, pastors and church leaders began to eye it, warily at first and then with downright hostility. In 1921, the Assembly of God organ, *Pentecostal Evangel*, attributed the wave of strikes that occurred after World War I to "Bolshevist influence." A Nazarene minister, noting the danger from Bolshevism, said that only a great religious revival that would make America truly Christian could dispel the threat. The Reverend A. G. Osterberg of Fresno noted that Communists had "flagrantly displayed bitter enmity to God and his followers" and denounced the "ungodly, un-Christian, God-hating, blaspheming crowd" that was falling in with it.[2]

Pentecostal patriotism in World War II cleared the way for all-out anticommunism by the denominations afterward. In the midst of the 1961 Berlin crisis, the *Pentecostal Evangel* reprinted an address by the Boston Congregational minister Harold J. Ockenga to the National Association of Evangelists on the "folly of coexistence." He called for "courageous action" in confronting communism. "Firmness is the only thing which communists understand. Firmness must be backed up by military strength and force. We may be thankful that our nation had courage enough to move into Korea, into Lebanon, into Formosa. . . . The same courage should be manifested in reference to Berlin. We should remind the communists of their treaties and of our rights, and declare that we will maintain access to Berlin whatever comes, even if this means using atomic weapons."[3]

In 1967, the General Council of the Assemblies of God struck the denomination's fifty-year-old bylaw objecting to "participation in war or armed resistance that involves the taking of life" and replaced it with a more neutral clause leaving it up to the individual to decide whether to fight.

On the home front, Pentecostal communities exhibited considerable paranoia about Communists. Whether church members or not, patriotic, politically conservative Okies generally were wary of anything with a Communist flavor. A few Holiness and Pentecostal pastors were sympathetic to the cause of unions and socialists and were known to have supported strikers in the textile mills of the Carolinas and the fields of California. But they were the exception.

The anticommunism of the churches was well in line with the broader ideology of the postwar United States. In a time of heightened ideological tension, U.S. political leaders seized on America's commitment to God, using it to draw a clear line between the nation and its Communist enemies. In 1954, Congress passed legislation inserting the phrase "under God" in the Pledge of Allegiance to the Flag, borrowing the phrase from Lincoln's Gettysburg address. Scores of religious organizations supported the action, and more than a million Americans wrote their congressmen to recommend a yea vote. Senator Homer Ferguson, the Michigan Republican who introduced the bill, noted that the addition of the two words would underscore the contrast with the Soviet government, "which rejects the very existence of God."

Two years later, "In God We Trust" was adopted as the national motto, and the phrase was placed on new paper money. Congressman Charles E. Bennett of Florida, a Democrat, said: "In these days when imperialistic and materialistic communism seeks to attack and to destroy freedom, it is proper for us to seek continuously for ways to strengthen the foundations of our freedom. At the base of our freedom is our faith in God and the desire of Americans to live by His will and by His guidance."[4]

Religion and respectability went hand in hand in Washington. President Truman attended church regularly; Eisenhower was baptized and became a member of the Presbyterian Church a few days after taking office. In the 1950s, the National Prayer Breakfast became a highly visible Washington institution, and Billy Graham developed a close personal relationship with Vice President Nixon. Aside from such concrete evidence of the commingling of God and country, government policy was firmly committed to upholding traditional family values in ways that were reassuring to conservative Christians.

Prayers and Bible reading had been a regular part of public school instruction since Colonial times. A national survey in 1946 showed that Bible reading was *required* in schools in thirteen states and authorized as a local option in twenty-five more. In 1960, one third of the nation's schools opened each morning with a devotional prayer.[5]

Abortion was illegal, and many books, such as Henry Miller's *Tropic of Cancer*, were suppressed on grounds of obscenity. It was forbidden to Catholics by their church to obtain civil divorces, and annulments were extremely hard to come by; fundamentalists generally condoned divorce only in cases of fornication and adultery.

American divorce rates remained remarkably constant in the 1950s, and most families still were made up of working husband and stay-at-home wife; in 1960, 70 percent of all married women were full-time homemakers.

The first signs of a change in the government's position as defender and ally of the "traditional" family appeared in the late 1950s. In 1957, the U.S. Supreme Court issued the first of a series of decisions that created new and more stringent standards for declaring works of literature or art obscene. More than thirty obscenity rulings eventually were reversed for failure to meet the new tests. In 1960, the Food and Drug Administration approved Enovid, a 100 percent effective oral contraceptive for women. Then in 1962 came the bombshell. The Supreme Court ruled that a nondenominational school prayer composed by the New York Board of Regents was an unconstitutional establishment of religion by the state. The decision was actually intended to protect minorities—there had been a long history of the Jehovah's Witnesses being harassed and arrested for refusal to salute the flag, for example. But many evangelicals, especially those from predominantly white Protestant communities, saw it differently—as an imposition of secular orthodoxy. A year later, the court, leaving no doubt that it meant business, ruled that reciting Biblical passages in school was also unconstitutional.

Oca described his feelings at the time: "When we see things like that coming up and see how desperate some of our people in government are and what they will do, the extent they'll go to stop God's work and stop prayer, then we know what some of them will do. We'll finally be like the Communist nation where no one will be allowed to pray. We can see the handwriting on the wall. They're trying right now, and they're not letting up."

The prayer decision added to his anxiety about the drift of American society. Looking back over the previous quarter century, he believed that the trouble for the American family began in World War II, with tens of thousands of women going to work. He saw a distinction between what some women were doing and Ruby, Cora, and Cleo working in the fields or in sheds. "They really had to work," he said. "But, boy, they was going to have their kids right by their side, like Ruby picking cotton back there at Twin Pines Ranch.

"When the women went off to work in the defense plants and all and making big money, they come home with their big check and first thing you know, the kids were bothering them. They were going one way and their husband going the other. I think a woman's place is in the home if she's got children, raising those children upright, taking care of her home, taking care of her husband, and I feel that if women throughout this country took their place at home directing their children there'd be a lot of jobs for men."

The arrival of rock 'n' roll in the 1950s was to Oca a direct challenge to the authority of the American family. For the first time, a truly national youth culture, separate from the adult culture, emerged, and the first clue to its emergence were the jarring, pounding rhythms of rock. Oca considered rock music to be "demon possessed."

Until 1964, it did not occur to him that the uneasiness he was feeling could be expressed through the political process. The two political parties did not leave much to choose between. Eisenhower was a moderate Republican who sought accommodation with the Soviet Union and refused to send American troops into Hungary to support that country's anti-Communist uprising in 1956. Supreme Court Chief Justice Earl Warren had been an "education governor" of California who had supported generous financing of the state's public school and university system and had presided over the prayer decision. He was a Republican.

Most Pentecostals were wary of political involvement of any kind. As late as the eve of World War II, Pentecostalism was still a small, poor movement on the fringes of American society and the conservative religious community. After decades of sectarian battling, there were twenty-six different Pentecostal sects, and most Pentecostals worshiped in small churches called "works" on the edge of towns or in the country. They lived in relative cultural isolation and seemed to prefer it that way. What theological education they provided for their clergy was in carefully supervised settings, such as ten-day Bible schools or, later, Bible institutes that offered a diploma but not a baccalaureate degree. The emphasis was on pastoral and missionary work. In 1939, Southern California Bible College did begin offering a bachelor of arts degree, but then only in Bible studies.[6]

Pentecostals found themselves estranged from and despised by other Protestants, including by non-Pentecostal fundamentalists. Most Pentecostals accepted the word of the Bible as literally true—the virgin birth of Christ, His physical resurrection, and His imminent, visible, and personal Second Coming.[7] Yet they were denounced by fundamentalists in mainstream denominations for the unpardonable vanity of believing that speaking in tongues was a sign of special favor. Some fundamentalist Bible colleges refused to admit Pentecostals. In 1928, the World's Christian Fundamentals Association wrote the

Pentecostals out of the fundamentalist movement, calling them "fanatical and unscriptural."[8]

By the time thousands of Pentecostals went off to World War II, however, leading Pentecostal denominations were becoming uncomfortable with their isolation. In 1943, several sought a rapprochement with their evangelical brethren. The Assemblies of God joined the brand-new National Association of Evangelicals, which promised to shun "bigotry, intolerance, misrepresentation, hate, jealousy, false judgment, and hypocrisy."[9] Then, in 1948, eight Pentecostal denominations with more than a million members founded their own organization, the Pentecostal Fellowship of North America. The platform sought to placate non-Pentecostal fundamentalists with a plank acknowledging the infallibility of scripture.

Fundamentalism was a key link between Pentecostals and the rest of the socially conservative American Protestant universe. Another was afforded by the healing revivals that began in 1947 and continued into the late 1950s. The appeal of Oral Roberts and other Pentecostal healers went far beyond denominational lines.

Roberts did not support political candidates or promote partisan causes. Yet like so many religious leaders before him, he rallied people and prepared them for broader involvement, participation, and engagement. His large grass-roots following, stretching from Georgia to the central valley of California, was one of the first culturally cohesive Sun Belt communities. The movement was anchored in Roberts's home base of Tulsa.

In planning his tent rallies, Roberts worked closely with local Pentecostal businessmen such as Demos Shakarian in Los Angeles. The Shakarian family originally were Armenian Presbyterians. After their arrival in America in 1905, they had gone into the dairy business outside Los Angeles, where they witnessed the Azusa Street revival. Demos Shakarian began sponsoring meetings of healing evangelists, claiming that his sister had been healed after a serious automobile accident and that his dairy herd had been saved from tuberculosis by Kelso Glover, the faith healer who cured Oca's eye during the 1948 revival at Fresno Memorial Auditorium.

Shakarian had in mind organizing hundreds of local fellowships of Christian businessmen, open to all denominations but led by Pentecostals. The formative meetings took place in Fresno after an Oral Roberts revival in November 1951. The businessmen convened their organizing meeting at the Belmont Inn in Fresno, selecting an "upper room"—a favored Pentecostal custom dating back to the Holiness days, when the faithful sought to dramatize their particular closeness to the lives of Jesus and the Apostles. Oca was present and became a charter member. Dick and Doris Tatham sang for the businessmen assembled for a breakfast. Oral Roberts was the main attraction, but those in attendance constituted the makings of Fresno's Pentecostal elite. Earl Draper, a local real-estate and insurance man who said he'd been cured of tuberculosis by the power of prayer was elected secretary. There were insurance and real-estate men like him, contractors, and owners of small and medium-sized retail stores.

Oca drove down to further meetings at Clifton's Cafeteria in Los Angeles and began to contribute regularly to Roberts's ministry. The men at these meetings called themselves the Full Gospel Business Men's Fellowship, and they represented a search by rising Pentecostals for self-respect and wider associations, on their own terms. Thousands of former field-workers, mechanics, and truck drivers, had now become self-employed farmers, contractors, and auto dealers.[10] But such people would have felt uncomfortable joining the Rotary, the Lions Club, or a political organization. The Full Gospel Business Men's Fellowship was quintessentially American. Its founding was a reminder of the counterforces that are steadily at work against the processes of homogenization.

The luncheon and dinner meetings revolved around business and the Lord, not politics. But the local fellowships provided a center for a new generation of religious businessmen with predominantly conservative outlooks. In 1954, Vice President Richard Nixon visited the organization's convention in Washington, D.C. Ten years later, speakers at meetings of the Full Gospel Business Men's Fellowship, which had now added the word "International" to its name, set a more political agenda. A speaker at a conference in 1964 declared that at the founding of the United Nations, U.S. leaders "accommodated [themselves] to the Russian Communists, and so dishonored God. And as we excluded the Bible from our schools so we did away with the last bulwark against the communist termites who are gnawing at the very foundations of our God-given Christian republic."[11]

Taking stands on the issues was one thing. Active partisan involvement in election campaigns was another. In 1947, the conservative theologian Carl F. Henry wrote "Uneasy Conscience of American Fundamentalism," in which he criticized the political apathy of religious conservatives. Their separatism from the political debate, he argued, let "modernists" set the national agenda. As a result, Henry warned, America was sliding relentlessly toward secularism.

Some were heeding his words. In 1956, *Christianity Today* magazine began publishing. Supported by the conservative oil millionaire

J. Howard Pew,[12] it offered an alternative to the line espoused by *Christian Century*, a well-established organ of the liberal Protestant churches. Pew also financed the Christian Freedom Foundation, whose goal was to train "real Christians" for public office. Its funding was later taken over by Amway Corporation president Richard DeVos, who in the late 1970s also became an influential figure in the conservative movement.

There was also the remarkable mass appeal of the nation's best-known evangelist, Billy Graham. Graham, unlike Roberts and the tent healers, was not Pentecostal, but many Pentecostals admired him. His Crusade for Jesus emphasized family values and subtly laid the groundwork for the "moral issues" to enter the national political debate. His statements in the 1950s sometimes echoed the John Birch Society line. He frequently attacked the United Nations, the United Council of Churches, and the New Deal, which he suggested had undermined laissez-faire economics, the Protestant ethic, and individual self-reliance. The home, he argued, was where the defense of the nation had to start since "one of the great goals of communism is to destroy the American home. If the Communists can destroy the American home and cause moral deterioration in this country, that group will have done to us what they did to France when the German armies invaded the Maginot Line."[13]

Oca saw nothing wrong with political involvement by Christians, though he believed in the imminence of Christ's return and the "rapture" of the church. "Our people have always looked for the coming of Lord," he said. "That's why we've always been very strict. We don't know the day or the hour the son of man cometh. But you will know the season." But the Bible, he said, instructed Christians to "occupy until He comes." In his opinion Christians had an obligation to defend their interests. "As long as we're here, we can't sit down and say, 'The Lord will be here in five years, so I'm not going to worry about foreign policy.' I felt that if the Russians came in and marched on our soil, I'd be one of the first to say, 'Give me a rifle.'

"I heard a lot of our preachers say, 'I'm ordered by my government to protect my country and I'm a full-blooded American.' . . . And I've heard them say, 'I'll defend my country, my wife and daughters from bein' raped and beat and killed, and our country taken over.' There's no way I'll set back and say I don't want to go out. I think I'm justified in the eyes of God to go out and do it. Because in the old Bible they had wars. God ordered the destruction of whole cities and every living thing in them."

His call to a more politically active life came after a heart attack he suffered in 1962 while cranking up a lawn mower outside his house. He was hospitalized for nineteen days and forced to slow down. But it didn't stop him. He had been supervising the conversion of a decommissioned county school into a mental hospital when he was taken ill; subsequently, he bought another school and a decommissioned hospital in Selma. He concluded the latter purchase in January 1963, paying $25,000 for yet another white elephant. It became part of Oca Tatham Enterprises. But as various health problems arose, Oca began looking for other less strenuous outlets for his energies.

He had been a Nixon supporter in 1960. Richard M. Nixon was a Republican, a Protestant, and a Californian, running against John F. Kennedy, a Democratic Catholic from the East. In Fresno, Oca's daughter Doris worked as a Republican precinct chairman in the Nixon campaign. But Oca came to admire President Kennedy, who proved his mettle with tough stands against the Russians during the 1961 Berlin crisis and the 1962 Cuban missile crisis. "I liked the way he came across," he said. "I thought in many cases his judgment was very good. I had respect for the Kennedy family, for his brother, his mother. And I remember saying, 'Well, you have to hand it to him, the Kennedy family as a whole looks like a pretty fine family, pretty clean. Good church people and good Catholics.' "

He was devastated by Kennedy's assassination in November 1963. Down in Delano, Cora Tatham cried as if she had lost one of her own sons. "There was no Democrat or Republican in me then," said Oca. "We lost our leader. I was hurt bad, and I didn't get over it in a day or two. I hurt a long time over that. You almost felt too sad to cry."

Within a few months, though, he found his first true political hero in Barry Goldwater.

Oca viewed Goldwater as a fellow free man of the Western Republic. When Goldwater used the words "freedom" and "liberty," Oca heard a theme that harked back to the days of the unsurveyed frontier. Goldwater wasn't talking about civil rights or the First Amendment, but about throwing off the straitjacket of government regulation and a class structure that denied opportunity to some. Goldwater's freedom implied social mobility based on individual enterprise rather than on credentials, status, or political connections.

The Arizonan was a new kind of Republican candidate. For the conservative Old Guard, anchored in the North and the Midwest, educated at Ivy League schools and the major state universities, supportive of civil rights and free market economics, the idea of an alliance with a radical, populist element centered in the South and the West and concerned mainly with cultural issues and anticommunism was disturbing. The Goldwater candidacy veered off on a whole new tangent, utilizing a range of issues that were new for a Republican, such as law and order, crime, and race, and that questioned the modus vivendi with the Soviet Union resulting from the United States' bipartisan foreign policy of containment rather than victory. Though crime rates in 1964 were small compared with what they would later become, crime emerged in 1964 as one of the new, soft issues. Supreme Court decisions such as *Miranda v. Arizona* and *Mallory v. United States*, which broadened constitutional protection for criminal suspects through the right to remain silent and to receive a speedy trial, angered many Americans. The crime issue, as Goldwater skillfully exploited it, resulted in a white mainstream backlash that set the pattern for subsequent reactions against laws and judicial decisions broadening the rights of blacks, women, and gays in the 1960s and 1970s.

Similarly, the new GOP hierarchy was able to make capital with white voters on the race issue. While Eisenhower had sent troops to protect the court-ordered desegregation of Central High School in Little Rock, Arkansas, Goldwater was one of only eight Republican senators to cast his vote against the 1964 Civil Rights Act. The vote, which was taken on July 2, 1964, just as the 1964 campaign was heating up, opened a new epoch for the Republican Party. A party that for a century had been associated with Abraham Lincoln and the emancipation of blacks was to become a home not only for unreconstructed racists, but also for millions of whites who felt threatened by the social revolution of the coming decade in all its forms, from forced busing to women's assertiveness. In the short term, the strategy was to prove disastrous. But it positioned the GOP to split the traditional Democratic coalition, enabling it to become a nearly all-white party with an ideological and cultural agenda accessible to millions of "traditional" voters.[14]

Goldwater, an Episcopalian with a Jewish father, did not make an overt appeal to the born-again Christian camp, as Reagan would do in 1980. His political strategists, including Richard Viguerie, did seek out fundamentalists such as Billy James Hargis. Goldwater, Oca knew, drank liquor.

That was a minor drawback, however, compared with Goldwater's virtues. First and foremost, it seemed to Oca that Goldwater could be counted on to deal with the Communists in Vietnam:

"I figured that the Democrats had always gotten us into war and the Republicans had got us out and, well, hearing Goldwater talk, he was tough. I believed he would do exactly what he said, he'd stop that war. Because when he was asked what he would do, he said, 'I'll go in and bomb hell out of them,' and I thought, that's the only way to stop it."

Goldwater had suggested that it might make sense to defoliate the North Vietnamese Communists' supply routes with low-yield atomic weapons. Oca, similarly, did not believe in "pussyfooting around." Goldwater was "a man who'd do what he said he'd do, and wouldn't listen to a bunch of junk, and be swayed. He'd just go out and take care of the problem. That's how I was sold on the guy. I figured that we were going to have to deal pretty tough with the Communists, and we could not deal with them from a Christian way, saying God bless you, you're a great guy, and you ought to quit fighting. You don't win wars that way."

In 1954, Goldwater had voted against the Senate's censure of Senator Joseph McCarthy and in fact had defended him as having "the strongest voice now speaking in America against communism." Oca believed that "McCarthy was probably nearer right than wrong. Our government had a lot of Communists in it." McCarthy had touched the populist heartstrings, but he hadn't been quite respectable enough to create a movement.

Soon after the Republican convention, Oca wrote out a check to the Goldwater campaign, his first gift of money to politics. Then he went down to Goldwater headquarters in Fresno and volunteered.

"It was the first time I'd ever been involved that heavy in my life, but I felt like I had something to work for because I disapproved of that war and the way it was being handled," he recalled.

FROM TIME TO TIME during that fall of 1964, Oca slid into his trademark Cadillac and headed out onto Highway 99. The cotton harvest was in full swing. In the flat fields on both sides of the road, bored-looking men in western shirts, jeans, and dark glasses loitered around metal cotton wagons full of the white cargo. Off in the hazy distance the Sierras were barely visible through a haze of dust stirred up by trucks and tractors.

Selma, Tulare, Tipton, Earlimart—the familiar little farming towns came and went. Oca exited at Delano and found a place to park on Main Street. Several new business propositions had been drawing him back to his mother's hometown lately. He had been talking to a man about buying a funeral home, and he was looking into a seventy-bed convalescent hospital, a proposal that had embroiled him in yet another collision with local authorities.

He gathered up an armful of books and walked into a store where he knew the proprietor.

"How many of these do you think you could give away to people who'll *read* 'em and not *burn* 'em?" Oca asked. The man looked at the cover: *The Conscience of a Conservative*, by Barry Goldwater.

"I figured you for a staunch Republican," said Oca. "I'm supportin' the guy. He said he'd go in and bomb hell out of the North Vietnamese, and I believe him. That's the only way to stop it, and I'm doing what I can."

He didn't give the owner time to reply. "Suppose I leave half a dozen. Just remember to tell 'em that the Democrats always get us into these things, and the Republicans get us out."

In Fresno he hooked up with other local Goldwater men and women, attended meetings, and lobbied friends. For the good of the cause Oca drove across town and gassed up at the service station owned by a black businessman who had been losing customers due to his support of Goldwater. Oca got several friends to buy their fuel there, too, and they kept the man in business for the duration of the campaign.

The Goldwater cause became a family enterprise. Bill Tatham joined the United Republicans of California, a group of young conservatives for Goldwater, and subscribed to *National Review*, the conservative magazine. He also joined a local Goldwater committee that included several druggists and a doctor.

While attending Southern California College as a freshman, Renee Tatham was elected president of the Costa Mesa Young Republicans, which spearheaded the local Goldwater effort.

Doris and Gordon Weaver, now living in the San Francisco Bay area, went all out for Goldwater. Gordon's sense of the Communist threat, first instilled in the churches his father pastored, had deepened during his experiences in the 1950s monitoring Soviet transmissions for the Army Security Agency on the East German border. He had almost taken a job afterward with the National Security Agency, the secretive government organization that monitors Communist communications and breaks Communist codes. Now Oca inundated the Weavers with stacks of campaign literature and copies of *The Conscience of a Conservative*. On Election Day, the two Weaver children paraded with "Vote for Goldwater" signs across the street from one of the polling places in San Pablo.

Goldwater's defeat was a bitter disappointment to the Tathams, who took no consolation from the fact that Lyndon Johnson was a man of the Texas hill country, with whom many Okies could easily identify, for they saw Johnson as a Washington insider, a president who had plans for a vastly expanded role for the central government and who stood on the opposite side of just about every issue from them. Doris even shed a few tears. It seemed "just like doomsday," she said, and she half expected something dramatic to happen if Goldwater lost. But life went on.

A year after the election, Oca and Ruby traveled to England with hundreds of other members of the Full Gospel Business Men's Fellowship International. Demos Shakarian, who led the group, borrowed a name from the Cold War and called it an "airlift." Shakarian dispatched "Love Jesus" squads to outlying towns and cities and offered free haircuts to British beatniks at the London Hilton. Oral Roberts, who had just founded Oral Roberts University in Tulsa, addressed the windup of the convention at Royal Albert Hall.[15] Oca purchased a bowler hat for himself and his sons and had his picture taken for his scrapbook.

LYNDON JOHNSON had won a huge victory in 1964, but four years later the Democrats surrendered the presidency to Richard Nixon. In that short period of time, the politics of the United States changed in fundamental ways. Henceforth, for at least the next generation, the Sun Belt would have a lock on the White House, much as the South had controlled most elections before the Civil War. After Kennedy, every elected president had strong associations with the Sun Belt—Johnson, Nixon, and Carter by birth, Bush and Reagan by adoption. The Republican Party succeeded in creating a remarkably durable presidential coalition, representing a broad spectrum of white America, ranging from the lower-middle class to the rich. The Democratic Party watched as its New Deal coalition of minorities, lower-income whites, and liberal elements of the middle class was torn asunder by the reaction to judicial and legislative developments. The Johnson presidency gave the country Medicare and Medicaid and continued the era of pork-barrel federal projects that had been so important to vulnerable geographies, such as California's central valley. Yet by recasting and vastly magnifying the role of the central government, through income redistribution programs and civil rights legislation, Johnson's legislative record awakened the slumbering hound of Jeffersonian populism. Between 1964 and 1968, the fundamental political premise of the New Deal was turned on its head. Millions of middle- and lower-middle-class whites suddenly felt threatened more by the poor than by the rich. And the poor now were no longer the distressed working class of the 1930s, but the white "crackers" in the South, the "hillbillies" on the Appalachian slopes—and especially the blacks and other minorities.

Johnson had envisioned the Great Society as a natural extension of the social-political agenda begun by Roosevelt. But working-class Americans resented income redistribution programs that favored people whom they found undeserving, programs designed by professors, urban planners, social-welfare workers, and international economists.[16] The scope of Johnson's legislative record was breathtaking. It included the Civil Rights Act, the Economic Opportunity Act, the Voting Rights Act, the Elementary and Secondary Education Act, model cities, and rent subsidies for low-income housing.[17] All told, the new laws added up to an unprecedented intervention by the federal bureaucracy and federal judiciary in schools, neighborhoods, hospitals, public facilities, and employment halls. But the costs and impact of these programs fell disproportionately on the white lower-middle class that for decades had been a core part of the New Deal constituency. Liberals designing the education and housing policies, for example, had the resources to send their children to private schools or live in neighborhoods far removed from urban ghettos. Working-class whites were more likely to attend schools affected by busing orders or to compete with blacks and Hispanics for jobs and housing.

The new situation was a unique opportunity for the Republican Party: for the first time since the New Deal, it could offer itself to the American people as the party of the average man. The demonstrations by students at the University of California in Berkeley in 1964 and the riots by poor blacks in Watts in 1965 focused attention on liberal privilege and black rebellion, the Achilles' heels of the Democratic coalition. The symbolism of the Democratic dilemma was stark: six days after a Democratic Congress passed the landmark Voting Rights Act of 1965, the rioting and burning began in Watts. The Democratic plan for peaceful change was stillborn. Disorders flared later in other cities, finally reaching to within a few blocks of the White House in April 1968. By then, the distinction between peaceful protest and unfocused revolt was blurring in the minds of frightened whites. The stage was set for the movement begun under Goldwater to escape at last from the economic issues, which Democrats had exploited so successfully for three decades. With the economy strong, it was possible for George Wallace, Richard Nixon, and eventually Ronald Reagan to shape a new kind of coalition politics that grouped voters by values and biases rather than by income.

Voting figures for the six counties in the southern part of the San Joaquin Valley in 1964, 1966, and 1968 told the story of this shift. Truman, a Missourian with strong Midwestern beliefs, had been popular with Okies. His folksy, direct style, uncomplicated religious and family values, and support for social legislation that rewarded the working and the deserving (such as the GI Bill) resonated with Okies. And when Okies turned out in large numbers to vote for Eisenhower, the war hero and former wartime commander, they did not alter their Democratic leanings.

In 1964, Johnson swamped Goldwater in all six southernmost valley counties. But two years later, Ronald Reagan, in defeating the liberal Democrat Edmund G. "Pat" Brown for governor, won all six. Then, in 1968, a fundamental realignment began. Hubert Humphrey, running for President against Richard Nixon, won Merced County, barely edged out Nixon in Fresno, Madera, and Kings, but lost Kern and was badly beaten in Tulare. The deeper one went into the Okie strongholds, the weaker Humphrey became.

Humphrey may well have been hurt by a small but decisive move by traditionally Democratic white voters to George Wallace, running that year as a third-party candidate on the ticket of his American Independent Party. Wallace polled between 7 and 11 percent of the total in each of the six counties in the southern valley, enough to shift the balance of power. If the Wallace vote had gone to Nixon, Humphrey still would have won Fresno County, that bastion of ethnic diversity, but he would have lost the other five. Four years later, Wallace was not on the ballot, and Nixon, running against the liberal George McGovern, captured the Wallace vote of the previous election.

In the next few years, Kern County voted more conservatively than the rest of California on a series of key state measures, including the death penalty, marijuana legalization, homosexual rights, and school busing. Country music, the cultural glue that linked Bakersfield with Nashville, reflected the increasing popularity of "traditional" views. Songs of such stars as Merle Haggard sprang to the defense of God, country, hard work, the patriarchal family, and, at least implicitly, the white community.[18] The new Republican presidential majority had coalesced.

Wallace had run as a segregationist in several northern primaries in 1964, but the complex response to his 1968 campaign could not be explained by racism alone. Quite aside from the issue of segregation, whose illegality and unconstitutionality had basically been decided by 1968, he painted a convincing picture of a privileged, coercive, liberal Democratic establishment—a *political* upper crust that many average voters perceived as more threatening than the *moneyed* upper crust of the Republican Party.[19]

Most Tathams apparently voted in 1968 for Nixon, not Wallace, but the populist element of the Wallace message held some appeal.

And the Tathams were not extremists. Oca considered the John Birch Society "a little wild . . . radicals." Goldwater was not a fanatic, but a friend of Jack Kennedy's, an easygoing Episcopalian, and a man from a comfortably affluent business family. (If proof of Goldwater's credentials as a social moderate were needed, he gave it in September 1981, in a stunning attack on the Moral Majority, pro-life, and other such New Right groups: "I can say with conviction that these groups have little or nothing to do with conservative or liberal politics.")[20]

The Tathams emphatically rejected racism. Pentecostals were, after all, people of Azusa Street. The Klan, along with all other secret societies, was forbidden to Pentecostals. Tathams had grown up in the presence of colored pastors—Oca had been saved in the colored church in Vian. It was a simple fact that Tathams believed in, and tried to practice, Christian brotherhood. Moreover, Oca was too much the free trader, the individualist, the believer in maximum social mobility to approve of segregation: an organized system in which one powerful group formally denied opportunity to another, weaker one. The stories that came alive for him were those of individual achievement, and the greater the odds, the more he celebrated the overcomer. He was a cheerleader for individual initiative and success, and his heroes included blacks who rose in the armed forces or who founded big churches. The lynching of blacks and the burning of black babies by the Klan, which he knew about from Tulsa days, sickened him. But that did not mean that Oca was free of prejudice, nor did it make him an enthusiast for civil rights enforced and imposed by the central government.

Since its founding in 1914, his church, the Assemblies of God had compiled an uninspiring record in addressing the problem of

racial segregation and civil rights. By 1914, white and black Pentecostals had divided their sects along racial lines. In 1939, the General
Presbytery disapproved the ordination of black men and women,
though the move may have been partly out of deference to the
Church of God in Christ, the leading black Pentecostal denomination.
The Reverend Bob Harrison was the Jackie Robinson of the Assemblies of God, the first black to attend an Assemblies bible college and
to be ordained after the war—but only in 1957, six years after he
applied. In the 1940s, the Assemblies actually had given consideration
to a proposal for a *segregated* black fellowship within the denomination. In 1965, at the peak of the civil rights movement, the General
Council adopted a resolution affirming civil rights. It urged members
to "discourage unfair and discriminatory practices" and asserted that
those in authority have a "moral responsibility toward the creation of
those situations which will provide equal rights and opportunities for
every individual." In 1968 the General Presbytery adopted a major
statement declaring that "the spirit of alienation, rebellion and racism
is a universal human weakness."[21] The statement seemed to repudiate
equally segregation (racism) and black violence (rebellion). The decla-
ration did not mention civil rights or social justice, though it did
pledge the denomination to "exert our influence as Christian citizens
to justifiable social action in . . . employment, equal opportunity and
other beneficial matters." Time and again black Pentecostal churches
pleaded in vain for more support in the area of civil rights from their
white brethren.

Oca said, "They could come in and we'd accept them as friends
and reverends, and, you know, treat them nice, but not license them."
He had heard stories about "the morals of those old-time black
preachers," though he was quick to acknowledge that white preachers
often left plenty to be desired in the moral sphere as well.

Goldwater's candidacy in 1964 had been a kind of political trump
card played against the Democrats, for it made it possible for whites
in the reborn Republican Party to take a principled stand against the
massive central government intervention on behalf of blacks and
minorities while credibly expressing opposition to racism and segregation.[22] Goldwater himself insisted that he was opposed to segregation. It was this position that individualistic Tathams, with their
intense suspicion of government, could legitimately assume.

Oca's concerns were deepened, he said, when blacks went "on the
rampage," beginning with Watts in 1965. He kept expecting them to
do something and "wondered why they *didn't* do something, like start

burning our churches." In most cases, though, the civil rights issues were not of pressing immediacy to him, Ruby, and their children. Having departed the small farming towns where whites, blacks, and Mexicans still competed for housing, jobs, and educational resources, they had created living arrangements that insulated them in most ways from the raging fires of race conflict.

Two years after Goldwater's defeat, Oca found yet another champion in Ronald Reagan. He volunteered in his campaign around Fresno, handing out buttons and bumper stickers and chipping in some money. This time he met less resistance from Okie friends about voting for a Republican.

That same year, Oca's daughter Doris and her husband, Gordon Weaver, found themselves drawn into one of the early skirmishes of the cultural wars.

Moving from Fresno to the San Francisco Bay area in 1962, the Weavers had found themselves in one of the crossroads of American ideology. Berkeley was just over the Oakland hills, Marin County just beyond that. There was the black ghetto in Oakland, the Students for a Democratic Society in Berkeley, gays mobilizing their power in San Francisco, Birchers in Livermore.

In 1966, the Weavers moved to the suburban town of San Ramón, on the east side of the Oakland hills, and enrolled their two oldest daughters in the San Ramón Valley Unified School District. The district was becoming a laboratory for testing some of the new ideas percolating through the education community. In 1964, Richard L. Foster was hired as superintendent. Foster was a believer in "student participation." He wanted to encourage even very young students to design their own learning styles. Though it was some years before mandated school busing, Foster also organized an impromptu busing program, taking black and low-income children from Oakland to spend the day at San Ramón's district high school in a program designed to deepen the social awareness of San Ramón's predominantly white children. Foster attributed the storm of protest over this plan to the racism of the suburban parents.

The good public school system, along with lower taxes and less polluted air, had been among the reasons for the Weavers' move to San Ramón. But Doris soon got wind of strange goings-on at Country Club Elementary School. Her daughter Gina had been coming home with stories of no assigned desks or places to study and children being allowed to study outside. Gina, it turned out, was in one of the new "unstructured" classrooms. Doris did some checking, and what she discovered made her angry. Some of the teachers, she learned, had received "sensitivity training," a phrase that connected in Doris's mind with hot tubs, Big Sur, and marijuana smoking. She and a small group of mothers began attending school board meetings and making their dissatisfaction known. Foster, she felt, had to be stopped.

Among the people from whom she received practical advice and encouragement over the next few months were members of the John Birch Society. Doris was not a member, but there was a Birch bookstore up the road in Walnut Creek, and an active chapter in Livermore, home of one of the country's leading weapons laboratories. Communist penetration of America's schools was a main concern of the Birch organization in that era, and some Birchers saw sensitivity training as a Communist trick to get Americans to let down their guard against hostile ideologies. From local Birch people, Doris received agendas of coming school board meetings and advice on how to deal with unfriendly school bureaucrats.

Doris and her group showed up at school meetings with clipboards and pens. "I don't care if you just write down zeros and x's, just act like you're taking notes," Doris told the mothers.

At one meeting with school officials, she spoke up, and some years later she paraphrased what she had said: "If we hear of one more thing happening, if anybody's clothes come off in the class, or if anything else like this happens, let me tell you there are enough mothers that are organized. We will have a mother in this class when it opens and when it closes, and every day we will have a tape recorder. We'll sit there and write everything that's said and draw pictures of what's happening. I think we can probably get a tape recorder in there because it shouldn't be a secret class. It's a public class, and we will tell you ahead of time if you need to know who's coming. We'll give you a schedule of who will monitor the class and if we find out it's happening in any other school or classroom, we'll get organized so that every room, if we have to, will have parents in it."

By 1968, the school controversy in Oakland was district-wide and bitter. Foster had his supporters. "Teacher-student-parent enthusiasm has grown tremendously in the three years Dr. Foster has been here. Students are developing an inner direction and real sense of responsibility under his administration," one parent said at a meeting reported in the Oakland *Tribune*. But a Danville parent charged that students had been exposed to "salacious" literature and left-wing speakers. Teachers, he said, "seem to encourage a sort of anti-parent, anti-America, we're-unfair-to-minorities, and the-war-in-Vietnam-is-illegal attitude."[23]

In October 1968, Gordon and Doris returned from a trip to Europe just in time to hear the news: Foster had announced he would resign at the end of the school year to take up a new offer at Berkeley.

It was a small triumph and a harbinger of the civil war among Californians still to come.

CHAPTER FOURTEEN

THE VALLEY: 1976

SPLASHING AROUND after school in the swimming pools of rich farmers in the early 1960s, Eldon Tackett's boy, Gene, sometimes got a peculiar giddy feeling. It wasn't until he was a Peace Corps volunteer in a small village in India that he began to understand what may have been behind those strange sensations: He had, he realized, "stepped off my allotted place in life." In the Hindu caste system this was a seditious act that could unbalance the whole social order. In the United States, it was just part of the dream.

In America, the son of an Okie who had picked oranges could aspire to anything. So one January day in 1976, Gene called his parents down to the Kern County courthouse in Bakersfield and asked them to stand by him while he announced that he was a candidate for the Kern County Board of Supervisors. A few reporters showed up and took notes. Gene, the former Peace Corps volunteer and ACTION worker, wore an open-necked shirt and suede jacket—somewhat unusual garb in a town in which the dress options usually came down to western shirts or coat and tie. He had made only one concession to convention: he shaved off his beard.

The Tacketts were not, as Gene put it, "part of the land-ownership group" in McFarland. His mother, Loretta, cleaned people's homes and took in laundry. His dad still worked for the SMUD irrigation district as a ditch rider, sometimes standing waist-deep in muddy water, bleeding from the sharp pieces of concrete chipped off by the jackhammering when he repaired a pipe. Gene, the Tacketts' only child, was a worker, too. When he had to choose between high school football or his after-school job bagging groceries, he kept the job.

The central valley had its caste system, of course. As far as Gene knew, his dad had never been invited to the home of one of the wealthy farmers. But the social structure of the valley towns was porous: the votes of rich ranchers' children had helped elect Gene president of the student body in his junior year at McFarland High School. And he had his dreams—almost all of them involved getting out into the world beyond the mountain ranges. Some Saturday nights he'd pick up his paycheck from the Farmer Boy Market and take his friend Cathy to dinner in Bakersfield—not to a pizza joint with the rest of the crowd but to a real restaurant where they were attended by waiters. Cathy, the daughter of a Bakersfield meat cutter, had big dreams, too. That was what made those evenings so magical. They shared their dreams and let the roller coaster of possibilities take them for a wild ride.

Not that Gene was unhappy with McFarland or his parents. Quite the contrary. His close-to-ideal childhood was one of the reasons he felt confident about moving out into the world.

He cherished his Oklahoma connections and identity, imprinted on him by many experiences, including visiting relatives in farm labor camps in the 1940s and 1950s. Their houses were smaller and warmer than what Gene was accustomed to, and the food cooking on the little stoves smelled different. He was only five years old and still living in Porterville when his Uncle Smitty taught him to say "Hubba! Hubba!" to the women who passed his parents' home on Hockett Street. Uncle Smitty had been hit with shrapnel during the war, and afterward he married several times, drank hard, and worked hard, too, building dams and canals. Uncle Smitty took Gene for wild rides along the ditch banks in his '49 Chevrolet convertible. Years later, when he had moved back to Oklahoma, Uncle Smitty wisecracked that the police were "so sorry to see me leave they chased me clear to Tulare County to try to get me to come back." The Oklahoma relatives who flitted through his life seemed to Gene like wonderful characters.

Gene grew up admiring the live-hard, die-young philosophy of

James Dean, who crashed and died in the foothills over the mountains from Bakersfield. But about the closest Gene came to rebel behavior himself was to take the family car to watch drag racing in Delano when he should have been at a school meeting. The truth was that neither McFarland nor his parents gave Gene much to rebel against. Eldon and Loretta raised their only child to be honest, responsible, hardworking, truthful, and caring. Beyond that, they didn't place too many limits. Eldon didn't consider it a sin if Gene necked in the used MG he had purchased with his own money. He wanted to teach his boy to be responsible, not to shelter him from the world. When a second cousin who was a reserve deputy sheriff held a showing of some blue movies that had been confiscated from a local citizen, Eldon did not object to Gene's tagging along. When the boy turned sixteen, the father gave him a pack of condoms and told him it was important to act responsibly.

Loretta, who had grown up in Baptist churches in Oklahoma, had childhood memories of brush arbors and preachers. Eldon was religious in his own way. It seemed to Gene that he had the fear of God, for he kept a small Bible in his car, stuffed in the crevice between the dashboard and the rearview mirror. But except for trips back to Oklahoma to visit Loretta's mother, the Tacketts did not attend church, though they dropped Gene off at the Baptist Sunday school. When Gene was saved, he didn't cuss for several months, but he felt uncomfortable with the talk against lipstick and dancing and with some of the hypocrisy. It seemed to him that some of the leading men of the church treated their wives differently at Sunday services than they did when they took them shopping at the Farmer Boy Market and let them carry all the groceries.

The closest Gene came to serious religious commitment was at the Pentecostal Church of God on the east side of McFarland, the church founded by the Tathams and their friends in the 1930s, where he went to please his girlfriend. Gene found it strange to talk about the upper room, where people spoke in tongues. But when the church had a contest to see which young Christian could bring in the most new people, Gene rounded up his parents and relatives and brought them down. Eldon stood in the rear, hands in pockets, nervously jangling his keys, until his boy collected the prize. Soon afterward, Gene broke up with his girlfriend and that was pretty much the end of his churchgoing.

After graduation he took his Lions Club scholarship and headed over the mountains to the University of California in Santa Barbara in his icebox-white MG. This was no Okie school. In Santa Barbara, "the valley" didn't mean Bakersfield, Fresno, and Stockton; it meant the San Fernando Valley, with all its wealth and sophistication. Gene loved college. It was 1961, and Americans of all backgrounds were beginning to take pride in their color and ethnicity. Gene felt he had something to be proud of, too, and he relished the fact he was an Okie. In his sophomore year he joined a fraternity, and the fun continued. He developed a wide circle of partying friends, drank beer, and fell in love with a woman from L.A.

It took him nearly five years to wake up from this Disneyland fantasy. He was still not close to graduating, had dropped out several times, and had abandoned plans to become a lawyer. He had worn out his welcome at Santa Barbara and was so stressed out after the L.A. woman rejected him that a doctor prescribed Librium.

The Peace Corps helped him get his life back on track. Gene trained for overseas service at the State University of New York at Albany, learning how to raise chickens. He became friends with a Harvard Law graduate by the name of David Copus; assigned to India, Gene and Dave ended up in Susundi, a tiny village of working-caste Hindus and Untouchables, located in a mango orchard at the end of a dirt road a few miles from the Ganges. They lived in an unfurnished fertilizer-storage building, a relic of a failed attempt to establish a farm cooperative. But they soon gave up on the improved outdoor cement latrine and followed the ways of the village.

Once a month, Dave and Gene bicycled to Gazipur and caught a coal-burning train to Benares, the city to which thousands came each day to sprinkle the ashes of their dead on the holy waters of the Ganges. They would order cold beer and sit on the veranda of Clark's Hotel, cadging meals and drinks from Western tourists eager to hear their stories of village life. On a few occasions, they boarded the train for Delhi, stretching out their sleeping bags in the third-class luggage racks.

Dave and Gene stayed for more than a year in Susundi and left with some achievements to show for it. They had introduced the farmers to new strains of wheat and potatoes. When the tour ended, Gene returned to the University of California in Santa Barbara. Motivated as never before, he devoured books on history, political science, and Indian religion until his twenty-sixth birthday took him beyond the age of draft eligibility.

He cut a strange figure on trips back to McFarland. Sunburned and bearded, he had taken to wearing Indian shirts and sandals around the house. On a trip home to Oklahoma with his parents, his hippie appearance was the subject of local talk. "Well, I've heard about 'em, but I never thought I'd see one," Gene overheard a farmer say.

Gene was no hippie, though. "You can cut hair; you can't cut off a drug habit," he told his dad. "I don't use drugs. I wouldn't want to ruin my life."

In 1970, with college and draft anxieties behind him, he rejoined the Peace Corps as a recruiter in Los Angeles. Two years later he was appointed director of the southern California recruiting office of ACTION, the federal volunteer agency that sought volunteers for the Peace Corps and for Vista and other domestic programs. Working for ACTION was a "religious experience," Gene said. "I felt everybody should be pulled out of McFarland and sent to India for two years, that the world would be better off for that. It was exhilarating."

As a top recruiter, Gene canvassed thousands of volunteers, meeting teachers, farmers, soil scientists, and toolmakers. He learned how to talk to reporters and editors on newspapers, and he discovered that he was good at talking about poverty, foreign assistance, and education. Recruiting trips often took him to California Polytechnic State University in San Luis Obispo, where there were people from all over California with agricultural or scientific backgrounds. Some of the teachers were former Peace Corps volunteers from Brazil and Venezuela, and they would get together, go clamming, or have big group dinners and watch slide shows about small-scale technology in Third World countries.

Gene involved his parents in his recruiting work. Eldon took future volunteers on tours of SMUD, and Loretta cooked meals for them. It was part of the training, Gene felt, for the young volunteers to be overwhelmed with hospitality, something that was likely to happen abroad. Sometimes the Tacketts would have a dozen people sleeping off a big home-cooked meal on the floor of their home on Sixth Street in McFarland.

In the middle of all this, Gene began to date a dark-haired former Peace Corps volunteer, Wendy Wayne, who had seen the world as a teacher at a "self-help" school in a tiny Kenyan village. Later she had explored her own Jewish roots during six months on a kibbutz in Israel. Wendy and her five siblings had grown up amid the swirl of parties and political fund-raisers attended by politicians and a Hollywood crowd at their parents' home in Cheviot Hills. Jane Fonda had rehearsed the show she did for the troops in Vietnam at the

Waynes' house. Wendy's mother had high ambitions for her children and for herself, and it took Wendy a long time after she decided not to become a doctor to stop feeling like a failure because she had disappointed her mother.

In 1975, Gene and Wendy quit their jobs and set out on a trip around the world that lasted nine months. They visited Hawaii, Hong Kong, and Thailand, slept on the windswept beaches of Malaysia's coast, and took in the sights of Europe. Gene planned to work in the 1976 presidential campaign of the Peace Corps' first director, R. Sargent Shriver. He even had a "Shriver for President" rubber stamp made and used it on the envelopes he mailed home. The United States, it seemed to him, was ready to make a fresh start in tackling the issues that most interested him: jobs, economic opportunity at home and better relations with the Third World. But Shriver's candidacy fizzled, and Gene found himself back at his parents' home in McFarland without a job. He looked into working for Senator Alan Cranston, who was mounting a bid for another term in Congress, but was told he lacked experience.

The turning point came when Gene looked up Bob Sogge, a former Peace Corps volunteer whom Gene had met when they were both doing recruiting in Los Angeles. Sogge was considering running for Congress in 1978.

"Why not run for county supervisor?" Sogge asked.

Gene experienced the feeling he got in the farmers' swimming pools. He wasn't sure whether he was even registered to vote in Kern County. It had always puzzled Gene why so few Okies were in local politics. He figured that a lot of his people still harbored feelings of inferiority and avoided situations that might expose their lack of education or sophistication. Gene went to the library and reviewed old issues of the Bakersfield *Californian*, trying to learn more about what a supervisor did. The more he read, the more excited he got. The supervisors had a say over the use of land—and thus over the oil, land, and agribusiness companies that dominated Kern County's economy and politics. They approved the budget and oversaw county assistance to the poor and the elderly, which meant that a supervisor could affect people's lives directly. It seemed a natural step from his work in ACTION and the Peace Corps. Then, too, it was a job. It paid $26,000 a year.

The Board of Supervisors technically was nonpartisan but everyone around McFarland knew that Gene and his family were Democrats, the very kind of homegrown moderate-conservative Democrats who had always done well in the central valley. Gene had grown up in a family in which the political ideology was the easygoing populism of the communities along the Friant-Kern Canal, an outgrowth of the east side's history as a place of smaller farms and ranches, some of which were run by successful Okies. The Bureau of Reclamation's 160-acre limitation on eligibility for federal irrigation water guaranteed that the small farm was at the center of the area's official ideology. Unofficially, many ways were found around the limitation, but even well-heeled grape ranchers on the east side felt small compared with the giant land companies and agribusinesses on the west side, around Tulare Lake and in southern Kern County. And some of the big farmers, such as Hollis Roberts, were Democrats.

Gene, like Eldon Tackett, was a Democrat, too. In 1960, Gene had joined a Young Democrats Club at McFarland High School and had gone door-to-door distributing Kennedy brochures. Usually the reception was warm, but sometimes the door was slammed in his face by a person saying, "I wouldn't vote for a Catholic." The night Kennedy won, Gene put on a coat and tie and went to the victory celebration in Bakersfield.

Gene followed Kennedy's presidency with growing enthusiasm. Kennedy stood up to the Communists in Berlin and Cuba, but Gene responded to the other part of the Kennedy message, which urged Americans to ask what they could do for their country and which became the spirit of the Peace Corps.

He learned of Kennedy's assassination in class at Santa Barbara, when the professor came in shaking with rage, shouting, "Those Texas newspapers killed him." Gene packed a suitcase and drove straight back to McFarland to watch the funeral ceremonies on his parents' television set. Most of the time he lay on the couch and felt like crying. It was the first important loss of his life, and it took a long time for the pain to go away.

THE LOCAL KERN COUNTY Republican organization had been slow to exploit the disaffection of the Truman Democrats. During the long dry years after World War II the organization had been little more than a club for a few retail businessmen and car dealers, but Reagan's election to the governorship of California in 1966 energized the party. Reagan's victory captured the imagination of William H. Park, a local geologist. Park himself had been born in Oklahoma, but he was not really an Okie. He wrote articles for oil and gas journals,

through which he was in touch with the big oil companies that dominated Kern County's economy. In 1966, he was elected to Bakersfield's city council and began to build the party from the ground up.
Two Republicans were elected to the state assembly in 1968 with
Park's behind-the-scenes help. Setbacks followed, but in the early
1970s a Bakersfield Community College professor by the name of
William M. Thomas joined the effort to strengthen the party's base.

A young conservative, Thomas turned out to be a gifted organizer
and savvy student of the electorate. (He was something of an Okie
himself, having come to California from Idaho during the war, and
he subsequently married a woman whose parents had arrived in
Porterville from Oklahoma about the same time as Gene's.) By the
1970s, Republicans were winning the Bakersfield congressional seat
and other local offices. When Gene announced his candidacy for
county supervisor in 1976, four of the five members of the Kern
County Board of Supervisors were Republicans.

One tactical problem for Democrats in the lower San Joaquin
Valley concerned Cesar Chavez and his United Farm Workers. Democratic office seekers wanted to endorse Chavez's goals. Though most
of the Hispanic workers in his constituency did not vote, they represented a large pool of future voters. Chavez and his lieutenants were
active in the local Democratic Party. The problem was that Chavez
and his union were disliked by many of the old-line Truman Democrats—the Okies and their descendants who still made up a big voting
bloc in the southern valley. Unlike whites such as the Oca and Ruby
Tatham family, who were moving up and out of the small towns into
the suburbs of larger towns and cities, the poorer whites still living
in the smaller towns felt doubly threatened by Mexican militancy.
Mexicans were beginning to move into formerly all-white housing
districts and to monopolize field work. Chavez's movement was over-
whelmingly for Mexicans, and whites did not feel welcome in it,
though many whites, such as Cleo's cousin-in-law Bill McKinney, still
worked in the field.

Gene had grown up in what would become the center of farm-
worker militancy, and of La Causa. Delano, a few miles up Highway
99 from his parents' home in McFarland, was Chavez's first headquarters. For a time Chavez had lived next door to Cora Tatham on Main
Street and had become a familiar figure in town, walking or driving
with men Cleo called "his bodyguards."

Cleo hated Chavez and his union. "I'd have worked for five dollars
less a day rather than have to work for *him*," she said. "I believe in

being under freedom and not bondage. I believe in the union. But my husband's union was different. I don't believe in pushing people into the union if they don't want to. That takes the freedom away from the other one."

She resented Chavez's tactics with the growers. "If he'd have went in there like a man ought to, and not started runnin' it over 'em, he'd have done all right. He ought to have went in there in a sensible way, and talked to them, and not just gone in and demanded."

Stories about Chavez and his men became part of the folklore of the older generation of whites in the valley towns. Cleo had heard about a farmer who had been run over by Chavez's men on his own farm, about Mexican and Filipino women who had flung hunks of blacktop at police cars; about Chavez's men blocking the entrances to fields. As Cleo saw it, Chavez "cut the white man out from working. The white man lost out in the grapes, and a lot of white people depended on that. If you were from Oklahoma and came out here, you didn't work. He didn't work nothing but Filipinos and Mexicans. It was a fight out in the fields. He came in here and was gonna run things. One of the Kennedys come out here and kissed Chavez. And I thought, Kiss that Chavez! That's the last thing in the world. Boy, people here was burned up. He was a stinker who stirred trouble."

Chavez's first big effort to force the California farmers to come to terms with his union—which involved an appeal to the public throughout the United States to support a grape boycott—had occurred while Gene was serving in the Peace Corps in India. In 1970, the year Gene went to work as a Peace Corps recruiter, Chavez and the growers reached an agreement and farmers came to Delano to sign the first labor contracts with the United Farm Workers. Gene was astonished to hear of Chavez's victory. From his reading of *In Dubious Battle*, John Steinbeck's fictional account of a failed apple strike, he had concluded that farm labor strikes were hopeless because there were always more hungry pickers than jobs. Yet it seemed to Gene that when the farm workers won, the whole valley won because higher wages would be good for the economy as a whole. Gene assumed that his dad would be on the side of the strikers, too. But when Gene came home, Eldon angrily denounced Chavez as a Communist. He had never told Gene the story of how he and a bunch of relatives and friends had helped to break the Mexican strike in Santa Paula in the early 1940s.

Gene did not have much sympathy for the anti-Hispanic attitude of the older generation of Okies. "At some point I realized that the

Okies were a little racist against Hispanics because everyone needs to look down on somebody," he said. "There was a sense of being a lower-class type person out here if you were from the Midwest, a psychological thing. Now *they* could turn around and be that way. They say the same thing about Hispanics that Californians used to say about the Okies—why do they come if they don't like the pay? Why don't they stop having so many children? Why is the state giving them everything? But the *farmers* have an economic interest in welfare and food stamps because that keeps their workers here in the off season. It comes down to a question of who is really being subsidized."

People came, struggled, moved up, and then others came and took their place—Mexicans following Okies, Hmongs following Mexicans, and so on. People who had been at the end of short-handle hoes now worked in office jobs in Bakersfield. The system worked, and Gene believed that government had helped to make it work. Government had outlawed the short-handled hoe, required portable latrines in the fields, passed laws protecting the unionizing efforts of farm workers, set safety standards for labor camps, and provided support for pickers in the off season.

In 1976, Chavez was pushing for adoption of Proposition 14, a statewide referendum that would have allowed his union to conduct membership drives on farm property. On this major issue in the election campaign, Gene did not take a position. He said it was a state matter, not one concerning his local district. It was prudent to keep his distance from Chavez. Early in his campaign, Gene did drive out to Chavez's Forty Acres headquarters, west of Delano, and met some of his people, though he did not meet Chavez. Gene wanted the Hispanic vote, which was substantial in his supervisory district. On the other hand, he understood that too close an association with Chavez would hurt him among the whites and Okies who were the core of his constituency. Already there were jibes from a few friends and relatives that he was too close to the Mexicans.

THE SUPERVISORY district in which Gene was running was itself as big as many congressional districts. It covered some 2,000 square miles and stretching from the farming towns alongside Highway 99 to the China Lake Naval Weapons Laboratory at the edge of the Mojave Desert. It included many of the 1930s "Okietowns," including the old Tatham base of Delano, Shafter (site of one of the big labor camps), parts of Wasco (where Oca had sold potatoes), and McFarland (where Pastor Tom Fuller had preached at the original Pentecostal Church of God).

Gene started his campaign with plenty of assets. Lots of people knew the Tacketts in McFarland and Delano: Eldon Tackett knew the farmers because of the water district, and Gene had bagged groceries for just about everybody in town. He also knew people in all the farming towns. Gene's Peace Corps experience helped him communicate easily with Mexicans and Filipinos. His girlfriend, Wendy Wayne, who was helping with the campaign, could have been taken for a Mexican with her dark complexion and Spanish-language fluency.

The incumbent, Republican Leroy Jackson, a much-decorated World War II navy fighter pilot, managed the China Lake Naval Weapons Laboratory, and his battle-scarred face was a plus in the eastern part of the district where military families lived. But Jackson was not well known in farming towns along the Friant-Kern Canal.

Gene held his first strategy sessions around his parents' kitchen table. His campaign cochairmen were the daughter of Gene's old boss at the Farmer Boy Market, and his friend Charlie Buchanan. Wendy came up from Los Angeles to be treasurer, and two Peace Corps friends, Sogge and Ed Lieberman (who had done a stint in Costa Rica), were there, too. Money came in from David Copus and some of his Harvard Law School friends.

Gene Tackett was a man of the center, a kind of political hybrid. He retained a good deal of the conservative cultural values of the valley—he opposed gun control, advocated stiff punishments to deter crime, and when he got word that a campaign worker had been seen smoking marijuana, Gene fired him. But he also represented the eclectic, open culture of the Pacific Coast and the Peace Corps. He was strong on women's rights and favored health care for the elderly. Borrowing from his idol, John Kennedy, Gene stressed the theme of generational vigor. He could "get things moving in the first district."

He wanted to walk every block in the district, and he started close to home. Eldon Tackett raised money for the campaign with yard sales of the plants he grew in kettles. Cleo Frost, whose son, Jerry, knew Eldon Tackett at SMUD, where they both worked, bought a coffee pot.

Gene paid a call on Jack Pandol, one of the east side's most successful grape ranchers and a Republican. "Support me or I'll cut your water off," Gene kidded. It was not possible for a Republican to support a Democrat overtly even in a "nonpartisan" race, but

Pandol, who knew Eldon, did the next best thing: he invited Gene to a candidates' night at Slav Hall. "If you work half as hard as your dad, you'll be a good supervisor," he said.

Shortly before the June 8 primary, the Bakersfield *Californian* endorsed Gene. Jackson narrowly defeated Gene in the four-way primary race, but the results were interpreted as making Gene an odds-on favorite to defeat Jackson in the two-man runoff in November.

Soon after the primary, Gene latched onto an issue and a cause. He came out against a proposed $7 billion nuclear plant for the southern San Joaquin Valley. The idea for the nuclear plant had been around for some time, but was given urgency by the huge rise in oil prices after the 1973 OPEC oil embargo. It was strongly supported by the big west side farm corporations and land companies, which envisioned the plant's giving cheap, inexhaustible electricity to the land served by the California Aqueduct, the west side's irrigation canal. And Pacific Gas and Electric sent its slickest lobbyists to the valley to promote the project, offering it as a cure to the most vexing problem faced by southern valley farmers: irrigation water with no place to drain. Even then, in the mid-1970s, this captive water was understood as an environmental threat, for it leached the soil's natural salts back to the surface of hundreds of acres of cropland. But if the irrigation runoff was used as the reactor's coolant, the water would then disappear into the atmosphere as steam.

But many of the east side farmers and a few of the more enlightened farmers in other parts of the county were suspicious. The Pandols, the Zaninoviches, the Robertses, and others like them got no water from the California Aqueduct, which operated in western Kern County on free-market principles. Moreover, a huge nuclear plant hardly seemed like an environmental solution, even to people who had been conditioned for decades to believe that engineering could do anything.

The campaign against the plant was led by a west-side rancher named David Bryant, whose Agriculture Protection Association warned that farmers faced ruin from the nuclear contamination of their soil and the commodities that grew from it. Bryant's tactic was eventually to persuade the Board of Supervisors to put the matter on a county-wide "advisory referendum," which, he gambled, could be won. A victory would give the supervisors the backbone to reject the necessary permit.

Gene drove out to Bryant's office on Pond Road in Wasco,

through leafy potato fields, to hear Bryant pitch his case. Bryant made a convert of him, and though the Central Labor Council denounced Gene's change of heart, the move was politically shrewd. The east-side farmers who lived in Gene's district were unenthusiastic about the plant and did not like labor unions. Meanwhile, the $7,000 that Bryant's groups raised for Gene doubled his campaign fund. And his stand made credible his assertion that he had "no vested interests with big business, big farms, or anyone"—unless one was so unchari-table as to suggest that the Agriculture Protection Association was such a group. It put him on the other side from Big Agriculture and Big Water, which was where he wanted to be.

In the context of the valley's politics, it also helped that the Demo-crats had nominated for president a born-again Southerner with whom thousands of valley residents could identify.

On the day that Jimmy Carter recaptured the White House for the Democratic Party, Gene easily defeated Jackson, 13,214 to 10,005. There would be a second Democrat on the five-member board of supervisors.

Gene's first symbolic act as supervisor occurred at Casper's, a downtown Bakersfield clothing store. He had dropped in at the invi-tation of the haberdasher to select the robin's-egg blue blazer that, worn with white pants and a plastic belt, was the standard uniform for a Kern County supervisor. Gene studied himself in the full-length mirror. He looked terrible in robin's-egg blue. He removed the coat, thanked the salesman, and left. When he did show up at the county offices to have his picture taken with the other four supervisors, he was not only minus the coat but minus a necktie, too.

Early the next year, Wendy and Gene slipped away to L.A. and got married. It was typically laid-back and low-key: in the middle of a big party for about 150 friends, they took their vows. Eldon and Loretta came down from McFarland and mingled with the young crowd.

Back at his job on the Board of Supervisors, Gene kept his prom-ise to David Bryant and voted for a county-wide advisory referendum on the nuclear plant. He had support on the nuclear issue from Republican supervisor Trice Harvey, whose farmer-constituents had little love for the giant nuclear project. The election was finally held in June 1978 and went against the utility. Pacific Gas and Electric withdrew its application with the Board of Zoning Adjustment for a conditional-use permit. There would be no nuclear power plant in the southern San Joaquin Valley.

Gene considered this a good start. But in the small print of the 1976 election returns, there were worrisome signs for Democrats. Proposition 14, the Chavez initiative, was smothered statewide. A Republican unseated a Democrat in one of Kern County's other supervisory districts. And Jimmy Carter was outpolled by Gerald Ford in the county by a margin of fifty-two to forty-five.

Chapter Fifteen

Brothers

WHILE GENE TACKETT was making new friends in the southern part of the valley, Bill Tatham was making money—and possibly a few enemies—up in Fresno. One day in May 1976 he pulled out of the lot by his office on Shaw Avenue at the wheel of his gray 450 SL Mercedes sports car when—thud! The brake pedal went to the floor. He flicked off the ignition switch, spun the wheel, and pumped the brakes. Nothing happened! He swung the wheel to avoid parked cars and curbs as the vehicle careened around the lot until he could bring it to a bouncing stop.

Bill waited until his heart rate slowed, then went back to the office and arranged for the car to be towed to Slavich Brothers, the local Mercedes dealer. The car, with 3,182 miles on the odometer, was almost new.

"Anybody out to get you?" asked the shop foreman who called from the garage after checking the car.

"Not that I know of," said Bill. A small threaded coupling was missing from the vacuum line, rendering the brakes useless and raising a question of whether it had been a mechanic's oversight or something more sinister.

The next morning, a friend from the sheriff's office telephoned. "Looks like it could have been an out-of-town job," he said. "Locals just cut the brake lines with tin snips."

No definite proof of foul play was ever found, but Bill believed that someone had indeed been out to scare him. He took it seriously enough to buy a .38 revolver, take out a firearms license, and do some practice on a pistol range. He posted a security guard outside his home, arranged for his twelve-year-old daughter to be escorted to school, and parked the Mercedes in full view of his private office.

He had another unnerving experience. The phone in his bed-room rang in the middle of the night. When he answered it he saw that one of the buttons was already lit up, indicating that the call was being placed from a phone he kept in the garden in the rear. All he heard was a click.

Whatever it meant, it was a kind of compliment. As his brother Gerald would jokingly remind him, Bill Tatham wasn't doing badly for someone one generation away from the cotton patch. Conceived in the Oklahoma of the Depression and born in a California tank house, Bill had felt the gentle pressure of his mother's cotton sack against him before he ever saw the world. But he had risen far above his humble background by the time of the brake trouble. In 1976, his holding company, Consolidated Industries, was worth several million dollars and had interests in equipment leasing, warehousing, health clubs, pharmaceuticals, and commercial real estate. His main holding, a nursing home chain called Belcor, operated twenty-one convalescent hospitals with more than 1,500 beds in California and was attempting a takeover of another chain.

He could afford a few indulgences, such as the Mercedes and the Portland Thunder, the World Football League team he briefly owned—and on which he lost a few hundred thousand dollars. The football escapade had earned him his first write-up in the Fresno *Bee* in 1975. "You couldn't call him Our Town's Howard Hughes," wrote sports columnist Omer Crane, "but we had to do some digging to get a 'make' on this lean ascetic with the mutton-chop whiskers and the steel-rimmed glasses. A very quiet operator indeed."[1] Bill acknowl-edged to Crane that he had made "an awful lot of money" lately.

In 1973, Bill and his wife, Earline, had moved into their new home on Van Ness Boulevard, north of Shaw Avenue. Van Ness *Boulevard* was not to be confused with Van Ness *Avenue*, a long street shaded by large evergreens, running south from Shaw Avenue. It was the abode of raisin magnates, cotton brokers, downtown businessmen, and Americans of Armenian descent who had done well in trade or retailing—of older Fresno money. But as the town began to spread north into the fig orchards and new wealth was amassed in real estate, contracting, and franchised businesses, a new street, Van Ness Boulevard, became the choice residence for the newly success-ful. It was also wide and shady, but the architecture of the homes was bolder and more contemporary. Parked out front were European sports cars, and in back were many tennis courts and pools.

A few older Fresno families also lived on Van Ness Boulevard—families such as the Robertses, who once had owned hundreds of acres of the fig orchards that were being torn out for residential housing. But most of the homes belonged to Fresno's newly arrived: developers such as John Bonadelli and Leo Wilson, the wheel manu-facturer John Siroonian, restaurateurs such as the DiCicco family.

Bill and Earline's house had three wings wrapping around an interior courtyard enclosing a kidney-shaped swimming pool, a raised flower bed with an inlaid Mexican tile wall, and a rare giant sago palm that Bill valued at $10,000. The couple spent long hours planning and decorating their home, returning from trips with ideas and materials, supervising the construction and landscaping.

Bill's success gave him unique status within a hypercompetitive family. He was fast becoming the new family hero, rivaling his father, the aging hero. The Tatham home environment had produced a brood of overachievers and strivers. When Dick enrolled at Bethany Bible College after high school, he signed up for twenty and a half units in his first semester—too heavy a load, as it turned out. As for Bill, he had his first stomach ulcers by the time he was twenty-five.

Oca Tatham was not a parent who dreamed of "my son the doctor." He didn't want to be outdone by anyone—*especially* his sons. When Bill and Dick were on the Clovis High School track team, he challenged them to footraces in his business shoes and relished beat-ing them. The message was that they would have to prove themselves. The acid test was how they handled money and what kind of business-men they were. They all worked for him, but he kept it businesslike. The boys got pocket money and lessons in hard work; he got cheap muscle. He gave them responsibility, turning a peach orchard over to Dick and Bill and allowing them to keep the proceeds of what they made on it or letting Dick sell cases of after-shave lotion that he'd acquired at the Cherry Avenue auction. When Dick was just out of high school in 1952, Oca put him on to a real find: more than a hundred surplus ice boxes, still in crates and unsold. Dick tried to take a leaf from his dad and went up to small towns in the Sierras to peddle them. But home refrigerators were coming in, and, though he made a few dollars, he couldn't unload the boxes, try as he might. Finally, he got Bill to help him tear them apart and sell them for parts—aluminum and insulation, metal screws and rubber—making a little on the scrap.

To Oca, a formal education was not seen as a particularly valuable asset. He was fond of reminding people that he had been to "Knocks University" and that none of his children had earned a bachelor's degree. Bill left high school convinced that "the other guys were a little more intelligent. I never did feel smart. I always felt there was a group of kids that were a lot smarter. It could be that we—and I'm not going to blame anything on our parents—were never told we were as smart as the other kids."

The children grew up feeling that they could *do* things, not that they *knew* things. Bill, Brenda, and Gerald all took classes at Fresno State or Fresno City, but none finished. Doris and Dick attended Bethany Bible College. Brenda and Renee attended the Assemblies' three-year Southern California College, but Renee dropped out after a couple of semesters. It was sixteen years before Bill finally amassed enough credits from Fresno City College, Fresno State, and San Jose State to get a two-year college certificate.

But Oca showed them that it was all right to plunge in. He had learned on the job, and he let them know he thought they could. Dick recollected how his dad always said, " 'Don't be afraid of developing land or building homes.' He showed us it was okay to try," Dick said.

They measured themselves against him. No matter how far they rose or how many miles away from Fresno they traveled or how old and sick he became, they would feel his presence, sizing up their financial decisions and their relationship with God. "Dad doesn't want us to fall behind." Dick was then fifty-five years old, and his dad was seventy-seven and recovering from quintuple heart bypass surgery.

DICK WAS EIGHTEEN MONTHS OLDER than Bill, but often found himself competing with him. Dick's whole first grade class was held back in Delano so he and Bill went through school in the same grade. In his junior year, Dick was called up to the varsity football team at Clovis, ahead of Bill, and starred as a quarterback and half-back. But in his senior year an injury forced him out of the lineup and he played only sporadically. Bill went in as halfback and got the headlines and offers of several football scholarships.

Dick dreamed of becoming a detective like Dick Tracy, his make-believe hero. But police work was considered out of bounds for a true-believing Pentecostal because it could require the taking of life. So Dick went off to Bethany Bible College to prepare to be a pastor, making Oca "a little proud."

After Bethany came a period of drifting between church and business, driving for Jack Kooken's trucking company, pastoring a country church that was using an abandoned roller-skating rink in the farming community of San Joaquin, and then setting up a patio and masonry supply business in Los Baños with Gerald. There were discouraging moments. At one point just two people were attending the church in San Joaquin, and the Sunday offering wasn't covering his gas. But then a whole new group of people started coming.

He still wasn't thirty when he arrived in Los Baños in 1962, but he'd acquired a wife, the former Grace Snelgrove and her three children from a first marriage and twin girls of their own. He was a kindly shepherd who'd found a flock of women to look after; soon he found a new congregation.

Dick was the son who seemed most eager to please his dad. He didn't resist Oca's advice, as Gerald was inclined to do, and he copied his dad's scrounging ways. But Los Baños was not a great success. He "felt maybe I had to prove something from a business standpoint in order to satisfy questions in my father's mind—and maybe my wife's, as to why I didn't make money like the rest of the family." Despite the sixteen-hour days, he lacked Oca's touch for managing money. When a call came for him to pastor an Assemblies of God church in Buhl, Idaho, he was ready. He stayed until 1969, when he answered another call from the Assemblies of God, this one to Lake Havasu City, Arizona.

It took a bold imagination to see possibilities of the town, a planned community being carved out of barren though beautiful desert on the east side of the Colorado River by oil magnate Robert P. McCulloch. The country had an eerie resemblance to the Golan Heights in the Holy Land. The lake was Dick's Sea of Galilee. The town was still basically a rock heap. Churches and gun stores faced each other oddly across boulder-strewn roads. Its main attraction was sunshine. (It would shortly have the London Bridge, dedicated in 1971, and the world's first air-conditioned beach, on the Havasu lakefront.)

The sun drew a mixed and incompatible crowd of motorcycle gangs and senior citizens in trailers: the young and the old and not much in the middle. It was basically a frontier town, with most of the characteristics. There were dopers hiding out from the law, retirees from Mafia families, women escaping from abusive husbands. It was the kind of place where a teenager rifling through his parents' drawers might suddenly come upon $10,000 in hundred-dollar bills stuffed under a shirt.

Driving there with his family the first time, Dick lost an axle on his trailer eighty-five miles from their destination. They left the trailer in the desert with all their things and Dick, six girls and his wife limped the rest of the way in a secondhand diesel Mercedes. The frontier preacher and his family lived in a trailer while Dick held services in an elementary school and lobbied with the McCulloch interests for ground for a real church. Sites had already been set aside for eight churches, however, and the Episcopalian McCullochs were unenthusiastic about having the "holy rollers." But Dick persisted. In the meantime, he helped to make ends meet by selling real estate on the side, which won him respect from the developers. Finally his requests for permits to build his church were granted.

Dick selected an unusual church design, utilizing three geodesic domes of a kind he had seen used by an auto repair shop in Yucca, and he got a salvage company in Fresno to donate an air-conditioning unit. He bought plumbing supplies through a Fresno supplier, wholesale. Volunteers worked weekends putting up sheetrock and tying in the struts for the dome. Two sheetrock workers were saved while working on the job and went on to finish the walls.[2] Several other volunteers accepted Christ before the ribbon was cut in November 1972. Though it was plain enough that it was a church, the building looked to some like a scale model of a nuclear reactor. If that connoted energy output, that was fine with Dick.

GERALD WANTED MONEY, status, and his dad's recognition, too, but he was reluctant to pay the price to get it. He wanted to be free and unobligated. Years went by, and, as he moved from job to job, he never bought a house of his own. He was caught up in a personal struggle. He questioned the family's preoccupation with the pocketbook. "Your money value has to be certified before your opinion counts for anything," he grumbled. Yet he admired Bill's financial success and would have liked it for himself. If only the price of freedom were not so high!

After high school, Gerald moved from job to job, doing construction, helping build a Central Valley Project pumping station, forming the partnership with Dick in Los Baños, becoming an estimator for a ceramic tile and masonry company. But he found a calling in brick-laying. There was art in constructing something that would be seen and used by thousands of people before it crumbled to nothing. It took a particular kind of integrity, too, since mistakes were easy to hide in buried foundations or improperly mixed mortar and would not show up for years. And it took art. A mason's motions had to follow a careful choreography; otherwise one's muscles and bones would tear and break. A specialized understanding of the climate came into it, too, because in the 115-degree noontime valley heat of the Southwest, one had to know tricks to keep the mortar moist.

In 1973, seventeen years after his high school graduation, Gerald received his contractor's license and formed his own company, Ger-aco. But he still had an "image" in the family that he couldn't shake. He was Gerald Tatham, the fellow who would not be tied down, the "black sheep" in the painting his sister Brenda kept in her living room, the perennial kid brother, the misfit who was always being told he would have made a fine teacher, a fine pastor, a fine this, a fine that.

Yet Gerald was liberated in ways the others weren't. For one thing, he seemed least affected of all the sons by Oca's measuring, evaluating, checking, sizing up. Gerald didn't cater to his dad. Some-times he even baited him. When Oca put a $2,800 chrome blower on his GMC pickup truck, Gerald suggested that he get a blower like that and put it on the church. Working on a construction job away from Fresno in the summer of 1967, he grew a beard.

"You look just like a filthy hippie," Oca told him.

"My beard makes me a hippie about as quick as your Honda makes you a Hell's Angel," Gerald shot back, a reference to the motorcycle his dad sometimes ran around on. Immediately, he re-gretted the comment. On the other hand, he noticed that nobody ever suggested that Bill's beard, with full muttonchops and a droopy handlebar mustache, made him look like a hippie.

Gerald vexed his close relatives, some of whom made reforming him a kind of permanent project. Yet Gerald, the high school outlaw, siphoning gas and getting into fights, was in a certain way an unfin-ished version of his father. The son was playacting—a California adolescent mimicking the dead-real experiences of a Depression sur-vivor who had to gouge coal and bootleg. But the connection could not be missed.

Still, he wanted the money and status that Bill had. He wondered:

Was there a shortcut to it? Perhaps there was, through creativity. The shortcut he tried to follow was Gera-Binder, an invention he thought of one day in 1973 while sitting on a riverbank with a couple of bricklayers. Transporting scaffolding was one of the headaches of contracting. The bands binding the scaffolding could break during shipment, and there would be fifty, a hundred metal frames shooting out of the back of a van at sixty-five miles an hour. Lying loose on a job site, they were always being stolen.

Gerald's patent was for a device that would bind scaffolding frames to make a securely bundled unit, easy to transport and difficult to steal. He used the Gera-Binder for his own jobs, and, as other contractors expressed interest, he took out U.S. and Canadian patents in 1975. He went to equipment shows and made the rounds of rental yards promoting the device. The president of Safway, the nation's largest scaffolding company, came up to Fresno to see it, and Gerald traveled to Oklahoma to scout out a centrally-situated distribution center. In his spare time he also worked on another new idea, a scaffolding plank made out of extrudable aluminum that would neither break nor slip. In 1974, Gerald went into production of the Gera-Binder, named his new company after his wife, and invested $85,000 in it. He planned to market the Gera-Binders for $33 apiece, building in a substantial profit margin. He was on a roll.

IT WAS CLEAR soon after Bill Tatham left high school that he had unusual gifts. After thirty months of accounting courses in Fresno and a management training program at R. J. Reynolds Nabisco Company, he went to San Jose State and while there was hired by Continental Can. By the time he was twenty-five he was overseeing a dozen accountants with college degrees, making $750 a month, and playing the stock market on the side.

Bill liked to work by himself in the quiet office on weekends. But otherwise he was miserable in corporate life. Being a supervisor meant attending social affairs, joining clubs, dealing with office politics, and knowing about office love affairs. For what? Bill knew college graduates who weren't making as much in a year as his dad did on a single deal. By the time his dad asked him to come back to the valley and work as administrator of Wish-I-Ah in 1960, Bill's ulcer doctor was advising him to look for another line of work.

Yet moving back proved traumatic for the young couple. The sanatorium in the Sierra foothills was far from the bright lights of the Bay, in Fresno. Bill called his former manager from a pay phone and inquired if the job was still open. It was, but Bill let the chance pass. They threw in their lot with Fresno County. He went to work for his dad.

Bill stayed on with the new owners after Oca sold six months later, but was already hatching a plan to become an independent nursing-home operator. This first entrepreneurial venture resulted in an embarrassing retreat. He had to turn to his dad for help. Bill had invested his savings in a decommissioned public school on South Elm Street in Fresno and set about converting it into a mental hospital. Just when all seemed clear, the staff of the county planning commission refused to issue a permit, citing the threat to patients from the chemical spraying of nearby grape vineyards.

It was a devastating blow that suddenly jeopardized Bill's life savings, and he called in his father.

"How much you got in it?" Oca asked. Oca agreed to buy the property from him. If Oca could somehow wangle a permit, he would lease it back to his son to operate. Oca hustled around, taking pictures of other nursing homes that were even closer to vineyards, measured distances, and obtained testimony from medical experts. Then he went out to the peach ranch of county supervisor Charles Preuss. "I could put it in *your* community," Oca mused. Charlie "looked funny," Oca recalled. When the case came up again, he had his approval.

It was during the rehabilitation of the school that yet another development jeopardized the project. Oca suffered his first heart attack. Now it was Bill's turn to take the lead. He worked alongside the carpenters and plumbers until the facility was ready. They called it Four Acres Sanatorium, and waited for patients to fill up the forty-four beds. Bill planned to take mainly "degreed" mental patients—those with less severe psychological problems, like alcoholics, elderly people, and others not requiring locked facilities. It was the low end of the market and qualified for government funding. But when he finally opened in 1962, he had exactly one bed filled and an around-the clock staff to pay. Gradually, the place filled up. Bill handled the bookkeeping, mailed the bills, and often drove patients to medical appointments himself. The following year he leased the former Selma Hospital from Oca as well. Soon he bought two more facilities. In 1965, Congress passed the Medicare and Medicaid legislation that financed the exponential expansion of the industry. Bill was in on the ground floor.

Meanwhile, he was dabbling in raisin ranching. West of Selma, he bought twenty acres of sandy loam with a well, planted Thompson's Seedless grapes, and signed up with Sun-Maid, the raisin co-op that his father-in-law used. That purchase was followed by several others. Bill was comfortable in cowboy boots, jeans, and open-necked western shirts, conversing with his Mexican farm manager. But grape farming, he soon discovered, gave sleepless nights if not ulcers. A year's work might be ruined by an untimely rain while the raisins were drying in their trays in the fields. The longer the grapes ripened on the vine, the higher the sugar content and value of the raisins, but the greater the risk of fall showers. Waking during the grape-picking season, Bill would listen to the rain on the roof, not knowing whether his crop had been spared.

Farming was a gamble. An investment in an almond ranch did not pay off because there was no bottom to the sandy soil and the irrigation water seeped into the ground before reaching the end of the row. By 1968, Bill was getting out of farming and being drawn deeper into the nursing-home business. Congress's enactment of Medicaid and Medicare was changing everything. Medicare covered the costs of a hundred days in an extended care facility for those over sixty-five, and federal Medicaid funds were available indefinitely to augment the state's contribution to the care of the indigent. Medicaid paid the way for the poor and built in a profit for the nursing-home operator. Medi-Cal, the California version of Medicaid, went into effect in March 1966. The following year, the number of nursing home patients in the state doubled.

By then Bill was operating four convalescent facilities, two of his own and two others leased from Oca. Despite the improved profit margins resulting from Medi-Cal, he was increasingly frustrated. There were unending "people problems"—nosy inspectors, nurses who came late for shifts or did not come at all, families who neglected their institutionalized relatives or, worse, pocketed the meager spending money that Medicaid allowed. One day a patient wandered off into a vineyard and died. And there was more and more red tape— state inspectors with different interpretations of the rules, threatening to shut down facilities if requirements were not met. For a man still in his early thirties, Bill was shouldering heavy responsibilities. He was running nursing homes, supervising the installation of irrigation pipe at the vineyards, setting up credit lines at banks, dabbling in real estate.

It seemed to Earline that her husband was always figuring— figuring on a napkin in a restaurant, even figuring at church. When he heard that raisins were going to $240 dollars a ton tomorrow, or when he started thinking about meeting his nursing-home payroll, out would come the pen. Finally, she told him, "You'll have our children doing that if you don't stop." He put away the pencil, but continued figuring in his head.

"Slow down," Oca told him. "You're going to have a heart attack."

Bill heeded his advice. In 1969, he sold his four operations to a publicly owned chain based in Los Angeles. Thanks largely to Medicare and Medicaid, publicly owned nursing-home companies were gobbling up smaller operators across the country and attracting the attention of Wall Street. Bill and Oca retained ownership of the nursing-home properties, leasing them to Century Convalescent Hospitals, Inc. Bill got stock in the company and took a job as a senior manager. Two years later, Century went out of business. The chains had expanded too fast, and the federal government, worried about the costs, was moving to get Medicare and Medicaid subsidies under control. In closing out its operations in 1971, Century cited a "significant decrease in the reimbursement rate for Medi-Cal."

The collapse of Century brought Bill back into the business of being a hands-on operator, for it left him with all his nursing properties, but nobody paying the rent. He had watched the shakeout carefully, and, by the early 1970s, nursing homes were once again becoming good buys. Forming a small, closely held corporation with Oca and several others, including his accountant, his stockbroker, his banker, and his friend and business associate Earl Giacolini, a Fresno County druggist, Bill began to expand. His new company was called Belcor, named for the Belmont and Cornelia avenues intersection in Fresno where one of the convalescent hospitals was situated. He already had begun to operate eleven of the hospitals in Century's bankrupt chain, including the four former Tatham facilities. Belcor acquired the operations of four other facilities from a Denver company, then two more in Stockton and Santa Cruz. Within a year Bill had bought out Oca and the partners, and was preparing to turn over the day-to-day operations of his chain to a staff headed by Clyde E. Dahlinger, a six-foot-two former football player.

Given the difficulties that he would have later with the bureaucracy in Sacramento, it was ironic that the California Department of Health was, in this earlier period, urging him to acquire more hospitals. Bill was to say that many of those he acquired resulted from the department "contacting me and telling me there is a facility that's available. They're losing it. They're really in trouble, and they'd give me the name of the owner and other information and suggest I go in, and they would give me an immediate licensing so that I could bill for Medicare, bill for Medi-Cal, and so on."

Bill could be an aggressive player, as he showed in taking over Clovis Convalescent Hospital, one of the best operations in the valley's health care system. In 1972, the landlord approached Bill about becoming the new tenant. The owner was dissatisfied with the present tenant, who allegedly had been late making some payments. Was Bill interested? He was indeed. The plan called for Bill to arrive at midnight and assume control. There were legal risks because the operator wasn't being notified, and Bill decided not to consult his lawyers. All they would say, he figured, was don't do it. Instead, he followed a script drawn up by the landlord's attorney.

Shortly before midnight, Bill, Clyde Dahlinger, and the landlord met at Bob's Big Boy on Blackstone Avenue and drove to the hospital. Bill and Clyde waited in the parking lot while the landlord went in and called the administrator at home. When the sleepy man arrived, the landlord advised him that the facility was being repossessed and that another operator was taking over. Clyde and Bill were introduced, and Clyde asked the staff to finish the night shift. The next day, Clyde offered everyone jobs, took an inventory, and had the administrator count the cash in the safe.

In 1973, Bill purchased most of the stock in a failed bank holding company. As part of the deal, he acquired the banking concern's equipment-leasing company, a printing center, and an insurance agency. Of special interest was the leasing operation. Nursing-home proprietors leased voluminous amounts of equipment, everything from beds and kitchen gear to trucks and cars. He could save money by setting up a leasing company of his own.

But there were also other advantages. Leasing companies are basically finance companies. They use bank credits to buy new equipment, which they rent to customers at a marginally higher rate of interest than they pay the bank. The U.S. tax code made the business highly attractive. Leasing companies were entitled to the investment tax credit on the furniture, vehicles, or equipment they rented out. On a million dollars' worth of telephone equipment installed in an office building, for example, a hundred thousand dollars could be deducted as the investment tax credit.

There was yet one more attraction: his leasing company was a source of cash with which to acquire more nursing homes. Through it he established large lines of bank credit at Security Pacific, Bank of

America, Wells Fargo, and other institutions. If he needed to put money down to buy a new convalescent facility, he would have one of his leasing companies buy all the equipment in the facility, and lease it back to the owners. That got cash into the owner's hands and became Bill's down payment on the real estate, buildings, and land— the owner didn't care where the money came from.

As Bill explained it: "I could go in with no money and take over— take over operations that were million-dollar operations."

The same year that Bill got into the leasing business he launched an unfriendly takeover of one of the largest nursing-home chains in California.

Hy-Lond Enterprises of Sonoma had started in the early 1960s as a small partnership founded by an Iranian-born Seventh-Day Adventist by the name of George Beitz and his brother-in-law, Jack Breitigam. With the encouragement of the Adventist Conference, they expanded their nursing-home holdings and brought in Middle Eastern investors, some with Adventist backgrounds. The most important outsider was Daniel Hasso, a wealthy importer and operator of stores in Kuwait and member of a fabled family of Iraqi merchant-princes.

From a few convalescent hospitals, Hy-Lond expanded steadily and went public in 1969. The company had several facilities in Fresno, and Bill wrote to Beitz for information about them. Hy-Lond hospitals had a good reputation for providing care in a clean, safe environment, but Bill concluded from the financial reports that they were overstaffed and loosely managed. The stock had soared as high as twenty-one dollars a share but was down to sixty-two cents by 1974. As a nursing-home operation, Hy-Lond seemed to be a money loser. But Bill had other reasons for being interested. Nursing homes, like parking garages, were real-estate businesses in disguise; nursing-home beds, like parking slots, paid the rent while the underlying buildings and real estate appreciated in value.

Hy-Lond also had losses and tax debits that could offset Belcor's profits, and it was a potential market for the pharmaceutical and distributing businesses that Bill had set up to service his nursing homes with drugs, medical supplies, bedding, frozen foods, meat, and janitorial supplies. He could roll Hy-Lond's balance sheets into a consolidated tax return for his own companies if he could obtain 80 percent of Hy-Lond shares, thereby qualifying for attractive tax possibilities.

Bill acquired a hundred thousand shares in Hy-Lond for sixty-two cents apiece. In late 1975, Beitz went to meet the mysterious man from Fresno. Bill offered him a golden parachute—a ten-year salary and an interest in Bill's pharmaceutical business in return for his help in taking over the company. But Beitz turned him down.

The first confrontation occurred just before Christmas 1975 at a board of directors meeting at a Holiday Inn in San Francisco. Bill nominated himself for the board of directors and used his 10 percent of the shares to get himself elected. He kept accumulating stock through tenders and courted members of the Hasso family. The Hassos, it was evident, were wavering in their support for Beitz. To some of the Hasso investors, Bill's cost-conscious style of management was just what was needed, and Bill's buying activity was increasing the price of publicly traded Hy-Lond stock. Bill tested his strength at a board meeting in October 1976 with a proposal to move Hy-Lond's bank accounts to his preferred bank in Fresno, a proposal which was approved. Two months later, he got Clyde Dahlinger elected to the board.

The showdown came in February 1977 at a meeting in the offices of Hy-Lond's attorney in the Trans-America Building in San Francisco. Beitz was confronted with the defection of the Hasso bloc, and resigned. Within a few months, Hy-Lond closed its headquarters in Sonoma and moved to Bill's brand-new office building in Fresno, at a choice site on the corner of Shaw and Fruit avenues. One of Bill's first moves was to get rid of the company airplane. Shortly after the coup, George Beitz resigned from the board of directors and sold his stock to Bill. In April 1978, Bill and Dahlinger were elected co-CEOs. Bill's hand-picked slate of directors included Doris's husband Gordon Weaver, his friend Earl Giacolini, Tom Nast of the Happy Steak restaurant chain, and other up-and-coming business friends.

The real treasure that Bill was unearthing in his nursing-home expansion was land and buildings.

The nursing-home business, he figured, was never going to be very profitable. Government regulation of Medicare and Medicaid rates would prevent any windfalls. But the business provided an extremely stable stream of cash that paid the mortgages on the land and the buildings that he acquired along with the beds and the patients. It was a far safer business than, say, owning shopping malls or office towers. The economy could go sour, and suddenly one would have vacancies. If the economy dipped into a deep recession, there would be more vacancies and the rents needed to pay the mortgages might not be sufficient. In the worst case, the real-estate entrepreneur could face bankruptcy. That wasn't likely to happen in the nursing home business subsidized by the government and serving an aging population in a country in which families no longer cared for their own elderly.

Once Bill had control of Hy-Lond, he embarked on a complex corporate restructuring aimed at improving the balance sheet of the new public company while moving the hospital properties and land under the control of his family holding company, Consolidated Industries. The steps served three purposes: they created a balance sheet that would be attractive for a potential buyer, increased the value of the stock (and with it Bill's net worth), and put the real estate under Bill's personal control.

Bill's renamed public nursing home company, Consolidated Liberty, Inc., reported hefty increases in pretax earnings, but the lion's share of the gains was attributable to the leasing, food service, telephone service, hospital management, and other operations. Earnings per share went from thirty-one cents to $1.89 between 1977 and 1979.

Bill used an array of specialists and troubleshooters to do the hands-on work, while he concentrated on several new investments in banking and construction, but he was in charge. Politely but firmly, Bill reminded "hired guns" of their place. Lawyers sitting in on meetings after they had finished their presentation were told to stay if they wished, but were reminded that the additional time was "not billable." Sometimes Bill drew up the legal briefs himself, while a lawyer cooled his heels outside, ready to come in to supply wording or a legal authority—but only when summoned.

One of the Hy-Lond people who was in on the takeover thought that "Bill had ice in his veins. . . . He acted like, 'This is what I need to do, and this is what is going to happen.' The people part of it didn't concern him. That was the feeling at Hy-Lond."

Some of the nursing-home staff also found Bill aloof and mysterious. He had a reputation as a "moral stickler" who disapproved of drinking and bad language. When there were staff meetings at the Shaw Avenue office, Dahlinger warned staffers to watch what they said in Bill's presence. Fortunately for the staff, perhaps, Bill did not seem to know very many people's names.

Staffers assumed that the pressure to hold down costs came from Bill, though no one could be certain. "We always had the impression that we were stone-cold broke," said an employee. The same worker remembers attending a meeting at Bill's office and wondering, "How can I go back and tell people we can't get more linen when there's all these Mercedes and antique clocks up here?"

Behind the beard and the steel-framed glasses Bill looked at the world with a steady, slightly disconcerting gaze, a taciturn Cherokee gaze. One sensed a difficulty with personal contact, a shyness, even a hint of some hidden hurt.

He was absorbed in what he was doing. Off the screen, the world almost seemed not to exist for him. Friends and relatives got used to Bill turning away from a conversation in midsentence, as his mind called him back to whatever deal was at hand.

Oca had been the hands-on operator, confident of his personal skills, less so of his technical ones. He checked the furnaces at Wish-I-Ah, prayed with patients, and dealt personally with late payers of water bills. He collared commissioners, buttonholed supervisors, stood belly to belly with building inspectors. And he had complete confidence in these personal dealings, perhaps because he knew he had it in him to be hard.

Oca personalized everything. As Bill's business grew in scope, he *im*personalized it, invariably using the plural pronoun "we" to describe the activities of his closely held, wholly owned family corporation: "we bought," "we sold," "we thought." In fact, there was no "we," just Bill pulling the strings behind the curtain. His organization shielded him to some extent from the messy human details: from decubitus ulcers, urine smells, disgruntled employees, confrontations with lobbyists for the elderly in the halls of the statehouse. To guard Consolidated Industries in which Earline and his children were the only stockholders, Bill paid men who, he sensed, could be harder men than he could be: his lawyer Gary Kerkorian, former all-American football player and backup quarterback for the Baltimore Colts, Clyde Dahlinger, and his banker, Henry Wheeler.

Bill was the man of imagination and vision who did his best work in the solitude of his office, surrounded by tax forms, legal briefs, and code books. He had perfect confidence in his ability to master the technical parameters of any problem. Working with a yellow pad, he could dissect a business, see how to tease profits from it by cutting costs, consolidating here, shedding a loser there, extracting the real estate, using tax credits from one business to offset profits in another. If the junk man disassembled things to maximize values, Bill's art was to *reassemble* things in a more complex and intricate pattern. Oca had thrived on the anarchic side of the American economy. Bill's art was to create logical patterns out of the confusion that his father had so cleverly exploited.

His natural skills enabled him to exploit the two relentless realities of the 1970s: inflation and a tax code so complicated that thousands of people spent their entire lives poring over it as if it were a Talmudic text. A new and enormously complex kind of arbitrage developed that involved buying and selling tax-loss businesses almost as if they were commodities. A statement that Bill's nursing-home company filed with the Securities and Exchange Commission referred to the "pass-through of refunds from carryback of consolidated net operating losses." Money-losing companies could be valuable assets in the tax game. In November 1977, Bill sold sell 44,000 shares of a company he had called Liberty Spas, which owned an athletic club on Blackstone Avenue. Subsequently, the buyers sued for $85,000, saying they thought they were getting a company with a net operating loss that could be used to reduce their tax exposure, when Bill's company had actually used the loss to reduce *his* taxes. The suit was dropped when the misunderstanding was cleared up.

Once Bill had the architecture clear in his mind, he went after what he wanted with single-minded determination. He said, "I don't go to some mountain and meditate for three days. I make a decision very quickly if I have the facts. I pick up the phone and call somebody and do it right then. I don't go home and sleep on it for three days and have a lot of meetings and talk about it. I know what I want to do."

What excited him was creating the deal. "Once a deal is done," he said, "you just have to close the escrow, and a bunch of recordings and checks change hands, and you end up with a building and lease it out, and somebody rents it from you, and you get a check every month for the next twenty years. When you get the idea, it's exciting. But when you do it, it's *not* exciting. Because it's all over."

The one flaw in Bill's expansion was a certain vulnerability to human factors. He kept his word and stuck to the letter of business deals, as his father had taught him. That others were brazen crooks was difficult for him to comprehend.

When things went right, the leasing business was extremely profitable, but there were risks. Customers sometimes defaulted, leaving the leasing company with used equipment for which the investment tax credit was no longer applicable. There was danger of fraud, from phony bills of sale to collusion to generate phony tax credits to arson against the leased equipment. Mafia involvement in the leasing business was widely suspected, and the Federal Bureau of Investigation believed that the Mafia operated in Fresno, which was only a two-hour drive from the Nevada line. "If they owe *you*, you'll get

paid—if you stay after them," a lawyer friend told Bill. "Just don't
owe *them*."

By 1976, Consolidated Industries had bank credit lines in the
high seven figures and was growing rapidly. Bill's scare on the parking
lot came while his leasing company was embroiled in a messy lawsuit
involving a Nevada hotel casino that was leasing furniture from him.
Payments from the hotel on some $400,000 worth of furniture had
stopped. The suit, in which Bill's lawyers alleged fraud and deceit by
the hotel, was eventually settled, but it cost him several hundred
thousand dollars.

Just as that dispute was being resolved, far more serious problems
developed with another batch of leases. In April 1976, Bill had agreed
to provide guarantees for another leasing company that was financing
the installation of phone equipment to small businesses around San
Francisco. What he did not know was that the vendor of the phone
equipment was having serious problems servicing customers and the
leasing firm was overextended. He first got wind of trouble when the
status report began coming in late from the company whose leases
he was guaranteeing. Some of the auto dealers who were supposed
to be renting the phone systems said they had never been installed.

Bill's in-house accountant, Dee Rowe, drove to Richmond in the
East Bay to take a look at the records. He reported back that some
of the telephone systems appeared to have been "double-funded"—
financed with several banks or leasing companies. Among the documents subsequently filed in connection with a lawsuit Bill brought
was a sworn affidavit from a bookkeeper for the vendor stating that
"certain lessees appeared in the portfolio of more than one financier."
During a phone conversation with the president of the vendor company, she recalled, "I specifically told [him] I was sending him a lease
which I believed was forged."

Several months later, the troubled vending company went out of
business. Bill had guaranteed the leases, and the collapse left him
with responsibility for servicing a tangle of leased phone equipment
all over California. It was bad enough that some of the leases he had
guaranteed were for systems that had never been installed. Now
companies with legitimate leases were threatening to withhold
monthly payments unless they got service. Bill hastily set up a telephone service company—an unanticipated expense that, he was to
say, cost him more than $1 million.

He was in for other unpleasant surprises. On a routine trip to
San Francisco one day, Rowe dropped in at an office building to

which Bill was leasing an electronic smoke detector system. As a friendly gesture Rowe inquired of the property manager how the system was performing. Rowe got the shock of his life. "We don't lease," the manager said. "We have a new system all right, but we paid *cash* for it."

Rowe, a thin, pale man in his early forties, excused himself and called Bill from a pay telephone. "I think we have a problem," he said. "They say they paid cash for the smoke detector system. If this guy is right we're in a lot of trouble."

Bill was bewildered. For many months he had been getting regular monthly rental checks for this particular smoke detector system; the San Francisco company that installed the equipment collected the monthly rental checks and routed them on to Fresno in the company's own envelopes. Whenever a question came up, somebody in Bill's office would call the telephone number listed on the correspondence and a secretary would answer.

It occurred to him that he was the victim of a scam. The equipment company had sold the installed smoke detectors to the owner of the building for cash and also sold Bill's leasing companies the same detectors. The equipment company was using Bill's own cash to pretend to make fictitious "monthly payments" from the building owners, who were none the wiser. Bill got the picture: eventually, the "monthly payments" would just stop and the perpetrator would vanish with the rest of Bill's cash.

Bill ordered Rowe to come home. Then he telephoned the FBI. It was a troubled period. In April 1978, Bill's leasing company was put on one bank's "watch list" pending an audit of its collateral. Bill still had plenty of good leases and nursing-home real estate to offer as collateral. Nevertheless, the situation created a momentary financial squeeze, as his banks shut down new financing while they evaluated Bill's problems.

Bill remembered it as "wartime." He hired private detectives and investigators to look into the people behind some of the companies and banks with which he had been dealing and worked closely with the FBI in an unfolding criminal investigation that eventually led to one criminal indictment and conviction.

Behind a reserved demeanor was a tough Okie, as customers and clients who were slow to pay learned. In those cases, Bill said, he had a man he called on to pay a visit to the deadbeat and "put his hand right on the till" if that was what it took.

In November 1979, Bill filed a civil suit against a Sonoma County businessman, charging fraud and misrepresentation in connection with a number of leases.

The following April, he sued the Bank of America, which had put Bill in touch with the other leasing company that had given him so much trouble. Bill's suit alleged conspiracy and sought compensatory damages. It charged that bank officials knew that the leasing firm was overextended, and that the bank secretly wanted to take over Bill's finance business. The bank denied all the allegations.

The 1978 difficulties with the leasing operation had been a rude awakening, and soon there was another.

In August 1978, the California Department of Health filed suit against Reedley Convalescent Hospital, one of Bill's original units, in order to recover penalties assessed the previous year when the facility was cited for failing to notify a doctor for more than a week after a patient developed a bed sore. A $5,000 penalty was reduced to $2,000 at a citation review conference, but, ten months later, the nursing-home company continued to protest the penalty and the state filed suit. The complaint was settled for $1,500.

More serious problems followed. The Santa Cruz County district attorney filed suit against Hy-Lond's Santa Cruz Care and Guidance Center after a patient who was supposed to be fed only pureed foods was found dead in bed with a banana in her throat. (The suit subsequently was dropped.) And in August 1979, a Hy-Lond hospital in Novato was cited for fifty violations. (Bill said the facility was operated by former Hy-Lond employees and he never recalled visiting it.) A subsequent suit brought by the Marin County district attorney was dropped after Hy-Lond agreed to pay $87,500 in penalties and $12,500 in administrative costs. Also in 1979, a registered nurse complained to the Fresno County board of supervisors that residents of two former Belcor mental-health facilities in the Fresno area were not being adequately protected from sexually abusive patients. Files at the Fresno office of the state Department of Health Services in Fresno noted too few janitors, too few nurses, and unlocked medication drawers.[3]

In July, the administrator of the Hy-Lond Convalescent Hospital in Santa Barbara resigned, charging that headquarters refused to respond to his concerns about low wages and high turnover. And in October, there was a strike at the old Four Acres facility, the original Tatham nursing home. The director of field operations claimed to have received an early morning phone call warning him that strike-breakers would have their tires slashed. A judge ordered the Service

Employees Union to reduce the pickets to two and allow access to the building. Bill issued a statement that he would never be "black-mailed."[4]

Under Bill and Clyde, the chain's approach to dealing with citations became a political issue in Sacramento. Clyde got things done. Those who saw him in Sacramento described him as a lay-it-on-the-line, cards-on-the-table guy. Bill said, "He didn't let bureaucrats cram things down his throat." According to Tom Truax, then the Sacramento lobbyist for the California Health Care Association, Dahlinger played a leading role in shaping the industry's positions in Sacramento, at a time when the legislature and consumer groups were pushing for regulation that the association considered overly onerous. The association responded by setting up a political action committee and getting involved in the drafting of legislation, such as new minimum-wage laws for nurses. Truax described Dahlinger as "bright" but "confrontational."

In dealing with the enforcement division of the state health department, Consolidated Liberty usually forced the state to go to court or to an appeals board rather than pay fines. Dahlinger encouraged nursing-home staffers to talk to their state senators and assemblymen to give them the company's side of the story. Bill and Clyde did not win all these battles. The Grey Panthers, the senior citizens lobby, was actively calling attention to what it believed were substandard conditions in nursing homes across the United States, and the California state legislature was feeling political pressure to toughen up. The association wanted higher rates for patients whose care was funded by the state and federal governments. In the end it accepted tougher regulations as the condition for getting them.

As difficulties with the state government mounted, it became clear to Bill that he would have to get even more deeply involved in the bureaucratic politics or sell. The chain had become an enormous headache. It had three thousand employees, gross revenues of fifty million dollars a year, and Bill and Earline owned it all except for the small amount of stock still in public hands. Bill asked Clyde to look for a buyer and the one he found was Beverly Enterprises, the largest nursing-home chain in California and one of the biggest in the United States. Bill personally negotiated the deal, in which Beverly agreed to take over operation of Hy-Lond's hospitals and become Bill's tenant.

In July 1978, according to a bank credit report, William R. Tatham already had a net worth of $10,307,121. The Beverly deal made him much richer. The sale was structured so Bill ended up with some

$13.8 million in cash and dividends, much of which he used to buy nine Beverly properties in California and elsewhere.

The press release announcing the sale stated that, as a result of the negotiations, Clyde would no longer serve with the firm. Clyde had been the company's man in Sacramento, and Bill said that officials would not transfer the licenses to Beverly with Clyde on board. Bill did not think the state legally could make such a demand, but if Clyde stayed, he said, there could have been no sale. If he went, it would look like he had dumped his top man.

Clyde went. "Clyde always acted in our interests," Bill said subsequently.

There was still the matter of outstanding violations. On November 21, 1980, the Department of Health Services issued a press release stating that as part of the sale, the buyers would pay the state $75,000 in civil penalties. It announced that four of the company's facilities were being placed on "probation," meaning that they faced a shutdown if Beverly was cited for major new violations. "The settlement enables the state to resolve long-standing citations for violations of laws and regulations designed to assure proper patient care without resorting to costly litigation," the announcement said.

Ten days later, the Fresno *Bee* began publishing a three-part series on the California nursing-home business, with special attention to the five mental-health facilities in the chain that Bill had just sold. In interviews with *Bee* reporter Royal Caulkins, Bill explained that he was unaware of problems such as the state's threatened withdrawal of the license of four of his facilities. "For all intents and purposes, I got out of operating nursing-homes in 1972," he said. That was the year he hired Dahlinger to run the operations. He went on, "I haven't even been in most of the facilities, to be honest with you." Members of the nursing-home staff confirmed that they had never seen Bill at one of the hospitals. "I honestly don't think Bill knew much about the nursing-home business," said a former staffer.

Nonetheless, Bill was stung by the stories, which were read by his family in Fresno. A few days later he took out a full-page advertisement in the *Bee* to "set the record straight." He said that Consolidated Liberty received on average fewer citations and fines than all other long-term health-care facilities in California, that he had sold voluntarily and not under duress from the state. And to refute the notion that his company put profit over patient care, he asserted that the five mental-health facilities in Consolidated Liberty had suffered a combined loss of $300,000 in 1980 and actually were being subsidized by the rest of the chain. He suggested that the state government should take back responsibility for these patients. This "open letter" concluded with Bill's thanks to employees in the mental-health facilities: "You have been subjected to harassment by government agencies and misguided citizens' groups, abused by patients, and now along with your former employer, publicly attacked by the Fresno *Bee*."

A few weeks after the sale there was a farewell luncheon for Dahlinger. It was a tense affair. Staffers were divided over whether Bill had jettisoned Clyde or whether Clyde had hurt Bill's good name in the community. Clyde was good-humored about it—he did not seem any worse for the experience, and neither did Bill, who came out of the transaction owning land and property that made him something of a real-estate tycoon.

Bill now owned forty-five nursing homes or mental-health care facilities in Sonoma, Petaluma, Napa, Santa Rosa, San Jose, Santa Clara, Stockton, Bakersfield, Modesto, and Merced—and as far away as Little Rock, Arkansas. He got a convalescent hospital in downtown Santa Barbara, located on property that he envisioned as a future major commercial development. He also picked up properties around Los Angeles and Sacramento. In Santa Cruz, his property overlooked the yacht club. In Burbank, it was near the studios of NBC.

It was the deal of a lifetime for a long-term strategist. Because of his financial success, Bill was usually seen as the son who was "following in his father's footsteps." Temperamentally, though, Bill was more like Ruby—quiet, controlled, a good listener. Oca and Bill, to be sure, both were loners who seldom took on partners, individualists who wanted to be in control of their own destiny, "low-tech" men who were successful in a world being transformed by science and high technology. California in their time became a center of leading-edge industries in aerospace, computers, and biotechnology. That Bill and Oca knew almost nothing about these industries was of no consequence to them. They had their ears much closer to the ground, and they sensed the opportunities in the businesses in which American fortunes have always been made: real estate, banks, drugstores, and health services.

Yet they approached business in fundamentally different ways. Oca was the short-term trader and thinker who acted and then imagined. Oca, a fellow who on a whim would pull off the road in a little Texas town and make a deal to buy cotton-harvesting machinery he didn't understand, saw the everyday human distractions of life as potential opportunities. Bill, a long-term planner and thinker, imagined first and *then* acted, collecting nursing homes with a grander scheme in mind. Bill thought of his dad as a "junk man." He was referring to the Delano days when his father was red-eyed from nights spent separating brass from iron. It was a kind of compliment—for he respected his dad—suggesting that Oca could find value in anything. But Bill was also making the point that he was different.

One day Gerald told Oca: "Dad, did you know that Bill's yearly income is more than your net worth?"

Gerald served as the messenger of the news that Oca had been outdone by one of his sons, Bill, and that another of them, Gerald, was enough of his own man not to be afraid to remind him of that fact.

All through 1976, Gerald had worked to promote sales of the Gera-Binder. A Los Angeles company was interested, but when Gerald visited, two of the top managers got into a fierce row right in front of him. A desk was pushed over and Gerald beat a hasty retreat.

Gerald flew to Maryland to meet with a senior official of a scaffolding company. There had been a misunderstanding. The man he was to see wouldn't be at the job for several days. Gerald flew back to California without a sale.

Technical hitches developed. The binder needed a special pin to secure it that added to the costs and made it more difficult to sell. Not wanting to be caught short of supplies when customers started calling, Gerald ordered a thousand made. But in 1977 construction eased off during an economic slowdown, and he was left with debts. He thought perhaps he had been "too independent" for his suppliers in insisting on keeping control of the business. "I was a very small nothing to them," he said. "They were very large manufacturers. And they did not want to buy a product that they could make so easily themselves."

The overall economic situation had hurt, too. Contractors were moving their equipment back to the yards, and customers for Gerald's binders suddenly were idle. Gerald wondered if his approach to the marketing had been wrong. Still, he believed he had "changed the concept of scaffolding." He had brought fresh thinking into a hidebound, self-satisfied industry. And then, he said, "they" had squashed him.

CHAPTER SIXTEEN

RESISTANCE

TO LIVE HAPPILY and successfully in California, one almost needed the inner resources of a space traveler. Whizzing along at close to the speed of light, the galactic voyager ages normally, but the world he sets out from is unrecognizable when he returns. That was an experience Californians had once every decade or so. The peninsula south of San Francisco, so recently full of apricot orchards and vineyards, had been transformed into the center of a new industry, unimagined in 1960. The small towns, dairy farms, and fruit orchards of Orange County had given way to clogged freeways, edge cities, and technology parks.

Oca Tatham in 1980 walked on an entirely different planet from the one he had arrived on in August 1934. He had seen the Third World become the First World in his own lifetime and had participated in that change. A true Californian, he took it in stride, rejoicing that housing was better, cars more reliable, roads wider, and tires safer. He didn't agree with what some people said—that growth, change, and material progress led to anxiety, self-questioning, and moral decay. Man could be healthier and better off without turning away from God.

He, for one, was determined not to be conquered by California, for, much as he admired his adopted state, he recognized the pitfalls. A culture in which every opinion was "valid" he viewed with continuing suspicion. One best kept one's guard up when people were constantly warming their hands over the bonfire of their yesterday's beliefs. Oca wanted a new car every year, not a new set of values. When it came to values he was still the junk man—he preferred his used.

In the eighteen years since a heart attack in 1962, he had successfully reordered his activities. His health wasn't conducive to his former, frenetic pace. Also, there were simply fewer niches in the economy after the mid-1960s for a businessman who used his kitchen table for his office. Rather than accommodate, he shifted to new, more promising arenas of individual enterprise, adventure, and personal initiative.

With the children grown up and income from various investments fairly steady, Oca and Ruby had the money, the time, and the motor homes to indulge an Okie passion for the open road. One time they took a slightly used twenty-seven-foot Pace Arrow motor home with an island bed to the Baja peninsula. Another time Oca bought a fishing boat with gorgeous leather seats, pulled it down to Mazatlán, and went after marlin and sailfish. Ignoring his heart problems, he took sky rides in a parasail pulled behind a powerboat along the beach.

He made his first trip to Mexico on New Year's Day of 1966, traveling at the invitation of a contractor friend who was involved in Christian works south of the border. He and the friend filled up a GMC pickup truck with clothes, bicycles, and sewing machines and drove for several days. Bill donated a couple of bikes. They announced to the Mexican customs man that they were going fishing (and later salved their consciences by doing so) and tipped him a few pesos not to raise the tarpaulin and levy duty.

They drove on to the new Assemblies of God Bible school in Durango. It was run by a remarkable woman, Margaret Klassen. She came from a family of German Mennonites who had left Russia in the 1920s and traveled to Canada, Mexico, and finally Kansas. The drought of the Dust Bowl years had driven them on to California, where they picked grapes and cotton and settled in Reedley, a large Mennonite community southeast of Fresno, above the aquifer. Margaret joined a Full Gospel tabernacle associated with the Assemblies of God and then, in the 1950s, followed her calling to an Assemblies orphanage in Acapulco. A Baptist businessman from Texas, with a broom factory in Durango, had donated the land for the Bible school.

All but one of the makeshift, lean-to buildings had been gutted by fire when Oca and his friend pulled in. Something about the charred buildings, the dirt floors, and the earnest-looking boys and girls in their clean white shirts and blouses touched a chord. Oca remembered: "The Lord said to me, 'They can't do anything, but you can.' I said, 'Okay, Lord, what does it cost?' Then I said, 'I'll build you a dorm, a new one for the boys.' "

The students were warming their beans and tortillas on a charcoal stove, and heating bathwater over a pit. But the children were clean in a way that an Okie who remembered the thirties could appreciate. "They wore white shirts. And I mean they were clean. It was amazing how clean those people were, with no water to stay clean, hardly."

Back in Fresno, he rebuked himself. "I'd say, I can't stand myself, hardly, living like I was living. Them little children—and me putting forth no effort, not sharing with them or anything."

The dormitories cost some $9,000, a considerable sum in those days. Along with money from Oca, the school got a regular monthly stipend from the Assemblies of God, someone from Mississippi paid for a small library, and several times a year, when he and Ruby went to Mazatlán, Oca would come over to the school for several days, a longish time for a man as restless as he was. Margaret Klassen remembers Oca sending offerings "right along."

The ground-breaking for the new Bethsaida Bible Institute took place later in 1966. Oca and Ruby drove over the mountains from Mazatlán bringing clothes. He was all business on the trips, a sharp-eyed building inspector poking around and complaining about Mexican building methods. He and Ruby went to Mexico three or four times a year after that. It was another semifrontier, a little like the unfinished California he had known in the 1930s and full of opportunity, too, in its own way.

On the trips to Mexico, Oca never felt quite right just lounging in the hotel or fishing. Leaving the hotel in Mazatlán, where waiters in white jackets served papaya and *huevos rancheros* to tourists on a broad veranda overlooking the sea, he gravitated to back streets and mud sidewalks where barefoot children and mothers half a generation removed from the backcountry begged for money. He thought: *How pleased the people in a place like this would be to have a church.*

He found himself in a sea of Catholic indifference. The Catholic Church had a large cathedral in Mazatlán, but it didn't seem to reach out to people the way Oca's churches did. Catholic worship lacked the flavor, emotion, and personal contact with the Lord that seemed to him to be the essence of a relationship with God. He couldn't comprehend a religion in which the priests "spied" on their congregation through the confessional. No wonder, he thought, that so many Catholic priests were becoming "born again."

He smelled opportunity. Through Margaret, he met a Mexican family that was part of a grass-roots Pentecostal movement in Mazatlán. Mercedes Díaz must have instantly ignited a spark of recognition. Like Oca's mother, Mercedes was a woman of mixed blood (one parent was Chinese), with five children and a troubled marriage, struggling in a society in the throes of radical transformation. She had become involved with Pentecostals in 1963, and, though she had been raised a Catholic, the experience changed her life. "My home and family changed and a new life started," she said. "Through the Assemblies of God I found the power to change my husband."

When Oca met her in 1969, Mercedes was going door to door in the little fishing village of Urías, near Mazatlán, praying for the sick and holding meetings in a shack with a dirt floor. Urías, crisscrossed by railroad tracks and marred by potholed streets, was poor. Oca was convinced that the Holy Spirit was the answer to the poverty he saw and that Mercedes was the agent of the Lord, generously spreading the Holy Spirit among the fishing people of the village.

Doors were slammed in her face, but a few people began to come to her meetings. What the services lacked in amenities they more than made up for in intensity. Someone played an accordion, and the music made them feel good. The Catholic neighborhood was not always hospitable to the singing, praying worshipers. Rocks were thrown, and a few car windshields were smashed. Mercedes went to the police for help several times, but getting little help she kept on anyway.

Oca gave Mercedes money to tear down the shack she had been using in Urías and put up a two-room chapel with brick walls and a cement floor. In 1977, the Iglesia de las Asambleas de Dios—the Church of the Assemblies of God—was ready. Eventually, a seven-foot-high brick wall with a padlocked gate was erected to keep out vandals.

"I couldn't believe all they had done," said Oca. "They'd made benches out of any size board. And dirt floors. I went in and they sang and played the accordion, and the people would come forward. Never would have known most of them were Catholics who didn't know what accepting the Lord was. They didn't know Jesus loved them like He does. They'd been taught to be scared to death of God. God'd get even with 'em if they'd done something wrong."

Oca and Ruby went with the Díaz family to the first big baptismal service. One of the preachers was an ex-prizefighter, Ramón Pérez, who had put away his gloves and picked up a Bible, much like M. D. Townsend, the prizefighting evangelist Oca and Ruby had known in the 1930s.

Not long after the Urías chapel was built, the Lord spoke to Mercedes and told her to build a larger church in a different place. In 1980, she bought several lots on credit in Mazatlán's bustling Emiliano Zapata district, a working-class neighborhood of alleys lined with car repair shops through which wafted the pleasant smells from a commercial bakery. There was a public housing development across the road. For Mercedes, a more ambitious phase of church building had begun.

Oca was no pastor. He fixed buildings for others to fill, as he had done with the nursing homes. If a church got built, people would come, the way patients had come to Wish-I-Ah. He imagined himself as a kind of corporal in the Lord's army and told a friend that his first thought every morning was "Here I am, Lord, reporting for duty." The Mexican churches bore witness to his *activity*. Those who professed that they lived for Jesus were a dime a dozen; it was a more select group that could give hard evidence of *doing* something for Him. His accomplishments in Mexico vindicated his principles, not himself. A part of Oca felt that the Lord was on the side of growth.

His belief in what he was doing gave him the will to drive the hardest of deals with local suppliers of bricks, cement, lumber, and building materials. Haggling with a Mexican merchant at a lumber-yard, he was not satisfied with the discount he was getting and appealed to the manager: "We are two old men at the end of our lives. What are we going to do with money now? This is for God." An extra 10 percent came off. Then Oca turned to the question of a discount on a box or two of common nails.

Some may have wondered how a man who pushed so hard to save a few pesos could call himself a Christian at all. Oca's explanation was that he was doing it for God. The money saved did not go into his pocket. Money spared on a roof was a head start on the pews. Out of all the money that Oca saved, another church would grow.

. . .

IN A SENSE, Oca had been traveling on the same old river ever since he was a boy, except that by 1980 it had become a wide body of water moving forward with its own power and energy. What had begun in the sticks and the slums was now being carried forward by educated Catholics and Episcopalians seeking a richer spiritual life and calling themselves "charismatics." The stream had grown big and broad. There was room in it for little sects with a narrow focus on personal purity, big cathedrals attended by thousands, television and radio shows, and seminaries and universities. Oral Roberts, the healer, was planning to build a great hospital. The wealth flowing in from real estate, oil, and new Sun Belt businesses was helping to finance huge, independent churches all the way from north Florida to Orange County.

Pentecostalism, it seemed to some observers, was emerging as *the* Protestant religion for an America passing out of the age of the printed word and into the era of electronic communication. Walter J. Hollenweger, author of *The Pentecostals*, an exhaustive study of the movement, noted the view of the Baptist theologian Harvey Cox that Protestantism would decline "unless it makes room within itself for other means of communication." That was precisely what it was doing. Pentecostalism, with its emphasis on feelings, personality, intuition, and body language was emerging as the religion par excellence of the media age.

In the little churches south of the border, Oca had gone back to the headwaters. In them he reconnected with an authenticity and intensity that he had known long ago and that he had feared was in danger of being lost. Yet he himself no longer attended a little church at home in California. In the 1970s he had begun going to Peoples Church, the largest and fastest-growing religious enterprise in Fresno. Wits nicknamed it "Heaven on Herndon." In fact, its physical appearance was somewhat otherworldly, set back from Herndon Avenue in the middle of open fields, swooping roofs making it seem ready to ascend in flight at any moment. Actually Peoples Church was solidly rooted in this world and had lost a good deal of the Pentecostal character it had when founded in turkey sheds in 1953. Services were more "Baptistic" than Pentecostal, it was said. There was a robed choir and some of the best church music in Fresno—but by the 1970s, there was no speaking in tongues at the main Sunday service.

Compensating for the diminished intensity was a variety of programs that would have made it the envy of a small-town mayor—

programs for the single, the divorced, the recovering alcoholic. The Fresno Christian Education System, run by an association of eight churches, housed its high school at Peoples Church. In June 1980, the church set up a crisis-intervention hot line. The church's non-profit foundation produced the Sunday services for television channel KJEO, the ABC affiliate in Fresno, bringing Pastor G. L. Johnson's sermons to an estimated 15,000. An independent, for-profit subsidiary produced a half-hour series for educational television called "Little People," a sort of "Sesame Street" teaching moral and religious values. A retirement center and theological seminary were planned.

Peoples Church lacked the flavor of the Mexican churches into which Oca was pouring his energies, but, as Oca well knew, it satisfied other needs. Much as he had loved the springtime freshness of the Pentecostal Church of God in McFarland and Calvary Tabernacle—much as he identified with the simplicity and intensity of the Mexican sects—he knew he couldn't go back.

No one knew better than he how fragile the little churches were. They lived always at the brink of crisis. Pastors came out of nowhere and, through charisma, through personality and will, dominated their parishes. In the eleven years Oca and Ruby had been at Calvary Tabernacle, there had been four pastors and steady turmoil. One pastor clashed with the deacons over church priorities; he wanted to invest in a radio station and left when the deacons refused. Claude Weaver took over in 1949, but the Ohioan's style, more businesslike than emotional, left many of the Southwesterners cold. He clashed with the deacons on various matters until Oca and Ruby and many others drifted away. Even his son, Gordon, then married to Doris, joined the exodus.

In 1956, a group from Calvary, including Oca, founded Northeast Assemblies of God on Chestnut Avenue. But after ten years, this church, too, was thrown into crisis. Gerald Tatham, setting out to disprove rumors that the pastor had been investigated by police for sexual advances on a male minor, discovered that there was, in fact, something on the police blotter. The suspect pastor had denied the charges and pleaded no contest. Being the church's youth leader Gerald Tatham prevailed upon his father to force the matter into the open with the church elders, for the deacons, including Oca, had been aware of the matter but had withheld the information from the full congregation to protect privacy. There were long, anguishing meetings at which the deacons weighed the need for charity and forgiveness against the need for forthrightness. Assemblies of God officials were brought in. The pastor, who never admitted the allegations, eventually took a position in another town. But the affair divided old friends and families. Gerald and Oca, by being among those pressing for the airing of the matter, had done what they thought was right, but not all agreed.

Even without such traumas, many Pentecostal youths felt hemmed in or uncomfortable in the little churches of their parents. There was still a good deal of commotion at Pentecostal services in the 1950s and 1960s, "a lot of things going on," as Bill Tatham's eldest son, Billy, remembers it at Northeast Assemblies. "You know, this lady with a tambourine and all this stomping and yelling and screaming, I mean singing loud and praising, I should say. And long services and falling asleep on the pews."

Church surveys showed then (and subsequently) that a great many second-generation Pentecostals did not speak in tongues, yet a church such as Northeast Assemblies still put a gentle pressure on the youth to "perform." At the same time, the musically talented younger Tathams were restive with the musical fare of the smaller churches. Gerald had begun listening to Mozart and Bach played by philharmonic orchestras in high school and had enjoyed the old hymns and liturgies of the traditional Protestant service. In the 1960s, his musical talents brought him to the attention of a woman called Audrey Meiers, who was establishing choir clinics to upgrade the quality of church music. In the 1960s, Doris sang with the Sacred Concert Society in San Francisco, which included many professional singers. Gordon's brother directed the group. Brenda—who sang solos at Clovis High, joined a madrigal group, and was a guest soloist in Handel's *Messiah* at Fresno's Full Gospel Tabernacle—wanted more than Northeast Assemblies offered. She and her kid sister, Renee, began attending services at Full Gospel Tabernacle, which had a more diverse musical program and attracted a white-collar crowd.

When Brenda was married in 1964, the wedding took place not at Northeast Assemblies, but at the Full Gospel Tabernacle. Soon after that, Bill and Earline Tatham began attending services at Peoples Church. Bill found "people I could be comfortable with," but the adjustment was difficult at first. "I had to get accustomed to things being more formal. It seemed that people participated less. There were more things done *for* you at Peoples Church. And it seemed that everything was organized orderly and planned."

Brenda and Jerry followed to Peoples Church, and eventually
Oca and Ruby came. At the services on Wednesday nights and Sundays, more and more old friends turned up: Jimmy Nichols, Oca's
old auction partner; Thurlow Hubbart, the mailman from Calvary
Tabernacle and Northeast Assemblies; Paul Wilcox, the contractor
who had helped him finish renovating a nursing home when he had
the heart attack in 1962. Only Gerald and Cora and Gerald's Uncle
Vernon and his wife, Dora, stayed with the smaller churches.

Pentecostals were moving up in the world, and some were distanc-
ing themselves from the culture that was represented by noisy meetings at little wooden churches on the edge of town. The sixties saw
thousands of Assemblies of God churches adopt new names such as
"Christian Center," the neutrality of which was meant to downplay
the "holy roller" connection. And as the social position of Pentecostals
changed, so did their needs.

In one respect, Peoples Church *was* a kind of Heaven for many
of Fresno's Pentecostals: it was a representative California institution
that was open to everybody, large enough to rise above the petty
quarrels that had splintered so many of the smaller churches. The
name itself had a kind of populist ring and was not one likely to be
found on an Episcopalian, Presbyterian, or even Baptist facility. Many
of the little churches resented Peoples Church's growing power in
the Fresno church community, but they could do little more than
look on.

Pastor Johnson appealed to Baptists who wanted a somewhat
freer style of worship, to Methodists who were disillusioned with
what they saw as the liberal bent of their denomination, and to the
nonaffiliated. Johnson said, "Here came Baptists, here came Methodists, here came Mennonite Brethren." A cross section of the business
community was represented as well. There was Edward Baloian, an
Armenian American who owned truck farms and packing sheds; Jack
Harvey, whose Harvey Byproducts processed dog food; Paul Read,
manager of the W. W. Lyles irrigation pipe company; the pharmacist
Earl Giacolini, Bill Tatham's sometime business partner; and other
self-made men, as well as influential local officials and politicians.

The church had come a long way since its founding in 1953 by
Floyd Hawkins, a "boy evangelist" from Oklahoma. The first build-
ings were the refurbished turkey sheds from which Hawkins's son
Wayne had scrubbed the bird droppings, symbolically eradicating the
shame that Floyd Hawkins felt about his "Okie-hick" background.
Hawkins was determined to make Peoples Church a dignified place

with the finest music and none of the holy roller ambience. He had
been on his way to achieving that goal when he stepped down for
personal reasons. After a brief hiatus following Hawkins's departure,
G. L. Johnson became pastor in 1963.

George Lee Johnson was a cordial, energetic man with considerable preaching gifts and a cornball sense of humor ("Good morning
from Fresno, home of the fruits and the nuts"). G.L., as everyone
called him, was one of Fresno's success stories. Immaculate in a three-
piece gray suit, he looked as if he had spent his whole life in front of
a prospering, growing congregation. To compensate for the first-rate
education he had never had, G.L. tried to read one or two books
a week on nonreligious subjects, devouring sociology, psychology,
economics, and biographies of a wide variety of contemporary per-
sonalities. His most prized possession, he told the Fresno *Bee*, was his
library; his favorite television program was "60 Minutes." His dream
was to found a theological seminary in Fresno that would draw scholars from around the country—and that, incidentally, would be his
legacy to posterity and the valley.

Hidden beneath a breezy exterior, however, was a driving ambition to erase his childhood pain and poverty. He had been born in
1928 in Houston, Texas. His father, a belligerent man who abused
G.L.'s mother, was a previously married Baptist minister. When G.L.
was only five, his mother left his father and went with her children
to live in a tiny community forty miles north of Beaumont. After that,
G.L. saw his father again only one time before attending his funeral
many years later. His father vanished from his life in 1933. "We
weren't poor—we just didn't have any money," G.L. liked to say
brightly about those times, reflecting the view of so many Depression
victims that only hoboes and tramps were truly "poor." His mother
"worked out," and as soon as he was old enough he began shining
shoes at a local drugstore. Eventually, his mother remarried and they
moved back to Beaumont. Evidently this was not a happy turn of
events for G.L. His new stepfather, no Christian, had a drinking
problem. The boy's best moments were spent at the local Baptist
church of his mother's. Before he was ten he was teaching Sunday
school and leading the singing.

Then his mother switched to an Assemblies of God church, one
of the works that had sprouted up in Texas many long years after
the religious revivals that had followed thousands of disoriented
sharecroppers and hill people into the oil patch after the Spindletop
oil strike of 1901. G.L. received the baptism of the Holy Spirit and

spoke in tongues on the day Hitler invaded Poland in 1939. It seemed
to the teenager that the "end times" were at hand. The news from
Europe, he said, "drove me to my knees."

From then on he was constantly in church. His gifts as a song
leader and Sunday school preacher caught the attention of a traveling
evangelist by the name of Elvis Davis. A year after the religious
experience ignited by Hitler's marauding armies, he began traveling
with Davis to country churches, preaching to the young people while
Davis ministered to the poor farmers. By the time he was fourteen,
G.L. was holding his own revivals and preaching around Beaumont,
attracting what he called "the steady, hardworking people, though a
lower socioeconomic level, the poorer classes of people, I'm sure."
He was also learning how to pick out a song on the piano and hit the
right notes on a trombone. But he wanted more. Halfway through
high school he transferred to the Assemblies of God's Southwestern
Bible Institute in Waxahachie, Texas.

For a poor boy with little chance for college, a Bible school offered
possibilities. "I'd made up my mind if I was going to be in the ministry
I wasn't going to be one of those guys who work in grocery stores all
week," he said. "I'm choleric. Hard driving. I rebelled against poor
quality." Southwestern was one of the Assemblies' first efforts to
give better groundings to its future pastors; it offered instruction in
Greek, vocal music, homiletics, interpretation of scripture, parlia-
mentary law, and something called "articulation."

G.L. seized the opportunity. On weekends he and his friends
would go into small country churches to sing, pray, and play music.
Many of the Waxahachie students had fathers pastoring churches,
and they wrote home about the exceptional preaching abilities of
their schoolmate G. L. Johnson. Invitations for him to come and
preach were soon forthcoming.

In 1947, at the age of nineteen, he finished at Southwestern. He
did a stint as a traveling youth worker, then as an occasional song
leader for Oral Roberts. Then came a kind of purgatory. The Assemblies sent him to Cleveland, Ohio, to be an assistant pastor in a church
attended by a mixture of families from the Appalachians and Eastern
Europe. G.L. did not like it. His fiancée, a woman who came from
the "more progressive" Dallas–Fort Worth area, was in Texas; in
winter there was the "snow and ice and coal smoke and soot and filth
of the East." He "yearned to see the setting sun on the plains, where
it was wide open and clean." The Cleveland experience convinced
him that he would not mourn if the eastern part of the United States
broke off and floated out to sea.

The Assemblies let him come back to Texas after seven months. He got married, and other assignments followed in Corsicana, Texas; Owensboro, Kentucky; and finally Tallahassee, Florida—"a very cultured city," with "very high-level people," according to Johnson.

The Tallahassee assignment posed an early test of his skills as a pastoral politician. Half the congregation were redneck and old-time Pentecostals, the rest were middle-class, many of whom worked at Florida State University. G.L. then began to evolve the philosophy that would guide his efforts to make churches grow. He planned to reach out to what he called "the salt, the bread and butter of America—the moral fiber and strength of this nation: the middle-class evangelical:

"You don't build churches in the lowest sections of the city, nor in the highest. You build on the forty-hour-a-week people. You build out of that hardworking, consistent person. The higher class people—they're going to the mountains or the coast on Sunday or flying across the country, whereas your middle class—they're consistent, faithful, dependable, hardworking people. . . . Where do our strong, fine leaders come from? I have a feeling they come from the lower middle classes more often than the upper classes. . . . Where do people in the ministry come from? Nearly all from middle or lower-middle classes—maybe the lower classes. People who've learned to hurt and life has made them discipline themselves into a structure that made them aspire to better things."

In 1961, G.L. moved to Fresno to help run the Assemblies of God Latin American Orphanage program. Like most Texans, he felt right at home in California's dry, sunny central valley. Traditional family and church values were important there, but people were energetic and wanted their institutions to grow. Two years later he became pastor of Peoples Church.

In 1971, Johnson made arrangements with Denman H. Mapson, a professional consultant, to advise the church on administration, management, and planning. Mapson had known Tammy Bakker while he was pastoring a church and serving as a district leader in north Minnesota. Later he had met Jim Bakker while executive of an Assemblies of God college in Minneapolis that both Bakkers attended. At Mapson's recommendation, Peoples Church set up a separate foundation, to which the Internal Revenue Service gave tax-exempt status as a charitable organization in 1972. One of the first tax-free gifts the foundation recorded was an automobile valued at $2,500, donated by Bill Tatham.

Mapson wasted no time in introducing modern administrative

practices and educating Pastor Johnson about the business fundamentals of running a modern church enterprise. Spiritual leadership
came first, but it was also crucial for the growth-minded pastor to
know something about tax law, zoning and planning, real estate, and
fiscal management. Mapson had the church's bookkeeping computerized on two main-frame computer terminals, which he set up at
Peoples Foundation and at Fresno airport, to facilitate time-sharing
with paying customers.

   Church membership was helped by G. L.'s regular radio broadcasts over local stations. Mapson and G. L. also discussed the possibility of using television to spread the message. Mapson and his staff
began to plan for the new property on Herndon Avenue in 1974,
and they discussed with G.L. the possibility of undertaking some
kind of commercial development along Herndon Avenue. Mapson
masterminded the fund-raising program for the big new Herndon
Avenue facility, using the catchy names "Possess the Land" and "Together We Build." A student of the tax laws, he pointed out to potential property donors that by giving to a tax-exempt charitable
organization they could deduct the full market value of the property
rather than the "book value," which usually was lower because it
counted depreciation on any improvements.

   Once the Herndon Avenue land was acquired, Bill Tatham gave
the project a boost with a $300,000 gift. Mapson and his staff handled
the design studies and selected Commercial Builders, of Wichita,
Kansas, whose president, Roe Messner, was one of the country's
leading builders of churches. The development provided opportunities for Fresno's entire evangelical community. The Fresno Christian
Education System could use the property that Peoples Church was
vacating on Cedar Avenue for its grammar school and the new Peoples facility could house a Christian high school.

   The most dramatic moment in the campaign came when a Madera rancher, Sherman Thomas, rose from his seat one Sunday,
walked down the aisle, and presented G.L. with a check for a million
dollars. It was spontaneous on Thomas's part, but, in fact, it was the
final product of a complicated set of transactions that Thomas had
previously set in motion by donating parcels of farmland to the foundation with the understanding that he would suggest a use for it later.
The check was made out to Peoples Foundation from a title company
and reflected proceeds from the sale of the farmland. The transaction
enabled the foundation to purchase and equip facilities for the Fresno
Christian Education System and to use those facilities as collateral for

additional projects. It was a very sophisticated business deal, and it showed how complex the financial operations of large, multimillion-dollar tax-exempt churches had become. The ribbon cutting for the new $4.5 million Herndon Avenue facility took place in June 1978. The same year Mapson was invited to become executive pastor.

G. L. Johnson had carried the church through a time of extreme turbulence. Around the time he took over, the charismatic renewal movement was starting to call Americans back to the miraculous, inspiring, and emotional in the Christian experience. Gerald Tatham had been directing the choir at the Full Gospel Tabernacle in Fresno one day when the hippie movement and the flower children showed up at the church door. Members of Tony Salerno's Agape Force, one of the alternative Christian groups that materialized out of nowhere, showed up. Gerald thought the girls looked "earthy" in their long dresses and brogans. Salerno had attended the Assemblies of God's Southern California College with Gerald's sister Brenda, and he was a sign of a new current in the Assemblies of God. Salerno rented an old building across from Fresno High School and filled it with his followers, including many former hippies.

Much of the charismatic movement seemed phony to Gerald. "The real Jesus People weren't the ones who floated through in the sixties," he said. "They were the Oca Tathams and Claude Baldwins who were there all along." Many of the kids in the Agape Force seemed to Gerald to be on ego trips. He saw defiance in the way they clapped in unison, raised their hands, and said "Glory" louder than anyone in the church, and it seemed to him they were saying, "*We* are holier than you are."

Yet he and Cora were intrigued. Gerald craved a balance between his church's emphasis on self-denial and the equally powerful Christian impulse toward charity. Gerald and Cora were interested in the wider range of spirituality described by Paul in his Second Letter to the Corinthians. This included subtler, less concrete manifestations than speaking in tongues, a more intuitive life of the spirit, as was meant by "word of knowledge," "word of wisdom," and "discernment of spirits."

Down in Orange County, Pastor Chuck Smith, a Pentecostal preacher, was baptizing the hippies who wandered along the Huntington and Laguna beaches or camped out in Tahquitz Canyon, stoned on marijuana or tripped out on acid. With this remnant Smith founded the church of the "Jesus people." In Fresno, there were religious "happenings": the Agape Force, seminars on "dancing in the spirit," *koinonia* groups, and Christian rock festivals. It was all part of a new awakening, a spontaneous search for fresh answers and direction in a time of cultural confusion. Catholics were buffeted by a Vatican that one year seemed to be open to social change and the next reaffirmed its stand against artificial birth control. Jews struggled with the moral dilemma of a warlike Israel risen from the ashes of the Holocaust. The Protestant community, ideologically disordered by civil rights advocates and anti-Communist crusaders, hungered for simple spirituality without ideology.[1]

The charismatic renewal stressed the healing, intuitive, and prophetic gifts that Protestants generally had dismissed as superstition and pseudoreligion. Pentecostalism, a folk religion of the materially deprived, inspired a mass religion of the spiritually deprived but often well-to-do. Charismatic groups appeared at the citadel of Catholicism, Notre Dame, among Phi Beta Kappa students at Yale, and in the High Church setting of an Episcopalian congregation in an affluent Los Angeles suburb. At Dick Tatham's Assemblies of God Church in Lake Havasu City, half of those joining were ex-Catholics. By the mid-1970s, the charismatic movement had touched millions around the world and had been accepted by the Vatican, Episcopalian bishops, and respected theologians. This turn of events perhaps could only have been fully appreciated by John Wesley himself, the Oxford-educated High Church Englishman who had grafted the ecstatic mysticism of Catholic divines onto the body of Protestantism to create the foundation of Methodism. Two centuries later, ecstatic experience again entered the hierarchical churches. In a sense, history was repeating itself.

In Fresno, churches died and were reborn in the turmoil. But Peoples Church kept its distance from the movement. "Where have they been all this time?" G.L. inquired of the Johnny-come-latelies. If imitation was the sincerest form of flattery, then "traditional" Pentecostals could be rightly proud of having been the first "people of the miracle." Yet some must have seen that the renewal movement was also a kind of trump card, played by Catholics and Episcopalians—representing historic tradition and, in the Episcopalians' case, the social upper crust. The newcomers came from traditions and ways of life that conflicted with the old Pentecostal code. Then, too, the new, independent churches bursting into existence suggested that the energy might be shifting elsewhere.

G.L. shunned the more exuberant charismatics. Indeed, said one observer, the church began to attract some "people who were not motivated in the areas of the Holy Spirit. . . . Peoples Church hung in solid and took in people who were not looking for hell, fire and brimstone, and the tongues. A lot of them didn't practice Bible studies, speaking in tongues, interpretation."

The dilemma was clear: to make Christianity "relevant"—or just to increase church membership—pastors had to appeal to the newly minted middle classes. Successful pastors had to be attuned, able to read the mood of their congregations. Johnson abandoned the condemnatory preaching once so common among old-time ministers. "Let 'em laugh. Let 'em cry. Let 'em worship," he said. "I'm not going to fight 'em."[2] He personally continued to speak in tongues—it was "good for my mental health," he stated—but he did not want members of his congregation breaking into tongues on Sunday morning.

Oca was proud of Peoples Church and of G.L., yet year after year he did not become a member. He had been disappointed by pastors and churches too often, and he didn't want to be hurt again. In any case, he considered himself still a little-church guy, and Peoples Church was a big institution. He gravitated toward intensity—toward places where people were hurting and hungry for the Lord, where there were "old-time songs with a message," where it was "real" and one sensed "the flow of the Holy Spirit." When it was like that, Oca said, he was ready to "go all the way."

It worried him that, in California, Christianity itself seemed in perpetual danger of becoming watered down. He knew, of course, that a great movement was not a monastery. It couldn't be built solely around denial. But it seemed to him that too many compromises were being made.

Everything that had happened since the presidential election of 1964 convinced him that resistance to the secular forces at loose at home and abroad had become more necessary than ever. "What's happened since World War Two is our homes went to pot, our kids went to the dogs, they've been on dope and everything else," he said. "You mention it, they've been doing it."

As a trader, poking around everywhere, Oca understood what a complex and varied world lay outside his door. Opinionated and judgmental as he could be, he was not intolerant. He was less interested in changing other people's opinions—a long and difficult task, as one who had spent his life witnessing to others well knew—than in making sure there was room for his own. In his own way he hated intolerance, whether it showed in friends from the Church of Christ who taunted his Pentecostalism or in a national media that ignored

religion and ridiculed TV preachers. Much as he might hope for
it, he doubted that Christianity would ever completely transform
America. What he really feared was that *America* would transform the
Christian people—that the flavor and intensity that he had staked his
life on would be swept away in a tide of secularism, government
bureaucracy, and colorless ideology.

The 1962 Supreme Court decision banning prayer in schools
continued to rankle him. "We wondered how far it's going to go when
they stop prayer in the school and they can have prayer in Congress.
They can't have it in school, where those little kids need it. They can't
have that. That's forbid. If they start in the schools and are able to
stop it in the schools, and a little girl can't even use a rosary, and
when they'll take men and jail them for months because they permitted prayer in the school or the Bible being read . . . when they'll jail
men for months in our country for that, we're in bad trouble."

Communism was gaining ground, having won Cambodia and
Vietnam in the 1970s. Oca's feelings about Vietnam remained bitter.

"Nixon went in and did what Goldwater said he would do. He
bombed them to lead them back into talks, if you remember. Twelve
days and nights of hell, fire, and brimstone on Hanoi. They wanted
to talk after five or six days and nights of that. He said, I don't think
you had enough yet. I think we need to go on now and give you
some more until you get ready to keep your word and know I mean
business.' And they knew he meant business and he quit. They were
at the meeting fast. And that's what I figured ought to have been
done and that's what Goldwater would have done. But Johnson, no.
Johnson didn't.

"Remember?" said Oca. "They were begging to release those
prisoners if we'd quit bombing them. They lied and said they'd release
them by Christmas and them Democrats said that's just political talk,
you know, they have reason to lie about it and you remember McGovern said, 'If I'm elected, I'll crawl all the way to Hanoi if I have to, to
stop this war—and I'll crawl waving a white flag.' And when they did
that, man, those guys in Hanoi just backed off, right then. Said, 'Hey,
we've got nothing to lose. Just wait another month or so and if he's
in, we've won the war. If we let it go like this, we'll never have to
give in.' "

Along with the foreign-policy developments since 1964, the
courts and Congress had issued a steady stream of rulings and laws
that made the federal government a guarantor of the rights of blacks,
women, gays, the handicapped, and minorities, while at the same

time continuing to redistribute tax money to the lower classes. As Thomas and Mary Edsall noted in their book *Chain Reaction*, from 1965 to 1975 the number of households on welfare went from slightly more than a million to almost 3.5 million. The Food Stamp program, which had served 4.3 million people in 1970, fed 17.1 million in 1975. At the same time, the relative tax bite of Americans was increasing (though less than was often asserted). From 1960 to 1975, the Edsalls noted, the maximum Social Security tax liability grew by 473 percent while per-capita income went up only 166 percent.

In roughly the same period, an outpouring of judicial decisions and laws seemed to many to be removing government as an ally of the traditional American family. Some religious fundamentalists believed that parts of the new body of law went against scripture. They cited Ephesians 5:23, "For the husband is the head of the wife, even as Christ is head of the church," to suggest that equal rights laws for women in the workplace and other venues went against Holy Writ. Others cited passages from Genesis, Leviticus, and Romans to argue that homosexuality was a sin, even as local jurisdictions passed ordinances protecting homosexuals and lesbians in housing, jobs, education, and public accommodations.

Divorce laws were liberalized in most states, which now had no-fault divorce, whereby courts did not so much dissolve marriages as give legal recognition to the fact of a marital breakup. *Editorial Research Reports* noted in 1973 "a diminishing regard for the 'till death do us part' mandate of the nuptial rite."[3] U.S. divorces rose from 264,000 per year in 1940 to 839,000 in 1972. (Throughout the 1970s, meanwhile, the rate of illegitimate births for both blacks and whites increased significantly.)

The nation's system of punishment was overhauled as a result of a prisoners' rights movement, a series of court rulings protecting various rights of criminal suspects and defendants, and a four-year moratorium on the death penalty from 1972 to 1976, which effectively took an estimated six hundred people off death row.[4]

In 1967, California's newly elected governor, Ronald Reagan, signed the legislation that marked the turning point on abortion, the Therapeutic Abortion Act. The law declared that an abortion was legal when performed by a qualified doctor, in a hospital certified by the American Hospital Association, to prevent mental or physical damage to the mother. By 1971, the number of legal abortions performed in the state had risen rapidly, reaching 116,000 that year.[5]

Although Reagan signed the bill, he used a veto threat to force the legislature to delete the word "fetal indications" from it, in deference to the predominantly Catholic antiabortion camp's contention that since an embryo was virtually a person, the phrase was an inappropriate one. Technically, the law did not permit abortion on demand, but it offered considerable leeway and protection to the medical profession, which lobbied hard for it. In 1973, the Supreme Court issued its *Roe* v. *Wade* decision that legalized abortion nationwide.

To conservative Protestants and Catholics, the new body of law represented a kind of betrayal by the powers that be. Until the 1950s, government had been an active ally of the traditional family, prohibiting and punishing conduct and activities that many Americans believed were detrimental to family stability. By 1980, everything had changed. Conservative Christians maintained they could have lived with the changes if government had simply turned neutral. But it seemed to have gone beyond that. The banishment of religion and religious discussion from schools and classrooms; legal action against Christmas displays on public property; government-funded abortion; school textbooks that seemed to inculcate a scrubbed, secularized version of American history; the teaching of values without any religious basis to them; sex education in the classroom—all seemed to say that America was moving away from God because the government had changed sides.

To some of the religious, the political activities of the nonreligious looked more and more like a coherent program based on a defined set of beliefs—in effect, a "religion."[6] Thus, the theologian Carl F. Henry would speak of secularism as "the new protected faith in America." Secularism, he and others argued, was triumphant in a way Christianity never had been because of the separation requirements of the Constitution, for secularism now seemed backed by the full power of the state.

In 1977, Jimmy Carter came to the White House supported by the votes and hopes of millions of evangelical Protestants. He was arguably the most religious President of this century, a born-again Christian and an active deacon in his local Baptist Church. His sister, Ruth Stapleton Carter, was a nationally known charismatic, and his vice president, Walter F. Mondale, was a preacher's son. Yet Carter turned out to be a disappointment to many evangelical Christians.

His closest advisers may have underestimated, or even missed altogether, the provisional quality of the evangelical vote for Carter in 1976. In his "Initial Working Paper on Political Strategy," written

just over a month after the election, on December 10, 1976, the
pollster Patrick Caddell mentioned Catholics, Jewish voters, black
voters, the labor vote, and the poor, but not the born-again vote,
other than to say, almost as an aside, that the President-elect had
done exceptionally well among "white Protestants." Carter's support
in the South, according to Caddell, "seems to have been based on
economic and class divisions." He noted that Carter ran well in southeast and central Ohio, without saying that one reason was his very
strong showing among born-again voters. The good showing there
he attributed simply to the large number of people with "some roots
in the South."

Carter gave senior government positions to people whom many
evangelical Christians considered to be liberal and secularist and
showed himself to be an old-fashioned Baptist separatist on church-
state issues. He probably was personally opposed to abortion. Moreover, he regularly signed appropriations bills containing Hyde
Amendment language that placed various restrictions on the use of
federal Medicaid funds for abortions. Nonetheless, during his term
hospitals continued to receive such funds for abortion counseling,
as well as for abortion procedures in some circumstances, such as
protection of the life of the mother. At the same time, the Internal
Revenue Service continued efforts begun under the Ford and Nixon
administrations to penalize private academies, including religiously
supported ones, that did not enroll black students.

Oca detested Carter. He blamed him for high interest rates and
a weak foreign policy: "I questioned so many times his being all that
born-again. Having him as our leader, I didn't trust him on anything
anymore."

Carter's presidency appears to have been the point at which millions of conservative Christians like Oca became terminally fed up
and began to think about what they wanted in political terms. Suddenly, the joining of populist religion and populist politics seemed
feasible.

The New Right became in the mid-1970s a kind of popular front
for the newer forces of resistance. Some had always resented the
upper crust and were now rejecting the very station that their new
wealth was giving them. Along with such people were working-class
Catholics who despised the vanity, wealth, and intellectual preten-
sions of the Vatican; Baptists who were angry at what they saw as
the compromises and accommodations among their fellow Baptists;
Southerners and Westerners who hated the condescension of conser-

vative intellectuals. Many were adrift on the surface of America:
Baptists who had been Catholics, Pentecostals who had been Baptists,
charismatics who had been nothing.

Paul Weyrich, who headed the Committee for the Survival of a
Free Congress in Washington, had grown up in a Wisconsin German
Catholic family. His father tended a boiler, and Weyrich emphatically
considered himself a populist. He had contempt for the mainstream,
East Coast–dominated Republican Party and said that he felt "closer
to William Jennings Bryan than to the Tories of whatever stripe."[7]
The Republican Party, he said, was made up of "effete gentlemen,"
and the old right was as "elitist as the liberal intellectuals. . . . they
don't know a thing about precincts and neighborhoods and they don't
want to know."

Although Weyrich himself was from the Midwest, a key aspect of
New Right influence involved the increasing power of the South. The
migration of millions of white Southerners to the West in the middle
decades of this century produced a tectonic shift in America's culture
and politics, one that was fully revealed only after 1964.

After the Civil War the South had been to a certain degree marginalized by poverty and its handling of the race issue. It was difficult
for non-Southerners to comprehend its complex outlook, culture,
and character because of those conditions. This changed. The civil
rights movement and court-ordered desegregation transformed the
South and removed the race question as a peculiarly Southern problem. The South and Southwest began to flex their economic and
industrial muscle. Northern factories moved south in order to take
advantage of its cheaper, nonunionized labor, while the South's continuing influence in strategically important committees of Congress
kept federal money flowing into the region for defense, space, water
projects, and highway building. (Reapportionment also increased the
political representation of the Sun Belt in the House of Representatives as its population growth outstripped that of the North and
Midwest.) The Sun Belt had always had oil and gas, soybeans and
cotton and rice. Soon it had auto and parts plants (Tennessee), space
industries (Texas), high tech (Texas), and banking (South Carolina,
Georgia, Florida, and Texas).

As Southerners moved west, their voice was more fully amplified
and the culture of the South and its neighboring borderlands, especially its religious culture, regained a weight appropriate to its size.
And in politics, notably in the selection of a President, it was the
linchpin of campaigns.

Along with the migrating people, an outlook and a particular way

Oca and Ruby Tatham in 1935

ABOVE LEFT: Cleo and friend in
1936. ABOVE RIGHT: Oca Tatham
in Oklahoma when he was about
twenty. BELOW: Cora Tatham
and her mother, Abigail
Sumpter, in Salisaw, Oklahoma,
1940

ABOVE: Ruby and Doris beside Ruby's first washing machine, 1935. ABOVE RIGHT: Oca hamming it up in California, 1934. RIGHT: Ruby and Oca with Doris and Dick on the beach near Los Angeles, along the way west, August 1934

LEFT: Hard times in Delano,
1936: (*left to right*) Vernon, Oca,
Ophelia (*child*), Walter (*behind
Ophelia*), Norma, Cora, and Cleo.
CENTER: (*standing, left to right*)
Wyvern Rogers with baby,
Walter Tatham, Cora Tatham,
Ophelia, Ruby with Oca, Jr.,
Oca with Dick, Granpa Rogers,
Melvina Robbins with baby, Sid
Robbins with young child, 1936.
All three babies died within a
few months. BELOW: The babies'
graves in 1936

TOP LEFT: Walter and Oca Tatham.
TOP RIGHT: Vernon Tatham with the
guitar he took to the army in World
War II. ABOVE: Oca and Ruby with
their children, ready for Sunday
morning church, 1943. ABOVE RIGHT:
Cleo Frost in front of her house in
Delano, 1992. RIGHT: Dick, Oca,
Gerald, and Bill Tatham, 1954

TOP: The church at San Juan and Kern streets in McFarland. Today boarded up but otherwise just as it was when Oca and the others built it in 1936. CENTER: Calvary Tabernacle in Fresno, the Tathams' church from 1944 to 1956. LEFT: Aerial view of People's Church, with parking space for 1,110 vehicles. The Tathams began attending in the 1960s.

RIGHT: Bill Tatham with Pat
Robertson. CENTER: Ona and
Oca (right) and friends (left) with
Jerry Falwell (center) at Falwell's
church in 1986. BOTTOM: Bill
Tatham (second from left) and his
son Billy (far right) after a New
York jury awarded the USFL one
dollar on its antitrust suit against
the NFL. USFL attorney Harvey
Myerson (center). Cotton merchant
Billy Dunavant of Memphis (left),
another USFL owner.

TOP: Billy Tatham and his fiancée, Susan McDannald, celebrating in Phoenix after an Outlaws victory, February 1985. CENTER: Oca's granddaughter Cindy Critchfield *(seated)* with *(left to right)* her son, Brent, husband, Bill, and daughter, Janée, 1992. RIGHT: Ona and Oca in Mexico on a recent trip

of life moved West, one that was peculiarly receptive to the populist messages of many different politicians, not only Reagan and Wallace, but also to protests such as California's Proposition 13 referendum measure, which in June 1978 rolled back real-estate tax assessments to 1976 levels and barred any new increases. These Southerners-turned-Westerners were generally receptive to the tax revolt, whose aim was to "starve" government of the tax funds it needed to carry through liberal programs. And they were generally receptive to candidates who appealed for a more moral, godly America.

Protestants, however, were, surprisingly, latecomers to the resistance of the 1970s. Born-again fundamentalist Christians tended to stick to their own knitting, raising their families, supervising their children, guiding their churches. *Their* children were not having abortions, giving birth to illegitimate babies, taking drugs, or marching in demonstrations—or so they maintained. Many born-again Christians felt that their most important contribution to a moral America came through imparting good, religious values to their children.

When a handful of Catholics, including Weyrich, began to wage fights against legalized abortion and for a constitutional amendment that would restore prayer in the schools, they did not get much Protestant help. In 1971, the Southern Baptist Convention, the largest Protestant group in the country, had passed almost unanimously a resolution upholding the right to have abortion if a mother was emotionally or physically endangered by having a child. Similarly, support for the Supreme Court's school-prayer decision remained strong in the Southern Baptist Convention through the 1970s.

Initially, the New Right offered itself to white Protestants not as an all-embracing doctrine or ideology, but as an ally in solving a particular problem. In August 1978, the Internal Revenue Service announced that it was proposing regulations to remove the tax exemption of private schools that practiced racial discrimination. The regulations merely codified the decision on this issue already made under the Nixon administration in 1970, in response to rising numbers of cases brought against these schools by civil rights groups. In 1976, while Gerald Ford was still President, for example, the IRS had lifted the tax exemption of Bob Jones University in Greenville, South Carolina.[8] Under the new rules proposed in 1978, the IRS would have authority to review the tax status of about 3,500 schools, most of them segregated academies formed after the government had desegregated public schools in the South. These hundreds of mainly white Christian schools attached to predominantly white congregations panicked. Some of them clearly had reason to believe that government had overstepped itself. These included schools in rural areas in which blacks were either few in number or attended their own churches. The IRS softened the proposed regulations the following February, and in September 1979 the Senate, led by North Carolina Republican Jesse A. Helms, voted to postpone putting the guidelines into effect for a year. Thereafter the issue became caught up in a protracted court battle in which attorneys for Bob Jones University argued that the University's practices were protected by First Amendment guarantees of religious freedom and civil rights attorneys argued that while the First Amendment should be protected in this as in all cases, it didn't extend to protecting allegedly religious positions that had secular consequences, such as segregation.

The IRS action was the catalyst that brought Catholic activists together with the hitherto apathetic Protestant groups. Congressman Philip M. Crane, an Illinois Republican, now accused the IRS of casting itself in the role of "social engineer,"[9] and, for the first time, conservative Protestants began to mobilize at the grass-roots level. When Weyrich addressed a meeting in Washington of some three hundred representatives of Christian schools in the National Christian Action Coalition, a predominantly Protestant group formed to fight the regulations, he was astonished at the reaction. "In all my years I had never seen a group as fired up as that," he recalls. The issue for the first time brought conservative Protestants into partisan political involvement, on the side of the GOP and against the Democratic administration that was forcing the issue. "[IRS Commissioner] Jerome Kurtz has done more to bring Christians together than any man since the Apostle Paul," said Robert Billings, Sr., director of the National Christian Action Coalition.[10]

Sensing that a turning point had come, Weyrich consulted Ed McAteer, a former marketing manager for Colgate-Palmolive who had gone to work in 1976 for Howard Phillips's Conservative Caucus, another New Right group. Phillips was Jewish and McAteer was a Baptist, but they saw eye to eye on politics. As a salesman, McAteer had made the acquaintance of hundreds of churchmen of every stripe and denomination.

The chief operative of Conservative Caucus was Richard Viguerie, a Louisianan of French Catholic background. His experience in right-wing politics dated back to the 1964 Goldwater campaign. He had a voluminous computerized direct mail system, built up from a list of donors to George Wallace's 1968 campaign. With McAteer's help, it seemed possible to put together a coalition of conservative

Catholics and Protestants that might rise above America's old religious animosities.

From an organizational standpoint, Catholics brought more than a thousand years of experience in the techniques of evolving coherent positions on public policies. Their presence in a political-religious movement would also be a kind of reassurance to those who doubted the commitment of Protestant fundamentalists to pluralistic democracy. (That very concern had once been directed at Catholics thought to be under the control of the Vatican, but it had faded after President Kennedy's election.)

The Baptists, America's largest Protestant denomination, brought two centuries of organizational experience and a vast grass-roots presence across the Sun Belt.

Pentecostals and charismatics added fire, emotion, and momentum. Their churches and denominations were the fastest growing in the nation. The Assemblies of God denomination's members and followers had grown from about 600,000 in 1970 to over a million in 1980, and the membership was continuing to grow at a rate that would allow the Assemblies to overtake the Episcopalian and Presbyterian denominations before 1990. In addition, hundreds of independent charismatic enterprises had been sprouting up.

Pentecostals dominated the exploding medium of television through the electronic ministries of such evangelists as Pat Robertson, Jimmy Swaggart, Oral Roberts, Jim Bakker, Paul Crouch, and others. Bakker, Swaggart, and Crouch were all affiliated with the Assemblies of God. (Crouch's Trinity Broadcasting Network, headquartered in an industrial park, between the offices of the Morton-Thiokol and Toshiba corporations, was well represented in southern California, Oklahoma, southern Florida, and southern Illinois. Crouch's father, A. F. Crouch, had attended the founding meeting of the Assemblies in Hot Springs, Arkansas, in 1914, and Paul's brother Phil had been president of the Assemblies of God's flagship institution, Central Bible College in Springfield, Missouri, before serving as business adviser to TBN. Paul's wife, Jan, a heavily madeup blond woman who appeared on Crouch's show with a beehive hairdo and sometimes a wig, was the daughter of Edgar Bethany, a founder of the Assembly of God's Southeastern College in Lakeland, Florida, and one of the leading early figures of the Pentecostal movement in Georgia.) Robertson, though a Baptist, professed to having been blessed by the Holy Spirit and to be Spirit-filled. Roberts was no longer strictly speaking a Pentecostal since he had shocked his followers by leaving

the Pentecostal Holiness Church and joining the Methodists in 1968.
Many Pentecostals had taken this as a repudiation,[11] but the charismatic influence in Roberts's institutions remained strong.

In recruiting Pentecostals, however, the political activists from
Washington did face several problems. Pentecostals had little or no
tradition of political involvement and were almost by definition ill
equipped to participate in a movement requiring group coherence.
Pentecostalism was, by definition, based on uniquely personal and
impenetrably private experiences. Moreover, the Pentecostal television showmen had ratings to protect and audiences to retain, and
they were reluctant to offend Democrats.

As the IRS furor was building, McAteer took Phillips, Viguerie,
and Weyrich to meet Reverend Jerry Falwell, pastor of Thomas Road
Baptist Church in Lynchburg, Virginia. During a nine-hour meeting
at the Holiday Inn in Lynchburg, the Moral Majority was born. They
talked and talked, for Falwell indicated interest while his adviser Jerry
Huntsinger kept telling him, "Your interest isn't politics."

Falwell acknowledged doubts about working with Pentecostals.
He had sworn never to allow a "tongue speaker" in his pulpit. Huntsinger had doubts about the reliability of the leading "political" Pentecostal, the Reverend Pat Robertson. Robertson, star of the "700 Club,"
which aired over hundreds of TV stations around the country, had
founded an independent news organization, Christian Broadcasting
Network, and on occasion he had his followers flood the White House
switchboard with calls. But Huntsinger worried: "You can't depend
on what Pat says, he'll wake up in the middle of the night and have
a vision."

It must have been one of the strangest scenes in the annals of
American politics: a couple of Catholics and a Jew providing the good
offices for Protestants to heal their differences and unite in a larger
cause. They listened with bemused fascination as two Baptists dis-
sected one of modern Protestantism's many doctrinal fractures.
There were yet deeper ironies. Nearly six decades earlier the moralistic wing of American Protestantism had achieved its last great victories: Prohibition in 1919 and the restrictive Immigration Act of 1924.
The first had been directed against Catholic *culture*; the second
against Catholic *numbers*. Now, moral Protestantism was so weak that
it required Catholics to revive its moribund spirit. Falwell agreed to
head the Moral Majority. Billings, who as director of the National
Christian Action Coalition led the fight against the IRS regulations,
became the first executive director.

In some ways Falwell was an unlikely choice to lead an ecumenical movement. His denomination was Independent Baptist—an especially zealous, sectarian group within the larger Baptist fold in the South. Independent Baptists generally hailed from the new aspiring classes in small, rural towns, mainly in the South. Many came from families in which a mother or father had arrived in church through some harrowing, life-changing experience. In experience and class outlook, they were closer to Pentecostals than any other religious group, a familiarity which perhaps explained their unrelieved enmity toward tongue speakers.

Falwell had attended Baptist Bible Fellowship in Springfield, Missouri, a seminary founded by followers of J. Frank Norris, a dark figure in American religious history who had towered like a black tornado cloud over the Baptist order in the South, especially Texas, in the first half of the twentieth century. Norris hated liquor, scientific research, the theory of evolution, and Biblical analysis, but more than any of those things he hated his critics and saw no evil in suppressing academic freedom in the interest of fundamentalist orthodoxy. His behavior eventually led to a break with the Southern Baptist Conference.

Yet in other ways Falwell's role was appropriate. All the processes underway in the churches for four decades had been promoting a fusion of diverse elements. Modern fundamentalism, whose ideas took shape at Princeton Theological Seminary in the north in the nineteenth century, had always cut across denominational boundaries, and now it could provide a common denominator between fundamentalist Pentecostals, Baptists, Presbyterians, and others. The charismatic movement, likewise, bound together traditional Pentecostals with new converts in the Catholic and Episcopalian churches. And the spirit of Vatican II eased contacts between Catholics and Protestants.

BY THE TIME of the 1980 election, the growing resistance to the social, racial, and cultural trends in American society was coalescing, and Ronald Reagan was poised to benefit. The Republican candidate for President was a divorced man who socialized with wealthy people in Hollywood and whose life-style was anything but a model of Biblical living. Yet to Oca and many of the Tathams, Reagan was almost family.

There were intriguing similarities between Reagan and Oca. They had been born just four months apart in 1911 in small communities in the middle of America, the sons of strong women and somewhat ineffectual fathers. The Depression, rather than World War II (in which neither served), was the seminal event of their lives. The Tathams were poorer than the Reagans, but Reagan, like Oca, had had to work as a boy. At one time he had sold homemade popcorn, just as Vernon Tatham had done at the Will Rogers Hotel in Claremore.

In their adopted state of California, they were self-made loners who succeeded without any clear plan other than a conviction that their futures lay in the unorganized frontier lands: Hollywood for Reagan, the unzoned farmland east of the Fresno city limits for Oca. Both were enormously self-sufficient: neither of them seemed to need other people except for functional reasons. Both had a rare quality of being adrift yet fully centered in themselves and alert for any stray opportunity that might come into range.

Politically, they were FDR voters who had drifted slowly but steadily away from the Democratic Party into the populism of the New Right as bad experiences with government fortified a dislike of governmental power, except as a mobilizer of American resources against the implacable enemy of individual initiative and personal liberty, communism.

Individualistic and unattached as he was, Oca was not a movement man by nature. But under the circumstances, he was convinced that his "Christian people"—those Baptists, Methodists, Mormons, even Catholics who had kept the faith—now had to stick together. In 1980, he joined the Moral Majority and supported Ronald Reagan for President.

G. L. Johnson, on the other hand, *was* a natural movement man. He did need people and sought to be part of something big and growing. In Tallahassee, he had joined the North Florida Chapter of Protestants and Other Americans United for Separation of Church and State, which opposed giving federal aid to Catholic parochial schools. He was briefly caught up in efforts by the city's ministerial association to calm the situation during a Negro bus boycott. His recollection of that was that he took a copy of the Atlanta Charter, a document drawn up in the Georgia capital during racial tensions there, rewrote it to fit circumstances in Tallahassee, and presented it to the ministers. They accepted it with a few revisions and issued it with their signatures, he said. Johnson did not advertise this civil rights role to his congregation, but even so, he said, he was criticized by "hotheads" for signing the resolution. "To me," he said many years later, "it was a conviction, probably a little pride, too. No one was going to tell me."

G. L. was still a declared Democrat in 1972, when he delivered the invocation at a Fresno dinner of Democrats for Nixon attended by former Texas governor John Connally, a Democrat-turned-Republican. The office of the pastor of a large Fresno church was an obligatory stop for aspiring politicians, and G.L. relished the contacts.

In 1975, Johnson delivered his first political message in the presence of members of the Board of Supervisors at the Fresno Convention Center. The title of the speech was "Détente: Godsend or Giveaway?" and its subject was appeasement of the Soviet Union. G.L. expressed concern that détente was luring the United States into a trap set by the Kremlin. It must have been an effective speech, for the same year John Garabedian, a Fresnan and member of the Republican State Committee, approached him about running for Congress. He declined, but didn't rule out speaking out on public issues. He was having second thoughts about his earlier involvement with Protestants and Other Americans United for Separation of Church and State. POAU had supported the Supreme Court decision outlawing prayer in the schools, and it later opposed the Moral Majority's social-legislation proposals.

"When the issues began to come up—prayer in schools, evolution, abortion, pornography, prostitution—we as moralists began to express our opposition to this, even though I was a pastor of a church," Johnson said. "Some will say the pastor has no right. He has as much right as anybody—not to speak for his church, but to speak for himself."

As Peoples Church gained prominence, Johnson began to move in a wider circle of ministers, some of whom were to play a prominent political role. He encountered Pat Robertson when the Virginia Beach clergyman was just starting his television ministry, which became the "700 Club." Robertson visited Fresno, and G.L. arranged for him to have breakfast with Bill Tatham. Johnson met Robertson again at a charismatic congress in West Berlin in 1978. Subsequently, they went together on visits to South Korea at the invitation of Korean evangelist Paul Yonggi Cho, whose 200,000-member congregation was affiliated with the Assemblies of God.

By the late 1970s, G.L. was involved with a group called Californians for Morality, which was taking stands on a wide range of matters, including the content of school textbooks and school prayer. Near the end of the Carter administration, he met Jerry Falwell, and

they established a strong relationship. Not long after becoming head
of the Moral Majority, Falwell arrived in Fresno and G. L. Johnson
became his guide, introducing him to local pastors and officials and
promoting his appearance at the Fresno Convention Center. The
meeting drew 6,000 people, far more than had been expected.
Henceforth, said G.L., "I became an influential factor in his thinking
in the central California area."

IN SORTING OUT their positions on issues involving religion and
the family, the Tathams, as usual, followed their individualistic bent.
During the coming decade, for example, different Tathams evolved
different positions on the abortion issue, which raised a conflict between the family's traditional distaste for governmental intervention
and its moral views.

Bill did not see what all the fuss was about sex education in the
schools. His children, he said, had never brought home anything that
he found objectionable. Doris, for her part, supported the Supreme
Court's 1962 decision on school prayer, a position that put her at
odds with her dad and her daughter Cindy. Living in the culturally
diverse Bay Area, the decision seemed correct. Doris couldn't imagine
a prayer that would satisfy old-stock American Christians, Buddhists
from Vietnam, Jews, and Hindus, all of whom attended the local
public schools. And how could non-Christian teachers lead her children in prayer? "You just can't legislate it," she concluded.

Doris, who had received help from the John Birch Society in
her battle against School Superintendent Richard Foster's permissive
educational policies in 1964, nonetheless remained strongly conservative. She and Gordon subscribed to *Human Events*, and after 1979
they were on Moral Majority mailing lists. Gordon gravitated toward
the libertarian side of the political spectrum. Doris considered the
liberal legislative and judicial record of the sixties and seventies—
such as lighter sentences for criminals—as a turn away from God and
religion. She trusted conservatives more than Democrats on issues of
war and peace: "I think the Right is less dangerous than the Left is.
They don't go bomb and kill, and do that sort of thing. Or at least
they do it with literature, trying to do it from a Biblical standpoint in
most cases."

She took the Goldwater line on civil rights, disapproving of segregation but showing little enthusiasm for the federal government's
massive intervention to promote black equality and rights. Christians,

she acknowledged, had taken part in the civil rights and peace movements of the 1960s and 1970s, but they were not the kind of Christians with whom she crossed paths. She therefore found it difficult to relate to those causes as "Christian" because, as she put it, "We don't know Christians who hold those views."

In 1972 she had worked for a Republican opposing Congressman Fortney H. "Pete" Stark, a director of the citizens' lobby Common Cause and a sponsor of the Northern California Civil Liberties Union, a Republican who had switched to the Democrats to protest Nixon's Vietnam policies. Stark provoked Nixonites by putting the peace symbol on the checks of his Security National Bank in Walnut Creek and then erecting a sign with the symbol in front of the facility. Gordon and Doris considered him "ultraliberal."

Stark's opponent, Lew M. Warden, Jr., was no born-again Christian and came across to Doris as a little rough-hewn. But he was a good campaigner with a handshake for everybody. Doris became one of his volunteers, helping to coordinate his campaign in Dublin, San Ramón, and Danville. Her middle daughter, Gina, helped her to canvas from house to house. In the end, Stark eked out a narrow victory.

What especially motivated Doris and Gordon politically were taxes and moral issues. In 1972, the family moved to San Leandro partly because it had a lower tax rate than where they had been living. Six years later they voted for Proposition 13, which mandated cuts in property taxes and checked California's spending for public services.

It seemed to Doris that "nine out of ten times when [legislation] has to do with a moral principle, it's Republicans who are sponsoring the bills, supporting them, and voting for them." She defined "moral principles" as those affecting the family, children, and the schools.

"God used to be in everything. He used to be in the Constitution, in God we trust, in the schools; it just seems that the Christian principles on which our laws are based are being lost."

Brenda English of Fresno canceled her subscription to *Cosmopolitan* when it changed its style from a woman's service magazine offering recipes and homemaking tips to a volume full of cleavage-displaying underwear and tips on how to please a man in bed. One day in 1976, she entered the Fashion Fair mall off Shaw Avenue with her daughter Kelly and perused the photographic exhibit on display. She liked the decorative quality and thought it made the mall look smart and sophisticated. Then she did a double take. One of the pictures showed a nude girl and boy, both seemingly young adolescents, walking through a field hand in hand. To Brenda, the photograph was so clearly erotic that she grabbed Kelly and walked straight out of the mall and to her car. Back home she called the mall manager.

"That's not a photograph that belongs in a nice mall," she said. "When you clean up your X-rated lobby I'll bring my family back." He promised to look into it, but Brenda wasn't finished. "I'm pretty sure I can get a whole bunch of mothers to come down there by five o'clock if that picture is still there," she said. Afterward she couldn't remember if she had used the word "picket," but she knew that was the implication. A few hours later she went by the mall and the picture was gone.

Gerald Tatham got a certain malicious pleasure parading his boa-constrictor-skin cowboy boots under the noses of Bill's secretary, who disapproved of clothing made from endangered species. One day he got a lecture from her after returning from a trip to one of the nursing homes that Bill rented out. "I've been out seeing twenty-year-olds whose minds have been messed up with acid. *That's* the real problem," he said.

Gerald resented "finger pointing" by liberals on such matters as America's policies toward South Africa. His wife, Cora, had read Alan Paton's *Cry, the Beloved Country* about conditions in that country, and the book had left her confused. She thought of the Biblical passage that said, "Each nation shall know what God's plan is." If the plan was for South Africa's white apartheid government to be overthrown, that would be revealed, but she worried that Communists were behind the opposition, just as they had "stirred up trouble in this country in the sixties."

If Bill was the pragmatist, Gerald the skeptic, and Doris the ideologue in politics, then Pastor Dick Tatham was the moralist. He and Grace raised a rebellious brood of daughters. At times he felt "humiliated when they disregarded my teaching." But Dick, like millions of American parents, saw his family's problems as part of a broader societal breakdown. Thus politicized, he turned his pastoral and entreprenurial energies against the enemy as he saw it. In 1979, he set up his New Life Christian School for kindergarten through twelfth-grade students at his church and bought some property from the Mormon Church for his Love and Care Preschool. New Life Christian had an initial enrollment of sixty-six students despite a tuition of eighty-five dollars a month. The schools were "an alternative" to the public schools with which he was disenchanted.

His substitute teaching at the local high school had given him a firsthand look, he said, at the drugs, poor discipline, and classroom talk of sex and pregnancy. One of his daughters came home from school one day and told him, "You can't touch me. The school says I can have you put in jail if you do."

"Humanism," New Deal ideology, and non-Christian educational views of such thinkers as John Dewey, author of *The Humanist Manifesto*, were a bigger influence in American society than many realized, Dick believed. He saw "an organized humanist movement that began in 1933 with a meeting of some of the national educators and some political leaders.

"*The Humanist Manifesto* is a reality that's influenced the youth of our nations and the schools, and it's contributed to a lot of our rebellion. I see humanism as saying you have your rights at the expense of someone else's. That is, I have my rights to do what I want to do as long as it doesn't hurt anyone else, even if it's in violation of Christian principles. The idea of that is we become a God within ourselves. A lot of things that happened in the sixties I feel came from humanistic teachings to do what you feel and it's okay."

Soon after Reagan's election, Doris hung a painting in their living room of the President-elect dressed for the ranch, in open-necked shirt and western-style hat. The picture occupied a place of honor. For Doris, whose candidate had lost in 1964, it was a validation of sorts.

CHAPTER SEVENTEEN

TRIBES

CORA TATHAM had passed away in Delano on February 26, 1976, at the age of ninety-five, leaving behind four children, seventeen grandchildren, and thirty-two great-grandchildren. She had been spry and active until the last few years, when she suffered from various complications resulting from a characteristic—but ill advised—burst of energy. Rushing into the street to break up a "war" between two great-grandchildren, she had broken a hip. Her health was troubled after that, and Cleo finally had to move her to Delano General Hospital. Several times they thought she was going and family hurried down from Fresno, but she hung on.

On one of those hurry-up visits Gerald stepped quietly into her room.

"Who is it?" Cora asked weakly.

"It's Dicky," whispered Gerald devilishly, seeing her eyes were closed.

"It is not," said the old woman sharply. "I'll kick you in the nose."

"She's not going anywhere," he told his relatives.

But finally the years just took her.

Cora had been a woman of rocklike constitution and unbending moral convictions, the kind to turn down government old-age assistance after the war to keep working at the Sierra Vista packing sheds, for she was still supporting several of Norma's children and needed the wages. She moved from Oca's former place on Glenwood Avenue to a house on Main Street. Wayne Frost treated her like his own mother. After Wayne came from his job at Hillcrest Sheet Metal, he and Cleo would pick up Cora and take her for a long drive. "Driving the country out," they called it. In 1962, she moved in with Cleo and Wayne in the home they'd bought in a new subdivision carved out of a vineyard north of town.

Cora stayed true to the old ways, faithfully attending the Calvary Pentecostal Holiness Church on South Main Street in Delano. That church took the place of the storefront the congregation had used before the war, which later became a barbershop and liquor store. Healing and miracles remained at the center of Cora's life drama. Near death, her "powers" still did not desert her. In the hospital one time, a woman brought Cora her sick child and begged for help. Cora laid a bony hand on the child's head and prayed. The woman reported that the child was healed.

To her great-grandchildren, she was "Old Granma Tatham," who gave them Indian dolls and encouraged them to be curious about their roots. She was the family's last remaining witness to the early history of the Sumpter and Tatham families. Dale Frost, a great-grandson who had taken the Frost name when he came to live with Cleo and Wayne, gave rapt attention to Cora's stories. The curiosity she sparked in him led him to major in history when he enrolled at California State College in Bakersfield.

Great-grandchildren whose parents had left the central valley got their first inkling of the family's history in California and in Oklahoma on visits to Cora and Cleo in Delano. Gina Weaver, living in an affluent neighborhood in the East Bay, relished those visits; she'd rub Cora's feet and back, and Cora called her "little nurse."

Cora represented the kind of tribal family that relied on collective strategies, mutual help, and a great deal of faith in the Lord to compensate for its lack of material advantages and self-confidence. When troubles came, she and her kin circled the wagons, and they extended a helping hand to others. While living in Delano Cora fed every hobo from the railroad station who came to her door, until Wayne shooed them away. "Cora Tatham can't afford to feed you," he told them. "You leave her alone."

She'd been foster mother to children all her life, taking in Arch

and Pearl when she was just married, then helping to raise various
of Uncle Willy's children, and finally taking in Norma's brood when
she was old herself. Cleo followed the same tradition, helping to raise
Dale along with her own boy, Jerry. Some said it was the way of the
frontier, but Dale suggested that fostering ran in the Indian blood.
(In addition to the Cherokee blood he had inherited from his Granma
Cora, Dale had Ottawa blood from his grandfather on his father's
side.) Cora and Cleo were proud of the Indian heritage and delighted
when Wayne, himself part Blackfoot, carved a twelve-foot totem pole
and set it up right outside the house in Delano.

In 1966, four years after Cora moved in with Wayne and Cleo,
Wayne died, the victim, probably, of his own Okie toughness. While
working at a job in Tehachapi he had stomach pains, but stayed to
see the job through. He slept overnight in a motel, treating himself
with Pepto-Bismol. When the pain got worse the next day, he managed to drive himself home after telling the crew to keep working.
He was purple in the face when Cora and Cleo helped him down
from the truck. Wayne lingered for two weeks after his appendix
ruptured.

Cleo was not quite fifty. Jerry was grown and out of school, but
Cleo's house was not paid for. She had a few thousand dollars from
Wayne's life-insurance policy and was immediately eligible for a Veterans Administration survivor's pension of sixty-two dollars a month.
But she wouldn't be able to draw her share of Wayne's Social Security
for another ten years and had no Social Security of her own coming
because the packing sheds had never taken out for it. She'd expected
Wayne's union pension, but when she went down to ask about it, the
man told her, "It don't fall to the wife." This left her with bad feelings.
"The union beat me out of that," she said. But she kept her sense of
humor. "They say money changes you," she said. "Well, I never did
have money so I never did change." She was sure God provided the
checks that sometimes came unexpectedly.

A year after Wayne passed on, Noel Dagenette died after a fall
downstairs in a Sacramento flophouse. Noel had pretty well abandoned his family after Norma's death and his trouble with drugs in
the 1940s, but family was family. Cleo arranged for Noel's body to
be sent down to Delano by train and gave the undertaker one of
Wayne's suits to dress him in. They buried him in a corner of Delano
Cemetery, a respectable distance from Norma's plot.

For Cleo and Cora, the survivors, it was a little like wartime all
over again. The women made their stand together. Cora, eighty-five
when Wayne died, could still cook, mend, and clean. They made

their food stretch. Cleo made quilts. Cora's only indulgence was an overfondness for cube steak. "Mama, I wish I had all the money you spend on that," she teased.

The government had improved the safety net of support since the 1940s. Cora, being a Tatham, had not felt overly friendly toward government, yet she thought it only right for government to act as a sort of neighbor who, at some point after a sickness or incapacitating injury, came by and took a turn feeding the horses or chopping a little cotton. The Johnson and Nixon years saw major new social legislation to help the poor and elderly, and Cora benefited. Medi-Cal, the California version of Medicaid, covered most of her medical expenses not paid by Medicare, and she also began receiving Supplemental Security Income, enacted by Congress in 1973 to guarantee sufficient cash benefits to the elderly, blind, or disabled to bring their total income three-quarters of the way to the poverty line. SSI was the safety net's safety net, and in its first year it caught two and a half million elderly Americans, including Cora Tatham. For Cora, there was no shame in the fact that, at the time of her death, she was receiving welfare. She'd spent her life looking after others and raising two generations of good citizens.

She was buried next to Walter in Delano Cemetery, a few feet from the graves of the three little Tatham and Rogers children who had died of fever within a week of each other in 1936. Uncle Willy Tatham lay close by, as did others from Drake's Prairie.

The Calvary Pentecostal Holiness Church put up a plaque in her memory in the entrance foyer. It showed a picture of Cora cutting what must have been one of her last birthday cakes and was simply inscribed: "Cora Granma Tatham, born in 1881, died in 1976." Oca said of her: "I think of my mother as a mother that stayed at home, wept over her children, did everything in the world she could to provide the very best food that she knew how to provide. She prayed for her family. She set the good example before them. She taught the family right from wrong. That's what I can say for my mother."

FROM TIME TO TIME, a magazine or newspaper in the valley would write an article about "the Okies today," and there would be anecdotes about those who had made it big—the rancher who owned the land where he had once picked cotton, the proprietor of an oil-drilling company who had arrived in California in the 1930s in a Hudson Super Six.[1] Humble dirt farmers such as Sherman Thomas in Madera were millionaires. Bill Elkins, who'd taken over the potato house from Oca in 1935, owned the leading tire dealership in Delano. Jack Kooken, Oca's wartime trucking friend, operated a long-haul trucking business in Stockton.

Yet such stories were the exception. Nearly every extended Okie family had stories to tell of the ruin and heartbreak wrought by alcohol, womanizing, divorce, and violence. Lonnie and Opal Rogers hadn't coped at all. Herman Morgan, Oca's truck driver and some-time handyman, waged a lifelong battle against the booze and the women. He tried hard to steer to the straight and narrow path, but time and again he fell back over the edge. His remarriage to Clara, shortly before he came to help Oca and Ruby at Wish-I-Ah, lasted about five years, but after Oca sold Wish-I-Ah, it broke up again. The 1960s were a hard time for them. Norman, their son, wrestled with a drug problem, and Herman wouldn't give up his trademark Camel cigarettes, despite his war wounds; he was in and out of VA hospitals with lung problems. The Tathams lost track of him. (Herman died in a VA hospital in Fresno on September 3, 1986.) Most of these Okie lives were like those of the tumbleweed that blew across the plains for a summer before drying out and falling back into dust. Of the people who came to California in Oca's Chevy truck, only Oca and Ruby became affluent.

Of the four nonfamily men aboard, one was dead by the time Cora passed on and a second would be within three years. Arley Land, who'd been at the wheel of the Chevy when it went off the road outside Albuquerque, had divorced Myrtle after the war; she'd moved to California with their daughter, but Arley stayed in Okla-homa, working for the city of Tulsa. He died of a heart attack in 1969. Bill Elbertson, who'd been so severely wounded in the Pacific war, eventually had married and settled down happily in Fort Smith, Arkansas. But his wife died in 1973, and on February 4, 1979, Bill shot himself to death at his home in Fort Smith and was buried next to his wife in the Fort Smith National Military Cemetery.

A third man, Dewey Rogers, Ruby's half brother, had simply vanished—a not uncommon fate for the tramps, hobos, and homeless who wandered across the surface of America in the 1930s and 1940s. He had moved back and forth between California and Oklahoma for years, taking a wife here and there and chasing women in between. Dewey was on hand in Collinsville in 1962 when Clara Rogers was sent home for burial, but that was the last time he was seen by Ta-thams. Efforts to find a death certificate were unavailing.

That left only Jim Anderson, who'd fared better. After the war Jim took jobs in heavy construction, working on the Saint Lawrence

Seaway project and building a radar station in Greenland. Jim and his first wife split up in 1952. He remarried and settled down in Benicia, on the northeastern shore of San Francisco Bay. He went fishing and hunting as often as he could. Joe Anderson, his son from the first marriage, was a specialty seed grower in Dixon, California, elected in 1980 to the city council as a Republican, and eventually elected mayor.

Lurking behind even the stories of material success one often found a tragedy of some kind that more than balanced the scales. Jack and Maxine Kooken would have given back all the money they'd made from Kooken Trucking Company to have their son, Albert, back, but Albert had been killed in 1962 when the tractor-trailer rig he was driving jackknifed and he was thrown out and run over by it. For months afterward Maxine sat and listened to the sound of the semis shifting down near the turnoff by their lot and thought she heard Albie coming home. At night she left the floodlights on in the lot for him. Jack had never been much of a churchgoer, but after that he went to Albie's church, the Church of Christ.

There were sadder stories even than that, ones that made people wonder what it was all for, the years of work and effort to make a better life. In the 1980s, the Yocum story would become the most famous of those stories. Hadley Yocum, a churchgoing, Arkansas-born dirt farmer, had left 140 acres of sharecropped cotton behind in Blaine County, Oklahoma, to come to California in 1937. He worked in the cotton fields and slept in a barn until he was ready to send for his wife, four sons, and two daughters. With forty dollars in their pockets they came looking for what they called "the Promised Land," but had to make do for a while in two unheated rooms in a labor camp. After the war the father and sons bought land and formed a farming partnership, putting in backbreaking years of work and eventually accumulating 5,000 acres of valuable land, rental properties, and restaurants. But they could not pass on the dream. One of Hadley Yocum's grandsons died of a drug overdose in 1972, another committed suicide, and in December 1983 still another grandson, then seventeen, would hire three friends to carry out a contract killing of his father and mother, with the apparent motive of getting his inheritance.[2]

THE EXTENDED TATHAM FAMILY had experienced no such Jobian tragedies. In fact, it showed a remarkable strength and resilience. Most of Cora's descendants had improved their material lot somewhat, and all but a handful were "in church." Yet most were still hemmed in by nagging, day-to-day needs, except now they lived from paycheck to paycheck instead of crop to crop. Tathams tended to prefer work that left them a degree of independence. Among Cora's descendants there were three independent contractors (Gerald Tatham, his cousin Kenneth Dagenette, and his Uncle Bill Thomas), a painter (Jerry Frost), a beautician and a bookkeeper (Norma's daughters, Catherine and Carol), a carpenter (Terry Tatham), and a preacher (Dick Tatham). The large corporation or institution did not attract many of them; they preferred things on a smaller scale. Compared to Oca and Ruby and most of their descendants, a number of other California Tathams seemed to have rather shallow roots in the new soil. For them, freedom of action meant no more than what it had for generations: the freedom to move on, and they did just that, fanning out to what remained of the American frontier. Alaska beckoned four of them: Cora's son-in-law Bill Thomas and her grandsons Kenneth Dagenette, Clifford Tatham, and Stephen Thomas.

Vernon remained close to Oca, staying put in Fresno with a job as night janitor at a vending-machine company, a position that gave him the run of the plant when "the big bosses" were not around. He liked it that way. His nickname was "Speedy." "If you smell smoke tell me and I'll cool my broom," he told a fellow at work. "They don't call me lightnin' for nothing."

Life had not been easy for him and his family. After his job on the Pine Flat Dam had ended, his work had been mostly seasonal—for several years he worked for a company that hung Christmas decorations for the city of Fresno—and unemployment compensation had to tide over his family between jobs. Dora turned down a job with Sears, with benefits and pension, because it was evening work and she needed to be at home with her three growing boys. So she took in piecework, cutting pads for air conditioners. But their situation improved in the late 1950s, when Dora took a part-time job at a laundry and joined the laundry union and Vernon got a job at a golf course, then found the permanent job at the vending-machine company. Eventually, Dora quit the laundry job and went to work as a night sales clerk for Ward's. By then Terry was in the army in Vietnam, Gary was in the air force in Germany, and Clifford was in Alaska working construction.

Their collective strategy kept them from ever feeling poor. The household ran like a co-op. Vernon couldn't afford to buy the older boys cars, so Gary paid for his by delivering the Fresno *Bee* and his parents helped with tires, gas, and car insurance. By the time their youngest son, Terry, was old enough for a car, they were able to buy him a 1964 Chevrolet.

Such generosity was always repaid. Gary learned to do the laundry and cook—even to make fudge. After they left home, Clifford and Terry bought their parents a couch and love seat, Terry installed tile counters in his parents' kitchen, and Gary helped his dad reroof his house. They were forever in and out of each other's homes, doing things for each other. Clifford came back from Alaska with a microwave oven for his mother, and Terry bought her a set of dishes with a yellow rose motif. When Terry's wife had her baby, Dora took off from work to help them.

OPHELIA'S HUSBAND, Bill Thomas, a skilled contractor, had ambition and a desire to improve himself. Bill was one of two among eight siblings to finish high school. He was a quick learner and easily picked up carpentry, carpet laying, and masonry. Ophelia bragged that her husband could handle a trowel like a professional the first day he tried.

The mild recession of the early 1950s had driven Bill to Alaska. He left Ophelia and the children behind while he took a job with Bechtel, building an air force barracks in Anchorage. Wages were double what they were in the Lower Forty-eight, but long hours left little time for hunting or fishing.

The first time he took the family up to Alaska, in 1958, he and Ophelia already had a son and a daughter; another daughter was born four years later. Sometimes the family stayed through the winters, hard and long as they were. But when the masonry work began to bother Bill's back, he enrolled in Fresno City College hoping to become qualified as an industrial arts teacher. He finished in 1971, but his timing was bad: the baby boom was over, high schools were closing, and teachers were out of work. And the Thomases were out of money.

Bill took out a loan and cashed in his life-insurance policy. He had heard there was a vacancy for an industrial arts teacher in Juneau, but they barely had the money to make the trip. Their car quit on the ferry trip from Seattle and had to be towed off the boat. Once in Juneau, Bill learned that the teaching vacancy had been filled. The next two years were nip and tuck. Bill's health improved somewhat, and he went back to work in construction. Norma's son, Kenneth, had caught Alaska fever, too, and Bill went to work for his construction company. Inside of three years Bill was on his own and making good money again. Still, it was hard going. The work days lasted fifteen hours during the construction season, and sometimes there would be bear prints on freshly poured concrete. But by the time they were ready to return to Fresno, Bill had $90,000 tucked away.

Back in Fresno he and his son-in law invested in six building lots and got a construction loan to put up thirty apartment units. They had a qualified buyer, and the work went smoothly. But by the time the units were ready, a hitch had developed: the new manager at the savings and loan wouldn't accept their buyer. Eventually, they sold the units, but the delays ate up all the profits and much of Bill's savings. The bank pulled back on other commitments for additional projects that would have made Bill financially independent.

Bill Thomas had come close, but the chance had been missed. He still didn't own a home of his own and had to keep hustling. He'd have to go back to Alaska again. Bill took it in stride; he'd kept his pride intact. Other than a couple of visits to the VA hospital and one unemployment check, he never asked the government for anything. Ophelia described him as a man who "always made sure the boss's tools were clean."

Down in Delano, Cleo made up for the loss of her mother and husband by pouring her love into her two grandsons. She felt a special connection to Rowdy, the younger of the two. He'd been born just two weeks after Wayne died. To Cleo, he was the life God had given her in place of Wayne's.

One day in 1978 Rowdy had told her, "Granma, you don't need to worry about getting old because I'm going to work and make you a livin' and we'll live together."

Cleo said, "Oh, baby, some little ol' gal will say I don't want your old granma here."

But Rowdy insisted. "I'll divorce her," he said.

Two days later the child was killed in a freak accident on the school playground. He was riding a motor scooter, lost control, and was thrown into a post. A neighbor told Cleo of seeing the figure of Jesus hovering over the little boy's crumpled body.

The death was hard for Rowdy's parents. Jerry Frost had a job at the SMUD water district where Eldon Tackett worked, but after the accident Jerry and his wife separated.

Cleo found consolation in her church. While other Tathams had moved "up" to the Assemblies of God, she stayed loyal to the Pentecostal Church of God in McFarland. It, too, had moved up in the world. It had relocated to a modern glass and brick facility a few blocks from where Eldon and Loretta Tackett lived.

Cleo did not have much use for big churches. "God was simple, God was meek. Jesus wanted everything for the common people," she said. "He didn't put on. He *walked* everywhere he went. Now those big churches, you don't feel no spirit in them. I can't go to them."

Vernon and Ophelia and their families also turned their problems over to Jesus. When Terry Tatham joined the army and went to Vietnam in 1968, Dora felt that "the Lord had his hand on him . . . a lot of prayers went up for him. When he said he worked in an air-conditioned place, we knew that God had answered our prayers." He came home safely.

Poems sometimes came to Ophelia in church. One poem was about how God is present even when He is silent. She got out her purse and started writing. She credited the Lord with making her feel safe when Bill was away on a construction job and she was alone in the house. She said, "God was real to me. It used to be I couldn't stay alone at night. We had Peeping Toms in the country. They wrecked my nerves. Listening to television one night I heard them say, 'There's somebody with a fear.' He said that God would bring angels to stand at each window and each door. God removed the fear from my heart. So I get by fine now."

THE OBVIOUS CANDIDATE to fill Cora's shoes in the family was Oca. He had the material resources, he had the self-confidence, and he was becoming a kind of patriarch in his own immediate circle of children, grandchildren, and great-grandchildren. But he wasn't cut out for the role of patriarch for the extended Tatham clan. It wasn't that he considered himself "better" than those parts of the family that were less affluent. He felt more at ease with plain people from Oklahoma (his cousins back in Sallisaw, for example) than with big shots. It was something else: the temperament and qualities that had got him the money kept him a little apart from his brothers and sisters and their families. He was the family hero. But he was too much his own man—too much the independent horse trader—to take on the collective responsibilities of a sprawling, extended family. He followed his own agenda.

The Oca and Ruby Tathams were becoming middle-class.

Oca's brother and sisters and their spouses worked as hard, or harder, than he did, and he gave them credit for that. But they didn't have his self-confidence, or a certain kind of imagination, or the competitiveness it took to completely master the larger world. After all, it had been his truck. He and his children were reaching out, developing a wider and wider range of business and social contacts, joining organizations, participating in charitable activities, and traveling. New associations began to replace the family's more exclusive ones. At the same time, the sense of obligation to an extended family of cousins, nieces, nephews, and aunts began to weaken. Cleo and Cora had held the pieces of the arc. But for Oca, the pieces of the arc were less interesting. For him, the future was in many ways more real than the past.

None of that diminished his strong attachments to the family. He and Ruby had taken in parents and relatives over the years, had slipped money to cousins, brothers, and sisters. Holiday gatherings at Oca and Ruby's drew a wide range of kin. In the 1970s, when Oca and Ruby were situated in a sprawling ranch house on Escalon Avenue in the Fig Gardens area of Fresno, fifty or more relatives might show up on holiday occasions. Those get-togethers were full of Okie stuff—practical jokes, skits, roughhousing, depanting unwary grandchildren, and photographing people in unflattering poses. Vernon, Dora, and their boys often came. Vernon participated in the antics and strummed his guitar. There would be enough pies, cakes, and food to fill the fifty or so children, in-laws, and grandchildren who had descended. On Christmas Eve, Oca dressed up as Santa Claus, and the newest grandchild would be selected to play the Christ child. Soon Gerald, Jerry English, and others gathered around Ruby's piano as Brenda played the old Gospel favorites, songs such as "How Great Thou Art," "Amazing Grace," "Standing on the Promises," and "Oh How I Love Jesus."

But in retrospect, it seemed that Brenda's wedding to Jerry English, which took place in 1964, had been a kind of social debut—a turning point in something of the same way that Jay Fuller's wedding to Helen had been in Delano in 1936. Brenda's wedding received a lengthy write-up and a picture on the social page of the Fresno *Bee*. The three-column photograph showed Brenda in a floor-length, hooped bridal dress, Jerry in white tie and tails, and half a dozen white-gloved nieces and nephews.

Brenda's design for the wedding demonstrated a flair for ceremony, which she later put to practical use as a wedding consultant for others. The *Bee* reported that the event had a French Revolutionary period theme: "In keeping with a wedding tradition of European royalty, six young relatives of the bride and bridegroom held garlands of white daisies. . . . Miss Tatham's peau de soie gown was fashioned with a bateau neckline and fitted bodice enhanced with seed pearl embroidered Alençon lace appliqués. The lace motifs were repeated on the front panel of the belled skirt. Seed pearls formed the coronet which secured the bride's bouffant floor-length veil. Miss Tatham held a cascade arrangement of stephanotis and white orchids."

It was not entirely due to Jerry that he and Brenda were living in a home in Fig Gardens, not far from Bill and Earline's. Brenda was ambitious. She worked as an Amway distributor and wedding consultant to supplement his teacher's salary and liked to fill up the house with Tatham relatives while she played the piano. She had the Tatham energy and confidence.

In some ways, only Dick and Gerald had one foot in the other, more tribal part of the family. Cora had taken particular pride in Dick, her preacher grandson. And Gerald the contractor, unattached and restless, gravitated toward his cousins and uncles—working at one time for his Uncle Bill Thomas and staying close to his Uncle Vernon and Aunt Dora, refusing year after year to join Peoples Church, preferring the blue-collar milieu of the smaller Pentecostal churches.

Yet Dick and Gerald, too, were Oca's sons. Dick was an organizer and entrepreneur, dabbling in real estate and the politics of Havasu Lake City's development and building the community's most talked about church. Gerald, the inventor, was too detached to be part of a tribe. He was the reporter, maintaining a distance from all camps.

The children of Ruby and Oca had energy and confidence, and as they improved their status, they developed an outlook that was distinctly middle-class. For upward mobility was giving them a stake in the *future* and weakening attachments to places and people left behind. They knew less of the family history than, say, Cleo. But, of necessity, they were concerned with things such as estate planning—Oca set up a "living will" for his children and grandchildren—investments, and taxes. Bill looked on his deal with Beverly Enterprises as a nest egg for posterity.

These changes made Oca and Ruby and their descendants feel more accountable for their *own* economic destiny. That in turn affected perceptions of government. Oca had readily accepted welfare in the thirties. But the more he and his children assumed responsibility for themselves, the less likely they were to consider government a friendly neighbor and the less kindly were their views of social services paid for by their taxes.

Ruby, more than Oca, was their ambassador to the middle-class world. She smoothed the path and, in a hundred different ways, gave them the green light to travel it. Ruby went on shopping sprees with Doris and listened approvingly to Renee's descriptions of her travels.

Oca wanted them to be careful with their money. Ruby wanted them to have it all. When Renee wanted to buy a sports car Ruby told her, "Do it if you really want to." Of Oca, Ruby said, "I'll handle him . . . I'll take care of it." Oca told Renee she should marry a Christian. Ruby hoped for that, too, but she also gave her daughter some other advice: "Marry a rich man." When Renee had her heart set on marrying the Vietnam vet who was not born again, Ruby slipped her the money for a wedding dress.

She encouraged the children to branch out, travel, move up in the world, get rich. Ruby went to Oca when Renee needed to borrow money for a down payment on her first house. She wanted a new Cadillac, and Oca bought her one in 1973, but when she sold it in 1978, she couldn't get him to buy her a new one again. He said an Olds was just as good. But she kept wanting the Cadillac.

Yet Ruby kept the connection to the other, tribal part of the family. Cleo thought of her as just another sister. Cora Tatham accepted her as a daughter and pressed a ring into her hand before she died.

Ruby had suffered from health problems for many years—varicose veins, goiter, eye problems, and back pain from the automobile accident in 1951. In 1981, she was diagnosed with cancer, a fast-growing thyroid variety. One of the first things Oca did was buy her the Cadillac she'd wanted for so long. He took her to Mexico in January, then on to Hawaii to attend a Jimmy Swaggart revival. By then she was suffering from pain, and they cut short the trip.

Oca hoped for a healing miracle—but he also scoured the country for miracle cures. He flew to Detroit to pick up several bottles of an under-the-counter drug not yet approved by the FDA. He rushed back to Fresno and gave her a dose of the black sticky substance, but it did no good. In April, she underwent surgery to the left side of her head and brain. Brenda sat with her in intensive care as Ruby tore at the bandages. For the next month she teetered close to death. When the doctors could do no more, the family moved her to a local nursing home. That same week Ruby made runner-up in the Fresno

Woman of the Year contest sponsored by the Fresno Chamber of Commerce. Some of her grandchildren had put her name in and collected signatures on a petition.

Shortly before the end, they put her in Saint Agnes Medical Center, a Catholic facility where, Oca was pleased to see, some of the nurses were charismatic. Oca slept little, except for spells of relief by Brenda and other members of the family. In the last days, Brenda decided that "the miracle was that she showed us how to die, beautifully, as a Christian woman should."

She went late on June 17, 1982. Brenda, Doris, Cora, and Earline were by her bedside. Ruby said, "Aren't the lights beautiful?" She took some short breaths and slumped and she was gone. While the doctors were still checking her, Brenda suggested that they sing. They sang "Trust in Jesus" and "Jesus Loves Me." Simple songs, thought Brenda, familiar and comforting ones that they knew from their childhood.

G. L. JOHNSON had already arrived when two assistant pastors came back from Perko's Restaurant with Oca. Soon there were fifteen or so people in the room, and they were still singing. Pastor Johnson asked if any of the children felt like saying what Ruby had meant to them. Brenda took the lead, saying Ruby had showed her how to work hard and serve others and her gift had been to help her when she couldn't help herself. They stayed with her for three more hours, unwilling to cover up her face until one of the pastors suggested they do it. Very Southern, thought Brenda.

G. L. preached the sermon at her funeral a few days later. Ruby, he said, had been a "Proverbs 31 woman," out of those passages that answer the question, "Who can find a virtuous woman?" He said, "It didn't matter whether the sun was shining or rain was pouring down, you knew if Ruby Tatham was in town that they were going to be in church. Over the years, of course, through various Providences, she was faithful to every one of those churches. She was a person who was reliable in her conviction. They said in other times, family members would get discouraged and say, 'It's no use, we have to give up, to quit.' She said no, 'We won't quit, we can do it by the help of God.' She cooked the meals, mended the clothes, and washed them. I wouldn't be surprised if right now she's busy, she's in glory. She's saying, I've got to get this mansion ready."

The family found a hundred dresses in her wardrobe, many with the price tag still on them. There were eighty-seven pairs of shoes, many never worn, and close to fifty purses. Doris said, "She wanted to have something in case they lost everything. . . . My mother reminded me of Tammy Bakker in that way." Time and again, Oca said, he'd shown Ruby their accounts, reassuring her that there was plenty of money. She would seem relieved, but only for a while. She remembered the Depression till the day she died.

After the burial, Oca went back to the big house in Fig Gardens. The Cadillac she had wanted, but had never driven, was parked in the garage. Alone in the big house, Oca felt at life's end. He drew the blinds and didn't come out.

PART FOUR

Chapter Eighteen

Keeping Score

BILL TATHAM'S improving fortunes in the late 1960s and 1970s were part of a quiet revolution that was redistributing money and power in hundreds of American communities.

Until the late 1960s, the economic and political power was "downtown." Fresno's movers and shakers were men such as Mayor Arthur Selland; Leon Peters, whose Valley Foundry company was the leading supplier of equipment to wineries; Lewis Eaton, chairman of Guarantee Savings, one of the southern valley's largest financial institutions; Louis Slater, who owned a furniture store and ran the Fresno Wells Fargo Bank; Abe Rodder, a prominent downtown merchant; Steve Pilibos, owner of the downtown Hilton Hotel; and the Levy family of Gottschalks, the city's leading department store. Many of these men had been outsiders once themselves. (Eaton's family name had been Einstein; Peters and Pilibos were of Armenian descent.) They were the inside power brokers working to get Fresno federal urban-renewal funds for a new downtown mall, civic buildings, and auditorium.

This whole structure began to shift with the pressure of commercial and demographic change in the 1960s. It was a chain reaction:

families moved to the suburbs, shops opened closer to the homes, offices opened closer to the shops, two-income families wanted the convenience of shops nearer the offices, and land for homes and businesses was cheaper on the edge of town than in the center. Out on Shaw Avenue, once a sleepy country road through the fig orchards north of town, Gordon McDonald from Santa Barbara began developing Fashion Fair, a mall that was anchored by leases from Weinstock's and J.C. Penney. The downtown interests fought the development, but the suburban developers had a majority of the votes on the city council as new constellations of economic power emerged on Fresno's northeast edge. Shaw Avenue gradually became a coveted location for Fresno County corporations. The brick-and-glass low-rise office buildings going up along it housed the companies that made the lower San Joaquin Valley go: farming corporations, consulting firms, insurance companies, real-estate brokerages. Bill moved into his handsome new office building at the southeast corner of Fruit and Shaw in November 1977. Meanwhile, Blackstone Avenue, from which Oca had once hauled the single-family homes he bought at auction, became the north-south commercial strip, lined with car dealerships, retail stores, fast-food franchises, and service businesses.

Retail stores like Weinstock's and Gottschalks, which had moored the old downtown, eventually gave in to the trend and built stores on the fringe while eyeing the possibility of expansion to other valley cities and communities. The power of downtown was diluted in other ways, too. Businesses unimagined a decade earlier sprouted on the fringes: computer stores, health clubs, printing and copying services. Newcomers like Leo Wilson and Gary McDonald, a former Baptist preacher, were making big money in land development. John Siroonian was building a small chrome and wheel shop into a company called Western Wheel and getting control of a major share of the country's aluminum wheel market. Fresnan Chic Brooks was expanding his restaurant chains, Perko's and Happy Steak. Bob Duncan, of Duncan Enterprises, was becoming a multimillionaire in the ceramics supply business. Bill Tatham was in nursing homes and equipment leasing, banking, health clubs, pharmaceuticals . . . just about everything. And except for his dad leasing him the two facilities at the very start, he had done it on his own. He was conscious of being part of something a little seditious. "Bill made it without *their* help," said a colleague who worked with him on real-estate deals.

By 1980 it was hard to say exactly where or what the center of Fresno was. Some suggested it was not a place at all, but the one institution that seemed to bring together all the diverse classes, ethnic groups, religions, cultures, and customs: Fresno State University's intrepid football team. Okies, Armenian Americans, "proud Portuguese"—everyone loved Coach Jim Sweeney's Fresno State Bulldogs. "Bulldogmania" was rampant. Nothing quite united the city like the team's Saturday date with destiny. Neon signs along Blackstone Avenue flashed "Go Dogs!," and "Dog Talk" on a Fresno radio station tracked the team's progress. Supporting Fresno football was a civic duty, a kind of philanthropic activity, and the more you did of it the bigger you were in the eyes of the community. At the games, people turned to see who had the best tickets on the fifty-yard line, much as operagoers at the old Metropolitan Opera had once craned their necks to identify the occupants of the Golden Horseshoe boxes to know who really counted. Those seats were for "high Fresno society," as one local businessman put it, partly in jest.

Supporting the Bulldogs bestowed status and helped an institution that belonged every bit as much to the whole community as, say, the symphony orchestra. Bob Duncan, the ceramics millionaire, devoted much of his philanthropic energy to the Bulldogs and was the principal figure in the Bulldog Foundation, which in many ways enjoyed the status of a symphony board or arts council. In 1978, Duncan's family contributed $757,000 to the construction of the new Bulldog Stadium. Bill Tatham was not on the board of the Bulldog Foundation, the absolute inner circle, but he was a foundation member, contributed at least one full football scholarship a year to the college, and gave more than $100,000 after the new stadium was complete. Bill had a large bloc of tickets on the fifty-yard line. He supported the Fresno teams, he said, "because they win." And by winning, and becoming ranked nationally, they gave Fresno itself a kind of national ranking, too.

Though Bill had chosen to remain in Fresno under the penetrating eye of his dad, he still wanted to be a Tatham on his own terms. Through football, Bill staked out his turf. Football, unlike dealmaking, required one to enter into a complex set of attachments. Bill, unlike Oca, wanted to *mesh*, to weave himself into a larger cloth. And it was no surprise that high-school football was his first success outside the narrow circle of Okies and Pentecostal churches. In the Clovis Cougar uniform, he escaped his sectarian background and charged into a world of which Oca knew nothing. Much later, in 1975, he took a stake in the World Football League. For Oca, it was a little like watching his son stand under a cold shower with all his clothes on tearing up hundred-dollar bills. But to Bill, losing the money was the price of admission to something bigger.

Bill's approach to pro sports was so different from his approach to business generally that it suggested some impalpable longing: perhaps a need for a weight in the community separate from nursing homes that got bad write-ups in the Fresno *Bee*, perhaps a need to assuage some very private hurt.

Only one other endeavor exposed these yearnings in Bill, and that was raising, with Earline, his three children. In one respect he simply wanted the best for them; in that sense, the expectations he had of them were a kind of generous pressure. In the subtle and sometimes not-so-subtle demands he made on them to succeed, he was appealing to the best in them. The children, like football, fit into Bill's desire to reach out. He fired them into the world like arrows on a string. He dreamed that one of the children would go to Stanford University, like his friend and lawyer Gary Kerkorian. He had never finished college and sometimes made fun of the college grads he bested in his deals—he would "take the deals and let them keep their degrees," he said. Yet he wanted his children to have the degrees. Once he was sure that they had high IQs, he let them know he expected them to do well. That, he made clear, meant getting good grades, going to college, and getting the advanced degrees in accounting or law that would make it possible for them to work for him. Tatham & Sons—or Tatham & Daughter—was not a notion that Oca had ever entertained; but Bill thought of it often. He had the same expectations for Renee as the boys. She had the "ability to do whatever she wanted, and I didn't want her to limit herself just because she's a woman. I wanted her to understand that she could do more. A woman ought to be able to decide for herself."

For the boys, Billy and Mike, football was the activity that first measured their Tatham qualities. Billy remembers that "a lot was expected." Both boys were stars at Bullard High School, the elite school serving Fig Gardens and the most affluent suburb. Bill attended not only games but practices of the Bullard Knights. And Earline was every bit as competitive, if vicariously, as her sons. She studied the game, learned the finer points, and became an energetic fan of Tatham football heroics. Her sons gave her plenty to cheer about. Billy played halfback for the Bullard team that won the North Yosemite League title and defeated its archrival, Clovis, 21–7. Afterward he was wait-listed for a football scholarship to Stanford. His dad did not hide his disappointment when, after Stanford turned Billy down, Billy quit the Fresno State Bulldogs following summer training camp. He felt burned out, and though he felt sheepish about not having pushed himself harder, Billy Tatham made clear that he was going to make up his own mind about such things.

Billy's kid brother, Mike, was the grittiest Tatham. A smallish, outwardly easygoing but fiercely competitive youngster, he turned into one of Fresno's two or three hardest-hitting defensive high-school backs. While Billy made local headlines as an offensive back with his quick cuts and fakes, Mike liked the way it felt to run full speed into an opposing pass receiver.

Mike played hurt. He broke his collarbone the first time in 1972. He separated it two years later, had surgery in 1975, but played anyway that year, separating it again. Mike then was chosen for the Fresno City All Star team that took on the county all-stars in September 1976. His surgeon strongly advised him against playing. "If you injure it again it'll be like sewing wet noodles together," the doctor said. City officials were not much more encouraging. Before they allowed Mike to suit up for the game, Bill had to sign a release relieving the city of any liability for serious injury to his son.

It was in the character of Tathams to do things they were advised against doing. Oca had done it all his life. Bill remembered his "raid" on Clovis Convalescent Hospital, which he had pulled off without talking to his lawyers. Now Mike wanted to play, and Bill and Earline did not try to stop him. Mike had something to prove—to his parents, his older brother, and the city of Fresno. He was, he said, the All-Star team's "slow white guy from the upper-class high school." The Fresno city starting line-up was heavily stacked with blacks from Edison High, including two who eventually went on to play in the National Football League. "I just wanted to see how I could do playing with those guys," said Mike.

He gave it all he had. But in the fourth quarter he landed on his shoulder under a pile of players and was taken from the game in agony. Bill and Earline drove him straight to St. Agnes Medical Center.

It was the start of a live-hard, play-hard period in Mike's life. A few months later, hurtling down a mountain during a ski vacation with several daredevil friends in Sun Valley, Idaho, he crashed head first into a fence, knocking himself unconscious and cracking two vertebrae. Bill and Earline brought him back to Fresno in an ambulance plane, and he went back to his old room at St. Agnes. The injury-prone Tatham was becoming a familiar figure to the nurses.

IF HIS CHILDREN were one passport to the world beyond Fresno, pro sports was another. Bill was brought into the World Football League in 1975 by Chris Hemmeter, a Hawaii hotel and shopping-center tycoon who owned a team in the league and wanted to keep it going after a disastrous first season. Bill agreed to buy out some Canadians and take a controlling interest in the Portland Thunder.

In one sense, new sports franchises were just another business venture. No doubt Bill calculated that it was a good, if risky, opportunity. The South and Southwest had a shortage of sports teams, since major-league football and baseball had refused to play in segregated public facilities. Although pro sports was being nationalized by all-weather domed stadiums and television, cities like Phoenix, Memphis, and Birmingham had no NFL teams.

But there was more to it than just the opportunity for very rich men to make still more money. Millionaires searching for something to do with their wealth could make more money with less risk investing elsewhere. In a sense, investment in a sports franchise was a kind of honest laundering: it glamorized unglamorous money. A sports team, like a newspaper, television station, or cable channel, captured the time and attention of average people. Men like William Randolph Hearst, Walter Annenberg, and John Hay Whitney—not to mention countless lesser men in cities all over the country—had bought newspapers as a way of translating ordinary money into influence, fame, and power. In the 1980s, this was done through the purchase of sports teams. Like newspapers, a sports team provided entertainment and—in a society increasingly starved for sports results—information. And who could deny that football in America was serving deeper emotional, if not spiritual needs and that it had become a kind of charismatic religion for the masses, a great revival under the tent, or the dome, concentrating every kind of human emotion into a three-hour event? Oca himself put it best: "They come halfway across the country to yell and scream, and then they call *us Pentecostals* fanatics!"

Not every new millionaire in America wanted to have his or her own team. One couldn't imagine a lone horse trader like Oca Tatham yearning for a place in the owner's box. Oca had made his money invisibly, and he spent it invisibly, too. He wasn't interested in glory; being a man who was never bored—who could find something of interest everywhere he poked his head—he didn't need a football game to keep his pulse beating fast.

The men and women who wanted to own a team were a special part of the millionaire community. Pro sports attracted jungle fighters and risk-takers: oil men, developers, heart surgeons, and trial lawyers, people who were never quite fulfilled, who wanted more of everything: more fun, more recognition, more challenges, more authority, more status—and more money.

Many of those in the WFL and the subsequent United States Football League were self-made men, but a good many were also the children of them: Donald Trump, whose father had been a business success long before Donald; Sam Battisone, Jr., who owned a team in the WFL and whose father founded the Sambo Restaurant chain; and Bill Tatham, whose dad had leased him his first nursing homes. Football was a kind of generational trump card for the sons. Investing in it was beyond the comprehension of successful fathers who probably disapproved but were not in a position to pass judgment.

In 1975, Bill formed a new Memphis football franchise, the Mid-South Grizzlies, with two partners, John Bosacco, a twenty-nine-year-old Philadelphia attorney and land developer, and John Bassett, then forty, the unofficial "dean" of the defunct WFL. Bassett had been involved in the WFL and was a great promoter. He had television stations in Canada and had married into the Carling beer family there. The NFL expanded in 1976 to two new cities, Seattle and Tampa Bay, and Memphis was on many short lists to get the next team. Bosacco, Bassett, and Bill soon applied for a franchise for Memphis in the National Football League.

The Grizzlies were an impressive team—on paper. The partners signed up top talent, including fullback Larry Csonka of the Miami Dolphins and star college quarterback Danny White, who later was quarterback for the Dallas Cowboys. The partners obtained pledges for 46,000 season tickets and received strong backing from Memphis businesses, the city government, and influential Tennessee politicians in Congress and state capitals. Bill, John Bassett, and the Memphis cotton broker William "Billy" Dunavant, Jr., sponsored an NFL preseason game between the Dallas Cowboys and the Detroit Lions that attracted more than thirty thousand fans. So the Grizzlies had the players and the potential fans. All they lacked was a league to play football in. When Bill and his partners presented their case to the NFL expansion committee in New York, the NFL turned its thumb down.

While Bill was waiting for the NFL to make up its mind about his football franchise, a partnership he was in with Sam Battisone acquired a controlling interest in the New Orleans Jazz basketball team in the National Basketball Association. In 1979, Battisone moved the Jazz to another sports-starved Sun Belt town, Salt Lake City. Then, in December of that year, Bill and the other Memphis franchise owners filed suit against the NFL, charging the league with breach of contract for refusing to allow their Memphis expansion and seeking $144 million in damages.

The United States Football League was formed while the partners were appealing a lower court ruling against them. Dave Dixon, the New Orleans promoter who acted as midwife for the new league, had toyed with the idea of starting a football league in the 1960s, until the NFL gave his hometown a franchise for the New Orleans Saints. What persuaded Dixon to try again in 1982 was cable television. The NFL had all three networks tied up, and were uninterested in televising another upstart league. But Dixon figured that with the arrival of cable as a serious competitor to broadcast television, the networks might just be worried enough about the competition to give a new football league a contract. Cable, therefore, made the USFL seem feasible.

The original owners included a number of men who were very wealthy but little known outside their business circles, big fish in relatively small ponds. There was Bassett; the Oklahoma oil man Walter Duncan; Marvin Warner, who had a big savings and loan company in Ohio; Bill Daniels of Denver, one of the pioneers of cable television; and a number of mall and real-estate developers, including Jim Joseph of San Francisco, Tad Taube of Oakland, Myles Tannenbaum of Philadelphia, and Alfred Taubmann, one of the biggest mall developers in America and soon to be a major shareholder of Macy's department stores.

Bill Tatham could have come in the first year, for he was flush with cash and assets. The Beverly sale had left him with real estate all over California and several other states. In 1981, he had sold the interest that he had acquired three years earlier in a Fresno savings and loan for a capital gain of about $1.8 million. In October 1983, the Bank of America agreed to settle the 1980 suit he had brought against it in connection with the alleged fraud against his leasing company. The settlement was sealed, so the terms were not known, but records filed with the Fresno County Recorder of Deeds show that subsequently one of Bill's companies received an $8 million loan from the Bank of America to finance a large garden apartment development on Cedar Avenue in Fresno.

Money was no problem for Bill in 1982, but he nevertheless sat out the first year of the league in the spring of 1983. As it happened, the USFL was moderately successful. The crowds in the warmer climes were fairly good and television ratings were better than anticipated. When the league announced plans to expand to eighteen teams in its second season, Bassett persuaded Bill to take a franchise that would begin play in the spring of 1984.

The USFL provided Bill with his first opportunity to work closely with one of his children. He needed a manager with the personal qualities to hire and fire coaches and players, massage egos, promote the team with the community, make deals with advertisers, and handle the press—skills which were not Bill's strong points. He could be the strategy man, staying in Fresno, controlling the purse strings, setting the objectives, and dealing with the league and the other wealthy owners, but he needed a somebody who could do the hands-on work for him.

The man he had in mind was his son Billy. Except for Pat Stroud, the oldest of Dick and Grace Tatham's six daughters, Billy was the oldest of Oca and Ruby's grandchildren, and though he was carefully groomed by Bill for the world of large institutions—he had a law degree from Pepperdine University in Malibu and an advanced accounting degree—Billy had perversely turned the tables on his dad. He took after his grandfather: he was a natural-born horse trader.

Before he was out of high school, he was doing a lively business buying and selling rifles and handguns, indulging an almost mystical enthusiasm for firearms. Perhaps, through the genes, some buried memory of the Oklahoma outlaw country had been passed down to the new generation, or perhaps it was the recollection of dinner-table stories of gunmen and sheriffs that kept the interest alive. Walter had owned a pearl-handled revolver; Walter and Oca had been deputy sheriffs in Oklahoma; Dick Tatham had followed Dick Tracy and dreamed of being a detective; and Dick was chaplain for the Lake Havasu City Police Department. Billy thought seriously about joining the FBI when he was recruited for it at law school. It seemed to him that the only people who were "doing things" were ministers, FBI people, and national politicians and that "the rest of us are just bumping into each other and getting up and going to work in the morning."

Living in Malibu and attending Pepperdine, he eased into the "recreational" gun trade, dealing in weapons that were advertised in gun magazines. There was, he discovered, "a ton of money in L.A. for exotic weapons," since the city was a magnet for the mercenary crowd. Billy bought a few semiautomatic MAC-10s, and pretty soon he was trading: "I bought a hundred Uzi barrels, thirty-five bucks apiece. Then a guy comes in and buys them all. Where are they going? Probably the Philippines. A guy calls and wants two MAC-10s."

This was racy stuff. Before the customer bought the MAC-10s he was called out of town, but he came back two months later, and Billy drove with the guns to a rendezvous on a street corner in the San Fernando Valley. The man showed up in a Raiders jersey and checked out the weapons carefully.

"It's none of my business, but what do you do?" Billy asked.

"Security consultation," he said.

"What government do you do it for?"

"Not ours."

"Where were you on the last trip?"

"Orient."

The federal government licensed regular firearms dealers, but much of the action in L.A. was between hobbyists like Billy, who figured they were too small-time to get a license. Still, it was a fine line between what Billy was doing and black marketeering, and there were risks.

One time he telephoned another hobbyist, whose wife answered and said her husband wasn't home.

Billy could hear the voice of his friend and some other men in the background.

"Tell that lousy liar to give me a call," he said and hung up.

Later the wife called back in tears. The voices in the background had been federal agents arresting her husband for illegal trafficking in firearms. Billy was scared.

The pride of his gun collection were his Ingram MAC-10 semi-automatic machine pistols with consecutive serial numbers. The MAC-10 looked as if it had been made for the make-believe world of television violence. A version with a silencer could be concealed in a "briefcase" and fired through a hole covered by a business card. The weapon had the potential for causing mayhem because it was inaccurate beyond point-blank range, but it was popular with dopers, motorcycle gangs, and gun fanatics.

Billy was on a visit home from Pepperdine Law School when he invited his dad, his Uncle Gerald, and kid brother, Mike, to try the weapon out. They stowed two of them in the family Blazer and drove out to a secluded canyon at the end of a dirt road. They pointed them at the side of a mountain and Gerald, a mischievous grin on his

face, squeezed the trigger. The canyon exploded. Clouds of dust
curled up from the side of the ravine. Laughing and whooping, they
dived for the car and piled in on the floor and across the seats as they
sped back to Fresno.

Billy half hoped some sheriff would stop them. He could imagine
his businessman-father and choirmaster-uncle being taken for a couple of right-wing crazies. Good, clean fun, he thought, as he doubled
over with laughter in the back. *Good, clean, Pentecostal fun!* It was a
splashy way of announcing that a new generation of Tathams had
arrived on the scene.

Late one afternoon, when he was living in Fresno after law school,
agents from the Federal Bureau of Alcohol, Tobacco, and Firearms
called on Billy. He'd bought and sold fifty or sixty MAC-10s in the
past three years, sometimes ten at a time from gun stores.

The agents asked to see his records, but Billy held his ground.
Not without a court order, he said. Finally, the agents backed off. "If
you're going to continue doing this, do yourself a favor and get a
commercial license," one of them said on the way out. Billy applied
the next day.

In Fresno after law school he worked briefly for an accounting
firm, then joined a law firm. But he was restless. He didn't want to
be a lawyer; he wanted to use the law like a sharp instrument to
promote the individualistic activities that interested him. So he was
pleased in 1982 when he got a chance to help with the California
Senate campaign of Barry Goldwater, Jr. In early 1983 his dad asked
him to go to San Diego to look into setting up a USFL franchise. He
was only twenty-nine and still very green, but he never hesitated.

In San Diego, he looked up Kenneth Rietz, a political and media
consultant he'd met working in politics the year before. Rietz had
directed Young Voters for Nixon in 1972. In the aftermath of Watergate, it came out that Ken had sent someone to infiltrate an antiwar demonstration in front of the White House during that year's
campaign. He had also "produced" the 1980 Republican National
Convention in Detroit, choreographing every event that occurred on
the platform in front of television cameras. More important as far as
Billy was concerned, Rietz had been a campaign consultant for the
mayor and three members of the city council, who voted on applica-
tions for leases to play at Jack Murphy Stadium.

Rietz was well aware of the difficulties faced by a USFL team
entering San Diego Chargers territory. The Chargers could not
openly oppose a spring football team because of the antitrust laws,

but the team had plenty of clout and, Billy believed, was ready to use it.

Initially, city officials seemed favorably disposed toward the new franchise. But in the next few weeks, two out-of-town soil experts whom Billy called on to evaluate the effect of spring football on the turf at Jack Murphy Stadium unexpectedly excused themselves, and the mayor, citing the concerns of the San Diego Padres baseball team about the turf problem, withdrew his support.

Billy did not mind the controversy and saw quickly that the battle would be fought with politics and PR. A few days before the June 14, 1983, meeting of San Diego's city council to decide on the stadium lease, Billy spotted former Chargers coach Sid Gillman at the San Diego airport. Gillman, a man credited with building the Chargers into an NFL force, was retired and about to be inducted into the Football Hall of Fame. Billy introduced himself and proposed a deal.

"Give me a call," said Gillman.

Billy and Rietz met him for a breakfast, and two days before the city council met, Bill leaked word to a friendly reporter that Gillman was coming to work for the new franchise. Having Gillman would make it a real San Diego USFL team and give it local credibility.

Earlier the Tathams had almost grabbed San Diego Chargers quarterback Dan Fouts, offering to pay him a $1 million signing bonus and $1 million for each of the next five years. It was quite an offer, considering the Tathams didn't yet have a place to play football, but it was the kind of deal that USFL owners were making in order to give their league prominence and attract interest from fans—and, more important, from television broadcasters.

USFL headquarters in New York scheduled a public relations event at Manhattan's "21" Club, at which the high point was to be the Tathams handing over a $1 million cashier's check to the NFL star. But the Tathams never got to New York.

The night before they were to leave with Dan Fouts for New York, the quarterback visited Bill and Billy in their hotel room in San Diego. The mood was relaxed. The million-dollar check was in Bill's briefcase, and the men sat on the beds, talking and watching Johnny Carson on television. Gradually, the mood shifted, becoming tense. The more Fouts talked, the more concerned the older Tatham became that he was looking for a way out. Fouts was worried what his teammates would think: with him, they had a chance to go to the Super Bowl; without him, there was not much hope of that. He had never been in the Super Bowl and still wanted a shot at it.

"Dan," Bill told him, "if you're uncomfortable with this, we don't want to do it. It's a lot of money for us and a lot for you." He told Fouts he had no objection if he made a phone call, and Fouts, sitting on the bed, dialed Charger owner Eugene Klein and arranged a breakfast meeting. Billy was sure that Klein, on the other end of the line, was promising to make Fouts the best-paid quarterback in football.

Then Fouts made another call, this time to his agent in New York. He had to move the phone away from his ear, and Billy could hear the agent screaming. Obviously, the agent was reaming him out, lacerating him for walking away from a $1 million deal.

The Tathams said good-bye to Fouts, packed their suitcases, and went to the airport with their check. It was not yet midnight, and Bill managed to charter a private plane to Fresno. He was fast asleep in his own bed a couple of hours later.

The next day Fouts called to say he was staying with the Chargers. Billy was angry, and he wondered if his dad hadn't been too nice to Fouts the night before. A wonderful opportunity for the hoped-for franchise in San Diego had slipped through their fingers—and, incidentally, a chance to "stick it to the Chargers," as Billy put it.

But his dad was in a Cherokee mode. At least, he said, Gene Klein would have to pay Fouts more money.

Rietz left for a European vacation the day before the city council vote on the application for a stadium lease, convinced that it would be approved. It wasn't. Chargers officials who crowded into the hearing room did not testify. Officially, the Chargers were neutral. Representatives of the San Diego Padres baseball team, however, spoke in opposition to the lease, citing concerns about the effect of spring football on the condition of the stadium turf. The final vote was five to three against the lease. All three favorable votes were cast by the council members for whom Rietz had been a campaign consultant. His other former client, the mayor, defected, citing concerns that spring football would conflict with his crusade to bring professional soccer to San Diego in the spring.

Assistant City Manager John Lockwood questioned whether Billy's subsequent criticism of the city was entirely justified: "Young Bill is a nice enough chap, but he gets emotionally involved and doesn't like to lose. To hint at anything else is a cheap shot."

IN JULY 1983, after a frantic search, the Tathams settled on Tulsa, Oklahoma, as a home for their team. It wasn't a major media market, but unlike San Diego, the welcome mat was out. The Tulsa *World* published articles recounting some of the family's cotton-picking-to-riches saga, and one article described Oca and Ruby as "Depression refugees." Ted Reed of the Fresno *Bee* filed a special report with the *World*, profiling the Tathams and quoting Oca: "That guy in *The Grapes of Wrath* started in the same town I left from and had a truck like mine, an old beat-up truck with a lot of people in it."

Almost from the beginning, Bill detected a coolness on the part of the old-line business and political establishment: during a meeting with Tulsa Chamber of Commerce officials, he was handed a soft drink and shown a long promotional film while the officials excused themselves to take care of more important business. Nonetheless, he heard comments such as "You came here because of your heart, not your head. You wanted to show that an Okie could make it." Well, Billy thought, it didn't happen exactly that way, but there was a lot of truth in it. He considered his "nationality" Oklahoman. For as long as he could remember he'd listened to his granddad's stories about outlaws roaming the Cookson Hills and the journey in the '29 Chevy truck in which they were almost killed in the pass east of Albuquerque.

They named the team after the cast of characters who had given Oklahoma such a distinctive image earlier in the century: the Outlaws. The team logo was the head of a man in a black cowboy hat with a black bandanna pulled up over his nose. Bill bought a live piranha, named it "Outlaw," and kept it in an aquarium in his living room.

Billy was soon spending sixteen hours a day at the team's impromptu headquarters, the Camelot Hotel. The walls of Billy's and Gillman's rooms were covered with charts. Through the fall of 1983 movie projectors ground away day and night showing game films. He was interviewing coaches, writing contracts, ordering tickets, giving interviews, lining up sponsors. And he loved it.

Except for trip to Tulsa to smooth over problems between Billy and Gillman, Bill stayed in Fresno, dealing with league headquarters and organizing the financing of the team. Gillman, the general manager, knew what it took to build a football team and he spent liberally on tryout camps and recruiting, but it was Tatham money he was spending. Billy, the president, asserted his authority over the purse strings. On his infrequent trips to Tulsa, Bill played the role of peacemaker. Gillman evidently felt abused by Billy, who had never been inside a professional football locker room. By Thanksgiving, Gillman had resigned.

Billy hired Coach Woody Widenhofer on the telephone. Widenhofer, defensive coordinator for the Pittsburgh Steelers, had just deplaned from a game on the West Coast when Billy reached him.

"Hello, Woody, this is Bill Tatham of the Oklahoma Outlaws. We need a head coach and would like you to consider it."

"I thought you guys just hired Jerry Rhome," said the sleepy voice, referring to the Washington Redskins coach with whom Billy had been dickering.

"Nope," replied Billy, who had not yet informed Rhome that he had lost patience waiting for him to make up his mind.

"What's your name again?" asked Widenhofer. "I'll call you right back." Woody wanted to make sure the caller was on the level. In their second call, Billy clinched the deal. "You're the guy for us," he said. "I can tell you're a good guy just from talking with you on the phone!"

Billy's blunt talk and impulsive ways endeared him to some of the Tulsa sportswriters, but foreshadowed problems later. Gillman had not felt well treated. Yet Billy had a close relationship with quarterback Doug Williams, one of only a few black quarterbacks in pro football when he came to the Outlaws from Tampa Bay in the NFL. At that time Williams was still absorbed by the personal tragedy of his wife's recent death; the Tathams were sensitive to his being away from his family and baby daughter, and they went out of their way to make him feel like a member of their own family. Bill and Earline, in Birmingham for a game early in the 1984 season, came back from a shopping spree with a doll for Doug's child. Williams said it was not something that usually happened in the NFL.

Williams was aware of the "redneck attitude" that held that quarterbacking was a "banking man's position"—in other words, a white man's job. Billy was nearly ejected from a game against the Tampa Bay Bandits as a result of an incident involving Williams. The game marked Doug's "homecoming" to Tampa Bay, and the fans heckled and booed him. During one series of plays, a Williams pass was intercepted, and a touchdown was saved when the quarterback knocked the ball carrier out of bounds. Whistles blew, and the referee penalized Williams for an illegal tackle. There were hoots, and beer was thrown while several security guards with badges looked on. Billy, who was close to the play, grabbed a guard and demanded his badge number. When Williams looked back he was amused to see the club president in the thick of the scuffle. That was young Billy Tatham, he thought.

The Outlaws' season officially opened in February 1984 with a

7–3 victory over the Pittsburgh Maulers. As an inauguration it was hardly propitious: the crowd at Tulsa's Skelly Stadium braved thunder, lightning, rain turning to snow, and temperatures with a wind-chill factor of twenty below zero, but as bad as the weather was, Billy had not been prepared for the low attendance. Only a little over 20,000 tickets were sold, and only 12,000 people showed up. The figures were disastrous—far below the 20,000 to 30,000 the Tathams needed just to break even.

On March 5, two games into regular-season play, Billy stunned Tulsa by announcing that the Outlaws would pull out unless a new all-weather dome stadium was constructed within the next three years. He estimated the price tag would be about $100 million. Skelly Stadium, a charming place for viewing a low-key college team, was ill suited to modern professional football; in Billy's view, it "stunk."

The Outlaws already had a following in the region's towns and farms, especially the blue-collar oil-and gas-field-workers. Billy or Widenhofer would often fly to small towns in Oklahoma, southern Kansas, or western Arkansas for promotional rallies, trips that Billy loved. He worked the towns like a politician, ducking into the Circle K's and Quik Trip's to shake hands and distribute Outlaws literature. At the rallies, he would stress the importance of Oklahoma to him and the Outlaws to Oklahoma. Oklahoma had a lot to be proud of, and it was time for the rest of the nation to stop kicking the state around. Oklahoma deserved a team. His speeches brought people cheering to their feet. In Collinsville, where his grandparents had lived for so many years in the shadow of the great BZ smelter, Billy arrived at an Outlaws rally with a police escort. A high school band played, and Billy talked about his bond with Oklahoma. One promotional tour took him to Sallisaw, where several relatives came and introduced themselves, one of them wearing an Outlaws jacket.

Billy also had the support of at least one influential Tulsa quarter: Oral Roberts. Billy had been born after the evangelist's great revivals his parents used to attend in Fresno in the 1950s. He remembered his mother and father had their first date at an Oral Roberts rally under a tent. But by the 1980s, Roberts presided over a nationally televised religious show that mixed entertainment with inspiration and the Word of God, a university with a library that attracted secular as well as religious scholars from around the country, and the City of Faith research center and 777-bed hospital. The City of Faith was the tallest building in Tulsa, and Oral Roberts University, a city within a city, was the leading attraction in the state. The value of his organizational holdings was estimated to exceed $1 billion.

Yet the former tent evangelist existed in a state of permanent crisis, each episode being resolved only at the last minute when God would save his latest project from almost certain bankruptcy by means of his followers' contributions. When Billy came to Tulsa, Roberts was in a new predicament: his new hospital—a controversial enterprise given Roberts's background in faith healing—was nearly empty and losing a million dollars a month. And there had been the 1979 divorce of his son and heir apparent Richard Roberts, not to mention a book written by Richard's former wife that described in detail her growing disillusionment with the materialism of Roberts's enterprises, underwritten with "seed-faith" contributions.[1]

Billy and his wife, Shauna, called on the evangelist soon after they arrived in Tulsa. Billy and Oral, an avid sports fan, exchanged ORU and Outlaws jackets at an ORU basketball game, and Billy jokingly dubbed Roberts the "number one Outlaw." Richard Roberts became a regular guest in the Tatham box at Outlaws home games; at a Jacksonville match, televised on the ESPN sports cable channel, he gave the invocation and got a thunderous round of applause when he prayed for an Outlaws victory. Billy did not tell him that the spectators were well primed by half-price beer night. The Outlaws lost anyway.

When stadium difficulties arose, it seemed to Billy that Oral Roberts was itching to help. He invited the Tathams and out-of-town relatives to lunch one day before one of the games; after the main course, he and Billy wandered over to the window and surveyed the vast expanses of the ORU campus.

"You know," mused Roberts, "there's one guy who could build you that stadium."

"Who?" asked Billy, thinking that perhaps he was referring to the Almighty.

"Oral Roberts," the evangelist said firmly. "I can see it right there," and he pointed to an empty expanse below. As Billy stared down, the dome, sparkling like crystal in the sun, seemed to materialize before his eyes.

Becoming increasingly animated, Roberts remarked that he could have the largest tent meetings in the country in the stadium. But then he caught himself. "I couldn't do it; it wouldn't promote what I'm trying to achieve here from a Christian standpoint, nor would it help my school. But you need somebody like me to do it."

Poof, thought Billy, still staring at the empty space below. What's for dessert?

The issue of where and how the dome stadium would be built

got a lot of publicity in Tulsa, but it was a sideshow to the politics that finally determined the destiny of the USFL. From the outset, the USFL owners had been in a bind: moderately priced players did not attract lucrative television contracts. But the owners' failure to hold the line on salaries increased the pressure on the league to obtain lucrative television contracts. That was not easy considering that the league played in cities like Tulsa, Oakland, Memphis, and Birmingham.

Donald Trump wasted no time establishing himself as the leading advocate of a new strategy of confrontation with the NFL. Experience showed that sports attendance and sports television ratings trailed off as the spring weather improved and people left their homes and apartments for their boats or beach houses. Trump favored moving quickly to a fall season, in which the USFL could battle head-to-head with the senior league and enter a court of law at the first hint of monopolistic activity. But not all the owners liked the idea of a fall season, which would force the league to compete for television time with college football and the NFL. As long as the league played in the winter and spring, the dog days between the regular football and baseball seasons, at least some television interest would be there. Evidence of that was the fact that in June 1984, after the end of the Outlaws' season in Tulsa, ESPN would sign a $70 million, three-year contract with the USFL.

For the Outlaws, a move to the fall would be disastrous since neither Tulsa nor Oklahoma had a stadium that wasn't already being used by college teams on Saturdays. Networks didn't want to televise football games played on ratty, torn-up turf, and the players' union wouldn't accept the risks of injury.

Billy fired off some hotly worded messages intended for Trump via the USFL's internal wire. It was fortunate, he wrote sarcastically, that "we lost sheep" have somebody to follow in the East. Most people didn't generally talk about Donald Trump that way, but when John Bassett saw the message, he fired off his own to Billy: "Bravo."

In Tulsa, the dome issue was becoming embroiled in politics. By May 1984, Billy was publicly attacking Mayor Terry Young for his lack of support and making comments to the press like "Skelly Field got one more season of professional football than it deserved." In the process, he was learning some things about Oklahoma.

Viewed from California, it was all one big state, but Oklahomans themselves knew that Tulsa and Oklahoma City were worlds apart. Tulsa was in many ways a Yankee city built with Eastern money to extract rich minerals resources, so it had a stuffy, starchy, rather Ivy League side, evidenced by the naming of Harvard, Princeton, Yale, and Boston avenues. In the decades since the Tathams had gone to California, Tulsa's oil-and-gas interests may have been dwarfed by bigger energy interests elsewhere, but it had become the financial, insurance, and service capital for the global oil-and-gas industry. It was a white-collar, managerial city full of technocrats and financial men, many of them born elsewhere. Affluent Tulsans banked and shopped in New York, secretly envied Dallas, and kept aloof from Oklahoma's farming and industrial towns. In Tulsa, billion-dollar drilling and pipeline deals were hatched over Scotch and dry martinis in private clubs high up in downtown skyscrapers and urbane promoters of art museums were likely to find a warmer reception than boosters of a professional football team.

Indigenous Oklahoma was to be found not in Tulsa but in its earthier sibling, Oklahoma City, with its tradition of cattle, cowboys, rodeos, and wheat. In Tulsa, Billy often felt he was the only one who wore cowboy boots. In Oklahoma City, people *did* wear cowboy boots, western shirts, and jeans. After all, it was the home of the Cowboy Hall of Fame.

Influential Tulsans did not like having the deficiencies of their city pointed out to them, least of all by a twenty-nine-year-old Californian. And they didn't like being threatened. Skelly Stadium was owned by the University of Tulsa, a private institution and jewel of the city. Billy's straight-from-the-hip comments did not sit well.

Soon he let it be known that the Outlaws had received feelers from a number of other cities interested in the franchise. He mentioned Honolulu and—unpardonable sin—Oklahoma City. "Some cities out there realize the value of a professional football team," Billy said. He later acknowledged that the remark went over "like a lead balloon."

In Tulsa, Billy was communicating with the mayor via telegrams. In Oklahoma City, he secretly met with the mayor and others, where the reception was much warmer. The idea for a domed stadium gained the backing of Oklahoma City's Edward L. Gaylord, publisher of the *Daily Oklahoman* there and an influential person in the state. Gaylord saw a domed stadium as a possibility that might keep Las Vegas from luring away the finals of the National Rodeo competition, in which he took an intense interest. Residents of Oklahoma City, it seemed to Billy, were "willing to roll up their sleeves and get the job done."

The one potential stumbling block was the University of Oklahoma Board of Regents. Memorial Stadium in Norman, home field of the famous Sooners football team, would be suitable as a temporary playing field until the Outlaws got their dome, and only the Regents could authorize a lease. But the Sooners were a religion in Oklahoma. The idea of another football team trampling sacred Sooner ground in Norman, even in the Sooner off-season, was bound to seem sacrilege to many. Another problem was political: two of the OU regents were Tulsans.

But Oklahoma City carried weight with the regents, too. As the Outlaws' season on the field went from bad to worse, Billy continued to negotiate secretly with Oklahoma City fathers. What resulted was the outline of potentially the sweetest deal that any USFL team ever saw: the city would use its influence to get the University of Oklahoma to lease Memorial Stadium to the Outlaws while the new stadium was being built, paying the team a relocation allowance and buying 10,000 season tickets in addition to what the Outlaws could sell. "If we have to lose this much money, at least we'll be appreciated," Billy told his dad, referring to the several million dollars that Bill ended up laying out for the 1984 season.

On June 24, the Outlaws finished the year with their tenth straight loss—Doug Williams had been hurt and sidelined midseason—to end with a 6–12 record. A few days later, Billy announced that Tulsa would not be the home of the Outlaws next season, but he didn't say where they would play. The next day, the Oklahoma City Chamber of Commerce announced it would study the feasibility of building a dome stadium and made clear that it was interested in a deal with the Tathams.

Inevitable recriminations followed in the Tulsa media. "We like the Outlaws, but we don't like Tatham," said one commentator, referring to Billy. News articles mentioning Billy's BMW and jokes about the young rich kid who turned cities against each other made their way into print. But the Oklahoma City power structure was still with the Outlaws.

On the day before a key regents' meeting on the Memorial Stadium lease, the Tulsa *Tribune* published a hard-hitting, critical article about Billy's management of the Outlaws, including four pictures of Billy on page one, which began, "Today, Tatham is cruising in his black BMW, scouting for a home for the gypsy United States Football League team." It was written by Mary Hargrove, an investigative city reporter, not one of the *Tribune's* more indulgent sports columnists. "He has been dubbed 'unpredictable' and 'a remarkable chameleon' who dabbled in empire building at the emotional expense of a city," she wrote. "He leaves behind a reputation with some for high-handedness, a multimillionaire who had to be badgered to pay his bills and casually broke promises." She went on to quote John Hamill, president of the Downtown Outlaws Club: "There is a feeling of sadness with a degree of bitterness, tempered by a sense of good riddance to the owner. The people in Tulsa don't like to be taken for rubes, and the feeling was that we have been taken."[2] And she identified the University of Tulsa and the local transit company as having had problems getting paid in a timely fashion.

Bill Tatham later said that all Tatham bills were paid, but the article was hardly the kind of publicity Billy needed for the meeting with the regents. The next day he found that someone had put copies of the article on the chairs in the conference room before the meeting started.

Hargrove covered the meeting.

"How can you face me after what you wrote?" Billy asked her.

"Show me anything that's inaccurate," Hargrove replied. Billy returned to his seat still steaming.

Billy had been arguing his case for an hour and a half when a courier arrived from the governor's office with a message asking the regents to negotiate a fair lease with the Outlaws. It would, he said, be in the interest of the state of Oklahoma.

On August 22, however, the issue became moot before a final vote was ever taken. USFL owners, meeting in New York, voted to play one final spring season and then switch to the fall; Trump had won. With that decision, Oklahoma City's interest in the USFL evaporated. The University of Oklahoma and Oklahoma City already had their fall football team: the Sooners, the greatest college football power in America. They did not want another fall football operation sharing the spotlight at Memorial Stadium. There would be no deal with the Tathams.

The departure of the Outlaws from Tulsa left ill feelings all around. Linebacker coach Jim McKinley filed a $25 million suit against the Tathams for breach of contract, and Woody Widenhofer, who was not rehired as head coach with the Tathams' new team, which would begin playing in Phoenix in early 1985, went on record in an interview with the Tulsa *Tribune* on October 25. Of Bill Junior he said: "He's willing to stamp on and move head coaches like they are a piece of meat." Gillman, who had clashed with Billy during the season, declined to comment. "I don't want to talk about the Tathams," he stated.

In the end, both Billy Tatham and Oklahoma received an education. "The Tathams and their team had a dramatic impact on the state," acknowledged Tulsa *Tribune* sports editor Steve O'Brien. "They sparked domed stadium studies in both Tulsa and Oklahoma City, heightened competition between the state's two major metropolitan areas, placed the University of Oklahoma in a politically awkward situation and created hostility in a solid group of fans." Downtown Tulsa Unlimited president Bill Fountain told the *Tribune* that Billy was "very personable and candid, but he reacted as a twenty-nine-year-old will. . . . Before you try to be an influence you have to play the games in a community."

An Oklahoma relative of Billy's, who raised bulls for rodeos northeast of Tulsa, said, "Billy could have had what he wanted, even the dome, if he'd gone about it the right way. But he threatened. These people are funny, whether they're plain old 'Okie' or what. You don't threaten them. Billy acted like a spoiled little rich kid."

"I probably was pretty outspoken," Billy admitted. "I said stuff that didn't make friends. But at that point we'd been screwed pretty good, so we went public and said, 'we need these things or we may have to leave.' All we were doing was putting it on the line, telling the truth. I mean, if I was trying to put anything over on those people, then I wouldn't have said a word and we'd have left when the season was over. Why put yourself through all that agony if it really wasn't for something you were trying to accomplish?"

The Tathams' red ink was to reach $4.2 million in just thirteen months, according to Bill. In the middle of the 1984 spring season, the suit that Bill and his partners in the Mid-South Grizzlies had filed against the NFL was dismissed by the U.S. Supreme Court. There would be no windfall there.

The blue-collar Oklahomans who had been the core of Outlaws support were big losers, too. But for decades wealthy outsiders had been coming to Oklahoma, promising the world and then abruptly pulling up stakes. At least the Outlaws were just a football team, not a zinc smelter.

Yet Oklahoma had touched a chord in Billy. His dad may have imagined that going to Stanford would launder the Okieness out of him, but Billy came away from the experience with his rough edges still unsmoothed. Individualistic, independent, stubborn, resentful of the upper crust, and unimpressed by titles or big institutions, he was pure Okie in many ways, a throwback whose BMW and California affluence were deceiving.

In his own way, he stayed loyal to Oklahoma, even though he was leaving it. One moment from the final days there lingered in his mind. In a store he encountered an Outlaw fan.

"You Mr. Tatham?" the hulking man asked.

Here it comes, thought Billy, expecting a tongue-lashing or maybe worse. "Yes, sir."

The stranger extended his right hand. "I just wanted to wish you all the luck in the world," he said. "I sure hope you guys make it."

It was one of the good memories that Billy took away from Tulsa.

IN JANUARY 1985, the Outlaws began the USFL's final season of spring play—in Phoenix. After a frantic search for a new home for the team, Bill had bought out the interests of a Phoenix heart surgeon and taken over the franchise in that city.

Before the season opened, Bill arranged an exhibition game at Bulldog Stadium in Fresno between his Outlaws and Tad Taube's Oakland team. Only 10,000 spectators showed up for the February game, a meager crowd compared with a typical turnout for the Bulldogs. But the gate covered the costs, and, by prearrangement with Fresno State, $10,000 of the proceeds went toward a new business school building, to be named for Leon Peters, Fresno's great civic leader.

Bill Tatham had brought the symphony to his home town.

Chapter Nineteen

Authenticity

NOTHING IN HIS LIFE had prepared Oca for the emotional ordeal of the first months without Ruby. He dreamed of cotton fields in the autumn, the brown stalks dabbed with white bolls, ready for the harvest. He hung a picture in his study of an abandoned church with weathered boards and a sign announcing "Closed for Rapture." Even God seemed to have fallen silent. His line to God had always been an action line, carrying specific instructions for doing. Suddenly, it was as dead as if the wires had been downed by an Oklahoma twister. He was ready for duty—but no orders came.

What came instead was a telephone call from Don Ghan, a friend from Peoples Church. Don had astonishing news: God had spoken to him in his prayers and left a message with him for Oca Tatham. He repeated the message as best he could remember it: "I sent an angel to you when I heard your cries, your prayers, saw your suffering, and your tears—except the angel couldn't get through. I have called you by name, because I have a plan for your life that nobody will know but you, but you were so low you couldn't hear my voice."

Don and Oca agreed it was unusual, though not unprecedented, for God to send messages through third parties. There was solid

Biblical example, in the tenth chapter of Daniel, where a man comes to Daniel in a vision and assures him his mourning has not been in vain and that his words have been heard and a plan will be revealed. Don and Oca read the passages from Daniel together. For the first time Oca felt his despondent mood lift a little.

Oca told the story of Don's message again and again, always using the same words and always in a very matter-of-fact tone, for in Pentecost such miraculous things were almost commonplace. In the first days after Don's visit, though, Oca still wasn't clear what the plan was for him. He had expected God to send him to Mexico to continue his work on Mercedes Díaz's new church, a charitable project he and Ruby had undertaken before her death. Slowly he began to understand that God, who was full of surprises, had something else in mind. He found his thoughts turning to a particular woman from the time when he and Ruby attended the Pentecostal Church of God in McFarland—to Ona Syers.

In those days Ona was married to Lowell Syers, who strummed his guitar to draw crowds for Jay Fuller's street preaching; Ona was the one who did Jay's laundry before he married. Things had gone sour for Ona and Lowell after they moved to L.A. Lowell drove a bus for Trailways, which kept him far from home for long stretches; he drifted away, and the marriage ended. Eventually, Ona returned to Delano and received her divorce. She worked in a school cafeteria and tended a soda fountain until, during a long spell of bad health, she sold her home and moved in with her in-laws. When she recovered her health, she worked at an orange stand, then at McDonald's. In October 1982, when Oca began thinking about her, she was working at a car wash.

Oca tried out the plan on Jay Fuller when he visited the preacher in Phoenix, where Jay was pastoring a small church.

"If I *did* remarry," Oca cautiously suggested, "I know who it would be." He watched Jay's reaction carefully as he mentioned Ona Syers. The little preacher brightened. "Well, she's one of the finest women in the world," he said.

Late one night Oca finally called her.

"Hello, Ona?"

"Yes."

"You'll be surprised who this is."

Ona had been asleep.

"Ona, this is Oca Tatham."

"Uh-huh."

"Ona, I've been praying, and He says it's part of His plan that we get together."

Ona was wide awake.

As Oca said later: "I knew God's will, and there's no use of me fooling around, 'n' I just claimed her at that point."

He was careful not to come on too strong, but he didn't want to leave Ona too much leeway either. "When can I come down?" he asked finally.

"Well," he said, "you really belong to me. The way God led me, you're the plan." He felt his grief lifting just a little more.

He took her to dinner at Bakersfield for their first date; their second was at Perko's in Delano. For a few days, they tried to dodge relatives, but then Gerald and Cora came down to talk to Ona, "to see if it was all right," Ona said. It was all right, and Ona reintroduced Oca to her five sisters and their husbands.

They were all Okie types—easygoing people who joked and told stories. Oca seemed relaxed around them. One of Ona's brothers-in-law, Bill Elkins, a tire dealer in Delano, was the man to whom Oca and Ruby had given their "furniture" of orange crates forty-seven years earlier.

To Ona's relatives, Oca was a prince in a Cadillac who came riding out of nowhere; she was his Cinderella. And he paid her the highest compliment: she was a clean woman. A clean person lived upright and did not smoke or drink. Oca bragged that Ona had "not had a coffee date in thirty years." She was Assemblies of God; all four of her children were "in church." Ione, her oldest daughter, who'd once been a child preacher, married a preacher's son, and a nephew sang on "Haven of Rest," a popular Christian radio show.

But Ona was no clinging vine. She was Ona Kirkpatrick, who'd handled a cultivator for her dad and had hoed, chopped, and picked cotton. She could cook biscuits, drive an automobile anywhere. Like Ruby, she was one of those pragmatic, competent women with a steady, quiet strength.

On January 29, 1983, a little over seven months after Ruby died, Ona's story had a happy turn. She and Oca got married at the Assembly of God Church in Delano. Oca's sons and Ona's daughters were grooms and bridesmaids; Gerald clowned, pretending to have lost the ring. Brenda helped Ona pick out a brand-new wardrobe for her all-new life.

After a short trip to Carmel, an anonymous well-wisher—Oca speculated it was Bill—upgraded them into the penthouse suite on the *Daphne*, the ship they had chosen for their Caribbean honeymoon cruise. Ona kept thinking she'd wake up to find it was all a dream and that she was late for her job at the car wash.

OCA'S HASTY REMARRIAGE was in many ways the highest compliment he could have paid Ruby: it showed that she had made marriage a happy institution for him. Oca meant no disrespect for Ruby or his children by taking Ona. He just didn't intend to mope around for the rest of his life like a sad old codger, fading quietly into the twilight.

The marriage began a kind of rebirth. Over the years Oca had been afflicted with various maladies: emphysema, heart trouble, gall bladder and kidney problems. He wore a hearing aid and took blood thinners to prevent clotting and embolism. But not too long before Ruby was diagnosed with cancer, he had himself anointed with oil by an old-time Methodist preacher who visited Peoples Church. "People were kneeling at the altar all the way across. It gave me a chance to search my heart and speak with the Lord. I didn't ask Him to do anything. I just said, 'I can't live without a heart, if You'll heal my heart I can live with the other stuff.' They prayed for me, and I didn't feel a thing, and anointed me with oil. Next day, I laid off half the medication and I felt fine. The day after that I laid off the rest. On the third day I said, 'Well, God, I believe you overhauled me.'" A while later, he said, his doctor took a blood sample and found it clean.

After he had begun courting Ona, he made changes in his life. He sold his house on Escalon Avenue, bought a condominium up the street, and outfitted himself with new clothes, including short-sleeved polo shirts and—to the amazement of his children—Levi's.

For in a way, Ruby's death simplified his life. It liberated him from having to be the patriarch of his large extended family, a role for which he was not temperamentally suited. Now he could just be himself, a plain man with an eighth-grade education who'd done all right. Visiting Doris after Ruby's death, he put her arms around her and hugged her. They were in the kitchen. "I almost dropped the frying pan," she said. He told Renee he loved her.

He was still Oca Tatham, confident of his own beliefs, but there was no pretending that everything was the same. He had received a lesson in human weakness: his own. The emotions that came to the surface after Ruby's death surprised him. Sorrow over loss was one thing, but he had indulged his grief, which had impaired his capacity to work and act for God. The ordeal had shown him he needed more than God; he needed some*one*, a wife, a companion. To the extent he'd believed he was above that, his pride was taken away. God didn't let him forget it, either. He often felt depressed, unable to control his emotion over the loss of Ruby, and Ona was generous and gave him room to grieve.

Through her, a woman out of the little church in McFarland that had been his first anchor in California, he reconnected with his past and was able to go forward again. Like Ruby, Ona represented a simpler and more authentic time, before big churches and wealthy preachers, when they were all dirt poor. And so did the churches in Mexico. Months before Ruby died, Oca had been waging a battle with himself over Mercedes Díaz's plans to build a big new church in Mazatlán. Mexican ways of building and doing business exasperated him. He worried about the project; it was out of control, and he was being dragged along. A local architect had designed a structure larger than Oca had envisioned, and, before Oca knew it, the foundation was already poured.

In Fresno he fumed and fretted, fearing he had a white elephant on his hands. Then on the night of October 9, 1981, the Lord spoke to him about the situation. "The first thing I heard was, 'The harvest is ready, will you help gather in the grain?' I started to reach up and shake Ruby when He said, 'Work until God calls you home.' I thought, Man, I'll get up and write that down word for word. The Holy Spirit spoke to my heart. Then the Lord started dealing with me. And I started complaining and said, 'Lord, I've been a loner all these years. I went down there to Mexico when I couldn't get help from anybody.' Then the Lord spoke smart and said, 'What about the money that's laying in your checking account? You're not even drawing any interest on that money.' And I said, 'Lord, I'll go in the morning and put the money in Peoples Church to be sent down.' And the Lord said, 'I'll take care of you.' "

Bill came over the next day and gave him a check for ten thousand dollars, his first gift to Oca's church work in Mexico. Oca called the surprise gift "an answered prayer."

The church took nearly six years to build and was the fruit of a monumental effort. Ruby did not live to see it completed; she died three years before. The Díaz family made enormous personal sacrifices: Mercedes' son Victor, who made a living taking tourists fishing, sold his house to pay off debts on the lots; Mercedes almost sold her house, but, she said, at that last moment, "God supplied the money."

Oca put nearly $80,000 of his own money into the building, including $20,000 for the roof. Peoples Church, Bill, Renee, and other American friends in California and Texas also helped.

It was the third Assemblies of God Church in Mazatlán. Most of the congregation was drawn from the neighborhood. They were people who worked at the local bread factory and tourist hotels or lived in the public housing development across the road. Mercedes' daughter Thersita, who graduated from Margaret Klassen's Bible school, helped with the preaching.

When Oca and Ona visited Mazatlán in the spring of 1985 only a few odds and ends were left to be done. It was one of the finest buildings around. Its white-stuccoed walls were clean and new; inside there were row after row of pews and a stage with a musical ensemble of drums and guitars off to one side. The words over the entrance read "Iglesia para La Gente"—The People's Church.

On a Wednesday evening on which Oca was invited to preach a sermon, he walked slowly forward, got up on the stage, and spoke into the microphone. "What's more important, to live for God or for ourselves?" he began, as Victor Díaz translated the words into Spanish for the Mexican congregation. "He's our sole repose. If we just continue to pray when God seeks it, it'll keep Him willing to do what He wants us to do, 'cause only what we do for Him will count. We only get one life, and it's up to you and me the way we live it. Jesus knows what we're doing and whether we're living for God or not. But you remember what the Word says: Greater is He that's within us than he that's in the world because it's Jesus who lives within our hearts, and we can't overcome the Devil, but Jesus is much stronger than the Devil. He laid down His life so we could be saved. He paid the price. Let's don't let Jesus die in vain for us."

The Mexicans waited patiently for Oca to finish and for Victor to translate: "It's always a blessing to be back here in this church. This is our home church in Mexico. We pray for you. All things are possible for those that believe in Christ."

The next day Victor drove Oca and Ona to the site of the next church-building project, in a town in the backcountry called Marmol, forty-five miles north of Mazatlán. The road wound through brush as thick as Ozark squirrel country until a yellowish plume belching up from the smokestack of Marmol's cement plant announced the town. Past the edge of the town, with its bean fields, weedy lots, and cinder-block houses, the town center showed fading paint peeling from stuccoed walls emblazoned with political graffiti. Across the town square, there were a few dilapidated stores and a run-down Catholic church. A block further, a stocky, mustached Mexican stood next to a freshly poured foundation, the site of the new Pentecostal church.

Oca, tanned, wearing a blue blazer and open-necked shirt, inspected the progress and bargained with the Mexican contractor about the price of a cement floor.

"Tell him he's doing it for the Lord, not for me," Oca said, his voice deep and resonant, friendly but uncompromising. He was a Tatham, doing what he did best.

"He says he loves the Lord, but he also has to feed his family," Victor interpreted.

Oca chipped off a piece of concrete from the foundation and grumbled that not enough cement had been used.

The conversation continued for another few minutes, until Victor, plainly uncomfortable with the haggling, said it would not do to humiliate the man, on whom so much depended. The price of pouring a cement floor already had come down from 100,000 to 75,000 pesos, a savings of fifty dollars.

"Well, it's only a couple of hundred dollars," said Oca, accepting the price at last. "It's better to let it go," he said, as if trying to convince himself. "It's better not to make him think we don't think he knows his job."

Still, it bothered him. "He's making good money, that guy is," said Oca when he was back in Victor's car, heading for the coast road again. The poor quality of the foundation work still aggravated him.

In May that church was finished, too. A friend of Oca's from Peoples Church in Fresno flew down to Mazatlán in a private plane, bringing two laborers to block the walls and put on the roof. They finished the job in four days.

FOR SOMEONE WHO COVERED as much ground as he did, Oca lived in a remarkably seamless world. He was a kind of middle man between times and places, with connections into the future and back into the past. Decades and geography overlapped in his life, and people and pieces from one place and time turned up in another. Yet everything he did reminded him how far he had come—and that he was still on a journey.

In October 1985, several months after returning from Mexico, Oca and Ona left Fresno again to take a trip, this time in a GMC pickup and Alpenlite fifth-wheel trailer equipped with gas stove, dining and sitting area, and a sleeping compartment up front. They were bound for Sallisaw, Oklahoma.

They drove down to Bakersfield, crossed the Tehachapi Mountains, and motored on to Barstow in the Mojave Desert, picking up Interstate 40, and crossed the bridge over the Colorado River into Arizona by Topock, at the same point the Okies had crossed heading west in the 1930s. After stopping by to see Dick in Havasu City they drove on, picking up Interstate 40, which had replaced the old Highway 66.

I-40 was the Sun Belt's Main Street, an east-west Mississippi of concrete, running from Barstow to Winston-Salem. In between, it flowed past Flagstaff, Albuquerque, Amarillo, Oklahoma City, Little Rock, Memphis, Nashville, and Knoxville. Just a few hours off the connecting interstates were Los Angeles, Phoenix, Dallas–Fort Worth, and Tulsa. The interstate was the connecting artery between the South and the West, transfusing the culture and outlook of the older region into the energy and vision of the newer one and reenergizing the South itself.

Many decades earlier, the regions served by the road were marked by scattered, disconnected communities: flinty, Bible-thumping Scotch-Irish in the Appalachian hinterlands; backcountry tenant farmers in Oklahoma and Texas; cotton pickers in southern California. But now, a traveler driving west was pursued all the way from North Carolina to the deserts of southern California by overlapping radio signals: country and Gospel sounds, preachers calling on Jesus, and broadcasters warning of the imminent threat of communism. I-40 had its own newspaper, the *I-40 Country News*, published simultaneously in El Reno, Oklahoma, and Hurricane Mills, Tennessee. It's motto was "If It's on I-40, It's News." A typical issue included a report on Ike Dale's Husky Truck Stop Appreciation Day in Amarillo, Texas, and a "North Carolina Calendar of Events."

People changed; the country changed. Approaching Sallisaw from the west on I-40, Oca and Ona left the Great Plains behind them and entered the rolling, wooded terrain of eastern Oklahoma. It bore little resemblance to the flat, windblown panhandle depicted by John Steinbeck. Plenty of people were still poor in Sequoyah County. Oca arrived back in the Ozark foothills, in a trans-Mississippi Appalachia of curvy roads, where people rocked away the hours on tumbledown front porches or poked around in vegetable gardens. County unemployment was considerably above the national average.

More striking than the enduring poverty, however, was the evidence of prosperity, a result of diversification into tourism, light industry, and new kinds of farming. Cotton had ceased to be grown commercially in Sequoyah County; now the bottomlands along the Arkansas River raised a more dependable commodity: soybeans. Eastern Oklahoma even had its own "seaport," Muskogee, just up the Arkansas River from Sallisaw on the McClellan-Kerr waterway.

The waterway was testimony to the benefits of pork-barrel politics and, in particular, to the power of the late Oklahoma senator Robert Kerr. Kerr had been a kind of Robert Moses of the wide-open spaces. Thanks to his efforts, inland Oklahoma was now connected by water to the booming Mississippi River trade, to the Gulf of Mexico—and to the world. Kerr Dam, south of Drake's Prairie on the Arkansas River, had been built in the late 1960s for the Arkansas Basin Project and had not been entirely welcome by local citizens, whose farmland was flooded. But it made the river navigable all the way to Tulsa.

Sallisaw land prices had soared with the opening of the state's first pari-mutuel horse-racing track at Blue Ribbon Downs on the western outskirts of town. "An Estimated $7 Million in Purse Money in 1984!" boasted the official racing pamphlet. Sleek quarter horses grazed in rolling pastures that looked more like Kentucky bluegrass than the dust country described in the opening scenes of *The Grapes of Wrath*.

To serve the weekend horse players from Tulsa and Oklahoma City, motels were going up outside Sallisaw along Interstate 40 at a furious pace, and stories circulated in town about folks lucky enough to have been sitting on the right land when the boom hit. In keeping with its up-to-date status, Sallisaw boasted a Radio Shack, a Wal-Mart, a karate school, and most of the rest of franchised America. Beer and wine could be purchased at local filling stations. (A movement in Sequoyah County to allow "liquor by the drink," which would have opened the door to the cocktail lounge, had narrowly been voted down.)

Sun Belt industry had arrived in Steinbeck country. Some Sallisaw residents worked at the Whirlpool washing-machine plant in Fort Smith just across the Arkansas border. Sallisaw could thank the environmental movement for one of its larger businesses, Holley Special Products, which turned out emission-control devices for automobile exhausts mandated for cars by states clean-air laws.

The largest employer in the county was the Kerr-McGee nuclear fuel plant in Gore, the town where Oca and Ruby once lived in a transient hotel and where Dick Tatham was born. Under government contract, the plant produced mildly irradiated yellow cake for its nuclear power plant at Oak Ridge, Tennessee. (Another Kerr-McGee plant in Crescent, Oklahoma, was the one made famous by Karen Silkwood.)[1]

Jim Mayo, editor of the Sequoyah County *Times*, credited the building of Interstate 40 (that passed Sallisaw a mile or so south of the courthouse) as *the* event which finally pulled Sequoyah County out of the Depression era. "It gave us a sense of optimism," he said.

The leg of I-40 from Fort Smith to Sallisaw was finished in 1969. Only then, as Oklahoma began measuring its progress not by barrels of oil pumped but by yards of concrete poured—for airports, highways, bridges, dams, and plants—did the movement of people to California finally end.

OCA AND ONA parked the Alpenlite in front of Cousin Leslie Tatham's place and prepared to stay for a few days. Leslie was a tall, slow-talking, friendly man whose handsome face had been chiseled by the more than four decades that had passed since he and Virble left Delano and returned to Oklahoma. They lived on a knoll close to town, on land that could have fetched a million dollars during the real-estate boom if he'd been willing to sell.

The two cousins lived very different lives, but they had a hundred stories to tell about relatives, cars, horses, and journeys. Oca and Leslie drove out to Brushy Mountain for a look at childhood haunts the second morning Oca was in town. It was still thinly populated. John Sumpter's house and the log house where Oca had been born were gone. Leslie pointed out this and that place, reminding Oca of the time a woman tried to have Walter Tatham arrested for disturbing the peace after he raced his mules down the road by her house.

Afterward the cousins drove on to Drake's Prairie. Almost all the old houses were gone; a tall stone chimney was all that remained of the Settingdown house, which had been one of the nicer homes. Leslie pointed out where Tathams had lived in this or that year before the great exodus west. There was nothing but grass where Walter and Cora had lived in 1933–1934 and from where they had set out to California in the Chevy truck.

They picked out places where friends had lived: the old Drake house, the Callaghans, the place Arch Tatham had purchased in the

Depression, the Eskews, the Lands. Then they stopped at the old Watts Church, which had been replaced by a new brick church a few dozen feet away.

On the way home they visited Leslie's brother Farris, who lived on the edge of Drake's Prairie in a beautifully situated home on a rise with a view of the rolling grassland. It was neat and well kept with grazing cattle, horse pastures, and white-fenced paddocks for quarter horses. They exchanged stories about particular horses with unusual gaits, and then Farris got out the picture he kept of James Oliver Tatham and his three boys, Walter, Willy, and Arch. It must have been taken right after they arrived in the Indian Territory in 1902. There were more stories about the Tathams and Drake's Prairie, or neighbors and kin long gone, of horses and wagons and seasons, until it was time to go.

Leslie and Farris Tatham had kept the faith in the way they knew. Farris's life, and that of his closest family, revolved around the Free Holiness church in Drake's Prairie, in which he was a leader. Back from the army after World War II, he had passed up a job offer from Southwestern Bell with a pension and a future; instead he became a self-employed carpenter. He wanted to be free to leave whatever he was doing to sing at funerals. He had a fine bass voice and was in demand as a soloist. His family quartet sang at funerals all over the eastern part of the state. His daughter worked in the town for the welfare department, lived at home, and played the piano for the church.

Summer camp meetings of the Free Holiness sect still had much of the old-time flavor, though the leaky brush arbor had gone the way of the kerosene lantern. Now meetings were held in a campground a few miles from Sallisaw, in an open facility with a metal roof and electricity. The evening meetings were softly lit with orange light bulbs and cooled by slowly turning fans. Free Holiness people came from as far away as California in vans, fifth wheels, and cars, ready for two weeks of prayer, fellowship, relaxation, and food. Between the marathon morning and evening meetings, they rested or helped themselves to meals from tables laden with meats, homemade pies, cakes and breads, and rich desserts.

Free Holiness people were no longer the poor folks from the holy roller church, yet many things were the same. At a summer camp meeting several months before Oca arrived in 1985, a blond woman who looked and sounded like Dolly Parton sang Gospel songs, while toddlers squirmed in their mothers' arms and older offspring sat quietly on benches. Grown men hopped and skipped up to the altar, where preachers stepped forward to lay hands on the sick or spiritually burdened, who testified in quavering voices. A pastor from California delivered his message in a shaking voice: "We don't need more education, what we need is old-time joy. If preachers don't have it before they get educated, they won't have it afterward. Drink the water! You'll be *satisfied*. Hugh Hefner, J. Paul Getty, what would it take to satisfy you? More! They're not satisfied. Money, women, power won't satisfy. Credit cards won't satisfy. Take a drink of the water!"

Membership in a Free Holiness church brought a rich reward: acceptance in a group and a purity and simplicity of life that was a dramatic contrast to the frenetic, electronic mass culture of the 1980s. Free Holiness followers stressed the importance of charity, honesty, simplicity, and neighborliness, and there was a warmth and intimacy that was lacking in the big, modern Pentecostal churches. Farris's wife, Oma, still made her own clothes from store-bought material rather than purchase store-bought dresses, and some families did not watch television.

Yet the sect was showing strains. The Free Holiness churches in Sallisaw and on the prairie had not grown much over the years, and in 1985 both were having difficulty recruiting pastors. Many of the stalwarts were still descendants of the founders, but their children were drifting away from Sallisaw and joining other churches and denominations. Of Leslie and Virble's six children, only two were still Free Holiness—one was a Baptist; another was a minister with the Assemblies of God and two others attended Assembly churches.

Remarkable as the Free Holiness sect was for its steadiness, it lacked the surging energy of the church it once had been. The shell was there but the vitality seemed to have drained away—or to have been dispersed to the contemporary churches with middle-class congregations rising across the Sun Belt. For some of the younger generation, the customs and dress codes—no neckties or short-sleeved shirts—seemed to have become an end in themselves. They seemed to make for a kind of cult of renunciation. Some in the younger generation found the Free Holiness interpretation of Scripture overly selective. Deuteronomy and Numbers admonish the godly to "build a parapet around your rooftop," yet Free Holiness adherents did not follow *that* injunction. Where, some asked, was the charity in shunning those who did not live up to every one of the group's exacting standards? A woman who was divorced after her husband deserted her was not allowed to sing in the Gospel group at meetings. Where was the kindness in that?

Oca understood on these trips back to Sallisaw how much California had worn away of what he took to be the unessential elements of his faith. He rejected the prohibition against wearing neckties (worldly adornments) and short-sleeved shirts (immodesty before the Lord). Experience had taught him that simply wearing a necktie did not compromise one's cherished principles. Even if he had stayed in Oklahoma, he probably would have been too much his own man to succumb to the conformity required for full membership in a Free Holiness church. He had succeeded by going his own way, by ignoring the constraints of any group.

On the Sunday after they arrived in Sallisaw, Oca and Ona attended a Free Holiness service in town with Leslie and Virble. In a quaking voice, Leslie gave testimony about a trip west to visit a son. Oca and Ona sat together rather than on opposite sides of the aisle, as the regular members did; he was an honored visitor from California, so allowances were made. He and Ona returned in the afternoon for Gospel singing, but at night they slipped away and attended the First Assemblies of God in Sallisaw, a brick church with a youngish, energetic pastor named Tackett—no relation, he said, to Eldon Tackett in McFarland, California.

It was a service that could just as well have been held at the Northeast Assemblies Church in Fresno. Men and women sat together in that church and the congregation was a mixture of middle class and working class. A woman spoke in tongues, and there was an "interpretation" by Pastor Tackett, who controlled the service as it progressed in orderly fashion through hymns and a liturgy. A man testified about his missionary work abroad, and at the end of the service there was an altar call, during which several young people "tarried," praying in hopes of breaking through to the higher spiritual experience of baptism by the Holy Ghost. Afterward Pastor Tackett greeted the congregation personally and Oca declared himself well pleased by the service.

SEVERAL DAYS LATER, Oca and Ona continued their journey, hooking up in Sallisaw with Ona's sister and brother-in-law, going on to Memphis to visit Buck Dodson from Delano days, and then keeping east on I-40. They were headed for the centers of electronic religion: Jim Bakker's Heritage Village in South Carolina, Jerry Falwell's church in Lynchburg, Virginia, and Pat Robertson's television studio in Virginia Beach.

To Oca, the success of the television preachers was quietly gratifying, still another reminder of how far he had come. He basked in the glow of their success—not as one awed by their celebrity, but as one who could say with no exaggeration that he helped make it happen. Indeed, the television ministries owed their existence to the subsidies and *effort* of millions of faithful, present and departed. The brightly lit studios, the churches with acres of sprawling parking lots, and the campuses with their fresh-faced, eager students—all were made possible by the long-term dedication of Christians like Oca and Ona. These centers were the finished product of the work begun by those who had picked up the burden in the heat of the day, material testimony to the effort of those who had lugged cotton sacks for an extra hour and given the proceeds to the local pastor; who had been in church on Friday night instead of at high school football games; who had raised their children right, worked hard, and kept the faith.

At the same time, Oca gave credit to the charismatic individuals who led the big churches and religious television ministries. They were like power stations, drawing in energy, focusing it, concentrating it, and then pulsing it back out in surges. Heritage Village and the "700 Club" were not like Rome or Jerusalem—centers of movements larger and longer-enduring than any pope or high rabbi. They were the incarnation of individual enterprise, and Oca appreciated them for what they were.

Oral Roberts had once been Oca's favorite, and he had supported Roberts as the evangelist widened his tent from county fairgrounds to national airwaves. As early as 1955, Roberts had begun telecasting weekly films of himself placing his healing hands on lines of supplicants in sweat-drenched tent revivals.[2] He founded Oral Roberts University in Tulsa in 1963 and four years later introduced a new and glamorous television show, using the World Action Singers, and a "new" Oral Roberts stressing success, happiness, and prosperity in the here and now. "Sunday Night Live with Oral Roberts" became one of the most popular religious shows on television.

Oca contributed to Roberts's seed-faith ministry for many years. But his support ended when, in 1977, Roberts claimed to have seen a nine-hundred-foot-tall Jesus in a vision and began soliciting donations to build a $150 million medical center. Oca could not bring himself to finance a hospital built by a man revered for the use of the healing power of prayer.

Subsequently, Oca switched his financial support to Jimmy Swaggart and Pat Robertson. Swaggart, who railed against modern psychology, the upper crust, and the accommodations that many, in as well as out of the Christian fold, were making with the world, captured Oca emotionally. Oca liked Jimmy for "telling it like it is." Oca respected Robertson, whose "700 Club" mixed inspiration with serious public affairs commentary from a Christian Right perspective and presented hard news gathered by the Christian Broadcasting Network.

Jim Bakker had never been one of Oca's favorite preachers, although he and Ona often watched Bakker's TV show, the PTL Club. He felt no emotional connection with Bakker. Their sojourn to Heritage Village took longer than they expected, due to a transmission problem with the pickup. Oca found Heritage Village a pleasant surprise; it was a kind of Christian Israel. Everyone was Christian. The guests of course were, but so were the waitresses in the cafeteria at the Grand Hotel, so were the guards at the RV court where Oca parked their fifth wheel, and so were the ushers at the PTL Club shows they attended.

Oca concluded that Heritage Village had its place: "When I go there and see what's happening I realize we have a lot of wealthy Christians today." But he didn't make a contribution. He had to think of his church in Mexico, "where some of those boys are probably still using a tree down there to preach under. So you got to use judgment, say, God, You help me to use this money the way You want it used. I'm not particularly interested in building up a kingdom here on this earth for Christian people, though I'm not criticizing them, you understand, I just think it's not my cup of tea, it's not something that God laid on my heart."

When Oca's transmission was fixed, he, his in-laws, and Ona headed up the valley along the Appalachians to Lynchburg and Jerry Falwell's Thomas Road Baptist Church. Now they were traveling in the heartland of Oca's forebears: the Scotch-Irish and English who had come out to the rim of the old colonial world before going west over the mountains. It had been there, in that very country, where the outlook and traditions of Ulster and the North British borderlands had first been stamped on the American continent. And it had been from there that the culture was spread south and west by a people who took along their shivarees, small churches, grass-roots doctrines, individualism, and stubborn refusal to be molded into the form desired by their "betters" in the ports and trading centers of the East.

In Lynchburg, Oca visited the campus of Falwell's Liberty University. The next day, a Sunday, they attended services at Falwell's church. Oca considered the historic divisions between Baptists and Spirit-filled Pentecostals now to have become "almost a thing of the past."

After the service, Oca waited to meet Falwell at the church door. Oca recounted the time he had met Bill Tatham in Fresno in 1984, when Falwell was touring California to rally support for the Reagan ticket. G. L. Johnson had invited Bill to fly on a private plane to San Francisco to fetch Falwell for an appearance in Fresno, and Bill had talked to the evangelist, a sports buff, about the Outlaws. Falwell had a photographer take a picture of him and Oca.

They drove on to their final destination, Pat Robertson's Virginia Beach televison studio. Oca was feeling tired, and the overcast sky over the Atlantic reminded him how far east he had traveled. He began to think about getting home.

Oca, his wife, and his in-laws attended a "700 Club" show. Robertson, they were told, liked the studio cool because the heat generated by the television lights made him perspire. Oca could see people in the audience grasping their arms, donning coats and sweaters as Robertson and his black associate Ben Kinchlow launched another edition of the "700 Club." Oca and Ona had trouble hearing, and the cold bothered everyone.

After the show they walked back to their trailers. There was an early hint of winter in the air, and the chill from the studio lingered. Oca remembered the apologetic words of their guide, so out of keeping in a Pentecostal setting: "Pat likes it cold." Pat was a "great guy," Oca said of the experience, but they might as well have been separated from him by a pane of glass.

CHAPTER TWENTY

SISTERS

IF CALIFORNIA in the 1970s and 1980s was a place where people bonded with each other through the ritual of personal confession—revealing their deepest neuroses to complete strangers at the first sip of their Chardonnay—then the Tathams belonged to a kind of California counterculture. Tathams considered it a little bit weak, and somewhat indecent, to speak too frankly of their personal misfortunes and problems, even—perhaps especially—to one another.

All the Tathams knew, for instance, that Cora and Walter had separated, yet Tathams generally passed over that fact quickly, with a reminder that the couple had never divorced, that Walter had sent her money and had visited her on holidays, and that he was buried next to her in the Delano Cemetery. Oca was ready to concede that he, Oca Tatham, had been a rotten, miserable sinner before finding the Lord. But personal confession was not his style: he did not regale his grandchildren with stories about youthful bootlegging or chasing women in cars whose tires came off on the turns. Honesty was a core Tatham value, yet issues that did not fit the image of what the family thought it should be were simply disremembered or disregarded. Tathams controlled their narratives, like tour guides leading visitors through a mansion where certain rooms are never entered.

The armor of silence and denial had been handed down from older generations of Tathams and Sumpters and came from the backcountry. In the hard conditions at the edge of the world it was best simply to endure what life threw at you and get on with it. If that wasn't possible, violence was an understandable, if not quite acceptable way of releasing one's feelings. One got a gun, as Altie Sumpter Byrd did when her husband strayed.

There was Christian virtue in silence and denial—and not just in the Tathams' church. If hope, faith, and charity were primary Christian qualities, then despair, the opposite of hope, was a work of the Devil. Worse: despair represented a personal rebellion against God's plan and, by implication, against His whole enterprise on earth.

For those like the Tathams who had grown up in a strict, perfectionist wing of Protestantism, dwelling on one's problems was strongly discouraged. To talk about oneself, rehash a truly embarrassing personal incident, or engage in too much reflection was to open a hairline crack through which doubt might enter. The sects celebrated *victory*—victory over alcohol, lust, the desire for material things, illness, and loss. In the holy roller works, people testified about action, not feelings—and especially about *God's* action, not their own. Tathams were part of a vast non-Freudian America. Oca's church and culture instilled an attitude of self-watchfulness, but did not encourage self-preoccupation or philosophical reflection. Not that an Oca Tatham lived an unexamined life. Oca constantly examined his actions and his thoughts about his actions, but impersonally, like a building inspector checking for cracks. The mysteries lay without, not within. Inexplicable forces wrought miracles and called forth signs, wonders, conspiracies, and coincidences. But those forces were external. Fundamentalist Christians did not view depression as a psychological condition, but as an indication that one had been entered by demons. Struggle, not insight, pointed the way to the cure.

The culture built toughness of character. On the other hand, a way of life in which candor and introspection were not encouraged left people and institutions vulnerable to innumerable cover-ups. No wonder so many deacon boards found it easier to shield a fallen pastor from his congregation than to bring out the facts and clear the air.

In the Tatham clan, it wasn't so much those matters involving clear moral failure that went unmentioned as the ones that were somehow awkward, ambiguous, or strange. Episodes that didn't quite fit the Tatham story as Tathams thought it should be were simply left out.

There was, for example, the tragedy that befell the family of Bill and Earline in 1972. They were living at the time at a house on Keats Avenue in Fresno, while waiting for the completion of their new home on Van Ness Boulevard. They were, in fact, over at the Van Ness property on the day that Mike came home one Saturday with a friend and began playing with a rifle that Mike and Billy used for shooting at targets. It was not unusual for young people in the valley to keep guns around, for the valley was full of wide open spaces, and was a paradise at that time for hunters and sportsmen, even young ones such as Mike, who was only thirteen.

Mike checked the rifle and it appeared to be unloaded. He cocked it and dry-fired it to make sure, before handing it to his friend, who aimed it out the window and dry-fired it. In the process of cocking and dry-firing, it discharged in Mike's hands and a bullet struck his friend. Apparently a live round had been jammed in the chamber.

Mike coolly called 911 and listened as the dispatcher told him to cover his friend with a blanket, and wait for the ambulance that was already on the way. Then everything became a blur. He was outside hailing some friends of Billy who were passing by in a car. Whether it was they or the dispatcher who called them Mike was never sure, but suddenly Oca and Ruby were there. He heard his grandfather's strong, deep voice, heard him taking control, and felt Ruby's arms around him, comforting him. His parents arrived home to find the ambulance and police cars outside. Their joy in finding their own son safe was was short-lived, for the next worst thing had happened. By the time Mike learned that the boy had died, he was heavily tranquilized and surrounded by more relatives than he knew he had.

In stoic, face-the-music Tatham fashion, the Tatham family attended the slain boy's funeral service. Mike held up well until the minister reminded the congregation that little Mike Tatham was a victim, too, and called for prayers for him. Mike rushed out of the church in tears. Even then, the Tathams summoned the courage to pay respects at the home of the dead boy's family after the service. It was a few days before Mike went back to school and when he did, he had to come home again. Emotions were raw, and when he learned that another boy at school had called him a "murderer," he fought it out with him.

Eventually the incident receded, and Mike learned to play a new role: that of the easygoing guy who helped relatives and friends forget the awkwardness they felt around him by laughing, talking and joking. For Mike, a long period of denial began. The incident was shelved, except that every so often Bill would ask him, "Are you all right?" And Mike would answer, "Sure."

Perhaps the emotional ambiguity surrounding the catastrophe made it especially difficult to deal with. Tathams were braced against death, illness, and economic setback, but an incident in which another person was the victim had more complicated emotional repercussions. No doubt Bill and Earline wanted to protect Mike, but their silence protected them as well. And although Mike might have believed he was being a good son by containing his own feelings, burying the incident required sacrifices on all sides. That was the Tatham way. But Mike would come to feel that the price paid for silence was too high.

In February 1979, there was another incident that didn't fit neatly into the Tatham story either: Oca and Ruby's youngest daughter Renee was assaulted and nearly raped while vacationing in Hawaii. She had gone to dinner with airline friends after a day of sun and surf and walked back to the hotel across the street with a younger man who was staying at the same hotel. She told the police that instead of dropping her off at her room as she had expected, he forced his way in, hit her in the face, and tried to rape her. Fending him off, Renee said, she escaped to a balcony, where she screamed for help while he ran off. He was arrested and charged a few hours later.

Though physically none the worse for the experience except for a swollen, bruised face and broken tooth, she was traumatized, shaken, and extremely nervous about how her family would react. She had reason to believe that the Fresno contingent did not approve of her tight skirts, dyed hair, and world-girdling life-style as an airline employee, and more than a day passed before she summoned up courage to phone her sister Doris. Doris called Fresno. It soon seemed to Renee that the family in Fresno was indeed having a hard time dealing with the news. Her dad and her brothers were angry at the perpetrator, but Renee believed, "They felt ashamed and that made me feel guilty. It was kind of like, 'The black sheep did it again.' It was shameful for people to know because it was breaking this Utopian view we had of our family. When I found out that some of our best friends in Fresno knew nothing about it, I was angry. I felt my family was ashamed of me."

It was Ruby who rose to the occasion. She had been reared in eastern Oklahoma and had "seen life." In her time, a young woman was lucky if she got a marriage proposal from the man who made her pregnant. Ruby went to a rape counseling center in Fresno and obtained information about the emotional phases through which a recovering rape victim passed so that she could recognize the symptoms in Renee and provide whatever support she could.

Ruby was the only member of the family who attended the trial in Hawaii. Renee feared that the defense attorney would try to discredit her morals and possibly bring up incidents from her past. All her life Renee had wanted to protect her mother, to shield Ruby from being disappointed with Renee. But if there was going to be anything like that, Renee decided, her mother was going to hear the details from her and not from some stranger. So the night before the trial, she sat Ruby down and went over her whole life, withholding few facts. The next day, the defendant was found guilty and sentenced to probation. The defense did not dredge up her past, but she never regretted the "heart-to-heart" with her mother.

Still, she wondered if it could ever have taken place in Fresno. For the dispersed Tathams, Fresno remained their city on a hill, the seat of moral authority and moral expectations, where the family felt it had to present itself in an unbending moral light. When Tatham children and grandchildren described the family, they often used the word "perfect." Bill's daughter said, "In my mind my dad was perfect." Her brother Mike, referring to his father and grandfather, said he "put those guys on a pedestal." His cousin Gina Weaver spoke of "our perfect little family."

Oca's judgment was a powerful force emanating from Fresno. He did not pry into his children's lives, but if information was volunteered, it became subject to his unsparing verdicts and opinions. He didn't demand to know who all Renee's girlfriends were, but when she confided that one of them was having an affair with a married man, he felt no qualms about condemning the woman's morals. The result was predictable: "Don't tell Grandpa," was the advice frequently given.

He didn't approve of Renee's dating a divorced man when she was living on her own in Fresno after turning twenty-one. And he flatly opposed her plans to marry a Vietnam veteran who was not a born-again Christian. After he was wounded, Renee had gone to the Bay area to be nearby while he recuperated at an army hospital, and the relationship continued when she took a job with an airline. But Oca didn't consider him a suitable husband.

"You're over twenty-one, so I can't stop you," he told her, "but I won't be there to give you away." She said she broke off the engagement for other reasons. Still, she added, "It cut my heart."

Fresno was a good place to be for Tathams who had no quarrel with Oca's moral judgments. Bill, a teetotaler who shared his father's strict views, could comfortably flourish there. Brenda liked the scale and style of the city. Dick, the preacher, left Fresno—but only to re-create a new version of it on the Arizona frontier. Gerald was *called* to Fresno. As the family's self-appointed but intensely loyal critic, he needed family close by so that he could nag at the big egos, poke fun at the petty hypocrisies—and, yes, enjoy some reflected Tatham glory. But his sister Renee could no more have stayed in Fresno than her dad could have remained on Drake's Prairie. Both needed a bigger playing field.

Renee was an independent-minded baby boomer born in 1946. Living at home in the early 1960s, she wore makeup and stretch pants, dyed her hair light blond, and "did all those ungodly things at an early age." When she turned twenty-one, she moved out of her parents' house to live on her own, becoming the first of the daughters who did not go straight from home to marriage. She did not consider her leave-taking a repudiation of the family. It was just a sign that, while she wanted to remain a Tatham, she wanted to do so on her terms.

Renee's oldest sister, Doris, could not have been more different. She was the self-sacrificing daughter who, when her mother was hospitalized, quit Bible school to take care of the family in Fresno. Yet the preacher's son she married, like Renee, could not stay in Fresno, either. Doris and Renee became the coastal sisters, living on the fault line of American culture and society. By 1985, both were feeling the tremors.

THE UNITED STATES ARMY gave Doris and her husband, Gordon Weaver, their first look at the wider world. Drafted in 1954, Gordon was assigned to an Army Security Agency unit in Fulda, West Germany, where he monitored Warsaw Pact communications. He and Doris lived off-post with a German family, and while Gordon kept track of Communist military transmissions, Doris took up photography and learned about the Catholic religious processions for which the city was renowned. They bought a secondhand Borgward and traveled to Italy, France, England, and Belgium for vacations. Someone snapped a picture of them holding hands under the palm trees on Capri.

After the bright lights of Europe, readjusting to Fresno was not easy. Friends and relatives got together for Rook, one of the few card games acceptable among Pentecostals, or fell asleep during Doris and Gordon's slide shows of Europe. For excitement, they joined a sports car club and went on all-night road rallies, winning trophies in time-and-distance contests that took them careening around roads all over the central valley in a sporty red Triumph 3. It was unusual entertainment by the staid standards of Fresno Pentecostals and revealing as well. The preacher's son had a flair for the adventurous, and so did his Tatham wife. Doris split the driving with Gordon and was as keen a competitor as he was.

Cindy and Gina, the two eldest of their three daughters, were born while Gordon completed a degree in accounting at Fresno State and worked in the circulation department of the Fresno *Bee*. When the Internal Revenue Service offered him a job in San Francisco in 1965, he leaped at the chance. The Weavers never came back to Fresno again except to visit. In Fresno, church activities had been mainly spiritual: revivals, missionary work, fund-raising. Bethel Temple, the church they attended in San Francisco, was led by an independent-minded Assemblies of God minister who encouraged people to have a good time together—ski in the mountains, visit the lakes, get together for special meals featuring the cuisine of a foreign country. They found themselves in a younger crowd of lawyers, contractors, and engineers, some of whom shared their love of sports cars and Europe. After several moves, the Weavers bought a new home with a view of the distant San Francisco skyline in the affluent Bayo Vista section of San Leandro, in the Oakland hills.

Gordon had been hired away from the IRS by a top Oakland accounting firm, Rooney, Ida, Nolt and Ahern, after a tough audit of one of the firm's clients. He had a sharp mind, knew the tax code better than most IRS men, and quickly grasped the fundamentals of complex businesses. He was also a prodigiously hard worker who often took time out only to attend Sunday morning church services. As well paid as he was, he spent lavishly: over the years he acquired a number of sporty, expensive cars, including a Mercedes, a Porsche, and a Jaguar, and pumped thousands of dollars into electronic gear and model trains, hobbies that he worked on in the basement of the family's San Leandro home.

Europe was a kind of magic kingdom for the Weavers, an escape that was even farther from Fresno than the Bay. They had their favorite places: Salzburg, Interlaken, villages in Switzerland, a little abbey in Austria. They liked to wander through castles or take in art exhibits. They loved the adventure of low-budget travel, of staying at out-of-the-way pensions and hotels, exploring the side streets and neighborhood bistros that were off the beaten track of ordinary tourists. They had their special "finds": a small hotel outside Baden-Baden, where the innkeeper would bring out a bottle of champagne to celebrate their arrival, or a restaurant on Lake Annecy, north of Chamonix. Usually they traveled with a well-thumbed copy of a Michelin guide, and no trip was complete without one splurge at a three-star listing.

RENEE WAS ALSO tasting the world beyond Fresno. In 1968, she was inducted as a flight attendant for Air West at a ceremony at Fresno airport, covered by a reporter for the Fresno *Bee*. She and her fellow inductees, he wrote in those days before reporters had to worry about sexual stereotyping in their writing, were "bouncy, perky, dimpled, dewy-eyed and all about twenty-one" in their "hot pink blouses and skirts above their knees."

After working for a year on flights up and down the West Coast, Renee took a job in customer relations at Hughes Airwest in the San Francisco airport. She was outgoing, cheerful, quick to take responsibility, and good with the VIPs who came through. One day she was in charge of the arrival of Lady Bird Johnson; the next she was running off to buy magazines for Bing Crosby. Gradually, her file became thick with laudatory letters from bosses and passengers.

She was young and single in the airline industry of the early 1970s, a certified member of what she called "the junior jet set." Crowded airports, deregulation, and layoffs were still years away, and Renee aquaplaned across California and the world. There were reduced-fare or free trips to Europe and Japan; shopping sprees in Athens, Rio de Janeiro, and Hong Kong; weekend flights to Hawaii to work on her tan; flyaways to the Mexican Riviera to "kick back," lie in the sun, and eat spicy shrimp. When she got bored she caught a cab and told the driver, "Take me to the airport."

She dated a string of wealthy star athletes. One was Daryle "The Mad Bomber" Lamonica, the all-pro quarterback of the Oakland Raiders, who had gone to Clovis High School with Gerald Tatham. After Lamonica, she briefly dated another quarterback, Marty Domres of the Baltimore Colts.

For the first few years Fresno, Renee hardly attended church at all. She drank wine—and other things, if offered—dated men who were not Christians, and had girlfriends who were having casual affairs with married men. Yet she wasn't rejecting the values she had learned as a Tatham; she was looking for ways to make them her own.

In the early 1970s, the search took her to Body Life, a program invented by Pastor Ray Stedmans, an Assemblies of God minister who had gone his independent way. Stedmans, who pastored Peninsula Bible Church in Palo Alto, wanted to make his church more "relevant" to the new generation of upwardly mobile professional people and academics in the Silicon Valley. Body Life referred to the "body of the church"—the members of the congregation—and stressed interpersonal relationships. Renee met a new circle of friends who were Christians or becoming Christians. Members became friends socially, going out together after church or getting together for Sunday brunches. Several times a week, Stedmans met with small Body Life groups. He used a Donahue-type format, working his way around the room with a microphone as people shared their personal experiences, needs, fears, and anxieties.

It wasn't easy at first for Renee to participate. She was unaccustomed, she said, to standing up in front of people and announcing, "I'm really in need right now, and I'm not in control." Tathams were supposed to be in control. But Body Life helped. "All of a sudden," she said, "I was realizing who I was and that I did love the Lord and the reason why and what He wanted of me and what was best for me and why it was best. Peninsula didn't tug on altar calls or try to get at people through hellfire and brimstone. It was wonderful Bible teaching about the love of the Lord and *possibility thinking*. They didn't say, 'We don't drink and we don't smoke and we don't chew and we don't dance.' They didn't have any of that, whereas the church I came from did, and I saw a lot of people that did those things who were just as good as I was and probably better in some respects.

"What attracted me were the things we *could* do. We could love each other! The Lord gives us so many possibilities. And it wasn't an emotional trip. It was more real than that. I listened to all these people sharing and loving and caring without the restrictions I had experienced before. It was just people, really open."

It was at Body Life in 1973 that she met Dave Kingman, the home-run slugger for the San Francisco Giants. After a couple of conversations at the Sunday night Body Life sessions, he called her for a date. It was exciting to sit in Kingman's box at the games and move in his entourage. Gifts from anonymous fans and admirers arrived mysteriously on the doorstep of his house or hotel room. Once Dave took Renee into a warehouse full of linens and told her to pick out anything she wanted. She was afraid she would be late to work, but she still had time to rush through, picking out enough rugs, sheets, and pillowcases to last a decade. Renee felt as if she were getting things she didn't deserve or shouldn't be taking. But part of her wished she had more time to choose carefully just what she really wanted.

DIFFERENT AS DORIS'S LIFE was from her kid sister's, she, too, was engaged in a search. She was still every whit the fundamentalist, Holy Spirit–filled Christian. Though the skeletal evidence of early man she and Gordon had seen in museums raised questions in his mind about the literal truth of the Genesis story, Doris's belief was unshaken. Miracles and healings, she found, were no less present in her busy life in the East Bay the they had been when she was a junkman's child. She had seen her mother healed of the goiter and was convinced of the power of healing in her own life.

For example, she said, "The Lord touched my arthritis." The doctor had told her the condition was incurable, but help came, she said, when she accepted that her "Heavenly Father was my physician."

"I could hardly comb my hair, or put my arms up above my waist. Every joint in my body was diseased. At the time I was doing tennis and taking golf lessons, and the doctor said, 'No more tennis, no more golf, all these things are just wearing out your sockets.' I had to wear low heels, sit a certain way, all these things to protect myself. So I really made it a matter of prayer, and I was prayed for by my friends. I went to the doctor about surgery, and they didn't want to do that. I had calcium deposits that was irritating the muscles, yet, all of a sudden, I started feeling great. I caught myself walking up and down the stairs instead of riding the stair glide we installed. It didn't hurt, and I started feeling great. I went to Europe and did the Eurail thing, went up and down all the stairs, walked day after day, and I came home and I said, 'If I can walk in Europe and go up and down those stairs, I'm not going to ride that stair glide,' so I had it taken off. " The aches disappeared, and she even gave up aspirin and her arthritis medication. Not long after that her dad was healed of his blood problems after the old-time Methodist preacher anointed him with oil.

In other ways, though, she and Gordon were changing. For one thing, they had begun attending the Cathedral at the Crossroads Church in Castro Valley, which was more often referred to as Neighborhood Church. Neighborhood belonged to the Christian Missionary Alliance denomination. It offered superior programs for the three Weaver daughters, but was non-Pentecostal.

For another thing, the Weavers were reconsidering some of the taboos they had learned as children. For years Doris had anguished about an incident that had happened just before she and Gordon had left Germany and the army. As a farewell gesture, the Italian man who ran their favorite pizza restaurant had reached for a bottle of red wine and poured glasses for them. Gordon and Doris glanced helplessly at each other and finally declined to sip the wine. Doris never forgot the crestfallen look on the man's face. If any sin had been committed at the pizza restaurant, Doris thought, surely it was their sin of self-righteousness. When they revisited Fulda in 1968, they went looking for him, hoping to explain the complicated rules of their church—and to drink a glass of wine with him. But he and the restaurant were gone. Back in the States, they decided it would be acceptable for them to drink wine.

Gordon had clients in the thriving California wine industry and occasionally was offered a sample of their vintages. The connoisseur of fine cars soon became a connoisseur of fine wines. On one occasion a client celebrating the completion of a complex tax return, invited Gordon and Doris to dinner and brought out his finest bottle of Château La Tour. And with great ceremony, the man uncorked the bottle and poured glasses. Slowly, he twirled the wine so that the light sparkled in the velvety liquid.

"This," he said with a flourish, "is civilization." Gordon understood. The wine was the culmination of years of trial and error with plant hybrids, soils, and distillation processes. Like a beautifully engineered European car, it symbolized the search for perfection that was the essence of civilization.

Although the wine-drinking issue was settled for Doris and Gordon, it remained a source of tension at ceremonial family gatherings. When Doris and Gordon's second daughter, Gina, was married in 1981, the festivities were planned in such as way to cause Oca and Ruby the least discomfort. Although there was a carafe of wine at each table and strolling violins, there was no dancing. Denial was the order of the day. Oca said later that he "pretended not to notice" that it was wine and not iced tea.

In the spring of 1984, Doris and Gordon celebrated their daugh-

ter Lisa's twenty-first birthday with a festive dinner at the Ahwahnee
Hotel in Yosemite National Park. Oca and Ona came up from Fresno,
and Gordon selected a single fine bottle of wine in honor of the
occasion. It seemed like a reasonable compromise; the wine would
add a celebratory flavor, but there would be no suggestion of drunk-
enness with half a dozen people sharing a single bottle. Oca sat
through the meal. This time he couldn't pretend not to notice. He
phoned Doris from Fresno: "Next time you're guzzlin' wine, count
us out."

To Doris, moderate drinking represented a breaking away from
restrictive, legalistic doctrines that no longer seemed appropriate.
But Oca did not view the prohibition against drinking as a legalism.
He had seen his Pentecostal community abandon many of the old
restrictions and did not disapprove. Ruby began wearing mascara
after the war. (Doris had felt like crying, she was so sure that her
mother was risking hell's fires. "I thought she was backslipping,"
Doris recalled. "I thought she wasn't a Christian anymore. Paint and
powder was a sin then. Then they started using powder.") Living in
a house on Indianapolis Avenue in Fresno, Oca had acquired a pool
table. Cora Sumpter and the old-time Holiness people had held to
the doctrine of no sex except for procreation. By the 1980s, not even
the use of birth control by married couples was an issue for most
Pentecostals. The old shibboleths simply fell away, often without anyone being much aware of it. Oca could accept this without feeling
that anything fundamental had been compromised.

But there came a point when a line had to be drawn. He came
from a background in which the church had been an institution of
denial and resistance, not just comfort and affirmation. The Bible,
he believed, contained *hard* truths as well as comfortable ones, a
notion that seemed difficult for Californians to swallow. "A lot of
people think that Christianity is for the weakling," Oca said. "But I'll
tell you it's different. It takes a man and woman, a real man and a
real woman, to really stick with it and live for God, turn all this stuff
down."

In the eastern Oklahoma he had known, drink had had all kinds
of demonic connotations, violent, sexual, and abusive. But his stand
against it involved deeper considerations still. For him, drinking
raised the ultimate issue for Christians and Jews. Abstinence was
essential for purity. And purity was a question of *character*. Regardless
of what the Bible said on the subject, it seemed to Oca that nondrink-
ers were those with the will power to say no. In that sense, the drinking

issue was central: it was tied up with his broader concerns about the drift of the family.

Oca felt that he had won the family the breathing space it had by not wavering from his principles. Now he stood squarely for resistance to the dangers posed by the family's improved circumstances and mobility. He worried about Bill's money and Renee's dating of non-Christian men; he fretted about the social ambitions of Gordon and Doris and about Brenda's new job as an insurance agent, which took up time that might better be devoted to her daughter and husband. He wondered about those European trips of Gordon and Doris and the sports cars that were popping up in front of some of his children's homes. Trips to Europe implied pure pleasure; his trips to Mexico were for the Lord.

Money, he knew, was dangerous because of the obligations that came with it, to lawyers, accountants, charitable organizations, and the whole regulated, bureaucratic system of California that he mistrusted. Wealthy as he was, he did not hold his money in high regard. Money was a sign of energy, competitive spirit, and, perhaps, God's expectations of him. It gave him a certain freedom of action, but it required humility before it. Oca Tatham did not want all the things that money could buy. His Cadillac was *practical*, the best car for a businessman who spent a lot of time on the road. A sports car, on the other hand, might suggest personal vanity and excess.

He kept reminding himself of the cautionary passage in the twelfth chapter of Luke about the rich man who, forgetting he could die that night, proposed to build bigger barns to store his fruits. When Brenda teased her father about the powerboat that he bought but seldom used, he didn't defend himself very vigorously. The point hit home.

BY THE MID-1970S, Renee was experiencing conflicts familiar to independent women all over America. Hughes Airwest urged her to accept a major promotion to manager of one of the airline's regional stations. The salary was enticing, but she couldn't quite imagine herself as a boss. She turned down the job. Then in 1977, after Kingman was traded to the San Diego Padres, Renee took the only available job in San Diego. It was a far cry from being a boss. She went to work outdoors on the tarmac, guiding aircraft to the gates, throwing bags, and unloading baggage holds. One week she had been working in her uniform at the San Francisco airport, smiling at travelers and small children and exchanging greetings with the airline brass; the next she was out with the gas fumes, noise, and grease of the blacktop, dressed in jeans and a yellow T-shirt, muscling baggage into the holds of DC-9's.

She was making history. The tarmac was traditionally a men-only area, and Renee was the first to breach the gender barrier. She figured it helped that she was no feminist; she took it for granted that women who walked into a "man's world" should expect difficulties. She was, she said, in favor of equal pay for equal work, but "not equal pay but special treatment." Women could "push it too far." She disapproved of the women who had protested at the San Francisco airport in the 1970s against an airline advertisement displaying a plane called *Linda*. Renee had been one of the airline employees interviewed for television during the demonstrations: "The women libbers got out there with their rollers and house dresses and I told the guys from TV, they're just horny old maids. They had no identity, they had no confidence in themselves, so they had to make noise." After a few weeks of tension, the men on the tarmac accepted her.

The airline business was changing. It was no longer the junior jet set. The energy crisis and the savage competition that followed deregulation under President Jimmy Carter was slashing profit margins and forcing mergers and layoffs. In 1980, Hughes Airwest merged with Republic Airlines, and suddenly the destinies of West Coast employees of Renee's former airline were under the control of executives in Minneapolis who knew little about the company or the pilots, managers, and employees who had built it. Soon after the takeover, Republic eliminated the paid lunch, reduced vacations, and abolished most overtime. Right before Christmas 1981, it announced a 15 percent pay cut. By then, many regular employees already had been replaced by "temporaries," and the union seemed powerless to stop it.

Renee blamed President Carter and the Democrats for the deregulation policies she believed were destroying the industry. She had spent the best years of her life working for a company that for all intents and purposes had vanished. In January 1983, Republic announced further sharp cuts in pay and benefits: wages were to be reduced an additional 23 percent, and the staff at the John Wayne Airport in Orange County was cut further. In 1983, Republic reported losses of $111 million, but Renee was skeptical about the company's rationale for the layoffs and pay cuts: "They played that game because all the airlines went through it, so everybody demanded the same. They pulled out a lot of roots. But it's all politics. It's not on an education basis that they hire people, it's not on their good work. It's on seniority numbers and politics."

With the help of a series of professional counselors, Renee had come to terms with the Hawaiian rape incident. She went to five therapists before finding the "right" one. They worked on her feelings of guilt, and the therapist helped Renee see that what had happened was not something that *she* had done wrong. She worked on learning not to blame herself. The therapy helped prepare her to make some new steps in her life. She left San Diego and bought a house with a pool in Mission Viejo, a short drive from the beaches in Laguna and a new job with Republic at John Wayne Airport. Renee was sure she could do well in public relations, and just in case the right opportunity came up, her longtime boss wrote her a rave recommendation, citing her "exceptional qualities" and adding that Renee was "genuine, empathetic and caring, and the response she elicits from our customers demonstrates these attributes."

The missing element in her life was a family. Why not have one? The right Christian man hadn't yet come along, but that wasn't necessarily a prerequisite. Tathams were unconventional. Years before, she had almost adopted a child from a Mexican orphanage. Oca had helped, paying a local pastor to find the mother in order to obtain her legal approval. But the mother, a prostitute, refused to give permission. Renee kept looking. Not long after moving to Orange County, she heard about an orphanage in Taiwan. In 1982, she adopted Melissa. With her new baby in her arms, she rushed back across the Pacific just in time to reach the bedside of her dying mother. She presented the child to the old woman, and Ruby smiled.

THE CRISES THAT CHANGED the lives of Renee and Doris came within two months of each other in the summer of 1984. One day in July, Renee was running after a passenger at the John Wayne airport when she tripped over a rope. She lay stunned for a few seconds. Her toes were tingling, and she felt dazed enough to allow someone to help her to her feet. For days, she suffered from headaches and a pain in her arm. A doctor took X rays and reported evidence of whiplash. In August, she went on sick leave and Republic sent her to a clinic where she took whirlpool baths to relieve the pain. Renee didn't work again until February 1985, but even then the pain continued in her arms and legs. That May she was hospitalized for ten days in traction and given steroids.

The accident had come at the worst possible time. She had no husband, and now she had a young child to raise and house payments to make. Her relationship with Dave Kingman had ended after many inconclusive years, and now the problems with her neck disrupted her plans to find a public relations job. The accident left her dependent on Republic's medical and disability plans.

Doris's crisis began that same September, shortly after she and Gordon returned from one of their trips to Europe. For years they had postponed redecorating their house, and while they were in Germany Doris had purchased curtain material. Flying home, Doris excitedly took notes as Gordon discussed his ideas about the colors of carpeting and wallpaper in their redecorated home.

Doris was still thinking about this while she ironed and folded Gordon's clothes and put them in the closet the way he liked. Then she heard Gordon at the door. He was home very early, and she supposed he was suffering from jet lag.

He came into the room and stood next to her. Suddenly, he said, "I came to get my clothes."

"Are you going to take them to the cleaners?" she asked, busy with his shirts.

"I'm taking everything," said Gordon. His voice sounded hollow and distant.

She stopped ironing. "Everything?"

"I came to get my things. I'm moving out," he said.

Doris figured she wasn't hearing him correctly. "You're what?"

"I'm in love with somebody else."

She had heard correctly. "Is it somebody I know?"

"You probably do."

Doris thought numbly: Her best friend? One of her sisters?

He said the name.

"I don't know her. Who is she?"

He told her.

"I need to sit down," Doris said. "I think I'm supposed to be asking you something, but I don't know what to say."

They walked to the living room and sat down stiffly.

"You can ask me anything," said Gordon.

Finally, she said, "How long has this been going on?" It sounded trite, Doris thought, like a line from a daytime soap.

"Two years."

Doris was still thinking like a wife. "But where will you stay? Who will do your shirts?"

"I'll stay with her."

"But what about the children? What about the grandchildren? What about all our trips?"

"You can have the family."

It wasn't Gordon speaking, it just wasn't. Not Gordon the dependable family man, the good provider, the churchman.

"You don't love me anymore?" she asked.

"I love you," said the strange voice.

"But you love her more?"

"Yeah."

Gordon collected some clothes and started to leave. Before he reached the door, Doris touched his face and kissed him. "Well, I still love you no matter what," she said. She thought his eyes filled with tears, but then he turned and left. She watched from the window as his Mustang disappeared around the corner and down the hill.

Alone suddenly in the quiet house, Doris wondered if she had been dreaming. Everything looked just as it had when she had begun the ironing. It was a clear day, and sunshine streamed through the big picture window. Across the gray water of San Francisco Bay the dim ridge of hills guarding the Pacific coast was easily visible.

She held her panic at bay. Her daughter Lisa came home after registering for college classes, disappointed that some were filled. Doris reassured her, "You'll get in later." Then she broke the news that Gordon had moved out.

She telephoned her other two daughters, who arrived a few minutes later. The four women sat in the living room of the Weaver home, talking, crying, and praying, and considered what to do next. Cindy arranged for them to go to the Assemblies of God Church in Oakland that she and her husband, Bill, attended. Gina was angry: her father was her hero; it was his example that had interested her in a business career. How could he spoil everything?

At Sequoyah Community Church, the pastor tried to lighten the mood, comparing Doris with the heroine of a TV show who did all the dirty work on the ranch while the cowboys had all the fun. He seemed noncommittal about the future of the marriage. This was not exactly what Doris had hoped for: she wanted to be told how her marriage could be saved in the age-old Christian way, with Gordon asking the Lord's forgiveness and Doris finding forgiveness in her heart for her husband.

She knew their marriage wasn't perfect. Gordon spent too lavishly on cars, hobbies, and travel, and she felt that she had become too much of a servant to his every whim. She was the one who called relatives and friends at the last minute to say they would not be coming because Gordon was working late. Though he was an excellent provider, he was a workaholic who left most of the child-rearing to her. At home he would disappear, tinkering with stereo gear or model railroad equipment in the basement. Doris knew that the women's movement preached that wives had a right to expect and demand emotional and sexual fulfillment from marriage. Still, Doris felt, if she was missing anything in life, it seemed unimportant compared with what she had: a solid life and three fine daughters. She was adamantly opposed to divorce. She felt simply that "sacred vows should be kept," and was ready to make her stand on those terms.

Gordon holed up in a room in Oakland. He had drifted into the affair. The relationship, he knew in his heart, was completely impossible; the woman was fifteen years younger than he, an unmarried professional, and not an active Christian. Yet perhaps because of the wide differences in their backgrounds, he thought, they enjoyed an easy communication, free of demands and expectations. Yet he felt deep remorse; he loved Doris. The right thing to do was to call and ask her if he could come home. After three days in the wilderness he did just that.

Almost at once, they began counseling sessions with an assistant pastor at Sequoyah. Doris and Gordon had come a long way just to be exposing themselves and their marriage in such a setting. Years earlier, when Doris was fighting Superintendent Foster, they had attended Pastor Rick Howard's Valley Christian Center Church in San Ramón. Gordon was church treasurer. Howard was a young Assemblies of God pastor with a reputation as something of a maverick in the denomination. As dean of men at the Assemblies' Evangel College in Springfield, Missouri, he had urged students to become involved with political issues like the war in Vietnam. At the church in San Ramón, Howard had begun getting together small "Faith and Work" groups, an experiment being tried in a number of "progressive" Assemblies churches. "Faith and Work" smacked to some churchgoers of the encounter groups that were springing up everywhere. Such right-wing preachers as Billy James Hargis were warning Christians against being seduced by modern psychology. Gordon and Doris were extremely dubious of what Howard was doing and said so. Howard responded by saying that these reactions were not at all unusual. Major Pentecostal denominations had rejected the doctrine of entire sanctification or total eradication of sin within the sanctified individual, but remnants of perfectionism remained, and, as Howard saw it, one corollary of entire sanctification was a high order of inner concealment. "The ultimate Pentecostal stance is you don't admit sin," he said.

Gordon and Doris had come out of that background. The Reformation had done away with the confessional booth and obligated every believer to deal directly with God. One took one's problems to the Lord, not to neighbors, relatives, or—least of all—social workers and psychologists. Yet in the 1970s and 1980s psychology slowly began to infiltrate the counseling programs of even the most conservative denominations and churches. Pastor Dick Tatham had taken psychology courses at the University of Idaho, and Renee had seen counselors after the Hawaii incident. Evangel College had a psychology department that sought to combine modern psychology and the Bible. The rationale was that churches should equip themselves "with the best tools available."[1]

Modern psychology was by definition at odds with binary Biblical notions of right and wrong, sin and purity. It looked at behavior on a case-by-case basis and seldom concluded that a problem as common and complex as marital distress was entirely one-sided. Where the goal of traditional church counseling was to put away "bad thoughts," modern psychology wanted to get them out on the table. Oca's favorite television evangelist, Jimmy Swaggart, representing the Southern and most culturally-conservative wing of the Assemblies of God, attacked psychology as a "false religion," a "worldly Pied Piper." The only answer to marriage problems, Swaggart insisted, was "fasting, prayer and application of the Word."

Doris was not a fan of Jimmy Swaggart's, but her own views were not so different. She liked the description of marriage the Christian writer and speaker Bill Gotherd used. Gotherd, she said, described it as a condition in which a man is under God's umbrella, the wife is under the husband's umbrella, and the children are under the wife's umbrella, and anyone who steps out from under the umbrella was going to get wet.

In the counseling sessions at Sequoyah, Gordon was aware of ideas that would have been considered heretical in old-line Pentecostal churches. The counselor wanted to save the marriage, but he conceded that some relationships might *not* be salvageable, a troubling point of view to Doris. On the other hand, she found the counseling sessions useful because they helped her to see she had fallen into some bad patterns. If Gordon "used" her, she had let herself become totally dependent on him.

Several mornings each week, Gordon left home before five o'clock and drove to his son-in-law's house to pray with him and another man. The family was in crisis. There were emergency family meetings and hours spent on the telephone, Doris talking to Cindy, Cindy talking to her husband. But Doris did not call the family in Fresno. She knew what the news would mean in Fresno: it would mean the end of the myth.

ON THE SURFACE, the family was at the peak of its success. Bill's ownership of a USFL team had made him a minor celebrity in Fresno. His son Mike had graduated from Pepperdine Law School and found a job with a top Fresno law firm. Gordon was in line to become managing partner at his accounting firm. In Lake Havasu City, Dick Tatham was extending his influence in and around his community through his church, his Christian schools and a Christian radio and TV station.

Underneath the surface, though, rivets were popping.

The family had been hit by a series of traumas and surprises. Ruby's death and Oca's sudden remarriage had been one. The children welcomed Ona as a companion for their father, but the speed of his decision had been a shock.

Far more disquieting was the epidemic of divorce among Oca's grandchildren. By the summer of 1985 six of their eleven marriages were ending or had ended in divorce. And one unmarried grand-daughter was about to have a child out of wedlock. No one in the family had experienced more sorrow with children than Pastor Dick Tatham and his wife, Grace. Donna's marriage in 1975 had been the family's first shock. She was several months pregnant, and to avoid "scandalizing" Dick's congregation, the wedding took place at Renee's in San Francisco. That marriage lasted nearly a decade. By the time Donna and her husband had split up, her twin younger sisters had divorced their husbands and a second marriage of one of the twins was coming apart. All the girls had strayed from attendance at their father's church.

Within the family, Dick Tatham had become a kind of Job, crying out in the Arizona wilderness above the River Colorado. He felt as if he would "faint" from the pressure, and asked God for strength to "hang on." He blamed society—and himself—for his family's predicament. He said, "I expected our kids to be in church every Sunday. They had no choice, and they rebelled against it. And that's what's happened in our society. But I'm afraid a lot of the time I put the ministry ahead of my kids. We were visiting hurting people, but our kids were hurting, too. You make a commitment to God, but if we neglect our own it's worse than being an infidel." He offered to resign from his pulpit, but the deacons wouldn't hear of it; several had problems with their own children. Divorce was the scourge of the age, and not even the traditional values of Tathams or of the Assemblies of God seemed able to stave off the troubles. Oca reacted with sadness to each new report. He prayed for the grandchildren and wept for Dick. And Dick's grief mingled with his own continuing sorrow over Ruby's loss. The family feared his condemnation, but the old horse trader surprised them. The moralist was also a man of the world. He took what was happening as a proof that the storm in the world was rising and was taking down even good people. His generation had made its share of mistakes, too, but now the Devil's snares had multiplied.

Dick was not alone in his sorrow. The marriage of Doris and Gordon's daughter Gina lasted only a little more than a year. Then one day in 1984, when Doris was still grieving over that, Earline phoned Doris from Fresno: Billy Tatham was separating from his wife.

Billy had met the former Shauna Joseph at Bullard High, Fresno's elite high school serving Fig Gardens and the city's affluent population of doctors, lawyers, and developers. There were sports cars in the school parking lot and parties with alcohol on weekends. At Bullard, Billy had realized that not everyone went to church four times a week or followed the rules he was taught at home and in church. It was a cynical time in the youth culture; drugs were accessible, hair was long, and Vietnam and Watergate were the headline news. "We used to go to Bible study and then go out and get smashed afterward," he said. "It was right at the end of the war and [the church youth leader] was trying to avoid the draft."

Billy made a smooth adjustment to Bullard. Soon he was "Wild Bill" Tatham, attending dances and parties, drinking beer, and growing his hair long with a part in the middle. He was a jock, a teammate said, "always in shape, lifting weights, and kind of wild and crazy." Bullard High served the more affluent classes, but it was also a melting pot of backgrounds that reflected the extraordinary mix of Fresno's population. Shauna was Catholic; her father's people were Portuguese from the Azores, and her mother's were Croatians from Dubrovnik.

When they met, Shauna and Billy were both questioning the

dogmas they had learned as children. Shauna, like so many young Catholics, was reevaluating the teachings that she had received at a Fresno parochial school. And Billy was rebelling mildly against the legalistic mores of his Pentecostal background. He and Shauna found neutral territory at Northwest Church, a nondenominational Fresno institution with Baptist leanings. To Billy, Northwest lacked "the warmth of Northeast Assembly, with the sense of closeness and love, and singing, and everyone having a good time. But it was sort of the fun without the seriousness. The music was tremendous. Modern. That church exploded."

The summer he graduated from Fresno State College, Billy and Shauna were married at Northwest Church. They wrote their own wedding vows. Shauna hoped to include a priest from Saint Thérèse's parish, but the parish said it would not be possible for a priest to assist at a Protestant service. Afterward there was a reception for four hundred people at the Piccadilly Inn. Bill and Earline would have preferred to keep it a "dry" occasion, but the bride's family stood by their Catholic tradition. There was wine and champagne for the guests and rock music for energetic young dancers, including the bride and groom. Bill Tatham picked up the tab.

By that time, experimentation with alcohol was becoming commonplace among Oca's and Ruby's grandchildren. Billy and Mike, who continued to live at home during college years in Fresno, found that the drinking issue was one on which there could be no meeting of the minds with their parents. The elder Tathams found cause, in the liquor smell on Mike's breath, to conclude that he had "something burning at him," and to tell him so. In retrospect Mike would come to believe that what was burning in him was mainly youthful curiosity.

"Some guys would get a bunch of beer and say let's tie it on, thinking: we're in college, we'll never have it like this again. Then you'd go home and take the heat. But for me it was just mainly curiosity. When you're raised as a Tatham, and then you hear that others in the family are *drinking wine*, that's enough to get your curiosity going."

In the early hours of a September 1978 morning, Mike was at the wheel of the family Blazer when it collided with another car in an intersection. Mike spent the night at St. Agnes hospital, but the other driver sustained more serious injuries. Mike had consumed two or three beers at a party, and had stopped at the Black Angus for a drink afterward. Fortunately for Mike, the Blazer was well insured, and the driver of the other vehicle had been drinking.

It was the second time that Mike had seemed to fling himself in the face of death. The first time had been just a little more than a year earlier when he had been skiing out of control in Sun Valley. He was, he would say later, "waiting for life to get even with me." Perhaps he thought he and not his friend should have taken the bullet in 1972. The Blazer incident pulled him up short. He had to stop hurting his parents.

Billy's and Shauna's marriage came apart during the Outlaws' ill-fated season in Tulsa. Shauna had taken a job as a nurse, and Billy had immersed himself in the football team. At the end of the 1984 season, he broke the news to his parents. Bill Senior and Earline took it hard. Divorce was something that was supposed to happen to others. Bill wished the marriage could be salvaged. Billy's decision brought feelings to the surface that usually stayed well buried in the Tatham family. Shauna's father had died when she was younger, and Bill had taken her under his wing, paying for some of her nursing education. Sometimes Bill and Earline wept during the blessing of the food, and Bill thought about getting counseling. Billy had made up his mind just as he had when he quit Fresno State football, and nothing would change that. In early 1986, he married Susan McDannald, whom he had been dating for more than a year. She had coordinated marketing and promotion for the Outlaws from 1983 to 1985 and had been married previously to a placekicker for the team while it was in Tulsa. Her family roots were in rural Missouri, but Susan was soaring beyond them. She had been Miss T.E.E.N. USA in 1980, and the year she went to work for the Outlaws she was a "top ten senior" at the University of Tulsa.

The divorces among the younger generation of Tathams marred the ideal of the perfect family. Doris, Renee, and others saw a connection between the troubles and Ruby's death. She had been their "center," the one in Fresno to whom they confided and with whom they prayed and gossiped. To Renee, she had been "a silent support, like holding somebody us up with her hands, and you take the hands away and we begin to fall. When they were gone you saw the unit becoming weak because it didn't have any support. It kind of fizzled."

BY THE SPRING OF 1985, Doris had come to the conclusion that her efforts to repair her marriage with Gordon were not working. He was still seeing the other woman, and when Renee came to visit her, she finally let out the secret that she had held so closely for months. After that she told Brenda and Jerry. They were all pillars of strength, calling her often, and also phoning Gordon to say they loved him, too, and were praying for him.

Doris had read a book that said if a relationship is not working, give the other person a chance to make a decision. Not long after letting Renee in on what was going on, she left a note for Gordon saying that if he was ready to make a "total change" he could contact her through Cindy. Then she got in her red Mercedes and drove to Fresno.

The two-and-a-half-hour trip was a little scary. Remarkably, it was her longest solo automobile trip in thirty-one years of marriage, and it made her realize how dependent she had become. Descending into the dry, flat valley, she sang and prayed out loud. The notion of herself fleeing *to* Fresno made her laugh. Yet there was something comforting about the valley, so much that was familiar: fields of alfalfa, advertisements for polled Herefords, lonely weathered barns, fading signs, farmyards full of rusting farm machinery. Reaching Highway 99, she maneuvered among the semis with their whip antennas whose drivers wore caps that said Sun-Maid on the front and tuned their radios to the doleful country and western music of California's agricultural heartland.

Doris dreaded the reaction of her dad and brothers in Fresno. She knew that her life-style—the trips to Europe, wine drinking, and expensive cars—was the subject of talk there. Still, they were her family, and they hadn't let her down so far.

She half expected that Gordon would have called by the time she pulled in at Brenda's home in Fig Gardens, but he hadn't. So she sat down and wrote a short essay about herself, calling it "Doormat—or Portrait." It ended with a prayer: "Create a newness. Forgive us and let us glorify You in all that we do. . . ." Just writing the words down seemed to help.

She planned to break the news to Oca and Ona over breakfast the next morning. She thought carefully about what to say, but when Oca began blessing the food, she blurted out everything through sobs. The condemnation she had feared did not come. Instead, they sat and talked and Oca told her he loved her. Soon Bill and Gerald came over; they hugged her silently—for the first time she could ever remember.

She stayed in Fresno a week, hoping Gordon would call. When he didn't, she drove home and called him at the office and told him, "You'd better find another place to sleep."

He moved into a small flat and for the next few months saw

her only once a week. They had begun attending Sequoyah, the Assemblies church, for it was comforting to be back in surroundings that evoked such strong memories from their youth. Also, they were not well known in the congregation, and could be more anonymous than at Neighborhood Church. So now, every Sunday morning, Gordon would arrive at the last minute and slide in next to her. When the service was over he left without saying a word. Sometimes he sent flowers or met her for dinner.

In September, he asked her to take him back. This time the relationship with the other woman definitely was over, he said. He took her to dinner at the Lakeview Club in downtown Oakland and gave her an emerald ring. But Doris set conditions: he had to give her room to be herself. Living alone for the first time in her life, she had felt a certain sense of liberation, much as she hated that word: "When I realized that for more than thirty years I had given in, kept my mouth shut, and not been myself, and I saw where it got me— that it didn't make him loyal to me, staying home, being faithful, keeping the peace—I saw that wasn't what made a good relationship. And I felt like I could be my Tatham self once again."

The psychologist they turned to next was a Christian, but he was not working directly for a church and practiced regular psychotherapy. He had the Weavers write answers to questions from a psychological profile test and then used the information they provided to probe their relationships. (Doris scored high on "caring.") At the twice-weekly sessions, he delved deeply into their Pentecostal childhoods and their relations with their parents and, after probing the sources of Gordon's workaholic tendencies, uncovered Gordon's efforts to win the approval of his minister-father. Doris, he found, wanted desperately to live up to the moral expectations of her family.

He gave Doris a copy of a book called *Own Your Own Life*. Doris liked parts of it. The book helped her understand that she wasn't responsible for the way her husband treated her, only for the way *she* reacted to him. This struck a chord. She realized she had to fight the impulse to "make everything okay." She had been "the fixer," the one who would "make everything right" and do anything to avoid disappointing friends or relatives.

One day she suddenly said to Gordon, "I don't give you permission for anything because that's not my position. I'm not your mother." She could hardly believe her own voice. But then she went on: "I don't give you permission. You do what you want to do. You have to decide." For the first time since her wedding day, she was pushing responsibility for the family back onto Gordon's shoulders. *Own Your Own Life* helped Doris see an important weakness in herself and pointed to a way of changing. Yet Doris also found parts of the book deeply troubling. It was, she concluded, "totally humanistic." The author quoted the Bible, but referred to certain passages as "myths," and he acknowledged that he was an admirer of Eastern religion.

Doris felt she would do almost anything to save her marriage. If counseling was what it would take, she would stick with it. But she kept wondering, as the expense of it mounted, When does the therapy start? When do we start working on putting the marriage back together? One day she got up enough nerve to ask the counselor the question. His answer stunned her. This *was* the therapy; they *were* working to save their marriage.

Doris was bewildered. The counseling didn't seem to be healing them; if anything, it was having the opposite effect. Yet Gordon felt the counseling was helpful, and Doris saw that it was enabling him to be less evasive about his feelings. Anger, negative emotions, everything was pouring out. But that only made the sessions all the more distressing to Doris. During their last visit, it almost seemed to her that satanic powers were at work. Gordon opened up and accused her of "turning the knife," dramatizing his point by a turning gesture of his hand. His face was flushed, and he looked at her with what she thought was hatred. Nothing had prepared her for that. She had been raised to "keep smiling," "look on the bright side," and "let God handle it." But what she was hearing was that Gordon did not *like* her; otherwise why would he be making such dramatic accusations? She thought, *If I'm that kind of person I'm rotten, insensitive, cruel. If I can have that kind of an effect on a person, how can I feel that God has forgiven me and given me His love and peace and joy? If Gordon feels that way why would he want to live with me, why would he want me to be his wife? If I'm that kind of person, how do I look in the sight of the Lord?*

She was sure the counselor was thinking, *No wonder he's in such bad shape if you do this to him.* Sure enough he was looking at her—as if she were a *witch!*

They stumbled out of the office.

"I don't think that way, and I don't feel that way, and I don't understand why you think I'm that way," she said.

Gordon made what seemed like a strange reply under the circumstances: "You're the most understanding person, you've been a wonderful wife, you've been supportive."

"Well," she said, "this is the last time I go to him. If I go through another session like this, we won't be together at the end of the day."

Whether Gordon agreed with her decision, he didn't say. "I'm not going back, either," he announced. Neither of them did.

She had moved quite a distance from the point at which she believed that saving her marriage involved nothing more complicated than forgiving Gordon for his sin. Yet there were boundaries she wouldn't cross. She didn't accept the whole superstructure of modern psychology with its relentless focus on flaws and weaknesses. When did it all end? Only after every mystery had been attacked and destroyed?

RENEE'S ACCIDENT and the ensuing problems gave her a chance, too, to reassess her life. It had not been the "all-out Christian life" that her parents had hoped for—that much she knew. Kingman had been a Christian, but in San Diego she had begun dating somebody who wasn't. "I had convictions," she said. "I just wasn't living all my convictions. I guess I compromised a lot to work in that lifestyle." Yet she didn't regret her experiences. She had associated with all kinds of people: gays, women involved in "crummy affairs" with married men, pilots cheating on their wives. They weren't what her dad would call "beautiful Christian people," but they were real. Jesus had gone among prostitutes and thieves.

What helped her most was South Coast Community Church, which she discovered about the time of her accident. Some people called South Coast the "yuppie church," but for Renee it was an antidote to the loneliness many complained of in what she referred to as "plastic" Orange County.

Orange County had once had a Middle America flavor to it. Before World War II, it had been a county of small towns with farms and orchards and ranches. With the arrival of defense and aerospace companies like North American Rockwell, Ford Aerospace, McDonnell Douglas, Hughes Aircraft, and Morton Thiokol in the 1950s and 1960s, Orange County became home to thousands of defense-industry families. It was this influx that gave Orange County its reputation as a place of sprawling suburbs, conservative politics, and traditional families. Then, in the late 1970s and 1980s, came a new wave of high-tech light industries, settling into neat, "smokeless" industrial parks. The construction boom obliterated farming communities and suburban villages, replacing them with mile after mile of high-rise office and apartment buildings, gigantic shopping malls, hotels, banks, and high-speed roads until it was all but impossible to tell where Irvine ended and Santa Ana began. There were almost as many jobs (1.6 million) in Orange County as there were people (1.9 million).

The high-tech influx changed the culture of the county once again. While it retained its conservative politics, it ceased to be a Middle American community of traditional family values. In the 1980s, nearly half the county's households consisted of single persons, either divorced or postponing marriage and child-rearing in order to enjoy the good life of southern California. The county was full of people just like Renee, people from "somewhere else" who had been places and done things—engineers, medical technicians, computer specialists, financial experts, brokers for national real-estate companies.

Such an environment presented new challenges and opportunities for churches. Within a few miles of each other in Irvine, Costa Mesa, Santa Ana, and Anaheim were half a dozen congregations that routinely attracted five to ten thousand worshipers every Sunday morning. From the Santa Ana Freeway, the cross above Reverend Robert H. Schuller's twelve-story Crystal Cathedral in Garden Grove was plainly visible. Not far away was John Wimber's Vineyard, from which a vast audience could observe the pastor performing modern-day miracles and healings in the very shadow of Disneyland's snow-capped Matterhorn. Close by in Fullerton was Charles "Chuck" Swindoll's First Evangelical Free Church, whose membership grew tenfold in a decade. West of the San Diego Freeway, in Costa Mesa, was the original church of the Jesus People, Chuck Smith's Calvary Chapel. And over on Bonita Canyon Road was Tim Timmons's South Coast Community Church.

Freeways made the churches possible. Half a million people lived within twenty driving minutes of each of them and a million within thirty. To the uninitiated, they often looked less like churches than stages for the media-wise celebrities who were their pastors: Chuck Smith was carried on Paul and Jan Crouch's Trinity Broadcasting Network; Schuller reached 7 million people on "Hour of Power"; and Timmons had been a guest on Pat Robertson's "700 Club."

But these were not Moral Majority churches. Orange County was Reagan country, but not Falwell country. The hip, world-traveling singles of Orange County did not welcome pastors telling them how to think politically. Moreover, to condemn divorcées, adulterers, fornicators, women who had abortions, people who would glance at a risqué magazine, users of alcohol and drugs, and gays would have been to write off much, if not most, of Orange County's new population. To criticize working mothers would be to question the county's economic underpinning.

The pastors did not condone the "permissive society." Chuck Swindoll "does not hesitate to tell us we are depraved," according to an associate. But Swindoll refused to preach against drinking, finding no conclusive scriptural prohibition against it, and he accepted three valid reasons for divorce. In examining their own lives, members of Orange County's middle class were prepared to admit that they had made mistakes. But they did not want to be condemned for the lives they had led. In 1985, Dallas Anderson was at work on a bronze sculpture for Schuller's Crystal Cathedral. When finished it would be called *Love Without Condemnation* and depict the scene described in the eighth chapter of John, in which the Pharisees bring an adulteress to Jesus and Jesus says: "He that is without sin among you, let him be the first to cast a stone at her."

Love Without Condemnation. It might well have been the creed of Orange County Christianity.

What people in Orange County plainly *were* looking for in their churches was what they were missing in their careers, communities, and homes: a feeling that their lives were meaningful; companionship; and help raising children in a turbulent time. In a society full of people who had tried astrology, karate, aerobics, est, and other outgrowths of the human potential movement, the church was often a last resort.

In many respects, the big, new churches of the Sun Belt were doing what the little Pentecostal works and storefronts had once done: serving as bridges for people in transition. What was the landscape of modern America? Divorce, drugs, corporate mergers, job insecurity. Millions felt that they were losing control over their lives, children, and economic destinies. Doris and Renee had advanced their material position only to find that the place they had reached was a shaky platform. Companies vanished, and people changed jobs, houses, places of residence—even wives. Those grappling with the changes formed a vast pool of potential converts to the new religions. *The inner light,* ignited by a charismatic spark, could shine a path through the confusion.

Each of the superchurches in Orange County had a different formula. John Wimber's Vineyard, which held services in a gigantic warehouse in an industrial section of Anaheim, did it through the excitement of "signs and wonders"—miracles of healing, exorcisms, speaking in tongues—the old Pentecostal system updated for a youthful, hip, relaxed group of worshipers excited by the hope that the supernatural would reach down to touch the secretary or the computer programmer, just as it had once reached down to touch people on Drake's Prairie.

"His style, cool, humorous, fatherly, is exactly pitched to baby boomers," *Christianity Today* magazine would write of Wimber in August 1986. "It is a style redolent of Ronald Reagan: an awfully nice neighbor leaning over the back fence, presenting what used to be considered extreme without sounding mean or pushy."

To counter despair, Schuller early in his ministry began emphasizing the "gospel of self-esteem," as he called it. He was a protégé of Norman Vincent Peale, author of *The Power of Positive Thinking*, a book that had sold millions of copies in the 1950s. Like Peale, Schuller was a pastor in the Reformed Church, and in the 1970s and 1980s his books also sold millions. Their titles were inspirational messages like *Tough Times Never Last But Tough People Do!*

THE SIZE OF the Orange County superchurches made them seem forbidding at first glance. Actually, they achieved the economies of scale enabling them to provide the specialized services their clientele wanted. There were programs for alcoholics, the newly divorced, the twenty-to-thirty set, the thirty-to-forty group, senior citizens, and single parents. Some pastors began to reach out to gays and even to offer job counseling and job placement services—something for everyone.

The pastors concentrated on an enormous pool of potential customers: the unchurched, the nonbelievers, the lapsed. When Schuller arrived in Orange County in the mid-1950s, he went door to door enlisting people to come to his services. If they already had a church he quickly moved on, but if they were churchless—and particularly if they had never had any experience with religion—he stayed and talked, inviting them to "come as you are in the family car" to *his* church, the Orange Drive-In. Traditionalists were shocked that the Word could be dispensed in a "passion pit," but Schuller's marketing gimmick worked. People did not have to dress up, they could stay inside their cars, and the children enjoyed going along for the ride. Soon Schuller built California's first "walk-in, drive-in" church. Designed by the "bio-realist" architect Richard Neutra, it was equipped with rollback glass panels that allowed drive-in patrons to watch Schuller while they listened to him over drive-in-style microphones. In 1980, Crystal Cathedral was completed. Designed by the well-known modernist Philip Johnson, its glass walls crisscrossed by white steel webbing rose twelve stories and reached back the length of one and a half football fields.

Renee seriously began looking for a permanent church after she adopted Melissa. She abandoned a small Assemblies of God church that mainly served "traditional" families and was "couples-oriented." When Oca visited, she took him to Chuck Smith's Calvary Chapel, and he loved it. It had a plain, blue-collar feel, but it wasn't quite right for her. She sensed some of the familiar rigidity. Eventually, she settled on South Coast.

Pastor Tim Timmons was a student of local attitudes. "The psychology of people living in this part of the world seems to be that you just can't hit them with a ton of bricks, a bunch of do's and don'ts. It wouldn't keep them here. You've got all these well-educated entrepreneurs making decisions all day long, and you come in and try to think for them? It doesn't go." South Coast was rapidly becoming the church of the latest wave of Orange County settlers: the cosmopolitan, well-traveled, self-motivated professionals.

Timmons came out of a strict Ohio Baptist religious background full of restrictions on drinking, smoking, dancing, and moviegoing, even roller skating ("dancing on skates"). "I felt that things were pretty screwy; I kept asking, 'Why?' Then as I went to college and kept asking those questions I realized that not much of that was Biblical—it was more cultural."

After attending an interdenominational seminary in Dallas, Timmons went home determined to "free these people from their rigidity." But he was "awakened real quick to the fact that they didn't *want* to be free." For a time he worked for Christian Crusade in Washington, D.C., but soon discovered an interest in and talent for psychology. He went to Dallas again, where he started a group called Christian Family Life, which held counseling seminars for married couples around the country, giving people "the Biblical game plan for marriage."

Timmons picked up on a 1960s word: relevant. To communicate with non-Christians he was convinced he would have to stop speaking "Christianese" and become more relevant. But he did not feel that he could put his ideas to work in the Bible Belt. "In Dallas everybody was a member of a church; it was very hard to reach the secular mind, the secular world, and I wanted to get to that mass that didn't go to church. And so, we moved to Orange County."

He and his wife arrived in Orange County in the mid-1970s and set up a counseling center. Soon they had more work than he could handle. Timmons also began pulling down fees as a motivational speaker at meetings of civic groups. "I wouldn't quote Scripture, I didn't mention Jesus' name. But I would give all these principles. And then in the end I'd say, 'Do you know where I get all this stuff?' And I'd say, 'Get your pen out. I want to give you the title of a book.' And they'd get their pens out at dental conventions, the round tables, it didn't make any difference. And I'd say, 'The book is Bible, B-I-B-L-E.' I wanted to plant a seed. I came to Christianity as a pragmatist, but I spoke of marriage and family because that's what I found worked. I found very quickly that that's not what they were after here. Businessmen wanted to know how to make money, and don't tell me how to be better off with my wife. So I went back to the drawing board, and I came out with the three basic priorities: there's who you are, your intimate relationships, and your business. And over the long term, your business is going to reflect your intimate relationships and who you are. So we've got to shore up these two before we can get to the third one. So I came back again and took them down. You want to make money. Yeah. You've got to get your intimate relationship because that'll help you care for your clients better, and you've got to be happy about who you are, and trying to show them happiness doesn't come through people, places, or things, but it comes through knowing who you are and being true to that."

In 1980, Timmons started his own church in Irvine with four hundred people; the congregation doubled within a few weeks and then doubled again. The church on Bonita Canyon Road adjacent to the University of California at Irvine could easily have been mistaken for a building in a high-tech industrial park but for the simple cross outside. The heart of the church was its programs, which were mixed Bible study and group therapy aimed at the 45 percent of the church members who were single. The programs included alcohol and drug recovery programs, overeater groups, and, later, a group called "Career Connections," which brought together area employers and church members who needed jobs. Timmons preached the "Gospel of self-actualization." His core message was that Jesus can make you feel better about yourself, which was both seductive and necessary for the upwardly mobile, professionally confident, but emotionally insecure people who poured into Orange County in the decade after 1975.

Reading Timmons's book *Hooked on Life* (written with Stephen Arterburn and published in 1985), one saw why Timmons, Schuller, and others who integrated psychology with religion were under fire from orthodox evangelicals like David Hunt, who claimed in his book *The Seduction of Christianity* that some of the new preaching crossed the line into secular humanism. True humanism, Timmons said, was Christianity—a statement that infuriated members of the Christian Right. In *Hooked on Life*, he went on for 181 pages before coming to the first sustained discussion of God.

Renee began going to South Coast Community Church while on sick leave in August 1984. She immediately got the warm feeling she had experienced at Body Life. She met real-estate brokers, registered nurses, engineers, a woman doctor, and several attorneys. People who had never been to church were in the congregation: Catholics, Baptists, Methodists, and every other denomination. They were looking for something more than the artificial, sexually charged singles scene at bars and nightclubs.

She threw herself into activities, attending Sunday night Bible-study classes that were an offshoot of a large singles group that met on Sunday mornings called "Focus 30" and, in anticipation of her fortieth birthday in 1986, "Focus 40" meetings, smaller "growth groups" usually held in someone's home. Along with her church, Renee had Melissa. One day in February 1985, before making her Fresno trip, Doris got a round-robin letter from Renee announcing that Melissa had been sworn in as a citizen at a ceremony at the Dorothy Chandler Pavilion in Los Angeles. Oca and Ona came down for the ceremony, and the three-year-old, looking perfect as a wax doll in a pink linen suit with matching pink bow in her hair, clutched her small American flag and danced around chanting "USA, USA!" Renee wrote:

> I ask for your prayers. I want to raise Melissa, understanding the responsibility for not just a United States Citizen, but a Christian Citizen. With the difficulty of youth I need your prayerful support to educate Melissa in the ways of our land and, most important, on the ways of our Lord. If God chooses for me to do this alone, as a single parent, then I will need divine leadership, in a big way. Each one of you are important to me, and I need your counsel, love and companionship, to help me be a better parent.

So many countries do not have the freedom of religion, open opportunity, and chance for educational advancement. Taiwan being one that is predicted to soon be under Communist rule is one we must pray for often. Someday I hope Melissa will realize this opportunity is probably one of the greatest in the world, to be a citizen, to be an American!

As 1985 wore on, Renee often telephoned Doris. They had become the embattled sisters, fighting to save Doris's marriage and Renee's independence. Sometimes they prayed together on the phone.

A few weeks before Thanksgiving of that year, Renee's neurosurgeon recommended an operation to relieve pressure on her spine. The outlook for saving her legs was good, but the operation was dangerous and difficult and people who underwent it often suffered chronic pain and discomfort. The surgery took place the week after Christmas, at the hospital of the University of California at Irvine. Gerald and Cora took care of Melissa in Fresno. The operation went as well as could be expected, but for once the Tatham support system broke down. Bill and Earline came down from Fresno on the eve of the operation, but they were obligated by family commitments to leave quickly. Doris couldn't come, for her daughter Gina had just had major back surgery of her own. Oca was recovering from a prostate operation.

The void was filled by friends from South Coast. An assistant pastor visited regularly, and one of the men from Focus 30 drove her home from the hospital. Church friends arrived with TV dinners and casseroles and helped her shower and dress. A man from the church drove her to doctors' appointments and to services and delivered a tape of Timmons's sermon if she didn't feel well enough to go. She also received several cashier's checks from anonymous benefactors.

To Renee, it seemed "the extended family that I guess the Lord wants us to have." She said, "I think what it taught me was that I have always had that extra happiness and love and joy because of my family. They have been my security blanket because of being single and I think what the Lord allowed me to learn is that my family is not going to always be there and geographically are not here, so that is not where my security is. I realized that's what the church family is there for."

The recuperation was slow and the pain was chronic, as the doctor had warned it would be. She hated taking painkillers; giving in to the pain seemed a sign of weakness, something that the family would not approve of. But there were times when she needed the relief.

She had filed a lawsuit against Republic, demanding compensation for the fall at the airport, and also a suit against a chiropractor who had treated her, but the litigation might drag on for years. Though still technically on medical leave, since May 1985 she had received no pay from Republic and was living off her savings, workmen's compensation of $896 a month, and union-negotiated insurance of $259 a month. She could not quit because her compensation claim against Republic might be jeopardized.

At a Super Bowl party in February 1985 she had met a friend by the name of Don. She was wearing her Outlaws shirt, and he was wearing one from Stanford, his alma mater. He was an engineer, fifty, divorced, and looking after his son and adopted daughter in a large home in Laguna Beach. Renee found it a pleasant change to share the experiences of single parenthood with someone without having the usual tensions of a "relationship."

Often they went together to South Coast or, because Don was a Christian, to "believers' meetings" at Chuck Smith's Calvary Chapel. At one of those sessions a man announced that he had a "word of knowledge"—a spiritual intuition—that someone among them was suffering from a neck problem. It took Renee a few moments to realize that the word of knowedge must have been about her.

A few months after she met him, Don learned that he was suffering from a malignant brain tumor and would not live more than a year. Don gave Renee power of attorney to manage his affairs, and after his brain surgery she and other friends from South Coast helped keep track of his bills and kept his books. Perhaps, she thought, God had given her a neck problem so she could care for Don while he was dying and that afterward God would heal her. But she naturally found it hard to deal with the senselessness of Don's tragedy.

Sometimes she would cry when she talked to Doris on the telephone. Then Doris would say, "Let's pray and ask the Lord for guidance and direction and peace." They found that it helped to admit they were both powerless to solve their problems. Doris would hang up the phone feeling as if they had given their pain to the Lord and could trust Him to shoulder it. She called it "lifting each other in prayer."

Although Gordon had moved back home, he still often seemed distant and absorbed by work, and his hobbies were untouched in the basement. The house redecoration project was on hold. Doris knew her daughters worried about her and that others wondered at the wisdom of her decision to take the "traditional" position on marriage instead of "letting it go." But sometimes Doris almost stopped caring. Lisa, her youngest daughter, told her, "Mom, you've got to decide what you're going to do and stick with it. You don't know where you stand, and you've got to decide: Can I put up with this the rest of my life? Can I live like this? Or would I be better off being alone and getting somewhere and at least knowing where I stand and know what's going on?"

In June 1986, Doris put the question to Gordon point-blank: "Are we going to make it?"

He was hopeful, and that helped. In September, they went together to Europe, once again spending most of their time in Germany. But the trip was not a total success, and several times it seemed uncertain whether they would complete it.

A month after coming home, Doris went by herself on a package-tour cruise in the Caribbean. It was a new experience, being on her own like that. She had a good time and even danced, for it didn't seem wrong. It lifted her spirits, so she was sure the Lord did not mind.

It was a melancholy time. Sometimes, she told a friend, she wanted to quit and "just go live in a little apartment with no controversy." She added with a smile, "I realize I'm becoming an eighties woman."

Gordon often dined at the Lakeview Club. The atmosphere was coolly elegant. The dining room possessed a good wine cellar, and Gordon was generous to friends and clients. He would call for a bottle of excellent vintage, and when the sommelier presented it, the label might still be dusty from the cellar.

Doris savored the good moments together with Gordon. One evening they listened to an Amy Grant record. It was just like the old days. But she often felt defeated and down. She had prayed, gone to church, fasted, and read every book the counselors had given her, anything to save her marriage. Now it was up to the Lord.

IN NOVEMBER 1986, Renee attended a pre-Thanksgiving lecture series at South Coast at which a motivational speaker named Terry Hershey coached the church's large singles population on how to "move on" after relationships ended. For one of the lectures he showed up in tennis shoes, slacks, and a striped blue and white tennis shirt, as informally dressed as the audience. Renee wore a sweater with peppermint stripes over a plain red skirt. Others wore jeans, sneakers, and even upscale jogging suits. Few neckties or jewelry were in evidence, and women outnumbered men.

Renee, just forty, was trim, attractive, and quick to smile. With her short blond hair and accented features, there was something brave but vulnerable about her. She looked a little like Mary Martin when she starred in *South Pacific*. But sometimes her face would become pinched with pain and discomfort in spite of herself.

Hershey's lecture began with a prayer: "Father, thank you that You don't quit on us." Then he launched into his subject for the evening. The key to moving on, he said, was to forgive—something he confessed to having had trouble with after the breakup of his own marriage. Hershey defined forgiveness for the audience: "I give up the right to hurt you back," comparing it to aerobic exercise. "You have to do it over and over—the payoff comes later," he said.

When he asked everyone to turn to his or her neighbor and share "something that occupies your thoughts," Renee blurted out that she was "owned by the expectations that others have of me." Near the end, when Hershey asked people to tell their neighbor what they had learned, Renee said she was "too quick to apologize for things that are not my fault." Hershey ended with a prayer: "Father, thank You for letting us know You think we're still okay."

Don had a second operation soon after that. It left him with speech and walking difficulties, and his doctor ordered a machine installed at his home to help him breathe. Renee sometimes went to Don's house with Melissa to sing what she called "praise music," songs like "Jesus Is the Sweetest Name I Know" and "Something Beautiful, Something Good." Singing to the sick was a Tatham tradition. Don would smile and try to say the words.

At the end of 1986, Renee had not received a regular paycheck from Republic Airlines for eighteen months and the money she was getting from unemployment compensation and disability insurance didn't cover her mortgage payments and living expenses.

To lift her spirits, she met a friend for cappuccino at the Dana Point Marina, a fifteen-minute drive from her house. The yachts and sailing boats docked at the marina always lifted her spirits. It smelled of the wide world and reminded her of the days when all she had to say was "Take me to the airport."

She still hoped she could find a Christian to marry, though sometimes she wondered if even a Christian man could live up to her father's expectations. She was making progress learning to deal with what she felt was the Tatham problem: covering up emotions and feelings and always trying to act "strong."

What choice did she have? "I'm not in control of my finances whatsoever, not enough to make decisions about what to do with the house," she said. "I have to get back to work and make a decision to do something else, and I can't live on borrowed money forever. My physical condition is out of control, and because of that a lot of my social situations are out of control. I'm not out there meeting people in an active world. I guess that's what the Lord wants for me—to find out my dependency isn't on my family, my dependency isn't on this house, my dependency isn't on my car. I think I've grown. I have friends all over the world, and I don't know if I'd go back and trade all that to be married and home. I wouldn't trade it."

The family began to encourage her to sell her home in Mission Viejo and return to Fresno where they could help her. Renee appreciated their concern but she couldn't see herself going back. In Fresno, she said, "I had a tendency to be what they wanted me to be and ceased being Renee." Also, Fresno was a place for "traditional families," and she and Melissa were not a traditional family. In fact, Renee said, she was "not traditional, period."

Chapter Twenty-One

Choice

A BRISK BREEZE blew off the Bay. Slivers of blue and gold gleamed through a leaden sky, providing some cheer for rush-hour motorists gridlocked on Interstate 880. At her home in a Castro Valley subdivision, Cindy Critchfield sent her husband off to his job as a construction supervisor and prepared for a morning of teaching elementary school children.

The oldest child of Doris and Gordon Weaver, Cindy was an attractive brunette with a Mariel Hemingway voice and the warm eyes of her mother. On that particular November day in the fall of 1987, she was simply dressed in a blue, one-piece jumpsuit. A necklace of carved wooden figurines, acquired on one of the family's periodic trips abroad, matched her short brown hair.

Breakfast done and dishes washed, she walked out of the kitchen, crossed the living room, and entered a side room where her "class" was already waiting: her son Brent, eight, and daughter Janeé, six. Her school in the home had begun.

There was a large map of the world, handmade charts, and pictures, some with questions in big letters such as "Can you generate electricity?" and "How do lungs work?" But Bible study was the first order of business. Cindy asked Janeé to read from the seventh chapter of Matthew until she came to the well-known passage "Ask, and it shall be given you. . . . For every one that asketh receiveth."

"What does that tell you?" Cindy inquired. The children squirmed in their seats. "Well, does it mean we can ask for *anything* we want?"

There were nervous giggles, and "Nos!"

Cindy suggested, "You have to ask *in God's will*; you can't ask for a hundred Cabbage Patch astronauts; other children would be envious, and you wouldn't want that many. You ask to find out what He wants you to have."

The morning wore on, with inevitable moments of frustration and laughter. Janeé could not find her place in the Book of Exodus. Brent, a precocious speller and reader, had trouble putting the final touches on the Puritan hat he was making for the approaching Thanksgiving celebration. Cindy offered suggestions but did not rush to help: these were opportunities for growth, for developing self-reliance, for the children to learn to think for themselves—the very opportunities Cindy believed were often lacking in regular schools, including the Christian school the children previously had attended.

They broke for lunch, and Cindy adjourned to fix macaroni and cheese in the kitchen, where a notice posted on the refrigerator said: "In this house, we obey our Lord Jesus Christ; we tell the truth; we consider one another's interests ahead of our own; we speak quietly and respectfully to one another." Lunch finished, Brent went upstairs to work with the family's Apple computer, preparing a paper about a summer trip to Brazil with his parents and grandparents. After a short rest, it was back to class and spelling tests for both children.

CINDY REMEMBERED EXACTLY when she and Bill had started rethinking the way they were living, a process that was to make her one of a small minority of American parents who educate their children at home. It was soon after the fall day in 1986 that her mother had called and told her that her father had left and asked her to come over right away.

She and her sisters had sat for hours with her mother and gone to Sequoyah Community Church to seek help from a pastor. The next day Cindy had jumped in her car and driven to her father's office in downtown Oakland.

It took all the courage she had. She was frightened of confronting her father, angry at him for creating the situation that required it, confused and shaken with conflicting emotions. "You're out of control," she told Gordon.

He looked down and seemed to be weeping. "I know," he said.

She had heard of legal and accounting gimmicks that men used to put their assets out of reach of women they left, and now she demanded to know if anything like that was going on. He assured her it wasn't.

The marital trouble of her parents had been what she called "a rattling" in her life: "It taught me not to just accept things the way they are. It made me think, Who is the God I'm supposed to be serving? I had this vision: we're climbing a hill for the Lord, but we're carrying all this baggage we think makes us happy. If only we could let go of it, we could run right up the hill."

About that time she and Bill attended a seminar about the possibility of home schooling for the children. Right after that, they started pulling plugs. Their three television sets went first. Bill had been coming home after work and the television sets would be blaring away with nobody watching. He would shake the stone dust off his boots and plunk himself down to watch the evening news. The news turned into "Wheel of Fortune," then the eight o'clock movie. Pretty soon it was time for bed. Cindy monitored their children's TV viewing carefully and put strict limits on it, yet she was disturbed about what *wasn't* happening when they were watching: the active learning, family discussions, or working on a computer.

The television sets went. Soon afterward, they decided to take the children out of their Christian school and teach them at home. Then Cindy signed up as a "home lobbyist" for Concerned Women for America, a grass-roots Christian Right organization that tried to influence legislation on abortion, pornography, and sex education.

She was not, she said, "going back to the woods." They weren't retiring to Drake's Prairie or, more plausibly, to some hilltop commune in Oregon. She and Bill were thoroughly at home in the East Bay's eclectic culture. They liked to travel and slip away for dinner at a Mexican restaurant, where Bill might drink a beer or even a margarita. She had nothing against that. She had *tried* to like wine, though it always made her dizzy. Yet she was more than a little ambivalent about the values of mainstream California, where so many people lived beyond their means, pursuing their self-interest and gratifying their egos. She couldn't imagine herself doing what her own dad did, spending $30,000 on a fast sports car or driving a

Mercedes as even her frugal mother did. She didn't believe in a vow of poverty—she and Bill were getting income from properties they rented out—but she plainly had her Grandfather Oca Tatham's appreciation of simplicity and authenticity. She shared Oca's determination not to be overwhelmed by California. "We live in the world," she said, "but there are parts of the world that are out of control. We reached the point where we asked ourselves, 'Is this the way we want to live?' "

Pulling plugs was Cindy's method for resolving the dilemma faced by her generation of Tathams: how to be a Tatham on one's own terms. Tathamism—a kind of tacit assumption of family loyalty, religious conviction, self-sufficiency, and individualism—was a given; the family did not breed the kind of outright rebels who reject or turn away from the values of their parents and family. Yet all the cousins were groping for their own style. For the grandchildren of Oca and Ruby, the quest seemed more difficult than it had for their parents. Tathams were becoming dispersed through the culture of California. Their parents had married men or women from the same Pentecostal or Okie background, but third-generation Tathams were marrying Catholics, Italian Americans, Californians. Billy's first wife had been Catholic; Cindy's kid sister Lisa would soon marry a man of Italian heritage, as would Bill and Earline's daughter, Renee.

At the same time, being a third-generation Tatham in California was to straddle a crevice that got wider and wider and a footing that got more and more precarious. The old legalisms, the code that had guided their grandparents, seemed moribund, even silly, to middle-class kids growing up in mainstream California. Yet what was to take its place? The more the family's will and inclination to enforce the old absolutes and certainties weakened, the more necessary it was for "Tatham values" to be rediscovered, reinterpreted, and expressed voluntarily. The pressures and tensions for the grandchildren were complex and ambiguous.

For Mike Tatham, the question was how to reconcile the ambitious, moralistic, striving Tatham part of his nature with the caring and compassionate qualities of his Graves grandfather. Mike had punched all the right tickets, following his older brother Billy to law school at Pepperdine University, and then, in 1984, to a large law firm in Fresno. He was on his way to making partner. But he reserved a corner of his heart for Granpa Graves, an ordinary working man and farmer whose greatest pleasure in life was to take his grandchildren fishing in the California Aqueduct. Granpa Graves was a man without an agenda, or a game plan for getting ahead; yet Granpa Graves—and Ruby Tatham, for that matter—had priorities that Mike admired. They never gave in to the rat race, it seemed to Mike. Brooding privately about the 1972 shooting tragedy, Mike felt pulled toward the values and spontaneous generosity of Ruby and Granpa Graves, and when both died within a few months of each other in 1982, he felt as if "something had been pulled from my stomach." What was appropriate for a Tatham? None of the cousins were morally condemning of beer or wine drinking. But for moralists like Bill and Earline, there was no compromising on the issue, and the drinking question became a source of generational tension.

Mike's new in-laws were strong Christians; but their religious values did not prevent his father-in-law from enjoying a cool beer after a day's work, and Mike enjoyed one now and then too. Gently but firmly, Mike's wife, Denise, urged him to begin a journey of self-discovery, in order to confront questions far more fundamental than whether to drink. The power and wealth of his parents was seductive. But whose rules should he follow? Was there any "one" rule that was right? What did it do for his integrity to hide beer if older Tathams were visiting, or to choose a Fresno restaurant where no older Tatham was likely to go to when he and Denise went out for dinner and perhaps a glass of wine? He asked himself, If you accept Christ, does that mean that if you drink you die? And why, if God is full of Grace? Character and faith were involved in the answers to such questions, it seemed to him.

What was a suitable role for a modern Tatham *woman*? In the older generation, Ruby had run stores, Brenda was an insurance agent, and Cindy's mother had been an independent travel agent for nearly a decade. Staying home was still an acceptable choice for Tatham women to make, but not many in the third generation were making it. Gina, Cindy's next-youngest sister, had an accounting degree and was helping to manage a small Bay Area computer company. A courageous young woman who had faced one operation after another to correct spinal and neck problems, Gina didn't begrudge her dad his pricey sports cars. On the contrary, she retained fun-filled memories of being his secret accomplice on a visit to a Porsche plant in Europe when she had snapped unauthorized pictures inside the factory and not been caught. Her youngest sister, Lisa, who had a 4.0 grade point average at San Leandro High School, was doing research at Stanford. Her cousin Renee, an accounting major, had been on the dean's list and a tennis star at Fresno State, rolling up a school record for the most wins for a woman. In the summer of 1987 she had worked in the Washington office of Congressman Tony Coelho. In Fresno, Brenda and Jerry English's daughter, Kelly, was California Bowl queen, with the pleasant duty of reigning over the Fresno State Bulldogs' biggest game of the year. She planned to go to college. Gerald and Cora's daughter, Caprice, worked at the Bank of America—she and her husband used day care after her first child was born. Patricia, the oldest of Dick and Grace's six daughters, was getting a job driving a Federal Express truck hundreds of miles over the Arizona desert. Donna, now separated from her husband, had headed off to college in Eureka with her three children to study biology and water quality. She wanted to "save the water in the West." Tatham women were also shaping their own individual responses to the sexual revolution: many of the granddaughters vowed to remain virgins until marriage, but at least one of the divorced granddaughters was living with a boyfriend.

As for the men, Billy Tatham was running a football team, and Mike would soon make partner. Mark and Jeremy, Gerald and Cora's boys, were still in school or college, and their son-in-law, Rebekah's husband, Jim Moriarty, was torn between a career in the ministry and one in business. In the fall of 1987, he was driving a potato-chip truck while Rebekah finished up her courses at Bethany Bible College.

Cindy did not condemn the choices being made in the family, but she questioned whether they were fully consonant with the religious values she had always believed the Tathams stood for. It seemed to her that too many friends and relatives were caught up in a rat race, working too many hours and buying expensive homes that saddled them with mortgage payments for the rest of their lives. Cindy could understand why a widowed friend left her young children in an after-school program while she studied for the accounting degree that would enable her to support them, but she was skeptical of many women's claims that they had to work.

Once she had been close to Billy; now that he was so heavily involved with football she had little to talk to him about when they met on holiday trips to Fresno. It seemed to Cindy, from the pain and heartache that so many of her cousins had suffered through, that the family was in danger of drifting away from God. She wasn't inclined to blame what was happening in the family on the Devil. In her view, it was more a matter of choice, of free will.

She did not believe she was making a "sacrifice" staying home with her children, but she knew the risks. To choose to teach one's children at home was to receive a very quick education about the power of government. Under California truancy laws the legal status of home-schooling families was ambiguous. But the risks, she thought, were worth taking for the sake of family self-sufficiency and independence.

Born in Fresno in 1956, Cindy, by her own account, had always been "a straight arrow." Doris and Gordon were very strict parents, and Doris taught her thrifty Tatham ways. She was allowed to attend the senior prom, but not weekly dances. Of the three daughters, she was the one whose life centered most closely around church. She accepted the Lord in kindergarten and was nine when she first spoke in tongues at Valley Christian Center. She felt "as if the Holy Spirit came over me and I felt I didn't know what I was saying. It just happened. It was a really neat experience. I felt close to the Lord at that time. But it wasn't like I was scared or anything." Afterward she periodically would speak in tongues. She could not imagine herself backsliding. Though unfamiliar with John Wesley and the doctrine of entire sanctification, her beliefs seemed redolent of Wesleyan certitude and purity. "Truly in my heart my desire is to serve the Lord," she said. "I can't imagine something happening to make me feel differently."

She met Bill Critchfield at Neighborhood Church. It was as if they had been drawn together by the music of an unseen harp. The Critchfields and the Tathams had remarkably similar family stories, but neither Cindy nor Bill knew it. Bill's father had followed his father from Missouri to California and eventually become an Assemblies of God preacher. When Howard Critchfield cooled on the ministry, he drifted into the real-estate business in the East Bay, accumulating dozens of rental properties and doing very well. Yet to him, the Weavers were different: they were the rich folk on the hill with the expensive foreign automobiles. "Cindy's not like us, she's not our type of people," he cautioned his son. He did not then know the story of how Cindy's grandfather had come out to California in 1934 in a battered Chevy truck loaded with poverty-stricken relatives and friends.

For his part, Gordon Weaver gave the young Critchfield what Bill jestingly called "the full storybook deal: What-are-you-going-to-do-with-your-life? And-how-much-are-you-earning? And-where-do-you-plan-to-live?" Gordon set up strict guidelines of how much his would-be son-in-law would have to earn before he would consent to his marrying his daughter: $1,500 a month. Bill, who had a real-estate license, passed the test. They were wed in 1976.

Soon after that, Cindy left her job as a dental assistant because of a health problem. Instead of returning to work, she volunteered at Neighborhood Church and with the Campus Crusade's "Here's Life America" evangelism program. While Bill worked in real estate—he had bought several properties from his dad and had refinanced them as prices shot up in order to buy several more—Cindy blanketed parts of Oakland with bumper stickers and billboards carrying Christian slogans.

The couple had big plans when they moved to San Diego in 1978. Bill had sold several properties, and they intended to use the proceeds to purchase a house and convert it into a residential home for the elderly. But this turned out to be a stressful project. Bill was having a difficult time in the business, and Cindy was having a difficult first pregnancy. The upshot was that Bill quit and put in for a forty-hour-a-week job at the ironworkers' union. It was three months before the job came through. Cindy looked back on that time, with so little money coming in, as one of the most exciting of her life. She kept a roaming Tatham eye out for bargains and bought everything on sale. "We were budgeted out," she said. "We had to rely on the Lord. . . . It was the Lord feeding the birds! One of the happiest times."

They came home to Oakland after three years. Bill, a big friendly man who took the world as he found it, got an ironworking job. The ironworkers were a tough lot: many of them had been in jail, and few knew that Bill was an evangelical Christian who taught Bible to his kids after work and almost never voted the "union ticket" at election time. Bill wasn't one to wear badges. When they asked him why he didn't swear, he answered that it was not his style. He did not share the joints that were sometimes passed around, but he would drink a beer after work with the blacks and Hispanics. They all earned good wages fastening fourteen-ton concrete or polished granite slabs onto the front of steel buildings. The hours left Bill time for the family.

Cindy began to give serious thought to teaching the kids at home after the family had gone on a low-budget trip to Europe in January 1986. Back at his Christian school, Brent had quickly caught up with the several weeks of studies he had missed, and Cindy wondered, What were they spending $249 a month for?

As a nonworking mother, she had the time to examine the educational options and she didn't much like them. At the public school, a single troublesome student disrupted a class she visited, and Brent was ahead of most of the children in his age group. Bill wanted to "go Christian," so in the fall of 1984 they had enrolled Brent in Redwood Christian School, where he quickly learned to read and was good in sums. But Cindy found the class "kind of wild." The school responded to discipline problems by canceling field trips and establishing what Cindy considered to be a rigid, competitive atmosphere: "You push them instead of being concerned about them. If they blow a play in football you yell at them instead of being concerned about how are they feeling now. They're already feeling like a fool out there."

The summer after the European trip, she and Bill attended Greg Harris's Christian Home School Workshop. Cindy was excited to learn that thousands of rural Americans had once educated themselves at home through correspondence courses—though of course Cindy and Bill, living in the middle of a great metropolis with many different schools to choose from, had very different motives. Harris said that home schooling produced more independent, "self-starting" children. Academic results were, he said, slightly above the norms for children in regular schools, in some cases dramatically better. Still, Harris made clear, home schooling was controversial: only about 200,000 families in the United States educated their children at home, almost all of them evangelical Christians. State governments had a legitimate concern about the quality of education the parents were providing. On the other hand, the public school systems often had less high-minded reasons for their hostility—declining enrollments meant less federal and state aid. In some states truancy laws were used to impose harsh penalties. In Alabama, several home-schooled children had been taken into state custody. A home-schooling family had been jailed in Idaho. In New York and Pennsylvania, where politically powerful educational bureaucracies wielded influence, the laws were most restrictive and home-schooling parents were required to obtain formal approval from local school superintendents. In New York, home schoolers were charged with child abuse rather than truancy, and there had been attempts by state welfare workers to seize children.

California law left home schoolers in a legal limbo. It allowed unregulated private schools but required teachers who did private "tutoring" to be certified. In 1986, the district attorney in Santa Barbara charged two home-schooling families with truancy, but a judge dismissed both cases. School Superintendent William Honig had said he was not against home schooling, and the Hayward school district truant officer had indicated he wouldn't make an issue of it. But Cindy feared the Alameda County school superintendent might carry out a threat to prosecute.

Cindy came from a family steeped in the intense individualism of a religious "out" group in which there was no shame in holding unconventional views. But even relatives who were accustomed to Cindy's independent streak were of different minds about her plans. Jerry English, her school-principal uncle-in-law in Fresno, had suggested it as a possibility; Doris and the Critchfields were supportive; and the idea was recommended on the popular religious radio program "Focus on the Family." But Gordon had reservations, and others suggested it was a mistake to "overprotect" the children. "It's a dog-eat-dog world out there, and the sooner they learn how to deal with it the better," a business friend of her dad's told Cindy. Cindy didn't agree with that kind of thinking at all. For heaven's sake, she said, they were talking about small children.

Cindy withdrew Brent from Redwood Christian School in the fall of 1986. She chose textbooks and a curriculum for him that she hoped would balance religious teaching with solid academic instruction. For science, social studies, and "Bible truths," she chose books published by Bob Jones University Press, which was associated with the fundamentalist college in Greenville, South Carolina. Scattered through these texts were comments and omissions that would have raised eyebrows in public schools. (The social studies textbook described Stonewall Jackson accurately—but perhaps incompletely—as a "Christian general" and characterized South Africa as a "beautiful country" while making no mention of its racial problems. It used Romans 13:1—"the powers that be are ordained of God"—as part of a lesson on civic obligations and cited other Biblical passages to define town government.) But whatever the drawbacks of the Bob Jones books, Cindy thought they approached learning more from a "thinking standpoint" than other Christian textbooks, and they helped the children achieve good test results. Cindy also selected a mainstream reading textbook published by William Morrow, *The Writing Road to Reading*, whose author, Romalda Bishop Spaulding, had a master's degree from Columbia University, and a geography book and a speller published by other commercial houses.

In June 1987 she nervously administered the Iowa Test in math, spelling, reading comprehension, and language skills to Brent and Janeé. Like many home-school mothers, she worried that the children might be falling behind, and as they worked away she felt butterflies in her stomach. But the results were reassuring: both children came out near the top.

Cindy rejected the notion that she was "sheltering" the children from dissident opinions. Quite the contrary, she insisted, she went out of her way to expose them to "both sides" of current topics: "By presenting them in the home and talking about it and working through with the kids and hearing their questions—that's an important part of family life. We try to let them know what's happening and not shelter them from what's happening. There's some stuff that they shouldn't hear, that they're not ready for. But we have candid discussions, even talk about abortion in our house. I think on the whole more issues should be taken up in the home. Obviously, things are being discussed in the classrooms."

She and other parents organized a spate of extracurricular activities. Brent was on the Castro Valley Soccer Club team. One night a week he went to Christian Service Clubs, a kind of Christian Boy Scouts. Janeé was in the Pioneer Girls. Cindy and other local home-school mothers organized trips and tours.

There had been only five other home-schooling families close by when Cindy started, but as the 1986–1987 school year progressed, the number grew and the families developed a special solidarity. But Cindy's decision cost her several friends who, she figured, were threatened by the Critchfields becoming "too radical." Some felt "condemned" by Cindy's choice, she admitted. This mystified and hurt her, but she was prepared to live with it. "We didn't preach to anybody," she said. "Hopefully, we're enough of a light so that if someone isn't being a good Christian they'll feel uncomfortable enough to make changes in their own lives."

Cindy admired the commitment of the other home-school women. One of the other women, a divorcee, had to drive a truck all day to support the family, yet found the energy to give the children their lesson when she got home. Demanding as it was, there were many side benefits. Their time was flexible. If the opportunity arose, they could take off for a trip anytime they wanted. During the spring and summer, the whole family got up at five o'clock and held school until ten. The rest of the day was free.

PULLING OUT the plugs coincided with other steps. For one thing, Cindy was back in the Assemblies of God Church, and had brought

Bill along with her. It had happened during their years in San Diego. She had gone one Sunday with her Aunt Renee, who had been in search of a good church herself. Cindy hadn't been to a Pentecostal church for years, but the moment she walked in, she felt at home. Worship was freer and more inspirational than at Neighborhood and had what she called a "sweet spirit." Some slipped into speaking in tongues. Cindy met former Lutherans, Catholics, Mormons, and people from families who had never attended church.

She was nervous about aspects of the charismatic services that might make Bill ill at ease, and sure enough, the first time she took him, a woman spoke in tongues. Cindy glanced sidewise at her husband, fearful that he would "freak out." But he seemed interested. "Wow!" he exclaimed as they left the service and went right along with her after that.

Back in the Bay area, they began attending Sequoyah Community Church. It was Assemblies of God, but Cindy was surprised to discover that articles from *Psychology Today* were sometimes discussed at Sunday school. "There's no hope in psychology," she said. "The hope's in the Lord." A church counselor had suggested to at least one couple that Cindy knew of that divorce might be an option. And in 1986 the church was thinking of letting divorced people serve on the deacon board. Eventually, she and Bill moved to another Pentecostal church and left her parents at Sequoyah.

The changes Cindy was making in her life spilled over into politics. As it happened, in the 1980s home schooling became one of the small but important causes of the Christian Right. An educational issue—the threat from Washington to remove the tax exemption for all-white Christian schools—had mobilized the religious community politically in the previous decade. Michael Farris (who subsequently founded a group called the Home School Legal Defense Association) once was executive director of the Moral Majority. He served as the lead attorney in the "Nebraska 7" case, in which seven fathers were jailed for sending their children to a church school that refused to obtain state certification. Raymond Moore, author of a number of books on home schooling, was a member of the Council for National Policy, a conservative umbrella organization of wealthy businessmen, New Right activists, and ministers.

Cindy was comfortable working for political causes. Political ideas and social issues had always been subjects of discussion around the Weaver home, and Cindy shared her parents' political conservatism. She had gone door to door with her mother in the Goldwater presi-

dential campaign when she was only eight years old and had read
John Birch Society materials that her mother had brought home
when Doris was fighting the battle against School Superintendent
Foster in the 1960s. At public school Cindy had never been afraid to
be associated with unpopular positions. She wrote papers and gave
speeches criticizing the "sex-ed fiasco" and the "sensitivity movement." And she did not agree with her mother's support of the
Supreme Court decision banning prayer in the schools. It had gotten
so that the word "Christmas" could not be used in public schools, but,
Bill Critchfield said gloomily, "They let you have meditation in PE
class and talk about getting in touch with your 'spirit guide.' " The
separation of church and state, Cindy believed, was central to America's decline. "You can't pull God out of things; that's the foundation
on which our country was set up. . . . We're not a Buddhist nation.
They [chose to] come to America."

By 1986, it seemed to many in the New Right that there was a
major disconnection between the conservative social agenda to which
President Reagan paid lip service and the overall mood spawned by
his free-market economic policies. The two Reagan administrations
lauded consumerism, accumulation of wealth, and a competitive,
predatory, unregulated business environment. The President might
talk about family, but Reaganomics encouraged acquisitive, hypercompetitive behavior that worked against the family. A generation of
young people felt pressured to buy bigger houses than they could
afford and rack up more credit card charges than they could pay off,
while the government itself built up a monumental public debt that
would take generations to clear. It was hard to see what was "pro-
family" about that. The moral and economic climate of the 1980s fell
short of what Cindy hoped for America. America, she believed, had
"strayed from Christian self-government. Everything moves out from
that. It comes back to having individuals who can govern *themselves*
first." She favored a saner, more democratic politics, a new politics
that would be far more morally and economically responsible.

President Reagan himself was too much an optimist to accept the
Christian Right's gloomy assessment of America's moral decline. To
Reagan, America was not declining; it was "number one." Yet Cindy
did not blame Reagan for the shortcomings of American politics and
society. Congress, Democrats, the media, and the bureaucracy were
equally to blame if not more so, she believed. "You can't pin this on
one person," she said.

While Cindy was exploring the educational options in 1986, Doris was attending several meetings at Neighborhood Church of an organization called Concerned Women for America. Doris considered CWA to be "up on things" and "interested in the curriculum that's being presented as far as humanism and that sort of thing." Bill's sister was on the local CWA committee and was in charge of keeping track of legislative issues.

CWA had been founded in 1979 by Beverly LaHaye, wife of a Baptist minister named Tim LaHaye who was also a leading player in the emerging coalition of Christian Right groups. CWA, which doubled in size every year, had nearly 400,000 members in 1986. It was interdenominational but most of the members were evangelical Protestants, and it was fast overtaking the liberal National Organization for Women (NOW) as the largest women's action group in the nation, appealing as it did to the many women who were worried about America's moral drift. It emphasized lobbying—a brochure showed how every woman could become a lobbyist without ever leaving her home.

Cindy had attended one of the first CWA meetings in San Diego in 1979, where Beverly LaHaye and Elizabeth Dole, the wife of Kansas Senator Robert Dole, spoke about alternatives to feminism. Cindy came away with a clear message: "We didn't have to go out and burn our bras and say we hated men. We could band together and have another voice, and that other voice didn't have to be the National Organization for Women."

CWA's slogan was "Come Save America." But CWA appeared indifferent to a great many of the concerns generally voiced about the state of the nation. CWA did not take stands on such public issues as racism, poverty, the environment, the exploding federal deficit, or the country's declining economic competitiveness, all of which arguably had a deep effect on the fortunes of the American family. Cindy did not see much connection between, say, environmentalism and her beliefs. Environmentalism and the pro-family movement shared a concern that the increasingly materialistic values in the society were harmful. But it was hard for Cindy to make that link. In Cindy's view the environmentalists were off base from a Biblical standpoint and their causes were puzzling. Man, she said, was "above the whales." God had created the earth for man to use; while she was willing to consider carefully the arguments of those who, for example, were trying to save California's giant redwoods, she was skeptical. She wanted to conserve what God had put in the womb, and environmentalists wanted to conserve what God had put on earth.

Nor could she make common cause with those who were trying to make American corporations more responsive to the needs of working families. She opposed the notion of federal laws requiring employers to guarantee leaves for working mothers. "I'm for mothers staying home with their children," she said.

CWA's agenda, however, fit her more focused concerns. Most of what CWA wanted was to safeguard and buttress the authority of the family. CWA was opposed to the Equal Rights Amendment, pornography, abortion, and sex-education courses in the schools that promoted birth control rather than abstinence. And it wanted to enlist government in its cause, an impulse among religious groups that was as old as America. Specifically, CWA believed that "government should intervene and take a stand on human life," according to a CWA representative.

As the Christian Right's emphasis on abortion grew, Cindy's interest increased. To Cindy, abortion was not a moral issue but a criminal one. "Just like I don't see the killing of the Jews as moral. That was criminal, too." She rejected the argument in favor of a woman's right to have an abortion as saying, "I'm all-important. They're saying, 'I'm going to get rid of this life because it's inconvenient.' But you can't just turn your back on it."

The abortion question seemed to Cindy to be at the very core of the American crisis. She remembered the childhood visits to Cora "Old Granma" Tatham in Delano, when Cora would relate how she had nursed her tiny, premature baby Cleo in a makeshift incubator made from a shoe box. Or perhaps it was Cindy's own sense of motherhood deepening as she took care of her baby daughter, Janeé, who had recovered from a life-threatening blood disease. She was convinced that Janeé's life was a miracle wrought by Brent's intense prayers.

The antiabortion movement, launched in a time that seemed to celebrate selfishness, hedonism, and greed, did make the effort to call Americans back to more responsible, accountable, and caring ways about children, whatever else its critics thought of it. Raising children required sacrifice, commitment, a generous heart—old American qualities that seemed absent from the 1980s climate of ego gratification, wealth accumulation, and self-fulfillment. Against the campaigns to broaden rights of all kinds, the pro-life forces were saying that with rights came responsibilities. Like no other cause, it united Catholics and Protestants, an essential requirement for strategists of the New Right. And once Catholic activists had awakened conservative Protestants to the issue in the late 1970s, the antiabortion crusade took off, mobilizing new voters and broadening the base of Reagan's constituency.

CWA could not take direct action to change the 1973 *Roe* v. *Wade* Supreme Court decision, which had protected a woman's right to an abortion. But the issue was nevertheless an effective drawing card for CWA membership, and CWA fought around the edges, highlighting candidates' positions on the question and getting active on matters such as requiring doctors and clinics to give parental notification when minors intended to abort their pregnancies.

Cindy began to go to CWA meetings in the fall of 1986, in the weeks before the midterm elections. Bill often came along, and was one of the few men attending. His political views were highly individualistic. He was a union man and a Republican, an evangelical Christian who drank beer and took a dim view of television evangelists who used scare tactics to raise money. He believed there was a place for government welfare administered to the truly needy, but it annoyed him to see Cadillacs pulling up in front of the food stamp distribution office near where he lived. Bill drove a van. And he knew of tenants receiving federal rent supplements who did not report their outside income. Yet a laid-off ironworker he knew had been too proud to seek public assistance when his unemployment checks stopped. The crew took up a collection for him.

At the CWA meetings, congressional and state candidates showed up, and during the 1986 campaign Christian Voice's "scorecard" on candidates was passed out. It reported that Los Angeles mayor Tom Bradley, who was running against Governor George Deukmejian, "supports homosexual life-style." Rose Bird, campaigning for reelection as California's chief justice, "opposes tough sentencing of repeat sex offenders," and Congressman Ed Zschau, a moderate Republican running against incumbent Democratic senator Alan Cranston, "supports spread of pornography."

Of more interest to Cindy was the local chapter of CWA's lobbying on local and state issues. She wrote to state legislators to protest school health clinics, which dispensed sexual information, and to oppose a bill prohibiting job discrimination based on sexual orientation and another to protect the jobs of persons with AIDS. CWA had targeted Assembly Bill 4328, which proposed three school-based health clinics from which students could be referred to doctors, abortion clinics, or Planned Parenthood without telling their parents. To CWA, these clinics typified the state's effort to undermine family authority and promote the idea that teenage sexual activity was inevitable. Cindy wrote to several legislators opposing the bill. It passed. But on October 30, a few days before the elections, Governor Deukmejian vetoed it.

Bill and Cindy also opposed enactment of a California statehouse perennial, Assembly Bill 1, which proposed to give homosexuals the same job protection as other minorities. It had passed both houses of the state legislature but been vetoed by Deukmejian in 1984. CWA opposed this "employment preference" measure for gays and also opposed several bills which, it contended, would give AIDS victims some of the same job protection as the handicapped. Bill Critchfield fantasized that a black welder with AIDS would soon be the best-protected worker in the state of California.

Sex education was one of the CWA's main preoccupations. Its strategy was to oppose statewide standards and to keep decisions on sex education at the local level, where parental and community lobbying was most effective. In 1987, the legislature passed a bill requiring the Departments of Education and Health Services to distribute currently available AIDS information to junior and senior high schools throughout California, but it also required the schools using the materials to send written notices to parents and to excuse students whose parents objected to the instruction. Nevertheless, CWA came down hard against it. Cindy and others wrote the governor urging that he veto the measure. He did so in September of that year.

Alameda County instituted its own AIDS education program during the 1986–1987 school year, but there was soon a battle over a film prepared in conjunction with it called *AIDS, Sex and Drugs*. Some parents, including ones who had nothing to do with CWA, objected to the film, arguing forcefully that it did not promote sexual abstinence and could be perceived as being "pro-homosexual." As a result, three editorial changes were made: a scene in which three girls were discussing sex and the importance of condoms was cut; an emotional scene showing a boy talking about his older brother, an AIDS victim, was deleted; and a scene promoting abstinence was added. It was a small but important victory.

There was additional controversy, and rumor, when word spread that a hot-line number on the packet of educational materials handed out to instructors connected callers to the San Francisco AIDS Foundation rather than to a school official. At Cindy's CWA chapter the word was that the schools had passed out a number for students to get in touch with "homosexual organizations."

Cindy did not see the film and had no children in the public schools, but she was convinced from all she had heard that the public schools were once again trying to promote the theme that sexual activity is okay for teenagers. The message, she believed, was: "If you are mature you are sexually active, so to be safe, use a condom." CWA responded by circulating a video that suggested abstinence was the best way.

That same fall of 1987, in Washington, the Senate Judiciary Committee, after days of testy hearings, rejected President Reagan's nomination of Robert Bork to the Supreme Court. CWA was unprepared for the intensity of the attacks on Bork and his position on abortion, and it was slow to respond. Still, Cindy sent handwritten letters to every member of the Senate Judiciary Committee; time-consuming as it was, she had been told that the handwritten notes carried more weight. The other CWA instruction was "No insults."

Bork's defeat left Cindy feeling bitter: "I felt like there were a lot of people who sat up there on their high horse. I just felt that those who were on the panel were doing a lot of mudslinging. Bork was painted as being a real fanatic who wouldn't give a viewpoint to the Constitution."

Soon after Cindy telephoned the office of her gynecologist. "Does the doctor perform abortions?" Cindy inquired of his nurse.

He did, she was told.

Cindy thanked her and explained that in that case she planned to find another doctor.

That was not quite as easy as she had expected. The "women's concerns" department of a local hospital was little help, and the person she spoke to seemed taken aback by her question. Eventually, she did find the kind of doctor she was looking for. "My waiting room is full of men and women who want children; in all good conscience I can't do abortions," he told Cindy. She wondered if it would be possible to develop a nationwide register of doctors who did not perform abortions. It would certainly dramatize the issue and might put some economic pressure on abortionist doctors.

Operation Rescue, the antiabortion group, was just beginning to organize the sit-ins and protests that would draw big headlines over the next years. But she and Bill decided against joining in an action aainst a Bay area abortion clinic. A representative had come to a CWA meeting and given out a telephone number, and he promised that the group did not use violence, only nonviolence borrowed from the civil rights movement. Cindy endorsed what Operation Rescue was doing and kept an open mind, but Bill was reluctant to become involved in a situation that might turn violent.

A FEW DAYS after the gray November day in Cindy's home-school classroom, the whole Weaver family journeyed to Fresno to celebrate Thanksgiving. Four generations of the extended Tatham clan gathered in a big room at Peoples Church. Along with relatives came in-laws and friends, until some seventy-five people were present. The theme was Okie. Bill showed up driving a 1934 Ford V-8 with spoke wheels that he'd bought from a dealer in the mountains. Somebody asked him when he planned to move into a tank house.

Oca, recently recovered from heart bypass surgery, seemed hail and hearty as ever, trading stories about famous Oklahoma outlaws with Jerry English's father-in-law, down from Oregon for the occasion. "A clean group of people," he said, sitting down for his turkey with all the trimmings. "Not one of 'em perfect. But clean people." Afterward the younger crowd adjourned for basketball and older folks carried on at Brenda and Jerry's place, where Brenda was at the piano and a roomful of Tathams, friends, and relatives sang one Gospel song after another.

The high point for Doris was the blessing of the food at the big turkey dinner at Peoples Church. Gordon had been selected to say the words. It was the family's way of letting him know that he still had his honored place among them. The moment spoke of healing. Indeed, the Weavers' marriage was on the mend, though Doris and Gordon were still taking things a day at a time. For the first time in a long while Doris seemed optimistic: they had plans for Christmas that Gordon would cook an English meal, with Yorkshire pudding. And in January they would celebrate their thirty-fifth wedding anniversary by sneaking away to a small hotel in San Francisco and playing tourist for a day, as they had often done in Europe. They even planned to take a Gray Line tour, disappearing anonymously in the crowds of out-of-town visitors.

Gina found that she was "looking up to my parents more now than ever. It takes a long time to work out all the problems of thirty-five years. They're the reason I can say, Yes, I would want to get married again. Because it can work. Look how they've handled it. They're happier now today, my mom and dad. They're different people. So it can happen. It's a real victory for them. I look at the rest of their lives together and think how fantastic it will be. And that's what I want."

Doris felt she could plan things again without some crisis interfering. It had been worth it. "If I had a chance to talk about this," she said, "I'd say, 'Don't dump your marriage.'

"We all like the fairy-tale story that ends when they all live happily ever after. It's possible. But marriage takes two to have that happy ending. I never gave up, except for about three days once, when I'd gotten worn down to where I needed some strength to fight on. I thought okay, I just went into neutral, and I decided, I can't fight. I just sort of went with the flow. But then we had a conversation and decided I wasn't going to give up.

"It was painful. In my case the simplest thing would have been to give up. People were telling me to give up, even church counselors. But I wanted to do what's right scripturally. The Lord promises He'll never leave you or forsake you. And I felt the only way to win was to come out with my family intact. Gordon is glad I hung in there. The family is still intact, and I'm a witness that it can be done. If you have an anchor you can sort of wait it out."

Cindy was feeling much better about her father, too. "It was a neat day when I could finally write my dad a letter on Father's Day. I could finally see that God had used it all. I was thankful for the outcome, that my parents were still together and that I have a deeper relationship with God."

That fall the Weavers' youngest daughter, Lisa, was married at a rooftop wedding ceremony and reception at the Kaiser Convention Center in downtown Oakland, "neutral" turf since the groom was Catholic. Gordon and Doris took dance lessons, and so did Cindy and Bill, determined finally to break with the old legalisms. But at the last minute, Gordon decided not to dance. "I know your dad's been unhappy with me for a long time," he explained. Doris was taken aback; she had made up her mind that she wasn't going to let her dad do this number on her this time. But he did anyway, without even trying!

Chapter Twenty-Two

Power Shift

THE POLITICAL EDUCATION OF Bill Tatham began when he was still a small-time nursing home operator. The Medicaid and Medicare legislation that helped finance the rapid expansion of the nursing-home industry was pending in Congress in 1965 when Bill got a call at home. The man on the phone was from the office of Congressman Wilbur Mills, the House Ways and Means Committee chairman who was engineering passage of the legislation. Based on the number of beds in Bill's nursing-home facilities, the caller said, Mills was counting on him for a political contribution in a specific amount. Mills was a Democrat and Bill was a Republican, but Bill wanted the law. He wrote the check.

From then on Bill understood that politics was more than a clash of ideologies. On another level it was just one more skill that a businessman needed to acquire.

Bill had the ancestral Tatham knack for hooking up with useful people. During Reagan's years as governor of California, he became acquainted with key evangelical Christians in the administration, including Herbert Ellingwood, a Yale graduate and a member of the Assemblies of God. Ellingwood kept in touch with the evangelical community while serving as Reagan's legal-affairs adviser and deputy attorney general, and he stayed on in the state administration after Democrat Jerry Brown became governor, working for the Republican attorney general, Evelle Younger.

Bill needed friends in Sacramento. His acquisition of the Hy-Lond chain in the mid-1970s had made him one of the largest nursing-home operators in California and a natural target of the Brown administration's campaign to clean up the nursing care business. The Democrats were pushing for tighter financial and regulatory controls, and Bill and Clyde Dahlinger often found themselves at odds with the authorities in Sacramento. Most of the pressure came from the Department of Health, but the attorney general's office also got involved. On a number of occasions, Bill said, he took his case to Ellingwood. Ellingwood couldn't call off the Health Department dogs, but, "We got a fair hearing as a result of the connection. Our side of the story got around in the attorney general's office. I was glad that I knew him, that there was a guy in Sacramento who could take our phone calls."

Bill was also being introduced to the national political scene through football. One day in the 1970s he went to Mississippi to see the late senator Jim Eastland on the veranda of his home. Eastland, a Democrat, was chairman of the Senate Judiciary Committee, which had considerable leverage over professional sports monopolies—like the NFL—through the antitrust laws it wrote, and this was at the time when Bill and his partners were seeking an NFL franchise for their Memphis Grizzlies.

The senator had been approached through cotton. Mississippi is a big cotton state, but Memphis is the center of the Southern cotton trade. Cotton's main man in Washington was Lou Barringer, of the L. T. Barringer cotton brokerage company of Memphis, a legendary figure who spent a good deal of every year living in a hotel in Washington and helping to write farm laws. Through Memphis friends, Bill met Barringer, who put him in touch with Eastland.

Bill went over to Eastland's place with his attorney and friend Gary Kerkorian. They drove down an old country road until they arrived at a large white mansion surrounded by huge live oak trees. The courtly senator beckoned them onto the veranda. The talk meandered over football and politics, and Bill recalled Eastland eloquently describing the Democratic Party's technique for getting out the black vote. At one point Eastland seemed to be weeping as he recounted the death of the slain civil rights leader Medgar Evers—against whose cause Eastland had once resolutely fought. But Bill couldn't be sure. Perhaps, he thought, the old man was just senile. After a while, they adjourned to a country club for dinner. Bill noticed that the waiters were all black. The NFL never did expand to Memphis, and Bill never found out whether Eastland lifted a finger on the city's behalf. Still, it was a day he wouldn't forget.

It helped persuade him that not all Democrats were like Jerry Brown. Democrats, Bill discovered, could often be more effective than Republicans at getting things done, especially in a Congress controlled by Democrats year after year. One Democrat whom Bill came to like was the California congressman Tony Coelho. Ideologically, they could not have been further apart—Coelho took liberal positions on issues like welfare and abortion—yet Bill identified with Coelho on a number of different levels. He sized up Coelho as a fellow outsider who was storming the ramparts of money, power, and fame from a base in the valley. And both of them were part of the generational and cultural power shift moving beneath the surface of America.

Tony and Bill shared an earthy, immigrant kind of background in the central valley and a strict religious upbringing. Tony's Portuguese-American father was a dairy farmer and a Catholic with traditional values. Tony's epilepsy had kept him out of the priesthood, so he sought out a political parish instead. In the 1960s he went to work in Washington for Congressman Bernie ("B.F.") Sisk, a powerful member of the Rules Committee. As Sisk's top aide, doing favors for people in the district, Coelho developed useful contacts in both parties.

Sisk quit in 1978, leaving a vacant seat. The Republican candidate was the air force hero and stunt pilot Chris Patterakis, who was something of a celebrity in the valley. But Tony, who decided to make a run for it, had been Sisk's man, and had done favors for hundreds of people. One of his acquaintances was Earl Giacolini, Bill Tatham's pharmacist friend and business partner, who had considerable experience in the politics of the central valley, through his activities as president of the California Pharmacy Association and member of the Sunsweet growers' cooperative. Both groups had funds that gave money to politicians. On trips to Washington and Sacramento, looking after the interests of the pharmacists and his fellow prune producers, he dropped by the offices of key lawmakers such as Sisk.

Bill had met Earl in 1962, when he was just starting out in nursing homes and ranching in Easton, in Sisk's district. Giacolini operated a small pharmacy that sold medicine to Bill's nursing homes. They became friends. Eventually both began attending Peoples Church and got to know the Reverend G. L. Johnson. In 1978, the year Coelho decided to run, Bill and Earl were forming a company together to open additional pharmacies and Earl was on the board of Bill's nursing-home company.

Giacolini arranged a small lunch for Coelho with Johnson and Bill after Coelho attended a service at Peoples Church. Whatever Tony said to persuade a die-hard Republican conservative, it did the job. Bill agreed to allow his name to be put on a list of Republicans for Coelho. In the November election, Coelho won with 60 percent of the vote.

Bill was less favorably inclined toward another Democrat who was running that year in another valley district. Congressman John Krebs from Fresno had been elected as a "Watergate baby" in 1974. A good-government reformer on the Fresno County Board of Supervisors, Krebs made a name for himself standing up to the real-estate developers who had been getting waivers of county requirements for roads, water, and sewer lines during the development boom in the late 1960s. He was supported by a reform organization, the Committee for Responsible Government, which was fighting to put controls on building in rural areas.

In 1978, his Republican opponent was Charles "Chip" Pashayan, whose father had a tire business in Fresno. Pastor Johnson sent Pashayan over to visit Bill Tatham at his new brick and glass building on the corner of Shaw and Fruit avenues. "Take a look at the records of the Board of Supervisors and the Planning Commission when Krebs was there," Bill told Pashayan. "See who was mistreated. That's where you'll get your contributors." Bill gave Pashayan's campaign a thousand dollars. Money also came in from the developers, farmers, and cotton brokers who considered Krebs too close to the liberal action group, National Land for People, then pressing Washington to enforce acreage limitations in the Westlands irrigation district in the western part of Fresno County. That fall Pashayan won an upset victory.

Tony Coelho did not forget Bill's early support when Bill called him in 1980 about a problem he was having bidding on a federal contract to build an IRS annex in Fresno. Bill owned property at Cherry and Jensen avenues, west of Highway 99 and the railroad tracks, but when the General Services Administration drew the boundaries in which the facility was to be located, Bill's property fell outside. In his call to Coelho, Bill noted that his holdings were inside

Tony's district. Bill recalls that he also contacted the black city council member Joe Williams, who represented wards with heavy concentrations of blacks and other minorities near Bill's property. Eventually, GSA readvertised new boundaries that took in Bill's holdings at Cherry and Jensen, and Bill's bid won. It was his first big government contract. That same year, he sent Coelho's campaign a check for five hundred dollars.

Bill stayed in touch with Coelho, and he used his help again several years later when the government threatened to foreclose on a series of Housing and Urban Development loans that Bill had taken over in the 1970s when acquiring some properties. According to Bill, he had done HUD a favor when he had assumed the loans. Many were months overdue, he said, but he quickly paid off the arrearages. But in the 1980s, he, too, fell a few weeks behind. When he did tender past-due payments, HUD officials refused to process them. Bill was tipped off by a local attorney with HUD contacts, who told him the government wanted to make an example of him.

Bill called Coelho after receiving a batch of foreclosure notices, and Coelho soon called Bill back. He had talked to a Fannie Mae supervisor. "Go ahead and send your checks," he said. "And do me a favor: Don't ever make a late payment on a HUD loan again."

In early 1981 Bill found himself in difficulties with the Federal Home Loan Bank Board arising from his purchases of stock in Fresno First Savings and Loan Association. Stockholders who accumulate more than 10 percent of the shares of an S&L are considered a bank holding company, with tax and financial disclosure consequences that Bill wished to avoid. Bill had acquired a stake of just under ten percent in 1978, becoming the largest single shareholder. But in 1979, he said, he was offered an additional forty-five thousand shares by a member of the Hasso family—the same family that had formerly been involved with the Hy-Lond nursing home chain. To avoid a problem, he had the stock placed in a trust for his son Billy. In March 1981, the staff of the Federal Home Loan Bank Board claimed that the purchase exceeded the limits. The Bank Board directed him not to distribute the forty-five thousand shares in the trust without prior written approval. The board also questioned Bill's contention that he had sent a letter notifying it that he was buying the additional stock.

For several months in 1981 the matter became embroiled in the planned sale of Fresno First to a San Diego S&L. The Bank Board's attorneys pressed Bill to turn over the profits on the additional 5 percent of stock to the other shareholders. Bill flew to Washington with a Fresno attorney for meetings and made clear he would fight any order to transfer the profits. But he did offer to sign a consent decree promising not to violate banking laws. On one Washington trip that Bill recalls, he stopped by at the Executive Office Building with his lawyer to see Herb Ellingwood, who was working for the Californian Edwin Meese, deputy counsel to President Reagan. Bill said he mentioned his problem with the Bank Board, but Ellingwood made no offer of help. In October, the Home Loan Bank Board approved the sale of the S&L. The regulatory climate was changing, and the matter died.

AT THE END OF 1984, the Tatham men settled on Phoenix as the new location for their homeless football team. Arizona was football crazy, but the USFL did not win any popularity contests there since Arizonans wanted the NFL, not the upstart USFL. So the arrival of the Outlaws was an irritation to Phoenix's downtown business establishment—utility executives, Republican lawyers and executives, and conservative Democrats.

To reduce pressure from the Arizona delegation in Congress to have the NFL expand to Phoenix, NFL Commissioner Pete Rozelle had not discouraged speculation that an NFL team might move there, and the arrival of a USFL team only seemed to confuse the issue. Phoenix romanced the Philadelphia Eagles, the Baltimore Colts, and the St. Louis Cardinals. Instead, it got the Outlaws. Young Billy Tatham felt as if he had landed in enemy territory. "It was like we were in a foreign country being shot at from all sides," he said.[1]

Yet what the Tathams wanted and what the Phoenix establishment wanted was the same. In the back of every USFL owner's mind was a vision of the Holy Grail: a seat at the NFL table where wealth, fame, and power met.

The Tathams' season in Phoenix in 1985 was a qualified success. The Outlaws, playing at Arizona State's Sun Devil Stadium, compiled a record of eight victories and ten defeats behind the quarterbacking of Doug Williams. Phoenix, unlike Tulsa, was an easy plane hop from Fresno and Los Angeles, and numerous Tathams came to sit in Bill's owner's box and root for the Outlaws. Home games were occasions for exuberant family get-togethers. After the biggest win of the first season in Phoenix, a 41–21 blowout of the Jacksonville Bulls before 34,000 fans, a dozen or so Tathams went off for waffles and ice-cream sundaes at Jerry's, a late-night family restaurant.

There was kidding about the scanty uniforms of the cheerleaders. "We changed the uniforms because of the banker . . . that's how deep our values are," Bill joked. "I bet the banker's a Mormon," he added as an afterthought.

Football politics was a contact sport. In October 1984, the USFL owners had authorized a new lawsuit against the NFL, this time an antitrust action against all twenty-seven NFL teams that sought $1.32 billion in damages. The USFL strategy, as dictated in New York by Donald Trump, seemed clear: to force the NFL into a merger that would bring as many as eight USFL teams into the NFL. When the USFL hired Harry Usher as its new commissioner in January 1985, his contract included bonuses if a merger was achieved.[2]

The USFL had a case. Armed with exemptions from antitrust laws provided by legislation, the NFL had concluded contracts with all three television networks for Sunday, Monday night, and Super Bowl coverage, giving it leverage over any network that might become too friendly with the USFL. Meanwhile it continued to stonewall on the promises it had made in 1977 to expand. Since no sports league could survive without television revenues, the USFL was in trouble. ABC had televised its play-offs in 1983 and 1984, but it backed off in 1985, prompting a lawsuit that produced a meager $2 million settlement. At the same time, the new NFL schedule reserved a series of excellent matchups in major markets for ABC's Monday night football program in the fall of 1985.

Whatever the merits of its new case, the USFL strategy for applying pressure on the NFL to expand did not work. The NFL refused to negotiate on the matter and the suit went to trial. On July 29, 1986, a New York jury ruled that the NFL did indeed "monopolize" pro football but awarded the USFL only one dollar in damages. Attorney Harvey Myerson had decided to make Trump his star witness in a blatant attempt to play to the sentiments of the local New York jury, calculating that a superrich, self-publicizing figure like Trump, comically emphasizing his wealth and power, would impress ordinary citizens of the great metropolis. Perhaps those qualities did impress the anxiously ambitious Myerson, but the tactic backfired. The jury might well have been more impressed by a plain-spoken fellow like Bill Tatham, whose family had personally lost millions in the quest to expand professional football to more cities. As one juror, Margaret Lillienfield, put it: "It wasn't a case of the little guys against the big guys; it was a case of the big guys against the big guys."

On August 2, 1986, Bill and Billy Tatham flew to New York to meet with the other owners. Everything was up in the air. There would be an appeal and a request for injunctive relief: specifically, the USFL would ask the judge to order coverage of the USFL season by one major network. But the immediate question was whether to proceed with the fall season, and a quick decision was required, as there was only a little over a month to go until the season's first kickoff.

There had been truth in what the juror had said about USFL "big guys." The millionaires who crowded into adjoining smoke-filled rooms at Manhattan's Meridien Hotel represented the new backgrounds and geographies that were storming the heights of American wealth and fame in the latest of the nation's unending power shifts: Trump, New York real-estate man Stephen Ross, Tampa Bay development mogul Lee Scarfone, Memphis cotton man Billy Dunavant, and Bill and Billy Tatham. But the millionaires were edgy. With the USFL, they had been reaching for the heart of the new success and status system. Now it was slipping away. They recognized the danger, for they, better than most, knew how quickly a rich man could be taken down by one really bad idea. Sam Battisone, the former World Football League owner and Bill's partner in the Utah Jazz basketball investment, had witnessed the failure of his family's fast-food chain, Sambo's Restaurants. Marvin Warner, the Ohio savings and loan operator who was one of the original USFL owners, had been indicted in 1985 for fraud in connection with one of the first big S&L failures. The bankruptcy and criminal litigation was to drag on for years.

The meeting quickly turned emotional. Total USFL losses since the start of play in 1983 were estimated at $200 million, and some of the owners could take no more. There were compelling reasons for going ahead with the fall schedule. The USFL had negotiated an $8 million ESPN contract for coverage of its fall season. The money would help reduce the owners' losses and weaken the NFL's argument that the USFL was nothing but a lawsuit. Ross, who had put up a reported $4 million for the Baltimore club, was yet to see his team take the field. No one present had more at stake in pressing ahead with the fall schedule than the Tathams. Phoenix was on everyone's short list for an NFL expansion team. And though Bill Tatham had been a thorn in the NFL's side, with his Memphis suit against the league in the 1970s, he was still well positioned to get a Phoenix franchise. The Outlaws had a 3,000-square-foot office in Tempe, Arizona, a thirty-year lease for Sun Devil Stadium, and a roster of high-priced players and coaches whom the Tathams believed were close to NFL caliber.

But then Trump dropped his bombshell. In many ways, Trump

owed his fame to the USFL. Before, he had been just a rich developer who put up big buildings. The New Jersey Generals and the USFL hoopla had helped him become a media darling. Now, having battered the owners with his ego for months and months, imposing his will on them as if they were a bunch of Sun Belt yokels, he was announcing he was tired of it all. Trump's team would not play.

Bill was dumbfounded, for the decision almost certainly spelled the end of the USFL. The ESPN contract depended on the availability of a New York television market. Billy surmised that "Trump had had his ego slapped around hard enough [at the trial], so he wanted to take his toy and go home." But Billy vented his anger mainly at Ross, who seemed to be supporting Trump's position. Ross was dapper in an expensive, hand-tailored suit, and Billy recalls, "I lost it . . . the last thing I said to him was, 'Why don't you just shut up?' Dad was sitting right between us. I could see Dad's muscles start to tense a little bit—wasn't sure whether it was to bail out or get in the middle. I had had it. Ross had an ego that was bigger than Donald's. Donald had earned the right. For Ross to tell us, that was too much to handle."

The vote to proceed with the fall season was five yes, two abstentions, and Trump voting no. The Big Apple had cast its veto. The fall season was dead. A dazed Bill Tatham walked out into a sea of television cameras and reporters.

Five days after the New York meeting, the Tathams released Doug Williams to the Washington Redskins. "The Tathams are the best owners I've been around," Williams said. "From mother, sister, brother, dad on down, the Tathams made me feel part of their family. They gave it that personal touch."

"I gained a good friend when I signed Doug," said Billy. "I think losing him is the thing that hurts the most."

The Tathams had paid their dues. Commissioner Harry Usher described Bill as "a guy who paid his share and did his share. When things are going down a rathole, you get a pretty good look at a fellow's character. Bill held up well." He regretted that the owners had received so little respect "for doing something very American, which was competing against something as big and powerful as the NFL."

UNTIL THAT SUMMER, Bill's football losses had still been a subject for family jokes—Mike kidded his dad about "violating your fiduciary responsibility to leave your kids a lot of money." Even with the losses, there was some psychic compensation. The Fresno *Bee*, which had stung Bill with its investigative articles about his nursing homes, rehabilitated him. "No Quit in Tathams" headlined a column soon after the New York verdict. "You want determination? Resoluteness? You're talking about William and Bill Tatham. They may be willing to give up millions. But never the dream."

But Bill's losses were stirring up some uneasiness in the family. Oca had always viewed football with a jaundiced eye. He could remember when Pentecostals were discouraged from even attending sporting events. Now football seemed to have become a kind of competing religion in his family. It bothered him that Bill often was unable to get back to Fresno after Saturday night USFL games in time for Sunday services at Peoples Church.

"That's enough about football, now let's talk about church," he said one night when conversation lingered too long on the USFL's battle for survival.

Oca also had doubts about the values that football instilled. He disliked the prayers for victory before games. "God doesn't take sides," he said. And as a businessman, Oca worried that Bill was squandering his wealth. His sons, he said, "did all right as long as they stuck to what I taught them." His own instincts as a horse trader made him wary of the kind of long-term commitments and entangling alliances required of a football owner. A franchise kept money tied up for years. Worse, one's success or failure hinged in part on the decisions of others. Trump, a wealthier man from the East, had controlled Bill's destiny.

An affidavit that Bill filed that October in connection with the USFL appeal stated that his cash losses attributable to the USFL came to $19 million. The foundation of Bill's wealth, the nearly forty nursing-home properties in California and elsewhere that he had retained in his 1980 deal with Beverly Industries, was intact. The properties were the true family jewels, the collateral on which his hopes for posterity rested, a kind of bank that could be drawn on for loans, deals, emergencies. As long as the facilities stayed rented, the leases would pay the debt on them. Given the demographics of America, with its aging population, that seemed a safe bet.

The situation was not immediately threatening, and Bill's businesses were arranged in such a way that football losses could offset profits elsewhere. Everything was tied together. Players could be "depreciated" for tax purposes, and football equipment—uniforms and pads, weightlifting machines, furniture for the club office—

could be leased to the Outlaws by one of Bill's leasing companies. Instead of Bill's writing a check out of his personal account, he could finance equipment through a bank line of credit to his leasing company, with five- or ten-year repayment terms. It cushioned the financial blow.

Bill was still very rich. Even so, in 1986 he was to some extent still living off the fruits of his successes between 1976 and 1981—the period between his takeover of Hy-Lond and the lucrative sale of his S&L stock in 1981. The team's enormous demand for money had forced him to sell several nursing homes and increase the mortgages on others, thereby raising the monthly payments on his debt. He was also dealing simultaneously with several other problems. One was a 1983 claim by the California Franchise Tax Board that Consolidated Industries owed nearby $1 million in state taxes for the years 1976–1980. In addition, there was his uncharacteristically ill-timed investment in a chain of banks in the southern valley. In 1981, he had purchased just under a one-fourth interest in Pacific Bancorporation, the holding company for First Community Bank of Bakersfield. But within three years, the value of his investment had declined precipitously due to the fading fortunes of the valley's core industries, agriculture and oil.

Bill placed several friends and business associates on the board, including Giacolini; Lyles, a Fresno businessman; William Buzick, previously chairman of the board of Consolidated Foods; and, briefly, D. H. Mapson, then Peoples Church's executive pastor. In 1984, the holding company announced a $6.2 million "loan loss" reserve to cover possible defaults. In June 1986, the bank's interest income was sharply down and the value of real estate it had acquired through foreclosures had climbed above $4 million. Belatedly, Bill had concluded that banks were a poor investment. Banks, he now understood, were in an unequal battle against competitors such as brokerage companies, which could operate nationwide without the restrictions or supervision of banks. But unloading his interest proved difficult. He cast around for Asian investors, but found no takers.

Overall he still sounded confident. "Some people still don't like to lose money at all. They feel like they're a failure if they take a loss. I don't feel that way. Nobody bats a thousand," he said. But in the fall of 1986, he no longer seemed invincible as he checked the Associated Press sports wire installed in his office for news about the USFL appeal. His brother Gerald noticed that Bill was taking a sudden interest in such mundane matters as electric bills and the cost of repairing leaky roofs of bank buildings. Gerald thought Bill was "a little humbler."

At times, he sounded fatalistic. "You just never really know if it's all going to work tomorrow, knowing that you owe millions of dollars, that you have millions of dollars in income from different sources involving a lot of long-term leases, knowing that some of those companies are not going to have stability forever. You see the thing getting into some big numbers, and as it keeps getting bigger, just a little bit at a time, it doesn't mean that it's better, just that if it fails it comes down a little harder. Just based on averages some of the guys we are dealing with will go down."

He saw himself as the son who *had* to succeed, for as he put it, "I always felt if I failed, everything the family had built would be lost and we would have to start all over again."

Unlike Oca, Bill Tatham had the natural instincts of a family patriarch. He was, in some ways, more like the family heads whom one met at ethnic gatherings in Fresno County. He took the long view—the dynastic view—in both his business and personal dealings. In business, he longed to own a football franchise that would be his children's and then, perhaps, their children's. And in relations within his own family, he looked far into the future. His children were directors of Consolidated Industries long before they were old enough for their decisions to have weight. "Bill Tatham & Sons & Daughter." That was a sign that Bill could imagine over his office door. He made the ultimate long-term investment, prodding his children toward college and advanced professional degrees, then supporting them lavishly with whatever money it took for them to attain their goals.

Bill increasingly was the Tatham who made decisions on behalf of the whole family, based on his perception of what would be good for the family's long-term interests. Should a reporter or an author be invited into the family's confidences for a story or book? Bill cast the key vote in such matters.

And within the family, Bill was the one to whom others turned. He was the brother who picked up the notes when someone faced a sudden financial setback, who paid for a plane to take Dick to a specialist in Los Angeles after he was diagnosed with a melanoma, and who bankrolled the college education of the children of in-laws.

He had been there again and again for Peoples Church. Bill was not one of those who advertised his contributions to the church and its related institutions, but they were considerable. Bill helped through complicated deals, property conveyances, swaps of notes, and out-right gifts—$300,000 one time, $50,000 another, and $100,000 an-other. A Fresno acquaintance described Bill as someone who "gave so quietly you never knew it," until you got on to some local board and discovered that Bill Tatham was a heavy contributor. That per-son, who with Bill had been in on meetings about the California Theological Seminary, was surprised to learn that Bill had contrib-uted in excess of $100,000 toward the seminary's library.

But by the second half of the 1980s, many of his breed of shrewd deal-makers and Sun Belt entrepreneurs were under financial strain. The Sun Belt was "overbuilt." There were too many malls, too many stores, too many banks, too many office buildings—and too many religious TV shows. For the preceding decade, growth had seemed as if it were a permanent condition of the Sun Belt. Abruptly, some were reminded that trees did not grow to the sky. Oil and agriculture, basic industries in California, Texas, Oklahoma, and Louisiana, were in trouble, and here and there the first signs of the S&L debacle and the coming real estate crash appeared.

Not surprisingly, some of the first warnings showed up in the sudden difficulties experienced by the superstars of the great Pente-costal ministries. Their growth, of course, was entirely derivative. The preachers had built big churches, hospitals, universities, and television networks from money supplied by others—by the "new people" making fortunes in real estate, oil, and business from Florida to Fresno. A Peoples Church, with all its ancillary services, was, liter-ally, built on the success of a Bill Tatham, an Earl Giacolini, or a Sherman Thomas. So the financial troubles of the religious superstars were an early indicator of a deeper, more fundamental weakness: a loss of confidence, a chilling sense that much of what passed for "wealth" was, in fact, a pyramid scheme. The unfolding crisis of the TV evangelists was the fish kill alerting the community to unseen toxins in the lake.

The ministries of the Pentecostal superstars had grown with the most astonishing speed, but they were vulnerable to their own ideol-ogy of miracles and endless possibilities, perhaps more so than other, less enthusiastic denominations like the Baptists. In the eighties, memories of the Depression faded and the sense of Biblical Immi-nence weakened. A humbling vision of the Lord's possible return at any moment was replaced by visions of power, fame, and worldly religious empires. The Pentecostal segment of the evangelical com-munity was the newest and least experienced, and, it soon appeared, was the most susceptible to fraud and mismanagement.

By 1985, Oral Roberts's City of Faith medical center was bleeding his empire of $1 million a month. The hospital and research center was described by one reporter as a "medical Potemkin Village," with hardly any patients.[3] In March, Jimmy Swaggart, the evangelist with the largest television audience, acknowledged that "the year's end caught us about $10 million in the red." He went on to say, "If ever there was a time we needed you to double your giving, it's this month. . . . The load is so heavy; won't you please help me carry it?"[4] In October, the Reverend Charles Blair's Calvary Tabernacle in Denver put on hold a $2 million fund-raising campaign for expanded facilities after protests that several million dollars were still owed for a 1976 church project that had resulted in bankruptcy and in the filing of criminal securities fraud charges.

In 1985, it was the turn of Peoples Church in Fresno to pay a price for an excess of temporal ambition. The problem was cost overruns on a 296-unit complex of retirement homes and apartments. Maple Village, located on land adjacent to the parking lot of Peoples Church, was a business venture launched by the church foundation. For some time it had been the subject of intense controversy in the church's inner councils. While some believed it was a shame not to exploit the church lands commercially, others felt the church had no business getting involved in such things.

Bill Tatham kept a watchful eye on everything the church and the foundation did. His friend Earl Giacolini was on the foundation board and pastors Mapson and Johnson consulted him on business matters. In 1982, in fact, they had proposed to the foundation that the retirement-home project be sold to Bill to develop privately, a step that would have allowed the church to make a graceful exit. Bill had experience; he was flush with money after the sale of his nursing-home chains. And as a private developer he could have taken full advantage of the tax code. But the foundation turned down the proposal. Bill speculated that his very willingness to take on the project may have persuaded some foundation members that they could do it.

In 1983, the Fresno city council authorized the issuance of $18.6 million in tax-free revenue bonds for the project. Maple Village was to have "a new senior life-style" in a "parklike setting." Unfortunately, the financial assumptions proved to be unrealistic. By the time the bonds were issued in late 1984, the project was already in trouble and Mapson and two others resigned.

Since 1983, the ever vigilant Fresno *Bee* had been probing some aspects of the foundation's activities, including its relationship with a for-profit television production subsidiary and its connections to several architectural and building contractors.[5] The foundation's 1984 tax return was difficult to follow. At the start of the year, it reported a net worth of $1.1 million, of which $350,000 had been loaned out. By the end of the year, the net worth had dropped to $869,866, with $912,198 loaned out. It was not clear to whom or for what purposes the loans had been made, but it was plain that the foundation was in an intense cash squeeze just as it faced huge new obligations from interest payments coming due on the retirement-center bonds.

Only one unit was rented when the first interest payment came due in 1985. Just before Thanksgiving, the church announced that the foundation was filing for protection under the bankruptcy laws. The unfinished project looked like a ghost town of white and beige two-story apartments. Everyone who came to services at Peoples Church drove right past it.

Some blamed Johnson for inadequate supervision, others thought it was the fault of Mapson. Still others pointed the finger at the church foundation's board, which included prominent Fresno businessmen. At board meetings leading up to the announcement, G.L. was sometimes so tense that he snapped a pencil in half. Much of what he had built was in jeopardy. Economy moves were undertaken well before the announcement. Broadcasts of his Sunday services were canceled, and the video, sound, and recording divisions of Peoples Foundation were put on the auction block.[6] The situation threatened the Fresno Christian Education System, the group formed by a number of Fresno churches to support a city-wide Protestant school system. Its main campus had been listed as collateral on the bankrupt retirement project. Madera rancher Thomas, the Peoples Church member who had donated $1 million to the school, said he had been unaware of that fact.[7]

The California Theological Seminary, which had opened in 1984, also was jeopardized. It was the first accredited seminary of its kind in the southern San Joaquin Valley and the fulfillment of a dream of G. L. Johnson. It was to be his gift to posterity. Peoples Church had contributed $1.5 million to the seminary, and the foundation had donated a $4 million piece of property that could be used either as collateral to raise needed capital or as a site for a future campus. Through G.L.'s connections, such Pentecostal notables as Pastor Glen Cole of Capital Christian Center, the largest Assemblies of God Church in Sacramento, and Pastor Tommy Barnett of Phoenix joined the seminary board. But the bankruptcy resulted in the seminary's losing the property, its principal asset. After that, it could only limp along until a plan was devised to save it. (The plan ended the seminary's formal connection with Peoples Church. It would become an extension school under the control of the Assemblies of God Theological Seminary in Springfield, Missouri, and the Church of God in Cleveland, Tennessee's School of Theology.)

In an interview with the Fresno *Bee* the week of the bankruptcy announcement, Pastor Johnson blamed others. "I'm not the final word. I'm not a dictator," he said. "I guess you're disappointed when you wake up and discover that you thought everything was going well—that you had delegated it to people—and you find it didn't go exactly like you thought it would."[8] G.L. said later that the board was not getting all the facts. Mapson, however, said that he had voiced personal concerns about the retirement center.

Mapson's replacement at the Peoples Church foundation was Bob Maddux, who had been in charge of the IRS office in Fresno that served the West Coast. After studying the books, one of the first things he did was go by Bill Tatham's office to discuss restructuring the foundation's debt. Bill agreed to help by purchasing sixteen acres of undeveloped farmland adjacent to the church, once reserved for a high school expansion. During the next two years G.L.'s pea green Mercedes was often parked in front of Bill's office while G.L. consulted Bill. Mapson—who had briefly served on the board of Bill's bank and had been chairman of the audit committee for the bank holding company—was given a temporary office in Bill's building after quitting Peoples Foundation. Bill's former nursing-home associate Clyde Dahlinger was brought in briefly to try to salvage the Maple Village project, and Mike Tatham for a while handled legal work for the foundation in connection with the bankruptcy. Gary Kerkorian, Bill's attorney, represented the separate interests of Peoples Church itself.

Gerald Tatham watched the troubles unfold with mixed feelings. He regretted the church's difficulties, for Peoples Church, with its array of educational and social programs, was a strong force for good in the community. Yet Gerald questioned the emphasis he saw at Peoples Church on material growth and expansion. In the 1970s, while working as the masonry contractor for the construction of the new church, he had had a falling out with Mapson and with the prime contractor, Wichita church builder Roe Messner. Messner, Gerald said, complained that the subcontractors were too slow. But Gerald said Messner's plans were the problem, and added that a city building

official told him approval to go ahead had been given on the understanding that more detailed plans would be submitted later. But
Peoples Church must have had friends at city hall, for the city did
not press. Gerald said he complained to Mapson, but nobody at the
church or in his family seemed to want to hear of problems. He
worked out his frustrations at the health club Bill owned, lifting
weights and doing fingertip push-ups until he was ready to drop.

Messner was appointed to the board of the California Theological
Seminary in about 1985. He was asked to resign in 1987, according
to a seminary official, after a top associate of television evangelist Jim
Bakker testified that Messner had supplied the $265,000 used to
purchase the silence of Jessica Hahn concerning her 1980 sexual
encounter with Bakker. Messner, according to the associate, had been
reimbursed by submitting phony invoices for work never done at
Bakker's Heritage Village.[9]

BILL MADE A POINT of distinguishing the church's problems from
his own. His losses, he made clear, were the result of a calculated
business gamble. And even after the disastrous meeting of the USFL
owners in New York City, he did not abandon his dream. Whether
or not the USFL won its appeal of the jury verdict, he and his son
still had a chance to get an NFL franchise there if the NFL bowed to
political pressures on it to expand to other cities. Phoenix was on all
the short lists to get an NFL team, if that happened.

Congress, where there was always sentiment in favor of expansion, still had political leverage on the league. The NFL had key
antitrust exemptions, and some of the owners argued that they
needed nothing else from Congress. But others wanted Congress to
allow the league more control over the owners' whimsical decisions
to move to other cities. The price of legislation that would permit the
league to impose more discipline on NFL owners, it was clear, would
be new NFL franchises in cities with political clout. Two senators
interested in seeing the NFL expand to cities in their states were
Dennis DeConcini of Arizona and Albert Gore, Jr., of Tennessee.
Both were members of the Senate Judiciary Committee, which wrote
antitrust legislation affecting professional sports.

Billy, in Phoenix, was personable, energetic, and quotable, and
he understood and enjoyed playing politics and sparring with the
media. He and Susan were social friends of such Republican political
comers as Arizona attorney general Bob Corbin and Congressman

John McCain, who in the fall of 1986 was running for the Senate. The ramrod-straight congressman, a Vietnam-era pilot who spent five and a half years in a Hanoi prisoner-of-war camp, was a conservative in the Barry Goldwater mold, and Billy was attracted to him. Billy and Susan contributed $3,000 to McCain's campaign, and Billy went on a live call-in program with the candidate, during which Bill praised McCain and McCain complimented Billy and the Outlaws. But as the campaign progressed, Billy also found himself supporting a less conventional politician, Evan Mecham, the maverick Republican candidate for governor. Billy went out one fall day to Mecham's campaign headquarters at Mecham's Pontiac dealership intending to spend a few minutes with him and drop off a small check. He stayed two hours; before leaving he tore up the check and wrote a larger one. The Outlaws' president, who had been fighting for recognition for two years from Phoenix's sporting establishment, found that he identified with Mecham, the political outsider. Neither was mainstream. Billy was Assemblies of God, Mecham was Mormon. "Mecham said that he was sick and tired of the state being controlled by the big power guys and making decisions for all of us," said Billy. "Well, the downtown guys had screwed us also, so we had something in common."

On election night, Billy and Susan went to dinner at McCain's house with twenty or so people, then returned with them to the Hilton Hotel downtown to await results. Billy shuffled between the McCain and Mecham suites, amused by the contrast. McCain's room was full of well-scrubbed Republicans in pin-stripe suits—and Billy had worn his pin-stripe for the occasion. Down the hall car dealers and self-made small businessmen congratulated Mecham. It looked to Billy "like an Assemblies of God Church twenty years ago."

He cultivated good relations between his organization and the new governor, and Mecham helped him when he could. Later, when Mecham caused a furor with his opposition to Arizona's celebrating the Martin Luther King, Jr., holiday and as other scandals emerged, Billy distanced himself from the governor, but he refused to disown him. Billy saw Mecham as the kind of "bigot you see in a lot of Democrats," but, he added, Mecham's enemies were the kind that "drank cocktails and would have preferred the governor to stay outside in an ice-cream truck."

Billy's other important friendship in Phoenix was with the Reverend Tommy Barnett, pastor of the First Assembly Church, the city's fastest-growing religious enterprise. It was a friendship indicative of the kinds of networks emerging in the Sun Belt in the late 1980s. Barnett, who had managed the growth of his church with considerably more skill than many other Pentecostal stars, was one of the first people the Tathams called on when they moved the Outlaws' franchise to Phoenix. As it happened, Barnett already had a Fresno connection, for he was on the board of G. L. Johnson's California Theological Seminary.

Barnett's father had been an early Assemblies preacher who had pastored a church in Kansas City for forty-five years. A short, peppery man, Barnett himself had been preaching since he was fourteen. He proudly told a visitor that he had been pastor of the big Assemblies of God church in Davenport, Iowa, When the Tathams arrived, Barnett had just completed a new $9 million facility, perched on Shadow Mountain outside the city. Barnett approached the challenge of increasing church membership like a politician plotting a voter registration campaign. His lieutenants divided up the city into a grid of precincts, assigned responsibility for evangelizing to block leaders, and sent buses into the ghettos to haul those without transportation to Sunday services. His goal, he said, was to make Phoenix a "Christian city" and to attract fifty thousand people each Sunday to his church on Shadow Mountain.

Billy was to say that Barnett not only "rejuvenated my relationship with Christ, but also became like a brother." He conducted the marriage ceremony for Billy and Susan. Billy credited the pastor with helping them get over the traumas of their divorces. He said, "The church was one of the few places I could go in Phoenix and not feel like people were trying to stab us in the back. He took us in like family." Barnett said of Billy: "He gave us his heart."

Barnett, like the Pope, had no divisions, but he did have a mighty pulpit, and he used it to help his friends. When Mayor Terry Goddard was quoted in the press expressing some glee at the jury's one-dollar-award decision in the NFL-USFL suit, Barnett reportedly called the mayor and told him, "You've lost ten thousand votes the way you treated Tatham."

"He felt we could use the franchise for Christianity," Billy said. "We could have cosponsored events on drugs and things. And we would have supported him on the moral issues." When Barnett needed $25,000 for a building fund, Billy gave it to him out of the team's coffers. "It was the best money we ever spent," he said.

The legal battle swirled on around the USFL antitrust suit through the fall of 1986. The league's attorneys were pressing for a court order that would require the NFL to expand immediately and award franchises to several USFL owners or, alternatively, limit the NFL to two television contracts so that one major network would be available for USFL games. The legal argument was that the NFL, by signing contracts with all three networks, had created a "shortage of football" on television. Arizona attorney general Corbin was among three state attorneys general filing friend-of-the-court briefs supporting the USFL. The others were Tennessee and Alabama, acting on behalf of Memphis and Birmingham. Several others also submitted affidavits, including Senator-elect John McCain.

By this time, Congressman Tony Coelho was majority whip in the House of Representatives, the number three position in the leadership. Coelho knew a good deal about the USFL's fight with the NFL, having once coordinated the House Select Committee on Professional Sports. Now, by coincidence, two important Fresnans had an interest in the USFL: one was Bill Tatham; the other was Samuel T. Reeves, head of Billy Dunavant's West Coast cotton operations. Reeves, a man of gracious Southern charm and an influential mover and shaker around Fresno, was believed to have an interest in the Dunavant group in Memphis that was seeking an NFL membership.

After the summer verdict in New York, Bill dined alone with Coelho at Nancy's Restaurant in Fresno and let his hair down about his difficulties with the NFL. "What can I do for you right now?" Coelho asked. Bill explained that he had gone to Phoenix hoping to discuss with DeConcinci the professional football bill that the senator was sponsoring in the Senate. DeConcini wanted an NFL team in Phoenix; the Tathams wanted to field that team. It seemed that they had similar interests. Yet DeConcini had dismissed him after a pro forma walk-through, Bill said. He seemed to be a cold fish who didn't like him. "I'll take care of it," Coelho said. Soon Billy succeeded in arranging a lengthy private meeting with DeConcini at a Phoenix hotel and was amazed at the senator's friendly demeanor.

Once during the fall of 1986, Bill and Sam Reeves drove out to Coelho's campaign headquarters in a small strip shopping center on Madera Avenue in Kerman. The atmosphere was "valley," with beer, enchiladas, and tortillas in the parking lot for the Mexican American, Okie, and ethnic types who dropped by. Bill and Reeves paid their respects and discussed the possibility of Coelho's submitting an affidavit to the New York court. Coelho was willing, but with the election coming up his advisers cautioned against helping two prominent local Republicans.

Eight days before Christmas, U.S. District Court Judge Peter K. Leisure in New York turned down the motion by the USFL to grant it relief. The appeal of the jury's one-dollar award would go forward, but the judge's ruling was a decisive, if not final setback to what remained of the USFL hopes. The Associated Press quoted Bill: "Obviously, we're disappointed."

It was a somewhat somber Christmas for the Tathams. Bill's sister, Renee, was in the hospital in Orange County after her neck surgery. On New Year's Eve, Central Bank took over Maple Village and foreclosed on other Peoples Foundation properties, including the main campus of the Fresno Christian Education System. Mike and Bill came and kept an eye on the proceedings, but there was nothing that either of them could do.

The Tathams still had their long-shot hope to save their football fortunes: that the NFL would pick Phoenix as an expansion city and accept the Tathams as the owners. There were no guarantees and all kinds of hurdles. But as Arizona *Republic* writer Bob Hurt put it, "Bill Tatham will play anywhere, including a supermarket parking lot."[10] While Billy worked the political circuit in Phoenix, Bill cultivated NFL owners.

Billy's first move in 1987 was to put together Arizonans for the NFL—ostensibly a community-wide effort to lobby for an NFL team but really more of a Tatham front. Howard McCrady, chairman of Arizona's largest bank, Valley National, joined after a call from his pastor—Tommy Barnett. The organization was housed in the law offices of Harry Cavanagh, who represented the Outlaws.

In mid-March, Billy and Outlaws coach Frank Kush flew to Hawaii for the NFL's annual off-season conference. Governor Mecham called ahead to ask the NFL to welcome the Tathams, but Billy's brief, impromptu meeting with Pete Rozelle was unfruitful. "I trust he'll understand if we don't roll out the red carpet," an NFL official told Hurt. Rozelle, evidently, had not forgotten that the NFL had been twice sued by Bill Tatham.

Billy stayed in the Phoenix news all spring, seeding ideas everywhere, stumping for a football team one day, an indoor soccer league the next. "Viewed suspiciously [at first] as a second-class carpetbagger peddling a third-rate product, Tatham couldn't even get the right people to answer the phone . . . Tatham has come a long way, baby!" wrote Phoenix *Gazette* columnist Joe Gilmartin.

In June Bill and Earline went to Washington for several days to visit their daughter Renee, who had a summer job in Tony Coelho's office. Bill attended Coelho's birthday cookout and made the rounds of a number of congressional offices, including DeConcini's, involved in legislation that would expand the NFL's antitrust protection. But nothing much was moving on the football front, and Bill waxed philosophical: "You have to believe in yourself. There's no point in doing this if you're afraid of the world of if you think the NFL owners are gods or that Washington is intimidating. They are human beings like the rest of us."

But things were slipping out of his control. Assuming the Tatham plan to own an NFL football team in Phoenix became a reality, the entry fee into the NFL would be around $75 million, a figure well beyond Bill's means after his USFL losses. He would have to have partners. One of those whom Billy checked out as a possible investor was Charles Keating, the Phoenix S&L magnate, but Keating wasn't interested. "I like amateur sports," he told Billy.

For a change of pace Billy and Susan Tatham traveled to Doug Williams's wedding in his hometown of Zachary, Louisiana. They were among the few white people in the crowd of more than four hundred people. Spotting Susan's blond hair, Doug thought how often he had been a "fly in white milk" and wondered mischievously how Billy and Susan liked it the other way around.

Congress was still the main pressure point on the NFL to expand, and the Tathams and others interested in expansion did what they could. In September, Bill and Earline contributed $2,000 to the campaign coffers of Senator Gore, and Billy and Susan chipped in $2,000 to DeConcini's political action committee and another thousand to Gore.

That November, Billy set out to impress Pete Rozelle when the NFL commissioner came to Phoenix to attend the annual sports banquet. Billy reserved fifteen tables and passed out Arizonans-for-the-NFL hats. Most of the Phoenix sports establishment was there, including Keith Turley, head of Pinnacle West (a venture capital offshoot of Arizona Power), Eddie Lynch of the Phoenix Metropolitan Sports Alliance, and Karl Eller, chairman of Circle K Corporation and a cofounder of the alliance. A local photographer took a picture of Rozelle in one of the hats. "We think we have friends in the NFL. We're satisfied we're in good shape," said Billy. But Rozelle was not born yesterday. He knew well enough who was behind Arizonans for the NFL.

The bad news came finally in January 1988, confirming months of rumors. Bill Bidwill, owner of the St. Louis Cardinals, came to

Phoenix for final talks about moving his NFL team there. A day later, Billy got a call from Mayor Goddard, telling him the Cardinals were coming to Phoenix. The Tathams' gambit had failed.

"He said he appreciated everything we'd done and that we'd laid the groundwork for the doggone thing," Billy said. At a press conference, Keith Turley, representing the Phoenix power structure that had finally realized its dream of getting an NFL team, was gracious to the Tathams. The Tathams, he noted, had receipts for the $20 million they had plowed into football in Phoenix. DeConcini telephoned to thank Billy for putting the community first, and Senator Barry Goldwater wrote Bill a letter saying he had tremendous respect for what he had tried to do.

It was small consolation for the years and the millions invested in football. And there may have been more than a little self-interest in Phoenix's kid-glove treatment of the Tathams. Bill still had a hold card or two, including his Phoenix football franchise. Possibly he could have used it to put up legal obstacles to the Cardinals' move. But as usual Bill was thinking about the future. Billy issued a statement saying he would be cheering from the stands like the rest of the fans.

It had been quite a five-year run, and they didn't want it to end. There would still be pressure in Congress for expansion of the NFL, and Oakland was in the running. It was a long shot, but Bill had friends there. Perhaps he could make it. Billy mused about making Doug Williams the first black in an NFL front office. He thought about starting up a new league. "If I had my choice I'd like to go after them again," he said. "Guys like Trump, we'd all like to give it another chance. It was really fun in the USFL. You had a team and you played every week. All the problems with coaches and the media—it was great. Fighting the NFL was fun, too."

Yet Billy couldn't resist making some final mischief in Phoenix. The Outlaws' stadium lease gave holders of Outlaw season tickets, some 15,000 of them, the right to convert to NFL tickets in the event an NFL team came to town. Those were tickets that Bidwill would have no control over, which pleased Billy since he relished the prospect of being a thorn in Bidwill's side. But not all the Outlaw fans wanted to watch what Billy called "the worst team in the NFL." As it happened, a thousand or so of those tickets ended up back in Billy's hands, some of which he gave to Barnett's church to sell, and the rest he sold himself. It was an opportunity that brought out the horse trader in him. Some in Phoenix speculated that Billy made at least half a million dollars selling the tickets that landed back in his lap.

He would not confirm the figure, but when he left Phoenix he seemed in no hurry to get a job.

BACK IN FRESNO, Bill Tatham swallowed his disappointment and began to return to the things he *could* control. In June 1988, the Fresno *Bee* carried a story about a major new business and real-estate deal: Bill Tatham had acquired Angelo Papagni's Madera winery and more than a thousand acres of grape vineyards around Madera and along Friant Road outside Fresno. The deal had been done with Aetna Life Insurance, which had foreclosed on the Papagni properties. The $12 million deal instantly made Bill's Consolidated Industries one of the top three grape-concentrate producers in California, according to the president of the processing subsidiary.[11]

It was an old valley story. As one family's fortunes declined, others were on the rise. Papagni's father had come to California in 1915 as a poor man and had painstakingly developed a vineyard. The Papagnis took pride in cultivating wine grapes of steadily improving quality. Eventually Papagni wines were sold at a few select stores in the East. Angelo Papagni was a great vintner, but he was not a great businessman. In the 1970s, he was caught up in the boom psychology of American agriculture and became financially overextended buying state-of-the-art wine-processing equipment. Then, suddenly, the combination of imported wine, rising interest rates, and his own overproduction squeezed him. With that, the horse traders moved in, as they always did.

Bill, the teetotaler, took a good deal of ribbing in the family about the winery. Under the deal that Bill made with him, Papagni could continue to use the winery to press grapes that he would grow on his former lands in Madera County, which he now rented from Bill. But Bill, who was embarrassed by the kidding, intended to sell all the grapes he pressed to the concentrate market.

One remaining worry was Cesar Chavez and the United Farm Workers. In 1983 Papagni's big farm in Madera had been targeted by the UFW for a union vote. The owner had "lost" the election, and for five years there had been long negotiations on the details of a labor contract. When Bill took over, the matter was still unsettled. Bill made some inquiries about farm labor law and then decided he was not going to make any concessions to the UFW. He gave notice to the Mexican farm superintendent and made plans to bring in his own workers for the pruning season.

Bill had big ideas for the five hundred acres of vineyards along

Friant Road. He might tear out the vines and create an upscale master-planned community complete with eighteen-hole golf course and office complex. He made contact with the Women's Professional Golfing Association about the possibility of using the site as a national headquarters.

The old Papagni vineyards and homestead occupied one of Fresno County's most picturesque settings. Located on a bluff above the San Joaquin River, it had something that was highly unusual in the pancake-flat valley: a view. Another point in its favor was that it was almost exactly halfway between downtown Fresno and the growing Millerton Lake state recreation area, and stood astride the path of Fresno's sprawling, northerly expansion. This sprawl had continued unabated for several decades, despite opposition from a vocal minority of county residents favoring "stable growth." First downtown had lost its battles to prevent the sprawl. Now the city was spilling out beyond Shaw and Blackstone avenues toward the river.

Smart developers bought cheap agricultural land in the path of the city's expansion, then applied pressure on city and county politicians for rezoning. The pressures (and the campaign contributions) were hard to resist. County population was growing as businesses were priced out of the real estate market on the Pacific Coast and retirees from Los Angeles traded in high-priced homes and condos for cheaper ones in the central valley closer to skiing, lakes, and mountains.

Bill had a grand design for what he had acquired.

"See how nice this is for developing?" he asked a visitor.

Oca, Bill acknowledged, was worrying again that his son was getting in over his head. Indeed, there were huge risks. And once again, as was so often the case in Bill's high-stakes endeavors, he realized his vision would involve politics. The area north of Copper Avenue, in which the Papagni property was located, was still earmarked for agricultural development under the existing General Plan for Fresno County. No doubt there would be opposition to intensive commercial development.

The state legislature had proposed a wildlife habitat for the area alongside the San Joaquin River. Although Bill's property on the bluffs was well away from the habitat, the state's proposal called attention to the environmental sensitivity of the entire area. In addition, land preservationists had been fighting developers over the rezoning of farmland for decades, so opposition from that quarter was almost a given.

The fate of the property eventually would be in the hands of Fresno County's five supervisors, who had the power to amend the General Plan. In his quiet way, Bill had already begun to court the votes.

The challenge excited him, and he was not unaware of the metaphor suggested by the purchase. It was quite an historical reversal—a character out of *The Grapes of Wrath* ending up with vineyards and grape presses of his own.

"It took fifty-four years," he said, counting back to his birth in a tank house on a cotton ranch in December 1934. His face was deadpan Cherokee, but his eyes twinkled.

CHAPTER TWENTY-THREE

THE VALLEY, 1988

FRUITS AND VEGETABLES shipped by truck today include ninety-six loads of carrots, eighty-eight loads of grapes, twenty loads of onions, one hundred seventy-two loads of potatoes, one load of radish, one load of chili peppers, fifty-seven loads of chippers, two loads of watermelon.

Kern District potato market: produce in short supply. Long whites, round reds, fifty-pound sacks, fifty to sixty russets, ten-pound bags baled.

Onion market: demand, reds fairly good, yellows moderate. Fifty-pound sacks yellow jumbos up three to two twenty-five.

Pepper market: demand fairly good, market higher.

Keep the Big Ten out of the Cotton Bowl: Use Puratron from Ciba Geigy. . . . Puratron is a restricted-use pesticide. Always read and follow label directions. . . .

It was noon on Election Day 1988 and the big news on Bakersfield radio was vegetable prices, not voter turnout.

Agriculture was as much the valley's lifeblood as it had been when the Okies came. Now, though, it was typically a big modern enterprise involving high risks and high rewards. Truck farmers grew a lengthy menu of high-value crops—celery, radishes, leeks, potatoes, tomatoes, beets, and onions—with a fast turnaround between planting and harvesting. They grew collard for "soul markets" in Oakland and Watts, bok choy for Korean groceries, cilantro for the Vietnamese and Thai restaurants of San Francisco Bay, and dill for the upscale trade. Farming "engineers" used laser beams to grade the land and pumped poison gases into onion fields to kill weeds.

Some things didn't change. Valley agriculture still required lots of hired labor because crops like grapes and melons defied efforts to devise mechanized harvesting techniques. Watermelon growers still used "thumpers," who could tell if a green melon was ripe by the sound it made when they tapped its side. Only now it was mostly Mexicans in the fields and the thumpers were mainly black.

The North Shafter Farm Labor Camp, operated by the old Farm Security Administration in the 1930s, was still going, its cabins resting solidly on cinder blocks that looked as if they'd been there when Steinbeck roamed the valley with a notebook. A long time ago it was a refuge for desperate Okies in need of shelter. In 1939, it served as the unofficial headquarters of striking cotton workers. Now the Kern County Housing Authority charged $105 a month to rent a cabin and the dusty pickups and beat-up campers with Texas license plates belonged to Mexicans, most of them from across the Rio Grande in Nuevo León state. Farther north, on the outskirts of Fresno, Hmong farmers from the highlands of Southeast Asia lovingly cultivated their plots.

TO ELDON TACKETT, all the change had not been for the better.

He had known the valley when it was a pristine frontier, teeming with game and wildlife—when hares big as doe jumped out of wheat fields and migrating ducks peeled off and fed in the swamps around Tulare Lake. Then you could see the snowcapped Sierra peaks from anywhere on the east side. Living in Porterville, Eldon would wander up into the hills and take potshots at quail and squirrel or help himself to a "shiner," an orange missed in the day's picking. Where orchards weren't planted, the wild wheat and oats grew waist-high.

Now everything had changed. A fellow was lucky to scare up a rabbit, and it was risky to eat a shiner because of pesticide residues. The water was polluted enough, Eldon knew, that many a farmer drank only bottled water. He could count on two hands the days in the year when the distant mountaintops peaked through the smog and haze over the valley.

Eldon had always lived close to the soil—in the orange groves, as a ditch rider for SMUD, and as a natural-born "green thumb" who grew tomatoes, peppers, and squash in his backyard. Now he worried about the environment. Now the run-off of irrigation water on the west side was causing major drainage problems. Kesterson Reservoir had become polluted with natural salts, and in fields where constant irrigation had caused these salts to leach back to the surface you could see white blotches like worn patches on an old pair of dungarees.

Eldon's hometown had become famous—for its "cancer cluster." Since 1985, McFarland had eleven cases of cancer in children and six deaths—four times the average for communities its size. Many blamed pesticides, but a state inquiry completed in January 1988 was inconclusive.

Some worried about the possibility of a new agricultural disaster—a "California Dust Bowl." They warned that without major changes in farming practices, it could happen.

Other changes made Eldon uneasy. It seemed to him that the farmers themselves had changed. In 1962, President Kennedy had detonated the dynamite charge that broke ground for the San Luis Dam, cornerstone of the federal-state water project that eventually brought water to irrigate the valley's dry west side.

In Kern County, the state of California owned the water and let huge agribusinesses buy it at cost.

Farther north on the west side, and along the Friant-Kern Canal on the east side, the water was federal and farmers had been required to divest themselves of holdings in excess of 160 acres. The DiGiorgios had sold theirs, and after 1977 the west-side farmers began selling theirs to conform to the limits. But these land controls, in Eldon's opinion, had not been effective. Farmers with smart lawyers evaded what limitations there were by setting up trusts and spinning off holdings to relatives, friends, and front companies, circumventing the spirit of reclamation law.

Eldon thought the farmers had become greedy. They enjoyed the generous benefits of price supports, subsidized irrigation water, and government relief payments, and when something bad threatened them, like the inspectors condemning a watermelon crop because of chemical residues, the federal government bailed them out. "Might just as well go out and buy a millionaire a big home as build him a big canal and give him the water," said Eldon. "Take the taxpayers' money and build something for the big shot, and foreign-ers getting half of it. Why raise a million bushels of wheat and give it to the foreign countries? We got to water that. We got to pay. Might just as well turn the whole valley into a single farm," he said.

Then there were the "giveaway programs"—federal and state strategies to ease poverty. To a resident of McFarland in 1988, gov-ernment programs were a vivid reality on all sides. On both sides of Highway 99 a Bakersfield developer subsidized by the Farmers Home Administration was putting in several hundred single-family homes for low-income families. Those who qualified could get low-interest loans with no money down and weren't required to pay higher com-mercial rates until they had the income to do so.

The Kern County Housing Authority operated low-rent apart-ments on the east side of the highway, and almost directly across Sixth Street from the Tackett residence was the McFarland Learning Center, which provided an "alternative" curriculum for pregnant girls, disturbed and difficult students, potential dropouts, and people who wanted to study English as a second language. In the Delano-McFarland area alone about five hundred families with children were on welfare, and more than four hundred, almost one family in ten, received food stamps.

Eldon could work out in his head what all that was costing the taxpayers—and those were only the programs for the *poor*. Uncle Sam was doing even better for rich farmers. Checks from the United States Department of Agriculture, Social Security, the welfare agen-cies, and coupons from Medi-Cal and the food stamp program greased the wheels of the McFarland economy as much as the money taken in by the local cotton gins, the orange processor, and the hay broker.

To Loretta Tackett that was a worrisome thing, for it was her belief that "when the government takes over everything, it's commu-nism as far as I can tell."

Federal intervention on behalf of minorities occurred as white numbers were diminishing in valley towns. By 1988, whites were a minority in both Delano and McFarland. In 1960, they made up nearly four-fifths of the population of McFarland; in 1980 it was a little over one fifth. Many second- and third-generation whites, like Gene Tackett, had moved away. Farm owners lived in Bakersfield and hired professional managers, often as not Mexican-Americans. The widening of Highway 99 wiped out a quarter of the downtown businesses.

Eldon saw a connection between the social programs enacted in the 1960s and 1970s and the population changes that put whites in the minority. Mexicans came to pick crops, stayed, got residency papers, and eventually drew welfare and unemployment. Cradled by the government's safety net, they stopped picking crops and a new wave of Mexican illegals arrived, ready to begin the cycle all over, while the white population dwindled. That, at least, was how Eldon saw it.

Eldon believed that "Americans would do the fieldwork if they'd shut off welfare. Instead, what they do is *raise* welfare 15 percent every year. Social workers come out and ask how much money you make? Why you can draw seven, eight hundred more from welfare! We was raised to work for what you get. We were taught that, and I still believe it. Giveaway is the ruination of the world. Make them do something for it, and they'll appreciate it."

There was little evidence, statistical or anecdotal, to support the view that Mexicans came to "get welfare." Californians had said the same thing about Okies in the 1930s. In fact, two-thirds of Kern County welfare recipients were *non*-Hispanic, and six out of ten of those qualifying for food stamps did not use Spanish as their first language. Those who took the risks and made the effort tended to share the qualities of earlier immigrants: they were people with a work ethic who wanted to improve their lot.

But it was not easy to convince whites like Eldon of this. Fairly often Eldon and Loretta visited Oklahoma, where both still had relatives, and from time to time Eldon would talk about moving back there for good. Oklahoma seemed "more open," Eldon said. A man could go hunting and fishing without getting permission.

TO GENE TACKETT, the California melting pot was wonderful. Gene believed that as more Hispanics obtained citizenship and voted, it would be a good thing for the Democratic Party in the southern valley in the long run. But he also knew that in the short run the party was in trouble. He needed to look no further than his father to see that. The "Truman Democrat" who had been Gene's model all his life had retired from his job with the water district in 1979, and the very next year he had voted for Ronald Reagan for President.

Now, eight years later, Gene was hoping that Michael Dukakis would reverse the Democratic Party's long downward slide. In 1987, he and Wendy discussed the choice of Democratic candidates and decided that Dukakis had many qualities they admired in a public official: competence, managerial skills, and a practical, problem-solving approach to government. Wendy liked Dukakis's progressive health care plan and felt a connection on a personal level to Kitty Dukakis who, like Wendy, was Jewish. So that summer, Gene picked up the phone, dialed 1-800-MIKE, and announced that he was ready to help.

In May 1988, he and Wendy attended the caucus at the Plumbers and Pipe Fitters Hall on Meany Avenue to pick candidates from the twentieth congressional district to run as prospective Dukakis delegates in the June Democratic primary. The hall was crowded with Hispanics who had come to support Daniel Ybarra, son-in-law of Dolores Huerta, cofounder of the United Farm Workers Union. Ybarra had bused in people from UFW headquarters in Keene. Only a few of Gene and Wendy's friends showed up, but after Ybarra gave a speech describing Gene as a friend, Gene won one of the slots and Wendy was picked as an alternate.

By the time of the primary balloting, Dukakis had the nomination sewn up, and it was no surprise to anyone that he got five of the seven delegates in the twentieth congressional district, the other two going to Jesse Jackson. What was remarkable, however, was the delegation's ethnic composition. The population of the district was about two-thirds white. But Gene was the only white of the seven delegates chosen to represent the local Democratic Party in Atlanta. The two Jackson supporters were black. And the four other Dukakis delegates were Hispanic, and included three with connections to the UFW.

Gene hated to think of the delegate-selection process in that light; the former Peace Corps member disliked separating people by groups. He noted that anyone could have run for delegate. Yet that was exactly the point: hardly any whites had run. It seemed that not many whites felt at home in the Kern County Democratic Party.

Gene was thrilled by the convention in Atlanta, where he rubbed shoulders with Hollywood celebrities like Morgan Fairchild and Joe Piscopo. Even before Dukakis's rousing acceptance speech, he felt this was the year for the Democrats to "pull it all together."

"It's a ticket we don't have to be embarrassed about," he said when he returned. "It could have coattails for other Democrats around here. That hasn't happened in a while."

At the age of forty-five, Gene's own elective career appeared to be over as a result of two solid defeats in bids for higher office. In 1982, while still a Kern County supervisor, he had run for Congress and lost. Two years later, rather than seek a third term as supervisor, he ran for State Assembly. After that second defeat, he started a private consulting business and spent a lot more time with his two boys, coaching soccer and T-ball. Wendy's nonprofit Community Connection for Child Care organization, which provided help of various kinds for working mothers and advocated such reforms as more day care at the job, had grown into a $3-million-a-year operation.

If his career in elective politics taught him one thing it was that being a man of the political center in Kern County was a difficult role. Twenty years earlier, his political views would have put him smack in the middle of the political consensus in the southern valley. Now he was strangely isolated—too liberal for many of the old Truman Democrats, too conservative for the party's more radical anti-business faction, and too white to be the flag bearer in a local party that was increasingly dominated by Hispanic activists.

Yet his political views had changed remarkably little over the years. He still considered himself a moderate conservative who opposed gun control, supported workfare, and approved of stiff punishments for criminals. At the same time, he believed government was basically a good institution that could help people solve problems. He wanted government to "bring people into the process," "help people help themselves," and "give everybody a piece of the action." Government was necessary as a sort of "referee," he said, to "protect me and my family from greedy people."

In office, Gene had been in his element connecting with organizations and issues—dealing with Senator Alan Cranston's office on the immigration problems of Filipino constituents in Delano, for example. He fought battles over chemical-waste dumps, zoning laws, and water rates—no problem was too trivial, not even crickets.

Late one evening a neighbor came to the door of his home in Oildale complaining about a cricket infestation. The neighbor led him outdoors to inspect a pile of the insects he'd swept up in his driveway. Gene circled the green heap, which glowed in the light of a street lamp. Back home, he fretted about the crickets, wondering what a county supervisor could do.

Gene's dedication made him the butt of his wife's April Fools' Day joke one year. Shortly after midnight, the phone rang and Gene tumbled out of bed to take the call. It was a woman who said she wanted to discuss a matter of urgent county business. Couldn't it wait until morning, Gene implored. The caller wouldn't be put off; she had to see him right away. Gene relented.

"You what?" Wendy exploded, pretending to be just waking up. "You've invited a strange woman over to our house in the middle of the night?"

Gene paced sheepishly for several minutes until Wendy felt sorry for him. "April Fool!" she laughed.

He took the joke in good humor, even as a sort of compliment.

His political models were the same ones they'd always been: John F. Kennedy, R. Sargent Shriver, John Steinbeck, and Eldon Tackett. Kennedy and Shriver were politicians who believed that public service was a high calling. Steinbeck's novels and his dad's whole life resonated with empathy for "the little guy."

Gene had voted against the budget of the Kern County Water Agency, which often was accused of being too close to the big landowners. He had successfully opposed the nuclear power plant and fought against the expansion of a hazardous waste-disposal site east of Bakersfield near the Kern River, fearing it might contaminate the river.

The latter fight became a cause for the environmental movement and the Sierra Club and quickly assumed partisan overtones. The disposal site was operated by the euphemistically named Environmental Protection Corporation—one of whose partners was chairman of the Kern County Republican Party. Gene was outnumbered by the county board's Republican majority, so the corporation got a conditional-use permit. But Gene subsequently testified against the decision at a hearing of the Regional Water Quality Control Board, and the state refused to issue the final permit.

Gene didn't automatically side with environmentalists. Farming and other businesses provided jobs needed for the county to prosper, and farmers on the east side like Hollis Roberts and the Pandols— people he had known since he was a boy—were not evil for wanting to protect their interests.

In 1982, Gene decided to challenge Congressman Chip Pashayan, the congressman whom Bill Tatham had helped get started in 1978. His seventeenth district had been redistricted to include the Okie-Hispanic towns in Kern County that were Gene's home base, and although Gene was the underdog, he figured he had nothing to lose. With the encouragement of Tony Coelho, Gene put together a low-budget, grass-roots operation that forced Pashayan to drain his political war chest.

Coelho opened doors for Gene in Washington, arranging a fast-paced three days in the nation's capital that involved numerous meet-

ings with labor unions and interest groups, including the National
Organization for Women, and he addressed the California Democratic congressional delegation at an informal breakfast meeting. As
his campaign progressed, thousands of dollars in campaign contributions poured in from out-of-state organizations like the National
Abortion Rights Action League, the National Education Association,
gay and environmental groups, and even the Brotherhood of Loco-
motive Engineers Legislative League based in Cleveland, Ohio. But
Gene fared less well in raising money locally.

In the end, money did matter. Pashayan outspent Gene three
dollars to one and took 54 percent of the vote. All in all, though, it
had been "positive," Gene said, and two years later his respectable
showing earned him the right to seek a seat in the State Assembly,
which many in California considered more important than a seat far
away in the U.S. Congress.

Gene felt that he had a fighting chance. Ronald Reagan would
head the Republican ticket in 1984, but the President's standing in
Kern County had been damaged by the deep recession being felt
in agriculture and oil. The Assembly incumbent, a fifty-six-year-old
petroleum geologist and native-born Louisianan named Don Rogers,
had been reelected two years earlier by only a slim margin. Rogers,
a Republican, was a fiscal conservative and tax cutter who hadn't, in
Gene's opinion, addressed the health and education problems of the
southern San Joaquin Valley.

Voter registration in the Thirty-Third Assembly District still gave
54 percent to the Democratic Party compared with 37 percent for
the Republicans, and to Gene the district was familiar territory. The
boundaries extended north from central Bakersfield to Tulare
County and encompassed the small farming towns of Shafter, Delano,
McFarland, Wasco, and Lindsay—Gene's home turf. It was full of
families like his own: people who had made the trek west, who still
went "home" to visit relatives in Oklahoma and Texas at Christmas,
who attended Pentecostal or Southern Baptist churches, and who
liked to hunt, fish, and listen to the music of Buck Owens and Merle
Haggard.

Gene stressed his Okie roots and the work-ethic values he had
been taught as a boy. "It took independence and a toughness of spirit
to come to California from Oklahoma," said a campaign brochure.
"It took a belief in the fundamental American principles of doing for
yourself and helping out your neighbors. Gene Tackett has faith in
the fundamental values his folks taught him, values they brought with

them from Oklahoma. The work ethic. Self-reliance. Local control. Focusing government on providing essential services. Respecting other people's money."

It was the same meat-and-potatoes pitch that had worked well for him when he ran for supervisor in 1976 and 1980.

His strategy for winning Hispanic votes required him to walk a tightrope. He had met Cesar Chavez's people during his first run for supervisor, but when he ran for Congress in 1982 he had passed word that he wanted no money from Chavez or his union. To survive, "I couldn't have a direct relationship with Cesar Chavez," Gene said.

At the same time, within the local Democratic Party Gene found himself to the right of a more radical camp allied with Tom Hayden and his "new politics." Hayden was a veteran of the left-wing Students for a Democratic Society and civil rights movement, and he had run a surprisingly strong race for the Senate in 1976. He organized a Campaign for Economic Democracy to perpetuate his influence in the state Democratic Party. One economic democracy concept that did not go over so well called for employees to be represented on the boards of corporations. Mainly, though, the organization attempted to address the growing concerns of Californians about the environment. CED pushed energy conservation and environmental and health initiatives and even persuaded Governor Brown to set up a special office on toxic chemical dump sites. The Democratic old guard in Kern County viewed the CED, which had strong support from Chavez's union, with extreme suspicion.

Gene had a cool relationship with the local CED leader, John Means. He had not given much support to Means when he ran for the Assembly in 1982, and that friction spilled over into 1984. When Gene began raising money for his own race against Rogers, he got a note from a Means supporter: "You screwed John, we're not going to help you."

Gene had a clear idea of what he wanted the main issue to be in his 1984 campaign: not the environment or the depravation of big corporations, but education. Gene believed that Rogers was vulnerable on this issue: he had abstained from voting on a key education reform bill, saying it would involve $466 million in new taxes. Instead, Rogers called for harder work, longer school days, and tougher discipline. Gene intended to confront Rogers on education, but to his astonishment the main issue of the campaign turned out to be Willie L. Brown, Jr., the black speaker of the State Assembly.

Early in the year, Brown had backed Gene with $37,000 from a

special political fund called 1984 Assembly Democrats and followed
up by sending one of his political operatives to work at Gene's Chester
Avenue campaign headquarters. By Labor Day, the Rogers camp was
hammering away at Gene for being a "puppet" of the liberal black
speaker. In fact, Brown had abruptly ended his support for Gene
and sent the campaign worker to a district that was more promising
for the Democrats. Gene was in a double bind, cut off from a major
source of funds but unable to say so publicly because it might brand
him a loser in the eyes of voters.

Rogers's campaign experienced no such trouble. By October,
his fund-raising was running $100,000 ahead of Gene's thanks to
contributions from medical, oil, and agribusiness interests. His financing included hefty contributions of $4,000 from the National
Rifle Association Victory Fund, $10,300 from the California Medical
Political Action Committee, and $15,000 from Tenneco West, Inc.

If running for office amid the conflicting political currents of
Kern County was not complicated enough, a whole new set of unanticipated issues entered the political debate: the emotion-packed
"social issues" of abortion, school prayer, child care, and gay rights.
There was no doubt where Gene stood on the social issues: he
was a liberal. The National Abortion Rights Action League had
kicked in $3,000 to his 1982 campaign. Gene, a strong supporter of
women's rights, had paid his respects to NOW during his 1982 trip
to Washington.

He believed that abortion should be seen as a health issue, not a
partisan political one. One of his senior campaign advisers in 1982
had been an antiabortion Catholic, and Bill Thomas, the popular
Republican congressman from Bakersfield, was pro-choice. But some
people were making it a partisan Democratic-Republican issue with
the goal of winning the religious fundamentalists' votes. In Gene's
view the argument contributed nothing toward solving the real problems: unwanted pregnancies, lack of child care, the dearth of prenatal
medical attention for the poor.

Gene hated the new "values politics" because, it seemed to him,
once an issue became ideological, real discussion ended. Day care was
a good example. "It's like a code word," he said. "It's perceived as a
socialistic notion. Opponents say the family is supposed to do that,
but the traditional family doesn't really exist anymore. The politicians
are way behind the people on this." Forcing religious and family
issues into election campaigns, Gene thought, perverted the debate
and led to a kind of moral McCarthyism: "The religious right have
the right to do what they want to do. Where I draw the line is when

they come over into my yard and put their belief system on me. And that's what happens."

Gene and Wendy were not members of a church or synagogue. Wendy had attended a lot of bar mitzvahs and Jewish weddings when she was growing up in Los Angeles, but her parents didn't practice Judaism. By the time she was old enough to make decisions about whether to attend school on Jewish holidays, she knew it would be hypocritical to stay at home.

A number of non-Christian artifacts graced the Tackett home in Oildale: a stone Buddha acquired by Gene in Nepal, a Javanese batik with a tableau of Hindu religious symbols, and a tapestry in silk representing Sira and Rama, the former a Hindu god, the latter the incarnation of one. The decorations reflected Gene and Wendy's eclectic experiences in the wider world beyond the central valley. The idea that they might raise questions about his and Wendy's "family values" seemed preposterous.

In the middle of October, Gene and Rogers squared off at a candidates' forum in Shafter. Settled by Mennonites early in the century, Shafter was strongly Republican and strongly conservative on the social issues. The inevitable question was asked: "Do you think taxpayer money should be used to pay for abortions?"

Rogers, a grave, thin-faced man, went first. He was opposed to abortion, so it followed he disapproved of government funds for clinics that performed them.

Then it was Gene's turn. "Well, I view it as a health care issue and if a person's health is jeopardized they should have the same right to an abortion whether they are rich or poor," he said. "It's an issue of conscience for women and men and not something that should be dictated."

He could hear what sounded like groans in the audience. Mike Bird, his campaign aide, looked glum.

"That means you're for abortion," said a local pastor who approached him after the meeting.

"I'm not *for* abortion," said Gene. "But I am for choice. That is the law of the land."

"Then you can't have read the Bible," said the pastor, and walked off.

"You're gonna have trouble on that," whispered Johnny Thomas, one of Gene's supporters locally.

Gene stared at him. "The Supreme Court has said that's the way it is. I can't change it," he said.

An even more uncomfortable scene followed at a candidate's

night in Bakersfield. A woman approached him and asked, "Why doesn't your wife have your last name?"

Gene was tired. "We're married," he said curtly.

The woman persisted. "In the Bible it says your wife takes your last name. You're not really married, are you?" She persisted: Were he and Wendy living in sin? Were their children illegitimate?

Rogers exploited the "family" issue in a late October mailing: "Dear Friend," it said, "As your Assemblyman I've been working hard to protect the traditional family values that have built our great land." The implication, of course, was that Gene Tackett would not work hard on behalf of families or that he didn't support "family values."

Gene smoldered, but he understood the sensitivity of the voters' feelings about these issues. When a gay group came to see him about supporting Assembly Bill 1, which provided job protection for gays, Gene turned them down. Personally, he believed one's sexual preference shouldn't limit opportunities, but he thought he could not be seen taking that position publicly. "There's no way a Democrat can support AB1 in Kern County and have any hope of getting to a position where he can do something," he told them.

On the Sunday before the election, Rachel Kennedy, a Catholic leader of the local California Pro-Life Council, set out with a friend in a car to the farming town of Lamont. They spent the morning putting pro-Rogers, anti-Tackett leaflets on cars parked in front of Catholic and Pentecostal churches attended by Mexican farm workers. Later, Kennedy said, "Tackett was superliberal and very pro-abortion." The effort in Lamont was intended to offset what she believed was Tackett's heavy spending of Willie Brown's money to win the Hispanic vote. It had been timed, she acknowledged, so that the Tackett camp would have no time to respond. The Rogers campaign, aware of what she was doing, had asked her not to distribute the leaflets in Bakersfield because it might be counterproductive; a good many Bakersfield Republicans supported abortion.

Republicans ended up with all five seats on the board of supervisors, control of the city council, both Assembly seats, and the congressional seat. In the heavily Hispanic fifth supervisorial district, Richard Ybarra, the Hispanic candidate, lost to a white woman conservative. Except for the venerable senator Walter Stiern, a kind of county institution, the county coroner would be the highest-ranking elected Democrat in Kern County. Gene was buried in a landslide. He collected just over 40 percent of the vote, though he salvaged some respect by carrying the Okie-Hispanic towns of McFarland and Delano in his supervisorial district.

In Sequoyah County, Oklahoma, which had given Harry Truman 68 percent of the vote in 1948, Fritz Mondale got just 37.2 percent in 1984.

BY 1988, Eldon Tackett was regretting his 1980 vote for Reagan. His political dander was up. "Reagan's brought the deficit so our grandchildren will be paying it off. He's got it so we can't pay the interest on the national debt. He's made more millionaires than there ever was."

But Eldon's support for Dukakis—"a greenhorn"—was soft. The Democrat who caught his attention was Jesse Jackson.

Jackson had made two dramatic visits to McFarland before the California primary and focused his rhetoric on the mysterious cancer deaths. Storming into Bakersfield May 19, he compared McFarland to Love Canal: "There's not only contamination, there's corruption," he told a Civic Auditorium audience. "No homeowner is protected until the children of McFarland are protected. No one can drink water and feel secure until there is no poisoned water anywhere where people drink water."

On June 5 Jackson returned to the valley to lead one of the biggest political rallies in McFarland's history, again addressing the cancer issue. He marched with Chavez, Texas agriculture commissioner Jim Hightower, and former New Mexico governor Tony Anaya, among people holding placards that read: "Jesse Cares About Children of All Colors."[2] Jackson attacked corporate agriculture, shouting, "Chevron, Tejon Ranch, Getty Oil, Shell Oil, McCarthy Joint Venture, Blackwell Land, Tenneco West, Southern Pacific Land—We demand a government of, for and by the people. Let this land be our land!"

His straight talk went right to Eldon Tackett's populist heart. Eldon pronounced himself not yet ready to vote for a black man for President, but if Dukakis lost, he figured he might support Jackson in 1992. But he was lukewarm, if not negative about Dukakis. As the campaign wore on, the Republican attacks on Dukakis's American Civil Liberties Union membership began to sink in. Mention of the ACLU raised Eldon's blood pressure. "They ought to blast them off the map," he said. "They're against everything's that's right." Eldon blamed the ACLU for preventing police officers from making drug and alcohol checks on drivers and indirectly for making the highways of Kern County less safe.

Eldon strongly disapproved of Dukakis's opposition to the death penalty. "You've got to fight fire with fire," he said, pronouncing the word with the Southwestern accent, "faar."

By October the Bush campaign was rolling in Kern County and Gene was no longer feeling so good about Dukakis's chances. One day, a group calling itself "victims of Willie Horton" visited Bakersfield.

"We need to do something," Gene said. "Maybe Kitty will come."

After watching the second debate between Dukakis and Bush with thirty or so friends at Shakey's Pizza Parlor at the Wild West Shopping Center, Gene acknowledged that his man had not done so well. "It was kind of like kissing your sister," he said. "He didn't show himself a lot different from the bunch. I'm not super turned on, but my faith is as strong as ever. He has the ability to make the hard decisions, but we need to change those folks who are undecided so we can win the election, and he probably didn't do that."

A television interviewer showed up and asked Gene some questions. Guidance on how to respond to the debate was not forthcoming from Dukakis's headquarters in San Francisco, so Gene improvised, sidestepping questions about the debate and focusing instead on Bush.

Somebody ordered hero sandwiches all around. It was turning into exactly the kind of campaign Gene hated: long on symbols—the flag, Willie Horton, the pledge of allegiance—but totally lacking in serious debate about where the country should be going in the 1990s.

"They're going to vote against somebody who doesn't support the death penalty because in their own mind they think if you execute people there's going to be less crime. I don't understand that logic, when all rational knowledge says that executing people doesn't cut back on the crime rate.

"They can come through now and look you in the eye and say Dukakis let Willie Horton out deliberately. There doesn't seem to be a way to succeed in the political business and be ethical. There's no citizen-politician anymore. They're so afraid of losing their jobs."

The week before the election, Dukakis arrived in Bakersfield to begin a whistle-stop train ride through the valley. Gene and the local Democratic organization prepared the event so that there would be good "visuals" at the train station. Gene had found a phrase, "Keep Hope Alive," he thought would contrast nicely with the negativism of the Bush campaign. At the same time, he was pushing a get-out-the-vote campaign in precincts where Mondale had scored well in 1984 and Alan Cranston in 1986.

He got to the station early and warmed up the crowd with chants of "On our side" and "We want Mike" and then drew cheers when he announced that a straw poll of high school students had "gone for Duke." Then the Duke himself arrived as the band played his theme, "Coming to America."

Standing alongside Dukakis, Cranston attacked the Bush campaign as a "despicable campaign of outright lies," and Dukakis finally used the "L word." He was, he said, "a liberal in the tradition of Franklin Roosevelt, Harry Truman, and Jack Kennedy." But when asked moments later whether he favored a nationwide grape boycott, he ducked: "I think I answered that question."[3]

Gene and Wendy got a dampener the next day when the Bakersfield *California* headlined: "3,000 Hear Whistle-Stop Speech; Many Lack Enthusiasm." Wendy was one of dozens of local Democrats who wrote to the paper complaining about what they thought was a misleading headline, but Gene refused to get worked up about it. Perhaps the reporters had picked up something they had missed. "I guess I'm kind of a Buddhist on these things," he said. "I just try to go on to what's next and not dwell on it too much."

THE FIRST INDICATION Gene had that Election Day was going badly came at around four-thirty in the afternoon when he called Dukakis headquarters in San Francisco. He had phoned earlier in the day, and the campaign worker answered with a crisp, "Dukakis for President, we're going to win." But this time, the last half of the sentence was dropped.

At five, Gene turned on the television set in his bedroom. It was just a few minutes after eight in the East, but as ABC came on with its Election '88 coverage, he heard Peter Jennings announce that the network had already tallied more than two hundred electoral votes for George Bush. As Gene watched, the Bush numbers climbed minute by minute. Soon the ABC election map showed a solid red South, denoting a Bush sweep. Worse, key states, Ohio and New Jersey, went to Bush.

Gene slumped on the leather couch, watching as the areas of red on ABC's map spread. New York for Dukakis! A faint hope, a dab of blue, but the Bush numbers resumed their steady climb. Gene kept switching networks. Shortly after six o'clock Pacific time, several hours before the California polls were due to close, Dan Rather of CBS announced: "It's over."

Gene and Wendy had hired a sitter for the children so that Gene could make the rounds of television stations and campaign headquarters. Wendy was still at Dukakis headquarters, helping with the phone banks. Gene hesitated before leaving the house. He was accustomed to losing—Democrats generally lost in Kern County—but he had joined a national campaign partly hoping to derive energy and purpose from a winning cause. Now that was not to be. "It kind of deflates you," he admitted.

Benjamin, their eight-year-old who had met Dukakis and been caught up in the campaign excitement, seemed unusually subdued. Dukakis had seemed like a winner at the airport. Now the television networks pronounced his defeat. It was something to think about.

Gene climbed into the station wagon and drove to Democratic headquarters on Seventeenth Street. Pulling in, he noticed someone had tried to scrape the Dukakis sticker off the bumper of the car parked in front of his. Inside, Wendy was still handling phones, making sure there was transportation for late voters; California wasn't lost yet. While Gene was there, an angry woman called to berate her about the campaign Dukakis had waged.

Gene didn't stay long. He headed back home for a quick bowl of chili. Wendy joined him just in time to watch Dukakis's concession speech on an old black and white television set in the dining room. The beaten candidate looked weary, but showed little emotion. As Wendy listened, she seemed to hold back tears.

Gene went out and pulled up his "Dukakis for President" sign from the front yard, a small symbolic act: it was time to put the campaign behind him.

But not quite. He got back in his car and headed for KGET-TV, the NBC affiliate where several present and former local politicians of both parties were milling around behind the cameras, waiting to be interviewed.

A Republican assemblyman who had been on the board of supervisors with Gene confessed to having put a campaign flyer on Gene's doorknob, and there was good-natured kidding about it. Gene and the others stood around as Congressman Bill Thomas exhibited the partisan edge that had made him such a formidable power in the southern valley.

"The Democrats will be trying to set the agenda even though they lost the election," Thomas said, sliding over the fact that Democrats had decisively won both houses of Congress. "George Bush was the only person that all Americans voted for."

There was little time for Gene Tackett, who gently disagreed with Thomas. "I'm not sure it's a mandate," Gene said. The fact that Congress was more Democratic than ever showed that voters were "hedging their bets."

Gene headed over to Marti's restaurant, where Democrats were holding an election night bash. Nobody was paying attention to the results of the state referendum that were flashing on a king-size TV screen. Waiters moved through the crowded rooms with pitchers of beer. Though some people were sad, considering the magnitude of the Dukakis defeat the crowd was in a good mood. One young woman with tightly curled blond hair was already looking ahead to a possible Dukakis run in 1992: "I think he's a person with a lot of feelings inside him."

Gene talked briefly with a black realtor who had been a Jackson delegate in Atlanta. The realtor said he might be prepared to support Gore in 1992 if that would enable the Democrats to regain the White House. That seemed hopeful.

"There's a lot more new people involved than I've ever seen before," Gene said excitedly. It was something to begin building on.

As he sat down for a taped interview with a skeptical radio reporter, Gene came back to the theme. Somewhere among the young volunteers Dukakis had drawn into the campaign, he said, were the future politicians who would lead the Democratic Party out of the wilderness.

The defeat he had felt watching the returns was already passing, and he began to look on the positive side. He recalled something that U.S. Ambassador Chester Bowles had told "India 34," his Peace Corps group, when it arrived in Delhi fresh from stateside training in 1966: "Bowles said you have a choice of being an optimist or a pessimist. He said it's the optimists who create the opportunities for better things to happen."

CHAPTER TWENTY-FOUR

UNCERTAIN VICTORY

MICHAEL DUKAKIS pushed all of Oca Tatham's panic buttons: Dukakis, the manager and technocrat, whose Bible was a book on Swedish city planning and whose ethnic and religious identity seemed to have been bleached right out of him.

The Massachusetts liberal's success in the spring and early summer of 1988 was part of an unsettling experience that repeated itself every four years in Oca's living room. Suddenly, an unfamiliar cast of characters paraded across his television screen: political pundits and pollsters, liberal Democrats, Republicans with Yankee accents and educations—all jockeying for power and influence over him and millions of those he called "the Christian people." The incomprehensible bureaucratic infrastructure of American politics was on display, reminding Oca that "the Christian people aren't very well organized." And in 1988 there was special reason to be uneasy: Ronald Reagan's presidency was ending.

The Reagan years had given confidence to millions of people who had felt on the fringe of American democracy for decades. Fundamentalism had been in the shadows after the humiliation of the Scopes trial in 1925, and the repeal of Prohibition in 1933. Then came the New Deal, with its giant government projects and social engineering intended to cure the Depression, suggesting that the American future was in the hands of big government and big institutions. The need to marshal resources for World War II and then for the Cold War helped to centralize power and consolidated the influence of unions, universities, media monopolies, and large corporations.

Then in the 1960s, the large bureaucracies and corporations began to stumble. Vietnam helped to cut down a particular elite. The war—initiated by a Harvard president and his Ivy League advisers and conducted by a defense secretary from the Ford Motor Company—was a failure. By the time the United States was extracting itself, the authority of big institutions was being challenged from the Left and the Right. American Protestantism spun off dynamic spiritual movements like bureaucratic corporations spinning off entrepreneurial start-up companies. Small economic, spiritual, and creative growth centers emerged, from Fuller Theological Seminary in Pasadena to Apple Computer in Cupertino. The United States began to be atomized, dismantled, and reassembled into a million support groups, self-help seminars, malls, boutiques, and electronic communities of satellite/cable television and FM radio. White Americans, in particular, began rearranging their lives around an increasingly privatized system of services: health spas, tennis clubs, private day care centers, religious TV, and a new menu of programs on paid cable channels. The "government" of many of these enterprises was hardly touched by traditional government, which found itself in direct competition with an expanded private sector for the limited incomes of citizens. Private security companies provided police protection, and whole suburban subdivisions were run by homeowners associations that had the power to tax (mandatory fees), legislate (rules and regulations), and exercise policing powers (deed restrictions for noncompliance with orders).[1]

The "Reagan revolution" was just that. It helped overthrow entrenched power, from the boardrooms of Fortune 500 companies to the budget committees on Capitol Hill. Antitrust restraints were eased to make possible the wave of corporate mergers, acquisitions, and buyouts, and the Justice Department began a sustained attack on federally mandated affirmative-action programs. The federal budget continued to grow steadily, mainly due to increases in defense spending and the rising costs of so-called entitlement programs like Medicare, but the portion of the budget allocated to discretionary

programs declined steeply. Although only two government programs
were actually abandoned—the Comprehensive Employment and
Training Act and Community Service Block Grants—spending on
welfare, housing, food stamp, and other programs for the needy was
effectively capped.

For Oca Tatham, who liked as little government as possible, it
was as though the caravan had finally caught up. The country was
described as "turning right." Yet Oca hadn't turned at all. He had
simply held his position and waited, perhaps thinking to himself,
Some day they'll have to reckon with us. For a while in the 1980s,
they did.

The Reagan years had been a kind of holiday for American
evangelicals. To Oca, having Reagan in the White House was the next
best thing to having someone right out of the Assemblies of God
there. Perhaps Reagan could have accomplished more, but Oca didn't
fault Reagan, given the forces that Oca believed were arrayed against
him. "The media's never favorable to Christianity," he said. "It scares
the Christians. They know they have the media one hundred percent
against them. Donahue will stick up for lesbians and homosexuals, but
you let a minister go in there, and they'll tear him up. It's television.

"We know there's a certain element that's fighting everything
that's good when it comes to Christianity," he continued. "They'd
throw Christianity out if they could. They're bitter men, bitter, bitter,
bitter. So the Christian people have got to stick together. If you're
Christian you better study the issues and see the guy you vote for
believes the way you believe."

Still, it was difficult to argue that the Reagan revolution was
also a moral revolution. It was a time of excess. Ostentatious houses
sprouted in vacation resorts all over the country. Greed (insider trading on Wall Street) and government lies (the Iran-contra affair) were
behind the scandals headlined in newspapers. The sturdy American
values of honesty and self-sacrifice seemed to have been devalued.

True, the secularists had received a sharp blow as everyone's
conscience was raised about abortion, pornography, and television
violence. Under Reagan, all federal funding for abortion counseling
ceased, thanks to a Republican-controlled Senate from 1981–1987
and the President's veto of certain appropriations bills. The Hyde
Amendment of 1976, named for Illinois Republican congressman
Henry Hyde, banned federal funding for all abortions except when
necessary to save the life of the mother and was tacked onto most
spending bills. After Reagan took office it became a cornerstone of

his antiabortion policies and was used to enforce an airtight ban on federal funding of such procedures.

Nevertheless, the conservative social agenda had not been achieved. The right to an abortion was still the law of the land. Much to Oca's dismay, a number of state governments continued to permit funding of abortions for the poor. Prayer was still outlawed in schools, more women than ever were leaving their children in day care centers to join the work force, and the rights and protection of homosexuals were expanded in many areas. Columnist Chuck Colson wrote in *Christianity Today* in 1988: "The anti-pornography campaign can claim a study commission but no legislation. Despite a zealous anti-drug campaign, crack and cocaine continue to kill our youth. Government grants subsidizing 7.1 million children a year—nearly half born out of wedlock—erode the traditional family, while long promised welfare reforms languish in the bureaucracy."[2]

For all the concerns expressed by liberals about the Christian right, that element had been slow to coalesce politically. Not until 1984, according to New Right leader Paul Weyrich, did fundamentalist Protestant pastors perceive that Reagan's presidency did not guarantee the success of their platform, and that they faced a long, sustained struggle. Weyrich found the Protestant pastors excessively "meek." While seeking Senate approval in 1981 of a constitutional amendment to restore prayer in public schools, Weyrich coached various pastors before they visited Washington to meet with Reagan, but once in the presence of the chief executive the preachers invariably held their tongues and praised him for the job he was doing. Loving your enemy didn't mean capitulating to them, Weyrich kept reminding them.

In 1984, efforts to register and politicize fundamentalist voters increased within Falwell's Moral Majority, the Reverend Tim LaHaye's American Coalition for Traditional Values, and his wife Beverly LaHaye's Concerned Women for America—the group in which Cindy Critchfield became active in 1986. By then, bonding between conservative pastors and businessmen was a political phenomenon. In 1981, LaHaye, Richard Viguerie, and others had brought together Texas millionaire Bunker Hunt, Houston businessman Bob J. Perry, and other wealthy men to create an alliance between New Right politics, Christian publishing magnates, and leading conservative pastors in an organization called the Council for National Policy. Pat Robertson was president one year. Members included Falwell, Tommy Barnett, Bill Bright of Campus Crusade, and Paige Patterson, Baptist president of the Criswell Center for Biblical Studies in Dallas.

Through the council, the preachers were exposed to conservative ideas and to tacticians with hands-on political experience. Speakers at the quarterly meetings included National Security Council aide Oliver L. North, United Nations ambassador Jeane Kirkpatrick and Congressman Jack Kemp. But in many ways the preachers were the key players. The organizers had the mailing lists, but the preachers had the followings. Jim Bakker endorsed Reagan and organized mass voter registration campaigns from his North Carolina facility. He developed a close relationship with George Bush, as did Jimmy Swaggart, briefly.

At the Republican Convention in Dallas in 1984, conservative Christians claimed a prominent place. Falwell delivered the benediction, describing Reagan and Vice President Bush as "God's instruments in rebuilding America."[3] Gary Jarmin of Christian Voice was quoted as saying, "We've taken over the GOP in many areas."[4]

The stepped-up grass-roots activity was felt in the Tatham orbit. One fall day in 1984, Bill Tatham got a call at his office from Pastor G. L. Johnson.

"How would you like to come up to San Francisco with us right now and pick up Jerry Falwell?" G. L. inquired.

Bill hesitated. He had come to the office in his preferred garb— jeans, cowboy boots, and open-necked shirt—hardly correct attire for meeting an esteemed Baptist preacher. But he doubted Falwell would take offense. "I'm on my way," he said.

Falwell had been traveling around the country, enlisting support for his "moral agenda" and Ronald Reagan's reelection and was lunching that day in Fresno with pastors from around the valley.

Two hours later, Bill was sitting on a private plane headed back to Fresno, talking football with the president of the Moral Majority. Bill had followed the political activities of Falwell, Robertson, and other ministers. He agreed with much of what they were saying, but he had reservations about pastors mixing in politics: "The church needs to worry about people's souls and most of the other things they [pastors] do are a waste. I mean, it's nice because you get people to come to church because they feel like there's a social status and for whatever reasons. It helps to keep the church together. But basically, if the guy gets his soul fed, that's what you're really there for."

A hundred and fifty protesters greeted Falwell outside the Piccadilly Inn—representatives of the local pro-choice movement, the

American Civil Liberties Union, and the United Methodists. Michael Loring, cantor emeritus of Temple Beth Israel, told a reporter for the Fresno *Bee* that Falwell's effort to "inject ultra-fundamentalist Christian religious doctrine into the laws and policies governing America's citizens" was "alarming and dangerous."[5] But this did not deter the enthusiasm of the Christian right. At the meeting, Falwell spoke, quoting back to the audience something Bill had said on the plane that day, mentioning Bill by name. This was a smart politician, Bill thought.

Falwell's main business was indeed politics, and he soon got down to it. A Reagan victory, he explained, would give the President the opportunity to name between two and five new Supreme Court justices and overturn *Roe* v. *Wade*, the 1973 decision that had legalized abortion. "There is a sleeping giant that began to awake in 1980, and it is standing up full-grown in 1984, and this nation will never be the same," Falwell said. Since 1979, he added, religious conservatives had registered five million new voters. "We don't break our backs to register people who will vote the wrong way. We're looking for people who know right from wrong."

DICK TATHAM, Bill's brother, was one of the evangelical pastors whom the White House and the New Right were recruiting to mobilize support for Reagan's 1984 reelection and for the administration's agenda in Congress. In 1983, with the help of a $25,000 loan from Oca, Dick had inaugurated the first Christian radio station in the desert and mesa between Las Vegas and the Mexican border. KNLB-FM, located in a building adjacent to his Christian preschool on property acquired from the Mormon Church, received news and nationally syndicated radio shows via the RCA Satcom III satellite. The radio station broadcast hard-hitting shows like "Talk Back with Bob Larson," in which Larson gave no quarter to homosexuals, gay ministers, child abusers, Satanists, or Christian rock musicians. The Bob Larson show soon became popular listening in the RV parks and on the assembly line of the local chain saw plant.

In 1985, Dick launched a low-power Christian television station, KAL-TV, whose programs augmented the five commercial programs available locally. He had pulled that off in typical Tatham fashion, scrounging surplus equipment at auctions, borrowing here and there, and getting a loan from Oca. The station aired programs from Paul Crouch's Trinity Broadcast Network, which sold time to Robertson,

Bakker, and Swaggart. In turn, TBN supplied substantial revenues back to KAL-TV by remitting some of the money collected from zip codes reached by Dick's transmitters.

Dick had attended a meeting of the National Religious Broadcasters in Washington in January 1983, wangling a free trip through a local friend who had him assigned to the NRB's security detail. The NRB was becoming a force in conservative politics since religious television was of key importance as an alternative media. When the White House began more actively to court the pastors through briefings with senior administration officials in Washington, Dick returned to Washington in May for a conference organized by the Association of Christian Schools. There, Deputy Under Secretary of Education Gary Bauer and others discussed a conservative agenda for education stressing school discipline, prayer, and the fight against drugs. The pastors were briefed on the President's position on church and state and about subversion of the church in Nicaragua.

That July, Dick returned to Washington again with a hundred or so other pastors, including Falwell, Swaggart, and G. L. Johnson, for a broader briefing. There was a reception in the Indian Treaty Room at the State Department attended by Vice President Bush and Interior Secretary James Watt (a member of the Assemblies of God). There were speeches by high-ranking administration officials and supporters including Faith Ryan Whittlesey, Reagan's assistant for public liaison; Bruce Chapman, deputy presidential assistant; and Surgeon General C. Everett Koop, who discussed abortion.

In one briefing that left a lasting impression on Dick, a State Department official from the Bureau of Refugee Programs discussed Communist insurgency in El Salvador, Nicaragua, and Guatemala and warned that it would lead to unrest in Mexico and, finally, to a flood of refugees into the United States. Dick left feeling physically ill. "The Communists are coming over from Mexico; Latin America is going," he said.

Back home in Lake Havasu City, Dick set up a voter-registration desk in the foyer of his church. He felt that he had to avoid taking a partisan position because of the diversity of political views in his congregation, but he felt that at least he was doing something.

In Fresno, meanwhile, Peoples Church was becoming more visibly a focal point for activism on social and foreign policy issues. Associate Pastor Dale McNeil, a retired air force lieutenant colonel who had flown a Bird Dog spotter plane in Vietnam to mark targets for U.S. fighter bombers, became a "political liaison" at the church.

Pat Clary, a former Catholic who directed the church's women's ministries department, was expanding the usual fare of Bible studies to include legislative and political action.

Another assistant pastor worked with Crisis Pregnancy Centers, an independent organization that counseled pregnant women about abortion alternatives.

Carol Magee, a church member, was involved with Interested Monitoring Persons Against Contemporary Textbooks, whose purpose was to eliminate "subliminal sexually-oriented" pictures and texts from schoolbooks. In 1982, the organization won a victory when the publishing company of Holt, Rinehart & Winston informally agreed to revise three illustrations for its new California reading textbooks.

A Peoples Church member, Donald Farrington, got his name placed on the November 1984 ballot by running as a write-in candidate for the State Assembly in the Republican primary. His district was a moderate-to-conservative farming area northeast of Highway 99, which had voted for the tax-cutting Proposition 13, a victim's bill of rights, Reagan in 1980, and Republican governor George Deukmejian in 1982 and against a gun-control initiative. But in 1982 it had elected an up-and-coming young Democrat by the name of Bruce Bronzan to the Assembly. Farrington's political views had changed little since he had been a campaign worker for Goldwater in 1964. He believed that the U.S. government helped Communists abroad and that Vice President Bush and Secretary of State George Shultz were "captives of the Council on Foreign Relations." In 1984, he hammered away at Bronzan for his support of the homosexual job-protection measure, Assembly Bill 1.

When Tim LaHaye arrived in Fresno for a fall speaking engagement at Peoples Church, Farrington met him at the airport and stayed close to him. On October 24, LaHaye returned to Fresno to address Farrington's supporters, calling on the "sleeping army of Christians to change the complexion of America by ousting the liberals in the American government."[6] Unless Christians were elected to office, he warned, America would continue on a decline that "will pass the Sodom and Gomorrah conditions."

But the small turnout of about 150 people was a disappointment, and Farrington garnered just over a third of the vote. In an interview with the Fresno *Bee*, Bronzan said, "I'm a Christian, but I have never believed that you should use that belief for political gain. I have no problem with different views and interpretations, but I do have a problem with those who think their view is the only view and they speak for everyone."[7]

Throughout 1985 and 1986, despite the problems caused by the Peoples Foundation bankruptcy filing, G. L. Johnson made occasional trips to Washington to attend briefings with administration officials. The briefings painted an increasingly bleak picture of the war in Central America, then a major preoccupation of the Reagan administration. Lieutenant Colonel Oliver North of the National Security Council staff—a member of a charismatic Episcopalian church in Virginia—was frequently a speaker at meetings of the Council for National Policy. And North spoke to visiting preachers in Washington, including Johnson, in June 1986. What North had to say shocked Johnson, and as soon as he got back to Fresno he arranged to deliver a special political address in downtown Fresno's civic auditorium.

Johnson and the other preachers had been shown satellite pictures of a submarine base in Cuba and a 10,000-foot runway under construction in Nicaragua. "My friends," he told the audience of a thousand people at the Civic Auditorium, "are you aware there is a gradual crumbling of democracy in Central America, as Marxism of the Soviet Union is moving in faster and faster every day? We have not been told how someone must stand up and declare that we are opposed to that and that it must be fought. We must somehow help the people who are standing up against these evil forces. For if we do not help them, you can be sure—as Colonel North told us—it will be necessary for our young men to go and fight, whether it is in Mexico City they fight or in San Antonio or San Diego."

Johnson's voice cracked with emotion: *"The fact is somewhere they must be stopped!"*

THERE WAS EXCITEMENT among the older generation of California Tathams when Pat Robertson announced in 1987 that he was planning to run for President. Robertson was Oca's favorite son. He already subscribed to the newsletter published by Robertson's Christian Broadcasting Network and tuned in to Robertson's "700 Club." Though unlikely, it was not impossible to imagine a charismatic Christian winning the White House. Governor John Ashcroft of Missouri was a member of the Assemblies (and, like Robertson and Bush, a Yale graduate).[8]

Ona, Cleo, Ophelia and Bill Thomas, and Vernon and Dora were also Robertson enthusiasts. But among younger Tathams, the support waned. Doris Weaver and her daughter Cindy liked him, as did Dick Tatham, but Bill, Gerald, and Renee had reservations.

Robertson's appeal was his intimate presence in the living rooms of millions of his viewers, his television congregation. Oca and Cleo called him "Pat," as though he were a member of the family. Television, Beverly LaHaye of Concerned Women for America observed, enabled Robertson to reach into "remote areas of the country, to farms and villages. . . . He's come into their homes, talked to them about their problems, ministered to them about finances, and become a friend to them. So when he says, 'Let's get you registered, let's get involved in politics, come to the caucus meetings,' they are willing to move and do things that they've never done before."

Yet Robertson was a difficult figure to place. Yale-educated and the son of a United States senator—the identical background as Vice President Bush—Robertson could have been anything, but chose to become a hero in the culture of religious people who emphasized the miraculous. In a sense, Robertson had chosen an unusual kind of downward assimilation as his road to fame and affluence.

He was a new kind of presidential candidate. Robertson prayed out loud on television that godly people would get elected to office and incited fears about an American education system that teaches "a philosophy that is amoral, anti-Christian, humanistic," which will "ultimately lead toward Marxism, socialism and a communistic type of ideology."[9] As he said, in February 1986:

"I think those Americans who cherish traditional values are looking for a candidate to represent their point of view and to stand tall on those matters. The major problem we face is the moral state of the people. I'm talking about the need for a spirit of reliance on God, a spirit of patriotism, a spirit of giving, a spirit, if you will, of self-sacrifice for noble goals. Unless we reinstate that spirit in our people we will continue to look to Washington for increasingly large handouts, bailouts and solutions.

"If all the evangelicals do is talk about prayer and abortion, without question it will become a very narrow special-interest group. But if they talk about moral renewal, if they talk about strong defense, if they talk about economic restraint, if they talk about the budget deficit—they will be reinforcing the mainstream."[10]

When Tim LaHaye originally approached Robertson about running, the television host had been reluctant to do so, and some thought with good reason. His ministry was successful, he lived well in a stately brick manor house, and his Christian Broadcasting Network gave him clout at the White House. He knew—or should have known—that the politicized fundamentalist element in the Republican Party had high "negatives" among voters.[11]

In some ways, it was true, the white Christian Right element in the Republican Party mirrored the black element in the Democratic Party: while both parties valued the hard-core support and passion these constituencies brought to their campaigns, neither party could afford to embrace them too warmly. Just as it was suicidal for the Democratic Party to be seen as "too black," it was also problematic for the GOP to come across as "too Christian." It was probably inevitable that both Jesse Jackson and Pat Robertson, the two men of the cloth running for high office, would finish 1988 feeling badly used by their respective parties.

Jesse Jackson came out of a culture in which ministers frequently served as political spokesmen and were expected to be involved in politics. Jackson was a black preacher from a humble background in the tradition of the late Martin Luther King, Jr., and he spoke movingly to the experience of all blacks. Robertson, a man of the upper crust, preached to a largely working-class and lower-middle-class white fundamentalist tradition that was extremely skeptical of politics, especially of ministers in politics.

Robertson had another problem: he was a charismatic who believed in miracles (prayer could influence a hurricane to turn away from Virginia and toward New England—a region which, unfortunately for Pat, also held presidential primaries). As a charismatic Baptist, Robertson could not count on the solid backing of conservative Baptists or other noncharismatic denominations. In a sense, he was a fringe candidate in a fringe constituency.

His campaign nonetheless began with high hopes. On February 2, 1987, Robertson addressed a standing-room-only crowd at Peoples Church and drew applause when he said that the first settlers "claimed this land for the Lord Jesus Christ." The Fresno *Bee* said Robertson's performance had "enhanced his credibility."[12] And Bill Tatham gave $2,000 to Americans for Robertson.

Subsequently, he agreed to underwrite a major Robertson campaign event in Fresno on July 20 as a favor to his friend Herb Ellingwood, who was managing Robertson's campaign. Some 1,500 people showed up at Selland Arena, many of whom wrote checks for $19.88 to Americans for Robertson. The event was a curious blend of political stumping and religious revival. Somebody "testified" about a healing from cancer; others spoke enthusiastically of Robertson's victory

in the Michigan straw-poll primary. The rally took place in the middle
of the Iran-contra hearings on Capitol Hill, and Pastor Johnson
closed the evening with a reference to it: "Ted Kennedy lets a woman
drown at Chappaquiddick and he serves in the U.S. Senate; Oliver
North tries to protect the nation from communism and he undergoes
a congressional investigation."

In Arizona, Pastor Dick Tatham and Billy Tatham were contacted
by Robertson's organization. Norman P. McClelland, president of
Shamrock Foods, who was managing the Robertson campaign, arranged for Billy to have breakfast with Robertson. Afterward Robertson went to a rally at Tommy Barnett's First Assembly Church. Billy
liked Robertson for passing up the easy life that his birth and education had assured.

Charles Roberts, another Shamrock Foods executive, flew over
to Lake Havasu City and asked Dick to head a Robertson campaign
group in Mojave County. Being a pastor, Dick felt that he could not
endorse a candidate, but he promised to help all he could.

Roberts' strategy was to recruit people to fill the precinct committee positions in hopes of taking control of the Arizona Republican
primary vote for Robertson. He met in Kingman with Dick and other
local pastors representing Baptist, Nazarene, and Methodist
churches. Some of the ministers liked Robertson, but none of them
were enthusiastic about lending their names to his campaign. But
back in Lake Havasu City, Dick and his church secretary got themselves elected to the Republican precinct committee.

As Robertson's primary campaign unfolded, it became clear that
an unusually large number of his supporters were members of charismatic churches or denominations. Ellingwood was in the Assemblies
of God; Pentecostal and charismatic leaders such as Oral Roberts and
Jimmy Swaggart declared for him.

"I feel as a charismatic leader that I have to support him," said
Vinson Synan, chairman of the North American Renewal Service
Committee, representing forty Pentecostal and charismatic organizations. "I don't think all will vote lockstep for Robertson, but many
will. . . . Most rank and file Pentecostals will go along with Pat."

But *outside* the charismatic fold it was different. Among Baptists,
the denomination that over the decades had remained most hostile
to Pentecostal doctrine, Robertson aroused emotions running from
the skeptical to the negative. A Spirit-filled Baptist minister was a
jarring notion to them. Tim LaHaye had helped persuade Robertson
to run, but by late 1987 he was backing Congressman Jack Kemp for

President and his wife, Beverly, was for Bush. She spoke of Robertson as a "good conservative" and a "friend," but she supported the vice president, as did Falwell (a Baptist), Ed McAteer, president of the Religious Roundtable (a Baptist), and Reverend W. A. Criswell, pastor of the 25,000-member First Baptist Church in Dallas, a center of the fundamentalist crusade to take over the 14 million member Southern Baptist Convention.

"Right now you see a crack within evangelicalism," said Paige Patterson of Criswell College in Dallas. "The charismatics are supporting Pat Robertson, but you see fundamentalist Methodists, Baptists, Mennonites, Churches of the Brethren, and so on supporting others." Patterson did not reveal whom he personally was backing, but he said it would not be Pat Robertson.[13]

To his followers, Robertson was simply a candidate who represented Christian principles. But many Baptists, whose denomination had played a leading role in securing the constitutional separation of church and state in the early republic, found aspects of Robertson's message disturbing. When Robertson spoke of the Founding Fathers, he seemed to some Baptists to mean John Winthrop and his theocrats in Massachusetts, not George Washington and American democracy.

"When I listen to Pat I don't hear mainline Republican thought as much as I hear a reconstructionist populism," said Ronald S. Godwin, senior vice president of the Washington *Times* and former executive director of the Moral Majority. Reconstructionism was a theology promoted by R. J. Rushdoony of the Chalcedon organization in California and his son-in-law Gary North of the Institute for Christian Economics. Rushdoony argued that constitutional democracy had failed and should gradually be replaced by Biblical law and a Calvinist-style rule by a "righteous elite."[14]

Herbert W. Titus, dean of the College of Law and Government at CBN University, who was well acquainted with the candidate's thinking and writing, strongly disputed that Robertson was a closet reconstructionist. Robertson, said Titus, emphasized the "Biblical legacy of the American Revolution" and was attempting to promote a "rediscovery of the godly heritage of American politics and law." Nonetheless, Robertson's views on some subjects were unsettling. He did not believe Supreme Court rulings to be the "law of the land" because they were not binding on the President, Congress, governors, and legislatures in the same way a "law" would be.

Robertson had set forth many of his views in his newsletter, which he wrote from 1977 to 1982. Discussing the budget deficit, for example, Robertson referred to Leviticus 25, which calls for cancellation of debts every fifty years. Robertson also expressed an interest in Biblical prophecy, citing the thirty-eighth chapter of Ezekiel as a guide to the future of the Mideast.[15] And he suggested that nobody "whose mind and body is not controlled by God Almighty is qualified" to govern. Acknowledging that he believed in a "limited democracy," Robertson said that government is "instituted by God to bring His law to people."[16] To a good many traditional conservatives, such views left doubts about Robertson's commitment to pluralistic democracy.

The primary season began with a surprising success for Robertson, who was second in the GOP primary in Iowa, trailing favorite son Senator Robert Dole of Kansas, but leading Bush. Then Bush won convincingly in New Hampshire, and as the primary campaign wore on, a series of gaffes and "funny facts," as the media called them, raised questions about Robertson's judgment and character. He stated that Soviet missiles were still in Cuba and that his Christian Broadcasting Network knew the whereabouts of U.S. hostages in Lebanon, but he offered no proof. There were also misstatements, later clarified or recanted, that he was a "tax lawyer" and that he was a board member of a "multimillion-dollar bank." After the March Super Tuesday primary, his candidacy was over. George Bush was the Republican nominee.

The end of Robertson's candidacy was a disappointment to the older generation of Tathams around Oca and Ona, but it was nothing like the defeat of Goldwater in 1964. Bill Tatham, for one, had few regrets. At the Fresno event in June 1987, he had found Robertson too "slick" for his liking, and his opinion did not improve when Robertson left him with more than $5,000 in unpaid bills after the event. Having agreed to underwrite it, Bill had no choice but to pay the delinquent accounts. At first he was mildly irritated. Then he was angry. Bill called Robertson's secretary in Virginia Beach; he called Ellingwood; finally, he called the Federal Election Commission in Washington to make sure that his coverage of the bills would not be interpreted as an illegal campaign contribution exceeding the limit allowed for individuals. Pastor Johnson phoned Robertson and asked him at least to call Bill and apologize. Robertson never called. Pat, Bill concluded, was "a jerk." By the end of 1987 Bill was leaning toward Dole, that flinty areligious pragmatist. But Bush would do, he said.

Shortly before Super Tuesday in the late winter of 1988, revelations about the private life of evangelist Jimmy Swaggart hit the headlines. On February 21, after several days of rumors that he had been with a prostitute in a Baton Rouge motel room, Swaggart confessed, sobbed, and begged forgiveness during a squalid, nationally televised program. Robertson supporters charged that the Bush campaign had leaked the story to the media to embarrass Robertson. A month later, the Assemblies of God suspended Swaggart from preaching for a year. Swaggart said he would not submit to the church directive.

Swaggart had long been a favorite of many of the older generation of religious Okies who had moved West. They identified with a poor boy who had risen above his humble roots, but who had never disavowed them. Swaggart's father had played the fiddle and bootlegged when Jimmy was growing up in Louisiana. Swaggart reached out to people who still attended small churches.

Oca had given more than $5,000 to Swaggart—money, he noted proudly, that went to a Swaggart program said to feed fifty thousand meals a day to hungry people abroad. But by late 1987, Oca's instincts convinced him that Swaggart was heading for trouble: "I believe he's got so big and powerful that people are looking more to Jimmy Swaggart than to the Lord." The revelations in early 1988 nonetheless stung Oca. His admiration for Swaggart being well known at Peoples Church, he took some good-natured ribbing about it. He saw, however, that the Lord was using the scandal "to impress on my mind to forgive and forget, to handle it like the woman who was caught in adultery. Jesus showed love without condemnation. That was how Jesus handled it. I'm handling it the opposite. The Lord has shown me how far off I am." To prove that he was learning, he sent a small gift of money to Swaggart's wife and son.

The scandal was the talk of Swaggart's older fans up and down the valley. Cleo and Ophelia burned up the phone lines discussing the affair. Ophelia felt "as if a knife had been put in me. I thought he preached the truth. But we can't get our eyes on people." She thought of the "little grandmothers" who sent money to those preachers and "they live like millionaires." She said, "If Jimmy Swaggart is hurting for money he should sell his house—or his son's millionaire house. When I heard I asked, 'Is there anybody honest in the world?' I hurt so bad. He's hurt millions. And they're crying, 'Forgive him, forgive him.' It made me deathly sick to hear that."

Ophelia's husband, Bill, was a lot harsher. "Billy says Swaggart is a dirty hypocrite," Ophelia said, "and that if he worked as hard as *he* did he wouldn't be out there huntin' those other women."

Cleo "tried to be broad-minded, but I'm going to tell you something. He got so much money, he begged all the time. He got Oca's money. Now he's caught between the wagon wheel and the mud. When a little small person comes up and gets a lot, it goes to their head. I don't believe you ought to call other churches names. He went after Catholics and everything."

To those outside the fold, the adultery of Jim Bakker, the peccadilloes of Swaggart, the financial difficulties of Roberts, and Robertson's political self-destruction seemed bizarre and outlandish. But for those within the fold, it was part of a natural cycle in which God cut down to size those who had lost track of their place and their mission. Periodic public displays of the Devil knocking the powerful off their high horses were a kind of rite, an essential sacrament reminding all, once again, that Satan was Lord of the world—an enemy who could raise his flag in the very center of the earthly kingdom. Witnessing the fall of Swaggart was like having the Lord at one's elbow saying quietly, "You see, you see."

Through such public embarrassments as the Swaggart affair, evangelical Protestants regained their balance and stability. The Catholic Church tended to conceal its scandals, quietly shunting morally wayward priests from one parish to another. Decentralized evangelical Protestantism had no way to restrain and check the populist heros who rose out of the ranks, so the Devil and publicity had to do the job. The scandals were a reminder to the flock of what Oca instinctively knew: *"God don't need Christian celebrities."*

Oca had seen it all, the con men and the charlatans, people he had trusted and believed in. He was a *collector* of disappointments. And in an important way, the fall of Swaggart conferred a certain confidence on the not-fallen. It wasn't Oca who slipped—he had "never let Ruby down," he said—but the celebrities. He didn't think of himself as *better* than Swaggart, only that Jimmy had followed the fault lines of his flaws while Oca had resisted more successfully.

THE PRESS AND TELEVISION COVERAGE of the dramas of Swaggart, Bakker, Roberts, and Robertson was a media circus that revived all the garish old caricatures of fundamentalist preachers as corrupt and phony con men. The stories had all the elements of a good scandal: sex, money, and betrayal. Yet the headlines obscured deeper truths. Individual preachers might disappear in a puff of smoke, but the religious movements out of which they had grown would remain and would continue to transform American politics and culture.

In August 1988, Cindy Critchfield joined a group organized by her Zion Fellowship Church at a large antipornography rally at the State Capitol in Sacramento. Some 3,000 people chanting "Remember in November" turned out to march in favor of toughening California's obscenity law and giving local communities authority to set their own obscenity standards.[17] An American Civil Liberties Union lobbyist called the law the protesters favored extreme and warned, "We'll be back to book burning," but the Assembly handed the demonstrators a lopsided victory. Cindy and Bill continued to discuss the possibility of joining Operation Rescue, the militant antiabortion group. Others like them did, and the organization gathered strength.

While evangelical denominations, including the Assemblies of God, added churches and members in the 1980s, they also showed heightened concern for poverty, hunger, drug addiction, and racial discrimination, more in keeping with the social mission of an older American Protestanism. To be sure, only one in a hundred Assembly pastors was black and the percentage of black parishioners in its ranks was minuscule. But by the late 1980s, one out of ten members of the denomination was Hispanic, as large numbers of Mexicans and other Latin Americans flocked to Pentecostal churches in the Southwest. Teen Challenge—an antidrug program for young men started in 1958 by an Assemblies of God pastor in Pennsylvania—was a nationwide program providing 107 residential treatment centers with more than a thousand beds by 1987. The efficacy of its AIDS testing and drug rehabilitation were recognized and documented by the National Institute on Drug Abuse and the Department of Health, Education and Welfare. In December 1990, several Assemblies of God congregations in the Chicago area purchased and began renovating four large buildings at the Robert Taylor Homes to minister to blacks in the nation's largest public housing project.[18]

Tathams believed in helping others, but directly, or through private organizations, not through government programs financed by taxes. In their churches and families, they carried on the tradition of back-country ancestors who helped neighbors and relatives through direct, individual action rather than through intermediaries in government or social service agencies.

Gary Tatham manned the crisis hotline at Peoples Church several nights a month.

Brenda English was president of the Evangel Home, an emergency shelter in Fresno for women fleeing spousal abuse or family problems who were referred to it by police and welfare and social service agencies. Most of the women at the shelter were young, single, and unmarried. The shelter subsisted on donations and the volunteer work of people from local churches, such as Peoples Church. "You'd swear it was run by a bunch of liberals," Brenda joked. "It takes Republican money to do a lot of things," she added. "Love is an action. It's doing something."

Doris Weaver supported Teen Challenge in Oakland and bristled at the suggestion that evangelical Christians were indifferent to social problems. "Just because you have a job working in a [government] agency doesn't mean you really care," said Doris. "They're pretty cold people, some of them. We do it with love. We see their plight and want to help. That's where Christianity comes in. People helping people."

Three mornings a week, Doris's daughter Cindy Critchfield went to a friend's house and made sandwiches for underprivileged junior high school students in Oakland's inner city. An organization called Morningstar Ministries, affiliated with the Pentecostal church she and Bill were attending, offered the sandwiches to the children of heroin addicts. It was an effort to reach the parents through the children, and one parent had in fact gone into rehabilitation as a result of the program's contacts with their child. Cindy thought it was scriptural to give food to the sick and hungry. Such charity had been at the heart of Christian social mission for centuries. In the Pentecostal denominations, helping the poor and the hungry had usually been subordinated to saving souls, but invariably, as church movements grew, the social mission grew with them. Cindy remembered how her Grandmother Ruby had taken people in, cared for sick relatives, opened up her house, and given clothes to the poor. One could imagine Cindy in the nineteenth century handing out soup, bread, and God's message at a Salvation Army kitchen. Cindy thought it would be nice if people got off heroin, but it was fine, too, if the sandwiches just made sure the children weren't hungry.

The Tathams did what they could for others—as much or more, no doubt, than many who wanted to alleviate poverty and solve social problems with government money. They belonged to a long and respectable tradition in American Protestantism which held that citizenship began with oneself and worked out from there. A Christian could not solve all the problems of the world. But by being born again, and by helping others to be born again, the Christian could take a small step to make the world a better place.

Evangel Home, Teen Challenge, the Love Line, and Morningstar

Ministries were several of the "thousand points of light" that Bush referred to in his praise of the volunteer spirit. The question was whether volunteerism could ever do more than scratch the surface of society's needs for drug treatment centers, better schools, medical care for the poor, better police protection for those living in fear in public housing developments. For the country, that issue would remain unresolved. But Tatham views on that subject were clear.

BUT AS FAMILIES EVOLVED, they changed, and as subsequent generations tried to come to terms with their time and place, the politics, religion, and culture of a region shifted in complex, unpredictable ways.

Within the Tatham family, one of the interesting stories was the subtle evolution of political attitudes from one generation to the next. Older members of the family tended to hold more dogmatic views. "If the Democrats get in, they'll try to put the Christians out of business," Oca said as the 1988 election campaign neared an end. It was, he added, "hard to find a Democrat who isn't for abortion, pornography, and soft on Communists. Real born-again Christians don't vote Democrat—if they read. They're not going to put a guy in there that's against Christianity.

"There's no way I [can] vote for Dukakis and be a Christian. The guy doesn't believe in saluting the flag, he believes in abortion. He believes in taxpayers paying the bill, the government picking up the tab for abortion. I don't go for his releasing these here guys on a lifetime sentence for the weekend. That guy'd never make a President we want."

Tathams were dispersed right across the economic spectrum, from the affluent (Oca), to the near-poor (Cleo). Yet political views remained remarkably constant. For Tathams, the voting issues were cultural, not economic. Only rarely, if at all, did Tathams vote Democratic now. And it was hard to imagine that pocketbook issues would take precedence over moral, religious, and cultural ones any time soon.

CLEO, A WIDOW WHO WAS ENROLLED in Medicaid, was no more favorable to the Democrat in 1988 than Oca. "That Dukakis is out to stop all religion," she fumed. "He's against the pledge of allegiance. He's a card-carrying member of the ACLU! I listened to

Duke on the news, and he was saying all that 'other one' would talk about was saluting the flag. You know what? When you can't salute the flag that's our freedom! Makin' fun of wantin' to salute the flag! That's our freedom when that thing quits wavin'. I just about fell over. He stands for stampin' out all religion. I wouldn't vote for him as scavenger man."

Ophelia's assessment of Democrats was even less charitable: "They can hardly be Christians when you see the things they support," she said.

Younger Tathams, nonetheless, were working out their politics in typically individualistic, Tatham fashion. Experience and the corrosive forces of California were having their effects.

For Tathams, the abortion issue posed a particularly agonizing conflict between the family's moral position and its deeply held suspicion of government meddling. Time after time, public opinion polls showed that most Americans disapproved of abortion, yet a solid majority did not believe the government should intervene in a woman's reproductive decisions.

One of those who was reluctantly coming around to that view was Doris Weaver. It had taken a lot of agonizing, and she was not entirely happy with her position. "It would be good to stop," she said, "but I don't know that legislating it would make a difference. We don't approve of it; I think we should withdraw the government money for it. But you're not going to change people by telling them what to do. It comes down to stopping it by being born again."

Similarly, her sister Renee was against the government making the choice for women. Years earlier, before abortion was legal, she had a girlfriend who had an abortion in Watts. Paint was peeling from the ceiling, and the circumstances were sleazy. After the procedure, the friend developed an infection and almost died. As Renee saw it, women were always going to seek abortions, so they might as well do so under safe conditions.

Bill Tatham took a middle-ground position. "If you ask me am I for or against abortion, I would say I'm against abortion," he said. "If you ask me are there some cases where abortion should occur, I'd say definitely. In other words, I wouldn't take a blanket position and say that all abortion is wrong." He appreciated specialized expertise and thought sex education in the schools was a "good idea if the teachers are well qualified and it's presented properly." He had no complaints about any teachings that his own children brought home from school.

Gerald also rejected a total ban on abortion. "The Bible says a child is from God, but until I hear it from the man Himself I can't accept that a baby conceived in a rape is a gift from God," he said. He would, he said, counsel a daughter to terminate such a pregnancy.

On other issues, younger Tathams were tending to make up their own minds, based on common sense and experience rather than political propaganda. Gary Tatham planned to vote for Bush, but not out of a "party line kind of thing." He considered the Bush campaign's use of the Willie Horton story a ploy that glossed over the serious underlying problem of overcrowded jails. "What really makes me mad is that the politicians started talking in 1978 about getting tough on crime. We were overcrowded then and we're overcrowded now, and they haven't given us any new prisons or more staff to handle it. It wasn't Dukakis's policy, but he got caught on this."

IN THE TATHAM FAMILY, Bush's victory in November was greeted with a sense of relief, but without excitement. Oca kept a photograph of George and Barbara Bush in his study on Palm Avenue, along with a number of the political testimonials he had received from a Republican Party grateful for his support over the years: membership in the Republican Presidential Task Force and *Who's Who in the Republican Party* and certificates from the Ronald Reagan Presidential Foundation, the National Republican Senatorial Committee, and the Republican Presidential Citizen's Advisory Commission.

George Bush was the best they could get. But he was not one of them. The unanswered question was, Who was he, this man who had once favored abortion and called Reagan's economic policies "voodoo" and pretended to be a good ol' boy from Texas? Was he authentic or a pre-Goldwater Republican dressed up in Reagan disguise?

The old backcountry American values that were so interwoven into the culture of the South and now the entire Sun Belt could now be felt in the politics and policies of government at every level. This Southern-based culture had won many important battles. But time and again in history, the South had not known what to do with its victories. What had the early victories of Lee's armies meant to the South in the end? So often the South's role had been to fight courageous delaying actions, but to lose the wars. Perhaps, with the immense population shifts of the twentieth century, that would change.

Or would it? Whether the evangelical revival could blunt the growth of a more secularized culture was questionable. The nation's universities, political establishments, businesses, and media remained unfriendly ground for evangelical Christians. In part, according to theologian Carl F. Henry, that was because the Moral Majority and groups like it had missed an opportunity. Men like Falwell had promoted fundamentalist rights rather than human rights, Henry argued. They had not found common ground with blacks, women, and oppressed people in the Third World based on a shared commitment to justice and dignity. Now, Henry feared, the moment may have passed.

In some respects, what evangelical Christians defined as traditional American values were more threatened than they ever had been. At least after the Civil War, the opposing force—the secular, industrial North—had been geographically separated. Within its own region, the South could impose its moral and cultural authority. Now the many strands of American culture rubbed against one another in every neighborhood. In California, on any street one could now find Hispanic Catholics from south of the border, Buddhists from across the Pacific, "secular humanists" with liberal points of view, Republicans who supported abortion—and perhaps doctors performing them. Those groups held their views with an intensity equal to the Tathams'.

History was on the move. Abroad, the great godless enemy was dying and disintegrating. The world was being transformed with breathtaking speed. Only one thing could be said with certainty. America would feel the change in the wind, even if not for a while. Nobody could prevent that, least of all George Bush.

CHAPTER TWENTY-FIVE

LAST PIONEER

"HUSH, YOU THING," said Cleo as her little dog jumped onto the sofa and barked a raspy, staccato bark. It was the same every day when the mailman brought the letters. The little dog kept jumping and worrying until the letter carrier went out through the metal gate by the climbing roses.

In the spring of 1988, the mailman delivered a disturbing letter. Along with the Medi-Cal stamps that she used to buy her heart medicine and pay her doctor, the California Department of Public Health sent a notice:

"Pursuant to California legislation enacted in 1981, Medi-Cal benefits received by a beneficiary after age 65 are recoverable after death under certain conditions," it said. "Recovery may be made from the distributee of the Medi-Cal beneficiary if he or she does not leave a surviving spouse, minor children or a totally disabled child."

Cleo read the letter again, resting her hands firmly on the table to quiet the trembling that had afflicted them lately. Medi-Cal, the state's version of the national Medicaid program for poor people, was notifying her that the government might take her house on Quincy Street after she died to recover its money.

Her late husband had bought the house, and she had promised him she would leave the house to their son, Jerry. Now the state of California was telling her she might not be able to keep that promise.

At seventy-two, vinegar still flowed in Cleo's veins. Her first instinct was to find out who was responsible and call them "everything 'cept something good to eat."

"That Deukmejian's got this state like Russia," she complained, referring to California's governor. "When you die nobody gets to leave anything to their children. It goes back to the state. That rotten outfit's trying to keep this whole thing quiet."

The stamps had been coming ever since she had signed up for Supplemental Security Income a decade earlier. Qualifying had not been easy: the state people insisted on seeing her checkbooks and tax records to prove that she had no more to her name than a home, a secondhand car, a wedding and engagement ring, and the $1,500 in savings that was allowed to be set aside for burial expenses. But the coverage provided a safety net; SSI recipients automatically went on Medi-Cal. The SSI allowance of $140 and Wayne's Social Security and VA survivor's benefit gave her a total of $598 in cash a month to live on. But nobody told her about the policy of taking over poor people's houses to recover the government's costs. In 1985 Oca had given her a few hundred dollars and told her to pay off the mortgage note a year ahead. Now the house might be lost anyway.

She wasn't afraid of dying. "Tell the truth, I'm not that anxious to hang around here," she said, discussing the implications of the state's notice about her benefits. "Noooo. Too much trouble ahead—more trouble than we can realize."

But she wanted to leave something of value to her son, Jerry. She hadn't come to California and scrimped and saved all her life, only to die a pauper. Jerry had had so many heartaches: Rowdy's accidental death and his divorce from his first wife. Cleo had stuck with him, as a widowed mother of an only child will. He was a good man who had had a run of hard luck. "This house is the only thing I have to leave my boy, and he needs it," she said.

As she shuffled about the house, she figured her options. Other than her house, her only asset was her '77 Oldsmobile with 150,000 miles on it. If she went off SSI, the Medi-Cal coverage would stop, but she could rent out a room to her niece Carol, have a garage sale, sell the car, or even make quilts again if she could only get her hands to stop shaking.

Of the car she said: "The insurance on that dude's killing me anyway."

If ends didn't meet, she could sell her house and rent. At least that would keep her house away from the government.

Still, her plan had drawbacks: her house was paid for. If she rented . . . well, rents always rose, and the interest she got from the proceeds of her home would be fixed. If she went off Medi-Cal, she'd have to pay her Medicare premiums out of pocket and buy a private health insurance policy to supplement Medicare.

Age had chiseled her features and etched lines in her face, the evidence of character and the tragedies that had crossed her path. Though her spirit was intact, the years had begun to give her body assertive little nudges. Now, when she had trouble signing checks at the bank because her hands shook, they told her not to hurry.

In 1985 she'd fallen from a ladder and broken her arm. Then, there had been a strange moment in church when the whole world suddenly went topsy-turvy. It was after that that she noticed the trembling in her hands. More recently, she'd been looking up into the branches of her plum tree, thinking about plum jelly, when everything went blank. The next minute, she was lying on the ground with a broken ankle, wondering how she could crawl to a telephone. A few months before the Medi-Cal notice came in the mail, she had begun taking medicine for heart flutters.

Cleo first heard about the state of California taking the houses of old people from her cousin Alma McKinney up the highway in Earlimart. She was especially close to Alma, the oldest of Arch and Winnie Tatham's children. She and Alma were the last of the original group of Tathams in California from Drake's Prairie. The others had gone back to Oklahoma, moved to Fresno or the coast, or died.

Once dozens of relatives lived in Delano and the surrounding smaller farming towns, but now there was just Cleo and Alma and Catherine and Carol, Norma's two daughters. Cleo and Alma often talked on the phone. A long time ago they had discovered a quirk in the local telephone system: calls from Cleo's home in Delano to Alma's home in Earlimart carried a toll charge, but the ones from Alma to Cleo were free. So when Cleo wanted to reach her cousin, she'd dial, let the phone ring twice, and hang up. That was their signal. Alma would call right back, and they would talk, gossiping, commiserating about their health or recalling old times on Drake's Prairie.

Alma's husband, Bill, became ill with heart and stomach problems in early 1987. Medi-Cal paid for most of the hospital costs, but when doctors couldn't help him anymore, Alma transferred him to a local nursing home. Care at the home was not covered by Medicare, and Alma had to bring in proof of her deeds before they would admit Bill as a Medi-Cal patient. A lien was placed on their home. Bill lingered only a week, but the lien on the house stayed. When Alma's sister Eureda came from Oklahoma to visit, the two of them made inquiries about getting it removed. The answer was discouraging. A computer in Sacramento had kept track of all of Bill's payments from Medi-Cal, and those would have to be paid back before the lien would be lifted.

It was distressing news for Alma. She and Bill had bought their house in 1949, all cash. They wanted to be near Bill's sons from a previous marriage, so Bill went to work once again for the Sierra Vista Ranch, installing irrigation pipe and doing "curvy plowing," a specialized technique for turning soil between the grapevines. The house was small, but they had fruit and nut trees in the backyard— lemon, orange, peach, and pecan.

With Bill gone, Alma wished she lived nearer their only son in Bakersfield or even with Eureda and her brothers in Sallisaw, but the lien made selling her house problematic. In any case, Alma reasoned, a house in Earlimart would never bring enough to pay for one in town.

To ease Alma's loneliness, Cleo would often drive up the few miles from Delano in her Oldsmobile to visit. Alma had never learned to drive, but sometimes she would take a Greyhound bus the thirty-nine miles to Bakersfield to see her son.

Alma was unhappy about the lien. "We wouldn't have gotten into SSI if we'd known," she said. "They changed it up. In Oklahoma you can stay for a year in the rest home, and that's a poorer state than this."

Of course, the state of California had its reasons. Medicaid had been a great step forward for the nation's welfare system. It allowed the elderly poor to live out their lives in the dignity of their own homes, and there were safeguards in the law that prevented a person's home from being taken from the family as long as either the husband or wife lived there. Ultimately, though, someone had to pay for the doctors, drugs, hospitals, and nursing homes—care the state provided. Was it right for taxpayers to pay rather than relatives? Why should taxpayers support a person in old age so their children could enjoy an inheritance?

As Medicaid costs rose, many states began looking for savings at the margins. The payments were so stingy already that many physicians refused to treat Medi-Cal patients, and state officials dared not cut the schedules further for fear of crippling the program. Instead, a tougher "Medi-Cal recovery program" was instituted in the early 1980s, one that was supported by Democrats as well as Governor Deukmejian and the Republicans. The Department of Public Health was under firm instructions to recover Medi-Cal money from the estates of beneficiaries.

In 1987, recoveries in the state of California reached $13 million and were projected to double in 1988 as a result of additional staff in the probate division of the Public Health Department. The collections division improved coordination with Social Security and welfare agencies, which, along with probate attorneys around the state, were a source of intelligence about the death of Medi-Cal patients.

The concept of recovering the cost of government benefits from poor people remained politically controversial, however. If the policy was to seek recovery from the estates of Medicaid and SSI recipients, what about the estates of wealthy farmers? Should farms be seized and sold by the federal government in order to recover what had been paid out in the form of crop disaster or flood relief or as Commodity Credit Corporation price supports? The sums of money involved were much larger in those cases.

And then there was the risk that a tough recovery policy might drive the needy off the Medicaid program altogether. A few days after Cleo got the notice, she decided not to keep her appointments that week with her doctor until she clarified her situation. She did not want to use any more Medi-Cal stamps until she found out what the letter meant.

ONE DAY in early July Cleo came back from town to find a package with a note from a woman named Beverly Livsay, who worked for the Senior Citizens Information and Referral Service, a local agency funded by the Older Americans Act. She had dropped by to talk, and since Cleo wasn't home she left her phone number.

Cleo would learn later that Livsay was the same woman who several years earlier had helped her fill out the forms to prove that her income was little enough to qualify her for a small property-tax reduction. The reduction brought the tax down from several hundred dollars to a manageable $150 a year.

Cleo called Livsay to tell her about her fear of losing her house.

Livsay listened carefully and asked for some financial information. She told Cleo she appreciated her desire to leave something to Jerry, but she strongly urged her to put herself first and not do anything hasty. "Think about the quality of your own life in the years ahead," she said. "You should be worrying about yourself. I'm sure your son will be able to provide for himself very well. Don't do anything without checking back with us."

At her suggestion, Cleo also called Jim Harvey, a lawyer with the Legal Assistance Office in Bakersfield. Harvey was knowledgeable about the problems Medi-Cal collections had created. Although the law had been on the books for seven years and the Public Health Department notified recipients several times a year to remind them of the recovery policy, families of SSI recipients were frequently unaware of it until the recipient died and relatives suddenly found a lien on their loved one's estate.

"My husband and I were always against welfare," Cleo told Harvey. "I don't want charity."

Like Livsay, Harvey advised Cleo to think carefully about her own needs before going off SSI and Medi-Cal, both excellent programs that had improved the quality of her life. If she still wanted to act, she should at least wait until the next SSI check came in and then notify the Social Security Office, at which time she should apply for an insurance policy issued by the American Association of Retired Persons.

Cleo was reassured by her conversations with Livsay and Harvey. For the first time she felt she had contacted people who really understood her concerns and who had specific ideas about what she could do. But she also knew that she was dealing with the poverty bureaucracy, and as a Tatham that made her uneasy. She would proceed her own, independent way.

She figured she could get at least $55,000 for her house, and that would give her more money—$3,000 or $4,000 a year in interest— than she was collecting from SSI. "That will get these saps off my tracks," she said.

She made plans for stripping off wallpaper and painting the inside of her house to get it ready to sell. Jerry, she said, could come up from where he was living on the coast to spruce up the outside with a fresh coat of paint. She would try to sell the things she had accumulated but could do without by putting together a garage sale. "People can do a lot of things to help themselves," she said cheerfully. She was fired up and talked about finding a mechanical quilter to speed up her quilt making, which she had always done by hand in the past. "They're not about to clamp me," she said defiantly. "I'm not going to sign any papers."

CLEO STILL HAD plenty of friends in and around Delano. Carol and Catherine lived in the vicinity, and Carol's grandchildren often visited, creating a commotion in the house, which pleased Cleo greatly. She watched the television news and religious programs, especially Pat Robertson's "700 Club," which was carried on Paul and Jan Crouch's Trinity Broadcasting Network out of Orange County. The ministers had become part of Cleo's extended family; it was Paul and Jan and Pat. She was proud of Pat Robertson and what he had done for Christians with his presidential campaign. "You can't beat Robertson for a good guy," she said. "He got up and told it like it was. Pat Robertson had the facts."

All through the summer she followed the political campaign. Before the Republican Convention Cleo was excited about reports that Bush might pick Governor Deukmejian as his running mate. She was still convinced that Deukmejian was behind the effort to increase Medi-Cal collections and saw a way to "get him out of here so maybe he won't be tryin' to steal all the old people's homes."

In the end, the choice of Dan Quayle as Bush's vice president seemed like a good one to her: he was young, handsome, and energetic, and his service with a noncombat National Guard unit during the Vietnam War only added to her admiration. It touched her isolationist, antiwar nerve. "Fact of the matter is, it wasn't that different in World War II," she said. "Nine out of ten if they'd had any pull wouldn't have went."

Generally, though, she was disillusioned with the present crop of Republicans. She called Reagan "The Laugher," never having trusted him after he had proposed eliminating the cost-of-living increase for Social Security recipients in his second year in office. She was not impressed with George Bush. "Bush will carry out just like the President because he doesn't know anything else," she said. She had just about made up her mind not to vote for anybody, but she worried about what Oca would think about that.

"We're livin' in the closin' days of time, folks," she said one day. "They're going to cut everybody down they can. It was the way they said it would happen. Now they're cuttin' the ministers down because we're livin' in the closin' days and gettin' ready for the big battle of Armageddon, when the Bible says they're going to try to turn everybody away from God. And if they can they will turn them away from the preachers.

"This thing's going to go the way God wants it to go," she said. "This thing's going to wind up when people least expect."

She thought she saw signs of the final unraveling at hand: "Los Angeles had more gang wars and murders than the whole state. I never even think of going to L.A., they've got too many gangs. When they're having them gang wars I don't know why they don't bring in the army."

The view from her living-room window was pretty much the same as it had been when Cleo moved in 1936. Yet Quincy Street and the neighborhood had changed considerably so that much of it was almost unfamiliar. Along the County Line Road into which Quincy Street dead-ended, there was a building boom going on, though the north side was still all grape vineyards and cotton fields. New apartments with shaded carports had gone up on the other side. But Quincy Street was still working-class, evident from the Mexican names on the post office boxes and the front yards full of vans and low-riders.

Cleo was friends with many of them. "Mexicans are the finest people you ever saw," she remarked one day, recalling the time she heard a lawn mower start up in her front yard and looked out to see a Mexican neighbor cutting her grass.

But sometimes there were beer cans littering Quincy Street in the morning. The Mexicans and Filipinos had big families with lots of young people, and that often meant trouble. The neighborhood had become a lot rougher. One time Cleo had stayed up all night with a loaded .10 gauge shotgun across her knees as someone fiddled for hours with the lock on her back door. Lately, she had taken to leaving the TV and lights on when she went to church. "There's so many old people being broke in on," she said.

Sometimes she would hear Mexican boys shouting insults at each other in the streets, "Okie!" they would cry, as if it were a bad word.

Lying in bed one night, she smelled a peculiar odor wafting through her window. Carol had spent the night, and she asked her what it was.

"That's a marijuana cigarette," Carol told her.

Cleo figured out they had poked their heads out the window and puffed on it so their mama wouldn't see them or smell it. It made a terrible stink. "My land, we'll soon be dizzy and drunk from pot smoke," she complained to Carol.

It worried her. "Mexico fills California full of dope. It's a dope den. But they's been boys come to our church and give their heart to the Lord and never did take another. There's some beautiful Mexican people, but I get tired of hearing I'm prejudiced. They do more for Mexican people than whites."

Alma also felt the quality of life had gone down in the valley towns: "It's a lot harder times here now. I'm not slurring nobody. They just don't have potatoes and things like they used to have for people to pick up in the fields. They don't have as many grapes. Things don't require as much work."

Alma had had her purse stolen from her house. She had come in from the store, left the screen door unlatched, and before she knew it, her purse and watch were gone.

Cleo didn't regret being where she was. She had been true to her word: she had told her dad in 1936 that she would never leave Delano, and she had stuck to that.

Still, she looked forward to her visits to relatives in Oklahoma and Kansas, where life hadn't changed so much and didn't seem so complicated. She especially liked going to the new brick Holiness Church in Watts with her cousins, who still lived on Drake's Prairie. It had a kitchen, and there was a piano and an organ. Her cousin Farris Tatham, Alma's brother, who years earlier had passed up good jobs to sing at funerals, still arranged the music, and his daughter Sue still played the piano and taught.

"Those kids are trained to sing," said Cleo. "They go to church just to worship the Lord. They just preach the word of God and salvation."

In the middle of Cleo's dilemma about the house, a bunch of Oklahoma cousins came out to California to visit Alma and make repairs on her house. Farris built a little shed for Alma's washer, which Cleo thought looked "fancy," and put lattice on the porch to keep it cool. Then they took Alma back to Sallisaw with them for a few weeks. It was a kind of family concern that Cleo didn't see much of nowadays in California.

By early October, Cleo had decided on a plan: she would go off SSI and Medi-Cal. Her niece Carol could move in with her, and pay a little rent, and that would help make up some of the lost SSI income. She was approved for a health insurance policy through the American Association of Retired Persons that cost $26 a month, which would help cover some of the expenses previously billed to Medi-Cal.

The idea of Carol moving in was appealing. They would be women banding together again, just like during the war and after

Wayne died. Carol needed a better place to live and raise kids than her trailer home; she could help with the rent and groceries, and Cleo could look after Carol's grandchildren.

On October 5, Cleo went down to the Social Security Office in Delano with the intention of getting her name off SSI. It was not a place she liked visiting. Most of the people waiting to get information were Mexican and could barely understand English. The women at the counter were all Hispanic, and there were signs in Spanish everywhere.

"I want to get off SSI," she said.

"What do you want off for?" the woman asked warily.

Cleo decided not to mention the notice that had come earlier. "Two reasons," said Cleo. "My niece wants to move in, and I want off."

When nothing happened after several weeks, Cleo telephoned the office and talked to a different person. This time, the woman filled out the forms and sent them over for Cleo to sign and return.

ON THURSDAY, November 3, Cleo drove over to pick up Alma, who was just back from Oklahoma. After stopping by Cleo's house for something to eat, Alma complained of a "crazy head" and Cleo took her to the hairdresser to get a permanent wave. Alma had been to the doctor several times about her sick spells, but he could find nothing wrong with her.

But the next day, Alma's neighbor called Cleo. Was Alma there? No, Cleo said, Alma wasn't, and she hadn't talked to her all day. The neighbor's call alarmed Cleo.

"Go over and see if the screen door is latched from the inside," Cleo instructed her. "If it is then call the police."

The neighbor phoned right back; it was latched from the inside.

Cleo jumped into her Oldsmobile and sped down Highway 99. A policeman was waiting outside Alma's house when she got there. With Cleo's permission he broke down the rear door, and Cleo followed him into the house. Inside the temperature must have been close to a hundred, and Alma was lying on the bed with her mouth open, the electric blanket turned up high. She was breathing, but unconscious. They rushed her to Delano Hospital in an ambulance and doctors diagnosed a stroke.

Eureda came out from Sallisaw, and the two women visited Alma several times a day at the hospital. She improved gradually, but it was clear she couldn't live by herself for a while. So the decision was made to take her back to Sallisaw, where Eureda would care for her in her home on Drake's Prairie—the home that Arch and Winnie first bought when they returned from California.

Alma's sudden departure saddened Cleo, but she tried not to show it. She knew Alma was in the best and most loving hands, and she prayed for her recovery. She would miss her cousin up in Earlimart and would miss calling her on the phone and letting it ring twice as their signal. She still had Carol and Catherine and their children, who were family, and other friends as well. And she had her Bible.

"I get up early and study that," she said. "Sometimes I make some toast, and I wear that Bible out. We're going to have to do that. The Bible says to hide the word in your heart. We need to study it so it's *hidden* in our heart, and if we don't, we're going to be in bad shape. We're livin' in the closin' days of time, folks, and gettin' ready for the battle of Armageddon." Then she added, "The spirit of God works in a real meek way, without any movement, and you can get your soul fed that way."

Oca stopped by from time to time, often when he and Ona were visiting Ona's son and sister in Delano or when Oca was driving south to see Dick in Lake Havasu City or Renee in Orange County. Sometimes after one of the visits, she would find a bill tucked underneath a saucer.

Cleo worried about her brother's gallivanting around in trailers and mobile homes, especially after his open heart surgery. "He ought to stop that scalawagging," she said.

But she knew that he was having his golden years and wouldn't stop for anything.

Brenda marveled that her dad "hadn't just burst at the seams emotionally" after Ruby's death, and she credited Ona for saving him. Brenda thought the marriage was "the best thing that could have happened to him."

"Dad, I'm glad you have Ona," Renee told him.

But there were still times when Oca felt depressed, and his face would become drawn as he remembered Ruby. Sometimes he wondered how it would be in Heaven, when all three of them—he, Ona, and Ruby—would be together. It wouldn't be awkward. "What a day it will be when my Jesus I see," he said. "You know, that's the song. And I think of that song and the meaning it has to me now, when I think of Ruby and think we'll be together forever. But neither will Ona be just the same, either, because you know jealousy between the two, it won't be. It'll all be glorious. What a day."

His life had gone fast now, he realized: "You're a young man, and tomorrow, just like they say, you're old. That's how fast it goes. And we realize only what we do for God is going to count, that's what it's all about. That's what gives you real joy and makes life worth living."

Some nights he was up until four in the morning, "praying and talking to the Lord and searching my life. And it's just wonderful. God will reveal to you your weakness and all your problems and lay it out, and it's you yourself sometimes who is your worst enemy, you know. It's yourself gets you in bad. So sometimes you gotta get yourself crucified and say, 'Lord, you control this ol' man, here,' y'know, Himself, and make sure that the Holy Spirit directs you and not yourself and all your selfish desires. And I follow that direction, see. That's the thing that Christians like."

"You know," he said one day, "in Oklahoma my dreams weren't large *enough*, really, and it turned out a hundred times greater, I guess, than I anticipated."

He went on: "I'm glad everythin' happened just the way it did. You see, I learned lessons that no money could buy. I look back and thank God for them because today I'm living for Him. If we'd had everythin' handed to us on a silver platter, we'd never have known what an answered prayer was. We wouldn't know what people meant when they said, 'God come to our rescue in time of need.'

"When you get so low-down to where you can't call on anybody but God and then when He supplies, you know where it comes from. I've seen people so burdened down with a need that they've come weeping before God, and God come to the rescue."

They had been down-and-out, no doubt of that, but "happy, yeah, happy we were. Potatoes and gravy for breakfast. Nobody complained. Now, people are ready to moan about anything. You know what? They were closer together, they respected one another a lot more then, and they loved the Lord a lot more then. They were faithful to the Lord."

Not everybody kept the faith the way his family had: He had "seen people come out here from the Middle West, work in the cotton field, and get them a good used car. And then they didn't need the Lord anymore. Can you imagine? They quit coming to church. They were spending weekends going all over California, exploring California."

Not Oca Tatham.

"I look back, and I think how it was almost a necessity to live for God. We didn't have everything, but we had peace and joy. Would you believe it, the hardships we had? Did you know we were bubbling over with joy? We were happier than those crooks in Oklahoma City . . . a lot happier than they were with their big Cadillacs and their millions of dollars of tax money."

Without God, he figured, he'd have ended up dead at a young age—or in an Oklahoma penitentiary. He was "a miserable sinner . . . without God at my side I'd 'a' never made it. Without Him, I'd be drifting like a ship upon the sea."

ONE EVENING IN NOVEMBER 1988, right after the election, Cleo and a friend took a drive out of Delano, down to McFarland—"ridin' the country out," she had always called it. It was dusk, and the sky over the coast range had a cool orange glow; the heat of the day settled back into the earth.

"Here's where my husband worked for years," she said as the car moved down the road.

Her eyes twinkled as she pointed out places on Main Street and on adjacent ones, like Glenwood, where Oca and Ruby had lived and kept junk out back.

"Swanee's was a drunk place, and that other one by it. Dewey Rogers came up here that first week, and they got old Dewey down and stomped him. That was a blacksmith shop, and that there was Tatham Tire and Wheel Exchange. The building on the corner, that one house was the only hospital they had. It was real neat then. And right here, Oca had his tire shop. He was a go-gettin' dude, boy.

"Bill Elkins was right here where this big store is, had a big tire shop and gas station. Saturday night people drove up and down. The grocery stores were all open, and all the girls and boys would go up and down the street.

"I lived right here where Sears is. That was all vacant lots then."

The car turned, and they drove down Glenwood, past the lot where Oca and Ruby and then Cora Tatham had rented. The old house had burned down. "See that tree. My mama planted that when it was like this," Cleo said, gesturing with her hand at knee height. Farther down the street, she pointed and said, "This old house sold candies and gum. Dick and Gerald bought them nickel cigars and got caught by Oca."

Cleo chuckled. "This right here was the cathouse. Them ol' boys rode into it."

The car passed the Manila Market where the Filipino owners had helped her and her mother during the war when their men were off fighting the Japanese, and then they passed the place where the sheds had been.

"These sheds was going all the time, but that old Chavez closed 'em down," she said softly.

She chuckled again. Here had stood the joint where Bill Elbertson, Dewey Rogers, and Jim Anderson had come up to see Delano the first week they were on the Twin Pines Ranch, after which Dewey escaped through a cotton field.

"Uncle Willy lived here at the end of the bridge they built over 99," she said. "Then it was all Russians. We lived at the end of the bridge. The new 99 took that house."

The car turned onto 99 to go the few miles to McFarland, and Cleo pointed down the road to Delano Cemetery. "There's galores of Chinamen buried there," she said. "They all died at once and got buried in one grave."

A mile or two north of McFarland, just west of the highway, was the old Twin Pines Ranch where they had turned in that August day in 1934. The Calverts left in the 1940s, selling it to some people called Bowman, who farmed it for years. Away to the east of town was the Holgren Ranch and the tank house where Oca and Ruby had lived and Bill was born.

At twilight, McFarland looked bedraggled, as if it had seen better days. It was fighting to keep its only bank, having already lost its hardware store. Some people speculated that some of the little farming towns wouldn't survive now that so many of the big farmers lived in Bakersfield or Fresno. Eventually, it might go back to wheat fields or orchards, some thought.

It was a melancholy notion. "There used to be shops and every kind of thing here," said Cleo.

At San Juan and Kern avenues on the east side of town, the church Oca had helped build in 1936 was still standing. Cleo noticed that someone had put up a cross at the entrance—"maybe Mexicans."

"All the people lived here's dead and gone," she said. "I knew everybody when we lived up here on Twin Pines Ranch. This church is the one we built with Jay Fuller. We got this bigger church during the war, and that there was Ona's house. This was fields, and they opened it up for lots—twenty dollars I believe you got a lot. We called it Tent City. Littlejohns was here, but Lands lived in Delano. And Aunt Myrtle, she worked her fingers off to pay for that."

Then it struck her, and she said abruptly, "All my friends, so many of 'em got killed." Soon she was talking on again about the people who'd lived in the little houses. As she chattered, the streets seemed to fill with shadowy figures—men in overalls and straw hats, barefoot children chasing dogs down the dusty shoulders. A man clutched a beer bottle by the neck, and men leaned over the hoods of jalopies or huddled on the steps of porches, drawing on their fags and gossiping in that distinctive, cordial accent.

For a moment it seemed—Okies! But no, it was only her imagination, excited by vivid recollections and the valley twilight. Most of the real Okies were gone. They had used this place only for a time, moved on, or died and left it to other people. One day these people would move on, too. The government would probably widen 99 one last time, leaving a few motels and franchised food stores along the access roads, and that would be that.

So it went in America. Once there had been dozens of Tathams living on the north banks of the Missouri but now they were all dead and gone. And what had they left behind? A few headstones overgrown with vines and brush, heaved crooked by winter frosts; a few scratchy marks scrawled by the census taker in the great census book.

Cleo had kept her vow. She had never left Delano. Now she was the last of her Tatham people left there—and one of the last from the great Oklahoma migration, for that matter. When she died a chapter would close, just as it had closed when they buried John Tatham in a grave somewhere east of the Appalachians. But the story continued. The Tathams were pioneers, and most likely always would be. They had plodded through the Cumberland Gap, drifted into the upper Mississippi Valley, wandered down into Oklahoma, and made it to California in a rattletrap truck with no front windshield. Now there were few physical frontiers left, but what others there were, Tathams would no doubt find.

In the cemetery by Delano, the dead had all been pioneers—unknown Chinese, Croatians from the sunny Adriatic isles, Russians, Italians, and Okies. Walter and Cora Tatham rested there side by side. Cleo often brought flowers to the gravesite, placing them carefully at her mother's headstone. The words on the stone told almost nothing of the story. Yet they formed the sweetest of all epitaphs:

CORA TATHAM, B. JOPLIN, MISSOURI, 1881

ASLEEP IN JESUS

EPILOGUE

WHEN I VISITED the Tathams in California for the last time, just before Christmas 1991, I was no longer the detached interviewer taking notes for a book that many in the family must have begun to doubt would ever be finished. Suddenly, there *was* a book, and it had become an active participant in the Tatham and Tackett sagas.

Typed chapters of manuscript, which I had mailed ahead, were circulating among parents, children, grandchildren, and cousins, causing a bit of a stir. Two of Oca's great-grandchildren, Brent and Janeé Critchfield, aged twelve and ten, had prepared family genealogies based on my descriptions of the early history of the Tathams and Sumpters, and they were ready for my inspection when I stopped by. Tathams, I gathered, were burning up phone lines discussing the pages.

I detected misgivings here and there, but mainly I sensed that the pages were helping to lift a burden from the family's collective shoulders. When I first arrived on the scene in 1985, the family was entering the period of self-discovery described in Chapter Twenty. There had been divorces, experimentation with alcohol and drugs in the younger generation of Tathams, and the family was confronting the gulf between its image of itself and the realities. Appearing at that particular moment, I was the nonjudgmental outsider in whom Tathams felt safe confiding. In fact, I sensed a hunger to open up. Tathams were close and supportive of each other, but I think many of them understood that an objective book could jog memories of things known but never really confronted.

I hadn't known Gerald Tatham more than a few minutes before he told me that his grandparents had separated. Gerald, I later understood, was arming me for my work. Now, scanning the first hundred pages of the manuscript, Gerald seemed pleased. "There's nothing like the truth," he said. History was being substituted for family myth.

Rather than being shocked to learn that Granpa drank moonshine, had an eye for women, and did a little bootlegging in his youth, several of Oca's children and grandchildren told me they had a new respect for him. To them, it made the life he had lived after his conversion so much more of an achievement. In a small way, perhaps, the chapters were laying lines of communication along which morning-glory vines could begin to grow.

A high point of the years spent writing this book came when I stopped by to see Mike Tatham at the Fresno law firm where he was now a partner. Mike canceled his luncheon plans and took me into his Palm Avenue office. By laying out the story of his grandfather, Mike said, the book indirectly was helping him continue a dialogue with his *own* father, Bill Tatham, Senior. He swiveled in his chair, talking slowly and deliberately. The book, he said, made his dad and granddad real people who "weren't perfect, either," and that was good.

Mike was pleased about his deepening relationship with his father. I gathered that during the previous year and a half he had begun to discuss the childhood shooting incident with his parents. He had concluded that, painful as it might be, he had to work through feelings that had been buried all these years.

A number of remarkable things had happened.

Not long ago, the father of his slain friend had invited him to lunch. It had taken courage for the man, but now, he told Mike, he could look him in the eye and say that he forgave him. If the father could let go of what had happened, Mike thought, perhaps the time had come for him to try.

With the help of a professional counselor and a pastor at Peoples Church, Mike delved deeply into his feelings. For a Tatham in Fresno to seek that kind of help was unusual, he knew. "The Tathamism thing is you're not supposed to have problems," he said in a subsequent conversation.

Through the help, other things were forced to the surface, and he began to separate who he was from the Mike Tatham who played a role for his parents and his church. In a powerful, rich family, which nonetheless was experiencing emotional traumas, such as Billy's divorce, Mike was expected to be the model son with no emotional problems. Now he refused to play that role.

"If you're a Tatham, the religion you inherit is almost too much to bear—I always struggled with that," he said.

The counseling, he said, was leading to a better relationship with his parents. After the tragedy, he said, "The relationship with Mom and Dad got frozen. They protected me and I obeyed."

Evidently their instinct was to try to protect him again when Mike sought help. "I had to tell them, 'All you can do is pray for me. This isn't something you guys can fix. It's a spiritual thing. Don't try to.' "

He credited Denise with helping him see that moving forward meant "letting go of the security of being the son of Bill and Earline, which due to their tremendous success is almost enough to pull you through life without trying—a dangerous and tempting gravity." His independence was paying off. "I can even tell Dad I think he's wrong," Mike said with a grin.

Bill Tatham, Senior, was finding that he, too, could ease up and let go. "People are looking at themselves and where they fit in," he said. "It's a little bit sobering."

Pastor Dick Tatham in Lake Havasu City could take satisfaction from having built a new community of Tathams on the Arizona frontier.

Like his distant ancestor Isaac Tatham, the first Tatham settler in Missouri, Dick was now surrounded by rafts of children and grandchildren. All six of the daughters of Dick and Grace were living in or around the town, along with nine grandchildren. On Christmas, nearly twenty children, grandchildren, sons-in-laws, and boyfriends would be coming to their home.

His elder-statesman's status was assured. He was president of the Lake Havasu City Ministerial Association, but now his Christian Assemblies Church, one of five in the early 1970s, was one of about forty. His radio and TV stations were growing, and his daughters seemed to be pulling their lives together. Several were attending his church regularly and said that prayer had become an important part of their lives. Donna, who had taken a job as coordinator of the city's recreation program, was making plans to remarry her second husband.

His kid sister, Renee, had married in the summer of 1990. Terry Yapp was a real-estate man whose family had come out from Kansas. She had met him at South Coast Community Church. Christian and well-to-do, he met with Oca's approval. Soon Oca was boasting to friends about the fat commissions his new son-in-law was earning.

Now they were involved with another huge Orange County religious institution, Saddleback Valley Community Church. Renee had joined the pastoral staff, visiting sick people in hospitals.

She described Saddleback as "upbeat rather than traditional . . . filled with baby boomers . . . with great music that brings the ceiling down, applicable sermons and no altar calls. . . . You have to make the decision yourself to put your life together."

Her neck pain was still chronic, and as of December 1991, her disability claim against Republic Airlines was still not settled. But life was good, Renee said. She was "doing a lot for other people. The Lord needs to sit on our hearts." Apparently, marriage agreed with her. But she could not bring herself to part with the Tatham name. She was "Renee Tatham-Yapp."

Renee's brother Gerald and his wife, Cora, had come down to visit recently and talked about this book—about where they all fit in. Renee said she liked the description of herself as a "seeker." "We're a more comfortable family now," she said. "It had reached a point where some things couldn't be covered up anymore."

I caught up with Doris Weaver at her home in the San Leandro hills. She and Gordon were in good shape, their marital troubles behind them. Doris was director of women's ministries at Sequoyah Church and occasionally counseled women about financial and marital problems. Whatever qualms she may have had about the book's revelations of her own and Gordon's difficulties a few years back were outweighed by her hope that it would "show that marriages can work out with God's help, as it did in our case." In that, she was expressing one of the deepest of Christian beliefs, that even one's troubles can be useful to God.

On the way to Fresno, I stopped in San Ramón to visit Cindy and Bill Critchfield at their new home in a comfortable suburban development. "You don't need an address," Bill had told me. "Just look for the only white pickup truck."

They were still content with the decision to home-school Brent and Janeé. Cindy, in fact, had become coadministrator of the American Christian Academy, an affiliation of ninety-four home-schooling families with 175 children. Bill was taking time off from the construction business to help, a luxury made possible by income from their modest real-estate holdings. Cindy was no longer active with Concerned Women for America, but she was continuing to support pro-family and pro-life causes, including a lobbying effort in Sacramento against a proposed school voucher system. The voucher system, she feared, was a very bad bargain: in exchange for government funds, the government would get more control over private education.

Their television set was still off, except for the few occasions when Bill succumbed to the temptation to watch a major sports event. (Afterward he always felt sufficiently "guilty," he confessed with a wry grin.) In fact, they were pulling out more plugs. They had stopped listening to music with a heavy background beat, and Bill had given up drinking beer. "I realized I was holding out areas for myself," he said. "The Lord calls you to different levels of obedience as you grow in your Christian walk." They had canceled their subscription to a daily newspaper because, Cindy explained, it was "biased against everything we believe in." She mentioned the local press's uncritical support of higher salaries for public school teachers and its negative portrayal of the Operation Rescue antiabortion group.

They had taken to celebrating the last Thursday in October as "Reformation Day," a counterevent to Halloween, which Cindy considered a celebration of Satan. While other children dressed up as hobgoblins, Cindy had Brent and Janeé discuss Martin Luther's Theses and write papers about individuals who had changed the world for the better.

Cindy's convictions had cost her another friend, one who had turned away from the Critchfields' door on Halloween on seeing that Cindy's children were not in costumes. "She called and said she didn't want to be my friend anymore," Cindy said. "I cried for a day. I wasn't standing in judgment. But what could I do?"

It was late when I left their house. The whole family came to the door to see me off and wished me a safe journey to Fresno through a foggy night. I knew that the views held by this family living in the house with the white pickup truck out front would be considered unconventional by millions of Americans. Yet in America, I was thinking, it was always the unconventional that provoked self-examination, and ultimately tested the nation's principles. In their comfortable suburb, Cindy and Bill were part of the infinitely varied tapestry of American life, culture, and ideas.

IN FRESNO, the Peoples Foundation was still facing legal action in connection with the troubles of the retirement village project, but Pastor Johnson was optimistic about the future. Peoples Church was still growing, the Christian high school was operating, and the former California Theological Seminary had been salvaged.

Gerald Tatham was excited about the prospects for his latest inventions: automatic closing and latching devices for sliding doors. He was gearing up to sell them in five states; more than 2,000 had already been produced and sold in California, Arizona, Connecticut, and the District of Columbia. He had demonstrated them before the Consumer Products Safety Commission in Washington. Gerald believed that the latcher would reduce the risk of children accidentally drowning in pools accessed through sliding doors. Gerald also figured that the closer device could mean millions of dollars a year in energy savings across the air-conditioned Sun Belt.

The family could use a "second hero," Bill had told him. It was a word of brotherly support. Now it was up to him.

With Kelly English off at Azusa Pacific University, Brenda and Jerry English were throwing themselves into Twenty Something Bible study group. Brenda had made contact with a long-lost cousin, a daughter of Lonnie and Opal Rogers in Bakersfield. The woman had married an Assemblies of God pastor, and Brenda was hoping she would give her testimony to the Twenty Something group about overcoming a neglectful and abusive home life.

Billy, back in Fresno, was becoming involved in the real-estate game. Some in the family were calling him "Little Oca." The old horse trader was pleased and boasted that Billy was "just like me. . . . He reads the ads in the *Bee* cover to cover just like I did."

As for Bill Tatham, the end of 1991 found him raising cash and consolidating his finances around his vision for a major development around the old Papagni vineyards and homestead off Front Road. He had sold or was in the process of selling a number of his real-estate properties, including his office building on Shaw Avenue, several of his nursing-home facilities, and two grape ranches in the Madera area. Now he was considering an offer to sell the building that he had built for and leased to the Internal Revenue Service. He had reached preliminary agreement to merge Pacific Bancorp, the bank holding company in which he was the largest shareholder, with Valli-

Corp Holdings Inc., another banking concern. The practical consequences were that the stock in the new, merged company would be
considerably more salable than the depressed shares of his own banking enterprise. An article in the October 30, 1991, Fresno *Bee* quoted
an analyst as saying that the merger, if finally approved, would be a
"mixed blessing" since investors had been expecting ValliCorp to find
a healthier institution with which to join forces. Bill, who had been
trying to ease out of the banking business for some time, saw it
differently.

In the fall of 1991, he commissioned architects to draw up several
alternative plans for an upper-income development, and he moved
his office to the former Papagni ranch house atop a knoll off Cooper
Avenue. Alone except for a secretary and undisturbed except for
occasional visits by lawyers and accountants, he planned strategy. The
project would require a change in the general plan, but Bill was
hopeful. The demographics of Fresno were on his side. Oca, of
course, was nervous that Bill was getting over his head again. He was
advising him to sell to someone with more experience, based on the
maxim that had always served him well: "Nobody ever went broke
making a profit." But Bill was in no hurry; he felt he could be patient.

Everyone remarked on the spectacular physical qualities of the
site. The view through the picture window of the former Papagni
home above the old man's vineyards was of a rolling European vista,
breathtaking in the otherwise flat environs of Fresno. In the fore-
ground were a row of well-pruned rose bushes, still blossoming in
December, and beyond that one could see clumps of lush orange
trees speckled with bright-colored fruits. Beyond the orange trees,
acres of grape vineyards spilled away almost to the river. Next to his
desk by the window, Bill kept a telescope mounted on a tripod from
which to survey his domain. There, he was like a pilot on the bridge:
Bill Tatham, master of Fresno, sailing into the future.

I DROVE DOWN Highway 99 to Delano to visit Cleo a last time, and
found her game as ever despite nagging problems with arthritis. She
had stuck to her decision to quit Medi-Cal, a true Tatham prizing her
independence over her security and counting on the Lord to make
up the shortfall. As we talked about the book, I wondered when and
if I would ever sit in her small kitchen again, drink coffee, and listen
to stories about the Dust Bowl migration.

In the many hours I spent with them, all the Tathams had been
unfailingly tactful when it came to personal matters of religion. They

accepted me for what I said I was, a "stuffy Episcopalian," and respected the distance my work as an author required. This time, however, Cleo must have sensed a more personal moment had arrived. It was a foggy night, as it often was in the valley in December, and, my eyesight not being the best, I expressed apprehension about driving as we parted. She stopped me just before the door, and taking my hands in hers she said, "Let's pray."

I bowed my head as her words came: "Heavenly father, protect Dan in his travels. Spread Your wings over him and see that he comes safe and sound to his destination. And bless his family, Oh Lord, that they may prosper and be well." It seemed like the most natural thing in the world. I thanked her, said good-bye, and stepped out into the foggy night feeling strangely comforted.

BACK IN BAKERSFIELD, I caught up with Gene and Wendy Tackett and their two boys. Gene was still doing consulting work, and Wendy continued to head up the Community Connection for Child Care. With their boys getting older, they were expanding their horizons. In the summer of 1989, the entire family went to Africa to attend the reunion of Wendy's Peace Corps group; now they were making plans to visit the Indian village where Gene had spent his Peace Corps assignment.

Next I drove to the home of Eldon and Loretta in McFarland to drop off copies of several chapters. Though I had given them less than an hour's notice, they were prepared with cookies, coffee, and Loretta's specialty, candied walnuts. As I sipped my coffee, Loretta peeked into the pile of manuscript. "That's right," she said, after perusing a page or two, "I cleaned houses in those days." There was no shame at all in her voice, but rather, I thought, an affirmation of the Okie work ethic. Eldon and Loretta Tackett had never asked for anything they wouldn't work for.

In a few days they planned to head back to Oklahoma for their annual Christmas visit to Loretta's mother and other family there. The jaunt would be a first for Eldon; at the age of seventy-three, he would be making his first flight on a commercial airliner.

Back in Fresno, I called on Oca before heading to the San Francisco airport. A few days earlier I had found him struggling with the fact that my book told some of the details of his "wild" youth. He was prepared to let the truth speak for itself—after all, he said, he was just a miserable sinner—but he wondered how the tales of his youth could serve the purpose of glorifying God. Whether the book made *him* look good did not concern him; he wanted it to make *God* look good to others. But as he had read more pages he realized that a book was more than just a bunch of facts; what counted was the overall effect. He began to see God's plan in the book, for it must have been Providence that led me to his family. Now he could understand what the book could do. "I can see how you go along and then you hit 'em with a miracle," he said enthusiastically. "Then you go along again and hit 'em with a prayer."

I treated Oca to a farewell lunch at Carrow's on Blackstone Avenue—a franchised family place that Oca favored for its coffee, waffles, and steak. Our conversation flitted from the continuing sins of Jimmy Swaggart, to pastors he had known, to Fresno real estate, to grandchildren. Afterward I dropped him back at his home. Standing somewhat awkwardly in the entrance hall, I expressed admiration for the rack of hats by the door. He took down a western-style number and fingered it; he'd had it more than forty years, he said, a real "prize possession." Picking up on the clothing theme, he led me back to his bedroom to look at some of his western boots. While searching for a particular pair, he came up instead with a pair of boots that Ruby sent him out to buy for himself when she was dying of cancer. He turned them over and felt the soft leather, and I was sure his mind was flooding with memories.

He led me to the door of the ground floor condo and there he stopped. "Let's pray," he said. He clutched my hands the way Cleo had done and began praying in a strong voice.

"Heavenly father, pour your blessings on Dan as he travels, and keep him safe. Protect him with Your love, oh Lord. And bless his undertaking with his book. Make this book a success, and bring a bounteous reward to Dan for all the work he has put into it. And may it glorify You, Lord, and may people see that it is only through Your grace that any of this could happen."

As I drove north on Highway 99 I wondered about the coincidence of the prayers two days apart. I was pretty certain that Oca and Cleo had not spoken to each other in that time. Perhaps some intuition had been transported between them—some word of knowledge. I did not rule it out. Such are the mysteries.

ACKNOWLEDGMENTS

This book was possible only through the cooperation and assistance of the Tathams, the Tacketts, and their many in-laws and friends. In countless meetings in homes, offices, cars, restaurants, and churches, they not only shared their story but also taught me many things about the importance of family. For the generosity, hospitality, and kindness of too many of them to name here individually, I am forever grateful.

Several should be mentioned, however. In every family there are one or two who become the keepers of the story. Two in the Tatham family whose memories are especially vivid are Cleo Frost and Leslie Tatham. Their accounts added detail and verisimilitude to portions of the saga that would have been almost a blank without their contributions.

I came close to abandoning this project on many occasions. Had it not been for the encouraging words I received at one of these low points from my erstwhile editor at the Washington *Post*, Richard Harwood, I would assuredly have done so. Other friends also offered indispensable encouragement from time to time, including Sidney Blumenthal, George Crile III, Noel Epstein, Joel Garreau, William Greider, Christopher Hitchens, Walter Pincus, and Julia Reed, among others. Perhaps it is no coincidence that most of them has known or is discovering the exquisite agony of writing a book.

Timothy Dickinson, who read large parts of the manuscript and offered both ideas and editorial comments, is in a special category. At every stage, he played a multifaceted role, simultaneously serving as supportive friend, tough critic, and one-man think tank. The book is orders of magnitude better because of him.

I am also grateful to a number of others for the ideas and insights that they provided. This is a book about migration, culture, religion, business, and politics. Relatively few historians and journalists seek out the complex relationships between these separate currents, and perhaps wisely so, for the weave is seldom easy to discern. A few who have focused on the bigger picture, and who shared some of their insights with me were David Barrett, Joseph Barton, Michael Cromartie, Tom Edsall, James Gregory, Carl Henry, E. Glenn Hinson, Ronald S. Godwin, Timothy Smith, and Grant Wacker. Sidney Blumenthal, Christopher Hitchens, and E. J. Dionne also helped me connect the story to contemporary politics and culture.

In doing research on families, one thing leads to another. The Tathams and Tacketts put me in touch with relatives and friends, thus constantly expanding my circle of contacts, and becoming my best research resource. Oca Tatham introduced me to Cleo Frost, who helped me track down Jim Anderson, one of the non-Tatham men on the truck in 1934. Similarly, Gerald Tatham, who has the instincts of a reporter, was able to help me locate people with whom his mother and father had been associated.

Barbara Tatham of Raytown, Missouri, is deserving of special mention. As the principal genealogist of the Tatham family that came west to Missouri through the Cumberland Gap, she is a reservoir of information about Tathams in the nineteenth century, all of which she shared with me. She also firmly corrected some of the pages I sent her for review.

This kind of networking generally proved more helpful than reading material in libraries, yet archives and libraries were also important in filling in background. I am especially thankful for the help provided by William Welge and Carolyn Graangard Smith of the Oklahoma Historical Society, Robert Priddy of Missourinet, R. Laurel Boeckman of the State Historical Society of Missouri, and Anne Thebeau, librarian of the Bakersfield *Californian*. The "Odyssey Project," an oral history enterprise of California State College in Bakersfield, was a rich source. The project interviewed many survivors of the 1930s migration to the southern San Joaquin Valley. Sharon Goldsmith set me up with the Odyssey Project material. Cecil M. Robeck of Fuller Theological Seminary in Pasadena provided helpful documentation about the Azusa Street revival and other historical events.

Vicki Warren, my occasional research assistant on this project, saved me hundreds of hours of time through her energetic work as sleuth and fact checker. Without her help the book still would not be done. Amy Pyle of the Fresno *Bee* provided technical help for which I was grateful, and Pam Keyes was also of assistance.

Everywhere I went I found a few people with specialized knowledge and a willingness to share it with a complete stranger. Jim Mayo, editor of the Sequoyah County *Times*, an unusually interesting small paper, gave me considerable background about the economy and history of eastern Oklahoma, and provided various other assistance. Joe Meredith provided insights and background about Fresno County politics and the movers and shakers of Fresno. Jimmy Baloian and John Blackburn showed me central valley agriculture from the ground up.

When one is on the road, one needs and appreciates the hospitality of friends and strangers, and I was fortunate in this regard. Old friends Ulla Morris and Bill Carter put me up and entertained me in Palo Alto on numerous occasions, and Drummy Hadley and Diana Hadley did so in the course of several lengthy sojourns in Arizona.

In Fresno, I received help, hospitality, and assistance from DeWayne Rail, teacher, poet, folklorist, and pigeon keeper, and his talented wife, Tori. They plied me with food and many insights into Okie culture—while providing a family atmosphere away from home. I hope that someday De-Wayne will write his own book about Okies.

In addition to writing this book, I have a full-time job. Without the indulgence of my editors at the Washington *Post*, I never could have found time to start—or complete—this project. In granting me a leave of absence— and then more leaves—they stretched every rule in the book. For their patience and confidence in me, I am forever indebted to Benjamin Bradlee, Leonard Downie, and Robert Kaiser.

This book started at Viking Penguin and moved with my editor, Elisabeth Sifton, to Alfred A. Knopf. There she nurtured the book through its many incarnations and provided her usual wise guidance and strong editing in the final phases. Her assistant, George Andreou, was also unfailingly supportive, patient, and encouraging. Elisabeth's departure from Knopf left a personal, emotional, and professional vacuum, and at another house I might have felt like an orphan. But the speedy assurances of Knopf's head, Sonny Mehta, that everything was on course showed why it is the dream of every writer to be published by Knopf, a house with a deserved reputation for treating authors well. In that period, as in several others, my agent, Amanda Urban, was a tower of strength. She has been one of my strongest sources of support throughout, and I thank her.

None of this would have been possible without the love and support of my wife, Elaine Shannon, who produced both a book of her own and a child while this work was in progress, yet accepted the trying role of author's wife as well. Her self-sacrifice and generosity are a constant marvel.

PART ONE

CHAPTER TWO: TUMBLEWEED

1. See James R. Green, *Grass-Roots Socialism* (New Orleans: Louisiana State University Press, 1978), pp. 323 ff. The Ku Klux Klan was active on the right and the Working Class Union on the left. The latter robbed banks and advocated violent revolution.

2. Peter H. Argersinger, "Pentecostal Politics in Kansas: Religion, the Farmers' Alliance and the Gospel of Populism," *Kansas Quarterly*, Vol. 1, No. 4, Fall, 1969.

3. See Grant Wacker's paper, "A Profile of American Pentecostalism," presented at the University of North Carolina, Chapel Hill, July 1981.

4. An excellent definition of Pentecostal religion is supplied by David B. Barrett, in the July 1988 issue of *International Bulletin of Missionary Research*, published by the Overseas Ministry Study Center in New Haven, Conn.

5. From Ira C. Brackett's description in *The History of Sequoyah County, 1828–1975*, Sequoyah County Historical Society, 1976.

6. By far the most exhaustive description of early Tathams that I could find was "Tatham Narrative, 1735–1983," published in 1987 in Raleigh, N.C., by B. Vincent Ballard of Cary, N.C. It covers the history of Tatham families

in Virginia and North Carolina. Ballard says it is conceivable that the "Thomas Tatham" who served with the Botetourt County militia under Captain Hawkins in the Indian Wars of 1790–1792 could have been a son of early settler John Thomas Tatham. He notes, however, that John's son Thomas would have been only fifteen, unusually young for enlistment. For assistance with the Virginia portion of the history, I am also greatly indebted to Barbara Tatham of Raytown, Mo., the principal genealogist of the Tatham family that migrated to Kentucky and Missouri.

7. Most of the history of the Tathams in Missouri presented here is based on meticulous genealogical research by Barbara Tatham of Raytown, Mo. Some details are from Missouri Historical Company's *A History of Carroll County, 1882*, St. Louis, 1881, and private records of J. J. McKinny, Hett Fisher, James A. Williams, and the Barrett-Neblock family, as well as the Carrollton *Daily Democrat*.

8. *The History of Sequoyah County*, published by the Sequoyah County Historical Society, 1976.

9. Collinsville *News*, November 25, 1915.

10. See Arrell M. Gibson's history of the Tri-State mining district in *Wilderness Bonanza* (Norman, Okla: University of Oklahoma Press, 1972), esp. p. 228.

11. Research by Pamela Keyes.

12. See Gibson, *Wilderness Bonanza*, pp. 164, 228.

13. See Leroy Wesley Hawkins, "A History of the Assemblies of God in Oklahoma: The Formative Years, 1914–1929" (M. A. diss., Oklahoma State University, July 1972).

14. Carl Brumback, *Suddenly from Heaven* (Springfield, Mo.: Gospel Publishing House, 1961), p. 67.

15. I. R. Wilcox, Weleetka, Okla., "Sallisaw Has a Bout with the Kimes Brothers," undated essay. Wilcox also provided the information in a telephone interview that Pretty Boy Floyd attended the trial of one of the Kimes Brothers and was "impressed."

PART TWO

CHAPTER FOUR: THE VALLEY, 1934

1. Anthony M. Tang, *Economic Development in the Southern Piedmont, 1860–1950* (Chapel Hill: University of North Carolina Press, 1958), p. 25. In the first four decades of the nineteenth century, considerably more independent pioneer farmers moved from the upper Piedmont areas of Georgia and South Carolina than moved in.

2. Lawrence Goodwyn, *Democratic Promise* (New York: Oxford University Press, 1976), pp. 25–33.

3. Frank Lawrence Owsley, *Plain Folk of the Old South* (New Orleans: Louisiana State University Press, 1949), p. 55.

4. John Updike, *Self-Consciousness* (New York: Ballantine, 1989), p. 134.

5. Some details about Acala cotton were provided by Scott Sanford, U.S. Department of Agriculture. Also helpful is John Turner, *White Gold Comes to California*, copyrighted by California Planting Cotton Seed Distributors, Bakersfield, Calif., 1981, and published by Book Publishers, Inc., Fresno, Calif.

6. There is an enormous body of literature and documentation on the early history of California water. A good summary of the valley and its early water history is contained in the *California Water Atlas*. Some history is also to be found in Senate Document 113, 81st Congress, 1946, agency discussions of the Central Valley Project.

7. Walter J. Stein, *California and the Dust Bowl Migration* (Westport, Conn.: Greenwood Press, 1973), pp. 36 ff.

8. Stein, p. 82.

9. For a full description of the labor situation in California in this period, see Carey McWilliams, *Factories in the Field* (Boston: Little, Brown, 1939), pp. 287 ff.

10. Interview with Dr. J. Thorner by the Odyssey Project, California State College in Bakersfield, 1981.

CHAPTER FIVE: THE HORSE TRADER I

1. A. James Reichsley, *Religion in American Public Life* (Washington, D.C.: Brookings Institution, 1985), p. 40.

2. Perry Miller, *The New England Mind: From Colony to Province* (Cambridge, Mass.: Harvard University Press, 1953), pp. 41–43.

CHAPTER SIX: IMMIGRANTS

1. James N. Gregory, *American Exodus* (New York: Oxford University Press, 1989), p. 25. Sources are Bureau of Agricultural Economics of the Department of Agriculture and 1937 federal unemployment census analyzed by the California Department of Industrial Relations and others.

2. See Gregory. Chapter one and the notes to chapter one contain exhaustive research on comparative pay and population movements.

3. Donald Worster, *Dust Bowl* (New York: Oxford University Press, 1979), p. 61.

4. Carey McWilliams, *Ill Fares the Land* (Boston: Little, Brown, 1942), pp. 17–18.

5. Hearings, U.S. Congress, House of Representatives, Select Committee to Investigate the Interstate Migration of Destitute Citizens, (Tolan Committee), 76th and 77th Congress (Washington, D.C., 1940 and 1941), p. 3003.

6. See Gregory, p. 153.

7. Delano *Record*, August 25, 1934.

8. See Gregory, all of chapter eight, for a full and moving description of the role of country music in the Okie culture.

9. James G. Leyburn, *The Scotch-Irish: A Social History* (Chapel Hill: University of North Carolina Press, 1962), p. 325.

10. Arrell M. Gibson, *Wilderness Bonanza* (Norman: University of Oklahoma Press, 1972), pp. 210, 229.

11. Dick Meister and Anne Loftis, *A Long Time Coming* (New York: Macmillan, 1977), p. 74.

12. Walter J. Stein, *California and the Dust Bowl Migration* (Westport, Conn.: Greenwood Press, 1973), pp. 257, 270–272.

13. Cletus E. Daniel, *Bitter Harvest* (Berkeley: University of California Press, 1981), p. 276.

14. Stein, p. 235.

15. Daniel, p. 281.

16. Stein, pp. 263, 274.

CHAPTER SEVEN: THE CHURCH

1. See James N. Gregory, *American Exodus* (New York: Oxford University Press, 1989), all of chapter seven, "Special to God."

2. George M. Marsden, *Fundamentalism and American Culture* (New York: Oxford University Press, 1982), pp. 72–80.

3. For a definition of Pentecostalism, see note 4, chapter two.

4. February 1986 interview with David B. Barrett, research consultant to the Southern Baptist Foreign Mission Board.

5. Vinson Synan, "The Quiet Rise of Black Pentecostals," *Charisma*, June 1986, pp. 45–55. Synan's article notes in passing that although the denomination did not play a major role in the black civil rights movements of the 1950s and 1960s, many ministers and members were involved in the struggle. The Reverend Martin Luther King, Jr., preached his last sermon at a Church of God in Christ temple the night before he was assassinated.

6. For a profile of Parham, see Robert Mapes Anderson, *Vision of the Disinherited* (New York: Oxford University Press, 1979), especially pp. 47–73.

7. For descriptions of Azusa Street, see Vinson Synan, *The Holiness-Pentecostal Movement in the United States* (Grand Rapids, Mich.: William B. Eerdmans Publishing Company, 1971), pp. 105–112; Anderson, pp. 66–71; and Frank Bartleman, *Azusa Street* (Plainfield, N.J.: Logos International, 1980).

8. Interview with Pastor Rick Howard of Peninsula Christian Church, Redwood City, Calif., November 1985.

9. Quoted by Grant Wacker in paper, "A Profile of American Pentecostalism," University of North Carolina, Chapel Hill, July 1981.

10. See Grant Wacker, "Patterns of Primitivism in Early Pentecostalism," Department of Religious Studies, University of North Carolina, Chapel Hill, February 1986.

11. See Cecil M. Robeck, Jr., introduction entitled "The Writings and Thoughts of Frank Bartleman," in *Witness to Pentecost*, ed. Robeck (New York: Garland Publishing, Inc., 1985).

12. Anderson, p. 123.

13. Synan, *The Old-Time Power* (Franklin Springs, Ga.: Advocate Press, 1973), p. 178.

14. Anderson, p. 191.

15. Wacker, "A Profile of American Pentecostalism."

16. Interview with Fred M. Spencer, Fresno, California, October 1985.

17. Gregory, p. 196.

18. Hearings, U.S. Congress, U.S. House of Representatives, Select Committee to Investigate the Interstate Migration of Destitute Citizens (Tolan Committee), 76th and 77th Congress (Washington, D. C., 1940 and 1941), p. 3000.

19. Ibid.

20. Walter J. Stein, *California and the Dust Bowl Migration* (Westport, Conn.: Greenwood Press, 1973), p. 169.

21. Nathan O. Hatch, *The Democratization of American Christianity* (New Haven, Conn.: Yale University Press, 1989), p. 216.

22. *Delano Record*, October 12, 1934.

23. William G. McLoughlin, *Revivals, Awakenings, and Reform* (Chicago: University of Chicago Press, 1978), p. 39. McLoughlin is referring to what he calls "the Puritan legacy."

CHAPTER EIGHT: WARTIME

1. Frank Carson, "The Grapes of Raps," *Collier's*, January 27, 1940, p. 67, cited in George Bluestone, ed., "The Grapes of Wrath," in *Steinbeck, A Collection of Critical Essays* (Englewood Cliffs, N.J.: Prentice-Hall, 1972).

2. H. F. Scoville's analysis on the transient relief program in Los Angeles County and California as a whole, transmitted November 3, 1939, and included in hearings, U.S. Congress, House of Representatives Select Committee to Investigate the Interstate Migration of Destitute Citizens (Tolan Committee), 76th Congress (Washington, D. C., 1940 and 1941).

3. Ibid., pp. 2991–2994.

4. Walter J. Stein, *California and the Dust Bowl Migration* (Westport, Conn.: Greenwood Press, 1973), p. 281.

5. Frank Bartleman, "The World Situation," circa. 1916.

6. See Cecil M. Robeck, Jr., introduction entitled "The Writings and Thoughts of Frank Bartleman," in *Witness to Pentecost*, ed. Robeck (New York: Garland Publishing, Inc., 1985).

7. Robert Mapes Anderson, *Vision of the Disinherited* (New York: Oxford University Press, 1979), p. 202.

8. Vinson Synan, "The Quiet Rise of Black Pentecostals," *Charisma*, June 1986, pp. 45–55.

9. Jay Beaman, "Pentecostal Pacifism: The Origin, Development, and Rejection of Pacific Belief Among Pentecostals" (diss., North American Baptist Seminary, April 1982).

10. Lately Thomas, *Storming Heaven* (New York: William Morrow, 1970), p. 334.

11. Beaman.

PART THREE

CHAPTER NINE: DESTINIES

1. For the best description of the people and geography of the Dust Bowl migration, see James N. Gregory, *American Exodus* (New York: Oxford University Press, 1989), all of chapter one, "Out of the Heartland."
2. Conversation with DeWayne Rail, July 1986.
3. Thomas J. Smith, in an interview with the Odyssey Project in oral history, California State College, Bakersfield.
4. Oliver Carlson, "Up from the Dust," *U.S.A.*, August 1952, pp. 97–104.

CHAPTER TEN: THE VALLEY, 1950

1. Walter J. Stein, *California and the Dust Bowl Migration* (Westport, Conn.: Greenwood Press, 1973), p. 56.
2. Marc Reisner, *Cadillac Desert* (New York: Viking Penguin, 1986), p. 181 ff.
3. Hearings U.S. House of Representatives, Select Committee to Investigate the Interstate Migration of Destitute Citizens (Tolan Committee), 76th and 77th Congress (Washington, D.C., 1940 and 1941), p. 3003.
4. Letter from Assistant Secretary of Agriculture Charles F. Brannan to Commissioner Michael W. Straus, Bureau of Reclamation, March 15, 1946. See Senate Document 113, 81st Congress, "Comments on the Comprehensive Plan for Water Resources Development in the Central Valley Basin of California."
5. See "Factual Data for Southern San Joaquin Municipal Utility District," prepared by the U.S. Bureau of Reclamation, on file with SMUD, McFarland, Calif.
6. SMUD minutes, May 1950.

CHAPTER ELEVEN: IDENTITY

1. Demos Shakarian, *The Happiest People on Earth* (Chappaqua, N.Y.: Steward Press, 1975), p. 113.
2. David Edwin Harrell, Jr., *Oral Roberts, An American Life* (Bloomington: Indiana University Press, 1985), p. 43.
3. David Edwin Harrell, Jr., *All Things Are Possible* (Bloomington: Indiana University Press, 1975), pp. 66–67.
4. Harrell, *All Things Are Possible*, p. 199.
5. Fresno *Bee*, October 19, 1958.
6. Dowie's activities are described in several papers by historian Grant Wacker, including "Marching to Zion: Religion in a Modern Utopian Community," published in the December 1985 issue of *Church History*, beginning on p. 496.

CHAPTER TWELVE: THE HORSE TRADER II

1. Eric Hoffer, *The Ordeal of Change* (New York: Harper & Row, 1963), pp. 57ff.
2. Fresno *Bee*, May 22, 1957.
3. Fresno *Bee*, July 8, 1958.

CHAPTER THIRTEEN: GOLDWATER MAN

1. Robert Mapes Anderson, *Vision of the Disinherited* (New York: Oxford University Press, 1979), pp. 196 ff.
2. Delano *Record*, October 14, 1934.
3. *Pentecostal Evangel*, July 2, 1961.
4. Richard V. Pierard, *The Political Role of Religion in the United States*, edited by Stephen D. Johnson and Joseph B. Tamney (Boulder, Colo.: Westview Press, 1986).
5. A. James Reichley, *Religion in American Public Life* (Washington, D.C.: Brookings Institution, 1985), p. 145.
6. William W. Menzies, *Anointed to Serve* (Springfield, Mo: Gospel Publishing House, 1971), p. 359.
7. Definition by Richard Quebedeaux, *The New Charismatics II* (New York: Harper & Row, 1983), p. 37.
8. Vinson Synan, *The Old-Time Power* (Franklin Springs, Ga.: Advocate Press, 1973), p. 186.
9. James Davison Hunter, *American Evangelism: Conservative Religion and the Quandary of Modernity* (New Brunswick, N.J.: Rutgers University Press, 1983), p. 41, as quoted in Reichley, *Religion in American Public Life*, p. 312.
10. David Edwin Harrell, Jr., *Oral Roberts: An American Life* (Bloomington: Indiana University Press, 1985), p. 153.
11. Walter J. Hollenweger, *The Pentecostals* (London: SCM Press Ltd., 1972), p. 468.
12. Richard V. Pierard, "The New Religious Right in American Politics," in *Evangelicalism and Modern America*, edited by George Marsden (Grand Rapids, Mich.: William B. Eeerdmans Publishing Company, 1984), pp. 165–168.
13. William G. McLoughlin, *Revivals, Awakenings, and Reform* (Chicago: University of Chicago Press, 1978), p. 189.
14. Thomas Byrne Edsall and Mary D. Edsall, *Chain Reaction* (New York: Norton 1991), p. 43.
15. Quebedeaux, p. 71.
16. Kevin Phillips, *Post-Conservative America* (New York: Random House, 1982), p. 34.
17. Edsall, p. 39.
18. James N. Gregory, *American Exodus* (New York: Oxford University Press, 1989), pp. 242–3.
19. Edsall, pp. 78–79.
20. Phillips, p. 50*n*.

21. Menzies, p. 372.

22. Edsall, pp. 32–46.

23. Oakland *Tribune*, June 23, 1968.

CHAPTER FIFTEEN: BROTHERS

1. Fresno *Bee*, August 20, 1975.

2. Ruth Lyon, *Pentecostal Evangel*, "Arizona's 'Church of the Domes' Attracts Attention," June 15, 1975, pp. 16–17.

3. Royal Caulkins, Fresno *Bee*, November 22, November 30, and December 1, 1980.

4. Ibid., and court documents on file, Fresno County courthouse, and interviews.

CHAPTER SIXTEEN: RESISTANCE

1. William G. McLoughlin, *Revivals, Awakenings, and Reform* (Chicago: University of Chicago Press, 1978), pp. 179–216.

2. Fresno *Bee*, November 17, 1974.

3. *Editorial Research Reports*, October 10, 1973, p. 779.

4. Thomas Byrne Edsall and Mary D. Edsall, *Chain Reaction* (New York: Norton, 1991), p. 111.

5. Kristin Luker, *Abortion and the New Politics of Motherhood* (Berkeley: University of California Press, 1984), pp. 88–100.

6. Dennis Vogt and Warren S. Brown, "Bottom-line Morality," *Christianity Today*, April 22, 1988.

7. Kevin Phillips, *Post-Conservative America* (New York: Random House, 1982), p. 48, taken from an interview with Richard Neuhaus in *Commonweal*, October 9, 1981.

8. Martin Schram and Charles R. Babcock, Washington *Post*, January 17, 1982.

9. Warren Brown, *Washington Post*, October 31, 1978.

10. Edsall, *Chain Reaction*, p. 133, citing *Conservative Digest*, August 1979.

11. Vinson Synan, *The Old-Time Power* (Franklin Springs, Ga.: Advocate Press, 1973), pp. 268 ff.

CHAPTER SEVENTEEN: TRIBES

1. Michael Fessier, Jr., "Grapes of Wrath, 1977," *New West*, July 18, 1977, p. 24.

2. See Richard Lee Colvin, "Dust Bowl Legacy," *Los Angeles Times Magazine*, March 26, 1989, p. 8, and Odyssey Project in oral history of California State College, Bakersfield, interview with Hadley Yocum, 1981.

PART FOUR

CHAPTER EIGHTEEN: KEEPING SCORE

1. See Patti Roberts, *Ashes to Gold* (Waco, Texas: Word Books, 1983).
2. Mary Hargrove, Tulsa *Tribune*, July 25, 1984.

CHAPTER NINETEEN: AUTHENTICITY

1. In 1990, the Nuclear Regulatory Commission began investigating reports that uranium was leaking into the ground and that workers may have been exposed. The plant, which was acquired by General Atomics in 1988, was ordered shut down in 1991 pending corrective action.
2. *Time*, February 17, 1986.

CHAPTER TWENTY: SISTERS

1. See review of *The Holy Spirit in Counseling* (Hendrickson Publishers), ed. Marvin G. Gilbert and Raymond T. Brock, in *Pentecostal Evangel*, June 15, 1986, p. 30.

CHAPTER TWENTY-TWO: POWER SHIFT

1. Phoenix *Gazette*, August 8, 1986.
2. Michael Janofsky, *New York Times*, June 8, 1986.
3. Paul Taylor, Washington *Post*, July 5, 1984.
4. *The Evangelist*, March 1985.
5. Royal Caulkins, Fresno *Bee*, February 19, 1983, August 14, 1984, and September 7, 1984.
6. Fresno *Bee*, June 30, 1985.
7. Fresno *Bee*, December 21, 1985.
8. Fresno *Bee*, November 23, 1985.
9. Art Harris, Washington *Post*, September 15, 1989.
10. *Arizona Republic*, March 15, 1989.
11. Fresno *Bee*, August 25, 1988, and June 6, 1989.

CHAPTER TWENTY-THREE: THE VALLEY, 1988

1. Marc Reisner, *Cadillac Desert* (New York: Viking Penguin, 1986), p. 385.
2. Bakersfield *Californian*, June 5, 1988.
3. Bakersfield *Californian*, October 31, 1988.

CHAPTER TWENTY-FOUR: UNCERTAIN VICTORY

1. See Joel Garreau, *Edge City* (New York: Doubleday, 1991), p. 187.
2. Charles Colson, "So Much for Our Great Awakening," *Christianity Today*.
3. *Newsweek*, September 17, 1984.
4. Sidney Blumenthal, "Righteous Empire," *The New Republic*, October 22, 1984.

5. Fresno *Bee*, September 20, 1984.

6. Fresno *Bee*, October 24, 1984.

7. Jim Boren, Fresno *Bee*, October 14, 1984.

8. Michael Barone and Grant Ujifusa, *Almanac of American Politics, 1988* (Washington, D.C.: National Journal, 1987), p. 664.

9. Myra McPherson, Washington *Post*, October 18, 1985.

10. *New Wine*, February 1986, reprinted from *U.S. News & World Report*, November 4, 1985.

11. Thomas Byrne Edsall and Mary D. Edsall, *Chain Reaction* (New York: Norton, 1991), pp. 208 ff.

12. Fresno *Bee*, February 7, 1987.

13. Washington *Post*, March 8, 1988.

14. Ibid.

15. Tom Reid, Washington *Post*, September 11, 1987.

16. Wayne King, *New York Times*, Nov. 27, 1987.

17. Sacramento *Bee*, August 5, 1988.

18. Letter to the *Wall Street Journal*, December 30, 1990, from Edith L. Blumhofer, project director, Institute for the Study of American Evangelicals, Wheaton College, Wheaton, Illinois.

SELECTED BIBLIOGRAPHY

PEOPLE, PLACES, AND MIGRATION

Billington, Ray Allen. *Westward Expansion: A History of the American Frontier*. New York: Macmillan, 1949.

Caro, Robert A. *The Path to Power*. New York: Vintage Books, 1983.

Collins, Henry Hill, Jr. *America's Own Refugees*. Princeton: Princeton University Press, 1941. •

Egerton, John. *Generations: An American Family*. New York: Simon & Schuster, 1983.

Federal Writers Project American Guide Series. *California*. New York: Hastings House, 1939.

———. *Oklahoma*. Norman, Okla.: University of Oklahoma Press, 1941.

Fischer, David Hackett. *Albion's Seed: Four British Folkways in America*. New York: Oxford University Press, 1989.

Gibson, Arrell M. *Wilderness Bonanza: The Tri-State District of Missouri, Kansas, and Oklahoma*. Norman, Okla.: University of Oklahoma Press, 1972.

Gregory, James N. *American Exodus*. New York: Oxford University Press, 1989.

Key, V. O., Jr. *Southern Politics*. New York: Alfred A. Knopf, 1949.

Kuznets, Simon. *Population Redistribution and Economic Growth of the United States, 1870–1950.* 3 vols. Philadelphia: American Philosophical Society, 1957–64.

Lemann, Nicholas. *The Promised Land.* New York: Alfred A. Knopf, 1991.

Leyburn, James G. *The Scotch-Irish, A Social History.* Chapel Hill, N.C.: University of North Carolina Press, 1982.

McFarland, Gerald. *A Scattered People: An American Family Moves West.* New York: Pantheon Books, 1985.

McWilliams, Carey. *Ill Fares the Land.* Boston: Little, Brown, 1942.

———. *Factories in the Fields.* Boston: Little, Brown, 1939.

Mills, Edwin W. *The Scotch-Irish Heritage of Missouri Ozarkians.* Osceola, Mo.: 1961.

Owsley, Frank Lawrence. *Plain Folk of the Old South.* Baton Rouge: Louisiana State University Press, 1949.

Reisner, Marc. *Cadillac Desert.* New York: Viking, 1986.

Stein, Walter J. *California and the Dust Bowl Migration.* Westport, Conn.: Greenwood Press, 1973.

Tang, Anthony M. *Economic Development in the Southern Piedmont, 1860–1950.* Chapel Hill, N.C.: University of North Carolina Press, 1958.

U.S. Congress. House. Select Committee to Investigate the Interstate Migration of Destitute Citizens (Tolan Committee). *Hearings.* 76th and 77th Congress, 1940 and 1941.

Worster, Donald. *Dust Bowl.* New York: Oxford University Press, 1979.

Woodward, C. Vann. *Origins of the New South, 1877–1913.* Baton Rouge: Louisiana State University Press, 1951.

CULTURE AND RELIGION

Ahlstrom, Sydney E. *A Religious History of the American People.* 2 vols. Garden City, N.J.: Image Books, 1975.

Anderson, Robert Mapes. *Vision of the Disinherited.* New York: Oxford University Press, 1979.

Balmer, Randall. *Mine Eyes Have Seen the Glory.* New York: Oxford University Press, 1989.

Bartleman, Frank. *Azusa Street.* Plainfield, N.J.: Logos International, 1980.

Eighmy, John Lee. *Churches in Cultural Captivity.* Knoxville: University of Tennessee Press, 1972.

Goldberg, George. *Reconsecrating America.* Grand Rapids, Mich.: William B. Eerdmans, 1984.

Harrell, David Edwin, Jr. *All Things Are Possible: The Healing and Charismatic Revivals in Modern America.* Bloomington, Ind.: Indiana University Press, 1975.

Hatch, Nathan O. *The Democratization of American Christianity.* New Haven: Yale University Press, 1989.

James, William. *The Varieties of Religious Experience.* New York: Penguin Books, 1982.

Jensen, Richard. *The Winning of the Midwest*. Chicago: University of Chicago Press, 1971.

Kelley, Robert. *The Cultural Pattern in American Politics*. New York: Alfred A. Knopf, 1979.

Kleppner, Paul. *The Cross of Culture: A Social Analysis of Midwestern Culture, 1850–1900*. New York: The Free Press, 1970.

Marsden, George M., ed. *Evangelicalism and Modern America*. Grand Rapids, Mich.: William B. Eerdmans, 1984.

———. *Fundamentalism and American Culture*. New York: Oxford University Press, 1980.

McLoughlin, William G. *Revivals, Awakenings and Reform*. Chicago: University of Chicago Press, 1978.

Menzies, William W. *Anoited to Serve*. Springfield, Mo.: Gospel Publishing House, 1971.

Niebuhr, H. Richard. *The Social Sources of Denominationalism*. New York: Henry Holt, 1929.

Quebedeaux, Richard. *The New Charismatics II: How a Christian Renewal Movement Became Part of the American Religious Mainstream*. San Francisco: Harper & Row, 1983.

Reichley, A. James. *Religion in American Public Life*. Washington, D.C.: Brookings Institution, 1985.

Smith, Timothy L. *Revivalism and Social Reform*. Baltimore: Johns Hopkins University Press, 1980.

Synan, Vinson. *The Holiness-Pentecostal Movement in the United States*. Grand Rapids, Mich.: William B. Eerdmans, 1971.

———. *The Old-Time Power, A History of the Pentecostal Holiness Church*. Franklin Springs, Ga.: Advocate Press, 1973.

Weber, Max. *The Protestant Ethic and the Spirit of Capitalism*. New York: Charles Scribner's Sons, 1958.

Weber, Timothy P. *Living in the Shadow of the Second Coming*. New York: Oxford University Press, 1979.

POLITICS AND REBELLION

Daniel, Cletus E. *Bitter Harvest*. Berkeley: University of California Press, 1982.

Edsall, Thomas Byrne, and Mary D. Edsall. *Chain Reaction*. New York: W. W. Norton, 1991.

Goodwyn, Lawrence. *Democratic Promise, The Populist Movement in America*. New York: Oxford University Press, 1976.

Green, James R. *Grass-Roots Socialism: Radical Movements in the Southwest, 1895–1943*. Baton Rouge: Louisiana State University Press, 1978.

Luker, Kristin. *Abortion & the Politics of Motherhood*. Berkeley: University of California Press, 1984.

Meister, Dick, and Anna Loftis. *A Long Time Coming, The Struggle to Unionize America's Farm Workers*. New York: Macmillan, 1977.

Neuhaus, John, and Michael Cromartie, eds. *Politics and Piety*. Washington, D.C.: Ethics and Public Policy Center, 1987.

Phillips, Kevin P. *Post-Conservative America*. New York: Random House, 1982.

Pope, Liston. *Millhands and Preachers*. New Haven: Yale University Press, 1942.

STEINBECKIANA

Benson, Jackson J., and Anne Loftis. "John Steinbeck and Farm Labor Unionization, The Background of *In Dubious Battle*," *American Literature*, May 1980.

Davis, Robert Murray, ed. *Steinbeck—A Collection of Critical Essays*. New York: Prentiss Hall.

PHOTOGRAPHIC CREDITS

For permission to reprint some of the photographs in this book grateful acknowledgment is made to the following: Fresno *Bee* (aerial shot of People's Church); Ron Riesterer (Cindy Critchfield and family); Rod Thornburg (Cleo Frost in Delano); Wide World Photo (USFL announcement).

A NOTE ABOUT THE AUTHOR

Dan Morgan has been a reporter, editor, and
foreign correspondent for the Washington *Post*
since 1963. His previous book, *Merchants of Grain*,
was nominated for the American Book Award.

A NOTE ON THE TYPE

This book was set in a digitized version of a type
face called Baskerville. The face itself is a facsimile
reproduction of types cast from molds made for
John Baskerville (1706–1775) from his designs.
Baskerville's original face was one of the
forerunners of the type style known to
printers as "modern face"—a "modern"
of the period A.D. 1800.

Composed by Crane Typesetting Service, Inc.,
West Barnstable, Massachusetts

Printed and bound by Fairfield Graphics,
Fairfield, Pennsylvania

Designed by Iris Weinstein

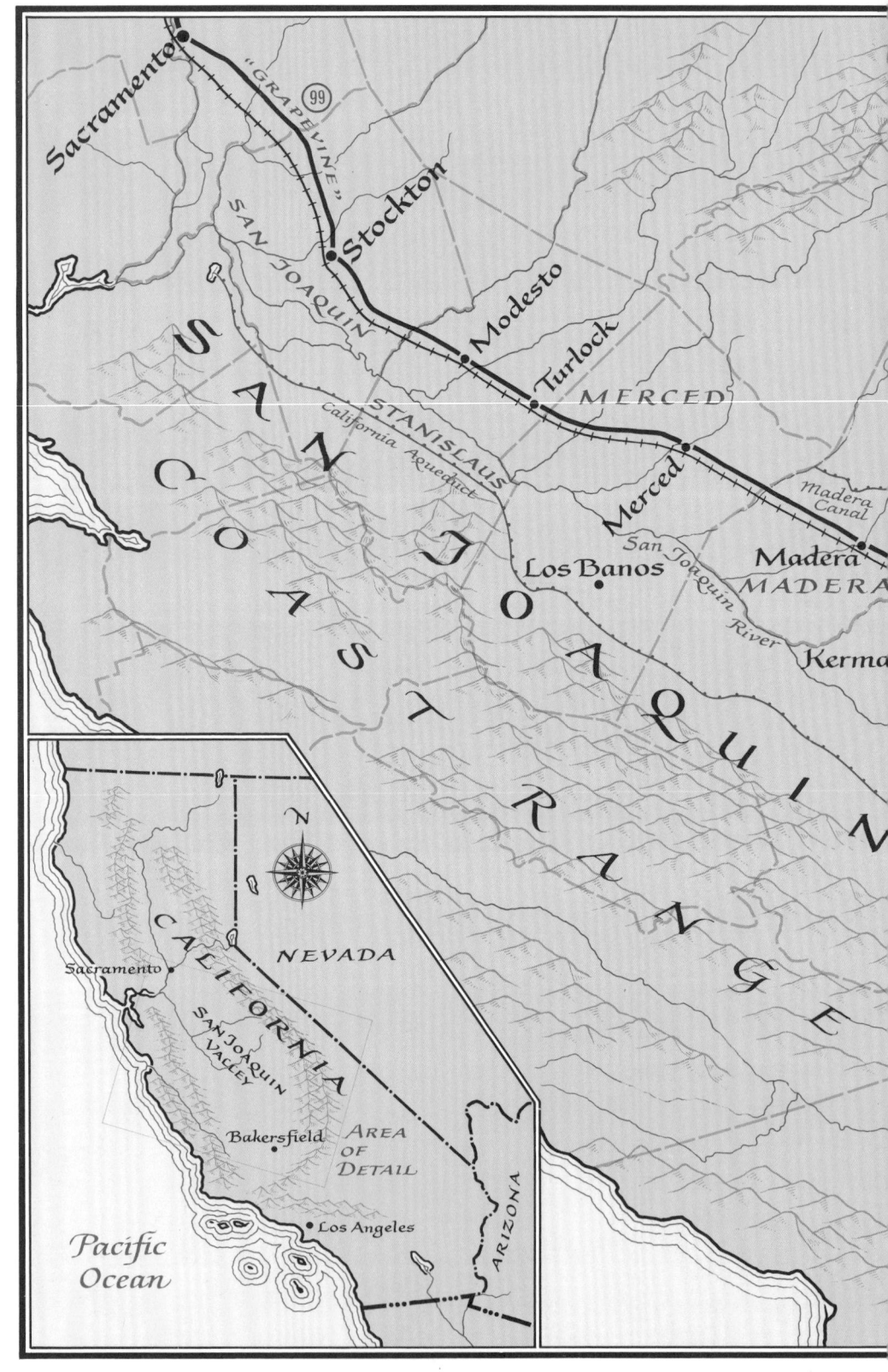